A Companion to John Wyclif

Brill's Companions to the Christian Tradition

A series of handbooks and reference works
on the intellectual and religious life of Europe,
500-1700

VOLUME 4

A Companion to John Wyclif

Late Medieval Theologian

Edited by

Ian Christopher Levy

BRILL

LEIDEN · BOSTON
2006

On the cover: 'The Trial of Wycliffe' (one of the Ford Madox Brown murals in the Great Hall of the Manchester Town Hall). Reproduced courtesy of Manchester City Council.

This book is printed on acid-free paper.

Library of Congress Cataloging-in-Publication Data

A C.I.P. record for this book is available from the Library of Congress.

ISSN   1871–6377
ISBN-13: 978-90-04-15007-2
ISBN-10: 90-04-15007-2

CONTENTS

LIST OF CONTRIBUTORS

MISHTOONI BOSE (Oxford, 1994) is Christopher Tower Official Student in Medieval Poetry in English at Christ Church, Oxford. Her research interests include late-medieval poetry in England and France, scholasticism and medieval intellectual life, the Wycliffite controversies and their aftermath, religious reform, and fifteenth-century literary and religious cultures. She has published on the writings of Reginald Pecock and is completing a study of writing and reform from Thomas Netter to Thomas More. Her most recent publication is *Vernacular Philosophy and the Making of Orthodoxy in the Fifteenth Century*, New Medieval Literatures 7 (2005). Her next project will examine the influence of Guillaume de Deguileville on late-medieval English literature.

ALESSANDRO D. CONTI (Pisa, 1980) is Associate Professor in the Faculty of Letters and Philosophy at the University of L'Aquila (Italy). His research interests include the tradition of commentaries on the *Isagoge* and on the *Categories* in late Antiquity and Middle Ages, and Realism in late Middle Ages. He has published editions of texts by R. Alyngton, J. Sharpe, W. Penygull, and Paul of Venice. Among his books is *Esistenza e verità: Forme e strutture del reale in Paolo Veneto e nel pensiero filosofico del tardo medioevo* (Rome 1996). He has been the Guest Editor of *Vivarium* 43.1 (2005), dedicated to Realism in late Middle Ages.

MARY DOVE (Cambridge, 1970) is Reader in English in the School of Humanities at the University of Sussex. She works on the medieval Bible and biblical interpretation, with a focus on the Song of Songs; she has edited and translated the *Glossa Ordinaria in Canticum Canticorum* (Brepols, 1997), and her study of Nicholas of Lyra's commentary on the Song of Songs is included in Krey and Smith (Brill, 2000). Her book on the Wycliffite Bible, *The First English Bible: The Text and Context of the Wycliffite Versions*, is scheduled to appear in 2007.

STEPHEN E. LAHEY, (University of Connecticut, 1997) is Lecturer in the Department of Classics and Religious Studies at University of Nebraska, Lincoln. He is the author of *Philosophy and Politics in the*

Thought of John Wyclif (Cambridge, 2003), and is engaged in writing a survey of Wyclif's life and thought for Oxford's Great Medieval Thinkers series, and in translating Wyclif's Trialogus. He is also an Episcopal priest, serving in three churches in the Diocese of Nebraska.

ANDREW E. LARSEN (UW-Madison, 1998) is currently a visiting professor at Marquette University. He is currently working on a study of academic condemnations at Oxford.

IAN CHRISTOPHER LEVY (Marquette, 1997) is Assistant Professor of Theology at Lexintgon Theological Seminary. He has published articles on various aspects of John Wyclif's thought. He has also published an abridged translation of Wyclif's *On the Truth of Holy Scripture* (2001); and a monograph on Wyclif's eucharistic theology: *John Wyclif: Scriptural Logic, Real Presence and the Parameters of Orthodoxy* (2003). He is currently completing a volume of medieval commentaries on the Epistle to the Galatians.

STEPHEN PENN (York, 1998) is currently a lecturer in the Department of English Studies at the University of Stirling. His research interests include medieval literary and linguistic theory; Latin writings of John Wyclif and the relationship between Latin and vernacular in the later Middle Ages. He has written several articles on medieval literary theory and late-medieval intellectual culture and is currently working on a collection of translations of John Wyclif's Latin writings (Manchester).

TAKASHI SHOGIMEN (University of Sheffield, 1998) is Lecturer in History at the University of Otago in Dunedin, New Zealand. His research interests include the political thought and ecclesiology of late medieval Europe and the comparative history of political and social thought, with particular emphasis on late medieval and early modern Europe and Tokugawa Japan. In addition to journal articles and book chapters, he has a forthcoming book, *Ockham and Political Discourse in the Late Middle Ages* (Cambridge University Press).

INTRODUCTION:
A COMPANION TO JOHN WYCLIF

Ian Christopher Levy

Perhaps no medieval theologian has experienced the ebb and flow of human affections to the extent that John Wyclif would endure. Both hailed and reviled in his own lifetime, he would later be held up as hero and villain after his death, only to be reclaimed and ignored intermittently over the centuries. This is not the place for Wycliffite historiography; the essays contained in this volume will speak to such questions within the confines of their particular topics. Wyclif's medieval and modern legacy is an interesting topic in itself, but suffice it to say here that the study of John Wyclif received its greatest boost in the late nineteenth century when a group of predominantly German scholars began to publish critical editions of his Latin works, covering the full range of this prodigious mind, thereby producing volumes of logic and metaphysics, christology, ecclesiology and politics, biblical exegesis, and sacramental theology, as well as a host of sermons. Whatever the shortcomings of these editions, they remain indispensable and will not be surpassed without a similar concentration of effort. All of this is to say that it is really only in the last one hundred years that the scholarly world has had access to these often massive works, in all of their complexity and subtlety. Wyclif's star began to be eclipsed, however, in the second half of the twentieth century when attention shifted to his Lollard followers. Scholars were now focusing their energy on popular heresy rather than the academic, on vernacular works rather than the Latin; one might say that Wycliffite studies moved from the Theology department across campus to the English department. This does not mean that Wyclif had disappeared from the scene; in fact, a series of essays greeted the six-hundredth anniversary of his death in 1984, in addition to a critical edition and translation of one of his most important metaphysical works (*De universalibus*). And in just the last decade there has been something of a resurgence evinced by translations, journal articles and monographs devoted to the many aspects of Wyclif's thought. This has been fueled to some extent by the broader advances made in the study of late medieval scholasticism. And so, now more than ever before, Wyclif is taking his place within the wider context of late medieval theology, metaphysics and politics. As the essays here should illustrate, Wyclif was a medieval thinker of the first rank, as deft and innovative as he was passionate and combative.

This book is specifically concerned with John Wyclif, the late medieval scholastic theologian. That point needs to be made at the outset, precisely because Wyclif's legacy is peculiar for a schoolman, inasmuch as his work spawned popular dissenting movements both in England with the Lollards, and in Bohemia among the followers of Jan Hus. To the Church authorities in the decades after his death Wyclif was the heresiarch *par excellence*, the progenitor of anti-authoritarian sentiment which was viewed as threatening both to crown and mitre. So it was that when the Council of Constance condemned Jan Hus in 1415, they drew up a list of forty-five Wycliffite errors deemed to be at the heart of the unrest. The leaders of the Conciliarist movement sought to reform the Catholic Church, but saw the Wycliffite and Hussite agenda as a recipe for anarchy. No doubt then, the role that Wyclif's ideas came to play among the English Lollards and the Bohemian Hussites in the years following his death is a complicated and fascinating topic, fully worthy of the scholarly attention it receives. Nor should we forget that many of the surviving manuscripts of Wyclif's Latin works were copied and preserved by the Hussites of central Europe. In that sense, Wyclif's "after-life" had a tangible affect on the Wyclif we have come to know through these writings. And so, focused as this volume is on John Wyclif, some of the essays do address Wyclif's influence across future generations, whether it be his logic and metaphysics among the fifteenth-century schoolmen, his role in the creation of the English Bible, or the response his work elicited from some very fierce opponents in his own lifetime and beyond.

This remains, however, a book about the life and thought of John Wyclif. That is not only because the Lollard and Hussite movements are broad and separate (though clearly related) topics which would require the sort of full-fledged volumes they are often accorded. More than that, the present volume is an effort to address John Wyclif on his own terms. It is imperative that students of both the Lollards and the Hussites have a firm grasp of what Wyclif himself actually taught on the wide range of topics which figured so heavily in these variegated movements. Only then can one assess the degree to which Wyclif influenced these later generations, and to what extent they diverged from the master. In fact, a wider gulf might emerge than previously imagined, thereby affirming the independent mind of those future Lollards and Hussites. No matter how the question of adherence cuts, it is still of vital importance to press beyond well-worn characterizations of Wyclif's theories and see what he said and why he said it. His own words, written in response to events in his own times—and read within the context of the ideas that shaped his mind—must form the basis of all assessments of Wyclif's place in history. It is in this vein that Wyclif should be allowed to assert his independence from those who came after him. It is generally agreed now that the old monikers of "Pre-Reformer" or "Morning Star of the Reformation" are ill-suited anachronisms. But if Wyclif is to take his place in the late medieval scholastic pantheon with the likes of Duns Scotus and William of Ockham, then he must be studied as a thinker in his own right, freed from the burden of his progeny.

Here then are eight substantial essays on major themes pertaining to Wyclif's life, writings and legacy, all of which take great pains to situate Wyclif firmly within his intellectual and historical context. Each essay is grounded not only in a rich use of primary sources, but the most current secondary scholarship as well. We hope that this collection will truly serve as a "companion" to students and professors alike, who will be able to turn to a given chapter and come away with a solid understanding of the topic at hand. Though it should be said that the chapters have been arranged so as to present a coherent narrative such as one might expect from a monograph. The copious and precise documentation provided in the notes should allow for each chapter to serve as a springboard for further research. Indeed, the scholars who have contributed to this volume share the common goal of making Wyclif better known and more widely studied.

In the first chapter, Andrew Larsen offers a comprehensive look at Wyclif's life and career, with special attention paid to the structures and processes of the late medieval university; for that is where Wyclif spent almost his entire adult life. Larsen also examines Wyclif's brief foray into international diplomacy as a representative of the Crown in its dealings with the papacy. University, Church, and Crown came to form that inexorable combination that characterized Wyclif's eventful career. Larsen makes it clear that in his dealings with the Duke of Lancaster, John of Gaunt, Wyclif was no mere pawn of this lay magnate, but rather an astute player who saw the potential benefits of this relationship for his own reform program. He also remarks on Wyclif's apparent willingness to compromise his strict requirements of just dominion for the sake of fostering such powerful patronage. No doubt, Wyclif was a "complex man," as Larsen observes. Clearly, he was an ambitious man endowed with tremendous intellectual capabilities as well as the charisma to rally his followers. And yet, while convinced of the rectitude of his own positions to the point of excessive antagonism, some rather pointed contradictions seem to arise which are impossible for historians to ignore. Larsen's careful analysis of Wyclif's life and times presents us with a vivid picture of this figure in all his complexity of motivations and ideals.

Alessandro Conti offers the fullest and most rigorous analysis of Wyclif's logic and metaphysics to date. Conti shows us that Wyclif was at once a product of a long tradition of metaphysical realism and a highly original thinker whose innovations were pursued by later generations at Oxford. As Conti writes, "Wyclif built up a metaphysics of essences, culminating in an ontological and epistemological primacy of universals over any other kind of beings, by which all the main and subsequent forms of realism were to be inspired." Conti contends that Wyclif's unique take on Duns Scotus's doctrine of formal distinction, and his own particular theory of predication, proved to be the mainstay of his legacy. In fact, "Wyclif's description of the logical structure of the relationship between universals and individuals demanded a redefinition of predication." Conti concludes his analysis of Wyclif with a look at the "Oxford Realists" who flourished in the first quarter of the fifteenth century and who partially modified Wyclif's system as they introduced a new "predication by essence, based on a partial identity between the entities for which the subject and predicate stood." Conti's presentation of Wyclif's logical/metaphysical legacy goes a long way to correct the conventional misunderstanding that Wyclif's intellectual achievements were consigned to an orthodox oblivion following the publication of Archbishop Arundel's Constitutions. In point of fact, the schoolmen of the next generation were quite capable of separating the wheat from the chaff, as it were, steering clear of Wyclif's ecclesiology while embracing his logic.

Stephen Lahey has written the first comprehensive treatment of Wyclif's trinitarian and christological thought. Apart from the introductions to the critical editions of Wyclif's *De Trinitate* and *De Verbi Incarnacione*, scholars have tended to bypass what to all accounts would be the foundational material of any medieval theologian. Lahey is in agreement with scholars who consider these works to have been part of Wyclif's lost commentary on Peter Lombard's *Sentences*, and he is thus keen to situate Wyclif's views within the late medieval Sentence-Commentary tradition. As one might expect, Wyclif's metaphysical realism comes to the fore on these topics, for Lahey notes that universals function as natures when Wyclif explains both the divine nature particularized in the three persons of the Trinity and the hypostatic union of divinity and humanity in the person of Jesus Christ. In fact, Wyclif contended that the chief threat to trinitarian orthodoxy in his own day was the rejection of real universals. Hence Lahey takes pains to contextualize Wyclif within the larger theological debates of the middle fourteenth century, and he believes that Wyclif's *De Trinitate* must be read as a response to the positions held by such scholars as Adam Wodeham and Robert Holcot. Against these *moderni*, Wyclif will take his stand with the likes of St Anselm and Robert Grosseteste. This is not to say that Wyclif locked himself away from more recent theologians, however, for Lahey shows how Wyclif follows Duns Scotus's explanation of the Incarnation, which likens the relationship of the divine and human natures to that of a substance and accident. Ultimately, Lahey observes that, for Wyclif, the Incarnation forms the focal point for ordering a Christian society, as it is here that the divine life and teaching is most fully communicated to the human race.

Takashi Shogimen places Wyclif's ecclesiology and political philosophy squarely within the traditions of the late Middle Ages, notably the papalist/anti-papalist debates, while comparing Wyclif more specifically with Marsilius of Padua and William of Ockham. He observes that whereas Ockham thought that the problems plaguing the Church of his own day were specific instances of heretical deviation from the proper ecclesiastical order, Wyclif attacked the very foundation of Church power itself. In that way Wyclif resembled Marsilius, but while Marsilius sought to instate a system built on popular consent, Wyclif looked instead to the divine will alone, thereby calling for a radically theocentric (as opposed to anthropocentric) ecclesiology. It is in this vein that Shogimen traces Wyclif's peculiar brand of grace-founded dominion bestowed by God upon faithful Christians apart from all human mediation. Shogimen comes to the conclusion that Wyclif chartered a "third way" of ecclesial governance that was opposed to both the papal and the Marsilian principles. Against the first, he placed the temporal above the ecclesiastical; while against the second he replaced the model of popular consent with a community of theologically astute believers endowed with divine grace.

Stephen Penn writes on Wyclif's sacramental theology, providing an analysis of Wyclif's understanding of all seven sacraments with careful attention given to their place within his ecclesiology. For, as Penn argues, much of what proved to be controversial in Wyclif's pronouncements about the sacraments spoke directly to questions of clerical authority. And yet, Penn points out that, no matter how far Wyclif pushed his criticism of contemporary sacramental practices (penance serving as a prime example), that was not what spelled his downfall; it was the rejection of transubstantiation that marked the end of his university career. Penn treats Wyclif's eucharistic theology at some length and concludes that while Wyclif's final position on this sacrament was not purely the result of his metaphysical realism— and was certainly indebted to scriptural authority—he could never have come to this position apart from such a strict adherence to this realist metaphysic, which in turn also sustained his doctrine of Scripture.

Ian Levy examines Wyclif's prescription for living the Christian life as manifested in the devotional practices and responsibilities of both clergy and laity. Levy covers a broad range of issues: Wyclif's relationship with the mendicant orders; the controversy over preaching rights; what constitutes good preaching (all points of contention with the friars); and questions of personal devotion involving pilgrimages, saints, images, prayer, indulgences, and funerals. In a more scholastic vein, Levy also examines Wyclif's theory of grace and merit, and thus the soteriological process by which the wayfarer hopes to reach the heavenly Jerusalem. Wyclif emerges from all of this as a critic to be sure, but not an extremist; indeed many of his views were tempered by a sober traditionalism that sought to redress some of the excesses of late medieval piety. A consistent aspect of Wyclif's call for clerical reform specifically, and the moral reform of Christendom generally, is the centrality of the poor and humble

Christ who serves as a model for all believers to imitate. At the heart of the Christian life for Wyclif was what he termed the "law of Christ," which translates into a "law of love" that is proclaimed in preaching and manifested in a life of charity.

Mary Dove offers a fresh perspective on Wyclif's understanding of Scripture as well as on his role in the production of the English Bible. Dove helpfully provides the proper historical context for both Wyclif's exegetical method within the tradition of medieval commenting and the vexing textual issues surrounding the Bible as a "book" which faced everyone from Stephen Harding to Roger Bacon and Richard Ullerston. In this vein, Dove remarks on Wyclif's "dazzling exegesis of biblical intertexuality" as he attempts to prove that both the Old and New Testaments are the thoroughly authentic word of God despite the possibility of any textual corruption in the time of Ezra or mistranslations at the hands of St Jerome. But no matter how much Wyclif would make of the indefectible Eternal Scripture, Dove contends that he never lost sight of the value of the texts themselves: "Wyclif's neo-Platonist concept of Scripture is grounded in the material presence of the Latin Bible." With respect to the production of the "Wycliffite Bible," which some modern scholars have tended to distance from Wyclif himself, Dove argues for Wyclif's initiation and supervisory role in a project that would have begun, she says, by the early 1370s. Dove devotes a substantial part of her essay to the production of this English Bible as she examines the principles of translation and glossing at work in the quest for what the Lollards would call an "open" or "trewe" version of the text.

In the final essay, Mishtooni Bose observes that, "the last word was an elusive prize in these [Wycliffite] controversies," which even the exhumation and burning of Wyclif's remains in 1428 could not bring to a close. Here Bose concentrates on the strategies employed by Wyclif's opponents in a series of texts written over the space of some sixty years. Though Wyclif was a life-long academic, Bose remarks that, "it was a hallmark of these controversies that they would call into question the already porous boundaries between the worlds in and beyond the schools." It is an ironic sign of such ambiguity, therefore, that the anti-Wycliffite Bishop Reginald Pecock would fall victim to the tension between the legislative and academic battle against heresy. An outstanding feature of the entire Wycliffite controversy, which Bose makes clear, is that each side of the debate relied upon the same sources of tradition (Scripture, Fathers, Canon Law). Thus the means of refuting Wyclif would have to turn more on the issue of method than material. It is fitting, then, that Bose would draw on the words of Thomas More who, in 1515, despaired of scholastic theology's ability to battle heresy effectively. For, as Bose concludes, it would not be the collective works of Radcliff, Netter, and Pecock that curtailed the spread of Lollardy, but a royal and ecclesiastical determination that was willing to resort to the most violent means if need be to enforce its will.

Bose's essay serves as a perfect coda to this volume, highlighting as it does the enigmatic legacy Wyclif bequeathed to churchmen and scholars alike. Wyclif could not be so easily overcome because, in the end, he could be so easily categorized. Every time we seek to assess Wyclif's ideas we are plunged into a world of complex questions that have yet to be sorted out fully, not only from an historical standpoint, but from a theological and moral standpoint as well. Wyclif was not only a controversialist; much of what he wrote aroused no suspicion among university and ecclesiastical officials. His theology was for the most part deeply traditional and orthodox, and his metaphysics inspired a new generation of thoroughly orthodox adherents. Nevertheless, he surely was a very controversial figure because, above all else, he brought to the fore the single most vexing issue of medieval Christendom: the issue of authority in the Church. This problem is still with us today and we seem no closer to solving it. Perhaps that is why we are still fascinated with Wyclif—for all of the solutions he proposed and the lingering questions he could never resolve.

THE LATIN WRITINGS OF JOHN WYCLIF

This list of Wyclif's Latin works is drawn from Williell R. Thomson's *The Latin Writings of John Wyclyf* (Toronto: PIMS, 1983). The numbering system is his, thus enabling readers to check details on the various works of Wyclif cited in this present volume. It should be noted, however, that recent research has called into question Thomson's dating of some of Wyclif's works, in addition to the fact that Wyclif seems to have revised his own writings in the last years of his life.[1]

Section A

1.	A1. *De logica*
2.	A2. *Logice continuacio*
3.	A3. *De logica tractatus tercius*
4.	A4. *De actibus anime*
5.	AS. *De proposicionibus insolubilibus*
6.	A6. *[Questiones et dubia super viii libros physicorum]*
	A7. *Summa de ente [Summa intellectualium]*
7.	A7.I.a. *De ente in communi*
8.	A7.I.b. *De ente primo in communi*
9.	A7.I.c. *Purgans errores circa veritates in communi*
10.	A7.I.d. *Purgans errores circa universalia in communi*
11.	A7.I.e. *De universalibus*
12.	A7.I.f. *De tempore [De individuacione temporis]*
13.	A7.I.g. *De ente predicamentali*
14.	AT.II.a. *De intelleccione dei*
15.	AT.II.b. *De sciencia dei*
16.	A7.II.c. *De volucione dei*
17.	A7.II.d. *De trinitate [De personarum distinccione]*

---

[1] See Anne Hudson, "The Development of John Wyclif's *Summa Theologiae*," in *John Wyclif: Logica, Politica, Teologia*, ed. M. Fumagalli, B. Brocchieri, and S. Simonetta (Florence, 2003), pp. 57–70; and Hudson, "Cross-Referencing in Wyclif's Latin Works," in *The Medieval Church: Universities, Heresies and Religious Life*, ed. P. Biller and B. Dobson (Suffolk, 1999), pp. 193–215.

Section B: Pastoralia: *Sermons, Commentaries and Practical Theology*

Section C: Materia ad hominem: *Correspondence and* Responsiones

Section D: Homo publicus: *General Petitions and Protestations*

Section E: Polemica contra Papatum *I:*
On Disendowment, the Schism, the Despenser Crusade

Section F: Polemica contra Papatum *II:*
On the *"Four Sects"* and the Secta Christi

JOHN WYCLIF, C. 1331–1384

Andrew E. Larsen

Fourteenth-Century Oxford

Oxford in the middle of the fourteenth century, the Oxford in which Wyclif conducted most of his career, was an institution in transition.[1] Down to the end of the thirteenth century, Oxford had operated largely in the shadow of its older sister, the University of Paris, so that intellectual activity at Oxford tended to mirror philosophical and theological concerns at Paris.[2] In England, a Parisian education was considered more prestigious than an Oxford education, to judge from the academic backgrounds of leading English ecclesiastics. But early in the fourteenth century, Oxford emerged from the Parisian shadow and began producing a large number of talented and distinctly English thinkers, including William of Ockham, Walter Chatton, Richard FitzRalph, Adam Wodeham, and many others. Whereas earlier scholars had often tended to begin their university education at Oxford and then move to Paris to finish it, by the 1320s, this was becoming uncommon, and a Parisian education was becoming less important for episcopal preferment, although an Oxford degree was hardly a guarantee to high office.[3] Intellectually, the period from 1315 to 1340 was, in William Courtenay's phrase, "the Golden Age of English Scholasticism."

But after this, Oxford began its decline.[4] This decline has traditionally been blamed on the Black Death, but in fact the Black Death does not appear to have hit Oxford heavily.[5] The mortality rate for

[1] My thanks to Kira Barnes, Anne Hudson, Ian Levy, Stephen Lahey, and Steve Muhlberger for helpful comments and advice on this essay.
[2] William J. Courtenay, *Schools and Scholars in Fourteenth Century England*, (Princeton, 1987), pp. 149–57.
[3] Courtenay, *Schools*, pp. 151, 154; Jean Dunbabin, "Careers and Vocations," in *The History of the University of Oxford*, ed. J.I. Catto and Ralph Evans, (Oxford, 1984), 1:565–605, at p. 590.
[4] Courtenay, *Schools*, pp. 327–48.
[5] William Courtenay, "The Black Death and English Higher Education," *Speculum* 55 (1980), 698–714; *Schools*, pp. 331–32, at pp. 702–5.

students and masters appears to have been closer to twenty percent than the forty percent average for the clergy. Nor were the 1350s a period of sharp decline in the volume of writings being produced; it is possible to identify more than a half-dozen philosophers and an equal number of theologians actively writing at Oxford during the decade. But the philosophical works of this period are mostly of an introductory level, while the theological works tend to be shorter. Wyclif's *De propositionibus insolubilibus* and *De logica*, which he explicitly says are written for beginning students, fit into this trend toward introductory philosophy.[6]

Rather than the Black Death, the decline of Oxford's intellectual life has its roots in the late 1330s and 1340s. The trend toward shorter and simpler philosophical works began in the 1330s, not the 1350s.[7] One cause is the declining recruitment among the Franciscans in the wake of the Poverty Controversy in the 1320s and 1330s. A reduction in the number of new Franciscan recruits in the 1320s and 30s meant a decline in the number of talented Franciscan students entering Oxford in the late 1330s and 1340s, with a corresponding decline in the level of intellectual ferment taking place there.[8] Another important factor in Oxford's decline was the development of alternatives to Oxford, including the expansion of Cambridge, and the rise of mendicant *studia* at London, Norwich, York, and elsewhere.[9] These developments would have taken time to be felt at Oxford, but they help explain the scholarly decline that was becoming pronounced by the 1360s. The Black Death may also have caused a drop in the number of masters of grammar who were responsible for training students before they entered the university.[10] This would have resulted in fewer and less well-prepared students arriving in Oxford in the later 1350s and afterward, which would have had an impact on the level of academic achievement. In the 1350s, there were also problems with so-called "wax doctors," mendicants who were granted exemptions from normal requirements such

---

[6] Courtenay, *Schools*, p. 349; Catto, "Wyclif," p. 190.
[7] Courtenay, *Schools*, p. 346. In some sense, the number of works produced in the 1350s represents a brief revival, not a new decline.
[8] Courtenay, *Schools*, p. 331.
[9] Catto, "Wyclif," pp. 176–8; Courtenay, *Schools*, pp. 88–117.
[10] Courtenay, "Black Death," pp. 706–7.

as regency by virtue of their political connections.[11] Such men, while probably few in number, would hardly have contributed to the intellectual life of the university in any meaningful way. Finally, by the 1370s, and perhaps as early as the 1350s, there was a shift taking place from theology to law as the "popular" subject. Law was replacing theology as the academic vehicle to episcopal appointment, so that talented and ambitious men who might have studied theology in the 1320s and 1330s were studying law in the 1370s and beyond.[12] By the 1350s, it was possible for a student to study law without having first received a masters of arts.[13]

This period was also a time of considerable controversy within the university (which may have in itself contributed to an academic decline by diverting scholars into internal disputes). The largest dispute centered around the quarrel between Richard FitzRalph, former chancellor of Oxford, now archbishop of Armagh and prominent preacher at Avignon, and the friars over issues of pastoral rights and duties.[14] In 1350, FitzRalph was preaching against the Augustinians in London, Coventry, and Deddington, and perhaps even at Oxford. He was supported by Adalbert Ranconis and Adam Easton, among others, while the Augustinian Geoffrey Hardeby led the friars' attack and sought to undercut FitzRalph's theory of dominion, which was the core of the attack on the friars and which was based heavily on Augustinian theology. Another Augustinian Friar, John Kedington, attempted to turn FitzRalph's arguments around by asserting that the mendicants had a superior dominion. For his efforts, the university forced Kedington to recant, fined him (and through him his entire order), and essentially ended his teaching career by forbidding

---

[11] See *Munimenta Academica*, ed. H. Anstey, (Rolls Series 50) (London, 1868), 1:206–8, (hereafter cited as "RS") for a complaint about two wax doctors; M.W. Sheehan, "The Religious Orders 1220–1370," in *The History of the University of Oxford*, ed. J.I. Catto and Ralph Evans, (Oxford, 1984), 1:193–221, at p. 208.

[12] Courtenay, *Schools*, pp. 366–8; John Fletcher, "Inter-Faculty Disputes in Late Medieval Oxford," in *Studies in Church History Subsidia 5: From Ockham to Wyclif*, ed. Anne Hudson and Michael Wilks, (London, 1987), pp. 331–42, at pp. 338–41.

[13] Fletcher, "Disputes," p. 338.

[14] Aubrey Gwynn, *The English Austin Friars in the Time of Wyclif* (Oxford, 1940), pp. 80–9; Katherine Walsh, *A Fourteenth-Century Scholar and Primate: Richard FitzRalph in Oxford, Avignon, and Armagh*, (Oxford, 1981), pp. 349–451; Carolly Erickson, "The Fourteenth-Century Franciscans and Their Critics: II. Poverty, Jurisdiction, and Internal Change," in *Franciscan Studies* 36 (1976), 108–47, at pp. 117–19; Catto, "Wyclif," p. 180–83.

him to teach without the unanimous opinion of the theology masters, the chancellor, and the proctors.[15] These debates over dominion were taking place during Wyclif's time as an arts student and must certainly have left an impression on him. Pastoral duties became a recurrent topic of discussion at Oxford in the next century, and not least in the thought of Wyclif.

The dispute between FitzRalph and the friars was only one aspect of the political tension within Oxford between the mendicants on the one hand and the regular and secular students on the other. The complaint over the wax doctors involved a protest against the mendicants violating the university's rules. In 1357, a Friar John was forced to apologize for having dishonored a Benedictine student, while another mendicant was required to apologize to the entire body of arts students for having disparaged them.[16] Kedington's censure, which was unusually severe, is best understood as the university making him the focus of hostility against the mendicants in general. Shortly before 1365, the university attempted to forbid friars from recruiting candidates who were under 18, but in that year, Urban V ruled against them, and in 1366, Parliament rejected the rule as well.[17]

In 1366, a dispute broke out between the Benedictine Uthred of Boldon and the Dominicans, led by William Jordan, that culminated in 1368 with Archbishop Simon Langham issuing a condemnation of articles connected to both men.[18] Significantly, this conflict coincides with a dispute between the Benedictines and the seculars over Canterbury College, a dispute in which John Wyclif played a key role.[19] A third censure followed, probably sometime in the mid-1370s, although Wyclif, our only source for this incident, does not include a date for it. A faction of seculars within the university, led quite

---

[15] For John Kedington's case, see *Munimenta Academica*, 1:208–11; Andrew E. Larsen, "The Oxford 'School of Heretics': The Unexamined Case of Friar John," *Vivarium* 37 (1999), 168–77.

[16] *Munimenta*, pp. 207–7.

[17] Sheehan, "Religious Orders," p. 208.

[18] For the Condemnations of 1368, see Mildred Elizabeth Marcett, *Uthred de Boldon, Friar William Jordan, and Piers Plowman*, (New York, 1938); David Knowles, "The Censured Opinions of Uthred of Boldon," in *Proceedings of the British Academy* 1951, pp. 306–42, and Andrew E. Larsen, *Popular and Academic Heresy Before the Time of Wyclif*, (Ph.D. diss., University of Wisconsin,1998), pp. 198–216.

[19] See below, p. 14.

possibly by William Barton, brought charges against an unidentified Franciscan who had preached about the "poverty and state of the primitive church" (*ex predicacione pauperatatis et status primitive ecclesie*).[20] From what Wyclif tells us, this must have been a formal censure, because the Franciscan was forced to publicly recant his ideas and assert the opposite in the church of St Mary's. Without knowing more about the case, it is hard to truly analyze this incident, but it is clearly part of the wider debate over clerical endowment, and like the other two censures, it is also clearly a reflection of tension between the orders at Oxford, although Wyclif seems to link the censure of the Franciscan to an attack upon himself.

In the entire first half of the fourteenth century, there was only one known academic censure, the Censure of 1315. But in the space of approximately 20 years, between 1358 and the mid-1370s, there had been three censures, all of which show signs of political motivation.[21] Most academic censures at Oxford have received a reasonable amount of scholarly attention, usually emphasizing the philosophical and theological issues involved, but there has been relatively little attention directed toward the motivations behind such condemnations. The unspoken assumption has tended to be that academic censure was primarily driven by a desire to suppress heresy and perhaps by a discomfort with the philosophical ideas that lay behind certain condemned propositions. However, to see the censures as only being about the suppression of heresy is to overlook important elements that drove censure.

To make sense of heresy charges and academic censures, it is useful to look at heresy charges from two angles.[22] Heresy can be viewed

---

[20] Wyclif, *De veritate Sacrae Scripturae* 14, ed. R. Buddensieg, (London, 1905), 1:356; Catto, "Wyclif," pp. 206–7.

[21] On the subject of academic condemnation, see William J. Courtenay, "Inquiry and Inquisition: Academic Freedom in Medieval Universities," *Church History* 58 (1989), pp. 168–81; J.M.M.H. Thijssen, "Academic Heresy and Intellectual Freedom at the University of Paris, 1200–1378" in *Centres of Learning: Learning and Location in Pre-Modern Europe and the Near East*, ed. J.W. Drijvers and A.A. MacDonald, (Leiden, 1995), pp. 215–28; *Censure and Heresy at the University of Paris 1200–1400* (Philadelphia, 1998), pp. 1–39; Gregory S. Moule, *Corporate Theory, Canon Law, and the Censure of Academic Heresy at the University of Paris in the Fourteenth Century*, (Ph.D. diss., University of Wisconsin, 1999).

[22] See Talal Asad, "Medieval Heresy: an Anthropological View," *Social History* 11 (1986), pp. 345–62; Andrew E. Larsen, "Are All Lollards Lollards?," in *Lollards and Their Influence in Late Medieval England*, ed. Fiona Somerset, Jill C. Havens, and Derrick G. Pitard, (Woodbridge, 2003).

from the accused's standpoint, with an eye to establishing the facts of the matter. What did the accused say or do that caused charges to be brought, and what did the accused mean by those statements and actions? To what extent might those statements or actions qualify as unorthodox by the theological standards of the time? Did the conclusion of the case reasonably reflect the accused's orthodoxy or lack thereof? But heresy charges can also be viewed from the top down, with an eye to understanding the actions of the authorities. Condemnation for heresy involved the exercise of ecclesiastical authority for specific reasons, which might involve a desire to protect the truths of Christian faith, but which might also involve other concerns.[23] Thus a whole second range of questions needs to be considered. Who brought the charges and why? Was the motive for the charges purely a concern for heresy, or were personal feeling or political factors involved? How did the accusers and authorities in the case understand the charges and issues at hand? Why did they reach the verdict they came to?

These are, of course, problematic questions. Sources often omit much of the information necessary to definitely answer them. Evidence is often biased, because it most commonly takes the form of charges brought by the accuser while omitting material from the viewpoint of the accused. In many cases, we have no information about who brought the initial charges. Nor is it always easy to determine whether a particular statement could be considered orthodox or unorthodox. This is particularly true in matters around academic disputes, since theological debate in universities often took place at the cutting edge of theology and about issues whose orthodoxy had not been definitively established. Classroom debate enjoyed a privileged status that might enable an accused to insist that a dubious statement in the classroom had been made as a quote of another's opinion (*recitative*), or that he had made the statement only for the sake of discussion (*disputative*), and that he had not actually asserted the statement to be true (*assertive*).[24] By at least 1330, it was standard at Oxford for scholars to take an oath before inception that they would not teach anything contrary to the faith, and that they would only discuss suspect ideas *disputative* and not *assertive*. This oath, called the *revocatio condi-*

---

[23] Asad, *Medieval Heresy*, p. 356.
[24] Thijssen, *Censure and Heresy*, p. 30.

tionalis, protected the scholar from accusations that he had pertinaciously defended a heretical idea by granting him a presumption of non-pertinacity, so long as he agreed to formally recant the suspect ideas with a *revocatio actualis*.[25] One result of this was to place the emphasis during accusations of suspect teaching on the ideas involved, which tends to obscure the identity of the person making the statement and of the accusers.[26] There is also a certain vagueness in the terminology employed in documents dealing with these cases. While there was a relatively sharp distinction between a statement that was heretical (*hereticus*) and one that was merely false or erroneous (*falsus, erroneous*), it is harder to see the technical distinctions between statements that were "close to intolerable errors" (*erroribus intolerabilibus proximi*), "openly wrong" (*apertissime iniqui*), "repugnant to the catholic faith" (*fidei catholice repunantes*), "scandalous" (*scandalum*), "ill-sounding" (*male sonans*), "offensive to pious ears" (*piarum aurium offensiva*) or a host of other terms that were used. For example, is a proposition that is "repugnant to the catholic faith" worse than one that is "openly wrong?" All of these were below the level of heresy, but some focus on the formal doctrinal content of the statement, while others emphasize a statement's potential to mislead the uneducated.[27]

Despite the difficulty in answering many of these questions, accusations must be viewed from both sides in order to make full sense

---

[25] Courtenay, "Inquiry and Inquisition," pp. 178–9: Moule, pp. 152–64.

[26] The case of Uthred of Bolden is unusual in that we know the identity of both accuser and accused; condemnations and censures issued in 1277, 1284, 1286, 1315, and 1366 all avoided specifying the identity of the author of the propositions, even in cases such as 1286 and 1366 when the condemning authority was the Archbishop of Canterbury acting outside of the university. In 1357, the author of the censured articles was partially identified (his last name and order being omitted but probably not intentionally), but in this case, the purpose of the censure was distinctly to punish John Kedington for having offended the university politically.

[27] There is also some vagueness in the terminology of condemnation. There is a tendency among scholars to distinguish a 'censure', which occurred within a university and which carried only the weight of the university masters and chancellor, from a 'condemnation', which occurred outside a university and had the authority of a bishop behind it. But a *censura* dealt with excommunication, interdict, or suspension of an individual, not with ideas. A better distinction would be between a prohibition (*prohibitio*), which forbids discussion or dissemination of an idea, regardless of its truth or falsity, and a condemnation (*condemnatio* or *reprobatio*), which declares an idea to be false and therefore beyond discussion or dissemination. But even here the actual usage of terms was not always consistent. When Archbishop Kilwardby issued his condemnation of thirty propositions, he used the term '*condemnatio*', but later said that he was only forbidding discussion of the propositions at Oxford, not condemning them as heretical. See Thijssen, *Censure and Heresy*, p. x.

of them. For a heresy accusation to occur and produce formal charges
of some sort, two conditions needed to exist. The accused had to
have said or done something which could reasonably be construed
as heretical by some standard. Heresy accusations rarely occurred
against those who were not in some way vulnerable to an accusation. The few exceptions to this rule are essentially political trials to
which an accusation of heresy has been added. In general, it was
necessary for an individual to make theologically dubious statements
of some sort before an accusation could occur.[28] A statement made
disputative or *recitative* would be less likely to produce an attack than
one made *assertive*, but which category a statement fell into could
be open to debate in many cases. But John Kedington, Uthred of
Boldon, and the unnamed Franciscan would not have been censured
if they had not made statements that were dubious enough to leave
them open to attack. Thus, such statements are a necessary cause
for formal heresy charges.

But theologically dubious statements were not by themselves a
sufficient cause for formal charges. Formal charges required that episcopal or university authorities have a desire or motive to intervene
and bring charges. In the absence of a motive to bring charges, they
did not occur. It is not enough to assume that bishops were automatically concerned enough about heresy to oppose it. Before the
late fourteenth century, English bishops as a whole seem to have
been generally disinterested in the problem of heresy; surviving episcopal records from the fourteenth century up to the 1380s reveal
only about a dozen cases in all, and this is not entirely explainable
with the argument that there simply was little heresy in England.
Thus in cases of heresy, we must ask why a particular bishop or
archbishop chose to bring charges. Was he sincerely concerned about
the theological issues? Did he have political or personal motives?
Was he under pressure from other authorities, either ecclesiastical
or secular, to bring charges, or not bring charges? In the context of
the university, dubious statements were made all the time in the
course of teaching activity. What caused a statement made *disputative*

---

[28] In the following discussion, I use the term "theologically dubious statements"
as a shorthand for statements which might be reasonably construed to fall outside
the bounds of orthodoxy; the term is not intended to argue that such statements
were, in fact, heretical.

to be treated as a statement made *assertative*? Why did John Kedington's statements during a determination arouse such a strong response? Why did the archbishop of Canterbury become concerned about Uthred's classroom theories only in 1368, almost a full decade after Uthred was a regent master? The answer in both cases is that wider political tensions made these two men lightning rods for censure. In a different political climate, it is possible that neither man's ideas would have provoked any formal action. To fully understand these censures, we must assess both the necessary and the sufficient causes, and not simply the necessary ones. And, looking forward a little bit, these distinctions can help us make sense of key moments in Wyclif's career.

If Oxford in the period from the 1350s to the 1370s was politically charged enough for different segments of the university population to orchestrate academic censure against their opponents, it becomes clearer why intellectual activity at Oxford was declining. Intellectual adventurousness was more likely to be punished in this period than it had been earlier in the century. An atmosphere of academic censure helped stifle intellectual discussion. It would be a mistake, however, to see this as the primary cause of the decline. Oxford may have experienced political tensions that occasionally erupted into censure, but there was nothing like an on-going academic witch-hunt. Archbishop Courtenay's purge was unprecedented, although not completely without foreshadowing.

John Wyclif's Early Life

Having considered the environment at Oxford in the later fourteenth century, let us now turn to the career of John Wyclif. The starting point for understanding Wyclif's early life is 1356, the first firm date we have in his life.[29] In the late spring of that year, he was already

---

[29] The most comprehensive study of Wyclif's life is still H.B. Workman, *John Wyclif: A Study in the English Medieval Church*, (Oxford, 1926; repr. Eugene, 2001) (hereafter cited as "Workman"), but at more than eighty years old, it is outdated on many points; similarly, Hastings Rashdall's entry on Wyclif in the *Dictionary of National Biography* is now obsolete and has been superseded by Anne Hudson and Anthony Kenny's article on Wyclif in the new *Oxford Dictionary of National Biography* (Oxford, 2004), 60: 616–30. Other important works on Wyclif's life include Gwynn,

a bachelor of arts.[30] Under normal conditions, that status took about five years to achieve, which would put his matriculation at approximately 1350, give or take a year. Since students normally entered Oxford at fourteen or fifteen, this would suggest that Wyclif was born c. 1335. The Black Death struck Oxford in 1349, and it has long been assumed that it severely disrupted the functioning of the university, which did not return completely to normal until 1353.[31] This means that Wyclif might have matriculated any year between 1346 and 1350, depending on how much progress he was able to make in his studies during the disruption. This in turn means that he might have been born as early as 1331, but it is difficult to see how he could have been born any earlier than this.[32] However, as already noted, in William Courtenay's analysis of the impact of the Black Death on Oxford, he found little evidence of severe disruption and a strikingly low mortality rate among university scholars,

---

Austin Friars, pp. 210–79; Joseph H. Dahmus, *The Prosecution of John Wyclyf*, (New Haven, 1952) (hereafter cited as "Dahmus"); K.B. MacFarlane, *John Wyclif and the Beginning of English Nonconformity* (London, 1952) (whose usefulness is restricted by its lack of footnotes); A.B. Emden, "Wyclif," in *Biographical Register of the University of Oxford*, (Oxford, 1957–9), 3:2103–6; J.A. Robson, *Wyclif and the Oxford Schools*, (Cambridge,1961), pp. 9–31; Anthony Kenny, *Wyclif*, (Oxford, 1985); and Jeremy Catto, "Wyclif and Wycliffism at Oxford 1356–1430," in *The History of the University of Oxford*, ed. J.I. Catto and Ralph Evans, (Oxford: 1992), 2:186–219. Also helpful are Geoffrey Martin, "Wyclif, Lollards, and Historians, 1384–1984," in *Lollards and Their Influence*, pp. 237–50, and Stephen E. Lahey, *Philosophy and Politics in the Thought of John Wyclif*, (Cambridge: 2003), pp. 9–23, both of which survey the historiography on Wyclif.

[30] Robson, *Wyclif*, pp. 10–14; see p. 10, n. 5 for the document itself. For a description of the arts curriculum and the time it took, see Courtenay, *Schools*, pp. 30–35.

[31] Workman, 1:82–3; M.J. Wilks, "The Early Oxford Wyclif: Papalist or Nominalist?," in *Church History* 5 (1969), 69–98, at p. 90 n. 2.

[32] Nineteenth-century scholars, such as Lewis and Lechler, tended to date his birth to 1324. More recently, 1327 has been suggested; M.J. Wilks, "John Wyclif, Reformer, c. 1327–1384" in *Dictionnaire de Spiritualité*, xvi, cols. 1501–1512, repr. in *Wyclif: Political Ideas and Practice: Papers by Michael Wilks*, (Oxford, 2000), pp. 1–15. These dates have the merit of putting him in his mid to late-50s when he suffered his fatal stroke and allowing him more time to produce his considerable volume of writings. But it is not impossible that a man in his late 40s could suffer such a stroke, and, as William Courtenay, *Schools*, pp. 348–49, has pointed out, Wyclif's academic output was probably produced in a shorter period than normally assumed. The primary objection to a date in the 1320s is that it puts his matriculation at some point in his early 20s, an unusually advanced age for a new university student and something for which there is no particular evidence.

which makes it improbable that Wyclif was significantly delayed in his academic progress.[33] Thus, on the balance, he is more likely to have been born around 1335 than 1330.

A second complicating issue is the question of his ordination to the priesthood. He must have been ordained as a priest by 1361 at the latest, when he received the living of Fillingham. However, a record exists of the ordination at St. Mary's Abbey, York, of "John, son of William of Wykliff," and "John, son of Simon of Wycliff'" in September of 1351.[34] In the wake of the Black Death, both of these men received rapid advancement through the lower orders of sub-deacon and deacon in the months before their ordination as priests. If Wyclif was born in 1335, he would have been sixteen years old, way too young for ordination, even during the crisis of the Black Death, when permission was given to ordain men as young as twenty-one.[35] If he was born in 1331, he would have been just old enough for ordination late in 1351 to be plausible, but as we have seen, 1331 is probably too early.

Working from a birth date somewhere between 1331 and 1335, we can fill in some gaps about his family, although we have to distinguish between multiple men named John Wyclif. The man traditionally identified as the famous John Wyclif was born in Teesdale, in modern-day Richmondshire, in the North Riding of Yorkshire, to the Wyclif or Wycliffe family, members of the lower gentry. His parents were Roger Wyclif, the lord of Wyclif, and his wife Catherine. They had an older son William Wyclif, who was married to a woman named Frances (and who also had a son named John), and a younger son John.[36] This John Wyclif, however, cannot be either of the men ordained in York in 1351, whose fathers were respectively William and Simon. By 1363, John the son of Roger had inherited the manor of Wyclif, and he and Catherine jointly disposed of the living of the local church in 1369, which suggests that they were mother and son, (which means it is unlikely that the famous John Wyclif was the son

---

[33] Courtenay, "Black Death," pp. 702–5.
[34] York, Borthwick Institute, reg. 10A, Reg. Zouche (York), fos 49v, 50r, 52r, 53r; Catto, "Wyclif," p. 187; Wilks, "John Wyclif," p. 1.
[35] William J. Dohar, *The Black Death and Pastoral Leadership: The Diocese of Hereford in the Fourteenth Century* (Philadelphia, 1995), p. 70.
[36] Workman, 1:37–42.

of the William who was the son of Roger).[37] From all of this, it should be clear that very few details of Wyclif's early life can be regarded as firmly established, and the problem is compounded by a large number of potential relatives, men who employ the name "Wyclif" in some capacity.[38] At this point, it is impossible to definitively say which of the four potential John Wyclifs we have looked at was the famous theologian, but the traditional identification appears most likely.[39]

As already noted, John Wyclif enrolled as an arts student in Oxford around 1350, and became a bachelor of arts by 1356 and a probationary fellow at Merton College, although for unknown reasons he apparently did not complete his probationary year. Within a year or two of this he incepted as a master; although the exact date of his inception is unknown, by 1360 he was listed as a master, holding the office of Master of Balliol.[40] The reasons for his move from Merton to Balliol are unknown, but probably have to do with the

---

[37] It is possible, though, that the John son of William who was ordained in 1351 might have been the famous John's nephew, but in that case he must have predeceased his father, since the manor of Wyclif passed to William's younger brother John and not to his son.

[38] John son of William cannot be the son of the William Wyclif who held the living of Wyclif from 1363 to 1369, because that William was a priest who obtained a license for non-residency in 1365 to study of Oxford (and was certainly too young to have an adult son in 1350, even if he had ignored his obligation to be celibate). This William was a fellow of Balliol in 1361 when John Wyclif was master of Balliol. Thus we can identify four distinct John Wyclifs, two or possibly three distinct William Wyclifs, a Simon Wyclif, and a Robert Wyclif who held the living of Wyclif in 1362, and who may or may not be the Robert of Wyclif who held livings at St Crux, Kirkeby Raveneswath, and St Rumbald in Yorkshire and who was nominated to a prebend in Dublin Cathedral. This Robert is likely a relative of some sort, since he acted as a mainpernor for the famous John Wyclif in 1371. For Robert Wyclif, see Anne Hudson, "Wyclif and the North: The Evidence from Durham," in *Life and Thought in the Northern Church c. 1100–c. 1700: Essays in Honour of Claire Cross*, ed. Diane Wood, (Woodbridge, 1999), pp. 87–103 at pp. 87–88. There are also at least two other John Wyclifs in Oxford in the 1350s and 1360s. We must either assume that the Wyclif family was an extremely large one, or more likely that "Wyclif" was in use by more than one family.

[39] Workman, Dahmus, and most other earlier scholars accept the identification with the John Wyclif who became the lord of Wyclif. More recent scholars, including Catto, Wilks, and Hudson and Kenny, all favor one of the two men ordained in 1351, but have not advanced any argument against the traditional identification. Since the men ordained in 1351 are unlikely candidates to be the famous Wyclif, we must also acknowledge that we cannot say when the famous Wyclif was ordained, other than that it was in 1361 at the latest.

[40] Robson, *Wyclif*, p. 13; Catto, "Wyclif," p. 187.

patronage of Archbishop Thoresby of York and the presence of other Yorkshiremen at Balliol.[41] The fact that he was made Master of Balliol suggests that Wyclif had some prior connection with Balliol, and thus it is possible that Wyclif spent at least part of his undergraduate career there, as would be typical for a northerner.[42] A year later, he resigned the Mastership of Balliol to take on the living of Fillingham, and a year after that he was unsuccessfully put forward for a canonry at York. During his regency in arts, he wrote his earliest extant works, including the first parts of *De logica* and *De propositionibus insolubilibus*.[43]

A year later, in 1363, Bishop Buckingham of Lincoln granted Wyclif a license for non-residency in order to study theology. The process of studying theology normally required a seven year period of study to become a bachelor, and an additional two years to become a master of theology, although this process was slightly compressed by the 1350s.[44] What we know of Wyclif's progression during this period fits well into this scheme. When his non-residency was renewed in 1368 he was not yet a bachelor; documents refer to him as a bachelor of theology in May of 1370 and in January of the next year, but in December of 1373, he is called a master, while John Kynyngham (Cunningham, Keningham) shifts from referring to Wyclif as "magister" in his first determination to calling him "doctor" in his second. Thus his inception must have occurred between mid-1371 and mid-1372.[45] In this period, he continued to write on logic, including the questions on Aristotle's *Physics*, the *proposiciones Wyclif in determinacione sua*, and the *Summa de ente*, but he also began writing

---

[41] Catto, "Wyclif," p. 187, Wilks, "John Wyclif," p. 1.

[42] The notion that Wyclif started out at Balliol, transferred to Merton after graduating, and then went back to Balliol is, however, a strange one. It is not easy to imagine a scenario that would justify this series of moves, unless we attribute it to his sometimes difficult personality. Such moves might have delayed his graduation by a year, thus making 1349 or perhaps 1348 the earliest reasonable matriculation date.

[43] Hudson and Kenny, "Wyclif, John," p. 622. In general, I have followed their dating in this article as being the most current available. See also Lahey, *Philosophy and Politics*, pp. 9–10, and W.R. Thomson, *The Latin Writings of John Wyclif*, (Toronto, 1983), pp. 1–39.

[44] Courtenay, *Schools*, pp. 41–42.

[45] CPL, 4:193; *Fasciculi Zizianiorum*, ed. Walter Waddington Shirley, (RS 5) (London, 1858), pp. 4, 14, 43; Robson, *Wyclif*, pp. 15, 163; Catto, "Wyclif," p. 188; Thomson, pp. 227–9 (but see Courtenay, *Schools*, p. 191, n. 59).

on theology (as would be expected), including *De composicione hominis, De benedicta incarnacione,* and the *Postilla in totam Bibliam.*[46]

During the start of his theological studies, Wyclif took rooms at what was then known as Queen's Hall, but in 1365 Archbishop Simon Islip appointed Wyclif Warden of Canterbury College.[47] Canterbury College was founded in 1361 as a mixed college of seculars and Benedictine monks from Canterbury intended to help meet the dearth of educated clergy resulting from the Black Death. This arrangement proved unworkable and in 1365 Islip reformed the college as a secular institution with new statutes. He appointed Wyclif as the Warden at the time of this reorganization, but Islip's actions angered the monks, who refused to accept Islip's violation of the original arrangements. When Islip died in 1366, the monks immediately appealed the matter to his successor, Simon Langham, who ruled in their favor, ordered the reinstatement of the college's original warden. Wyclif and the other seculars refused to accept this ruling, and when Langham ordered their expulsion, Wyclif appealed the matter to Pope Urban V. Wyclif remained resident at Canterbury until 1370, when Urban ruled in Langham's and the monks' favor and ordered Wyclif and the others to vacate the college, which they did. Given Wyclif's conflict with Langham during this period, his renewal of non-residency in 1368 seems prudent.

Wyclif's contemporary and one-time friend, the Franciscan William Woodford, asserted that this conflict was the origin of Wyclif's animosity against the mendicant orders, and Thomas Walsingham makes a similar accusation.[48] While most scholars have tended to accept this claim, it is worth keeping in mind that it was made retrospectively by someone hostile to Wyclif, and Woodford's statement that Wyclif's teaching was the product of corruption and disappointment is clearly intended to undermine Wyclif's criticisms. Wyclif's only

---

[46] Hudson and Kenny, "Wyclif, John," p. 622.

[47] The details of this conflict are to be found in H.S. Cronin, "John Wyclif, the Reformer, and Canterbury Hall, Oxford" in *Transactions of the Royal Historical Society* 8 (1914), 55–76; see also Workman, 1:172–94; Robson, *Wyclif,* pp. 15–17; Catto, "Wyclif," pp. 187–88. Rashdall rejects the identification of Wyclif the Reformer with Wyclif the Warden of Canterbury Hall.

[48] *Fasc. Ziz.,* p. 517; Thomas Walsingham, *The St Albans Chronicle: The Chronica Majora of Thomas Walsingham,* ed. John Taylor, Wendy R. Childs, and Leslie Watkiss, (Oxford, 2003), pp. 74–5; Workman, 1:186.

direct comment on the conflict occurs in *De ecclesia*, where he says that Islip wanted "*pure clerici saeculares*" at the college and that Islip sinned by appropriating a parish church, but that Langham sinned more greatly by changing the arrangement.[49] He does refer to Langham as "Antisymon", contrasting Langham unfavorably to Simon Islip and drawing a parallel to 'antichrist' and perhaps Simon Magus as well. This rhetoric is a foretaste of Wyclif's later invective, and given the lengths the suit went to, hard feelings are understandable. But it is still a stretch to connect the antimendicant sentiments Wyclif showed later in life to this incident. He was still on good terms with the mendicants as late as 1379, years after the final verdict on Canterbury College. And it is important to remember that Wyclif's primary opponents in this dispute were not mendicants, but Benedictines.

Service to the Crown

It seems likely that Wyclif entered royal service for the first time sometime shortly after the final verdict in the dispute over Canterbury College. We know that in 1371 he served as an executor for William Askeby, the Chancellor of the Exchequer, and he may have come to the Crown's attention with the help of Richard, Lord Scrope of Bolton, who owned land in Richmondshire.[50] The same year, the Crown granted Wyclif a portion of the tithes of Ludgershall, where he was serving as rector.[51] There is no clear evidence that he was directly serving the Crown before 1374, but he claims to have been at the Parliament of 1371, where he heard an argument for the partial disendowment of the Church advanced by two Austin friars.[52]

---

[49] Wyclif, *De Ecclesia* 16, ed. J. Loserth, (London, 1886), p. 371; Cronin, "John Wyclif," p. 68; Workman, 1:193; Catto, "Wyclif," p. 188.

[50] Catto, "Wyclif," p. 199 n. 83; Hudson and Kenny, "Wyclif, John," pp. 617–18.

[51] E 159/147, Commissiones, Easter; George Holmes, *The Good Parliament*, (Oxford, 1975), pp. 167–68.

[52] Wyclif, *De civili dominio* 1, ed. Johann Loserth, (London, 1900), 2.7; see also Aubrey Gwynn, *English Austin Friars*, pp. 212–16. Catto, "Wyclif," p. 200, n. 83, rejects the notion that Wyclif was present at the Parliament of 1371, but Workman, 1:210, Gwynn, *Austin Friars*, p. 213, and Holmes, *Good Parliament*, p. 168, all feel that he was present. If he was not present on Edward's business, we are left with the small question of why the Crown granted him the tithes of Ludgershall just a few months later.

Wyclif's presence at this Parliament is most easily explained by the idea that he was serving the Crown or perhaps Lord Scrope in some capacity at the meeting, although his presence at this Parliament is not provable. Scrope was one of the leaders in an attack on the dominant roll of the higher clergy in English government. As a result of this attack, Bishop Wykeham surrendered the office of chancellor and Bishop Brantingham the office of treasurer, which was given to Scrope. The anticlericalism of this Parliament was to continue through the later Parliaments of the decade.

In 1374, Wyclif was appointed to a royal commission to discuss the question of papal provisions.[53] Papal financial demands had been a source of considerable concern in England since the late 1360s, and Edward III renewed the Statutes of Provisors and Praemunire in 1365. In 1373, Parliament had complained that papal provisions were undermining the rights of patrons and were impoverishing the kingdom. In May, a council was held to discuss the conflict over papal demands, including a demand for tribute based on King John's submission to Innocent III.[54] At the council, Uthred defended papal exactions, while Friar John Mardisley opposed him on the point. Wyclif may have been present at this discussion, based on evidence in his *Determinatio*, in which he responds to the arguments of the Benedictine theologian Uthred of Boldon and another monk, William Binham.[55] Binham's argument in the *Determinatio* deals with the tribute, which suggests that his argument was produced in relationship to the council. Wyclif's response to Binham was based, so he claims, on an argument "which I have heard was given in a certain council."[56] The language is ambiguous about whether Wyclif heard the arguments in person, or simply learned of their substance, and while we

---

[53] See Workman, 1:218–56, for a good explanation of the mission to Bruges, but Holmes, *Good Parliament*, pp. 7–62 provides a fuller look at the political issues surrounding it. See also Dahmus, pp. 4–5, and W.A. Pantin, *The English Church in the Fourteenth Century*, (Cambridge, 1955), pp. 87–91. The grant of power to the commission can be found in the *Calendar of Patent Rolls, Edward III, 1370–74*, p. 462.

[54] *Eulogium (historiarum sive temporis)* ed. F.S. Haydon, (RS 9) (London, 1858–63), 3:337–9; Workman, 1:228–30; Holmes, *Good Parliament*, p. 14; J.I. Catto, "An Alleged Great Council of 1374," *English Historical Review*, 82 (1967), 764–71. The *Eulogium* dates the Council to 1374, but Catto persuasively argues that it must have occurred in 1373; Workman's treatment of the incident is thus out of context.

[55] Wyclif, *Determinacio Johannis Wyclif ad argumenta magistri Outredi de Omesima monachi*, in *Opera Minora*, ed. Johann Loserth, (London, 1913), pp. 405–30.

[56] Wyclif, *Determinacio*, in *Opera Minora*, p. 417, 425.

cannot know for certain that he was there, he refers to himself in the *Determinatio* as a *"pecularis regis clericus,"* which seems to indicate special service to the Crown. It would also help explain his choice to be part of a second delegation to respond to Gregory's demands. However, as we shall see, the dating of the *Determinatio* is a complicated matter, and it is unwise to make an argument about Wyclif's service to the Crown based on this text.

An initial delegation from Edward III to Pope Gregory XI at Avignon demanded that the pope should cancel all currently unfulfilled reservations and should give up the practice of reservations and provisions. This commission, which included Bishop Gilbert of Bangor, Sir William Burton, Uthred of Boldon, and John Sheppey, a doctor of civil law, failed to resolve the matter. As Catto points out, Uthred's participation in the delegation was highly diplomatic, and probably intended as a gesture of moderation.[57]

In July, Edward sent the second delegation to Bruges to meet with papal delegates. The commission was lead by Bishop Gilbert and William Burton, but Uthred was not included, and Wyclif took his place.[58] The other members were Juan Guttierez, an agent of John of Gaunt, Simon de Multon, doctor of canon law, Robert Bealknap, a justice of the assizes, and John Henington, who is otherwise unknown. Departing in July, Wyclif was back in Oxford by September, and the delegation achieved nothing of note.[59] We know nothing of Wyclif's role in this meeting, but it has been speculated that Wyclif's views of papal provision may have contributed to the mission's failure.

In August of the next year, a third delegation was appointed. It included Burton, Guttierez, and Multon, and although John Gilbert was not formally a member, he remained active in the negotiations. Bealknap had become chief justice of common pleas, and was thus replaced, as apparently was John Henington, for unknown reasons.

---

[57] Catto, "Great Council," p. 771.

[58] On June 3, he was sent a letter summoning him to a council presumably related to this mission; the record of the letter's sending is at E 403/451.

[59] See A.K. McHardy, "John Wycliffe's Mission to Bruges: A Financial Footnote," *Journal of Theological Studies* 24 (1973), 521–22, for a brief discussion of the financing of his trip. He returned owing the Crown more than £7, which suggests that he returned sooner than expected and thus was expected to repay the excess amount he had been given. He did not repay until 1382; Holmes, *Good Parliament*, p. 20.

Wyclif was also replaced, and while we have no information about why, it is commonly thought that his opposition to papal provisions may have been the main reason. The new commission was led by Bishop Houghton of St David's and Ralph Erghum, John of Gaunt's chancellor. This new delegation was largely under the direction of Archbishop Simon Sudbury, who had just been translated from London to Canterbury with papal permission, and John of Gaunt.[60] Although there is nothing to suggest that Wyclif and Gaunt met at this time, Gaunt must certainly have become aware of Wyclif's participation in the second delegation (especially if Wyclif had played a role in the commission's failure to reach an agreement).

Gaunt's involvement in the second Bruges conference is key to understanding it. By 1374, he was emerging as one of the leading advocates for a peace treaty with France, which was to be negotiated under the auspices of Gregory XI.[61] But for this deal to work, the dispute over provision had to be resolved. The reformulated delegation dutifully negotiated a concordat to resolve the disputed issues, although it was not until 1377 that all the details had been finalized. Gregory XI settled a series of lawsuits over benefices in favor of the royal candidates, revoked a general reservation of benefices held by pluralists, and agreed to a series of episcopal appointments that suited the Crown, while Edward authorized the collection of a much-needed subsidy.[62] While these are not insignificant, neither side conceded anything of real consequence regarding future provisions, and the issue was to remain a problem in Anglo-Papal relations for another generation.

Wyclif's Livings

This is a convenient point to survey the livings associated with Wyclif. As already noted, in 1361, he received the living of Fillingham in

---

[60] For a brief biography of Simon of Sudbury, see Simon Walker, "Simon Sudbury," in the *Oxford Dictionary of National Biography*, 53: 271–73.

[61] Holmes, *Good Parliament*, pp. 49–56; Anthony Goodman, *John of Gaunt: The Exercise of Princely Power in Fourteenth-Century Europe*, (New York, 1992), pp. 53–55.

[62] Thomas Rymer, *Foedera, Conventiones, Literae, et Cujuscunque Generis Acta Publica*, (London, 1709), 3:1037, 1072; Pantin, *English Church*, pp. 90–91; Holmes, *Good Parliament*, pp. 46–49.

Lincolnshire, which was in the possession of Balliol College, and he appears to have resided there until 1363, when he obtained permission for non-residence to study theology. In 1362, the university unsuccessfully put his name forward for a canonry at York; he was turned down, but Urban V instead granted him a prebend at Aust in the church of Westbury-on-Trim. Wyclif failed to arrange a vicar for the church, although he appears to have held this benefice down to the time of his death.[63] Soon thereafter, perhaps by August of 1362 and certainly by that time the next year, Wyclif inherited the manor of Wyclif.[64]

Wyclif's status as a non-resident pluralist who failed to provide a vicar for his church has occasioned many comments, since it is incongruous to find a prominent critic of the Church being guilty of such an offense. Most scholars rise to Wyclif's defense on this point, and indeed it is important to realize that the system as it then existed placed Wyclif in something of a bind.[65] His income from Fillingham was probably barely sufficient for him to maintain himself at Oxford (although his income from the manor of Wyclif, if he held it, and the tithes from Ludgershall are generally overlooked when calculating his finances), and his income from Westbury was small enough that it would have been expended had he appointed a vicar. Had he done his duty as a priest, he would have had to leave Oxford, while pursuing his studies meant neglecting his parishes. Thus, as an absentee pluralist, he was arguably being pragmatic in accepting a system that he was not in a position to change. It is also possible that he had not come to completely oppose such practices at this point. But later in life, while still an absentee pluralist, he repeatedly denounced absenteeism. In *De veritate Sacrae Scripturae*, he insists that appointing a vicar does not absolve a priest from his duties.[66] In *De potestate papae*, he condemns prebends who fail to fulfill their

---

[63] Workman, 1:153, 156–71, Robson, *Wyclif*, p. 14.

[64] CPL, 4:193; Workman, 1:40–1; M.E.H. Lloyd, "John Wyclif and the Prebend of Lincoln," *English Historical Review*, 61 (1946), 388–94.

[65] For defenses of Wyclif's pluralism and non-residency, see Workman, 1:161–9; MacFarlane, *John Wyclif*, pp. 23–27. Workman argues that Wyclif's failure to provide a vicar was not due to a lack of concern but rather to an inability to find a suitable vicar owing to the problems created by the Black Death, a reasonable but entirely speculative argument.

[66] Wyclif, *De veritate* 26, 3:37.

obligations.[67] And in *De blasphemia*, he argues that non-residence cannot be justified by either studying at a university or serving in secular matters.[68] While Wyclif may have been being pragmatic early
in his career, it is hard to avoid the sense that his later denuncia-
tions have an odor of hypocrisy to them.

In 1368, shortly after renewing his license for non-residency, he
exchanged Fillingham for the living of Ludgershall in Buckingham-
shire.[69] At some point in 1373, Wyclif received a reservation for the
prebend of Caistor at Lincoln, but although the reservation was
renewed later that same year with permission to hold it in plurality
with Westbury, in 1375 it was given instead to Philip de Thornbury,
the illegitimate son of an English mercenary captain active in Italy,
much to Wyclif's bitterness.[70] Wyclif does seem to have actually held
the prebend for a brief time, because in 1378, his name appears on
a list of men who owe debts relating to first fruits.[71] Regardless of
whether he received Caistor or not, in April of 1374, Wyclif received
Lutterworth from the crown.[72] The timing of the grant is interesting, because it comes just before Wyclif's first definite act of service
to the Crown, namely the second Bruges delegation. Since it is
improbable that Wyclif would have been compensated for service he
had not yet performed, the grant of Lutterworth seems to reinforce
the notion that he was already in service to the Crown by 1374,
and the grant has generally been understood this way by scholars.[73]
Having received Lutterworth, Wyclif resigned Ludgershall, perhaps
as late as early 1376.[74] At the end of his life, he appears to have
held the manor of Wyclif and the livings of Westbury and Lutterworth.
In the matter of the Lincoln prebend, we must again acknowledge
a certain element of hypocrisy in Wyclif's character. At the same

---

[67] Wyclif, *De potestate papae* 12, ed. J. Loserth, (London, 1907), p. 359.
[68] Wyclif, *De blasphemia* 12, ed. M. Dziewicki, (London, 1893), pp. 178–79.
[69] Workman, 1:195.
[70] John Wyclif, *De civili dominio* 17, 3:334; *Calendar of Entries in the Papal Registers
Relating to Great Britain and Ireland* (hereafter "CPL"), 4:193; Workman, 1:203–206;
Dahmus, pp. 3–5.
[71] Vatican Archives, Collectorie 12, fol. 182; Holmes, *Good Parliament*, p. 176.
Unless we assume that the list was compiled in error, this document resolves the
uncertainty about whether Wyclif ever actually held the prebend.
[72] *Calendar of Patent Rolls, Edward III, 1370–4*, p. 424.
[73] See also Workman, 1:209; Dahmus, p. 3; and Holmes, *Good Parliament*, pp.
168–69.
[74] Workman, 1:209.

time that he was opposing the papal right of provision at Bruges, he was anticipating a prebend by virtue of that same right, and later expressed bitterness at his failure to receive it.

There was also a curious incident involving the prebend at Westbury in 1375. In November of that year, a clerk named Robert Faryngton was granted a patent for Westbury, less than two weeks after the Crown had issued a document confirming Wyclif's tenure there.[75] In December of 1376, Wyclif was reconfirmed in his prebend at Westbury when John of Gaunt informed the council that Faryngton had received the grant on the mistaken impression that it had been vacated, presumably by the recent grant of the prebend at Caistor.[76] Workman argues that Wyclif was restored to Westbury and held it until the end of his life, which seems correct. Earlier scholars, such as Rashdall, saw Wyclif as resigning Westbury to avoid pluralism, but Workman sees the incident as a simple error which was corrected by help from his patron, John of Gaunt. Holmes, on the other hand, reads the incident as happening because Wyclif was currently out of favor because of the shifting policy toward the papacy, and sees Gaunt's intervention the next year as evidence that Wyclif was back in favor and useful to Gaunt.

There is one other matter of preferment to consider. According to Thomas Netter, Bishop Hallum of Salisbury claimed that Wyclif became a critic of the church because he was passed over in 1375 for appointment to the bishopric of Worcester.[77] John Gilbert had been translated from Bangor to Hereford, and Ralph Erghum had been appointed to Salisbury, both by way of the papal provisions that they had opposed at Bruges but that the final concordat ultimately permitted, while Wyclif, whose presumed opposition to provisions may have cost him his place on the third delegation, received nothing. On the surface Hallum's statement reflects a disparity in the way the delegates were rewarded for their efforts. But on deeper examination, Hallum's charges ring false. That Wyclif might have hoped for a bishopric eventually is not unreasonable, but it is unlikely

---

[75] Workman, 1:169–70; Holmes, *Good Parliament*, p. 177

[76] The papal document confirming the prebend at Caistor specifies that Wyclif may hold it in plurality with Westbury.

[77] Thomas Netter, *Doctrinale Antiquitatum Fidei Catholicae Ecclesiae* (Venice, 1757–59), 1:560, 934; Workman, 1:252–3; Dahmus, p. 6.

that he particularly had his eye on Worcester in 1375. There had already been a nomination to the office made in 1373, and during this period, Wyclif was expecting the much lesser office of prebend of Caistor. Clearly, the story owes its genesis to a desire to discredit Wyclif by attributing his motives to revenge and bitterness, much like the motives cited by Woodford and Walsingham in relationship to the conflict over Canterbury Hall. While both incidents may have contributed to Wyclif's attitudes toward the Church (and in the case of the bishopric of Worcester the matter is far from likely), it is simplistic to suggest that they were the foundation of his criticism. But, given the contradiction between his actions and his arguments, it is easy to see how such stories could originate.

The Determinatio

After his return from Bruges, Wyclif returned to Oxford, again, taking rooms at Queen's College. It was either now, or within the past year, that Wyclif may have issued a first draft of his *Determinatio* against Uthred of Boldon and William Binham. The work is undated, and its dating has been the source of some debate. In the nineteenth century, it tended to be dated to 1366, but Loserth advanced a date between 1374 and 1376.[78] Workman places in later in 1374, and sees it essentially as a product of Wyclif's dissatisfaction with the events of the mission to Bruges. His chief reason for dating it after Bruges is that, had Wyclif published the work before Bruges, he would have been too obviously a partisan to participate in the delegation.[79] McFarlane dates it ambiguously in the period after 1372.[80] Dahmus follows Workman, and points out that in the *Determinatio*, Wyclif accuses Binham of attacking him at the Curia in the hopes of having Wyclif deprived of his benefices, which Dahmus took to be a reference to Wyclif's loss of the Caistor prebend.[81] Holmes places it in 1373, and sees the grant of Lutterworth and Wyclif's appointment to the second delegation as rewards for his defense of

[78] Rashdall, "Wycliffe," pp. 1119–20; Loserth, in *Opera Minora*, pp. xlviii–xlix.
[79] Workman, 1:231, 257.
[80] McFarlane, *John Wyclif*, p. 62.
[81] Dahmus, pp. 22–23.

the royal position in the dispute with the papacy.[82] It has been demonstrated that portions of the work respond to William Woodford's *De dominio civili clericorum*, which was written in mid-1376, and that it is likely that the *Determinatio* as we have it dates from 1377.[83] But, given Wyclif's penchant for revising earlier writings, it is possible that he wrote the *Determinatio* in 1373 and then subsequently revised it in 1377.

The date of the *Determinatio* is a matter of some importance, because it influences how we understand Wyclif's public stature and his relationship to Crown in the period from 1373 to 1377. If he published some version of the work in 1373, his appointment to the second delegation was, as Holmes argues, likely made with the full knowledge of his position on matters and must represent a certain hardening of royal attitudes after the failure of the first delegation. Workman's argument that Wyclif could not have been an avowed partisan before his trip to Bruges does not work; the redating of the Great Council of 1374 to the previous year demonstrates that an avowed partisan like Uthred of Boldon could be appointed to the delegation.[84] Dahmus's suggestion that Wyclif wrote after the loss of the Caistor prebend is stronger, but unproven; we have no actual evidence that Binham did complain to the Curia, or if he did, that it had any connection to the granting of Caistor to Philip Thornbury.

The other argument for dating the *Determinatio* to the period before the Bruges conference is that in the text, Wyclif refers to himself as a *"peculiaris regis clericus,"* by which he seems to mean that he is one of the king's own clerks.[85] As we have seen, such a description fits what we know of Wyclif's service to the Crown in the period leading up to the conference. In the period between September of 1374 and September of 1376, however, Wyclif does not seem to be actively serving the Crown, and if the dispute over the prebend at Westbury is any indication, he may have been out of favor at court. If such a reading is correct, then we must consider that Wyclif's opposition to papal provisions was well-known before 1374 and was probably

---

[82] Holmes, *Good Parliament*, pp. 168–69.

[83] E. Doyle, "William Woodford's 'De dominio civili clericorum' against John Wyclif," in *Speculum* 52 (1377), 329–36, at pp. 63–4; Anne Hudson, *The Premature Reformation: Wycliffite Texts and Lollard History*, (Oxford, 1988), p. 64 n. 26.

[84] See n. 53 for Catto's redating of the Great Council.

[85] Wyclif, *Expositio textus Matthei XXIII* 3, in *Opera Minora*, p. 322.

a factor in his selection for the second delegation. But Wyclif was certainly serving the Crown in 1377 and could certainly have described himself as a royal cleric during that time, so this piece of evidence is also unreliable. Ultimately, the issue must be regarded as unresolvable, even though it leaves us with a regrettable uncertainty about how to understand the Bruges delegation and Wyclif's function in it.

John of Gaunt and Wyclif

The concordat reached at Bruges in 1375 increased the unpopularity of John of Gaunt and, combined with an irruption of the Black Death and more than a decade of poor harvests, helped produce the Good Parliament, which opened in April of 1376.[86] When Chancellor Knyvet announced the need for a subsidy, the Parliament balked. The Commons appointed its first Speaker, Sir Peter de la Mare, who in conjunction with Bishops Wykeham and Courtenay and others led an attack on several royal officials, as well as Edward III's mistress, Alice Perrers. It then turned its attention to papal financial exactions and proposed the expulsion from England of all the pope's collectors and proctors. It finished its work with a call for annual Parliaments and a proposal to enact a formal Council of State chosen by the Commons. In many ways, the Good Parliament should be read as a reaction by the Commons against Gaunt's power and pro-papal policies

At this point, in early June, the Black Prince, who was the main supporter of the Commons in its actions, died, and John of Gaunt, Prince Edward's younger brother, moved into a position of dominance over the government. In July, under Gaunt's influence, the Crown rejected most of the proposals and dismissed Parliament. Most of the attacked officials returned to their posts, Alice Perrers returned to her place at court, and Peter de la Mare was arrested and imprisoned in Nottingham Castle.

---

[86] For the Good Parliament, see Workman, 1:266–74; Holmes, *Good Parliament*, pp. 100–194; John Taylor, "The Good Parliament and its Sources," in *Politics and Crisis in Fourteenth Century England*, ed. John Taylor and Wendy Childs, (Gloucester, 1990), pp. 81–96; and Goodman, *John of Gaunt*, pp. 55–60.

What role Wyclif may have played in these events, and what his relationship with John of Gaunt was like during this period is unclear, but there is no evidence that he was actively serving Gaunt or the Crown in the period between his return from Bruges and the end of the Good Parliament. Indeed, in many ways, the difficulty that Wyclif had in defending his Westbury prebend suggests that he was out of favor with Gaunt in 1375 or perhaps that Gaunt permitted an attack on Wyclif's prebend as a gesture toward the papacy.

However, after the Good Parliament, the situation changed. Gaunt came to consider a strong Anglo-Papal alliance a liability. Gregory had gotten bogged down in a war with Florence and was to die early in 1378, having managed to reoccupy Rome. Gregory's influence over northern European politics declined as result of his preoccupation with Italy, particularly since, by moving back to Rome, the papacy was sacrificing some measure of its influence in France. And, as the Good Parliament had shown, anti-papal feeling was strong in England. Consequently, Gaunt had little to lose and something to gain by throwing his support toward the anti-papal position.[87]

John of Gaunt's reputation has suffered almost from the time of his death, and most historians of the nineteenth and early twentieth century were hostile to him.[88] He has generally been seen as unscrupulous, grasping, and corrupt, and even the more moderate scholars have little positive to say about him. In September of 1376, John Wyclif was summoned to meet with the royal council, presumably at Gaunt's bidding.[89] Significantly, a few months after this meeting, Gaunt intervened with the council to support Wyclif's claim to Westbury, the first clear sign of royal support that Wyclif received since returning from Bruges, and the first definite connection between Wyclif and Gaunt. We know from Walsingham that Wyclif began preaching against the clerical leadership of the Church in the later part of 1376 and early 1377.[90] The scholarly interpretation of these facts popular before the middle of the twentieth century was that Gaunt summoned Wyclif from Oxford and persuaded the scholar to

---

[87] Holmes, *Good Parliament*, p. 166.
[88] See Goodman, *John of Gaunt*, pp. 15–41, for a good survey of the historiography on Gaunt.
[89] F. Devon, *Issues of the Exchequer*, (London, 1837), p. 200.
[90] *St. Albans*, pp. 76–77.

launch the preaching campaign in London, hoping that such a gesture would win him popular support among the Londoners for his
planned attack on Bishop Wykeham.[91] Consequently, there has been
a tendency to assume that Gaunt somehow persuaded Wyclif to start
preaching against the established church, and that Gaunt was cyn-
ically using the politically naïve Wyclif as a pawn in his larger political schemes.

As Dahmus points out, however, scholars have generally accepted
that Gaunt had fairly cynical motives while overlooking Walsingham's
statement that Wyclif was seeking support from Gaunt.[92] If we accept
that Gaunt was the force behind Wyclif's summons to the council
and the main reason Wyclif initiated his preaching campaign in
London, we must also acknowledge that Wyclif was more than a
tool of Gaunt. Assumptions that Wyclif was politically naïve and
therefore unwittingly being used by Gaunt simply do not square with
the career of a man who had associated with the government perhaps as early as 1371, who had probably attended Parliament as a
royal official, and who was appointed to an important diplomatic
mission in 1374.[93] Gaunt may have initiated the arrangement, but
we must consider Wyclif essentially an ally rather than a simple tool.
Here again we must acknowledge a certain inconsistency in Wyclif,
that he championed his theory of dominion in support of a man
whose notorious adultery would certainly have deprived him of
dominion.[94]

Furthermore, as Stephen Lahey has demonstrated, it is a mistake
to see Wyclif's interest in *dominium* as a radical deviation from his
earlier scholarly thinking.[95] Rather it was a development out of his
realism, and it was a growing strand of his thinking by 1373.[96] He
may have produced a first draft of the *Determinatio* in 1373, and at

---

[91] Workman, 1:275–82; Holmes, *Good Parliament*, pp. 166–67. The only major
scholar to reject this interpretation is Dahmus, pp. 7–19, who argues that this interpretation is based too much on Walsingham's hostile and unreliable evidence, and
that the motives ascribed to Gaunt are problematic. But Dahmus does not explain
why Wyclif was called to the council, why Gaunt supported him in the matter of
Westbury, or why Gaunt appeared with him in February.

[92] Dahmus, pp. 16–17.

[93] See, for example, Workman, 1:276.

[94] Dahmus, p. 18.

[95] Lahey, *Philosophy and Politics*, passim.

[96] Hudson and Kenny, "John Wyclif," pp. 622–23.

least part of his *De dominio divino* also probably dates from this period, and this may well have contributed to his appointment to the second delegation in 1374.[97] The fuller version of that work and its companion piece, *De civili dominio*, were certainly taking shape by 1376, and at least part of the latter work is likely to have emerged from a series of lectures in 1375 and 1376. *De mandatis divinis* and *De statu innocencie* also date to 1376. Walsingham, in a picturesque phrase, says that Wyclif had been "barking at the Church in the schools for many years in single acts," and he tells us that Wyclif had gained followers in London (a fact confirmed by the Londoners' intrusion at the Lambeth trial).[98] As we shall see, by November of 1376, word of Wyclif's teaching had reached the papal court, and Adam Easton, in his enormous *Defensorium*, refers to Wyclif as a "notable master of theology" and "notable and famous."[99] Knighton says that Wyclif was "the most eminent theologian of the time, considered second to none in philosophy, incomparable in scholastic learning," while the author of the *Eulugium historiarum sive temporis* says that he was called "the flower of Oxford" (*dictus flos oxoniae*).[100] From all of this, it is clear that by 1377, Wyclif was a well-known figure, at least among intellectuals, political figures, and the London crowd and the suggestion that he was an obscure academic prior to 1377 is hard to support. It cannot be the case that Gaunt simply asked Wyclif to produce a theoretical justification to support Gaunt's political agenda, which is what the earlier picture of their relationship essentially suggests. Rather Gaunt must have turned to Wyclif knowing that the scholar maintained theories congenial to Gaunt's agenda. How Gaunt learned of Wyclif's ideas is uncertain; he may have learned about them during Wyclif's participation in the Bruges conference, but that is certainly not the only possibility.

---

[97] Catto, "Wyclif," p. 200; Lahey, *Philosophy and Politics*, p. 10.

[98] *St. Albans*, pp. 74–75. "Aggregaverat ideo sibi quemdam pseudotheologum, sive, ut melius eum nominem, verum theomachum, qui iam a multis annis in scolis in singulis actis suis contra ecclasiam oblatraverat . . ."

[99] Margaret Harvey, "Adam Easton and the Condemnation of John Wyclif, 1377," in *English Historical Review* 113 (1998), 321–334, at p. 323.

[100] Henry Knighton, *Knighton's Chronicle*, ed. and trans. G.H. Martin, (Oxford, 1995), p. 242: "doctor in theologia eminentissimus in diebus illis, in philosophia nulli reputabatur secundus, in scolasticis disciplinis incomparabilis." *Eulogium*, 3:345. Such praise from chroniclers who hated Wyclif is surprising, but Wyclif's reputation for learning probably rests more on the volume of his output rather than the content of his thought; Courtenay, *Schools*, p. 355.

Wyclif, for his part, must have seen Gaunt as the closest thing to a champion of his theories that he was likely to find. If he sincerely believed that Gaunt was a reformer, he must have been deeply disappointed by the end of his life. As Gaunt's most recent biographer has pointed out, Gaunt's primary political position was the defense of the Crown and its authority, and it was this that led him to seek support from Wyclif.[101] Nor was Gaunt a religious radical; in his personal religious life he appears entirely orthodox apart from his support for Wyclif.[102] But his support for Wyclif was not completely due to politics. Knighton tells us that Gaunt believed the Lollards to be "God's saints" (*sanctos Dei*), and Walsingham says that Gaunt spoke highly of Wyclif's honesty and knowledge.[103]

The Confrontation at St Paul's

Let us now turn to the dramatic events at the Cathedral of St Paul in London on February 19, 1377.[104] Wyclif was summoned to appear before the assembly of bishops at St Paul's, to answer questions about his teachings. This was not a typical episcopal inquisition, which would have been presided over by Bishop Buckingham of Lincoln, who was Wyclif's superior as rector of Lutterworth; rather, it was called and presided over by Archbishop Sudbury in his capacity as metropolitan ordinary of the province of Canterbury, with the other bishops, most prominently Bishop Courtenay, acting as his assessors.[105]

---

[101] Simon Walker, "John of Gaunt," in the *Oxford Dictionary of National Biography*, 30:174–183, at p. 182.

[102] Goodman, *John of Gaunt*, pp. 243–44.

[103] Knighton, *Knighton's Chronicle*, p. 312; *St. Albans*, pp. 76–79; Goodman, *John of Gaunt*, p. 241.

[104] The events are described in *St. Albans*, pp. 80–85; and also in an English transcription of the same work, the "Transcript of a Chronicle in the Harleian Library of Mss No. 6217, entitled 'A Historical Relation of certain passages about the end of King Edward the Third and of his Death'," ed. Thomas Amyot, in *Archaeologia* 22 (1829), 204–84, at pp. 253–9; a rather different version of the events can be found in Walsingham's *Historia Anglicana*, ed. H.T. Riley, (RS 28) (London, 1863–76), 1:235; an independent account of the incident can be found in the *Anonimalle Chronicle*, ed. V.H. Galbraith, (Manchester, 1927), pp. 103–4; see also Workman, 1:284–88; Dahmus, pp. 28–29. Finally, there is a confused account by Walsingham, which conflates the St Paul's trial and the Lambeth trial, contained in the Short Chronicle version of his *Chronica Majora*, in *St Albans*, p. 985,

[105] Dahmus, pp. 35–6; Henry Ansgar Kelly, "Trial Procedures against Wyclif and

Walsingham reports that Archbishop Sudbury had to be pushed into the affair by the other bishops, and the archbishop's reluctance perhaps accounts for his virtual invisibility in the records of the trial. Wyclif appeared, accompanied by Gaunt and Henry Percy, who was the newly-appointed marshal, as well as four Oxford theologians, one from each order of friars.[106] The cathedral was extremely crowded, which reinforces the impression that Wyclif was well-known by this time and that his trial was a cause célebre. According to Walsingham, Wyclif's party had to push through a large crowd to get inside, where the crowd was just a bad. This caused Percy, whom the *Anonimalle Chronicle* describes as carrying a club, to order people out of the way, and Bishop Courtenay advised him not to invoke royal authority in the cathedral.[107] Courtenay also commented that had he known how Percy would behave, he would not have permitted Percy to enter the building. Gaunt replied that they would do as they pleased, regardless of what Courtenay wanted.

When Wyclif's party reached the Lady Chapel where the hearing was to occur, Gaunt, Percy, and the assembled bishops were seated, and then Percy advised Wyclif to sit as well. This remark angered Courtenay, who immediately responded that it was contrary to law and reason that one who had been summoned before the bishop for questioning should sit. This quickly developed into a loud argument between Percy and Courtenay, and then Gaunt joined in as well. He threatened Courtenay, telling him that his parents would not be able to help him, to which the bishop replied that he put

---

Wycliffites in England and at the Council of Constance," in *Huntington Library Quarterly* 61 (1998), 1–28, at p. 4. For Bishop Courtenay, see Joseph H. Dahmus, *William Courtenay, Archbishop of Canterbury, 1381–1396*, (London, 1966), passim; R.N. Swanson, "William Courtenay," in the *Oxford Dictionary of National Biography*, 13:687–92.

[106] The presence of theologians, rather than lawyers, in Wyclif's defense is unusual; see Kelly, "Trial Procedures," p. 4.

[107] The *Anonimalle Chronicle* presents the conflict differently, saying that Gaunt ordered Percy to arrest those who opposed Wyclif, which prompted Courtenay to threaten to excommunicate whomever tried to arrest anyone in the cathedral. It omits the quarrel over seating; *Anonimalle*, p. 103. It is difficult to square the two different accounts of the events. The Anonimalle version of the exchange between Percy and Courtenay makes more sense, but historians have generally accepted Walsingham's version as the more accurate, perhaps because it goes into more detail. It should be noted, however, that Walsingham's version is clearly colored by his hostility to Gaunt. Goodman, *John of Gaunt*, pp. 60–61, favors the *Anonimalle* version over Walsingham.

his trust in God. Then Gaunt threatened to drag Courtenay out of the cathedral by his hair. Walsingham's version suggests that this exchange took place quite openly, while the *Anonimalle Chronicle* seems to say that it occurred in a private conversation between Gaunt and Courtenay. The gathered crowd began shouting their defense of Courtenay (which shows that the conversation was overheard), and the meeting broke up in disarray.

Most scholars, such as Workman, who have looked at the St Paul's meeting have argued that the charges were brought against Wyclif for political reasons, primarily to embarrass Gaunt.[108] Indeed, Workman attempts no discussion of what the actual charges were, presumably because Walsingham says only that he was examined about "amazing things, which had proceeded from his mouth, taught to him, it is believed, by Satan, the adversary of the whole Church."[109] In essence, this approach concentrates on the sufficient cause of the summons to St Paul's, while de-emphasizing the necessary element of theologically dubious statements. In such a controversial and highly public setting, it is impossible to think that Courtenay did not have a reasonable list of charges to bring against Wyclif, but this is the impression that Workman leaves by not addressing the issue of what charges were being brought.

Dahmus rejects Workman's approach, arguing that the summons was driven entirely by doctrinal concerns stemming, most likely, from the content of Wyclif's preaching in London over the past few months.[110] He suggests that Wyclif was to be questioned about a list of articles based on his recent preaching, including that the pope had no special authority to excommunicate, that property could not be given to the church in perpetuity, and that temporal authorities had the right to confiscate property from possessioners, ideas that can be found in the *Determinatio* and that Walsingham links to Wyclif's

---

[108] Workman, 1:284; Rashdall, "Wycliffe," p. 1121.

[109] *St. Albans*, pp. 80–1: "Die igitur Jovis proxima ante festum Cathedrae Sancti Petri, appariturus erat filius perditionis, Johannes W[icliffe] coram episcopis, ut ibidem conveniretur super mirabilibus, quae de ejus ore processerant, ut creditur, docente eum Sathana, totius ecclesiae adversario."

[110] Dahmus, pp. 18–27. Some of these sermons survive in the *Sermones Quadraginta*. See John Wyclif, *Sermones*, ed. J. Loserth, (1888–90), 4.197–492; William Mallard, "Dating the *Sermones Quadraginta* of John Wyclif," *Medievalia et Humanistica* 17 (1966), 86–105; Siegfried Wenzel, "A New Version of Wyclif's *Sermones Quadraginta*," *Journal of Theological Studies* 49 (1998), pp. 155–61.

preaching in London.[111] Dahmus has essentially focused on the necessary cause of the summons, and his approach quite rightly draws attention to the fact that accusations of heresy require some grounding in theologically dubious statements. However, by rejecting the political motive for the summons, Dahmus has thrown out the sufficient cause for the argument. If political motives played no part in the summons, why did the summons happen the way it did? Why were they brought early in 1377, at a time when the bishops must certainly have known about Gaunt's support for Wyclif? At a time when the episcopate was embroiled in a conflict with Gaunt, why did they allow themselves to be diverted into examining heresy charges? If this was just a heresy trial, why was Sudbury reluctant to commit to it, and why were the proceedings atypically presided over by the archbishop and not the bishop of Lincoln? Why did Gaunt provide Wyclif with so much support? If Wyclif and Gaunt had no arrangement before February of 1377, how are we to explain Wyclif's summons to the council and Gaunt's subsequent decision to intervene in the matter of Westbury, followed soon by Wyclif's decision to begin preaching his political theories in London? It could be argued that Wyclif's preaching had created enough of a stir to force Courtenay and the other bishops to act, but to strip the incident of the obvious political elements is to miss the deeper context of the situation and to leave many important questions unanswered.

Thus we must see the incident at St Paul's as founded on Wyclif's teachings, stemming perhaps from the *Determinatio* but more likely from statements made over the winter of 1376 during his preaching in London. The *Anonimalle Chronicle* explicitly says that Wyclif was summoned to answer for things he preached in London, and also describes these points as "articles", indicating that this was a formal session at which Wyclif's teachings were to be condemned. But the charges also represent the conflict between Gaunt and the bishops, and as such were a clear attack on Gaunt. If Wyclif were found guilty of heresy at St Paul's, Gaunt could reasonably have been accused of being one of Wyclif's protectors (*fautores*).[112] Thus it was

---

[111] *St. Albans*, pp. 74–77.

[112] The only author who clearly treats the incident from both sides of the problem is Catto, "Wyclif," p. 204. His account emphasizes the political nature of the charges, but places it solidly in its larger theological context.

in Gaunt's best interest to ensure that Wyclif was not found guilty, and his confrontation with Courtenay reveals the larger conflict going on.

The morning of the confrontation at St Paul's, a bill had been introduced in Parliament to transfer control of London's government from the lord mayor to a royal official and to subject London to the jurisdiction of the marshal, Henry Percy. As a result of this, the citizens of London were already upset when the meeting at St Paul's occurred, and Gaunt's threats toward Courtenay were the last straw.[113] Rioting broke out. The next morning, on news that Percy had already acted on his new powers by arresting someone, a mob of citizens attacked Percy's house and freed the prisoner. Gaunt and Percy prudently withdrew from the city to Kensington, and when the mob descended on the Savoy Palace, it lynched a priest who had dared to publicly condemn Peter de le Mare, whom the Londoners had hoped to liberate. Bishop Courtenay, however, arrived at the scene and was able to calm the crowd and persuade it to disperse. What Wyclif was doing during all of this is unknown. He seems to have been ushered out of St Paul's by Gaunt's men, but his whereabouts and actions in the period immediately after the meeting at St Paul's are unknown, and he does not appear to have made any direct reference to the whole incident in his writings.

The Papal Condemnation

A few months later, on May 22, 1377, Pope Gregory issued a series of bulls against Wyclif.[114] Word of the aborted trial at St Paul's had evidently not reached Gregory, because in the first bull, *Regnum Angliae gloriosum*, he castigated Sudbury and Courtenay for having offered "no resistance that we know of," (unless this was a veiled criticism

---

[113] Workman argues that word of this bill reached St Paul's just as Gaunt was having his confrontation with Courtenay, but Dahmus, pp. 31–2 dismisses this as unfounded. The *Anonimalle Chronicle* says that the rioting broke out because word circulated that Gaunt had either threatened or beheaded Courtenay; *Anonimalle*, p. 114.

[114] *Register of Simon Sudbury* fols. 45v–6; *St. Albans*, pp. 174–93; *Hist. Ang.*, 1:345–53; David Wilkins, *Concilia Magnae Britanniae et Hiberniae*, (London, 1737), 3:116–7; see also Workman, 1:293–300; Dahmus, pp. 35–49, which includes translations of all the bulls; and Kelly, "Trial Procedures," pp. 4–7.

of the failed trial). He sent them a list of propositions attributed to Wyclif and ordered them to secretly investigate the matter and then arrest Wyclif on papal authority and extract a confession from him. They were ordered to restrain anyone who tried to object, on pain of ecclesiastical censure, and get the assistance of the secular authorities for the proceedings. In a second bull, *Nuper per nos*, Gregory dealt with the possibility that Wyclif might go into hiding; Sudbury and Courtenay are enjoined, both together and separately, to publicize a warning that Gregory was determined to prosecute Wyclif and cite him to appear before the pope within three months. Anticipating the possibility of royal interference, the third bull, *Super periculosis*, ordered Sudbury and Courtenay to speak with King Edward, Joan the Princess of Wales (the widow of the late Black Prince and mother of Edward's grandson and heir), and other nobles and royal counselors, assuring them that Wyclif's teachings were "contrary to the faith" and urging them to support Wyclif's prosecution. (Interestingly, *Super periculosis* makes no direct reference to John of Gaunt, despite his prominence in the government at the time.) In support of this, Gregory sent a fourth bull, *Regnum Angliae quod altissimus*, to Edward himself, informing the king of the instructions to Sudbury and Courtenay and asking Edward to assist them.

The fifth bull, *Mirari cogimur*, was sent to the chancellor of Oxford and the university as a whole. Gregory chastised them for allowing heresy to grow unchecked at Oxford, and for allowing matters to reach such a state that Rome had to act before Oxford did. The chancellor and university were ordered, under threat of the deprivation of all privileges and favors granted by the papacy, to forbid conclusions and propositions that sounded contrary to good works and faith, regardless of "the curious shuffling of words or terms." They were also ordered to arrest Wyclif and turn him over to Sudbury and Courtenay, along with any who might be tainted by Wyclif's errors.

There has been considerable discussion over the years of who informed Gregory of Wyclif's teachings. Those who would normally be the most likely suspects, the English bishops, are not likely to be responsible; if they were, it is hard to imagine that Gregory would have said that nothing had been done about Wyclif (unless, as mentioned, we see those comments as veiled criticism of the failed trial).[115]

---

[115] Workman, 1:296; Kelly, "Trial Procedures," p. 4.

Wyclif himself complains in *De ecclesia* that he had been misrepresented by "boys" to a "black dog" named Tolstanus. He also describes how Bishop Thomas Brinton of Rochester informed Wyclif that his views had been condemned and says that Brinton had received a copy of the list from his brothers. [116] Given Brinton's apparent glee in reporting the condemnation to Wyclif, we may suspect that the bishop was not a disinterested observer, and may well have been involved in what Catto sees as a co-ordinated campaign against Wyclif by leading monks. [117] Brinton was later to direct at least five sermons against Wyclif, some dating from 1382–83. [118] Brinton was a Benedictine, and therefore could be derided as a "black dog," but it is difficult to derive "Tolstanus" from "Brinton." Workman suggests that Tolstanus was Uthred of Boldon, also a Benedictine, but Dahmus rejects the suggestion, and deriving "Tolstanus" from "Boldon" is not much better than getting it from "Brinton". [119]

The most likely candidate for Gregory's source of information, however, was Adam Easton, an English Benedictine at the papal court. By November of 1376, word of Wyclif's ideas had reached Easton, who requested that the Abbot of Westminster supply him with information about Wyclif's teachings, and, as noted, Bishop Brinton and other Benedictines may well have orchestrated an effort to supply Easton with enough information to secure Wyclif's condemnation. [120] From Easton's writings, it appears that he received a copy of at least the first book of *De civilo dominio*, as well as various *dicta* of Wyclif. [121] From these materials, Easton seems to have compiled the list of conclusions that Gregory sent to Sudbury and Courtenay. In particular, Gregory's fifth bull attributes some of Wyclif's thought to Marsilius of Padua, an author Wyclif is unlikely to have read, but whom Adam Easton certainly had, since he cites *Defensor pacis* in his *Defensorium*. [122] Easton requested his information several

---

[116] Wyclif, *De Ecclesia* 15, pp. 354–55.

[117] Catto, "Wyclif," p. 204.

[118] Roy Martin Haines, *Ecclesia anglicana: Studies in the English Church of the Later Middle Ages*, (Toronto, 1989), pp. 209–13.

[119] Workman, 1:296; Dahmus, p. 37.

[120] W.A. Pantin, *Documents Illustrating the Chapters of the English Black Monks, 1215–1540*, (Camden Society, Third Series), 54 (1937), 3:76–7; Holmes, *Good Parliament*, p. 167; Harvey, "Easton," p. 321.

[121] Harvey, "Easton," pp. 322–23.

[122] Harvey, "Easton," p. 326, Dahmus, p. 38.

months before the aborted trial at St Paul's, which would explain why Gregory felt that nothing had been done. Finally, it is more reasonable to derive "Tolstanus" from "Easton" than from either of the other two choices.

There is also some confusion about how many propositions were actually condemned in the list Gregory sent with the bulls. Walsingham says that twenty-three propositions were condemned.[123] The list of propositions included in Sudbury's register has nineteen propositions, and Wyclif's response included in the *Fasciculi Zizaniorum* refers to nineteen conclusions.[124] But Wyclif's *Libellus* mentions only eighteen conclusions.[125] Walsingham's number is perhaps indicative that several lists of Wyclif's *dicta* were sent to Easton.[126] Dahmus argues that Wyclif chose not to respond to item seven in Sudbury's list because he felt it was embarrassing and indefensible.[127]

Although Gregory issued the bulls in May of 1377, they were not publicly known in England for several months. Sudbury and Courtenay only formally acted on them in December, but Wyclif was informed by Bishop Brinton of the condemnation some time during the Parliament of that year, which sat between October 13 and November 28. Wyclif describes Brinton as excitedly telling him, publicly in Parliament, that his teachings had been condemned, which suggests that Brinton only learned of the condemnation during the session.[128] There are several possible reasons for this delay.[129] It is possible that Gregory delayed in sending the bulls out, but it is more likely that they may have taken a longer than normal time to reach England. As Dahmus points out, three months was not enough time for word to reach Gregory of the aborted trial at St Paul's, so travel conditions in 1377 may have been particularly disrupted. War with France broke out again in June, and the French immediately began raiding the Channel ports, which might well have impeded a messenger traveling from Rome. A more serious complication, and one that

---

[123] *Hist. Ang*, pp. 324–5; *St. Albans*, p. 985.

[124] *Reg. Sudbury*, fols 46–46v; *Fasc. Ziz.*, p. 484.

[125] *Fasc. Ziz.*, pp. 245–57.

[126] Harvey, "Easton," p. 323. Harvey also includes a very helpful appendix comparing the list in Sudbury's register to Walsingham's list, to the *Libellus*, and to Easton's work.

[127] Dahmus, pp. 51–52.

[128] Wyclif, *De Ecclesia* 15, pp. 354–55.

[129] See Workman, 1:300; Dahmus, pp. 55–56.

certainly delayed matters, was the death of Edward III and the accession of Richard II, in June and July respectively. It was unclear what
arrangements would be made to rule England until Richard reached
his majority, and in such an environment, the bishops must certainly
have felt that it would be imprudent to pursue charges against Wyclif
when there was a real possibility that Gaunt would dominate the
government. During the first royal minority since the Conquest, that
of Henry III, a regent had been appointed, and the obvious candidate for the position now was Richard's uncle John of Gaunt. Gaunt,
however, was too unpopular, so instead the fiction was established
that Richard was old enough to govern on his own, and a series of
Continuing (or Continual) Councils was appointed to conduct the
day to day business of the Crown. The first Continuing Council was
immediately established until Parliament could meet, when a second
Continuing Council could be appointed to govern for the next year.[130]
Thus the bishops seem to have waited until Parliament was underway and it was clear that Gaunt would not dominate the second
Continuing Council, which was to govern England for the next year.
Finally, it is possible that Sudbury and Courtenay were in fact taking action secretly, as commanded in the first bull, although it is
hard to imagine that they needed to investigate the charges against
Wyclif, given that they had been prepared to act already in February.

The first evidence for the publication of the bulls comes from the
incident already mentioned. Richard II's first Parliament convened
in mid-October, and Wyclif was present in some capacity when
Bishop Brinton taunted him about the condemnation. This raises the
question of why Wyclif was at this Parliament. He had attended previous Parliaments as a royal clerk, so his presence may be that simple. But two documents he produced appear to be connected with
this Parliament. The first is a work included in the *Fasciculi Zizaniorum*,
entitled *Libellus magistri Johannes Wycclyff, quem porrexit Parliamento Regis
Ricardi contra statum ecclesiae*.[131] There is no date attached to it, but
given that it represents Wyclif's response to Gregory's condemnation, the Parliament referred to must be either the October Parliament

---

[130] On the Continuing Councils, see Saul, *Richard II*, pp. 27–29. It is important
to distinguish the Continuing Councils from the Great Council, which was essentially the House of Lords meeting with the king in an extra-Parliamentary session.
The Continuing Councils were a smaller, temporary, body with appointed membership.
[131] *Fasc. Ziz.*, pp. 245–57; see Workman, 1:308, 311; Dahmus, pp. 56–57.

of 1377 or the Gloucester Parliament of 1378. There is some doubt about whether the title of the *Libellus* is accurate; there is no record of any address by Wyclif in the Parliamentary rolls for either Parliament, and both Workman and Dahmus take the view that the *Libellus* was not in fact presented to any Parliament. But there is no mention in the rolls of Wyclif speaking at the Gloucester Parliament in 1378 either, and we know from other sources that he did, so it is unwise to lay too much emphasis on this point. It seems best to assume that the title of the *Libellus* is accurate and that Wyclif hastily wrote the *Libellus* during the October Parliament and presented the document to members of Parliament in some way. This could only have happened, however, if Wyclif received a copy of Gregory's condemned articles (which, as we shall see, is likely).

The other document that may be connected to this Parliament is the *Responsio* included in the *Fasciculi Zizaniorum*.[132] According to the document's rubric, Wyclif was asked by Richard II and his great council (*per Dominum Regem Angliae Ricardum Secundum et magnum suum consilium*) whether it was lawful for the kingdom to withhold funds from the pope, owing to the need for defense, even if the pope threatened censure. Parliament had already brought up the same issue in connection with the military expenses mandated by the renewed French attacks. It is unlikely that Wyclif was formally called on by Parliament, since there is no record of such in the Parliamentary rolls and the rubric specifically mentions the Great Council rather than Parliament. Nor is it likely that it was the Continuing Council that asked his opinion, since Bishop Courtenay was prominent in that body.[133]

In the *Responsio*, Wyclif argues that the Crown might lawfully withhold money needed to defend the kingdom. He also challenges papal authority to impose an interdict, since God would not recognize an unjust censure, and asserts that Christians have no obligation to give money to the pope, but rather that alms are given voluntarily.

---

[132] *Fasc.Ziz*, pp. 258–71; see Workman, 1:302–4; Dahmus, pp. 57–61.

[133] Dahmus, p. 59, argues that the Great Council did not ask Wyclif's opinion either, and apparently feels that the rubric is another error. But if this is correct, it is unclear why the document was created in the first place, and the last sentence strongly suggests that the document was formally presented to some governing body. Anne Hudson dates the *Responsio* to November, 1377, and therefore seems to accept that it was formally presented. See Hudson, *Premature Reformation*, p. 64.

Dahmus argues that the *Responsio* reaffirms most of the propositions condemned by Gregory.[134] Thus Wyclif must have had access to Gregory's list of condemned propositions, which increases the possibility that the *Libellus* was written during the October Parliament. The Council responded to the *Responsio* by imposing silence on Wyclif concerning the issues involved.[135] Since the *Responsio* is essentially Wyclif's defense of the condemned propositions, the Council essentially sided with Gregory and supported the condemnation, or at least chose not to challenge the pope on the issue.

Attempts to Condemn Wyclif

The immediate sequel to these events in October and November was the publication of Gregory's bulls, which reached Oxford shortly before Christmas. Sudbury and Courtenay must have judged that the Council's rejection of Wyclif's arguments marked a reasonable moment to take action, and it is not impossible that Courtenay might have engineered the incident with the *Responsio* as a prelude to taking formal action against Wyclif. Over the course of 1377, there was considerable controversy at Oxford over Wyclif's recent teachings. His positions were attacked by William Woodford, William Binham, Nicholas Radcliffe, and possibly William Barton and Uthred of Boldon, as well as by an unidentified Irish monk and others.[136]

But when the Chancellor, Adam of Tonworth, received *Mirari cogimur*, the masters of Oxford took a decidedly nuanced approach to their orders.[137] Wyclif's supporters argued in the congregation of regents and non-regents that it was illegal to imprison someone simply on the order of the pope, for that would admit that the pope held dominion over England. However, the university officials feared for its privileges, and the vice-chancellor, an unidentified monk, "asked and ordered" Wyclif to stay in Black Hall under house arrest, so that the university would be seen to be following the pope's

---

[134] Dahmus, pp. 60–61.

[135] As Dahmus points out, most of Wyclif's earlier biographers have passed over this silencing without comment.

[136] Catto, "Wyclif," pp. 205–7.

[137] *Eulogium*, 3:347–8; *St. Albans*, pp. 174–5; *Hist. Ang.*, 1:345. See also Workman, 1:306–7; Dahmus, pp. 61–4; Catto, "Wyclif," pp. 207–8; Kelly, "Trial Procedures," pp. 7–8.

instructions. This evidently all happened in the same assembly. The university then convened an inquiry into the condemned propositions. Although we have few details about this proceeding, the fact that the regent masters of theology examined a formal list of propositions and then delivered a verdict to Chancellor Tonworth leaves little doubt that this was a formal investigation into charges of heresy. Somewhat surprisingly, the regent masters rejected Gregory's condemnation and declared the propositions to be true, although they admitted that they were "offensive to pious ears." This slight condemnation prompted Wyclif to respond that the truth should not be stifled to avoid offence.

About the same time as these events happened, there was an incident between a group of students and some men of the royal household, in which the students lampooned the men in verse and fired some arrows at the window of their lodging. Tonworth and his proctors were summoned before Bishop Houghton, the chancellor of England. Houghton tried to depose Tonworth, who bravely responded that he could not be deposed because he held his office from both king and pope. Houghton deposed him anyway, daring him to get satisfaction from the pope, and threatened the status of the university itself. At this point Tonworth prudently resigned his office. Wyclif was released from house arrest and the unnamed vice-chancellor was arrested for having dared to arrest Wyclif. Although these two events co-incided, they appear to be essentially unrelated.[138]

Several points are noteworthy about this set of events. First, this incident marks the only time that a pope directly intervened in theological matters at Oxford. Such unprecedented action put the university in the difficult position of having to find a way to satisfy two conflicting authorities, and Wyclif's supporters quite successfully identified and exploited the point of conflict between those two authorities, with the ultimate result that the vice-chancellor was imprisoned for taking action against Wyclif.

Second, this incident again demonstrates the importance of distinguishing between necessary and sufficient causes in heresy prosecutions. While Wyclif's dubious theological statements provided a

---

[138] On this second incident, see *Eulogium, 3:348–9*; Rymer, *Foedera*, 4:32; and Wilkins, *Concilia*, 3:137. Workman, 1:306–7, links the two events, but Dahmus, pp. 63–64, argues that this is a mistake.

necessary cause for the formal inquiry at Oxford, papal authority was not sufficient to produce a formal condemnation because the masters were too concerned about royal authority. The fact that Wyclif's supporters exploited the conflict between royal and papal authority meant that the masters hesitated to issue any but the most tepid rebuke to Wyclif, even though a condemnation could reasonably have been issued on theological grounds and even more reasonably on the grounds of the papal condemnation.

Third, there is the question of why the Crown intervened at Oxford. If the final sentence of the *Responsio* is accurate, and there is no clear reason to doubt it, the Great Council had just rejected Wyclif's *Responsio* and censured him. So the government's decision to depose Tonworth and imprison the vice-chancellor requires some explanation. It is possible that we should see the Continuing Council as so divided over Wyclif that its decisions on him were in a state of flux as Gaunt's supporters, including Adam Houghton, and Bishop Courtenay struggled for dominance. Gaunt himself was not formally a member of the Continuing Council, but continued to exercise considerable influence.[139] But there is no direct evidence for such a struggle. Rather, the Crown's intervention is more likely to have been initially unrelated to Wyclif. The first we hear of Houghton's involvement comes not in conjunction with Wyclif's house arrest, but with the altercation between the students and the royal officials. Wyclif's supporters may have taken advantage of having Houghton's attention focused on the university to persuade him that the imprisonment of Wyclif was another affront to the Crown.

Not long after this, before March 27, 1378, Wyclif appeared before the assembled bishops at Lambeth. Sudbury had summoned him to appear at St Paul's by mid-January, but that meeting seems to have been postponed for reasons that are unclear.[140] Wyclif himself commented that he feared for his life, because he believed that Sudbury

---

[139] Early in 1378, the Great Council granted him control of the subsidy for national defense purposes. Walsingham says that the Council agreed to this arrangement reluctantly, but were unwilling to oppose him on the issue. He was also actively attending Council meetings in March, April, and June. See *St. Albans*, p. 219; Goodman, *John of Gaunt*, p. 73.

[140] See Dahmus, pp. 66–68, for a discussion of when the Lambeth trial occurred, why the venue was moved and whether any meeting at St Paul's ever occurred. For the trial itself, see *St. Albans*, pp. 197–211; *Hist. Ang.*, 1:356–63; Workman, 1:307–9, Dahmus, pp. 68–73; Kelly, "Trial Procedures," p. 8.

planned to meet with Pope Gregory to plan Wyclif's death.[141] According to Walsingham, on the day of the trial, the bishops received an agent of Princess Joan, Sir Lewis Clifford, who instructed them not to pass formal judgment on Wyclif. Despite this injunction, they pressed on with the matter, but the meeting was also disrupted by a group of Londoners, who forced their way into the chapel where the assembly was taking place and protested in support of Wyclif.

The Lambeth trial focused on the nineteen articles condemned by Gregory. Walsingham includes Wyclif's *Declarationes*, which make up his formal response to the condemnation. As Dahmus has pointed out, this document represents a moderation of his earlier positions, and Walsingham states that Wyclif qualified his ideas in a way he had not done when he had preached those ideas openly.[142] Ultimately, the bishops appear to have followed the line of the Oxford masters, since they issued only an order not to preach such ideas to the laity, but ruled that the articles were true.[143] Essentially, the bishops ruled that the statements were not heretical, but that they could be misleading to the uneducated.

Exactly why the bishops reached this conclusion is unclear in the sources. Walsingham first emphasizes the political elements of the trial when he describes the interference of Princess Joan and the Londoners, but he also says that Wyclif deluded the bishops into accepting his articles. Yet it is inconceivable that Bishop Courtenay would have simply been persuaded that Wyclif's ideas were acceptable. Rather, the decision must have been made for essentially political reasons stemming from Princess Joan's intervention. Whether Joan took action on her own or was acting to convey John of Gaunt's concerns is unclear; both options are plausible.[144] Regardless, the bishops at Lambeth took a position which mirrors both the Great Council's decision a few months earlier and the Oxford masters' decision, namely that Wyclif was not to speak about such issues but was not to be punished either. The Lambeth trial was the third unsuccessful attempt by Wyclif's opponents to condemn him in just over a year. Pope Gregory's death shortly after this third attempt, compounded by these failures, seems to have removed some of the

---

[141] Wyclif, *De veritate* 14, 1:374.
[142] *St. Albans*, pp. 210–11; Dahmus, pp. 68–69.
[143] *St. Albans*, pp. 210–11; *Eulogium*, 3:348.
[144] Dahmus, pp. 70–71.

pressure on Wyclif by reducing the impetus to seek a condemnation of him, an effort that was not truly to revive until 1381.

The Gloucester Parliament

In August of 1378, a scandal erupted in the form of the Hauley-Shakyl Affair.[145] Hauley and Shakyl had fought at the battle of Najera in 1367 and captured the count of Denia. Although Gaunt acquired the primary interest in the count's ransom, Hauley and Shakyl were permitted to keep hold of him and later on his son Alphonso, who was offered as a surety that the count would pay his ransom after his release. By 1377, Hauley and Shakyl were still holding Alphonso and waiting for their share of the ransom. But the Crown at this point ordered the two men to release Alphonso into royal custody, apparently because it was planning on releasing Alphonso as part of its diplomacy. Unwilling to lose their money, Hauley and Shakyl refused, and even defied a Parliamentary order, and were imprisoned in the Tower of London. But in August of 1378, they escaped and fled for sanctuary to Westminster Abbey. Sir Alan Buxhill, the Keeper of the Tower, took a large force of men (Walsingham says fifty) with him to the Abbey. He was able to trick Shakyl into leaving the Abbey precinct and so capture him, but Hauley remained inside, so Buxhill sent soldiers into the Abbey. Hauley was found listening to Mass, and, after an argument, he tried to flee. The soldiers chased him twice around the choir and then cornered him near the altar, where they slew him, as well as a clerk who had tried to protect him. Hauley's body was dragged through the church and cast into the street.

Sudbury, rather timidly, waited three days before issuing a general excommunication against the unknown perpetrators of the crime.[146] Courtenay's response was more aggressive. He excommunicated Buxhill by name and everyone else involved, but exempted the king, the queen mother, and Gaunt. Gaunt was out of the country at the time, but was widely blamed for the events anyway, and the issue

---

[145] For the whole affair, see *St. Albans*, pp. 236–45; *Anonimalle*, pp. 121–2; Workman, 1:314–6; Dahmus, pp. 74–5; and Nigel Saul, *Richard II*, (New Haven, 1997), pp. 36–38.

[146] *Reg. Sudbury*, fol. 49v; *St. Albans*, pp. 242–45.

revived the conflict between him and Courtenay. After some quarrelling between the two men, during which Gaunt threatened to forcibly bring Courtenay from London to Windsor, Parliament was summoned to meet at Gloucester, well away from the scene of the crime and the London mobs that were riled up against Gaunt.

One of the Crown's primary items at the Gloucester Parliament was a proposal to restrict the right of sanctuary in cases involving debt. Walsingham claims that the Crown planned to push for the disendowment of the Church, but there is nothing to support such a wild notion and it is best understood as a rumor Walsingham reported simply because of his hostility to Gaunt.[147] To help advance this case, Gaunt turned once again to John Wyclif. Wyclif is not mentioned in the Parliamentary rolls, but the *Anonimalle* Chronicler says that Wyclif and a second unspecified doctor spoke so persuasively in support of the Crown's position that no one was able to argue against them.[148] Furthermore, Wyclif seems to have incorporated his arguments at the Parliament into the *De ecclesia*, which he says was written at both the order of the king and the decision of the Duke of Lancaster.[149] How Parliament received Wyclif's arguments is unknown; the Gloucester Parliament was dissolved without enacting any legislation to limit the power of sanctuary, but a year later at the next Parliament, the right of sanctuary was restricted.

The Gloucester Parliament marks something of a turning point in Wyclif's life, because it appears to mark the end of Wyclif's formal service to the Crown. There is no evidence that Wyclif ever again acted as a royal clerk. The decline of the alliance between Wyclif and John of Gaunt is perhaps best understood as a mutual parting of ways. For Gaunt's part, Wyclif had become something of a liability over the past two years. He had been formally condemned by the pope and had been the focus of three attempts by Church officials to condemn him in England. He had occasioned a significant dispute between Gaunt and Courtenay. And while he had provided some helpful intellectual weight to a few of Gaunt's projects in Parliament, the duke may simply have felt that he could find other scholars who would be just as useful but less controversial. Wyclif,

---

[147] *St. Albans*, p. 246–47; Dahmus, pp. 76–77.
[148] *Anonimalle*, pp. 123–24.
[149] Wyclif, *De ecclesia* 12, p. 266.

on the other hand, must have realized that Gaunt was not a reformer at heart, and he may have been frustrated by the silence imposed on him by the Great Council, the Oxford masters, and the bishops at Lambeth. Regardless of the exact motives, it is clear that the close connections between the two men declined after the Gloucester Parliament.

Wyclif's whereabouts over the next two years are uncertain, but on the balance he appears to have spent at least some of that time in Oxford. He was definitely living in Oxford by August 1380, since he is recorded as having rooms there at that time.[150] Although he may have been at Lutterworth for part of this period, he probably preached at least one sermon (and perhaps as many as four) at St Mary's Oxford in August of 1379, and he may have preached another in the same church in August of 1378, making it likely that he was primarily based in Oxford rather than Lutterworth during this period.[151] It was during this period that he developed his criticism of the contemporary Church to its fullest form, attacking the mendicants, denouncing clerical pluralism and absenteeism, actively calling for the disendowment of the Church, and rejecting the doctrine of transubstantiation. Much of *De ecclesia* and *De veritate Sacrae Scripturae* date from this period, as do *De officio regis*, *De potestate papae*, and *De simonia*.[152]

Barton's Censure

Sometime early in 1381, perhaps March or April, Oxford Chancellor William Barton (or Berton) assembled a committee to examine and censure Wyclif's position on the Eucharist.[153] As mentioned earlier,

---

[150] *Second Report of the Royal Commission on Historical Manuscripts*, (London, 1874), p. 142. Dahmus, pp. 79–80, suggests that this means that Wyclif was not in Oxford prior to this date and that, since he took rooms for one year, that he ceased his association with Oxford in August of 1381. While an ingenious reading of the entry, it goes beyond the document.

[151] Mallard, "Dating the *Sermones Quadraginta*," pp. 97, 101.

[152] Lahey, *Philosophy and Politics*, p. 10; Hudson and Kenny, "John Wyclif," p. 622.

[153] *Fasc. Ziz.* pp. 110–13; Workman, 2:141–45; McFarlane, 97–8; Dahmus, pp. 129–34; Catto, "Wyclif," pp. 213–4; Hudson and Kenny, "Wyclif, John," p. 619; Ian Levy, *John Wyclif: Scriptural Logic, Real Presence, and the Parameters of Orthodoxy* (Milwaukee, 2003), pp. 232–39. The date of this action is unclear. It must certainly have occurred before May 10, 1381, when Wyclif responded to it, but how much time he took in responding is not known. Workman says that Barton summoned the committee in the spring of 1380, but that it did not issue its statement until

Barton had already engineered the censure of one Franciscan's ideas sometime in the mid-1370s, and he had also determined against Wyclif.[154] If the *Fasciculi's* information is correct, Barton did this in reaction against a series of conclusions Wyclif had arrived at earlier the same year.[155] The *Fasciculi* lists twelve conclusions ascribed to Wyclif, and then says that during a public determination Wyclif had posited three conclusions that represent the essence of the first twelve conclusions. Exactly what these two lists, of twelve conclusions and three conclusions, represent is unclear; they may simply have been extracted by the author of the *Fasciculi* or some other scholar from Wyclif's works or they may represent the formal list of propositions that Barton's committee examined.[156] The two articles that Barton's committee condemned represent the substance of the first two items on the list of three conclusions, but they do not exactly reproduce items on either list.

Barton's twelve-member committee, which was dominated by theologians but also included two canon lawyers, was made up of six friars representing all four mendicant orders; two monks, one Benedictine and one Cistercian; and four seculars, including fellows of Merton and Oriel. Thus the committee was structured to include representatives of all the major segments of the university. Such a committee was in keeping with the general precedent at Oxford for academic censures; in 1315, when Oxford had censured a series of Scotist propositions regarding the Creation, the committee involved had included all the regent masters of theology, thus representing

---

late 1380 or early 1381. This seems too long a process, and there is no clear reason for saying that the committee began its work early in 1380. McFarlane dates the statement to "mid-winter 1380–1", Dahmus prefers early 1381, and Hudson and Kenny say May 1381, which would mean that Wyclif wrote his response very quickly.

[154] *Fasc. Ziz.*, p. 241. For Barton, see "Barton, William," in Emden, *BRUO*, 1:124; and Jeremy Catto, "Barton, William," in the *Oxford Dictionary of National Biography*, 4:215.

[155] *Fasc. Ziz.*, pp. 104–9.

[156] While the *Fasc. Ziz.* has been ascribed to Thomas Netter of Walden since the sixteenth century, it has become clear that this is erroneous. The author may have been Netter's fellow Carmelite, John Keninghale, but this is not proven. See James Crompton, "Fasciculi Zizaniorum I" and "Fasciculi Zizaniorum II," *Journal of Ecclesiastical History*, 12.1 (Apr 1961), 35–45, and 12.2 (Oct 1961), 155–66; Anne Hudson, "Netter, Thomas," in *Oxford Dictionary of National Biography*, 40:444–47.

all the major segments of the university.[157] We do not have detailed information about the make-up of other committees involved in academic censure between 1315 and 1381 (such as the censure of John Kedington in 1358 and the attempted condemnation of John Wyclif in 1377), so we cannot know how standard such a committee's membership was and how much it might reflect Barton's desire to pack the committee against Wyclif.

Barton's committee issued a formal censure of two of Wyclif's propositions as erroneous, avoiding any mention of Wyclif's name or those of his followers. Barton prohibited the discussion of the ideas, under threat of imprisonment, suspension from the university, and excommunication. Those who heard such articles discussed were commanded to flee the discussion under pain of excommunication. Previous censures had normally included a *prohibitio* on discussion of propositions, but imprisonment is unprecedented as a penalty connected to condemnation (although Wyclif's house arrest in 1377 offered a model, even though it preceded the inquiry and was not a consequence of it). Excommunication was likewise unprecedented for a censure within the university, although in 1285 Archbishop Pecham, acting outside the university, had excommunicated Richard Knapwell for violating a previous academic ban (which had not actually involved excommunication as a penalty).[158]

There is disagreement about how unanimous the committee was in its vote. The *Fasciculi* says that the censure was unanimous, while Wyclif says that the verdict was seven to five.[159] Dahmus reconciles this contradiction by saying that the initial reaction of the committee was divided but that it finally came to a unanimous vote for censure.[160] But Robert Rygge, one of the secular theologians on the committee, was subsequently a supporter of Wyclif, and it seems

---

[157] For the Condemnations of 1315, see *Munimenta*, 1:100–2. See also William Courtenay, "The Articles Condemned at Oxford Austin Friars in 1315," in *Via Augustini*, ed. Heiko A. Oberman and Frank. A. James III, (Leiden, 1991), 5–18; Girard J. Etzkorn, "Codex Merton 284: Evidence of Ockham's Early Influence in Oxford" in *From Ockham to Wyclif*, ed. Anne Hudson and Michael Wilks, (Oxford, 1987), 31–42; and Larsen, *Popular and Academic Heresy*, pp. 143–55.

[158] For the condemnation of Richard Knapwell, see Larsen, *Popular and Academic Heresy*, pp. 126–42.

[159] *Fasc. Ziz.*, p. 113; Wyclif, *De blasphemia* 6, p. 89.

[160] Dahmus, p. 132. Gwynn, *Austin Friars*, pp. 259–60 suggests that Wyclif overestimated the size of the minority that voted for him.

unlikely that he would initially support Wyclif, then vote against him, and then change his mind to support him again. Furthermore, Levy points out that the first of the two censured propositions, that the substance of the material bread remains after consecration, could well have aroused resistance, since by itself it had long been considered orthodox.[161] So it seems likely that the committee was not as unanimous as the document asserts. Additionally, it is clear that the concept of unanimity was important in academic condemnations. In the first condemnation at Oxford, in 1277, Archbishop Kilwardby brought together all the masters of Oxford, regent and non-regent, to issue his condemnation. In 1315, the committee was so concerned to maintain unanimity that it obtained assent to its censure from a master of theology who had been absent and suspended from the university at the time of the censure, while in 1358 the chancellor decreed that John Kedington should never teach in the university again without the unanimous support of the masters of theology. Thus, the most likely explanation for the discrepancy is that Barton's committee was divided in its vote, but having made the vote the committee publicly emphasized its unanimity, perhaps to avoid a political rupture within the university, but more likely because unanimity was a standard element of the rhetoric of censure.

The author of the *Fasciculi Zizaniorum* somewhat improbably depicts word of the censure reaching Wyclif at the moment he was teaching the censured ideas in the classroom. Wyclif, upon hearing the news, was confused, but then asserted that "neither the chancellor nor any of his allies" (*nec cancellarius nec aliquis de suis complicibus*) could change his opinion on the issue. Dahmus insists that this was the first Wyclif learned of the committee, and that Wyclif was shocked by the verdict.[162] It is unlikely, however, that a formal university committee would have operated in complete secrecy, and if this story is anything more than sheer invention, it is a striking coincidence that Wyclif should have been teaching his views at the moment the censure was announced. Rather, we must assume that Wyclif and the rest of the university knew about the committee, in which case Wyclif's choice of subjects on that day probably represents a gesture of defiance. His confusion stemmed not from surprise that the

---

[161] Levy, *John Wyclif*, pp. 233–35.
[162] Dahmus, p. 132.

committee had been meeting, but rather surprise at its verdict. He must have believed that a majority of the committee would support him, or else that they would hesitate to formally censure him, as had happened back in 1377 at the university and also at St Paul's and Lambeth. He must have expected his political connections to protect him as they had before. Having been censured, his first recorded action after announcing his defiance was to appeal the verdict to the Crown, presumably because he thought that Gaunt would have the action overturned, as Houghton had overturned his house arrest in 1377.[163]

Wyclif's appeal to the Crown was handled by Gaunt, which is unsurprising, given his previous support for Wyclif. What is surprising is that Gaunt went to Oxford in person to talk to Wyclif, indicating that the duke took the matter quite seriously. Exactly what passed between the two is unclear, but Gaunt commanded Wyclif to not speak about the condemned matters, and Wyclif may have promised his patron not to discuss transubstantiation outside the classroom.[164] In ordering Wyclif to be silent, Gaunt was following a policy that he had been maintaining since the start of Richard II's reign, namely that he would not allow Wyclif to be directly attacked, but he also would not allow Wyclif to voice radical opinions. At first glance, this seems a radical turn-about from the situation in late 1376 and early 1377, but it is easily understood in terms of Gaunt gradually distancing himself from Wyclif's beliefs. For political reasons, though, allowing Wyclif to be condemned would have opened the door for Gaunt's enemies to attack Gaunt for having been one of Wyclif's *fautores*. Additionally, as already noted, there is good reason to think that Gaunt genuinely respected Wyclif, and this may have encouraged him to continue protecting Wyclif after any political danger to Gaunt had faded.

However, Wyclif soon defied both the censure and Gaunt's injunction, by issuing his *Confessio* on May 10 of 1381.[165] This was a lengthy statement clarifying and defending his position on the Eucharist, and it provoked considerable response, including a very long refutation

---

[163] *Fasc. Ziz.*, p. 114.

[164] Dahmus, pp. 133–5; Wyclif, *Joannis Wiclif Trialogus* 4.36, ed. G Lechler, (Oxford, 1869), p. 375. Hudson and Kenny, "Wyclif, John," p. 619, feels that this promise may have been given to the committee at some point.

[165] *Fasc. Ziz.*, pp. 115–32.

by John Tissington, one of the committee members who presumably voted for the censure, and an even longer work by Thomas Winterton, who identifies Wyclif's position as heresy but overall adopts a moderate position regarding Wyclif himself.[166]

The Peasant Revolt

Wyclif's actions over the summer of 1381 are unknown, but his attention was certainly focused in part on the Peasants' Revolt that broke out in June of that year.[167] Walsingham, Knighton, and the *Fasciculi* all link Wyclif to the rebellion; Walsingham lists Wyclif's heresies as the first of three causes for the rebellion, and says that Ball taught the heresies of Wyclif; Knighton describes Ball as the precursor to Wyclif the same way that John the Baptist was precursor to Christ; and the *Fasciculi* includes a supposed confession by Ball linking Wyclif directly to Ball and the Revolt.[168] These sources all reflect a general sense that Wyclif was connected with the Revolt in some way, but there is no reason to think that Ball was in fact personally connected to Wyclif.[169] Ball's "confession" was written twenty years after the fact and no earlier source knows anything about it. Had Courtenay possessed any real evidence for Wyclif's complicity in the Revolt, it is unimaginable that he would not have attempted to charge Wyclif as a criminal. For much of the twentieth century, scholars rejected any connection between Wyclif and

---

[166] *Fasc. Ziz.*, pp. 132–238; Workman, 2:146–47.

[167] For the Peasants' Revolt of 1381, see Rodney Hilton, *Bond Men Made Free: Medieval Peasant Movements and the English Rising of 1381*, (London, 1973, repr. 1986), pp. 137–232; E.B. Fryde, *The Great Revolt of 1381*, (London, 1981); Steven Justice, *Writing and Rebellion: England in 1381*, (Berkeley, 1994); Margaret Aston, "Corpus Christi and Corpus Regni: Heresy and the Peasants' Revolt," *Past and Present* 143 (1975), 3–47; Saul, *Richard II*, pp. 56–82.

[168] *St. Albans*, pp. 500–3; *Hist. Ang.*, 2:11–12; *Knighton's Chronicle*, p. 242; *Fasc. Ziz.*, pp. 273–74.

[169] Walsingham rightly notes that Ball had been preaching seditiously for twenty years at the time of the Revolt, and this is confirmed by the fact that he had been excommunicated by three different archbishops of Canterbury, three bishops of London, and the bishops of Lincoln and Norwich; see A.K. McHardy, *The Church in London 1375–1392* (London, 1977), p. xviii; Aston, "Corpus Christi," pp. 20–23. As early as 1364, Ball was denounced to Edward III has a preacher of heresy; *Patent Rolls of Edward III*, 12: 476. This makes clear that Ball was active as a heretic more than decade before Wyclif's thought began to radicalize.

the Revolt.[170] More recently, though, there has been a tendency to highlight the conceptual connections between Wyclif and the Revolt and to admit that Wyclif's teaching may have indirectly influenced the events. As Hudson points out, even when he condemns the Revolt for going beyond the law, he still manages to condemn the clergy as deserving of what happened. [171]

Wyclif was working on *De blasphemia* during this summer, since he begins discussing the Peasants' Revolt in the middle of the text.[172] By the end of the summer, however, he must have been under considerable pressure, both because of the controversy surrounding his views on the Eucharist and because of the accusations that he had been involved in the Peasants' Revolt in some way. He appears to have left Oxford permanently for Lutterworth in late 1381; the last evidence for him at Oxford comes from October 22, 1381, when he left a copy of the *Decretum* on deposit at the university.[173] By February of 1382, when the friars appealed to John of Gaunt against those who were slandering them, they identified Nicholas Hereford as their chief enemy; had Wyclif still been at Oxford, the friars would likely have mentioned him instead of Hereford.[174]

The Blackfriars Council

In the wake of the Peasants' Revolt, Wyclif's old nemesis, Bishop Courtenay, was promoted to Archbishop of Canterbury to replace the murdered Archbishop Sudbury. This certainly boded ill for Wyclif, especially since Gaunt had sent the new archbishop a gift of a dozen live does, a gesture that suggests Gaunt was seeking a better relationship with the man he had quarreled with so publicly.[175] Courtenay was formally translated to Canterbury on September 8, 1381, but he did not receive the pallium until May 4, 1382. Until his formal investment, he refused to undertake any official acts, including performing the wedding of King Richard and Anne of Bohemia (although he did perform Anne's coronation).

---

[170] Workman, 2:237–8; Dahmus, p. 82; Fryde, *Great Revolt*, pp. 17–18.
[171] Hudson, *Premature Reformation*, pp. 66–9; "Wyclif, John," p. 619; Justice, pp. 75–101.
[172] Hudson and Kenny, "Wyclif, John," pp. 623–24.
[173] British Library Royal MS, 10 E ii.
[174] *Fasc. Ziz.*, p. 294; Dahmus, p. 134.
[175] Goodman, *John of Gaunt*, p. 284.

During the period between elevation and investment, Courtenay certainly had reason to be concerned about the spread of heresy. The new chancellor of Oxford, Robert Rygge, began showing definite pro-Wyclif leanings at least by early May, appointing Nicholas Hereford and Philip Repingdon to preach the official Ascension Day and Corpus Christi Day sermons at Oxford.[176] Exactly when Courtenay learned of these events is unclear, but he had at some point warned Rygge that Hereford was suspected of heresy. Courtenay must also have known that Wyclif had submitted another document, the *Imprecationes*, to the Parliament that convened on May 7. In the *Imprecationes*, Wyclif returned to the relationship between the Church and the Kingdom of England, offering arguments that money should not be sent to Rome, that England owed no prelate obedience unless such obedience fit with Christ's law, and that non-resident foreign clergy should not be allowed to hold benefices, and that those who were excommunicated should not be arrested.[177] He also published a *Complaint*, in which he argued that members of religious orders should be allowed to leave them, that the clergy could be deprived of both property and tithes, and that his understanding of the Eucharist should be openly taught in the churches. Parliament did not respond to these works.

One of Courtenay's first official acts after receiving the pallium was to summon a council to meet at London Blackfriars on May 17.[178] This summons must have just preceded Wyclif's latest attempt to influence Parliament and Wyclif's efforts must have confirmed Courtenay's sense that immediate action was necessary. The composition of the council was certainly to some extent slanted against Wyclif, since of the sixteen masters of theology, fifteen were friars who could be counted on to oppose the increasingly anti-mendicant Wyclif. There were twenty-one other friars and a monk on the council, as well as fifteen seculars.[179]

---

[176] *Fasc. Ziz.*, pp. 296–300; see Anne Hudson, "Wycliffism in Oxford 1381–1411," in *Wyclif in his Times*, ed. Anthony Kenny, (Oxford, 1986), pp. 68–84, at pp. 68–9; Catto, "Wyclif," pp. 214–15.

[177] *St. Albans*, pp. 582–87; see Workman, 2:250–52.

[178] On the Blackfriars Council, also known as the Earthquake Council because of a large earthquake that struck London while the council was meeting, see *St. Albans*, pp. 596–602; *Fasc. Ziz.* pp. 272–4; Wilkins, *Concilia*, 3:157–8; Workman, 2:266–9; Dahmus, pp. 89–99.

[179] For a discussion of the composition of this council, see Workman, 2:253–66;

Although the *Fasciculi* says that Wyclif was present, this is almost certainly a mistake; the articles condemned by the council make no mention of Wyclif, and requiring Wyclif to be present would have raised the possibility that his patron Gaunt would intervene as had happened at St Paul's and Lambeth. The omission of Wyclif's name from the articles is almost certainly intentional. By omitting Wyclif's name, Courtenay was able to condemn Wyclif's ideas without provoking a fight with Gaunt. While Gaunt was less likely to intervene at this point, Courtenay's prudence here seems justified, given the failure of the trials at St Paul's and Lambeth.[180]

On May 21, the Council reconvened after a four-day hiatus to consider the articles Courtenay had presented to them. The meeting was interrupted, not by Gaunt or angry Londoners, but rather by an earthquake, which Courtenay quickly interpreted as an omen foreshadowing the purging of heresy from the realm. Then the council discussed the articles they had been given and condemned twenty-four of them, ten as heretical and fourteen as erroneous. The ten heretical articles cover the Eucharist, the power of clergy to perform sacraments, confession, obedience to the pope, clerical temporality, and the curious thesis that God must obey the Devil.[181] The fourteen erroneous articles deal with excommunication, unauthorized

---

Dahmus, pp. 90–93. Courtenay was certainly careful to make sure the council would not be divided the way Barton's committee had been, but it is unlikely that any general council of English ecclesiastics would have approved of Wyclif's teachings unless considerable pressure had been applied, as it was at Lambeth.

[180] There is also an illuminating parallel to this condemnation. In 1285. Archbishop Pecham of Canterbury issued a condemnation of 12 Thomist propositions drawn from the writings of the Dominican Richard Knapwell and excommunicated Knapwell. The Dominican Prior Provincial of England, William of Hotham, objected that as Knapwell was a Dominican, the only person with jurisdiction over him was the Pope. To get around this obstacle, Pecham issued a second condemnation based on the first, but omitting the name of Richard Knapwell. Instead, the condemnation includes a blanket excommunication of all who might affirm them, publicly or privately. For the whole case, see Larsen, *Popular and Academic Heresy*, pp. 137–42.

[181] Different versions of this list offer varying readings of this article, ranging from 'debet' to 'debeat' to 'debent', and the interpretation of this article consequently varies. Workman, 2:268, connects it to Wyclif's theory of dominion. Wyclif understood it in a historical sense, that Christ had obeyed the Devil in allowing the Devil to transport him and in washing Judas Iscariot's feet while the Devil was in the apostle; see *Sermones*, ed. J. Loserth. (London, 1889), 3:467–8; Kelly, "Trial Procedures," p. 9.

preaching, the rights of sinful clergy to temporalities and tithes, the efficacy of clerical prayer, and various aspects of religious orders.

As Dahmus points out, the articles condemned by the Blackfriars Council are essentially unconnected to the list condemned by Gregory four years earlier.[182] Only item eight on the Blackfriars list corresponds to anything on Gregory's list. The differences in the list largely reflect the increasingly radical nature of Wyclif's thought in the period after 1377. That Courtenay did not include Gregory's list within his own is easily explained; the papacy had already condemned those ideas, so it would have been superfluous for Courtenay to have done so.

Wyclif, in a response to the Blackfriars Council that is undated but was probably issued soon after the condemnation, says that some of the articles were rightly condemned, but that no one had actually maintained them, and that the Council had falsely attributed heresies to orthodox men in order to damage their reputations.[183] He goes on to say that the friars had persuaded the bishops to help them malign Christ, his saints, and the doctors of the Church as heretics, and that they had published their own particular doctrine of the Eucharist. It is clear that the majority of the condemned articles were connected to Wyclif's thought, while items six, ten, sixteen, and seventeen may not have been Wyclif's ideas, but rather those of his followers.[184]

Five days later, Parliament finally responded to Wyclif's writings and to the Blackfriars Council by issuing a statute requiring royal commissions be sent to the sheriffs and other royal officials to arrest all unauthorized preachers and their supporters. The bishops were empowered to certify someone as an unauthorized preacher and to start the machinery for their arrest.[185] A month later, on Courtenay's request, the Crown issued its own letters patent that revised the somewhat clumsy process prescribed by Parliament.[186] The Crown

---

[182] Dahmus, pp. 95–96.

[183] *Fasc. Ziz.*, pp. 283–85.

[184] Dahmus, pp. 96–98.

[185] *Rotuli Parliamentorum; ut et Petitiones, et Placita in Parliamento Tempore Richardi II*, ed. J. Strachey, 1767, 3:124–25.

[186] Wilkins, *Concilia*, 3:156; *Calendar of Patent Rolls, 1381–85*, p. 150. See also Dahmus, pp. 99–101; H.G. Richardson, "Heresy and the Lay Power Under Richard II," in *English Historical Review* 51 (1936), 1–28, at pp. 7–10.

issued commissions to Courtenay and his suffragans to arrest those who preached or maintained the conclusions condemned by the Blackfriars Council and to hold them until they recanted their errors. The Crown's subjects and officials were ordered to assist the bishops in their efforts and specifically warned not to assist, advise, or favor such heretics, on pain of confiscation of property. This patent represents a considerable revision, both of the system for punishing heretics as it had existed in fourteenth-century England and of the statute issued by Parliament a month earlier. In addition to the slow and sometimes ineffective process of signification for excommunication, the normal vehicle for arresting heretics, and in place of the slow and bureaucratic method allowed for by Parliament, the episcopate could now simply arrest those it deemed to be heretics on the basis of a royal commission to do so. However, this does not represent a wholesale abrogation of royal authority over the process. The letters patent specifically included a provision for the king or his council to intervene and release episcopal prisoners. Additionally, as the system evolved, the commissions were issued to a particular bishop and lapsed when that man was no longer bishop of that see, so that a new commission had to be obtained every time a bishop either died or was translated. This gave the Crown a measure of control over the process; had the Crown concluded it had conceded too much power, it could simply have allowed the commissions to lapse without renewing them. It is also interesting to note that Parliament was unhappy with the modification to their statute. The Parliamentary session ended on May 22, so that Parliament was not meeting when the letters patent were issued on June 26. When Parliament reconvened at Michaelmas, the Commons protested the letters patent on the grounds that the system required them to justify themselves more than their ancestors had been accustomed to, and that the system bound them more to the prelates.[187] They were promised that the system would be repealed, but this never happened. There is no reason to think that this protest was in any way intended as support for Wyclif; rather Parliament was protesting the increased authority of the bishops and perhaps the Crown's overturning of a statute passed by Parliament.

---

[187] *Rot. Parl.* 3:141; Richardson, "Heresy," pp. 8–9; Dahmus, pp. 137–38.

Well-armed by the new commission and largely fortified against the sort of interference he had encountered in 1377 and 1378, Courtenay began to target the incipient Lollard movement at Oxford. But the events that ensued are part of the wider story of Lollardy rather than the personal history of John Wyclif, and so are only summarized here.[188] Courtenay wrote to Peter Stokes, his main informant on events at Oxford, detailing the Council's decision and forbidding the teaching of those errors, either in the schools or outside them. Courtenay also wrote to Rygge, requiring him to publish the condemnation, but Rygge permitted Philip Repingdon to preach his scheduled Corpus Christi Day sermon, in which he aligned himself with Wyclif's position on the Eucharist. Rygge accused Stokes of infringing on the university's privileges and went so far as to gather a band of armed men to physically prevent Stokes from publishing the condemnation.

Stokes continued to confront Rygge and determined against Repingdon, but left Oxford fearing violence. On June 12, Courtenay reconvened the Blackfriars Council, at which Rygge and his two proctors appeared as defendants vehemently suspected of heresy, accused of favoring the heresies of Wyclif, Hereford, and Repingdon. Rygge submitted immediately, while his two proctors both took some time before doing so. Rygge was required to publish the condemnation at St Mary's, Oxford, and not to interfere with those acting on Courtenay's behalf or to allow Wyclif, Hereford, Repingdon, John Aston, or Laurence Bedeman to teach or preach in Oxford. The next day, the royal council issued Rygge a stern warning, insisting on the publication of the condemnation, and on June 15, Rygge did so, although he injected some of his own unauthorized comments as he read the statement. In all of this, the conflict between seculars on the one hand and monks and mendicants on the other is quite clear; Stokes was a Carmelite, while Rygge, Aston, Hereford, and Repingdon were all seculars. After Rygge's reading of the statement, the secular students angrily accused the monks and friars of trying to destroy the university, and those students in orders feared for their lives. The Cistercian Henry Crump was suspended for

---

[188] For these events see Dahmus, pp. 101–28, Hudson, "Wycliffism," pp. 70–75; Catto, "Wyclif," pp. 214–8; Kelly, "Trial Procedures," pp. 10–20.

disturbing the peace and calling those who supported the condemned articles "Lollards."[189]

Hereford and Repingdon attempted to get Gaunt to intervene on their behalf, and Gaunt listened to their arguments, but was outraged by their opinion about the Eucharist. After lecturing them on the correct understanding of the matter, Gaunt ordered them to accept Courtenay's authority. The two men appeared before a third session of the Blackfriars Council but refused to sign a submission. They responded a few days later, but their answer was considered insufficient and evasive and they were condemned. Aston, who also appeared with them, disputed with the archbishop (in English, for the benefit of the laity present), and Courtenay condemned him as a heretic and turned him over to the secular authorities. In the autumn, Repingdon renounced his support for Wyclif, while Hereford fled the country, only to wind up in a papal prison before later returning to England. Aston published a defense of his position from jail, but eventually recanted.

In mid-July, the Crown wrote to Rygge ordering him to uncover any supporters of Wyclif, Hereford, Repingdon, and Aston, and to investigate the writings of Wyclif and Hereford. In November, Courtenay convened what was essentially the final session of the Blackfriars Council, this time in Oxford. He appointed a commission to root out any scholars who might maintain any of the condemned articles, and he received the recantation of Repindgon, Aston, and Bedeman. Having thus completed an aggressive purge of Wyclif's supporters, he closed the session.

Through all of these events, Wyclif's ideas occupied a prominent position, but he himself played no known role in the events. He seems to have already left Oxford for Lutterworth, and Courtenay's orders forbidding that Wyclif be allowed to teach are more precautionary than intended to prevent something that was actually happening. Courtenay made no known attempt to take action against Wyclif outside the university during the period when Rygge, Repingdon, and the others were being disciplined.[190]

---

[189] That at least is the traditional reading of *Fasc. Ziz.*, pp. 311–12. Wendy Scase has recently argued that in fact Crump called the Lollards (that is, those who were supporting Wyclif and his ideas) heretics; see Wendy Scase, "A Wycliffite Libel and the Naming of Heretics," pp. 19–21, in *Lollards and their Influence*, pp. 19–36.

[190] Knighton, *Chronicon*, p. 252, asserts that Wyclif was present at the November

Why Courtenay let Wyclif ultimately go unpunished is not certain. It was standard in academic condemnations at Oxford to condemn ideas and specific articles rather than individuals, so we can understand why the university itself took no further steps after Barton's censure, but the matter was hardly limited to the university, and some academic disputes had been taken out of the university to the archiepiscopal court before (the cases of John Kedington and Uthred of Boldon being the best examples). So Courtenay's failure to pursue Wyclif requires some examination, even if we cannot arrive at a definite conclusion.

In an undated later to Bishop Buckingham, Courtenay refers to Wyclif as "the Antichrist," so it is clear that he remained hostile to Wyclif.[191] Dahmus argues that the letter makes reference to some restriction Buckingham placed on Wyclif in his capacity as Wyclif's superior for Lutterworth, and Catto specifically suggests that Buckingham may have warned Wyclif to moderate his language on the Eucharist. Thus it is possible that Courtenay was satisfied with Buckingham's actions and Wyclif's continued silence on this issue, but given the fervor with which Courtenay went after Wyclif's supporters at Oxford, it seems unlikely that he had no interest in taking the matter further. It is very hard to escape the conclusion that Wyclif escaped punishment due to Gaunt's patronage. But it is not clear whether Gaunt was actively preventing Courtenay from attacking Wyclif or if Courtenay simply decided it would be prudent not to attempt anything so long as Wyclif was not attracting attention to himself. Since the middle of 1377, Gaunt had consistently followed a course of requiring Wyclif to be silent, but not permitting any formal action to be taken against the man himself, and Wyclif's unmolested retirement fits into that same pattern.

Interestingly, in January of 1382, the Exchequer decided to collect the more than £7 Wyclif still owed the Crown as the result of the mission to Bruges. Wyclif paid the sum owed in June of that

---

synod at Oxford, and that he made a recantation. But the details of this claim contradict the evidence at several points, and the document that Knighton interprets as a recantation is, in fact, a reaffirmation of his position on the Eucharist; Dahmus, pp. 136–37.

[191] Wilkins, *Concilia*, 3:168–9; Dahmus, 138–39, Catto, "Wyclif," p. 218. The letter probably dates to the fall of 1382 or shortly before then.

year in Leicestershire, which strengthens the impression that he was at Lutterworth.[192] Whether this sudden drive to collect such a long-standing debt is just a manifestation of tardy bureaucratic efficiency, or if it represents some loss of royal favor, is unclear.

Wyclif's Last Years

At Lutterworth, Wyclif spent much of his time revising his older works, thus clouding our understanding of the evolution of Wyclif's career and thought.[193] He also penned a number of new works, including the *Trialogus*, the *Dialogus*, the *Opus evangelicum*, *De citationibus frivolis*, and the *Sermones viginti*, and does not appear to have been out of touch with major political currents and academic developments at Oxford, despite his retirement. Indeed, the *Sermones viginti* are unlikely to have been intended as sermons to be preached to his unlettered congregation at Lutterworth and seem intended for a university audience.[194] Henry Knighton and other later authorities assert that Wyclif translated the Bible into English during this last period of his life, but there has been some scholarly debate over the role Wyclif played in the translation; Hudson and Kenny feel that the question of Wyclif's participation is "irretrievable," while Conrad Lindberg sees Wyclif as directing the whole project.[195]

It is also worth commenting here about Wyclif's declining relationship with the mendicants.[196] For most of his life, Wyclif appears

---

[192] McHardy, "Mission," p. 522.

[193] Hudson and Kenny, "Wyclif, John," pp. 621–22.

[194] Hudson and Kenny, "Wyclif, John," p. 623.

[195] Knighton, *Chronicon*, pp. 242–4; Hudson, *Premature Reformation*, pp. 240–1; Hudson and Kenny, "Wyclif, John," p. 623. For a more detailed look at this complex issue, see Mary Dove, "Wyclif and the English Bible," elsewhere in this volume.

[196] For Wyclif and the friars, see Gwynn, *Austin Friars*, pp. 210–79; Carolly Erickson, "The Fourteenth-Century Franciscans and their Critics," parts 1 and 2, *Franciscan Studies* 35 (1975), 107–35, and 36 (1076), 108–47; Edith Wilks Dolnikowski, "FitzRalph and Wyclif on the Mendicants," *Michigan Academician* 19:1 (1987), 87–100; Thomas Renna, "Wyclif's Attack on the Monks," *Studies in Church History Subsidia 5: From Ockham to Wyclif*, ed. Anne Hudson and Michael Wilks, (London, 1987), pp. 267–80; Geoffrey L. Dipple, "Uthred and the Friars: Apostolic Poverty and Clerical Dominion between FitzRalph and Wyclif," *Traditio* 49 (1994), 235–58; Ian Christopher Levy, "Texts for a Poor Church: John Wyclif and the Decretals," *Essays in Medieval Studies* 20 (2003), 94–107.

to have admired the mendicants, particularly their original ideals.[197] He is known to have read at least one Spiritual Franciscan treatise, the *Vade mecum in tribulatione* of Juan de Pera-Tallada. During his regency, he enjoyed a friendly rivalry with the Franciscan William Woodford, since Woodford says that he used to send Wyclif a notebook with arguments in it, and Wyclif would write responses to the arguments in the book and send it back.[198] The year before Wyclif issued his *Determinatio* (and therefore in 1372 or 1376), he was engaged in a controversy with Woodford on the issue of civil dominion and the right of the clergy to own property. Later on, Woodford was to accuse Wyclif of making the attack out of malice, but at the time the debate seems to have been a civil one, although we might see it as the first cooling of their friendship.[199] In the 1370s, Wyclif was also on good terms with the Augustinian Thomas Winterton, another friar who was to write against him in 1381.[200]

By the late 1370s, however, Wyclif's relationship with the friars was becoming more complicated. In 1377 four mendicants accompanied him to St Paul's, and a year later he complained about the condemnation of the unnamed Franciscan by William Barton. The same year, according to the author of the *Eulogium*, Wyclif "greatly commended the religion of the Friars Minor, saying that they were most dear to God."[201] In 1381, he referred to them as his "dear sons in the mendicant religion." When Wyclif received news of Barton's condemnation, he was teaching at the Augustinian school at Oxford, which would have been unlikely if he had become fully antimendicant by that time. Yet in 1379, he was beginning to be more critical of the Franciscans, urging them to defend the bull *Exiit qui seminat* (the bull of Pope Nicholas III in which he declared that the Franciscan life of poverty was founded on the Gospels and strengthened by the life and teaching of Christ and the Apostles) and warning that if they did not, the Church would be at the mercy of lying hypocrites.[202] In 1380, he began a series of sermons that

---

[197] Workman, 2:97–98.
[198] Dahmus, pp. 19–20.
[199] Dahmus, p. 25.
[200] Workman, 2:146–7; Gwynn, *Austin Friars*, pp. 225–26.
[201] *Eulogium*, 3:345: "Johannes Wicclif magister in theologia dictus flos Oxoniae determinando disputavit contra possessiones immobiles ecclesiae, religionem Fratrum Minorum multum commendans, dicens eos esse Deo carissimos."
[202] Levy, "Texts," p. 101.

regularly used friars to illustrate immoral behavior, and by 1381, when he was writing *De simonia, De apostasia,* and *De blasphemia,* he was denouncing the evils of the friars; this became a common theme of the writings of his last years.[203] By this time, many mendicants had begun attacking Wyclif. Barton's committee had included six mendicants. In June of 1381, in response to Wyclif's *Confessio,* Woodford delivered the lectures on which his *Septuaginta duo quaestiones de Sacramento Altaris* was based; this work condemned Wyclif's teachings and attributed Wyclif's attack to corruption and disappointment stemming from the controversy over Canterbury College.[204] About the same time, Winterton issued his *Absolutio,* in which he rejects Wyclif's ideas as heresies, but hesitates to call Wyclif himself a heretic because, he says, he does not know if Wyclif intends to obstinately defend his errors or is ready to be corrected.[205] In February of 1382, the four mendicant orders sent a letter to Gaunt in which they identified Wyclif as the author of the Peasants' Revolt, and the friars played a very prominent roll in the Blackfriars Council later that year.

The reasons for Wyclif's break with the mendicants are clearly complicated. Walsingham and Woodford tied Wyclif's hostility to the dispute over Canterbury College.[206] While this drawn-out lawsuit may have tarnished Wyclif's views of the mendicants somewhat, it clearly cannot be the main cause of the break, given that the dispute was settled years before the break happened and that the real dispute was with the Benedictines. Carolly Erickson has suggested that it is chiefly due to the criticism he had received from the mendicants concerning his theological speculations, pointing out that both FitzRalph and Wyclif transferred their hostility toward the theories of some mendicants to the mendicants themselves after being attacked by the mendicants.[207] This certainly explains the somewhat hysterical tone of his last works, but Wyclif's break with the mendicants clearly precedes the attacks on him in 1382. Woodford and Winterton's attacks on him in June of 1381, if Wyclif was aware of them, provide a slightly more immediate motive, but while the collapse of the relationships with his one-time friends might have contributed to his

---

[203] Dolnikowski, "FitzRalph," p. 95.
[204] Workman, 2:186–88.
[205] *Fasc. Ziz.,* pp. 181–238; Gwynn, *Austin Friars,* pp. 225–26.
[206] See above, pp. 13–14.
[207] Erickson, "Fourteenth-Century Franciscans," pp. 120–22.

bitterness, it cannot explain matters by itself, nor does frustration over Gaunt's refusal to support him. Edith Wilks Dolnikowski has suggested that the roots of Wyclif's antimendicancy lie in FitzRalph's influence on Wyclif's early thought, while Geoffrey Dipple has connected them to the thought of Uthred of Boldon.[208] Although Wyclif did not begin to articulate his antimendicant theories until the late 1370s, his early adherence to FitzRalph may have conditioned him to move toward antimendicancy when things did not go as he had expected.

Why he began developing his antimendicant thought in the late 1370s is less clear than why it blossomed in the early 1380s. Wyclif must have become increasingly frustrated by 1381. In the late 1370s, his fortunes had been riding high; he had dodged three attempts by authorities to condemn him, he was an advisor to one of the most powerful men in the kingdom, and he must have hoped that his criticisms of the Church were about to bear fruit in the shape of real reform, especially since at the Gloucester Parliament it appeared that the king had at least listened to Wyclif's arguments about disendowment. Then in 1381, everything suddenly began to fall apart. He was startled by Barton's condemnation and Gaunt's refusal to intervene. Woodford not only attacked him but impugned his motives, and he began to be blamed for the Peasants' Revolt. To a proud and combative man, all this must have been deeply frustrating, and it is easy to see how he might have felt that it was the fault of the mendicants, who had failed to live up to the standards of St Francis. Certainly his disappointment and frustration increased in 1382, after he was condemned by the Blackfriars Council and Parliament refused to respond to him, and it is even possible (though hardly provable) that the stress and frustration of these two years contributed to the health problems that eventually took his life.[209]

Pope Urban VI summoned Wyclif late in 1383 to appear before the papal curia.[210] Little is known about this incident, but in *De citationibus frivolis*, Wyclif explains that he cannot go because he is "disabled and crippled" and because the Crown has prohibited him from going, and in a letter to Urban, he states that God "has obliged me

---

[208] Dolnikowski, "FitzRalph and Wyclif," pp. 92–3; Dipple, "Uthred," pp. 256–58.
[209] McFarlane, *John Wyclif*, p. 85.
[210] For Urban's summons, see Dahmus, pp. 139–48.

to the contrary."[211] The statement that God has not allowed it seems
to refer both to his physical infirmity and the royal prohibition,
rather than to an argument that God requires him to reject the
authority of the pope on this point. Whether the royal prohibition
he refers to was a particular prohibition on Wyclif or rather a general prohibition on papal appeals is unclear, but the former is more
likely. Given the tone of *De citationibus frivolis*, it would appear that
Wyclif's stance on the papacy had moderated somewhat at the end
of his life.

Sometime in 1382, Wyclif appears to have suffered a stroke that
severely weakened him for the rest of his life. This partial paralysis
did not prevent him from writing, but it may have made it difficult
to fulfill his pastoral duties, and he apparently hired a curate named
John Horn to assist him. Horn lived into his eighties, and in 1441
he is recorded by Thomas Gascoigne as testifying to Wyclif's last
days.[212] According to Horn, Wyclif was hearing mass on December
28, 1384. At the exact moment of the elevation of the host, he
suffered a stroke that paralyzed him and left him unable to speak.
Three days later, on December 31, he died. The date of his death
is confirmed by the record of the appointment of his successor, but
the rest of Horn's statement is uncorroborated. The general picture
of paralysis is supported by Wyclif's own statement in *De citationibus
frivolis*, as well as by Walsingham, who says the attack of paralysis
happened on December 29 (St. Thomas Becket's day), but Horn's
story of Wyclif suffering his fatal stroke at the moment of elevation
is highly suspect, since it seems to criticize Wyclif's rejection of transubstantiation.[213] Nevertheless, Horn is recorded as swearing to the
story's veracity and, while improbable, the story is not impossible.
Wyclif was buried, probably in the churchyard, and since he was
not under any excommunication at the time he would have received
a normal burial service.

---

[211] John Wyclif, *De citationibus frivolis* 4, in *Polemical Works in Latin*, ed. R. Buddensieg, (London, 1883), 2:556; *Fasc. Ziz*, pp. 341–42.

[212] John Lewis, *The History of the Life and Sufferings of the Reverend and Learned John Wiclif*, (Oxford, 1820), p. 336; Workman, 2:316; Hudson and Kenny, "Wyclif, John," p. 620.

[213] *St. Albans*, pp. 736–39; *Hist. Ang.*, 2:119–20.

After Wyclif's Death

Wyclif's story does not completely end with his death.[214] In 1395, Archbishop Arundel, the chancellor of England, ordered an examination of the *Trialogus* for heresy.[215] A year later, Arundel convened a synod that condemned eighteen articles drawn from the *Trialogus*, and the next year, a commission upheld the condemnation when a group of canon and civil lawyers complained that these eighteen articles were still being maintained at Oxford. In 1406, a document was issued in the name of the chancellor and the assembled masters of the university that praised Wyclif and asserted that he had never been found guilty of heresy and that his body had never been exhumed or burned. This document was sealed with the university's seal, and then sent to Prague, in support of the Hussites.[216] Thomas Gascoigne claimed that Peter Payne had stolen the seal and written the document himself, and the fact that the then-chancellor, Richard Courtenay, was almost certainly away from the university at the time makes the incident suspect, but it is possible that Payne somehow obtained the consent of the university masters.[217]

In 1407, Arundel issued the Constitutions of Oxford, which prohibited the reading of any work of Wyclif's, including translations of the Scriptures, until they had been approved.[218] Two years later, he ordered the university to establish a committee of scholars to examine Wyclif's writings for heresies and errors.[219] In 1411, the committee finally sent him a list of 267 heresies and errors. Arundel condemned the articles, required every member of Oxford to swear an oath renouncing them, and then submitted the list to Rome.[220]

---

[214] For this summary of events, see Dahmus, pp. 151–4; Catto, "Wyclif," pp. 233–4; Kelly, "Trial Procedures," pp. 20–26.

[215] Rymer, *Foedera*, 7:806.

[216] Wilkins, *Concilia*, 3:302; Hudson, *Premature Reformation*, p. 100.

[217] Thomas Gascoigne, *Loci e libro veritatum*, ed. J.E.T. Rogers, (Oxford, 1881), p. 20; Hudson, *Premature Reformation*, pp. 100–1. Catto, "Wyclif," p. 242, seems to suggest that control of the seal was lax enough that a faction at the university might have legitimately used the seal.

[218] Wilkins, *Concilia*, 3:317; John D. Mansi, *Sacrorum Conciliorum Nova et Amplissima Collectio* (Venice, 1784), 26:1031–46 (note that the individual constitutions have different titles in this version); Workman, 2:355–7; Dahmus, p. 152; Catto, "Wyclif," p. 244.

[219] Wilkins, *Concilia*, 3:322; Dahmus, pp. 152–53.

[220] Wilkins, *Concilia*, 3:339–49; Workman, 2: 366; Dahmus, p. 153; Catto, "Wyclif," p. 248.

As a result, in 1412, John XXIII presided over a council that condemned the *Trialogus* and the *Dialogus*, as well as other works of Wyclif.[221] The Council of Constance took up the issue and appointed a committee to review the works of Wyclif and Hus. The committee's report prompted the Council to first condemn forty-five articles, including the twenty-four articles of the Blackfriars Council, and to later condemn a total of 260 articles. Wyclif was declared a heretic and it was decreed that his bones should be dug up and cast out of hollowed ground.[222] At the time this was not done; no papal order on it survives, and Philip Repingdon, now bishop of Lincoln, apparently disregarded the Council's decree. Eventually, in 1427, Pope Martin V ordered Repingdon's successor to follow through, and in 1428, Wyclif's bones were dug up and burned, and the ashes scattered in the river Swift.[223]

Conclusion

Wyclif's overall personality remains hard to grasp, in part because there are so many uncertainties about the facts of his life, but he was clearly a complex man. He was obviously highly intelligent and well-educated, one of the great minds of his generation, (indeed, Knighton describes him as the pre-eminent theologian and philosopher of his day) and had he not become embroiled in religious and political controversy, it is easy to imagine that he might have risen quite high in the English Church, even in an age when theological activity was no longer a guarantee to preferment.

He was also a bold man, able to confront at different turns his peers, university officials, bishops and archbishops, and even the Duke of Lancaster. This boldness must have developed out of a sense of the rightness of his convictions, but it is also reflective of a strong quarrelsome streak in him. Throughout his life as we know it, he

---

[221] Henry Finke, *Acta Concilii Constanciensis* (Muenster, 1896), 1:124, 162–3; *CPL*, 6:174, 343; Dahmus, p. 153.

[222] Mansi, *Sacrorum Conciliorum*, 27:632–4; Dahmus, p. 153.

[223] *CPL*, 7:23. To make sure the order was carried out, letters were also sent to the Archbishop of Canterbury, Duke Humphrey of Gloucester, and other members of the Royal Council. The thoroughness of these letters suggests that someone in England had complained to the papacy that Wyclif's remains had not been dug up.

was engaged in disputes of various kinds, intellectual, legal, political, and religious. It is tempting to look to this quarrelsome element of his personality for explanation of some of the more obscure turns in his life, such as his failure to complete his probation at Merton or his removal from the Bruges delegation. But his convictions were not so strong that he was unable to overlook certain contradictions in them, such as his own absentee pluralism, his unsatisfied desire for papal provision, or Gaunt's scandalous personal life. It must be admitted that he was guilty of some inconsistency on these matters.

He possessed at least some measure of political savvy, developed in part through his service to the Crown, and this enabled him to navigate the political arena well enough that he essentially escaped punishment for his ideas and dodged three attempts to condemn him before university and episcopal authorities finally engineered a strong condemnation of his teachings. Despite his inconsistencies, he was able to inspire his followers to defy the established Church, although with much less success than he himself did. He must have been an effective preacher, to judge from the evidence that he was popular with the London crowds, and the dedication of his immediate followers is certainly due to his combination of intellectual ability and personal persuasiveness. While it is perhaps difficult to like him as a person, it is hard not to be impressed with his accomplishments and the legacy of his thought.

WYCLIF'S LOGIC AND METAPHYSICS*

Alessandro D. Conti

Wyclif's logical and metaphysical theories are, at the same time, the final result of the preceding realist tradition of thought (Wyclif himself presents the nucleus of his metaphysics, that is, the theories of

---

* Among the very large body of writings produced by Wyclif, both in Latin and English, the following are examined here in order to reconstruct his logico-metaphysical theories:
- *De logica* (*On Logic*—c. 1360), in *Tractatus de logica*, ed. M.H. Dziewicki, 3 vols. (London, 1893–99), 1:1–74;
- *Continuatio logicae* (*Continuation of <the Treatise on> Logic*), in *Tractatus de logica*, 1: 75–234, and vols. 2–3 (date of composition: about 1360–63 according to W.R. Thomson, *The Latin Writings of John Wyclyf: an Annotated Catalog* [Toronto, 1983], pp. 5–6; but between 1371 and 1374 according to I.J. Mueller in the philological introduction to his critical edition of Wyclif's *Tractatus de universalibus* [see below], pp. xxxv and xxxvii–xxxviii);
- *De ente in communi* (*On Universal Being*—c. 1365), in S.H. Thomson ed., *Johannis Wyclif Summa de ente, libri primi tractatus primus et secundus* (Oxford, 1930), pp. 1–61;
- *De ente primo in communi* (*On Primary Being*—c. 1365), in *Summa de ente, libri primi tractatus primus et secundus*, pp. 62–112;
- *De actibus animae* (*On the Acts of Soul*—c. 1365), in M.H. Dziewicki ed., *Johannis Wyclif miscellanea philosophica*, 2 vols. (London, 1902), 1:1–160;
- *Purgans errores circa universalia in communi* (*Amending Errors about Universals*—between 1366 and 1368), in M.H. Dziewicki ed., *Johannis Wyclif de ente librorum duorum excerpta* (London, 1909), pp. 29–48;
- *Purgans errores circa universalia in communi*, chs. 2–3, in S.H. Thomson, "A 'Lost' Chapter of Wyclif's *Summa de ente*," *Speculum* 4 (1929), 339–46 (The MS Cambridge, Trinity College, B.16.2, used by Dziewicki for his edition of the work, lacks the second chapter and the first section of the third chapter. S.H. Thomson integrated the text on the basis of the MS Wien, Österreichische Nationalbibliothek, 4307)
- *Purgans errores circa veritates in communi* (*Amending Errors about Truths*—c. 1367–68), in *Johannis Wyclif de ente librorum duorum excerpta*, pp. 1–28;
- *De ente praedicamentali* (*On Categorial Being*—c. 1369), ed. R. Beer (London, 1891);
- *De intelleccione Dei* (*On the Intellection of God*—c. 1370), in *Johannis Wyclif de ente librorum duorum excerpta*, pp. 49–112;
- *De volucione Dei* (*On the Volition of God*—c. 1370), in *Johannis Wyclif de ente librorum duorum excerpta*, 113–286;
- *Tractatus de universalibus*, ed. I.J. Mueller (Oxford, 1985) (date of composition: about 1368–69 according to W.R. Thomson, *The Latin Writings*, pp. 20–24; but between 1373 and 1374 according to Mueller in the philological introduction to his

universals, as intermediate between those of Thomas Aquinas and Giles of Rome and that of Walter Burley)[1] and the starting-point of the new form(s) of realism propounded in Europe between the end of the fourteenth and the beginning of the fifteenth centuries.[2] However, significant studies dedicated almost totally to the analysis of the main features of Wyclif's philosophy have appeared only in

---

own edition of the treatise, pp. xix–xxv)—English Translation by A. Kenny, with an Introduction by P.V. Spade, *On Universals* (Oxford, 1985);

- *De materia et forma* (*On matter and form*), in *Johannis Wyclif miscellanea philosophica*, 1: 163–242 (date of composition, between late 1370 and early 1372 according to W.R. Thomson, *The Latin Writings*, pp. 35–36, but about 1374–75 according to Mueller in his introduction to the critical edition of the treatise on universals, p. xxxviii).

Many of these treatises were later arranged as a *Summa*, called *Summa de ente* (*Summa on Being*), in two books, containing seven and six treatises respectively. On the complex questions concerning structure and purpose of the *Summa de ente*, see J.A. Robson, *Wyclif and the Oxford Schools* (Cambridge, 1961), pp. 115–40, and W.R. Thomson, *The Latin Writings*, pp. 14–35. Many of Wyclif's edited works were produced between the end of the nineteenth and the beginning of the twentieth centuries by the members of the Wyclif Society. Notwithstanding their ground-breaking efforts, some of their editions are inadequate. The problems with the manuscripts of Wyclif's writings are declared in their introductions, but further insufficienses were noted by W.R. Thomson, *The Latin Writings*, *passim*. For the insufficienses of Dziewicki's editions of the treatises on logic (*De Logica* and *Continuatio logicae*) see also N. Kretzmann, "Continua, Indivisibles, and Change in Wyclif's Logic of Scripture," in *Wyclif in his Times*, ed. A. Kenny (Oxford, 1986), pp. 39–41.

[1] Cf. *Tractatus de universalibus* (sixth treatise of the first book of the *Summa de ente*) 4, pp. 86/40–87/59: "Ut aliqui dicunt quod omnis substantia est singularis et, ut universaliter apprehenditur, est universalis, sicut opus dicitur humanum et res visa, intellecta vel aliter extrinsece denominata ab humanitate, visione et intellectione extra opus. Et ista sententia imponitur Sancto Thomae, Aegidio et multis aliis. Secunda via dicit quod universale non est aliquod suorum singularium, cum communicabilitate, participatione vel praedicabilitate, prioritate naturae, insensibilitate et quotlibet aliis differentiis distinguatur ex opposito a singulari. . . . Et illius opinionis videtur fuisse Magister Burleigh et multi alii. . . . Ego autem per medium incedo concordando extrema, et concedo cum prima opinione quod omne universale est singulare et econtra, licet distinguantur formaliter ab invicem."

[2] See below, pp. 118–25. On Wycliffism in Oxford between fourteenth and fifteenth centuries see: A. Hudson, "Wycliffism in Oxford 1381–1411," in *Wyclif in his Times*, pp. 67–84; M. Keen, "The Influence of Wyclif," in *Wyclif in his Times*, pp. 127–45; and J.I. Catto, "Wyclif and Wycliffism in Oxford, 1356–1430," in *The History of the University of Oxford*, ed. J.L. Catto – R. Evans, 2 vols. (Oxford, 1992), 2:175–261. Quite suprisingly Wyclif did not espouse the cause of realism in his youth, but only later. Indeed, at the beginning of his studies, he sympathized with nominalist views (a fact that can explain the hint of fanaticism which sometimes can be perceived in his extant writings)—see S.H. Thomson, "The Philosophical Basis of Wyclif's Theology," *Journal of Religion* 11 (1931), p. 89; Robson, *Wyclif and the Oxford Schools*, pp. 144–45; G. Leff, *Heresy in the Later Middle Ages*, 2 vols. (Manchester, 1967), 2:501.

the last few years.[3] Prior to Mueller's edition of his *Tractatus de universalibus* in 1985, medieval scholars and historians of ideas had generally given too little attention to Wyclif's logico-metaphysical views, focusing instead on his theological and political doctrines. His contemporaries, on the contrary, were much more interested in his logical and metaphysical theories, that they (rightly) perceived as an absolute novelty.[4] In fact, he elaborated a form of intensional logic where the main relation between beings (*entia*), the relation from which any other stems, is that one of formal distinction, conceived

[3] See N.W. Gilbert, "Ockham, Wyclif and the *via moderna*," in *Antiqui und Moderni: Traditionsbewubtsein und Fortschrittsbewubtsein im späten Mittelalter*, ed. A. Zimmermann (Berlin, 1974), pp. 85–125; A. Kenny, *Wyclif* (Oxford, 1985), pp. 1–30; P.V. Spade, "Introduction", in John Wyclif, *On Universals*, Text translated by A. Kenny, with an Introduction by P.V. Spade (Oxford, 1985), pp. vii–l; A. Kenny, "The Realism of *De Universalibus*," in *Wyclif in his Times*, pp. 17–29; P.V. Spade – G.A. Wilson, "Introduction", in *J. Wyclif Summa insolubilium*, ed. P.V. Spade – G.A. Wilson (Binghamton, NY, 1986); V. Herold, "Wyclifs Polemik gegen Ockhams Auffassung der platonischen Ideen und ihr Nachklang in der tschechischen hussitischen Philosophie," in *From Ockham to Wyclif*, ed. A. Hudson – M. Wilks (Oxford, 1987), pp. 185–215; A. Kenny, "Realism and Determinism in the early Wyclif," in *From Ockham to Wyclif*, pp. 165–77; G. Leff, "The Place of Metaphysics in Wyclif's Theology," in *From Ockham to Wyclif*, pp. 217–32; A.D. Conti, "Essenza ed essere nel pensiero della tarda scolastica (Burley, Wyclif, Paolo Veneto)," *Medioevo* 15 (1989), 235–67; A.D. Conti, "Logica intensionale e metafisica dell'essenza in John Wyclif," *Bullettino dell'Istituto Storico Italiano per il Medioevo e Archivio muratoriano* 99.1 (1993), 159–219; A.D. Conti, "Analogy and Formal Distinction: on the Logical Basis of Wyclif's Metaphysics," *Medieval Philosophy and Theology* 6.2 (1997), 133–65; M.J.F.M. Hoenen, "Jean Wyclif et les *universalia realia*: le débat sur la notion de *virtus sermonis* au Moyen Âge tardif et les rapports entre la théologie et la philosophie," in *La servante et la consolatrice. La philosophie dans ses rapports avec la théologie au Moyen Âge*, ed. J.-L. Solère – Z. Kaluza (Paris, 2002), pp. 173–92; A.D. Conti, "*Annihilatio* e divina onnipotenza nel *Tractatus de universalibus* di John Wyclif," in *Wyclif: logica, teologia, politica*, ed. MT. Fumagalli Beonio Brocchieri – S. Simonetta (Florence, 2003), pp. 71–85; Z. Kaluza, "La notion de matière et son evolution dans la doctrine wyclifienne," in *Wyclif: logica, teologia, politica*, pp. 113–52; E. Michael, "John Wyclif on Body and Mind," *Journal of the History of Ideas* 64 (2003), 343–60; L. Cesalli, "Le 'pan-propositionnalisme' de Jean Wyclif," *Vivarium* 43.1 (2005), 124–55; P.V. Spade, "The Problem of Universals and Wyclif's Alleged 'Ultrarealism'," *Vivarium* 43.1 (2005), 111–23. Among earlier studies only the following can be mentioned: M.H. Dziewicki, "An Essay on Wyclif's Philosophical System," in *Johannis Wyclif miscellanea philosophica*, 1:v–xxvii; S.H. Thomson, "The Philosophical Basis," pp. 86–116; L. Baudry, "A propos de Guillaume d'Ockham et de Wiclef," *Archives d'histoire doctrinale et littéraire du moyen-âge* 14 (1939), 231–51; Robson, *Wyclif and the Oxford Schools*, pp. 141–70.

[4] Cf. Robson, *Wyclif and the Oxford Schools*, pp. 118, 218–46; Hudson, "Wycliffism in Oxford 1381–1411," pp. 67–84; Keen, "The Influence of Wyclif," pp. 127–45; E.J. Ashworth – P.V. Spade, "Logic in Late Medieval Oxford," in *The History of the University of Oxford*, 2:50–62.

as the measure of the coincidence of the metaphysical components of two things (*res*). Consequently, starting from the definition of being (*ens*) as what can be signified by a complex expression (*significabile per complexum*), Wyclif built up a metaphysics of essences, culminating in an ontological and epistemological primacy of universals over any other kind of beings, by which all the main subsequent forms of realism were to be inspired.

Late medieval Nominalists, like Ockham and his followers, discriminated between things as they exist in the extra-mental world and the notions and schemata by means of which we grasp and signify them. For instance, according to the *Venerabilis Inceptor*, there are in the world only individuals belonging to two different genera, that is, substance and quality; on the contrary, the concepts by which they are understood and designated are both individual and universal, and of ten different genera (the ten Aristotelian categories: substance, quantity, quality, relation and so on). Nor do the relations through which we connect our concepts in a proposition correspond to the real links which connect individual objects in a state of affairs. Thus, our knowledge does not reproduce the world and its objects, but merely concerns them. In his maturity, Wyclif maintained that such an approach to philosophical questions was misleading and deleterious. Many times in his works he expressed the deepest hostility to such a tendency.[5] He thought that only on the ground of a close isomorphism between mental language and the world could the signifying function of terms and propositions, the possibility of definitions, and finally the validity and universality of our knowledge be accounted for and ensured. He firmly believed that mental language was an ordered collection of signs, each referring to one of the metaphysical constituents of the world (individuals and universals, substances and accidents, concrete properties, such as being-white, and abstract forms, such as whiteness), and that true propositions were like pictures of the inner structure and mutual relationships of such things. So the main characteristics of his own form of realism, to which all his contributions can be traced back, are the trust in the scheme object-label as *the* fundamental interpretative key of any semantic problem, and a strong *propensity* towards hypostatization: Wyclif <1> methodically replaces logical and epis-

---

[5] See for instance *Tractatus de universalibus* 3, pp. 77, 82; 8, p. 175; 15, p. 357.

temological rules with ontological criteria and references, <2> tries to find ontological grounds for any kind of logical distinction he introduces, and <3> develops his system of logic as a sort of componential analysis, where things substitute for lexemes and ontological properties for semantic features. As a consequence, like Walter Burley, he thought of logic as turning on structural forms and relations, existing in the world and totally independent of the mental acts by which they are understood:[6]

> Even though no created nature ever did any thinking, none the less there would be species and genera truly shared by their individuals; thus it does not depend on any created intellect that it is common to every fire to be fire, and so with the other substances.

His own formulation of the Scotistic formal distinction and his peculiar analysis of predication (certainly Wyclif's most conspicuous legacy to the thought of his times) are logically necessary requirements of this approach. In particular, <1> formal distinction is the tool by means of which the dialectic one-many internal to the world objects is regulated: it explains *why* things are at the same time things and atomic states of affairs, and *how* different items can constitute just one thing. <2> Wyclif conceives of predication as a real relation holding between metaphysical entities really or formally distinct from each other.

In what follows, <1> a glimpse into his logico-metaphysical world shall be offered together with <2> a short account of its most significant semantic entailment, the theory of supposition, and <3> an outline of the further developments of his main philosophical doctrines between the end of the fourteenth and the beginning of the fifteenth centuries. Thus, the first section of this chapter will be dedicated to the analysis of the twin notions of identity and distinction, viewed in their conceptual ramification, since they are the main tool of the logical machinery drawn up by Wyclif in order to solve the chief metaphysical problems inherited from the Scholastic tradition of thought. The second section will deal with the concepts of being and truth in their mutual relations. The reduction of being to truth

---

[6] *Tractatus de universalibus* 3, p. 79/196–200 (Kenny's translation p. 23): "Etsi nulla natura creata intelligeret, non eo minus forent species et genera communicata vere suis suppositis, ut non dependet ab intellectu creato quod commne est cuilibet igni esse ignem et sic de aliis substantiis."

(achieved through the definition of being as signifiable by a complex expression—*significabile per complexum*), the novelty of Wyclif's doctrine of transcendentals, will be examined. In the third section, I shall sketch his solution of the question of the composition of essence and being in creatures. In the fourth section, I shall discuss his theory of universals, focussing on the problem of the relations between universals and individuals. In the fifth section, I shall be concerned with the very core of Wyclif's philosophy, his analysis and divisions of predication. The sixth section will explore his general ideas about analogy, the logical counterpart of the doctrine of being. The seventh section will expound his central theses on the nature, reality, and mutal distinctions of the three main kinds of accidents: quantity, quality, and relation (*ad aliquid*). In the eighth section, his theory of supposition will be considered. And finally in the ninth section I shall illustrate the general position concerning predication, identity and distinction (or difference) held by the most important "school" of later medieval realists: the so called "Oxford Realists," a group of thinkers influenced by Wyclif's logic and ontology.

1. *The logical basis of metaphysics: identity and distinction*

The tool Wyclif utilises in building up his system is the *formal distinction*, a "family" of partial-identity-concepts (since no essence is totally identical with any other) that he draws from Duns Scotus's twofold notion of formal distinction.[7] Wyclif defines the notion of

---

[7] Duns Scotus gave two different definitions of formal distinction. He describes it in the *Lectura* (book I, d. 2, p. 2, qq. 1–4, ed. Vaticana, 16:216) and in the *Ordinatio* (book I, d. 2, p. 2, qq. 1–4, ed. Vaticana, 2:356–57; book II, d. 3, p. 1, q. 6, ed. Vaticana, 7:483–84) as a symmetrical relation between two entities which cannot exist separately (two entities x and y are formally distinct if and only if <1> both of them are constitutive elements of the same reality, but <2> neither of them can exist by itself, nor <3> is part of the definite description of the other); but in the *Reportata Parisiensia* (book I, d. 33, qq. 2–3, and d. 34, q. 1, ed. Vivès, 22:402–8, and 410) he defines it as an a-symmetrical relation between a whole reality and one of its constitutive elements (an entity x is not formally identical with another entity y if and only if <1> y is not part of the definite description of x, but <2> x and y are one and the same thing in reality). Scotus uses these two rather different notions of formal distinction in order to illustrate respectively <1> how the genus and the specific difference, and the specific nature and the individual difference are linked together, and <2> the relations which hold between the divine nature and

formal distinction (*distinctio*, or *differentia, formalis*) for the first time in the *Purgans errores circa universalia in communi* and six years later in the *Tractatus de universalibus*.[8] The two formulations differ from each other in some crucial points, and are both inadequate, as Wyclif's explanations of the different kinds of distinction are rather unclear. In the *Purgans errores circa universalia in communi* we read:[9]

> It must be noted that difference, or distinction, can be taken in six senses, and consequently identity too. <i> Some things differ because of their supposits. And this in two ways: or <i.a> so that they are different singular essences, like two men; or <i.b> so that they are the same singular essence, like the three divine Persons, or three things of the same soul <that is, memory, reason, and will>. <ii> Some things differ by nature; and this in two ways: or <ii.a> so that they are the same singular supposit, like matter and its substantial form, and human nature and divine nature in Christ; or <ii.b> so that they are totally separable from each other, like form and alien matter. <iii> Some things differ in species, . . . such as man and donkey. <iv> Some things differ because of the inner genus, or highest genus, such as spirit and body, substance and quality. <v> Some things differ more than in genus, such as categorial beings and extra-categorial truths. <vi> And finally some things differ because of a difference of reason only.

---

its three Persons, and between the human soul and its faculties. On Scotus's theory of formal distinction see M. McCord Adams, "Ockham on Identity and Distinction," *Franciscan Studies* 36 (1976), pp. 25–43; P. King, "Duns Scotus on the Common Nature and Individual Difference," *Philosophical Topics* 20 (1992), 51–76; S.D. Dumont, "Duns Scotus's Parisian Question on the Formal Distinction," *Vivarium* 43.1 (2005), 7–62.

[8] I follow Mueller's dating for the *De universalibus* instead of W.H. Thomson's. On Wyclif's theory of formal distinction see Spade, "Introduction," pp. xx–xxxi, and Conti, "Analogy and Formal Distinction," pp. 158–63.

[9] *Purgans errores circa universalia in communi* (fourth treatise of the first book of the *Summa de ente*), 4, p. 38/20–42: "Notandum quod sextupliciter potest accipi differencia vel distinccio aliquorum, sicut et idemptitas. <i> Aliqua enim distinguntur suppositis, et hoc dupliciter: <i.a> vel sic, quod sint diverse essencie singulares, ut duo homines; <i.b> vel sic, quod sint eadem essencia singularis, ut persone divine, et tres res eiusdem anime. <ii> Aliqua autem distinguntur secundum naturam, et hoc dupliciter: <ii.a> vel sic, quod sint idem suppositum singulare, ut generaliter materia et sua forma substancialis, et natura humana, ac natura divina in Christo; <ii.b> vel sic, quod sint omnino separabiles, ut forma et materia aliena. <iii> Aliqua vero distinguntur specie, . . ., ut homo et asinus. <iv> Aliqua autem distinguntur genere intrinseco vel generalissimo, ut spiritus et corpus, substancia et qualitas. <v> Aliqua autem plus quam genere: ut ens predicabile, et veritas extra genus. <vi> Set postremo distinguntur aliqua solum secundum racionem, quando sunt idem essencialiter sine distinccione reali, unum tamen non est formaliter reliquum, ut communius et suum per se inferius. Possunt autem omnes iste differencie reduci ad differenciam secundum rem, et differenciam secundum racionem."

> It happens when they are the same in essence, without any real dis-
> tinction, but one differs formally <that is, by means of a form> from
> the other, like more common and less common. All these differences
> can be reduced to these two: real difference and difference of reason.

According to this text, there are two main types of difference, seemingly the same as those recognized by the moderate realists of the
end of the thirteenth century: the real difference (the cases i–v) and
the difference of reason (*secundum rationem*)—or formal difference, as
Wyclif will call it later on (the last case). But: things are distinct in
the first way when <1> each one can exist without the other (cases
i, ii.b, iii–v), or <2> being complementary, have got dissimilar natures
(the case ii.a). Things are formally distinct from each other when
they are one and the same essence in reality, but their own formal
principles are not the same—as it happens to a nature and its instantiations (that is, its *supposita*). Hence, Wyclif's real difference and
difference of reason are not the same as the traditional ones. Wyclif's
real difference, in addition to the Aristotelian numerical, specific,
generic, and *plus-quam* generic differences,[10] also covers the Scotistic
formal distinction as defined in the *Lectura* and in the *Ordinatio*—considering that the second sense of the *differentia secundum supposita* (the
case i.b) is a reformulation of the first kind of Scotus's formal distinction, where the first two requisites have been so modified: two
(or more) entities differ *secundum supposita* if and only if they <1> are
the same single essence; but <2> can be regarded as independent
realities. As far as the difference of reason is concerned, it is evident that it does not mean real identity and conceptual distinction,
as it was commonly maintained, but it is a sort of transcription of
the Scotistic formal distinction as defined in the *Reportata Parisiensia*.
In the *Purgans errores circa universalia* Wyclif was therefore trying to
incorporate the novelties of the Scotistic approach to the problem
of identity and distinction into the traditional Aristotelian framework.
   In the later *Tractatus de universalibus* Wyclif was to modify his attitude, adopting the opposite point of view, as he attempted to include
the Aristotelian theory within a Scotistic context. He now claims that

---

[10] According to the common view, the *plus-quam*-generic difference was the
difference which held between the *res* of the sub-lunar world and the heavenly ones,
as the former were conceived of as corruptible and the latter as uncorruptible. In
Wyclif's view, this difference holds between the categorial beings and the non-categorial ones, as the former have a distinctive nature and the latter do not.

there are three main types of difference (or distinction): <1> real-and-essential; <2> real-but-not-essential; and <3> formal, or of reason (*formalis vel secundum rationem*).

He does not define the real-and-essential difference, but identifies it through a rough account of its three sub-types. The things which differ really-and-essentially are those things which differ from each other or <*a*> in genus, like man and quantity, or <*b*> in species, like man and donkey, or <*c*> in number, like two human beings.[11]

The real-but-not-essential difference is more subtle than the first one, since it holds between things which are the same single essence, and really differ from each other nevertheless—like memory, reason, and will, which are one and the same soul, and the three Persons of the Holy Trinity, who are the one and same God.[12]

The third main type of distinction is the formal one. It is described as the difference by which things differ from each other even though they are constitutive elements of the same single essence or supposit ("The third difference is the formal difference, or difference of reason,[13] by which things may differ even though they are all alike within the same single essence or supposit.")[14] According to Wyclif, this is the case for: <1> the concrete accidents inhering in the same substance, as they coincide in the same particular subject, but differ from each other because of their own natures; <2> the matter and substantial form of the same individual substance; <3> what is more common in relation to what is less common, like <*a*> the divine nature and the three Persons, <*b*> the world and this world; and,

---

[11] Cf. *Tractatus de universalibus* 4, pp. 90/122–91/130: "Notandum primo quod 'diversitas' vel 'distinctio' multipliciter intelligitur, . . . Aliqua enim differunt secundum genus, quae est maxima differentia rerum per se in genere, ut homo et quantitias, alia in specie, ut homo et asinus, et alia in numero, ut Petrus et Paulus. Et quaelibet talis est differentia essentialis."

[12] Cf. *Tractatus de universalibus* 4, p. 91/131–37: "Secundo differunt aliqua differentia subtiliori, licet sint eadem essentia singularis. Ut tres res spiritus creati, scilicet memoria, ratio et voluntas, distinguuntur realiter, licet sint eadem substantia, sicut spiritus increatus est tres res, quarum quaelibet est idem spiritus. Ista autem differentia est realis, licet non essentialis vel substantialis."

[13] Here Kenny translates '*differentia secundum rationem*' as 'notional difference', and '*ens rationis*' as 'notional entity', but I prefer the "standard" translations ('difference of reason', 'entity of reason'), since they are closer to the Latin expressions.

[14] *Tractatus de universalibus* 4, p. 91/138–40 (Kenny p. 29): "Tertia est differentia formalis vel secundum rationem, qua res differunt, licet conveniant in eadem singulari essentia vel supposito."

<c> among the categorial items belonging to the same category, a superior item and one of its inferiors:[15]

> <Formal difference, or difference of reason> can be subdivided into many kinds. Thus some things differ in accidental form while being alike within the same subject. Thus quantity, quality, relation and the other categories, if they coincide in the same particular subject, are all the same in particular subject, even though in their natures they differ in category. . . . In the second place some things differ formally, or by a difference of reason, when they are the same supposit, but incomplete natures. These natures may be very unequal, like matter and substantial form. . . . In the third way things may differ as more common and less common. Thus some people maintain a distinction of reason between the divine nature and person, since the nature can be common to many persons, but not the person. A second instance of this distinction is that between this world, and world as such: by God's power, we believe the species world is capable of more than one instantiation, even if not simultaneously or successively. . . . A third instance is the way in which the superior universal and its inferior are distinguished: they can be common to a greater or lesser extent. And this is the way in which genus differs from species, and in general every superior from its inferior.

This account of the various types of difference is more detailed than the preceding one, but not more clear: what is the difference between the definition of the real-but-not-essential difference and that one of the formal difference? What feature do all the kinds of formal distinction agree in? In any case, some points are obvious: <1> the real-and-essential difference matches the traditional real difference; <2> the real-but-not-essential difference and the first sub-type of the

---

[15] *Tractatus de universalibus* 4, pp. 91/138–92/166 (Kenny pp. 29–30; for the differences between this translation and Kenny's see above, n. 13): "Differentia formalis vel secundum rationem capit multiplicem divisionem, ut aliqua differunt secundum formam accidentalem, licet conveniant in subiecto. Ut quantitas, qualitas, relatio et cetera genera convenientia in eodem subiecto singulari, sunt omnia idem subiecto singulari, licet in suis naturis differant in genere. . . . Secundo differunt aliqua formaliter vel secundum rationem quando sunt idem suppositum sed naturae incompletae quantumcumque dispares, ut materia et forma substantialis. . . . Tertio modo differunt aliqua secundum rationem communioris et minus commune. Et sic ponunt quidam distinctionem rationis inter naturam divinam et personam, cum natura sit communicabilis multis personis, non sic autem persona. Secundo sic distinguitur mundus simpliciter ab isto mundo, cum species mundi creditur de Dei potentia posse plurificari etsi non simul vel successive. . . . Tertio sic distinguitur universale superius et suum inferius; secundum rationem amplioris communicabilitatis. Et sic differt genus a sua specie et generaliter omne superius a suo inferiori."

formal difference (that is, the distinction which holds between two—
or more—concrete accidents of the same singular substance) are two
slightly different versions of the Scotistic formal distinction as defined
in the *Lectura* and in the *Ordinatio*; <3> the third sub-type of the formal difference is a reformulation of the Scotistic formal distinction
as described in the *Reportata Parisiensia*.

In relation to the analysis proposed in the *Purgans errores circa* universalia the main apparent dissimilarities are the following: <1> there
are three general kinds of differences instead of two, since the second case of the *differentia secundum supposita* of the *Purgans errores* has
become the real-but-not-essential difference of the *Tractatus de universalibus*—as the examples employed show. <2> Notwithstanding the
presence of the qualification of "real", the real-but-not-essential
difference is closer to the formal difference than the second case of
the *differentia secundum supposita*, since in the *Tractatus de universalibus*
the term "essence" has the technical meaning of real entity with a
given nature.[16] <3> The first case of *differentia secundum naturam*, that
is, the difference between the matter and the substantial form of the
same individual substance, is seen as a sub-type of real difference in
the *Purgans errores* and as a sub-type of formal distinction in the
Tractatus de universalibus.

Like Duns Scotus before him, by means of the formal distinction
Wyclif was trying to explain how it is possible to distinguish many
different real aspects internal to the same individual thing, without
breaking its unity (the passage is from one to many). For that reason, Wyclif's formulation of the difference-theory and his theory of
universals and predication are linked together. Difference (or distinction) is defined in terms of partial identity, and is the main kind
of transcendental relation holding among categorial beings, since in
virtue of its metaphysical composition every categorial item is at the
same time partially identical-to and different-from any other belonging to the same category. As a consequence, the criteria for absolute
distinction are stronger than the traditional ones for real distinction:
within Wyclif's system, two things can be qualified as absolutely distinct if and only if they belong to dfferent categories. On the other
side, the definitions of the main kinds of difference do not exclude

---

[16] See below, pp. 89–91.

(indeed, in some case they imply) the possibility that two different items share one (or more) forms or essences. Thus, in Wyclif's view, the degree of distinction between two things must be read as the inverse measure of their partial identity. For instance, if we compare the list of the forms and levels of being which constitute Socrates and those which make up the universal-man (*homo in communi*), it is evident that they differ from each other; but it is also evident that Socrates and the universal-man, if considered from the point of view of their whole metaphysical composition, are partially the same, or only formally distinct, since the two lists of their constituents are identical for a long section. More generally, when among what differentiates two things there is the individual existence (*esse existere individuum*), they differ essentially (*essentialiter*). If the things at issue share the same individual existence and what differentiates them is (at least) one of their concrete metaphysical features, then they differ really (*realiter*); whereas, if what differentiates them is one of their abstract metaphysical components, then they differ formally (*formaliter*).[17]

2. *Being and truth*

1. In building up his own ontology, Wyclif takes many aspects from Duns Scotus's conception of being, but he <1> reverses the relationship between being and the true (*verum*); and <2> uses a little more traditional conceptual machinery for expounding the relations among being, God, and creatures.[18] The cornerstone of Wyclif's metaphysics is the notion of being (*ens*) as a truth (*veritas*) which can be signified by both a simple and a complex expression, while the general principle which leads him in his description of the inner structure of the reality is that of the homology of mental language and the world, according to which our thought spontaneously models itself on reality, so that the contents and articulations of our ideas are fully objective.

---

[17] On further developments of Wyclif's theory on identity and distinction see A.D. Conti, "Sviluppi e applicazioni della distinzione formale scotista ad Oxford sul finire del XIV secolo," in *Via Scoti, Methodologica ad mentem Joannis Duns Scoti*, ed. L. Sileo, 2 vols. (Rome, 1995), 1:319–36, and below, pp. 121–23.

[18] See below, pp. 103–7.

Not only, like Scotus, does Wyclif claim that the notion of being is the main object of our intellect, he also states that being is an extra-mental reality proper to everything (God and creatures, substances and accidents, universal and individual essences) according to different degrees, since God *is* in the strictest sense of the term and any other entity is (something real) only insofar as it shares the being of God in accordance with its own nature, value, and position in the hierarchy of creatures.[19]

The constitutive property of such realities is the capacity of being the object of a complex act of signifying (*omne ens est primarie signabile per complexum*).[20] Therefore Wyclif extends the set of referents of the term "*ens*" to include in addition to <1> the categorial beings (*entia praedicamentalia*): <2> all that is *in potentia* in its causes; <3> all the intelligible beings which are only in God as something producible by Him; <4> non-categorial (*extra genus*) principles, like God, the unity, and the point; <5> privations; <6> collections and groups of things, like villages, towns, cities, lands, and religious orders; <7> states of affairs, both atomic and molecular; <8> past and future states of affairs (*praeteritiones* and *futuritiones*), not seen as *res* that have been real and will be real, but regarded as real in the present as past and future truths; <9> the (molecular) states of affairs which are signified by negative true sentences; <10> hypothetical and tautological truths; and <11> such *res* as death, sin, and the false (*falsitas*) itself.[21]

---

[19] Cf. *De ente in communi* (first treatise of the first book of the *Summa de ente*), 1, pp. 1–3; 2, p. 29; *De ente praedicamentali* (fifth treatise of the first book of the *Summa de ente* according to Robson, *Wyclif and the Oxford Schools*, p. 119, but seventh treatise according to W.R. Thomson, *The Latin Writings*, pp. 26–27), 1, pp. 2–3, 13; *Tractatus de universalibus* 4, p. 89; 7, p. 130; 12, p. 279; *De intelleccione Dei* (first treatise of the second book of the *Summa de ente*), 5, pp. 97–100; *De materia et forma*, 6, p. 213.

[20] Cf. *De ente in communi*, 3, p. 36/11–26: "Ex istis palam sequitur advertenti quod omne ens est primarie ens signabile per complexum verum et econtra, et per consequens communius quam est ens non est possibile quicquam esse. Prima pars patet ex hoc quod omne ens esse est primarie signabile per complexum. Set omne ens est ens esse juxta proximo dicta, igitur illa pars vera. Non enim esset ens verum, nisi esset signabile per complexum verum, set omne ens est verum, ut prius patet ex dictis, igitur et cetera. Et ex istis elicitur quam amplum sit ens, quia tam amplum sicut est primarie signabile per complexum. Voco autem signabile quod habet aptitudinem ut significetur, ut est omne ens, et patet quod omne ens est primarie signabile per complexum, quia omnis veritas est sic signabilis: omne ens est veritas, igitur et cetera." Cf. also *Logicae continuatio*, 3, 1, 2:6; *De ente primo in communi* (second treatise fo the first book of the *Summa de ente*), 1, p. 70.

[21] Cf. *De ente praedicamentali*, 1, p. 2/26–33: "Pro declaracione istius materie oportet

This choice implies a revolution in the standard medieval theory
of transcendentals, since Wyclif actually replaces being with true.
According to the common belief, among the transcendentals (*ens*,
unum, *verum* etc.) being was the primitive notion, which all the others stemmed from by adding a specific connotation in relation to
something else, or some new determination. So *verum* was nothing
but being itself considered in relation to an intellect, no matter
whether divine or human. In Wyclif's view, on the contrary, being
is no more the main transcendental and its notion is not the first
and simplest, but there is something more basic to which being can
be brought back: the truth (*veritas*) (or true—*verum*). According to him,
only what can be signified by a complex expression is a being, and
whatever is the proper object of an act of signifying is a truth.
"Truth" is therefore the true name of being itself:[22]

---

supponere, quod ens dicatur de omni signabili per complexum, et sic quoddam sit
ens actuale vel existencie, quoddam ens potentiale, quod habet esse in causis secundis,
que possunt ipsum actualiter producere, et quoddam ens est, quod solum habet esse
intelligibile in Deo, ut omne, quod solum Deus potest producere, et non actualiter
existit." Ibid., p. 5/1–19: "Istis suppositis patet, quod restringendo ens predicamentale ad illud, quod per se est in aliquo decem predicamentorum, sunt quotlibet encia, quorum nullum est formaliter ens predicamentale, ut patet de Deo, unitate
et puncto, cum aliis principiis extra genus. Secundo patet idem de quotlibet priva-
cionibus, que, quamvis non sint aliquod 10 generum formaliter, tamen omnia sunt
accidentia substancie, cui nata est forma inesse, cuius est privacio. Tercio patet idem
de aggregatis per accidens de multitudinibus et multis similibus, que oportet omnem
loquentem ponere, ut patet tam de artificialibus quam naturalibus, Quarto patet
idem de pretericionibus, futuricionibus, potenciis et negacionibus, que, quamvis dicerentur accidentia vel posteriora ipsis subiectis secundum esse intelligibile, tamen non
possunt dici accidere alicui substancie secundum esse existere. Et idem patet de
aggregatis ex veritatibus ypoteticarum, cuiusmodi sunt veritates coniunccionum, dis-
iunccionum etc." See also *Purgans errores circa veritates in communi* (third treatise of the
first book of the *Summa de ente*), 1, pp. 1–2; and 3, p. 10: "Item, cum omne ens sit
veritas; et peccatum, falsitas, vanitas, et talia detestanda et ficta sunt encia; videtur
quod sunt veritates."
[22] *Tractatus de universalibus* 7, p. 139/330–42 (Kenny pp. 54–55; for differences
between this translation and Kenny's see above, n. 13): "Nam aliqua veritas est per
se in genere et aliqua non. Et de illa loquuntur philosophi vocantes illam 'ens rationis.' Nec obest de eadem re secundum rationem disparem habere varium intellectum, ut concipiendo Petrum esse animal, quantum, album, patrem generantem,
fatigatum in lecto hodie iacentem, divitem, intelligo decem genera sed complexe ut
sunt veritates apud considerationem meam. Et eadem decem praedicamenta alias
intelligo incomplexe. Nec variantur res illae propter variationem intellectus mei, sed
circumstant illas rationes ex quibus capitur variatio intellectus complexi et incom-
plexi, qui non potest Deo competere."

Some truths are *per se* in a category and others are not. It is of the latter that philosophers are talking when they call them "entities of reason." It is no objection that one can have different thoughts of the same thing under different aspects. Suppose I call to mind that Peter is an animal, so big, white, a father, a begetter, tired, lying today in bed, rich—when I do all this I am thinking of the ten categories, but in a complex manner as truths in my thought. At other times I think of the same ten categories in a non-complex manner. But these things are not altered because of the change in my thought; they are the context of those aspects from which the changes between complex and non-complex thought take their rise. All this is something that cannot apply to God.

From the semantic point of view this means the collapsing of the fundamental distinction of the common Aristotelian theory of meaning, that one between simple signs or expressions (like nouns) and compound (or complex) signs or expressions (like propositions).[23] From the ontological point of view this entails the uniqueness in type of the *significata* themselves of every class of categorematic expressions:[24]

Proposition, broadly speaking, is a being which signifies in a complex manner. Therefore everything which is can be called a proposition, since everything which is signifies in a complex manner that it is <something real>.

Within Wyclif's world it is the same (kind of) object which both concrete terms and propositions refer to, as the individual substances have to be regarded as (atomic) states of affairs. According to him, from the metaphysical point of view a singular man (*iste homo*) is nothing but a real proposition (*propositio realis*), where the actual existence in time as an individual (*ista persona*) plays the role of subject, the common nature, that is, human nature (*natura humana*), plays the role of predicate, and the singular essence (*essencia istius hominis*), that is, what by means of which this individual is a man, plays the role of the copula:[25]

---

[23] See for example Aristotle, *Categories*, 2, 1a 16–19; 4, 2a 5–10; *De interpretatione*, 1, 16a 9–16.

[24] *De logica*, 5, 1:14/1–3: "Proposicio large loquendo est *ens complexe significans*; et sic, quia omne quod est significat complexe se esse, omne quod est satis bene potest dici proposicio."

[25] *De logica*, 5, 1:15/12–22: "Proposicio realis est, ut *iste homo, iste lapis* etc. quia sicut in alia proposicione est subiectum et predicatum et copula, sic in *isto homine* est dare istam personam, que est pars subiecta speciei humane, que est tamquam

Real proposition is <something> like *this man, this stone* and so on, as in *this man* there is a subject, a predicate, and the copula just as in <any> other proposition: this individual, which is a part of the <whole> substrate <of existence> of the human species, is the subject; the human nature, which is essentially present in this man as his <characteristic>, is the predicate; and the essence of this man is the real copula which connects this man with his nature. And as in the artificial proposition the predicate is said of the subject, so in the real proposition at issue this man is essentially and really the human nature.

2. This position has also important consequences for the problem of the truth of propositions.[26] In the Middle Ages there were three predominant approaches to the problem of truth: ontological (proper to authors like Augustine, Anselm, and Grosseteste), epistemological (proper to authors like Thomas Aquinas and Giles of Rome), and linguistical (proper to nominalist thinkers like Ockham and Buridan). According to the first theory, the truth is a thing's being in accordance with the idea in the mind of God. According to the second, the true and the false are properly not in things, but are about things, as the truth is the result of an act of judgment of the intellect which states the combinations or separations found in things themselves. According to the linguistical approach, defining truth is identical with indicating the rules for establishing the truth of propositions, since only propositions are the bearers of truth-value.

Wyclif's theory derives from Grosseteste's doctrine, that he interprets in the light of his notion of being as *significabile per complexum*. In Wyclif's view, a proposition is a well formed and complete speech, which signifies the true or the false, and can be perfectly understood.[27]

---

subiectum; et est dare similiter naturam humanam, que essencialiter inest isti homini tamquam predicatum, et realiter predicatur de isto homine. Et est dare essenciam istius hominis, que est realis copula copulans istum hominem cum sua natura. Et sicut in proposicione artificiali predicatum dicitur de subiecto, sic in ista proposicione reali iste homo est essencialiter et realiter natura humana." In the later *Materia et forma* Wyclif <1> develops at greatest length the idea that in all things the essence corresponds to the Godhead, the matter to the Father, the form to the Son, and the compound to the Holy Spirit; and <2> calls matter, form, and the compound taken together "the created trinity."

[26] On Wyclif's theory of truth see Cesalli, "Le 'pan-propositionnalisme' de Jean Wyclif," pp. 124–55.

[27] Cf. *De logica*, 5, 1:14/4–10: "Sed multo contraccius diffinitur proposicio vel describitur, secundum quod est oracio artificialiter inventa, sic: proposicio est *oracio indicativa, congrua, verum vel falsum singificans, et perfectum intellectum reddens*. Vel: proposicio est <o>*racio indicativa, congrua, significans complexe sicut est vel sicut non est*."

Like Grosseteste,[28] he claims that every (linguistic) proposition has a twofold signification: natural and artificial. In its natural signification a proposition means nothing but its own existence, and therefore it is always true; in its artificial signification a proposition signifies what is or what is not, and it may therefore be true or false.[29] According to Wyclif, there are five kinds of propositions: <1> mental, <2> spoken, <3> written; <4> real, and <5> the signified propositions (*et quinta proposicio est sic esse sicut proposicio significat*).[30] The real proposition—as we have already seen—is nothing but any individual thing in the world, while the signified proposition seems to be any actual situation connected with individual things:[31]

> The fifth <kind of> proposition is a truth signified *a parte rei*, like this truth, that man is, is a complex truth, because it is a complex true <thing>. And this is the cause why it must be called "proposition."

A proposition is true if and only if it describes how things are arranged in the world; in other words, if and only if its own primary *significatum* is a truth[32]—and the primary *significatum* of both simple and complex signs is that which the sign at issue is chiefly taken to mean.[33]

Despite appearances, Wyclif's opinion on this subject is not just a new formulation of the theory of the *complexe significabile*. It is true

---

[28] Cf. Robertus Grosseteste, *De veritate*, in *Die Philosophischen Werke des Roberts Grosseteste*, ed. L. Baur (Münster i. W., 1912), pp. 135–36.

[29] Cf. *De logica*, 5, 1:14/13–19: "Sed notandum quod duplex est primaria significacio: scilicet, naturalis et artificialis. Primaria significacio naturalis proposicionis est illa mediante qua proposicio significat naturaliter se ipsam. Primaria significacio artificialis est illa mediante qua proposicio significat ex imposicione idiomatis veritatem sicut est, vel sicut non est." See also *Purgans errores circa veritates in communi*, 3, pp. 10–13. We find this same distinction in Alyngton's *Litteralis sentencia super Praedicamenta Aristotelis, de complexo et incomplexo*, in A.D. Conti, "Linguaggio e realtà nel commento alle *Categorie* di Robert Alyngton," *Documenti e studi sulla tradizione filosofica medievale* 4 (1993), 249–50.

[30] Cf. *De logica*, 5, 1:14–15.

[31] *De logica*, 5, 1:15/23–25: "Quinta proposicio est veritas significata a parte rei, sicut ista veritas: *hominem esse*, est veritas complexe, quia verum complexum; et hec est causa qualiter debet dici proposicio."

[32] Cf. *Logicae continuatio*, 1, 1, 1:76/9–14: "Pro quo sciendum est quod universaliter et convertibiliter, si aliqua proposicio significat primarie sicud est, vel si suum primarium significatum sit veritas, tunc est vera; ut ista est vera: *omnis homo est*; quia primarie significat quod omnis homo est, et ita est quod omnis homo est."

[33] Cf. *Logicae continuatio*, 1, 1, 1:76/21–23: "Et voco primarium significatum signi cuiuscunque, quod primo et principaliter apprehenditur toto signo."

that, in Gregory of Rimini's view, <1> the *complexe significabile* is not *one* thing in the world, but an arrangement of things in the world, and <2> in order for there be a *complexe significabile* it is sufficient that there is one thing in the world, since the existence of that thing gives rise at least to this state of affairs (or situation): that that thing is—which differs from that thing, though it is not another entity[34]—but, according to the supporters of the *complexe significabile* theory, the same *res* which are signified by simple concrete terms are signified, in a different way, by complex expressions (that is, by propositions). In Wyclif's thought, on the contrary, there are no simple things in the world which correspond to simple concrete terms, but simple concrete terms designate *real propositions*, that is, things that are at the same time atomic states of affairs. Wyclif derives the notion of real proposition from Walter Burley. Nevertheless, his view is sensibly different from that of the *Doctor Planus et Perspicuus* for many aspects. According to Burley the *propositiones in re* are the *significata* of statements, just as individuals (both substantial ones and accidental ones) are the *significata* of discrete terms and universal forms the *significata* of common abstract terms. In fact, Burley's world consists of macro-objects, really existing outside the mind, each made up by a primary substance and a host of substantial and accidental forms existing in it and by it. Primary substances, substantial and accidental forms are simple natures, belonging to ten different types of being, or categories. So the macro-object (e.g., Socrates or Coriscus) is not a primary substance (as the primary substance, that is, being-this-man, does not contain the whole being of the macro-object), but an ordered congeries of categorial items. Within the macro-object Burley distinguishes two different definite aspects of it: the aggregates and the real propositions (*propositiones in re*—a sort of states of affairs). The former are what is signified by common accidental terms such as "white", and the latter what is signified by ordinary (philosophical) sentences such as "Socrates is white" ("*Sortes est albus*"). An aggregate is nothing but the union of one of the countless accidental forms of a macro-object with its primary substance; and a real proposition is the union of two forms of a macro-object (one of

---

[34] Cf. Gregory of Rimini, *Lectura super I Sententiarum*, prol., q. 1, a. 1, in *Lectura super I et II Sententiarum*, ed. A.D. Trapp—V. Marcolino *et alii*, 6 vols. (Berlin and New York, 1979–84), 1:8–10.

which must be substantial) with and by means of the primary substance.[35] Wyclif's real proposition is everything which is, as everything save God is compound (at least of potency and act),[36] and therefore can be conceived of and signified both in a complex (*complexe*) and in a non-complex manner (*incomplexe*). When we conceive of a thing in a complex manner we think of that thing considered according to its metaphysical structure, and so according to its many levels of being and kinds of essence. From this point of view, even the abstract forms, like humanity (*humanitas*), are a sort of states of affairs, because of their own inner organization and make up (e.g. humanity is equal to the "sum" of the form of animality and that of rationality, which combine as potency and act respectively). As a consequence we can refer to the same entity by means of various types of terms: abstract nouns (like "humanity"), concrete nouns (like "man"—"*homo*"), infinitive expressions (like "being a man"—"*hominem esse*"), and complex expressions (like "universal humanity"—"*humanitas communis*", "universal man"—"*homo in communi*", and "the species of man"—"*species hominis*"), which therefore are synonymous:[37]

> Every universal is a form, a truth, or state of things capable of being signified by a complex, just as being a man is a common nature in which all men, in virtue of their species, resemble each other, and correspondingly with other things. That is why professional philosophers have called universals by abstract names, like "humanity" "equinity" and so on for other species.... So someone who wants to be made

---

[35] Cf. Walter Burley, *Expositio super Praedicamenta Aristotelis, prooemium*, chs. *de substantia, de relatione*, and *de priori, passim*, in *Expositio super Artem Veterem Porphyrii et Aristotelis* (A.D. 1337), ed. Venetiis 1497. On Burley's position concerning the meaning and truth of propositions see A.D. Conti, "Ontology in Walter Burley's Last Commentary on the *Ars Vetus*," *Franciscan Studies*, 50 (1990), 125–36; A.D. Conti, "Significato e verità in Walter Burley," *Documenti e studi sulla tradizione filosofica medievale* 11 (2000), 317–50; L. Cesalli, "Le réalisme propositionnel de Walter Burley," *Archives d'histoire doctrinale et littéraire du Moyen Age*, 68 (2001), 155–221.

[36] Cf. *De ente praedicamentali*, 5, pp. 38–39.

[37] *Tractatus de universalibus* 3, p. 70/13–19 (Kenny pp. 19 and 21): "Omne universale est forma, veritas vel dispositio significabile per complexum, ut esse hominem est natura communis in qua omnes homines specifice conveniunt, et correspondenter de aliis. Unde periti philosophantes vocaverunt universalia nominibus abstractis, ut 'humanitas', 'equinitas', et ita de aliis speciebus." Ibid., 74/88–94: "Volens igitur manuduci in notitiam de quidditate universalium debet intelligere confuse et abstracte idem per genus et speciem quod intelligit primo per complexum, cuius subiectum est terminus specificus vel terminus generis, ut idem est species hominis et hominem esse, idem genus animalis et esse animal. Et utrumque illorum est commune suis suppositis."

acquainted with the quiddity of universals has to think confusedly and abstractly, by genus and species, of the same thing as he first thought of by means of a complex whose subject is the specific or generic term; thus the species of man is the same as there being a man, the genus of animal is the same thing as being an animal. And each of these is common to its supposits.

On the ontological side, the result is that Wyclif's (metaphysical) world consists of molecular objects, that is, single items classified into ten different types or categories. These metaphysical items are not simple, but composite, because they are reducible to something else, belonging to a different rank of reality, and unable to exist by itself: being and essence, potency and act, matter and form, abstract genera, species and differences. For that reason, everything one can speak about or think of is both a thing (or molecular object) and a sort of atomic state of affairs,[38] while every true proposition expresses either an atomic or a molecular state of affairs, that is, the union (if the proposition is affirmative) or the separation (if the proposition is negative) of two (or more) things.

3. Wyclif's world is ultimately grounded on divine essence, thus there is a close connection between any kind of *truth* and the divine ideas.[39] Divine ideas play a threefold role in relation to God and creatures: they are <1> the specific essences of individual things themselves, considered according to their intelligible being in the mind of God; <2> God's principles of cognition of creatures; and <3> the eternal models of creatures. If we also take into account that in his opinion <4> divine ideas are really the same as the divine essence and formally distinct from it, and <5> this distinction originates from their being efficient (con)causes in relation to the different kinds of creatures, we can easily realize why Wyclif's position on this matter leads to heretical consequences from the point of view of the catholic theology: <1> metaphysical and theological necessitarianism; <2> restriction of divine omnipotence; <3> negation of the process of transubstantiation in the Eucharist.[40] In fact, Wyclif

---

[38] Cesalli ("Le 'pan-propositionnalisme' de Jean Wyclif") appropriately qualifies Wyclif's ontology as a (form of) "pan-propositionalism."

[39] Cf. *Tractatus de universalibus* 15, pp. 371–74; *De materia et forma*, 2, pp. 170–76. On Wyclif's theory of divine ideas see Robson, *Wyclif and the Oxford Schools*, pp. 171–76; Leff, *Heresy in the Later Middle Ages*, 2:500–10; Herold, "Wyclifs Polemik gegen Ockhams Auffassung der platonischen Ideen," pp. 185–215.

[40] On Wyclif's form of necessitarism and its theological consequences see Conti,

defines ideas as the divine nature in action, since they are the means by which God creates all that is outside Himself. In this way, any distinction between the ideas as pure *rationes* and the ideas as *exemplaria*, stated by Thomas Aquinas in his *Summa theologiae* (I, q. 15), is abolished. Furthermore, ideas are the constitutive principles of divine nature, essentially identical with it. Thus divine ideas become as necessary as the divine nature itself. On the other side, ideas are the first of the four levels of being proper to creatures.[41] Because of the necessary links between <1> the divine essence and the eternal mental being that every creature has in God, and <2> this first level of being of creatures and the remaining three, for God to think of creatures is already to create them. But God cannot help thinking of creatures, since to think of Himself is to think of his constitutive principles, that is, the ideas of creatures. Therefore God cannot help creating. Indeed, He could not help creating just this universe. As a consequence, everything which is is necessary, and a necessary object of God's volition: the three spheres of possible, existent, and necessary totally coincide. As a matter of fact, Wyclif, having defined necessary truths as those truths which cannot not be the case, <1> distinguishes between absolutely necessary truths and conditionally (or relatively—*secundum quid*) necessary truths, and <2> tries to show how relative necessity is consistent with supreme contingence.[42] He thought that such distinctions enabled him to maintain simultaneously the necessity of all that happens and human freedom;[43] and many times he affirms that it would be heretical to say that all things happen by *absolute* necessity; but his attempt failed in achieving its goal.

According to him, absolutely necessary truths are such truths as <1> those of theology (like the real proposition that God exists), that are *per se* necessary and do not depend on something else; <2> those of geometry, that neither can, nor ever could, nor ever will be

---

"*Annihilatio e divina onnipotenza*," pp. 71–85. On the connection between his form of realism and his own formulation of determinism see Kenny, "Realism and Determinism," pp. 165–77. On the links between his realism and his eucharistic doctrine see Leff, *Heresy in the Later Middle Ages*, 2:549–57; P.J.J.M. Bakker, "Réalisme et rémanence. La doctrine eucharistique de Jean Wyclif," in *Wyclif: logica, teologia, politica*, pp. 87–112. See also Kenny, *Wyclif*, pp. 68–90.

[41] See below, p. 93.
[42] Cf. *Logicae continuatio*, 1, 11, 1:156–65.
[43] Cf. *Tractatus de universalibus* 14, pp. 333–47.

otherwise, even though they depend on something else (*est ab alio sed non potuit non esse*); and <3> the past and present truths (like the real proposition that I have existed—*me fuisse*), that cannot be, but might have been otherwise (*per accidens necessarium, quia est necessarium quod potuit non esse*). On the contrary, relative necessity applies to those events that must follow certain conditions in order to be or happen—so that any contingent truth is relatively necessary if considered in relation to its conditions.[44] In its turn, relative necessity is divided into antecedent, consequent, and concomitant. <1> A certain truth is an antecedent relative necessity when its existence causes the existence of another contingent truth (*antecedens ut causa contingentis, inferens posterius naturaliter*). An instance of such a necessity is the necessity of volition, as where my unconstrained will or the unconstrained will of God is the cause which necessitates something else.[45] <2> A certain truth is a consequent relative necessity when its existence is caused by an antecedent (relative) necessity. And finally, <3> a certain truth is a concomitant relative necessity when it merely accompanies another true event.[46] These features proper to the relative necessity are not opposites, and the same truth may be necessary in all the three ways.[47] Wyclif insists that all three kinds of relative necessity are contingent truths in themselves,[48] yet he was unable to show how this is possible. He thought he had an explanation, but he was mistaken. In his *Tractatus de universalibus* (where he uses all these distinctions in order to try to solve the problem of the relationship between divine power and human freedom), he openly maintains that <1> in relation to the foreknowledge of God every effect is necessary to come about,[49] and <2> the Aristotelian prin-

---

[44] Cf. *Logicae continuatio*, 1, 11, 1:157.

[45] Cf. *Logicae continuatio*, 1, 11, 1:158/22–24: "Aliqua sit talis necessitas *volicionis*; ut si volicio mea vel volicio Dei sit causa necessitans aliud non coacta."

[46] Cf. *Logicae continuatio*, 1, 11, 1:157/26–35: "Si autem sumatur necessarium secundum quid, hoc contingit tripliciter: vel quod sit necessitas *antecedens*, vel *consequens*, vel *concomitans*. *Antecedens* ut causa contingentis, inferens posterius naturaliter; ut *Deum velle Sor esse* se habet ad *Sor esse*. Et dicitur necessitas, antecedens, quia necessario, illo positio, ponitur Sor esse: et illud est necessitas consequens. Necessitas concomitans est veritas contingens determinate concomitans alteram; ut *me esse tecum in hoc instanti*, et omne contingens determinate verum."

[47] Cf. *Logicae continuatio*, 1, 11, 1:157–58.

[48] Cf. *Logicae continuatio*, 1, 11, 1:158/3–6: "Conveniunt autem omnes iste necessitates in hoc quod sunt absolute contingentes et condicionaliter vel secundum quid necessarie; ut *equus est necessarius* ex supposicione, puta *ad equitandum*."

[49] Cf. *Tractatus de universalibus* 14, p. 333.

ciple that everything which is, when it is, necessarily is (the well known formulation of the diachronic contingence), applies also to what will be and has been.[50] Taking into account that God himself cannot begin or cease actually to know or will something, and thus He cannot change from knowing that *p* to knowing that not-*p* (where *p* is a given truth), nor from volition to non-volition or *vice versa*,[51] the logical result is that in Wyclif's world nothing may happen purely contingently.[52] It is true that Wyclif insists that even if God can never change from volition to non-volition, the fact that God wills *p* is in itself contingent, if *p* is not a theological truth,[53] but, like Bradwardine, he maintains that God's antecedent will is naturally prior to what He foresees. Given that <1> God is immutable, and hence that the divine power is not affected by the passage of time, and <2> divine ideas, within Wyclif's system, are as necessary as the divine essence itself, the logical consequence is that, despite Wyclif's claims to the contrary, the whole history of the world is determined from eternity. As a matter of fact, Wyclif's conditional (or relative) necessity is as necessary as his absolute necessity: given God, the world's entire history follows.[54]

3. *Essence and being*

Among the many sets of beings (*entia*) that Wyclif lists, the most important one is that consisting of categorial items. They are characterized by <1> having a nature, and <2> being the basic components of finite (molecular) beings or atomic states of affairs.[55] These categorial items, conceived of as instances of a certain nature, are called by Wyclif "essences" ("*essentiae*"). An essence therefore is a being which has a well defined nature, even if the name "essence" does not make this nature known:[56]

---

[50] Cf. *Tractatus de universalibus* 14, p. 334.

[51] Cf. *Tractatus de universalibus* 14, p. 335; see also *De volucione Dei*, 3, p. 149.

[52] On this subject see Kenny, *Wyclif*, pp. 31–41.

[53] Cf. for instance *De volucione Dei*, 7, p. 192.

[54] I am grateful to Ian Levy for calling my attention to this problem.

[55] Cf. *De ente praedicamentali*, 1, pp. 1–6.

[56] *De materia et forma*, 4, p. 185/21–24, and 31–33: "Suppono igitur quod nomen *essencie* sit commune ad significandum naturam, quacunque qualitate substanciali vel

> I therefore assume that the name "essence" is a common name which signifies a nature as determined by a substantial or accidental quality whatsoever. . . . But <the name "essence"> does not say *what* a thing is; it only says that a thing *is*—which is the first inquiry about a thing, according to the second book of the *Posterior Analytics*.

So the term "essence" is less general than "being" ("*ens*"),[57] but more general than "quiddity" ("*quidditas*"), since <1> every essence is a being, and not every being is an essence, and <2> every quiddity is an essence, and not every essence is a quiddity, since individual things are essences, but not quiddities. In his *Tractatus de universalibus* Wyclif, speaking of substances, distinguishes between singular essence (*essentia singularis*) and quidditative essence (*essentia quidditativa speciei vel generis*). The singular essence is the form which in union with the matter brings the substantial composite about. The quidditative essence <1> is the type that individuals instantiate, since it makes singulars the kind of things they are; <2> it is present in the individual (with which it is really the same and formally different) as the main constitutive part of its nature; and <3> it discloses the inner metaphysical structure of the substantial composite.[58] Consequently he identifies essence with the essential being which is ontological prior to the quiddity of a thing.[59]

In view of his position on the problem of being and his own conception of essence, Wyclif maintains no real distinction between essence and being.[60] Since, according to him, being is a *genus ambiguum*[61] (that is, it is possessed by the categories in different ways: directly [*per prius*] by substance and secondarily [*per posterius*] by accidents) it is the stuff that the ten categories modulate according to their own

---

accidentali qualificatam. . . . Non enim dicit, *quid* res est, aut *cuiusmodi* est, sed solum dicit quod *est*; que est prima questio de re, ex secundo *Posteriorum*." Cf. also *De ente primo in communi*, 3, pp. 88–89; *De ente praedicamentali*, 5, p. 43; and 5, *appendix prior*, pp. 44–45; *Tractatus de universalibus*, 7, pp. *universalibus* 7, 128–29.

[57] Cf. *Tractatus de universalibus* 6, p. 123/305–10: "Omne ens est esse. Omnis essentia est ens. Igitur omnis essentia est esse. Minor patet ex hoc quod multa habent esse quae non habent formaliter essentias, ut patet de privationibus et peccatis ac de aliis veritatibus extra genus. Ideo, ens est superius essentia."

[58] Cf. *Tractatus de universalibus* 1, pp. 15–16; 6, pp. 116–124, *passim*.

[59] Cf. *Tractatus de universalibus* 7, p. 129.

[60] On essence and being in Wyclif's thought see Kenny, *Wyclif*, pp. 21–22; Conti, "Essenza ed essere," pp. 244–51; Conti, "Logica intensionale e metafisica dell'essenza," pp. dell'essenza," 171–81.

[61] See below, p. 103.

nature, so that everything is immediately something which is.[62] The essences of creatures do not precede their beings, not even causally, as every thing is (identical with) its essence. The being of a thing is brought into existence by God at the same instant as its essence, since essence without being and being without essence would be two self-contradictory states of affairs. In fact, essence without being would imply that an individual could be something of a given type without being real in any way, and being without essence would imply that there could be the existence of a thing without the thing itself.[63]

As a consequence, the *pars destruens* of his theory on being and essence is a strong refutation of the twin opinions of Thomas Aquinas and Giles of Rome. Although Wyclif does not name either the Dominican master or the Augustinian one, it is nevertheless clear from the context that their conceptions are the object of his criticisms. Aquinas had postulated a real composition of essence and being in creatures, in order to account for the dependence of the world upon God at a merely philosophical level. He thought that because the essence of a creature receives its being from God, essence and being are distinct from each other, but related one to the other just as potency (essence) and act (being). Giles pursued the same line of thought, as he admitted a distinction between essence and being as between thing (*res*) and thing.

Wyclif objects to Aquinas that his theory is self-contradictory. In fact, if being is the act peculiar to essence, being is logically posterior to essence. Therefore, given a created essence A and its own act of existing B, since A is logically prior to B, A should have got a being before B having affected it. We can consider this new being of A we have found, and wonder whether it is identical with B or not. If it is, then B is not posterior to A—a result which is in contradiction with the necessary consequence of our assumption. If it is distinct from B, it is prior to B; and then B is accidental in relation to A—an outcome which is in contradiction with our assumption.[64]

---

[62] Cf. *De ente praedicamentali*, 4, p. 30; *Tractatus de universalibus* 7, p. 130.

[63] Cf. *Tractatus de universalibus* 6, pp. 122–23.

[64] Cf. *Tractatus de universalibus* 6, pp. 121/263–122/277: "Cum esse sit actus essentiae, patet quod nullo modo praecedit sed potius sequitur suam essentiam cuius est proprium esse, sicut dicunt loquentes in ista materia. Sit igitur A creata essentia et B eius esse formaliter consequens, sed posterius origine vel natura. Et patet quod Deus scit A esse pro illo gradu prioritatis super B, quia aliter non foret verum

Against Giles' formulation of the theory of the real composition of essence and being, Wyclif observes that if a creature (*homo*) and its being (*hominem esse*) are really distinct as thing and thing, then either <1> they differ as two individual substances, and so they are mutually independent, or <2> one of them is naturally prior to the other, and so one entails the other (without being entailed). Both consequences are false, because they contradict the truth that an essence and its being reciprocally imply each other, like a thing and the fact that it is real.[65]

The essence of a thing is therefore really (*realiter*) identical with its being. Yet, because of the complexity of the metaphysical composition of the finite being, such a statement is insufficient for adequately answering the question about the connection of essence and being. Since within every creature there are two different kinds of essence and four levels of being, the identity between essence and being cannot be complete; for this reason, Wyclif speaks of a formal difference (*distinctio* or *differentia formalis*)[66] between essence and being in crea-

----

quod A est prius B. Ex quo sequitur quod A habet esse pro illo gradu prioritatis. Quaero igitur: Utrum illud esse sit B vel esse prius B? Si B, sequitur oppositum dati. Si esse prius B, tunc B est esse accidentale adveniens anti in actu. Consequens iterum contra datum, quia supponitur quod B sit esse substantiale primum quod habet A post esse intelligibile aeternum."

[65] Cf. *Tractatus de universalibus*, 6, pp. 120/221–121/253: "Si homo et hominem esse simpliciter distinguuntur, tunc vel sunt omnino distincta ut duo supposita separata, sicut Petrus et Paulus, vel aliter se habent in quodam ordine naturali. Et per consequens vel sunt aequeprimo natura, vel unum prius et reliquum posterius. Primo modo non potest poni, cum tunc essent impertinentia et neutrum sequens ad reliquum. Quod est notorie falsum, cum formaliter mutuo se inferunt. Si secundo modo, tunc oportet quod hominem esse, quod sit A, sit prius quam homo, quod sit B, vel econtra, cum impossibile sit duo poni in eodem gradu numero ordinis naturae... Sed non potest poni quod A sit posterius B, quia tunc A esset accidentale homini, et, per consequens, praesupponeret hominem. Et cum nihil praesupponit hominem, nisi quod praesupponit eum in existentia, sequitur quod A prasupponeret hominem in existentia. Consequens falsum, cum A sit simpliciter hominem existere. Igitur, non praesupponit hominem existere. Nec requirit ad hoc quod ipsum sit hominem esse cum sit hominem esse, nec econtra homo praesupponit hominem esse, quia nec quoad consequentiam nec quoad causam. Non quoad consequentiam cum mutuo formaliter se inferunt, nec quoad causam quia tunc ex hoc quod est ita quod homo est, homo est. Et sic foret reciprocatio causarum in eadem linea naturae in infinitum, quod est impossibile, cum in mutuo se inferentibus illud quod est simplicius est causaliter prius. Et per consequens prius foret homo quam hominem esse si distinguuntur. Quod notum est esse falsum, cum hominem esse nec potest poni passio hominis nec aliquod novem generum accidentis."

[66] Sometimes he uses also the expression 'difference of reason' (*distinctio rationis*) with the same meaning.

tures. In fact, from the extensional point of view, being and essence of creatures are equipollent, as every being is an essence and *vice versa*; but, from the intensional point of view, there is a formal difference, since the being of a thing presupposes its essence and not *vice versa*.[67] As a matter of fact, finite beings have four distinct levels of being (*esse*), or reality, of which the most important one is that essential.[68]

The ideal being (*esse ideale*) that every creature has in God, as eternal objects of His mind and the means by which He creates all that is outside Himself. This first level of being proper to creatures is really and essentially the same as the divine essence.

The potential being that everything has in its causes, both universal (genus, species) and particular. This second level of reality is closely connected with the nature of the individual substance on which finite beings are founded, and is independent of its actual existence. It is called by Wyclif "essential being" ("*esse essentiae*" or "*esse in genere*") as well. As the first level of being just mentioned has no distinct reality from God, the main level of being proper of a thing is this second one, the *esse essentiae*, since it causes a thing to be what it is.

The individual existence (*esse existere individuum*), that is, the actual existence in time of a finite being as an earthly object (*res*).[69]

---

[67] Cf. *De materia et forma*, 4, pp. 184/18–185/4: "In qualibet autem creatura est distinccio, saltem racionis, inter *esse* et essenciam, . . . Ideo dicunt quod essencia, ens et *esse* differunt secundum racionem, sicut lux, lucens et lucere. Quidquid autem sit de hoc exemplo et sensu concedendum de esse et essencia, videtur mihi quod omne *esse* sit essencia, et econtra; distingwuntur tamen secundum racionem in creaturis, cum *esse* habitum per formam aut racionem specialem alicuius generis presupponit essenciam, et non econtra; cum *esse* contracte dicit huiusmodi racionem. Exemplum est de specie et individuo, que distingwuntur secundum racionem incommunicabilitatis, tamen omnis species est individuum, et econtra."

[68] In his *De intelleccione Dei*, 5, pp. 101/31–102/7, Wyclif speaks of three main levels of being, as in this work he equates the *esse accidentale* with the *esse existere*: "*Esse intelligibile* creature est eius *esse* supremum; quod *esse* est eternum in hoc quod deus eternaliter intendit illam creaturam existere tempore suo; et post illud *esse*, sequitur *esse possibile* creature in caussis secundis ordinatias a deo ad producendum creaturam in tempore suo; et illud est temporale medians inter *esse intelligibile* et *esse existere*; 3° vero sequitur *esse existere* vel *esse* accidentale creature in suo genere." On this passage see Leff, *Heresy in the Later Middle Ages*, 2:502–3.

[69] Cf. *Tractatus de universalibus* 7, p. 127/54–64: "Tertio habet creatura esse existere individuum, secundum quod esse incipit et corrumpitur pro suo tempore. Et solum illud esse acceptant moderni doctores <*that is, Ockham, Buridan and their followers*>. . . . Aliud enim est esse et aliud existere."

The accidental being (*modus essendi accidentalis substantiae*) caused in a substance by the inhering in it of its appropriate accidental forms.

Thus, as far as the *pars construens* of his theory concerning the relationship between essence and being is concerned, Wyclif holds that <1> the ideal being is formally distinct from the singular essence; <2> the actual existence is formally distinct from the universal essence; and <3> the singular essence is formally distinct from the actual existence:[70]

> Every creature has many kinds of being, at least one of which is distinct from essence. Take a given Peter: it is certain that his ideal being is distinct from his particular essence. And again his particular existence, which is the being of existence and being thus and so, is distinct from his quidditative essence in species or genus. And so with other cases. . . . It is clear that Aristotle spoke truly when he said that the existence of a particular is distinct from its essence or quiddity; I myself think that this is true even of the angels. But the difficult point is whether the particular essence and its existence are distinct. The Solemn Doctor seems to say that they are, just as light and shining are distinct from each other. . . . And this opinion seems to have greater plausibility when you take essence not as it is often taken, for the quiddity of things, but for essential being preceding the quiddity of a thing. . . . In such cases therefore there is a distinction of reason.[71]

If one takes into account the real identity of being and essence, the last distinction is problematic. The key to the solution of this problem lies in the fact that Wyclif establishes a close connection between singular essence and essential being, on the one hand, and a real identity between universal and individual (that is, between universal

---

[70] *Tractatus de universalibus* 7, pp. 128/80–130/118 (Kenny pp. 49–50): "Quaelibet creatura habet multa esse quorum aliquod et essentia distinguuntur; ut notato Petro certum est quod esse suum ideale distinguitur a sua essentia singulari. Et iterum existentia singularis, quae est esse existere et sic esse, distinguitur a sua essentia quidditativa speciei vel generis. Et ita de aliis. . . . Et patet quod Aristoteles verum dicit quod esse existere singularis et sua essentia vel quidditas distinguuntur—quod ego credo esse verum de angelis. Sed difficultas est utrum essentia singularis et suum existere distinguuntur. Et videtur Doctorem Solemnem dicere quod sic, . . . Et ista sententia videtur habere maiorem colorem intelligendo essentiam non pro quidditate rei ut saepe sumitur, sed pro esse essentiali praecedente quidditatem rei. . . . Est igitur in talibus distinctio rationis."

[71] Here Kenny translates '*distinctio rationis*' as 'mental distinction', but such a translation, acceptable for any other medieval author, is misleading for Wyclif, as in his view the *distinctio rationis* is the same as the *distinctio formalis*, and so an extra-mental relation, totally independent of our mind.

essence and singular essence), on the other hand. The essential being is the level of being which matches singular essence, while the actual existence is in a certain way accidental to the singular essence itself.

Wyclif's strategy concerning the question of the composition of essence and being in creatures, which was taken up by Paul of Venice in his *Summa philosophiae naturalis* (AD 1408) some thirty years later, can be summarized in the three following steps: <1> extension of the range of the notion of being; <2> sharp distinction between being and existence, as the former is the universal condition of every kind of reality and the latter the mode of being peculiar to individual substances; <3> assimilation of the distinction between essence and being to the distinction between universal and singular.[72] Since the last point is connected to Wyclif's theory of universals and it cannot be properly understood without knowing his position on this topic, Wyclif's theses about universals and singulars need to be analyzed now.

4. Universals

Wyclif characterizes his opinion on universals and singulars as intermediate between those ones of Thomas Aquinas and Giles of Rome and that of Walter Burley:[73]

> Thus, some say that every substance is particular, and is universal only by being apprehended universally; just as an artefact is called human, on the basis of a humanity outside itself, and a thing seen, or understood, or otherwise described on the basis of something outside itself. And this opinion is attributed to St Thomas, Giles and many others. The second way says that the universal is not any of its particulars since it is contrasted with a particular because it is common, or shared, or predicable, and is prior by nature and imperceptible by senses and different in many other ways ... And this opinion seems to have been held by Master Walter Burleigh and many others ... I, for my part, take a middle way, reconciling the extremes; I agree with the first

---

[72] See below, pp. 97–99.
[73] *Tractatus de universalibus* 4, pp. 86/40–87/9 (Kenny pp. 27–28). For the Latin text see above, n. 1. On Wyclif's theory of universals see Spade, "Introduction", pp. xviii–xx; Kenny, *Wyclif*, pp. 7–17; Kenny, "The Realism of *De Universalibus*," pp. 17–29; Conti, "Logica intensionale e metafisica dell'essenza," 181–89; Spade, "The Problem of Universals," pp. 111–23.

opinion that every universal is particular, and *vice versa* though the two are formally distinct from each other.

Like Giles, whom he quotes by name, Wyclif recognizes three main kinds of universals: <1> *ante rem*, or ideal universals, that is, the ideas in God, archetypes of all that there is; <2> *in re*, or formal universals, that is, the common natures shared by individual things; and <3> *post rem*, or intentional universals, that is, mental signs by which we refer to the universals *in re*. The ideas in God are the causes of the formal universals, and the formal universals are the causes of the intentional universals. On the other hand, just like Burley, Wyclif holds that formal universals exist *in actu* outside our minds, and not *in potentia*, as "moderate" realists thought—even if, unlike the *Doctor Planus et Perspicuus*, he maintains that they are really identical with their own individuals.

In addition to this partition of universals, standard in the Middle Ages, Wyclif introduces another one, which was very successful among his followers, based on the different functions that universal essences perform. He divides universals into <1> universals by causality (*causatione*), <2> universals by community (*communicatione*), and <3> universals by representation (*repraesentatione*). Anything which can bring about several effects is a universal by causality; any essence shared by many things at once is a universal by community; and any sign of the universals *communicatione* is a universal by representation. The first two kinds of universals are such in a strict sense, whereas the universals of the third kind are universals in an equivocal sense, only in so far as do they refer to the "real" universals:[74]

> There are three kinds of universal in general. The first is universal by causality, in the way that the most universal cause is God, and after him created universal things in accordance with the order in which

---

[74] *Tractatus de universalibus* 1, pp. 15/6–16/16 (Kenny p. 1): "Triplex est maneries universalium in genere. Primum est universale causatione, ut Deus est causa universalissima et post eum res universales creatae secundum ordinem, quo originantur a Deo. Secundum est universale communicatione, ut puta res communicata multis suppositis, ut natura humana et aliae naturae generales et specificae. Tertium est universale repraesentatione, ut signa priorum universalium quae *aequivoce* dicuntur universalia, sicut homo pictus *aequivoce* dicitur homo." Kenny's translation has been slightly modified, as I prefer to translate "*aequivoce*" litterally as "equivocally" instead of interpreting the latin adverb in a stronger technical way, as Kenny (who translates it as "by analogy") does.

they take their origin from God. The second is universal by community, a thing, for instance, shared by many supposits, such as human nature and other general and specific natures. The third is universal by representation, like the signs for the universals already mentioned, which are called universals *equivocally* in the way in which a picture of a man is *equivocally* called a man.

Since this division is based on the different functions an universal essence can accomplish, its principles are not mutually exclusive, so that one and the same universal can be placed into two (or more) branches of the classification at the same time—as in the case of God, who, according to Wyclif, can be considered an universal by causality and by representation. Moreover, it is clear that <1> the universals *ante rem* and *post rem* of the first division are universals by representation; <2> the universals *in re* are universals by community; <3> all the genera and species belonging to the ten categories, which are universals by community, are universals by causality too, as they are causes of their own individuals.

This last statement sheds light on the problem of the ontological status of the formal universals and their relations with the individuals. According to Wyclif, who depends on Avicenna, the formal universals are common natures, or *veritates*, in virtue of which the individuals that share them are exactly what they are—just as the human species is the truth or form by which every man formally is a man. *Qua* natures, they are prior, and so "indifferent", to any division into universals and individuals. Universality (*universalitas* or *communicabilitas*) is as it were their inseparable property (*quasi passio*) and not a constitutive mark of the nature itself.

As a consequence, the formal universals can be conceived of in two different manners: as first intentions, or as second intentions. In the first case, they are natures of a certain kind and are identical with their own individuals (for example, *homo* is the same thing as Socrates). In the second case, they are properly universals (that is, something that can exist in many things and can be shared by them), and distinct from their own individuals, considered *qua* individuals, because of the opposite constitutive principles: *communicabilitas* for universals and *incommunicabilitas* for individuals. Therefore, universals are really (*realiter*) identical-to, but formally (*formaliter*) distinct from their individuals. In fact, universals are formal causes in relation to their own individuals, and individuals material causes in relation to their universals, since individuals are *partes subiectivae* of the universals.

Thus three different kinds of entities can be qualified as formal universals: <1> the common natures instantiated by individuals—which are things of first intention; <2> the form itself of universality which belongs to a certain common nature when seen in its relation to the individuals—which is a thing of second intention; <3> the thinkability proper to the common nature, by which it is a possible object of our mind:[75]

> In an analogous manner "universal", interpreted formally, says three things: first the nature, which is a thing of first intention, secondly the possibility of being common to, or being predicated of many supposits, which is a thing of second intention; and thirdly the thinkability which is proper to the intellect, since a universal thing is uniquely thinkable in so far as it is non-sensible by a bodily sense.

Wyclif accepts the common realist account of the relationship between universals and singulars, and tries to improve it by defining more accurately its logical structure. The formulation he adopts—universals and individuals are really the same, but formally distinct—is only another way of saying that universals and individuals are the same identical things if conceived as first intentions, and differ from each others if conceived as second intentions—a thesis already found in Albert the Great's *Liber de praedicabilibus* (tr. 2, ch. 5). According to Wyclif, universals and individuals are really the same, but formally distinct, since they share the same empirical reality, which is that of individuals, but considered as universals and individuals they have opposite basic principles: the natural-tendency-to-be-common (*communicabilitas*) for universals and the impossibility-of-being-common (*incommunicabilitas*) for individuals. This means that not all that is predicated of individuals can be directly (*formaliter*) predicated of uni-

---

[75] *Tractatus de universalibus* 2, p. 64/278–285 (Kenny pp. 15–16): "Correspondenter 'universale', formaliter intellectum, dicit tria: primo naturam quae est res primae intentionis, secundo communicabilitatem vel praedicationem de multis suppositis, quae est res secundae intentionis, et tertio intelligibilitatem propriam intellectus cum res universalis sit appropriate intelligibilis sic quod insensibilis a sensu corporeo." This analysis of the referents of the term '*universale*' is similar to that of Scotus (cf. Duns Scotus, *Quaestiones super universalia Porphyrii*, q. 3, in *Opera Philosophica* [St. Bonaventure, NY, 1999], 1:19–20). The only remarkable difference concerns the third sense of the term. In fact, according to the *Doctor Subtilis* 'universal' interpreted formally says the three following things: <1> common natures; <2> properties of second intention, like being-a-genus, being-a-species, and so on; and <3> the entities which are made up by the union of a common nature with one of these properties of second intention.

versals and *vice versa*. Wyclif thought that a universal of the category of substance could directly receive only the predications of substantial forms more common than itself (that is, those forms which are put on a higher level in the *linea praedicamentalis*).[76] On the other hand, the accidental forms inhering in substantial individuals could be predicated of the substantial form itself that those individuals instantiate only indirectly (*essentialiter*), through and in virtue of the individuals of that substantial form.[77] So Wyclif's description of the logical structure of the relationship between universals and individuals demanded a redefinition of predication.

5. *The coincidence of logic and metaphysics: the theory of predication*

In order to achieve this task, Wyclif introduced new kinds of predication, unknown to Aristotle,[78] to cover the cases of indirect inherence of an accidental form in a substantial universal admitted by his theory of universals. In his *Tractatus de universalibus* he distinguishes three main types of predication, that he conceives as a real relation which holds between metaphysical entities:[79]

---

[76] Cf. *Tractatus de universalibus* 11, p. 239/43–48: "Oportet notare quod universale non recipit aliquam absolutam praedicationem formalem prout distinguitur ab aliis, nisi praedicationem sui generis, ut species humana est animal, corpus, substantia et ens, sed nec est alba nec nigra nec quomodolibet absolute accidentata."

[77] Cf. *Tractatus de universalibus* 11, p. 240/51–59: "Non est aliquod genus vel individuum accidentis, quin ipsum sit vere praedicabile tam de universali quam de individuo substantiae, diversimode tamen quia utrobique in concreto: de individuo formaliter et de universali secundum essentiam. Ut species humana, quamvis sit risibile, quantum et quilibet homo qualitercumque accidentatus, non tamen est risibilis, quantitative divisibilis, accidenter qualis vel quomodolibet aliter accidentata." See also *Purgans errores circa universalia in communi*, 3, p. 35.

[78] Cf. *Tractatus de universalibus* 1, p. 37/276–279: "Aristoteles autem non admisit praedicationem nisi formalem, vel per se vel per accidens. Ideo conceditur quod Aristoteles ignoravit dictam praedicationem <id est: secundum essentiam>."

[79] *Tractatus de universalibus* 1, pp. 27/157–28/169 (Kenny p. 4): "Tertio diligenter est notandum de triplici preadicandi manerie, scilicet de praedication formali, de praedicatione secundum essentiam et de praedicatione secundum habitudinem. Talis autem praedicatio principaliter est ex parte rei. Et hinc philosophi non loquuntur de falsa praedicatione signorum nec de praedicatione negativa, nec de praedicatione de praeterito vel de futuro, quia talis non est ex parte rei, sed solum vera praedicatio, licet vere ex parte rei una res negatur vel removeatur a reliqua, ut homo ab asino et sic de aliis veritatibus negativis. Solum autem illud quod est forma praedicatur realiter de subiecto." Kenny translates '*praedicatio secundum essentiam*' as 'essential predication', but in Aristotelian and common medieval contexts this

Thirdly, we must note carefully the three different kinds of predication, namely formal predication, *predication by essence* and habitudinal predication. All such predication is principally in the real world. And this is why philosophers do not speak of false predication of signs, nor of negative predication, nor of predication about the past or the future, because that is not in the real world; only true predication is in the real world, though truly in the real world one thing is denied or removed from another, as man from donkey and similarly with other negative truths. But only that which is form is really predicated of a subject.

In the *Purgans errores circa universalia in communi* they were the following: formal predication (*praedicatio formalis*), predication by essence (*praedicatio secundum essentiam*), and causal predication (*praedicatio secundum causam*); on the contrary, in the *Tractatus de universalibus* causal predication has been replaced by habitudinal predication (*praedicatio secundum habitudinem*)—a kind of predication that Wyclif had already recognized in the *Purgans errores circa universalia*, but whose position within the main division of the types of predication was not clear. In the *Tractatus de universalibus* formal predication, predication by essence, and habitudinal predication are described as three non-mutually exclusive ways of predicating, each more general than the preceding one (or ones). We speak of causal predication when the form designated by the predicate-term is not present in the entity signified by the subject-term, but it is something caused by that entity. No instances of this kind of predication are given by Wyclif.[80] Formal predication, predication by esence, and habitudinal predication are defined almost in the same way in the *Purgans errores* and in the *Tractatus de universalibus*.

Formal predication is that predication in which the form designated by the predicate-term is directly present in the entity signified by the subject-term. This happens whenever an item in the catego-

---

expression has a different meaning from the technical one the formula '*praedicatio secundum essentiam*' has in Wyclif (as a matter of fact, the common medieval essential predication is equivalent to Wyclif's first sub-type of formal predication), so I prefer to translate it in a (sligthly) different way. On Wyclif's theory of predication see Spade, "Introduction," pp. xxxi–xli; Conti, "Analogy and Formal Distinction," 153–58.

[80] In the treatises on universals of two of his Oxonian followers, William Penbygull and Roger Whelpdale, however, we find this example: "*Dies est latio solis super terram*"—and nothing prevents us from assuming it as appropriate for Wyclif as well. See Conti, "Analogy and Formal Distinction," p. 155, and below, p. 121.

rial line is predicated of something inferior, or an accident of its subject of inherence. In fact, in both of them, the subject-term and the predicate-term refer to the same reality in virtue of the form connoted by the predicate-term itself:[81]

> Formal predication is predication in which there is predicated something which formally inheres in a subject. By "formally inhering in" I mean something which identically applies to the subject in respect of the notion by which it is, as "a divine person is God" "man is an animal" and "Peter is musical", and in general whenever a superior is primarily and *per se* predicated of its inferior, or an accident of its subject.

To speak of predication by essence it is sufficient that the same empirical reality is both the real subject and predicate, even though the formal principle connoted by the predicate-term differs from that connoted by the subject-term. "God is man" and "The universal is particular" are instances of predication by essence. In fact, the same empirical reality (or essence) which is a universal is also an individual, but the forms connoted by the subject-term and by the predicate-term are different:[82]

> Predication by essence[83] is predication in which the same essence is the subject and predicate, even though the notion of the predicate differs from the notion of the subject, as in "God is man", "Fire is water", "The universal is particular."

Finally we speak of predication *secundum habitudinem* when the form connoted by the predicate-term does not inhere, directly or indirectly, in the essence designated by the subject, but simply implies

---

[81] *Tractatus de universalibus* 1, pp. 28/171–29/178 (Kenny p. 4): "Est autem praedicatio formalis praedicatio qua praedicatur formaliter inexistens subiecto. Et voco 'formaliter inexistere' illud quod identice convenit subiecto secundum rationem qua est, ut 'Persona divina est Deus', 'Homo est animal' et 'Petrus est musicus', et breviter quandocumque per se primo superius praedicatur de suo inferiori, vel accidens de suo subiecto." See also *Purgans errores circa universalia in communi*, 2, in S.H. Thomson, "A 'Lost' Chapter of Wyclif's *Summa de ente*," p. 342.

[82] *Tractatus de universalibus* 1, p. 30/194–198 (Kenny p. 4): "Praedicatio vero secundum essentiam est praedicatio in qua eadem essentia est subiectum et praedicatum, licet alia sit ratio praedicati quam sit ratio subiecti, ut hic: 'Deus est homo', 'Ignis est aqua', 'Universale est singulare.'" See also *Purgans errores circa universalia in communi*, 2, in S.H. Thomson, "A 'Lost' Chapter of Wyclif's *Summa de ente*," pp. 342–43.

[83] For the translation of the technical formula '*praedicatio secundum essentiam*' see above, n. 79.

a relation to it, so that the same predicate may be at different times truly or falsely spoken of its subject, without there being any change in the subject itself. According to Wyclif, we use such a kind of predication mainly when we want to express theological truths, like these: that God is known and loved by many creatures, and brings about, as efficient, exemplar, and final cause, many good effects.[84]

It is evident that habitudinal predication does not require any kind of identity between the entity signified by the subject-term and the entity signified by the predicate-term, but formal predication and predication by essence do. So the ontological presuppositions of the most general type of predication, implied by the other types, are completely different from those of the other two. This fact explains why the Oxford philosophers of the following generations tried to improve Wyclif's theory of predication by excluding habitudinal predication and redefining the other two kinds of predication in a slightly different way.[85]

The final result of Wyclif's "revolution" was therefore a fully developed system of intensional logic, which his followers added to (or, better, allowed to overlap with) the standard extensional system, inherited from Aristotle. As a result, <1> the copula of the propositions which they deal with cannot be extensionally interpreted, as it does not mean that a given object is a member of a certain set, nor that a given set is included in another, but it means degrees in identity; and <2> individuals and universals, considered as metaphysical compounds, appear to be hypostatisations of intensions, since individuals come from the *species specialissimae* by means of *rationes suppositales* just as species come from superior genera by means of the *differentiae specificae*. Only in virtue of renouncing an extensional approach to the matter were Wyclif and his followers able to give a logically satisfactory solution of the problem of the relationship between universals and individuals, which had always been the most difficult issue for medieval forms of realism.

---

[84] Cf. *Tractatus de universalibus*, 1, p. 34/235–41: "Tertia est praedicatio secundum habitudinem ex qua secundum genus adveniente subiecto non oportet ipsum ut sic esse proprie mobile, ut contingit rem intelligi, amari, varie causare et acquirere sibi ubicationem, quandalitatem et quotlibet relationes rationis, sine hoc quod ipsum ut sic moveatur vel sit mobile." See also *Purgans errores circa universalia in communi*, 3, p. 34.

[85] See below, pp. 119–21.

6. *Being, God and creatures: the doctrine of analogy*

If being is a reality, it is then clear that it is impossible to affirm its univocity.[86] Duns Scotus thought of being as simply a concept, therefore he could describe it as univocal in a broad sense (one name—one concept—many natures). Wyclif, on the contrary, is convinced that the *ens in communi* is an extra-mental reality, so he works out his theory at a different level in relation to Scotus: no more at the intensional level of the *ratio* connected with the univocal sign (*univocum univocans*), but at the extensional one of the *res* signified by the mental sign, considered as common to different entities according to different degrees of participation. For that reason, he cannot utilize Aristotelian univocation, which hides these differences in sharing. He prefers to use one of the traditional notions of analogy, since the being of God is the measure of the being of the other things, which are drawn up in a scale with the separate substances at top and matter at bottom.[87] Therefore he qualifies being as a genus, still ambiguous (*genus ambiguum*)—borrowing an expression already used by Grosseteste in his commentary on Aristotle's *Posterior Analytics*.[88]

Wyclif's denying the univocity of being does not mean, however, that the analogy of being implies an ordered multiplicity of meanings, as in Aquinas's commentary on the *Sentences*,[89] but a single meaning only, corresponding to a unique reality. Since Wyclif hypostatizes the notion of being and considers equivocity, analogy, and univocity as real relations between things, and not as semantical

---

[86] Cf. *De ente praedicamentali*, 3, p. 27.

[87] Cf. *De ente praedicamentali*, 3, p. 25/3–12: "Constat namque ex predictis, quod esse generativum est analogum, et constabit, quod nec ens in sua maxima communitate, nec accidens est genus logicum, <scilicet natura positiva multis speciebus univoce communicata,> cuius potissima causa est analogia. Ideo distinguendo genus amibuggum, de quo Lincolniensis I *Posteriorum* capitulo 5°, a genere loyco, cuius generativum est quodlibet predicamentum, videndum est, quomodo stabilietur genus loycum." Ibid., p. 29/7–13: "Proporcionaliter ut aliquid est reliquo perfeccius est ipsum magis ens, ita, quod summe ens est Deus, et gradatim alia, ut sunt ipso plus aut minus participancia Deus enim, ut copiosius vel minus copiose communicat bonitatem suam creaturis, quibus illabitur, facit eas proporcionabiliter magis et minus entes. Ipse enim est metrum aliis, ut sint, et ut tnate sint."

[88] Cf. Robertus Grosseteste, *Commentarius in Posteriorum Analyticorum libros*, 1.5, ed. P. Rossi (Florence, 1981), pp. 118–19.

[89] Cf. Thomas Aquinas, *In I Sent.*, d. 19, q. 5, a. 2.

relations between terms and things, his analogy is partially equivalent to the Aristotelian univocity:[90]

> It is certain that Aristotle's description of equivocals, univocals, and
> denominatives concerns extra-mental things (which are called "equiv-
> ocals" in accordance with those principles), and only secondarily the
> nouns of the things. . . . It is certain that there are extra-mental things,
> some of which are attributed equivocally, some univocally, and some
> denominatively to <other things which play the role of> substrate;
> and such things are believed to be the equivocals, univocals, and
> denominatives—because of them and in virtue of a relationship of sim-
> ilarity, the signs <which refer to them> are called equivocal and uni-
> vocal.

In fact, according to the standard interpretation of the opening passages of the *Categories* (ch. 1, 1a 1–6 and 6–12), equivocal terms are
correlated with more than one concept and refer to a multiplicity
of things belonging to different genera, whereas univocal terms are
correlated with only one concept and refer to a multiplicity of things
belonging to one and the same species or genus. Within Wyclif's
system, three facts differentiate *genera ambigua*, like being, from *genera
logica*, like substance (in other words, analogy from univocity): <1>
the logical genus shows the inner nature (*quidditas*) of its inferiors
(that is, the things of which it is predicated), but the *genus ambiguum*
does not; <2> every logical genus is immediately divided into two
inferior species by two opposite differences, which do not belong to
that genus, while being cannot have such differences, since anything
falls under it; <3> the ways in which a logical genus and a *genus
ambiguum* are common to their inferiors are different: the inferiors of
a *genus ambiguum* (or *analoga*) share it at different degrees of participation (*secundum magis et minus* or *secundum prius et posterius*), whereas
the inferiors of a logical genus (or *univoca*) share it all in the same
manner and at the same degree of participation.[91]

---

[90] *De ente praedicamentali*, 2, p. 15/17–28: "Ideo certum est, quod descripcio Aristotelis
de equivocis, univocis et denominativis consonat rebus extra, que dicuntur equivoca secundum istas raciones et consequenter nominibus rerum, . . . Certum est, quod
est dare res ad extra, quarum alique equivoce, alique univoce et alique denomi-
native competunt subiectis; et ille supponuntur esse equivoca, univoca et denomi-
nativa, et consequenter racione illorum signa dicuntur similitudine equivoca et
univoca."

[91] Cf. *De ente praedicamentali*, 3, p. 27/27–31: "Videtur michi, quod sufficit ad
racionem generis logici, quod sit natura positiva multis speciebus communicata sine
participacione sue essencie secundum magis et minus, et illam ultimam differenciam

Wyclif admits three main types of equivocity: by chance (*a casu*), analogical (which is similar to the traditional deliberate equivocity), and generic—only the generic one compatible with the univocity proper to the *genera logica*.[92] Equivocals by chance are those things to which it happens that they have the same name, but with different meanings and/or reasons for imposition. Those things are analogical which have the same name and are subordinated to a single concept, but according to different ways. Analogical things share therefore the nature signified by that name according to various degrees of participation. For this reason they differ from generic equivocals, which share the same generic nature in the same way, but have distinct specific natures.[93] Wyclif appears to depend here

intellexi superius per 'univoce communicari.'" Ibid., 4, pp. 30/1–32/33: "Ex istis facile est videre, quod nec ens, nec accidens in sua maxima comminitate sit genus loycum, quamvis utrumque illorum sit genus ambiguum. De ente ponuntur communiter triplices raciones. Prima ad hoc, quod sit genus loycum, oporteret quod diceret quiditatem sui subiecti; sed non sic facit ens in sua maxima communitate respectu alicuius, ideo nulli est, ut sic, genus loycum. . . . Secunda racio sumitur ex eadem radice. Nam omne genus natum est habere duas differencias sue divisionis et speciei constitutivas, sed sic non potest ens habere in sua maxima communitate; ergo non potest esse genus logicum. . . . Omnis differencia generis dicit aliquid extra racionem eiusdem generis, et implicat ipsum habere contrarium, a quod differt; sed nichil potest esse extra racionem entis, sicut nec ens potest habere contrarium, ergo ens in sua maxima communitate non potest habere differenciam. . . . Tercia racio, quare ens non est genus, tacta est superius, scilicet, quod ens equivoce communicatur suis inferioribus secundum magis et minus, quod alienum est a genere loyco."

[92] The division of the equivocals into *aequivoca a casu* and *aequivoca a consilio* is due to the Neoplatonic commentators of Aristotle. It was introduced into the Latin world by Boethius (see his commentary on the *Categories, de aequivocis,* in PL 64:166B–C). The semantical structure of the two groups of equivocals is the same (one name, many concepts, many natures), but in the case of the deliberate equivocals concepts (and therefore natures) are related to each other, so there is some (good) reason for the homonymy. In the late Middle Ages a new kind of deliberate equivocity was worked out, much more similar to Aristotelian univocity than to the standard Neoplatonic deliberate equivocity, and substantially identical to analogy by priority and posteriority (*per prius et posterius*), as it was based on the following semantical structure: one name, one concept, one nature, but shared according to different ways.

[93] Cf. *De ente praedicamentali*, 2, pp. 16–17, 18–19, and 21: "Tercio notandum, quod tres sunt gradus equivocacionis et univocacionis, et per consequens equivocum et univocum contingit in eodem analogo suis gradibus convenire. Quoddam enim est equivocum sine analoga conveniencia equivocatorum in illo equivoco, ut casualiter vocatur unus homo propria nominacione Felix, et alius, quia beatus, dicitur felix; nec est aliqua analogia vel commune proprie intencionis conveniens illis, secundum quod uterque dicitur felix, et taliter sepe contingit in nominibus propriis. . . . In secundo gradu equivocatorum sunt analoga, sive secundum esse, sive secundum operacionem vel aliam proprietatem accidentalem, ut ens contingit analoyce substancie

on Burley's prologue of the last commentary on the *Physics* (AD 1324), where the *Doctor Planus et Perspicuus* affirms that the term "being" is at the same time univocal and equivocal. It is univocal broadly speaking as a single concept is associated with it; it is equivocal, but not most strictly, because this single concept is predicated of the categorial beings in different ways: directly of substance and secondarily of accidents. Unlike Burley, Wyclif hypostatizes the notion of being, and does not seem to allow a distinction between deliberate equivocity using two concepts and the kind of equivocity which involves only one concept. On the other hand, he keeps the same explanatory scheme, since he also confines the Aristotelian definition of equivocity to chance equivocity and considers the other forms of equivocity as equivalent to the Aristotelian univocity.

In Wyclif's view, the *ens in communi* is the main constituent of the metaphysical structure of each reality, God included, since He is being. On the other hand, being is a creature, the first of all the creatures, and God should share it, for the twofold reason that <1> being is the most common reality, predicated of all, and <2> (according to Wyclif) to-be-predicated-of something means to-be-shared-by it. As a consequence, something would be for some aspect over-ordered to God and common to Him and his (other) creatures, and so the greatest possible diversity (that one between God and creatures) would admit a form of univocal (that is, formal) identity.[94] To solve this problem, Wyclif notes that something common can be univocally shared by its inferiors (*univoce participari suis inferioribus*) in two ways: either in virtue of the various differences (*secundum racionem differencie*) which modify it, transforming it into its inferiors, or in virtue of its transcendental nature (*racione transcendencie*), as a basic reality that inferior realities incorporate without modifying nor transforming it.[95] Being *qua* transcendental (*ens transcendens*) is common to

---

et accidenti, cum substancia sit per se ens; et accidens est ens, quia substancie formaliter inheret, et talis analogia est inter Deum et quodcumque causatum, inter ydeam et ydeatum, et breviter inter quodcumque ens intelligibile et actuale causatum extra Deum est talis analogia secundum operacionem proporcio-nalem. . . . In tercio gradu sunt omnia genera, ut innuit Aristoteles VII *Phisicorum* 31°, ubi dicit genus esse tacenter equivocum."

[94] Cf. *Logicae continuatio*, 3, 2, 2:37–38.

[95] Cf. *Logicae continuatio*, 3, 2, 2:38/10–14: "Dupliciter commune possit univoce participari suis inferioribus: vel secundum ractinem differencie, sicut universalia participantur a suis individuis; vel racione transcendencie, ut ractione essendi, sicut analoga participa<n>tur."

God and the creatures in this second way only[96]—that is, it can be predicated of everything and anything can be predicated of it according to the predication by essence only. In fact, what Wyclif says in order to better clarify his statement shows us that the relationship holding between the *ens transcendens* and any other being is a relation of partial identity (Wyclif speaks of transcendental identity— *transcendens idemptitas*),[97] which rules out that two things standing in such a relation to a third one, more general than them, can be formally identical to each other. He explains that it is true that <1> anything is the transcendental being, and that <2> the transcendental being is God, and therefore that <3> anything is the transcendental being which is God (*quodlibet est ens transcendens, quod est Deus*), but this conclusion does not mean that anything is God, in the sense of being formally identical with God; it simply means that something, that is, the transcendental being, partially identical to anything, is also partially identical to God.[98]

7. *The accidental forms*

Since Wyclif thought of substance as the ultimate substrate of existence and subject of predication in relation to anything else, the only

---

[96] Cf. *Logicae continuatio*, 3, 2, 2:38/14–17: "Primo modo non est ens univocum, quia sic esset genus. Sed secundo modo satis univoce participatur, cum significat omnia illa sub eodem signo naturaliter representata."

[97] Cf. *Logicae continuatio*, 3, 2, 2:39.

[98] Cf. *Logicae continuatio*, 3, 2, 2:38–39. At the beginning of the fifteenth century, two among Wyclif's followers, the English William Penbygull and the German Johannes Sharpe, tried to solve a similar aporia (focussed on the consequent superiority of a creature, that is the *ens in communi*, over God Himself) in two different ways. Penbygull, in his treatise *De universalibus* (in A.D. Conti, "Teoria degli universali e teoria della predicazione nel trattato *De universalibus* di William Penbygull: discussione e difesa della posizione di Wyclif," *Medioevo* 8 [1982], pp. 200–1), denies that the property of being more general implies natural priority. According to him being is a more general reality than God, and so over-ordered to Him, but in spite of this fact God is clearly naturally prior and infinitely more perfect than it. Sharpe, in his *Quaestio de universalibus* (ed. A.D. Conti [Florence, 1990], pp. 106–10), distinguishes between *communicatio* (that is, generality) and *participatio* (that is, ontological participation). He considers the latter simply as a sub-case of the former, since according to him a reality *x* is shared (that is participated) by a reality *y* if and only if: <1> *x* is more general than *y*, and <2> *x* is cause of *y*. Therefore, being would be more general than God, but its reality is not shared by Him, as the *ens in communi* is not the cause of God.

way to demonstrate the reality of the items belonging to other categories was to conceive of them as forms and attributes of substance.
Accordingly, he insists that quantity, quality, and relations, *considered
as accidents*, are forms inherent in the composite substances.[99] In this
way, Wyclif wanted to safeguard the reality of accidents as well as
their (real) distinction from substance and from each others, while
at the same time affirming their dependence on substance in existence.

7.1: *The absolute accidents: quantity and quality.*

Among the nine genera of accidents, quantity is the most important
one, as it is the basis of all further accidents, because every other
accident presupposes it. Indeed, quantity orders substance for receiving quality and the other accidental forms.[100]

In his commentary on the *Categories* (ch. 10, § 4) and in the first
part of his *Summa Logicae* (pars I, ch. 44) Ockham had claimed that
it was superfluous to posit quantitative forms really distinct from substance and quality, since quantity presupposes what it is intended to
explain, that is, the extension of material substances and their having parts outside parts. As an accident, quantity presupposes substance as its substrate of inherence. Like Burley,[101] Wyclif also denies
that material substance can be actually extended without the presence of quantitative forms in it, thereby affirming their necessity,[102]
and consequently he tries to confute Ockham's argumentation.[103] He
admits that the existence of any quantity always implies that of substance, but he also believes that the actual existence of parts in a
substance necessarily implies the presence of a quantitative form in
it, distinct <1> from the substance (say Socrates) in which it inheres,

---

[99] Cf. *De ente praedicamentali*, 6, p. 48. See also *De logica*, 3, 1:11–12.

[100] Cf. *De ente praedicamentali*, 6, p. 48/–11: "Post substanciam sequitur quantitas,
que est immediatum et proximum genus accidentis; repugnat enim genus substancie esse integrum, nisi fuerit tam substancia corporea quam incorporea, et per consequens tam quantitas continua quam discreta. Et quod sit prior qualitate, patet ex
hoc, quod qualitas quecumque presupponit quantitatem, ymo eadem species quantitatis, ut corporeitas, est disposicio ad quotlibet genera qualitatum, causans figuram,
aciem etc. Ideo solet dici, quod quantitas sit basis cuilibet alteri accidenti."

[101] Cf. Walter Burley, *Expositio super Praedicamenta Aristotelis, de quantitate*, fol. e3va.

[102] Cf. *De ente praedicamentali*, 6, p. 50.

[103] Cf. *De ente praedicamentali*, 6, pp. 50–58.

and <2> from the truth, grounded on the substance at issue, that this same substance is a quantified thing (*est res quanta*).[104]

He does not give us any sound metaphysical reason for this preference. Nevertheless, it is easily understandable, when considered from the point of view of his semantic presuppositions, according to which, the reality itself is the interpretative pattern of our language. As a consequence, the structure of language is a mere mirroring of that of reality. In Wyclif's opinion, therefore, some entities must correspond in the world to the abstract terms of the category of quantity (like "*magnitudo*")—entities really distinct from the things signified by the substantial terms. In any case, the most important evidence he offers for proving his thesis is a sort of abductive reasoning, whose implicit premise is the following inferential rule: if we can recognize a thing as *the* same thing before and after its undertaking a process of change, then what is changed is not the thing at issue, but a distinct entity really present in that thing as one of its real aspects. The second (explicit) premise is the observation that men are of different size during their lives. And the conclusion is that those changes are due to an accidental form distinct from the substances in which it inheres.[105]

Immediately after quantity, quality comes.[106] Following Aristotle (*Categories*, ch. 8, 8a 25), Wyclif defines quality as what in virtue of which substances are said to be qualified.[107] The chief feature of Wyclif's treatment of quality is his twofold consideration of quality as an abstract form and as a concrete accident. In the *De ente praedicamentali* he clearly states that quality is an absolute entity, with a well determined nature, and really distinct from substance.[108] Furthermore,

---

[104] Cf. *De ente praedicamentali*, 6, pp. 51–53.

[105] Cf. *De ente praedicamentali*, 6, p. 50/1–11: "Quod homo si quantus est veritas presupponens hominem esse, et potens deesse ab homine, ipso permanente, ergo distinguitur ab homine, et certum est, quod talis veritas inest homini accidentaliter, ergo est accidens homini, et ad nichil pertinencius deserviret, quam ad quantificandum hominem, cum ipsa posita est homo sic quantus, et ipsa ablata desinit esse sic quantus; ergo talis veritas est accidens, quo subiectum est formaliter et accidentaliter quantum; et tale describitur esse quantitas distincta; ergo est dare huiusmodi quantitatem."

[106] Cf. *De ente praedicamentali*, 7, p. 61.

[107] Cf. *De logica*, 3, 1:11/24–25: "Qualitas est *forma denominans subiectum esse formaliter quale*, ut color, albedo, caliditas, etc."

[108] Cf. *De ente praedicamentali*, 7, p. 61. See also *De logica*, 3, 1:11.

even if incidentally, against Burley,[109] he notes that qualitative forms can admit a more or a less (*suscipiunt magis et minus*), since the *propria passio* of the category of quality is to be more or less intense.[110] By contrast, in the *De actibus animae*, he seems to conceive of it as a mode of substance, without an actually distinct reality.[111] Truly, there is no effective difference between the theses on quality maintained in those two works, but only a difference of point of view. As what he says about the real-and-essential distinction and the first sub-type of formal distinction makes evident, quality considered in an absolute way, according to its main level of being, is an abstract form, really distinct from substance; yet, if considered from the point of view of its existence as a concrete accident, it is not *really* distinct from the substance in which it is present, but only *formally*. In the latter case, it is a mere mode of the substance, like any other concrete accident. In fact, in the *De ente praedicamentali* Wyclif speaks of quality, using the abstract term, while in the *De actibus animae* he constantly utilises concrete expressions, such as "*quale*" and "*substantia qualis*."[112]

7.2: *Relations and Relatives*

Aristotle's treatment of relations in the *Categories* and in the *Metaphysics* is opaque and incomplete.[113] Because of this fact, in the Late Antiquity and in the Middle Ages many authors tried to reformulate the doctrine of relatives. Wyclif's attempt is one of the most interesting among those of the whole Middle Ages, as he very likely was the first medieval author able to work out a concept of relation conceived of as an accidental form which is in both the relatives at once, even though in different ways.[114] Consequently his relation can

---

[109] Cf. Walter Burley, *Expositio super Praedicamenta Aristotelis, de qualitate*, fol. g1ra.

[110] Cf. *De ente praedicamentali*, 3, p. 28.

[111] Cf. *De actibus animae*, pars ii, 4, pp. 122–23, and 127.

[112] On this subject see Conti, "Logica intensionale e metafisica dell'essenza," pp. 201–6.

[113] The main reasons for this weakness are the following: <1> Aristotle speaks of relatives and conceives them as those entities which not-absolute terms of our language refer to he does not have any notion of relation; <2> he does not discuss the question of the reality of relatives; <3> he does not clarify the connection between the two difinitions of relatives he proposes in the seventh chapters of the *Categories*; <4> he does not give any effective criterion for distinguishing relatives from some items belonging to other categories.

[114] Wyclif's treatment of relations and relatives in the *De ente praedicamentali* is

be considered the ontological equivalent to our modern functions with two variables, or two-place predicates, whereas all the other authors of the Middle Ages had thought of the relations in terms of monadic functions:[115]

> <Relation> is different from quality and quantity, since it presupposes them just as what follows by nature presupposes what precedes. Quantity and quality are, in a certain way, absolute entities, but relation *qua* such is <a sort of link> between two things.

As it has been already said, Wyclif thinks that the items directly falling into any categorial field are simple accidental forms, therefore he distinguishes between relations (*relationes*) and relatives (*relativa* or *ad aliquid*)—these latter being the aggregates formed by a substance, a relation, and the foundation, or support (*fundamentum*), of the relation. Accordingly, the relationship between relation and relatives is, for him, similar to the ones between quantity and what is quantified, and quality and what is qualified. The relation is the very cause of the nature of the aggregates (that is, the relatives) of which it is a constituent; yet, unlike the other accidental forms, relations do not directly inhere in their substrates, but are present in them only by means of another accidental form, that Wyclif, following a well established tradition, calls "foundations of the relation" (*fundamenta relationis*). In his view, quantity and quality only can be the foundation of a categorial relation.[116] Thus, according to Wyclif's description, in the act of relating one substance to another four different constitutive elements can be singled out: <1> the relation itself (for instance, the form of similarity); <2> the foundation of the relation, that is, the absolute entity in virtue of which the relation at issue is present in the two substances correlated to each other (in

---

divided into two parts: in the first one (the seventh chapter of the book), he expounds his own theory; in the second one (the eighth chapter), he summarizes and discusses the essentials of Ockham's (but the *Venerabilis Inceptor* is not quoted by name) doctrine. Unfortunately the eighth chapter is incomplete, since our unique MS of the work is disfigured by considerable gaps here and there. On Wyclif's theory of relations see Conti, "Logica intensionale e metafisica dell'essenza," pp. 206–9.

[115] *De ente praedicamentali*, 7, p. 61/8–11: "Distinguitur autem a quantitate vel qualitate, cum presupponit ipsas tamquam posterius natura; quantitas eciam et qualitas sunt modo suo absoluta, sed relacio ut huiusmodi est inter duo extrema." See also *De logica*, 3, 1:11.

[116] Cf. *De ente praedicamentali*, 7, pp. 61–62.

this case, the form of whiteness which makes the two substances at issue similar to each other); <3> the subject of the relation (or its first extreme—*extremum*), that is, the aggregate compound of the substance which denominatively receives the names of the relation (in our example, the substance which is similar to another, say Socrates) and of the foundation of the relation ; <4> the second extreme (of the relation), that is, another aggregate compund of a substance and its own foundation, that the subject of the relation is connected with, (in our example, a second substance which is, in its turn, similar to the first one, say Plato).[117] The *fundamentum relationis* is the main component, since it <1> joins the relation to the underlying substances, <2> lets the relation link the subject to the object, and <3> transmits to the relation some of its properties. Even though relation depends for its existence on the foundation, its being is really distinct from it, as when the foundation fails the relation also fails, but not *vice versa*.[118]

Some rather important conclusions about the nature and the ontological status of relations and relatives follow from these premisses: <1> relation is a truth (*veritas*) whose kind of reality is feebler than that of any other accident, as it depends upon the simultaneous existence of three different things: the two extremes (of the relation) and the foundation. <2> A relation can (indirectly) inhere in a substance without any change in the latter, but simply because of a change in another one. For example: given two things, one white and the other black, if the black thing becomes white, then, because of such a change, a new accident, that is, a relation of similarity, will inhere also in the first thing, apart from any other change in it. <3> All the true relatives (*propria relativa*) are simultaneous by nature,[119] since

---

[117] Cf. *De ente praedicamentali*, 7, p. 62/10–13: "Relacio autem proprie dicta est respectus unius substancie ad aliam in suis accidentibus absolutis fundatus qui eo ipso ponitur, quod illa sunt posita, et illa quartum predicamentum." Ibid., p. 63/1–5: "Pro quo dicitur, quod extrema relacionum proprie dictarum, per se in genere existencium, sunt aggregata per accidens ex substanciis et fundamentis relacionum, ut quantitate, vel qualitate, et illa extrema sunt, quibus positis sequitur relacio propria."

[118] Cf. *De ente praedicamentali*, 7, pp. 62–63, 64, and 67.

[119] Cf. *De ente praedicamentali*, 7, p. 64/4–9: "Patet quod omnia propria relativa nedum dicuntur ad subsistendi convertenciam, verum eciam sunt simul natura. Alia autem relativa racionis, quamvis, in quantum huiusmodi, dicuntur ad subsistendi convertenciam; tamen unum est communiter reliquo prius tam tempore, quam natura."

the real cause of being a relative is relation, which at the same time (indirectly) inheres in two things, thereby making both ones relatives.

Like Duns Scotus, Wyclif divides relations into transcendental and categorial relations,[120] and, moreover, like many of his predecessors and contemporaries, among the latter he contrasts real relatives (*relativa secundum esse*) with relatives of reason (*relativa rationis*), or linguistic relatives (*relativa secundum dici*).[121] Wyclif defines real relatives as those aggregates <1> made up of a substance and <2> an absolute accidental form (quantity or quality), <3> whose reality consists in being correlated to something else;[122] if one of these three conditions is not fulfilled, we will speak of relatives of reason.[123] In this way, Wyclif eliminates from the description of the relatives of reason any reference to our mind, and utilizes objective criteria only, based on the framework of reality itself. In fact he maintains that there are three kinds of relations of reason, each one characterized by the occurrence of at least one of these negative conditions: <1> one of the two extremes of the relation is *not* a substance with its foundation; <2> both the extremes of the relation are *not* substances; <3> there is *no* foundation for the relation, or it is *not* an absolute accident—that is, a quantity, or a quality.[124] The strategy which supports this choice is evident: Wyclif attempts to substitute references to mental activity by references to external reality. In other words, he seeks to reduce epistemology to ontology, in accordance with his realist program.

---

[120] Cf. *De ente praedicamentali*, 7, pp. 61–62.

[121] Cf. *De ente praedicamentali*, 7, pp. 62–64.

[122] This definition is drawn from Aristotle, *Categories*, 7, 8a 31–32.

[123] Cf. *De ente praedicamentali*, 7, p. 63/1–8: "Pro quo dicitur, quod extrema relacionum proprie dictarum, per se in genere existencium sunt aggregata per accidens ex substanciis et fundamentis relacionum, ut quantitate, vel qualitate, et illa extrema sunt, quibus positis sequitur relacio propria. Ubi autem deficit aliqua particula illius condicionis, vocantur relativa secundum dici vel relativa racionis, quod contingit tripliciter."

[124] Cf. *De ente praedicamentali*, 7, p. 63/9–27: "Primo, quando unum extremum est substancia, habens fundamentum, et reliquum non, ut gracia, qua creatura racionalis est grata Deo.... Secundo modo est relacio racionis inter extrema quorum uterque deficit esse substanciam, ut inter quecumque accidentia et inter personas divinas. Sed tercio est relacio racionis inter substancias, quarum utraque deficit (definit *ed.*) fundamentum, ut caput et capitatum. Non enim est dare quantitatem aut qualitatem fundamenta talis relacionis, ad que posita ipsa consequitur; sed capitacio requiritur continuacionem et actuacionem, et talia vocantur specialiter relativa secundum dici in *Praedicamentis* capitulo de ad aliquid."

8. *The theory of supposition*

The relationship between thought and reality was a focal point of Wyclif's reflection. On the one hand, Wyclif believed that thought was linguistically constrained by its own constitution; on the other hand, he considered thought to be related to reality in its element and structure. Hence he deemed language, thought, and external reality to be of the same logical coherence. The theory of supposition was intended to provide an account of the different roles that words (or phrases) can have in relation to language, thought and external reality when they appear as terms in propositions.

In his treatise on logic, Wyclif defines supposition as the signification of one categorematic[125] extreme of a proposition (subject or predicate) in relation to the other extreme.[126] This definition, which is drawn from Burley's *De suppositionibus* (AD 1302), is quite different from the standard definition of supposition, as it seems to equate signification and supposition. On the contrary, according to the most common view, which went back to Peter of Spain's *Summulae logicales*, *significatio* and *suppositio* of terms were clearly distinct functions, inasmuch as the latter presupposed the former, since <1> signification consisted in the relation of a linguistic sign to the thing signified apart from any propositional context, and <2> a word capable of standing for something else or for itself in a proposition had first to have signification. Thus, in a realist context, supposition serves to tell us which things are involved in the truth-conditions of a given proposition: whether it be expressions, real universals, or individuals.

Wyclif's account of the divisions of *suppositio* is similar to that proposed by Walter Burley in his *De puritate artis logicae tractatus longior* (between 1325 and 1328). At the very beginning, Wyclif divides supposition into <1> improper (*impropria*), in which a term stands for

---

[125] One of the most important divisions of words in medieval linguistics was that into categorematic and syncategorematic terms. The former are those words that have meaning in their own right (for instance, the term '*homo*'); the latter, those words that are meaningful only when joined to words of the first kind (for instance, the term '*omnis*'). See G. Nuchelmans, *Theories of the Proposition* (Amsterdam-London, 1973), p. 124.

[126] Cf. *De logica*, 12, 1:39/14–17: "Supposicio est significacio termini kategor <emat>ici qui est extremum proposicionis, in comparacion ad aliud extremum. Et est extremum in proposicione subiectum vel predicatum."

something different from its primary *significatum* by special custom (*ex usu loquendi*), and <2> proper (*propria*), in which a term stands for something by the virtue of the expression.[127] In turn, proper supposition is divided into <1> material (*materialis*), when the term stand for itself or its sound (as it occurs in "'I' is a pronoun" or "'Iohannes' is trisyllabic"), and <2> formal (*formalis*), when the term stands for what it signifies.[128] Formal supposition is twofold: simple (*simplex*) and personal (*personalis*). Like William of Sherwood and Peter of Spain, Wyclif affirms that the supposition is simple when the term stands for a real universal only (*solum assertive supponit pro re universali ad extra*), as it occurs in "Man can be predicated of every man" ("*homo predicatur de omni homine*"), and personal when it stands for one or more individuals (*pro uno singulari vel pro multis*). In the first case, the supposition is personal and singular (*suppositio personalis singularis*), as it occurs in "this man is" ("*hic homo est*"); in the second one, it is personal and common (*suppositio personalis communis*), as it occurs in <1> "these (men) are" ("*isti sunt*"—*suppositio personalis communis distincta*), or in <2> "every man is" ("*omnis homo est*"—*suppositio personalis communis universalis confusa distributiva*), or in <3> "both of them are one of the two" ("*uterque istorum est alter istorum*"—*suppositio personalis communis universalis confusa tantum*), where the expression "one of the two" has supposition merely confused, since none of the two can be both of them (*quia non est dare aliquem istorum qui est uterque istorum*).[129] Finally, Wyclif divides simple supposition into equal (*equa*) and unequal (*inequa*). There is simple equal supposition when a term stands for the common nature that it signifies, as it occurs in "man is a species" ("*homo est species*"); there is simple unequal supposition when a term stands for a less common nature than that which it signifies, as it occurs in "substance is a species" ("*substancia est species*").[130]

Wyclif takes a resolutely realist stand, as its own formulation and division of supposition (where simple supposition is described as that possessed by a term in relation to a universal outside the mind), and his discussion of the sophism *I promise you a coin that I do not promise*

---

[127] Cf. *De logica*, 12, 1:39.
[128] Cf. *De logica*, 12, 1:39.
[129] Cf. *De logica*, 12, 1:40.
[130] Cf. *De logica*, 12, 1:40.

make evident.[131] Like Burley[132] before him, in his *Logicae continuatio* Wyclif defends the claim that what is explicitly promised in such a promise, "I promise you one or other of these coins I have in my hands" ("*promitto tibi alterum illorum denariorum in altera manuum mearum*"), is the universal-coin, and not a singular one, even if I can fulfil the promise only by giving any singular coin, since a universal cannot be given or possessed except by a singular.[133] Thanks to his distinction between simple and personal supposition, Wyclif is able to explain from a semantic point of view the difference between promising a coin in general and promising a particular coin: in the first case the term "coin" ("*denarius*") has simple supposition, and therefore the proposition is true if and only if what is said is true of the universal-coin; on the contrary, if the term "coin" has personal supposition (more precisely, personal and singular supposition), the proposition is true if and only if what is said is true of *a* particular coin. According to him, by promising a singular, a universal is promised *secundarie* and *confuse*, and conversely.[134] So, given two coins in my hands, the coin *A* and the coin *B*, the proposition "I promise you one or other of these coins" is true, even though, when asked whether I promised the coin *A*, my answer is "No", and so too when asked whether I promised the coin *B*. In fact, according to Wyclif, what I promised is the universal-coin, since the phrase "one or other of these coins"

---

[131] Cf. *Logicae continuatio*, 3, 3, 2:55–72. See also *Tractatus de universalibus* 7, pp. 133–135; and 8, *passim*. On Wyclif's discussion of this sophism see S. Read, "'I promise a penny that I do not promise.' The Realist/Nominalist Debate over Intensional Propositions in Fourteenth-Century British Logic and its Contemporary Relevance," in *The Rise of British Logic*, ed. O.P. Lewry (Toronto, 1985), pp. 335–38.

[132] Cf. Walter Burley, *Expositio in libros octo Physicorum Aristotelis, prologus*, ed. Venetiis 1501, fol. 8vb.

[133] Cf. *Logicae continuatio*, 3, 3, 2:62/17–34: "Nemo placitans pro communi promissione denarii vendicat illum denarium vel illum, sed vendicat quod debetur sibi denarius: quod fuit promissum. Sed quia tale commune non potest dari vel haberi nisi per singulare, ideo requiritur promittentem dare singulare; et tunc sequitur ipsam, dando universalem, impleri promissionem. Non enim potest quandoque dari vel promitti singulare, nisi in sic faciendo involvatur universale; quia omnes tales predicaciones secundum habitudinem suscipiunt universale a suis singularibus. Et sic conceditur quod habeam communem denarium per ante (si habeam aliquem denarium) non tamen ex illa promissione, ideo vendico illud commune michi dari ab illo qui sic promisit; quia, si posset michi dare illude sine denario singulari, placet michi. Sed cum non potest, ex dacione sua multiplicius habeo illud commune. Quotquot enim denarios quis habuerit, tottupliciter habet communem denarium."

[134] Cf. *Logicae continuatio*, 3, 3, 2:64.

has simple supposition and therefore stands for a universal, however restricted in its instantiations to one or other of the two coins in my hands.[135]

This does not mean that the universal-coin is a sort of third coin over and above the two coins in my hands. Wyclif had already rejected this mistaken conclusion in the previous chapter of the *Logicae continuatio*. He argues that to add the universal-man as a third man to Socrates and Plato, given that there are only these two individual men in the world, exhibits a fallacy of equivocation. When a number is added to a term of first intention[136] (like "man"), the presence of this numerical term modifies the kind of supposition from simple to personal; but one can refer to a universal only with a term with simple supposition. As a consequence the universal cannot be counted with its individuals—and in fact any universal is really identical to each one of its individuals, and so it cannot differ in number from each of them.[137]

A close similarity between Wyclif's distinction between universals and individuals and Frege's sense (*Sinn*)/reference (*Bedeutung*) dichotomy seems to emerge from Wyclif's theory of supposition considered together with his own belief on universals and predication.[138] The

---

[135] Cf. *Logicae continuatio*, 3, 3, 2:67.

[136] In the *Logicae continuatio* (3, 3, 2:64/21–29) Wyclif distinguishes terms of first intention from those of second intention in this way: "Isti termini, 'universale' et 'singulare', sunt termini 2ᵉ intencionis, connotantes communicabilitatem et incommunicabilitatem. Vocatur enim signum, terminus prime intencionis qui significat suum significatum, non connotando racionem universalitatis vel singularitatis; ut isti termini: 'homo', 'animal' etc. Et vocatur terminus 2ᵉ intencionis qui connotat alterum istorum, ut isti termini 'universale', 'singulare', 'genus', 'species', 'substancia prima', et 'substancia 2ᵃ.'" So, according to him, a term is of first intention when it signifies what it signifies without connoting either universality or singularity, whereas a term is of second intention when it connotes one of these two opposite properties. See also *Tractatus de universalibus* 2, p. 65.

[137] Cf. *Logicae continuatio*, 3, 2, 2:48/19–32: "Tunc dicitur quod terminus numeralis, additus termino prime intencionis, limitatur ad significandum numerum primo modo dictum <scilicet acce-ptum pro multitudine singularium>. Unde, sicut terminus distribuens limitat speciem specialissi-mam ad supposicionem personalem, ita ille terminus numerlis limitat terminum prime intencionis, et specialiter speciem specialissimam, ad supposicionem personalem. Cum ergo homo communis sit quilibet hominum singularium, non ponit seorsum in numero cum illis; ideo existente *omni homine*, *Sorte* vel *Platone*, non superest 3ᵘˢ homo communis ab illis, sed est uterque illorum, et non esset tercius, nec esset 3ᵃ persona hominis. Et per idem non oportet, ubique ubi est unus homo, esse duos homines."

[138] Cf. Read "'I promise a penny that I do not promise'," pp. 348 and 354.

relationship which holds between universals and singulars within Wyclif's system appears to be analogous to that which connects sense and reference in Frege's. <1> First of all, like that of Frege, Wyclif's semantic theory embraces both individuals and other sorts of thing. <2> Frege describes referents as objects of a certain kind, and the senses as ways of picking out these objects, and Wyclif represents universals as the *significata* of common terms (like "man") that, because of their presence in them, allow picking out the members of the class of things which form the extension of common terms themselves (the relation of real identity and formal distinction between universals and individuals). <3> According to Frege, senses are not mental images, but something objective, already existent in the world, and in Wyclif's view universals are entities entirely objective and totally independent of our minds, since they actually exist outside our minds before any act of understanding.

9. *Wyclif's legacy: the Oxford Realists on predication, identity, and distinction*

Such a resemblance between these features of Wyclif's system and Frege's most important semantic distinction <1> confirms the strength and originality of Wyclif's logico-metaphysical intuitions, and <2> is a further element which helps us to realize the fascination that his thought exerted on many late medieval authors. Specifically, the so called "Oxford Realists" (the Englishmen Robert Alyngton [+ 1398], William Milverley, William Penbygull [+ 1420], Roger Whelpdale [+ 1423], and John Tarteys, the German Johannes Sharpe [+ after 1415], and the Italian Paul of Venice [1369–1429]), were strongly influenced by his logical apparatus and metaphysical formulations.[139] According to these authors (who in their works show

---

[139] All those philosophers studied and taught in Oxford: Alyngton at Queen's College, Penbygull at Exeter College, Whelpdale at Balliol and Queen's Colleges, Tarteys at Balliol College; Paul of Venice at the Augustinian *studium* from 1390 to 1393. On their lives and works see A.B. Emden, *A Biographical Register of the University of Oxford to A.D. 1500*, 3 vols. (Oxford, 1957–59), *sub nominibus*. For analyses of their main works and doctrines and information on Wyclif's influence see: Conti, "Teoria degli universali e teoria della predicazione," pp. 137–66 (at pp. 167–203 critical edition of Penbygull's *De universalibus*); A.D. Conti, "Studio storico-critico," in Johannes

the closest familiarity with Wyclif's writings)[140] universals and individuals were really identical but formally distinct, and predication was a real relation between things. Partially modifying Wyclif's doctrine, they <1> introduced a new type of predication, called predication by essence (*secundum essentiam*),[141] based on a partial identity between the entities for which the subject and predicate stood; and <2> redefined the traditional post-Aristotelian categories of essential and accidental predication in terms of this partial identity. Furthermore, three of them, Penbygull, Sharpe, and Paul of Venice, starting from Wyclif's characterization of identity and distinction, formulated new definitions of these transcendental relations, which are the main tools that they utilized in building up their own metaphysical systems.

In particular, Alyngton,[142] and some years later Sharpe,[143] Milverley,[144] and Tarteys,[145] divided predication into formal predication and predication by essence (*secundum essentiam*), that Alyngton calls also "remote inherence" (*inhaerentia remota*). Predication *secundum essentiam* shows a partial identity between subject and predicate, which share some, but not all, metaphysical component parts, and does not

---

Sharpe, *Quaestio super universalia*, pp. 209–336, on Sharpe and the other Oxford Realists; A. de Libera, "Questions de réalisme. Sur deux arguments antiockhamistes de John Sharpe," *Revue de métaphysique et de morale* 97 (1992), 83–110; Conti, "Linguaggio e realtà nel commento alle *Categorie* di Robert Alyngton," pp. 179–241 (at pp. 242–306 partial edition of Alyngton's *Litteralis sententia super Praedicamenta Aristotelis*: chs. 2: *de subiecto et praedicato*; 3.1: *de regulis praedicationis*; 3.2: *de complexo et incomplexo*; 4: *de numero et sufficientia praedicamentorum*; and 7: *de relativis*; and the first section of 5: *de substantia*); A.D. Conti, *Esistenza e verità: Forme e strutture del reale in Paolo Veneto e nel pensiero filosofico del tardo medioevo* (Roma, 1996); A. de Libera, *La querelle des universaux. De Platon à la fin du Moyen Age* (Paris, 1996), pp. 402–28, on Sharpe; A.D. Conti, "Paul of Venice on Individuation," *Recherches de Théologie et Philosophie médiévales* 65.1 (1998), 107–32; A.D. Conti, "Johannes Sharpe's Ontology and Semantics: Oxford Realism Revisited," *Vivarium* 43.1 (2005), 156–86.

[140] Alyngton's commentary on the *Categories* heavily depends on Wyclif's *De ente praedicamentali*; Penbygull's treatise on universals is openly a defence of Wyclif's view on universals and predication; the metaphysical convictions which are at the basis of Paul of Venice's philosophy are an original version of the most fundamental theses of Wyclif.

[141] Paul of Venice calls this new kind of predication "identical predication" (*praedicatio identica*) see below, pp. 123–24.

[142] Cf. Alyngton, *Litteralis sententia super Praedicamenta Aristotelis, de substantia*, p. 289.

[143] Cf. Sharpe, *Quaestio de universalibus*, pp. 89–91.

[144] Cf. Milverley, *Compendium de quinque universalibus*, in Sharpe, *Quaestio super universalia*, Appendix II, pp. 160–61.

[145] Cf. Tarteys, *Problema correspondens libello Porphyrii*, London, Lambeth Palace 393, fols. 204(235)r–v, and 209(240)r–v.

require that the form connoted by the predicate-term is directly present in the essence denotated by the subject-term. Formal predication,
on the contrary, requires such a direct presence. If the form connoted by the predicate-term is intrinsic to the nature of the subject,
then the predication is a formal-and-essential predication (*formalis
essentialis*), while if it is extrinsic, the predication is a formal-and-accidental predication (*formalis accidentalis*). "Man is animal" ("*homo est
animal*") is an instance of formal-and-essential predication; "Socrates
is white" ("*Sortes est albus*") is an instance of formal-and-accidental
predication.[146] Unlike Wyclif, who applied predication by essence to
second intentions only, these later philosophers thought that it held
also when applied to first intentions. So they affirmed that it was
possible to predicate of the universal-man (*homo in communi*) the property of being white, if at least one of its individuals was white.
However they made sure to use as a predicate-term a substantival
adjective in its neuter form, because only in this way it can appear
that the form connoted by the predicate-term is not directly present
in the subject, but it is indirectly attributed to it, through its individuals. Therefore they acknowledged the proposition "*homo in communi est album*" as a true one, if at least one of the existing men was
white. According to them the formal-and-essential predication and
the formal-and-accidental predication would correspond to Aristotle's
essential and accidental predication respectively. But, as a matter of
fact, they agreed with Wyclif in regarding predication by essence as
more general than formal predication. As a consequence, in their
theories formal predication is a particular type of the predication by
essence. This means that they implicitly recognized a single ontological pattern, founded on a partial identity, as the basis of every
kind of predicational statement. But in this way, the *praedicatio formalis essentialis* and the *praedicatio formalis accidentalis* are very different
from their Aristotelian models, as they express degrees in identity as
well as the predication by essence.

---

[146] Really, unlike Alyngton, Penbygull, and Whelpdale, Sharpe does not explicitly divide formal predication into formal essential and formal accidental predication; moreover, as is evident from his formulations, he introduces another interpretation
of the distinction between formal predication and predication by essence, according to which the two kinds of predication at issue are complementary and mutually exclusive, since, according to this second reading, predication by essence *excludes*
that the form connoted by the predicate-term is *directly* present in the essence signified
by the subject-term see Sharpe, *Quaestio super universalia*, p. 91.

By contrast, Penbygull[147] and Whelpdale,[148] who almost certainly belong to the same generation as Sharpe, were closer to Wyclif's teaching as manifested in the *Purgans errores circa universalia in communi*, since they divided predication into formal (*praedicatio formalis*), by essence (*secundum essentiam*), and causal (*secundum causam*). Predication by essence shows a partial identity between subject and predicate, which share some, but not all, metaphysical component parts, and does not require that the form connoted by the predicate-term is directly present in the essence denoted by the subject-term. Formal predication, on the contrary, requires such a direct presence. And there is a causal predication when the entity signified by the predicate-term is not present in any way in the entity signified by the subject-term, but the real subject has been caused by the real predicate—"*dies est latio solis super terram*" is an example of this kind of predication.

Both these interpretative schemes of the nature and kinds of predication (that worked out by Alyngton and that elaborated by Penbygull and Whelpdale) are ultimately grounded on a notion of identity that is necessarily different from the common one—according to which two things a and b are identical if and only if for all P, it is the case that P is predicated of a if and only if it is predicated of b. So Penbygull and Sharpe put forward new criteria for identity and distinction.

Penbygull[149] <1> distinguishes between the notion of non-identity and that of difference (or distinction); <2> denies that the notion of difference implies that of non-identity; <3> affirms that the two notions of difference and real identity are logically compatible, thus admitting that <3.1> there are degrees in distinction, and <3.2> that the degrees of distinction between two things can be read as the inverse measure of their (partial) identity; and <4> suggests the following definitions for these three notions—non-identity, difference (or distinction), and (absolute) identity:

---

[147] Cf. Penbygull, *De universalibus*, pp. 186–8.

[148] Cf. Whelpdale, *Tractatus de universalibus* in Sharpe, *Quaestio super universalia*, Appendix IV, pp. 190–92.

[149] Cf. Penbygull, *De universalibus*, pp. 184, and 189–90. On Penbygull's theory of identity and distinction see Conti, "Teoria degli universali e teoria della predicazione," pp. 153–6.

<4.1> *a* is not-identical with *b* if and only if there is not any form
    F such that *F* is present in the same way in *a* and *b*;
<4.2> *a* differs from *b* if and only if there is at least a form *F* such
    that *F* is *directly* present in *a* but not in *b*, or *vice versa*;
<4.3> *a* is absolutely identical with *b* if and only if for all forms *F*,
    it is the case that *F* is present in *a* if and only if it is pre-
    sent *in the same way* in *b*.

Sharpe's theory of identity and distinction[150] is even more complex
than Penbygull's, as it combines those of Duns Scotus, Wyclif and
Penbygull himself. <1> Like Penbygull, he considers identity and
distinction (or difference) as the two possible inverse measures of the
coincidence of the metaphysical components of two given entities.
Moreover, <2> he speaks of formal and real (or essential) identity,
formal and real (or essential) distinction (or difference), and <2.1>
states that formal identity is stronger than real (or essential) identity,
since the former entails the latter, while real difference is stronger
than formal distinction, since the latter is entailed by the former.
<3> Finally, he admits degrees in formal distinction (*distinctio formalis
consistit in gradibus*), as he recognizes two different types, the first of
which comes very close to that proposed by Scotus in his *Ordinatio*,[151]
while the second is drawn from Wyclif's *Tractatus de universalibus*:

<3.1> two entities *x* and *y* are formally distinct₁ if and only if <i>
    both of them are constitutive elements of the same thing, but
    <ii> neither of them can exist by itself, nor <iii> is part of
    the other;
<3.2> two entities *x* and *y* are formally distinct₂ if and only if <i>
    there is at least one *P* such that *P* is predicated of *x* and not
    of *y*, or *vice versa*, but <ii> *x* and *y* are really identical, since
    one is a constitutive element of the other.

The first type of formal distinction holds among things such as the
intellective faculties of the soul, whereas the second holds between

---

[150] Cf. Sharpe, *Quaestio super universalia*, pp. 91–92, and 98; and *Quaestio super libros
De anima*, q. 2: "utrum potentia intellectiva distinguatur ab essentia animae", Oxford,
New College 238, fol. 236r–v see Conti, "Johannes Sharpe's Ontology and Semantics,"
pp. 173–5.
[151] See above, n. 7

such things as the essence of the soul and its intellective faculties or a species and its individuals, and as a consequence it is crucial in order to give a logically satisfactory account of the relationship between universals and individuals, which had always been the most difficult issue for any form of medieval realism.

Yet, among the Oxford Realists, the most original was Paul of Venice, whose analysis of predication and definitions of identity and distinction are partially different from both those of Wyclif and of his English followers. Paul divides predication into identical and formal, and defines them in a slightly different way in relation to his sources.[152] To speak of identical predication it is sufficient that the form signified by the subject-term of a (true) proposition and the form signified by the predicate-term share at least one of their substrates of existence. This is the case of propositions like "man is (an) animal" and "the universal-man is something white" (*"homo in communi est album"*). One speaks of formal predication in two cases: <1> when for the truth of the proposition it is necessary that the form signified by the predicate-term is present in all the substrates of existence of the form signified by the subject-term in virtue of a formal principle (declarated in the proposition itself) which is in its turn directly present in all the substrates of existence of the form signified by the subject-term. This is the case of propositions like "man is formally (an) animal", "Socrates *qua* man is an animal." <2> Or when the predicate of the proposition is a term of second intention, like "species" or "genus." This is the case of propositions like "man is a species", "animal is a genus."[153] As it is evident, identical predication is extensionally defined, whereas formal predication is intensionally defined, since formal predication entails a relation modally determined between the subject-thing and the predicate-thing. In fact, the formal predication presupposes that there is a *necessary* connection between the subject-thing and the predicate-thing of the given proposition. For this reason Paul denies that sentences like "(what is) singular is (what is) universal" (*"singulare est universale"*), that Wyclif acknowledged as true ones, are true propositions. For Wyclif the

---

[152] On Paul of Venice's theory of predication see Conti, "Studio storico-critico", pp. 318–22; and Conti, *Esistenza e verità*, pp. 119–28.

[153] Cf. Paul of Venice, *Summa Philosophiae Naturalis*, p. vi, 2, ed. Venetiis 1503, fol. 93vab; *Quaestio de universalibus*, in Sharpe, *Quaestio super universalia*, Appendix V, pp. 201–2.

sentence at issue is an example of predication by essence, but for Paul of Venice it is an example of formal predication, and no individual *qua* individual is an universal, and *vice versa*, as no second intention intensionally considered is any other second intention. As a consequence, Paul rewrites the preceding sentence in this form: "(what is) singular is this universal" ("*singulare est hoc universale*"), where the presence of the demonstrative "this" modifies the kind of predication from formal to identical. So corrected the sentence is true, since it signifies that a certain entity, in itself singular, is the substrate of existence of an universal essence.[154] As a result, Paul builds up a mixed system, where the copula of the standard philosophical sentences which he deals with can have a three-fold value: it means a partial identity between the subject-thing and the predicate-thing, in the case of identical predication; it means a necessary link between forms, in the case of the first type of formal predication; it means that the subject-thing in virtue of itself necessarily is a member of a given class of objects, that the predicate-term of the proposition labels and refers to, in the case of the second type of formal predication—that is, when the predicate is a term of second intention.

As far as the twin notions of identity and distinction (or difference) are concerned, the Italian master recognizes two main types of identity and distinction:[155] the material (*secundum materiam*) and the formal (*secundum formam*) ones. There is material identity when the material cause is the same, or in number (it is the case of the same thing called in different ways) or by species (it is the case of two objects made of the same kind of stuff). There is formal identity when the formal cause is the same. This happens in two ways: if the form at issue is the singular form of the individual composite, then there is an unique object known in different ways; if the form at issue is the common essence instantiated by the singular form, then there are two distinct objects belonging to the same species or genus.[156] Specularly, there is material distinction when the material cause is different, so that the objects at issue are separable entities; and there is formal distinction when the formal cause is different. This hap-

---

[154] Cf. Paul of Venice, *Quaestio de universalibus*, pp. 206–7.

[155] On the notion of formal distinction in Paul of Venice and his sources (Duns Scotus and Wyclif himself) see Conti, *Esistenza e verità*, pp. 20–31.

[156] Cf. Paul of Venice, *Lectura super libros Metaphysicorum Aristotelis*, book V, 2, 3, Pavia, Biblioteca Universitaria, *fondo Aldini* 324, fol. 185ra.

pens in two ways: if the material cause is also different, then it is a particular case of material distinction. If the material cause is the same, then a further analysis is necessary. If the material cause is the same by species only, then it is an improper case of formal distinction; but if the material cause is the same in number, then there is properly formal distinction, since the forms at issue have different definite descriptions, but share the same substrate of existence, so that they are one and the same thing in reality—for example, this is the case of the two properties of being-capable-of-laughing (*risibile*) and of being-capable-of-learning (*disciplinabile*), which are connected forms instantiated by the same set of individual substances.[157] Material distinction is a necessary and sufficient criterion for real difference, traditionally conceived, whereas there is formal distinction if and only if there is one substance in number (that is, material identity in the strict sense) and a multiplicity of formal principles with different descriptions instantiated by it. Paul therefore inverts the terms of the question in relation to Wyclif's approach, since Paul is attempting to reduce multiplicity to unity (the passage is from many to one). What Paul wants to account for is the way in which many different entities of a certain kind (that is, of an incomplete and dependent mode of existence) can constitute one and the same substance in number.

In conclusion, Wyclif's logico-metaphysical system, however rigorous in its general design, contains, as we have seen, some unclear and aporetic points, that, a few years later, his followers attempted to remove. All the same, Wyclif's philosophy has, directly and indirectly, exercised an enormous influence on the forms of later medieval realism, since <1> he pointed to the general strategy Realists of the end of the Middle Ages were to adopt; <2> his main intuitions concerning universals, individuals, and predication played a large role both in logic and metaphysics of the Oxford Realists; and <3> his inspiration can be traced in many of the basic categorial views of Alyngton and Paul of Venice. The originality, sophistication, and complexity of Wyclif's system, on the one hand, and its impact on the doctrines of so many authors of the later Middle Ages, on the other, testify and explain the high significance of Wyclif's philosophical work in the history of medieval thought.

---

[157] Cf. Paul of Venice, *Lectura super libros Metaphysicorum Aristotelis*, book V, 2, 3, fol. 185rb.

WYCLIF'S TRINITARIAN AND CHRISTOLOGICAL THEOLOGY

Stephen E. Lahey

1. *Locating Wyclif the Theologian in his Oxford Environment*

Anyone familiar with amateur photography can imagine standing in a darkroom, watching the slow resolution of a picture as it sits in its chemical bath. First the main outlines of the image emerge from a blank background, and only gradually do the details follow. Frequently the content of the picture is only recognizable when all the details are clear, when what appear as large, oddly shaped objects resolve into distinct, recognizable ones. Such is the case with understanding of Wyclif's earlier, theological works. Without a familiarity with the details of fourteenth-century Oxford theology, its main players and positions, and their complex understandings of the relation of logic to theology, the writings of one particular theologian are likely to confusing at best, recognizable only by broad outlines that may or may not have anything to do with the actual positions he takes. While some treatises of his *Summa de ente*, such as *De universalibus* or *De composicione hominis* might arguably be generally comprehensible apart from the mid-fourteenth century dialogue, others, notably *De Trinitate*, are not.[1]

A study of Wyclif's theology must consider a wide range of subjects, including issues of philosophical theology like his discussion of the necessity of created action and the freedom of human willing, his conception of how Being as such relates to the divine being and created being, and the nature of divine knowledge and willing.

---

[1] It is a stretch to claim that *De universalibus* is comprehensible apart from the atmosphere in which it was written, but it at least articulates an ontological position recognizable to those familiar with medieval arguments about universals. Professor Breck's summary of the argument of his otherwise excellent edition of *De Trinitate*, is almost impenetrable from a theological standpoint, largely because scholarship had not yet caught up to the treatise's content when he published it. See Johannis Wyclyf, *Tractatus De Trinitate*, ed. Allen duPont Breck (Colorado, 1962), pp. xxi–l.

It would have to address Wyclif's complex understanding of how divine law relates to justice in creation with regards to the law of Moses, and more widely how the law of Christ applies in human *dominium* relations. Wyclif's ecclesiology and its ties to his understanding of the pastoral offices and the sacraments would need to be incorporated into the study, as orthopraxy figures very importantly in Wyclif's theological vision. Finally, Wyclif's conception of the ontology of Scripture and how its truths must be understood and realized in the world would figure significantly in a study of his theology. If such a study is more imaginable now than it was a century ago, when the Wyclif Society edited most of his latin works, this is because scholars have been studying many of the topics listed with the care they require. This chapter will, I hope, contribute to that project by introducing two subjects essential to any Christian theology, namely, the nature of the Trinity and of the Incarnation.

Three treatises of the *Summa de ente* deserve our attention: *De Trinitate, De composicione hominis*, and *De Incarnacione*, all composed between 1370 and 1372. Scholars have noted these treatises' likely function as *Sentences* commentaries, required of all candidates for the degree of a Doctorate in Theology. Such commentaries were generally also the place for taking up one's lance against rival philosophical and theological positions. So it will be important to see how Wyclif's positions on how the three divine persons relate in one nature, and how two natures relate in the person of the Incarnate Word function as likely responses to the *Sentences* commentaries of earlier Oxford luminaries such as Adam Wodeham and Robert Holcot. Wyclif envisioned his theology as a return to the orthodoxy of earlier figures such as Anselm, Augustine, and Robert Grosseteste, as is clear to anyone who has read him. These theologians endorsed a philosophical position more consonant with realism than with the conceptualism prized by many thinkers in early fourteenth-century Oxford. Wyclif expressly intended to show how ontological realism explicates the complex realities of the divine being and its assumption of a human nature in these treatises, and so our interest is in understanding both how realism functions in his philosophical theology of divine persons, and how his thought relates to that of his likely opponents.

In both the metaphysics of the Trinity and of the Incarnation, a universal functions as a nature. In the Trinity, the divine nature is the universal, for which there are three particulars, namely the three persons, each of whom is divine through their instantiation of Divinity. In the Incarnation, the creature Jesus Christ is the result of hypostatic union of the Word, God the Son, with the nature Humanity, a universal by community, in the physical body of the man Jesus. In Christ, the part that normally is played by the created soul in a human being is played by Humanity, although this does not mean that Christ lacked a soul of any kind. In both the Trinity and the Incarnation, it will turn out that Wyclif's conception that the aggregate being arising out of the union of two distinct beings is itself something bearing ontological weight plays a part.

2. De Trinitate: *The Divine Nature as Universal, the Divine Person as Particular*

2.1. *Situating* De Trinitate

While much scholarship remains to be done, we can now identify at least some of the arguments to which *De Trinitate* contributes. This allows us to do more than describe it as what a realist theologian would say about the logical problems inherent to the doctrine of the Trinity. A key problem will be to identify theologians, or if not, positions connected to theologians against whom Wyclif argues; simply to refer to his opponents as "the *Moderni*" is by no means adequate, for everyone engaged in theology during the period fit that bill. It was not until the Council of Constance that the term was used especially to refer to the Ockhamist position.[2] Wyclif himself only occasionally names his opponents throughout his works, and not at all in *De Trinitate*; he uses the term '*Moderni*' very generally in this treatise, and includes among the *antiqui* everyone from Augustine to Scotus. At present, there are no published editions of *Sentences* commentaries of Wyclif's contemporaries, theologians such as Nicholas Aston, Richard Brinkley, Johannes Klenkok, and Uthred of Boldon, and relatively few of his predecessors in the decades before the Black

---

[2] Neil Ward Gilbert, "Ockham, Wyclif, and the 'Via Moderna'" in *Antiqui et Moderni: Traditionsbewußtsein im späten Mittelalter*, Miscellanea Mediaevalia Band 9 (Berlin, 1974) pp. 85–125.

Death.[3] Until more editions are available, our understanding of Wyclif's arguments will remain limited to broad outlines of positions. We may be able to guess at details, for instance, why Wyclif emphasizes ontology and speaks less about epistemic justification, but for the present, our picture of Wyclif's theology continues to emerge.

Thomson dates this treatise to 1370; Robson categorizes the treatise as the fourth tractate of the second book of the *Summa de ente*, following *De intellectione Dei, De scientia Dei, et De volucione Dei*. The tractates consequent are *De Ydeis, De potencia Dei productiva ad extra*. In his "Wyclif and the Augustinian Tradition" Gordon Leff views the treatise as valuable as a touchstone for Wyclif's "original theological position," as it was prior to the more combative treatises of the *Summa Theologie*.[4] He describes the main theme of the treatise to be that reason is a positive aid to faith, the function of which is to provide evidence of the divine Trinity through the signs available in creation. By providing fallen man the wherewithal to recover sufficient understanding of the world to appreciate revealed truth, reason complements faith. Likewise, Leff notes Wyclif's argument that some element of faith is evident in every act of knowing. In every act of knowledge that does not entail direct experience of the thing known, a degree of faith is necessary in the evidence presented to the individual knower for the evidence to be believed. This Leff characterizes as Wyclif seeking "to show where faith and reason converge, while reserving for faith what is distinctive to it. By making it accessible to natural experience in its different modes he has allowed reason a far fuller role in theology than the majority of medieval thinkers have."[5] Leff notes that Wyclif exceeds thirteenth century notions of natural theology by arguing that human reason can demonstrate God's triune nature sufficiently to convince any rational criteria,

---

[3] See William Courtenay, *Schools and Scholar in Fourteenth Century England* (Princeton, 1987) for an introduction to the bibliographic information available. J.A. Robson's *Wyclif and the Oxford Schools* (Cambridge, 1961) remains the best introduction to the milieu in which Wyclif wrote. I have made use of Robert Holcot, O.P. *In Quatuor Libros Sententiarum Quaestiones* (Frankfurt, 1967; a reprint of the 1518 edition), Adam Wodeham, *Lectura Secunda in Librum Primum Sententiarum*, ed. Rega Wood and Gedeon Gál, (St. Bonaventure, 1990), and Michael Dunning's as yet unpublished edition of Richard FitzRalph's *Utrum mens humana sit ymago Trinitatis increate*, (*Sent.Liber 1, Questio 5*).
[4] Gordon Leff, "Wyclif and the Augustinian Tradition," *Medievalia et Humanistica*, ed. Paul M. Clogan (Cleveland, 1970), pp. 29–39.
[5] Leff, "Wyclif and the Augustinian Tradition," p. 36.

given an understanding of the authoritative witness of revealed truth. But to contrast Wyclif with Aquinas and Scotus on the one hand, and Ockham on the other, as Leff appears to be doing, is to look past the tremendous amount of theology done in Oxford from the 1320s to the 1360s. Leff's description makes Wyclif appear to be a weird proto-rationalist, or perhaps an idealist of some sort, neither of which is accurate.

A good approach for understanding what a theologian thinks regarding reason's limits in matters of faith, and for seeing how he envisions a formal theology ought proceed would be to investigate his Commentary on the *Sententiae in IV Libris Distinctae* of Peter Lombard.[6] This is true, at any rate, for an identifiable period in Oxford. Before the 1280s, only those of Richard Fishacre, Robert Kilwardby, and Richard Rufus of Cornwall survive.[7] The period between Ockham's lectures on the *Sentences* in 1317–1319 and Bradwardine's *De causa Dei* in 1344 has been described as a Golden Age of theology in Oxford, and *Sentences Commentaries* abound from figures of this period, notably those of Adam Wodeham (d.1358) among the Franciscans, and Robert Holcot (d. 1349) among the Dominicans.[8] The last decade of this period is particularly rich, for Wyclif's immediate intellectual forbears, including Richard Brinkeley O.F.M., Richard FitzRalph, and Thomas Bradwardine, leave record of some activity with the *Sententiae*.[9] But after 1344, things appear to have changed.

---

[6] See Marcia Colish, *Peter Lombard* (Leiden, 1994). See also Philipp W. Rosemann, *Peter Lombard* (Oxford, 2004).

[7] See Rega Wood, "Early Oxford Theology," in *Medieval Commentaries on the Sentences of Peter Lombard: Current Research*, ed. G.R. Evans (Leiden, 2002), pp. 289–343.

[8] See Chris Schabel, "Oxford Franciscans after Ockham," in *Medieval Commentaries on the Sentences*, pp. 359–77. For Wodeham, see Courtenay,'s *Adam Wodeham* (Leiden, 1978); for Holcot, the best treatment remains Fritz Hoffman, *Die theologische Methode des Oxforder Dominikanerlehrers Robert Holcot* (Münster, 1972). For bibliography for both, see *A Companion to Philosophy in the Middle Ages*, ed. Jorge Gracia and Timothy Noone (Malden, Mass., 2003), pp. 84–5, 610.

[9] See Raymond Edwards, "Themes and Personalities in *Sentence* Commentaries at Oxford in the 1330s," in *Medieval Commentaries on the Sentences*, pp. 379–93. Edwards emphasizes the centrality of biblical exegesis and preaching in the choices and approaches of commentators in this period, which should be borne in mind for Wyclif's own approach. For a general outline of the topics discussed in FitzRalph's *Sentence* commentary, see Gordon Leff, *Richard FitzRalph Commentator of the Sentences*, (Manchester, 1963). For Thomas Bradwardine, see Jean-François Genest, "Les Premiers Écrits Théologiques de Bradwardine: Textes Inédits et Découvertes Récentes," in *Medieval Commentaries on the Sentences*, pp. 395–421, and "Le de Futuris Contingentibus de Thomas Bradwardine," in *Recherches augustinienne* 14 (1979), 249–336. For what

Commentaries no longer encompass as many of Lombard's *distinctiones* as they had previously, tending instead to address several large questions.[10] In addressing one or two questions where previously the commentator might have examined a dozen, the post-1344 commentator took the opportunity to engage in analysis of much greater detail. Further, whereas earlier the tendency had been to refer to one's opponents as "*quidam*," by this period it was much more common for one's opponents to be named, and his works accurately cited.[11]

The realist position was most dramatically made by Bradwardine in his *De causa Dei*, but it was generally the tenor of Oxford metaphysics in the 1360s, an articulation of the responses to Ockham made by Walter Burley (d. 1344) and Walter Chatton (d. 1343). Wyclif's position in *De Trinitate* appears to be a response to the kinds of positions held by Adam Wodeham and Robert Holcot, who both denied the inclusion of theology among the sciences. The vigor of Adam Wodeham's rejection of Walter Chatton's position in his *Sentences* commentary [I.d.1 q.2] might lead one to imagine that Wyclif's position is a direct response to Wodeham's, on Chatton's behalf.[12] Given the lack of edited *Sentences* commentaries of the period following Wodeham and Holcot at Oxford, it is impossible at this point to prove or disprove such an hypothesis; the best we can do in this discussion is to hold Holcot and Wodeham as proponents of the kind of position against which Wyclif argued.

While scholarship has made some headway in the past two decades in understanding the Commentary tradition of this period, there remains no serious attempt to include Wyclif in this tradition. Wyclif certainly would have lectured on the *Sententiae* in the course of his studies, and demonstrates familiarity with Lombard throughout his

---

remains of Richard Brinkeley's *Sentence* Commentary, see Zénon Kaluza, "L'oeuvre théologique de Richard Brinkley, OFM," *Archives d'Histoire Doctrinale et Littéraire du Moyen Age* 56 (1986), 169–273.

[10] Paul J.J.M. Bakker and Chris Schabel, "*Sentences* Commentaries of the Later Fourteenth Century," *Medieval Commentaries on the Sentences*, pp. 426–64.

[11] Damasus Trapp, "Augustinian Theology of the Fourteenth Century" *Augustiniana* 6 (1956), 146–274; William Courtenay, *Schools and Scholars*, esp. pp. 327–55.

[12] For Wodeham's special animus against Chatton, see Adam de Wodeham's *Lectura Secunda in Librum Primum Sententiarum*, vol. 1, ed. Rega Wood and Gedeon Gal (St. Bonaventure, NY, 1990), pp. 12–16.

works.[13] Aside from Robson's suggestion that Book 2 of the *Summa de ente* contains the body of Wyclif's 'lost' Commentary, the only reference to Wyclif's having published anything on the *Sententiae* can be found in Harris's 1886 introduction to *De benedicta Incarnacione*, wherein he endorses an unknown cataloger's account of the contents of Oriel 15, in which that treatise is included.[14] I believe that Robson's suggestion is correct; many of the criteria for post-1344 Commentaries are met in *De Trinitate*. The treatise is rich with references to specific works of authorities such as Augustine, Anselm, and Grosseteste, as well as to more recent luminaries such as Aquinas and Scotus. References more recent than the late thirteenth century are almost non-existent, though; FitzRalph and Bradwardine are the only figures mentioned by name. It is difficult to imagine Wyclif formulating the arguments of the *Summa de ente*'s treatises without specific opponents in mind, but his references to them are restricted to 'doctors of signs' or 'a certain doctor'.

The body of the treatise appears to wander from topic to topic, but the argument can best be understood as extended commentary on Distinction 5 of Book I, "Whether the divine essence generates the Son or was generated by the Father." The most fully developed section of the treatise is Chapter 16, in which Wyclif engages in recognizably scholastic formal reasoning addressing this question, referring twice to Lombard's treatment of it. His argument rests on points made in the previous fifteen chapters, ranging from the relation of reasoning to faith in the doctrine of the Trinity through consideration of the formal distinction of Scotus, and the right relation of language to object and idea in such a discussion. While Leff and others have emphasized Wyclif's reliance on Augustine's *De Trinitate* for the doctrinal content, Scotus's *Sentences* Commentary figures importantly in key points of the argument.

Wyclif's approach focuses more on ontology and the signification that underlies theological truth, suggestive of a desire to order theology and philosophy like that of twelfth-century theologians such as Anselm or the Victorines. In contrast, Richard FitzRalph shows much

---

[13] H.B. Workman, *John Wyclif: A Study of the English Medieval Church*, 2 vols. (Oxford, 1926), 1:96–7.

[14] See Robson, pp. 134–5, also W. Thomson, p. 15. Thomson notes further that Wyclif structured the *Trialogus* according to Lombard's *Sententiae*.

less interest in this, at least as regards formal trinitarian theology.[15]
De Trinitate's twentieth century editor, Allen DuPont Breck, describes
it as "not a pioneering work in the sense that it strikes at the heart
of any doctrine or practice with something basically new to say."[16]
He is right, for Wyclif's description of the Trinity does not diverge
from a fairly standard Scotistic depiction of three persons formally
distinct from one another, identical with the Divine Essence. But it
would be premature to suppose that this makes the treatise valuable
only as a set-piece within Wyclif's *Sentences* Commentary; *De Trinitate*
may well be a part of Wyclif's attempt to put Bradwardine's *De
causa Dei* on firmer metaphysical and theological ground, and his
explanation of the relation of faith and reason is an important part
of that enterprise. Bradwardine's efforts were very much directed
against thinkers such as Holcot, his associate in the de Bury circle,
and Adam Wodeham.[17] In his 1993 study of Holcot, Leonard Kennedy
comments that Bradwardine's anti-Pelagian arguments lacked noticeable effect; if *De Trinitate* is in fact directed against these thinkers'
positions, as I believe it is, the effect was noticeable indeed.[18]

2.2. *Faith and Reason as the Starting Point*

De Trinitate is divisible into four sections. In the first, Wyclif considers the relation of faith and reason, and explores an analogy useful
in understanding the distinction of persons within the Trinity. In the
second, he considers the relations between the divine persons, and
the way language limits our understanding of those relations. Next,
he examines the syllogism Wodeham considers to be valid about the
Father and the Son being of the same essence, and uses arguments
about universals, reference, and the formal distinction to extricate
the faithful from Wodeham's mistake. Finally, Wyclif presents a dis-
quisition on generation within the divine being that can only be the
fruit of his commentary on Bk.I, Distinction 5. The last chapter con-

---

[15] I am grateful to Michael Dunning for the use of his unpublished edition of
FitzRalph's Sentence commentary, the use of which has greatly assisted me by filling
out the brief picture of his commentary on Book 1 given in Leff, *Richard FitzRalph*.

[16] Breck, 1962, p. viii.

[17] See Heiko Oberman, *Archbishop Thomas Bradwardine: A Fourteenth Century Augustinian*
(Utrecht, 1957), pp. 43–8.

[18] Leonard Kennedy, *The Philosophy of Robert Holcot, Fourteenth Century Skeptic* (Lewiston,
1993), p. 140.

siders the spiration of the Holy Spirit from Father and Son, sum-
marizing the arguments levied against "the Greeks" who reject the
filioque clause in the Nicene Creed.

The treatise's beginning provides a strong indicator that *De Trinitate*
represents the beginning of Wyclif's Sentence Commentary. Rather
than beginning as Augustine did in his *De Trinitate*, with a brief discussion as to the utility of theological speculation and its place within
the life of the faithful, the first four chapters of Wyclif's treatise
stoutly defend the position that an act of faith is involved in every
act of reasoning, making faith absolutely central to any form of reasoning. Readers unfamiliar with the Sentence Commentary tradition
that had developed in Oxford in the early fourteenth-century might
be forgiven for wondering why Wyclif expends such energy arguing
for a rational analysis of matters of the faith. In 1317 William
Ockham had begun his own lectures on the *Sentences*, in which he
argued that natural reason is ultimately unable to encompass the
mysteries of the faith with the security and extent that his predecessors Aquinas and Scotus had imagined possible. While he stopped
short of holding that faith and reason were two separate spheres
between which fruitful dialogue is possible, not all who were to follow were as cautious.[19] During the two decades that were to follow,
Oxford theologians vigorously examined the possibility that theology
really isn't even a science at all. Most notable of these were Adam
Wodeham and Robert Holcot, and William Crathorn.

Adam Wodeham, Ockham's student and friend, attacked the arguments of his fellow Franciscan Walter Chatton with notable vigor.
Chatton had argued, as Wyclif would, that a return to the safety of
theological tradition and scriptural foundation would best serve the
needs of the day.[20] Wodeham argued against the possibility of using

---

[19] See Alfred Freddoso, "Ockham on Faith and Reason," *The Cambridge Companion
to Ockham*, ed. Paul Vincent Spade (Cambridge, 1999), pp. 326–49. See William
Ockham, *Summae Logicae Pars Prima Tertiae Partis*, c. 1: "Et sic articuli fidei nec sunt
principia demonstrationis nec conclusiones, nec sunt probabiles, quia omnibus vel
pluribus vel maxime sapientibus apparent falsi, et hoc accipiendo sapientes pro sapientibus mundi et praecise innitentibus rationi naturali, quia illo modo accipitur 'sapi-
ens' in descriptione probabilis."

[20] See Courtenay, *Schools and Scholars*, pp. 265–6; also Gracia pp. 674–5. The
influence of Chatton on Wyclif deserves much fuller consideration than is possible
here, where Wyclif's more immediate opponents are of interest. See *Reportatio in I
Sent.* Dist. 1–9 and Dist. 10–48, ed. See Girard Etzkorn and Joseph Wey (Toronto,
2002).

the fruits of natural reasoning to broaden our understanding of the divine, rejecting as many of Chatton's attempts at natural theology as was necessary to emphasize this impossibility. While a conclusion reliably attained using one form of science may seem applicable in another field, it would be foolhardy to assume that this holds across all the rational endeavors we suppose are sciences. We may presume that two diverse lines of argument lead to the same conclusion, as in the famous five ways Aquinas uses to demonstrate God's existence, but "diverse sciences do not prove formally the same conclusion through the same medium, unless by mendacity."[21] Scientific reasoning's ability, for example, to construct arguments demonstrating the existence of an infinite being may entice one to suppose that it can demonstrate God's existence, but the God it constructs is ultimately nothing in comparison to the God of theology. There is no possibility of reason establishing the falsity of the apparently valid syllogism "This thing is the Father; this same thing is the Son; therefore the Father is the same as the Son", for by Aristotle's rules, the conclusion follows neatly from the premises. "And thus unless through our faith it were known that one thing is three things, we would believe firmly the aforesaid sophism to have been well argued."[22]

Robert Holcot's position was that what is evident as scientific knowledge is born from demonstrative arguments; no faith is involved in the process. His argument is that theology could only be considered a science if it conformed to one of the three senses in which the term *scientia* is understood. In the broadest sense, it is firm adhesion to the truth, and in this sense theology is a science. But the question of the basis for that adhesion then arises. If the assent is based in evident knowledge of some truth grounded in empirical data, or in necessary first principles, then one cannot include theology among the sciences, for no viator can claim empirical knowledge nor intuitive comprehension of supernatural truths as necessary first principles.[23]

---

[21] Adam de Wodeham, *Lectura Secunda in Librum Primum Sententiae* 1.3.12, p. 1:247: "Et ideo ad variationem mediorum secundum speciem variatur actus sciendi secundum speciem, et diversae scientiae non probant formaliter eandem conclusionem per idem medium, nisi mendicando."

[22] Ibid., 2.1.13, p. 2:25: "Et ideo nisi per fidem nobis innotuisset quod una res est tres res, credidissemus firmiter sophismata praedicta bona fuisse argumenta."

[23] See Holcot's denial of the possibility of establishing God's existence through

But the matter is more complex than this; Holcot is not suggesting that formal reasoning has no place in theological investigations. While he is clear that the Catholic ought accept as true on authority of Scripture or the Church propositions that might otherwise be rejected, one can—and in some cases must—use logic to investigate theological statements and arguments. With heretics, it is best to stick to analysis of the forms of arguments they use, and leave the divergence in content to ecclesiastic authority Theologians must be well versed in logic, though, as sophistic arguments frequently arise that require careful parsing. In some cases, he continues, good reasoning can break down when addressing particularly difficult subjects, as with the nature of the Trinity. The syllogism 'this thing is the Father', 'this same thing is the Son', therefore 'the Father is the Son' is perfectly acceptable by Aristotle's reasoning, yet the consequence cannot be accepted, even if the premisses are. Understanding the limits of human logic, he suggests, is one of the first requirements of theological investigation.[24]

Another Dominican, William Crathorn (fl. 1330–1331) has recently gained some scholarly attention for his unique epistemological positions. In his Commentary on Book I of the *Sentences*, he argues that our knowledge of perceptible objects arises from our perception of sensible species, which have all the characteristics of the objects they represent. That is, the sensible species of a cat that I see has, just as the cat does, a tail, white fur, a pink nose, and so on. Holcot thought Crathorn's position was ridiculous, but given its similarity to that argued by philosophers three hundred years hence, it has recently garnered scholarly interest.[25] Crathorn's influence on Wyclif is likely to have been noteworthy, despite the two decades separating them, given the many subjects on which they directly disagreed. Crathorn's *In Primum Librum Sententiarum* follows Lombard's first book

---

unaided reason in J.T. Muckle, C.S.B., "*Utrum Theologia Sit Scientia* A Quodlibetal Question of Robert Holcot, O.P.", *Mediaeval Studies* 20 (1958), 127–53, at p. 144: "non habemus ab aliquo philosopho demonstrative probatum quod aliquis angelus est, neque de deo, neque de aliquo incorporeo."

[24] *Quodlibet* 87, '*Utrum haec est concedenda: Deus est Pater et Filius et Spiritus Sanctus*', in Hester Gelber, *Exploring the Boundaries of Reason: Three Questions on the Nature of God by Robert Holcot OP* (Toronto, 1983), pp. 34–36.

[25] See "On the possibility of infallible knowledge," *In Sent.* Q.1, R. Pasnau, transl., in R. Pasnau, ed., *Cambridge Translations of Medieval Philosophical Texts*, vol. 3, *Mind and Knowledge* (Cambridge 2002), pp. 245–301. See also Gracia and Noone, pp. 692–3.

only nominally, ranging across a host of issues that would, later
occupy Wyclif's attention. In addition to extended discussions of
mereology, indivisibles, and continuous motion, he lists five kinds of
Universals, including things universal by causality, by perfections,
and by similitude, but explains that logically speaking, the only real
Universals are signs or representations of things.[26] He is in agreement with Wodeham, Holcot, and Ockham that human reason cannot establish the existence of God as we understand the divine
through revelation. "I say then that it cannot be known by us in
this life properly said that there are not many gods, although according to the truth of things there are not many gods, but only one
God who is Father, Son, and Holy Spirit."[27]

One might conclude that by the 1330s, theology had become a
pallid version of what it had been twenty years before. The approaches
of Wodeham and Holcot predominated at Oxford in the years before
Black Death, and Courtenay notes that "theology as a science, its
practical or speculative nature, and its subject" had generally ceased
to be a matter of discussion.[28] Had a general air of skepticism settled over the university? While John Mirecourt and Nicholas of
Autrecourt were to be condemned in Paris in 1347, their condemnations were based less on a fear of the possibility of a theology-
killing skepticism in their views and more on personal and political
differences with the theology faculty there.[29] Skepticism was not the
problem; change in interests and methodology, more than anything
else, seems to have led pre-1349 Oxford to follow Wodeham's and
Holcot's approach regarding theology. Even thinkers one might expect
to have opposed the separation of theology from the sciences seem
to have occupied themselves with other concerns; Bradwardine's monumental *De causa Dei* is predicated on the idea that philosophy and

---

[26] Q.II, pp. 153–154; and at p. 182: "Iam ostendum est quod universale non sit
res extra animam, sicut aliqui imaginatur," in Fritz Hoffmann, *Crathorn Quäestionen
zum Ersten Sentenzenbuch, Beiträge zur Geschichte der Philosophie und Theologie des Mittelalters*
NF 29 (Munster, 1988).

[27] Ibid., Q.4, pp. 305–6: "Dico igitur non potest sciri a nobis in vita ista scientia proprie dicta quod non sint plures dii, licet secundum rei veritatem non sint
plures dii, sed unus deus tantum, qui est Pater, Filius, et Spiritus Sanctus."

[28] Courtenay, *Schools and* Scholars, p. 255.

[29] J.M.M.H. Thijssen, *Censure and Heresy at the University of Paris 1200–1400* (Philadelphia, 1998), pp. 73–89.

logic can defend theological truth, but he does not go out of his way to establish this.[30]

Wyclif does not appear to have been the first to resurrect the issue, though; in the early 1350s, the Franciscan Richard Brinkley addressed the question "Whether the Christian sect depends on faith or reason as its foundation" in his *Sentences* Commentary. Had Brinkley's *Sentences* Commentaries survived, we would be in a position to compare the force of his arguments against those of his Wodeham, but all that remains appears to be an *abbrevatio* prepared by Etienne Gaudet, a Parisian scholar in the 1360s.[31] Here, Brinkley is reported as arguing against philosophers who believe "that man should believe nothing, unless what ostensive reason is naturally able to conclude for itself to be the truth. And because they do not know how to prove evidently that there is another life, they establish for themselves this present one on its own."[32] Brinkley argues that man can, by evident reason, infer that human life is itself ordered to another life than the present. Do other sects (*i.e.* religions) have differing conceptions of how reason ought guide the faithful? Brinkley argues that every sect believes its foundational principles to be the truth, and uses these principles to construct rational arguments in favor of their sect. Unfortunately, what we lack are his conceptions of the interrelation of faith and reason that support these assertions. Gaudet reports him as having begun the question by arguing that the human will determines what the intellect will decide upon, and as having then presented arguments against this position. It is very tempting, given Wyclif's own arguments, to fill in the blanks in Brinkley's question, and have him hold that there is an element of faith in every act of reasoning. This would allowing us to recognize the compatibility of faith and reason as both matters fit for scientific exploration,

---

[30] "*De causa Dei praefatio*, pp. 5–6: "Indagare siquidem causas naturales entium et propinquas, difficulatatem non modicam continet et laborem; quanto magis totam universitatem harum causarum, volatu mentis corruptela corporis aggravate transcendere, et usque ad impenetrabile penetralecausarum supernaturalium, altissimarum, inaccessibilum et invisibilum penetrare, ipsasque velut nycticoracis oculo caligante perspicaciter intueri . . ." See also Oberman, *Thomas Bradwardine*, pp. 22–7.

[31] See Kaluza, "L'oeuvre théologique de Richard Brinkley, OFM."

[32] Kaluza, ibid., p. 227: "Circa quod est opinio philosophorum quod homo nihil debet credere, nisi quod ostensiva ratione naturaliter poterit sibi concludi esse verum. Et quia aliam vitam concludere evidenter nesciunt, praesentem pro fine sibi stauunt."

as Wyclif was to argue. But in the *abbrevatio* of the question that
follows, Gaudet describes Brinkley as "touching upon the incom-
possibility of reason and faith," which suggests that he followed his
Franciscan predecessors in seeing the two as separate. So while Wyclif
was likely influenced by Brinkley's logic, he probably wasn't influenced
by his understanding of the relation of reason to faith.[33]

A more notable connection can be made between Wyclif and
Nicholas Aston, who was a fellow at Queen's College from 1350,
and Chancellor of the University from 1359 to 1361.[34] Aston was,
like Wyclif, extremely sensitive to the centrality of logical analysis of
language in theological argument. Like Wyclif, he demonstrated no
interest in epistemology, preferring instead to apply philosophical
logic to ontological problems without reference to the questions of
knowability and certainty that occupied theologians in the 1320s and
1330s. More importantly, Aston followed Burley in arguing for the
reality of Universals, and again like Wyclif, articulated an approach
directly challenging those who would hold that truth lies in propositions, not in things. "Aston does indeed have a very strict definition
of truth, for he has identified the truth of any proposition, syllogism,
or argument with God."[35] For our discussion, Aston is most notable
for having formulated a proof for God's existence in response to
what he saw as a logically confused argument Bradwardine had made
in *De causa Dei* I.1.[36] Bradwardine's argument, itself a variant of
Aquinas's third argument in *Summa theologiae* Ia Q.2 a.3, from the
possible to the necessary, fails, Aston argues, because it fumbles on
possibility. Despite its supporters, the argument cannot be recognized

---

[33] "Et tangitur de incompossibilitate scientiae et fidei . . . deinde respondetur ad
quasdam rationes seu argumenta quae videntur probare oppositum quaestionis ex
incompossibilitate fidei et scientifici assensus." From *Utrum regulae sectae Christi et eius
propria principia per se sufficient ad aliquam conclusionem mere theologicam scientifice cognoscen-
dam*, Ibid. p. 229.
[34] See Courtenay, *Schools and Scholars*, pp. 333–46; Zénon Kaluza, "L'Oeuvre
Théologique de Nicolas Aston," *Archives D'Histoire Doctrinale et Littéraire au Moyen Age*,
48 (1978), 45–82. Joel L. Bender, *Nicholas Aston: A Study in Oxford Thought after the
Black Death* (Ph.D. diss., University of Wisconsin, 1979) contains the fullest discussion of Aston's life and thought, as well as an edition of eight questions from Aston's
Sentences Commentary.
[35] Bender, p. 183; art. 4, l. 519–22, in Bender, p. 422: "Ideo dico quod conse-
quentiae bonae et formali, syllogismo bono, vel argumento bono, vel propositioni
cuius contradictorium contradictionem includit, nihil in re correspondet nisi Deus . . ."
[36] Bradwardine, *De causa Dei* 1.1, p. 2B, also I.11, p. 198D.

as valid. The *falsigraphicus* [literally, mistake-writer] who jeers at such arguments would rightly assert that Bradwardine's argument allows for a contingency to God's existence that is not commensurate with revealed truth. Rather than pursue Aston's argument, it is sufficient to note that Aston's extended discussion gives evidence of a shift in interest in Oxford in the 1350s, back to subject matter in formal theology consonant with late thirteenth-century thought. This was likely strongly influenced by Bradwardine; following the Black Death, arguments for God's existence were once again on the docket at Oxford. If Aston's *falsigraphicus* is related to those Wyclif would later call "doctors of signs", then it is clear that Wyclif's theological positions were very much in step with those of his fellows at Oxford.

We can know confusedly that God's existence is demonstrable, Wyclif begins, and that the triune nature is recognizable as a result of this demonstration, but can we know God as the blessed experience in the divine vision?[37] When human reason establishes God's existence, it also establishes the triune nature of the divine essence, even if the demonstrator is unaware of this feat. Authorities such as Anselm, Augustine, the Victorines, and Grosseteste all argue that the Trinity is evident through recognition of trinities in creatures, which serve as natural signs by which human reason may deduce syllogistically the divine Trinity.[38] This is effectively described in *Liber de causis*, proposition 6, who says that sensible effects brought about by secondary causes make us stammeringly to name God in His causes.[39]

---

[37] *De Trinitate*, 1, p. 1. See *De Actibus Anime, pars secunda* 3, pp. 107/35–108/21: "[Q]uod deum esse est primum notum a quocunque cognoscente, non tamen est explicite cognoscibile, nisi a re racionali . . ."

[38] Peter Lombard, *Sententiae* 1.3.1. In FitzRalph's commentary on the *Sentences* 1.5: "Whether the human mind is an image of the uncreated Trinity", he argues that the mind's inability to understand the uncreated Trinity militates against this, but concedes that on Augustine's authority in *De Trinitate*, 14 c.15 it can be argued that the mind's ability to worship and participate in uncreated wisdom. "That mind is image of God for which it is receptive and can be a participant." The remainder of FitzRalph's commentary addresses real distinction between memory, understanding and will, between the acts of these powers, particularly between acts of cognition and of memory, and between acts of cognition and willing. Wyclif does not appear to have made use of this in his argument in *De Trinitate*.

[39] "The first cause transcends description. Languages fail in describing it only because of the description of its being. For the first cause is above every cause and is described only through the second causes which are illumined by the light of the first cause." Prop. 6, *Liber de Causis*, in *St. Thomas Aquinas Commentary of the Book of Causes*, trans. Vincent Guagliardo O.P., Charles R. Hess, O.P., Richard Taylor

One can summarize the argument much as one argues from motion to prime mover. We recognize that the soul in creatures is composed of a triune nature, in which memory, reason, and will define the singular essence. This phenomenon, like motion, demands a like, three-fold intelligence that is itself necessary and immutable. Therefore, God has a three-fold nature.[40]

Augustine's example should be our guide, Wyclif explains. His arguments show how reason allows us to recognize the divine truths woven into creation, but in each case the faith must serve as foundational. "This is generally said, that no one can assent to this deduction [of the three-fold divine nature from perceived created trinities] without faith, and so it is not merely natural, and is not demonstrated in the natural light."[41] But if faith is the foundation, is it not then the case that demonstration through natural reasoning is impossible? All reasoning demands some sort of non-rational assent, Wyclif argues, either before or outside of the reasoning process, to conditions that serve as evidence for the reasoning to take place. Learning to read, or to speak, requires a degree of faith in the teacher. The absence of the light of faith infused in the mind allows one to give assent to many ideas, but in each case, the mind craves evidence of some kind. Testimony of authority counts as such even in matters otherwise neutral, so assent can be given in these matters from the authority of scripture or teaching that will be, in light of divine reality, rationally clear to all. Truth is manifested in three kinds of light: divine nature or supernatural disposition, the light of reason or some

---

(Washington, 1996, p. 45). Compare to Wyclif's affirmation of impossibility of human language referring to God in *De Incarnacione* 7, p. 115/15–21. On this topic, see the discussion of analogy and God-talk below.

[40] *De Trinitate* 1, pp. 1–3. Contrast with Adam Wodeham, *Sententiae* 1, D.2, Q.1.14, p. 29/69–75: "Although in the truth of things, 'God exists' bears along with it 'the Trinity exists', nevertheless the soundness of this consequence is not evident . . . this term 'God' and likewise this term 'prime mover' in these propositions supposit for the Trinity, but this is not evident. And thus it does not follow that the Trinity's being might be proven evidently from creatures . . ." Also, contrast with William Crathorn, *Q.7 Utrum omnis creatura rationalis sit imago trinitatis*, where he argues that while in the powers of the soul there is an image of God, it is mistaken to conclude from this that the created being gives evidence of the Trinity of divine being. See Hoffmann, *Crathorn*, pp. 331–51.

[41] *De Trinitate* 1, p. 3: "Hic dicitur communiter, quod nemo potest sine fide prima assentire isti deduccioni, et ideo non est mere naturalis, et sic non demonstratur in lumine naturali."

other created power, and the light of faith in universal truths that are not evident to natural light.[42] All can converge in the human mind to allow one to give assent to a truth of faith.

Later in his life, Wyclif makes much the same argument at the beginning of his instruction on the Trinity in *Trialogus*, where he has his foil *Pseustis* argue a simplified version of the Ockhamist position. His champion *Phronesis* responds, "It is impossible for the faithful or the heretic to know something, unless they know it fundamentally through faith; because just as nobody knows letters—that one is A, the next B, and so of other—unless they believe, so nobody by their senses knows anything sensible, unless first truth speaks and teaches that, that a thing is sensible in one way or in another."[43] We do not degrade natural deduction simply because we give our assent to faith to augment that reasoning process. Further, faith is not judged to be better relative to the wealth of evidence available; the faith of a rich man with a Bible is not superior to that of a poor man without one. Not all acts of faith result in immediate understanding. Sometimes we believe something, yet never understand it, while in others, we come to an understanding immediately on giving assent to it, and in still others, what is believed is only understood after thought. This shows that not all faiths are of a kind.

But are they always present in any act of knowledge? And if so, and if faith is a virtuous qualitative *habitus*, which all theologians recognize to be a theological virtue, can we know anything without the assistance of grace, which is necessary for any theological virtue?[44] Wyclif is not forthcoming in his position on the place of illumination in knowledge here; we must deduce his allegiance to Augustine, Grosseteste, and Bonaventure. Their position was that every act of understanding entails the divine illumination of the mind, an active involvement of the light of Truth in each case of our apprehension

---

[42] *De Trinitate* 1, p. 5. Wyclif argues that just as sunlight is to moonlight, so is supernatural light to the light of natural reason. See *De Trinitate*, p. 6.

[43] *Trialogus* 1.6, ed. Gotthard Lechler (Oxford, 1869), p. 55: "Impossible est fidelem vel haereticum quidquam cognoscere, nisi per fidem fundamentaliter illud cognoscat; quia sicut nemo cognoscit literas, quod una est A, reliqua B, et sic de ceteris, nisi credat: sic nemo sensu cognoscit quodcunque sensibile, nisi prima veritas illud dicat et doceat, quod illud sensibile sit illud vel hujusmodi."

[44] *De Trinitate* 1, p. 14 for faith as theological virtue. On the need of Grace for any virtuous act, see *De dominio divino* 3.4–5.

of the truth. Aquinas and Scotus limited the need for this illumination to the sphere of revelation, arguing that the unassisted human
reason is capable of accurately perceiving the truth about things in
this world without the need of divine assistance. Faith factors into
this question when truths understood by pagans such as Aristotle
must be explained; Aristotle lacked the Christian faith, yet reasoned
out the truth of things in the world. This led Aquinas to conclude
that one could not have faith and knowledge about the same thing.
Faith requires assent without evidence, while knowledge entails having that evidence.[45] Henry of Ghent [d. 1293] is the last widely studied philosopher to have argued the need for divine illumination before
Nicholas of Cusa in the fifteenth century. By the shape of Wyclif's
arguments here, it is difficult to avoid concluding that he followed
Henry, Bonaventure, and Grosseteste in arguing the need for divine
illumination. "For it is impossible for a creature to know anything
unless it knows it through grounding from the authority of God
teaching and moving to assent."[46]

All that we understand, then, requires some faithful assent of the
human mind, some acquiescence to evidence that might be doubted.
In the case of understanding objects we perceive, our intuition of
sense data entails faith of a kind, which kindles growth of knowledge as our experiences increase. Gradually the knowledge we acquire
becomes fodder for the aggregation of sense experiences into judgments we make about the world, which judgments would be impossible without the fundamental faith we have in the individual
experiences. If this is a real quality, and not just a fiction we invent
to explain our knowing, then it must be like the other aspects of
our knowledge of things, it must be in itself something predicable
of the human mind, an act as such that may be identifiable in every
act of knowing.[47]

---

[45] *Summa theologiae* 2:2.1.4. See Joseph Owens, "Faith, Ideas, Illumination, and
Experience," *Cambridge History of Late Medieval Philosophy*, ed. Anthony Kenny, Norman
Kretzmann and Jan Pinborg (Cambridge, 1982), pp. 440–59.

[46] *De Trinitate* 2, p. 19. "Nam impossible est creaturam quicquam cognoscere nisi
cognoscat illud per locum ab auctoritate dei docentis et moventis ad assensum."

[47] For Wyclif's consideration of the ontological status of mental acts, see *De Actibus
Anime pars prima*, pp. 1–57, although he has little to say there about the relation of
faith to the reasoning process. See *Dialogus* 12 for a brief discussion of the difference
between opinion and faith.

Faith has a natural place in all our acts of understanding, great and small, and if we can claim to have an accurate explanation for even the least act of understanding the simplest thing, we should also admit to the possibility that great truths of faith, such as the Trinity, may be explored and understood by human reason.[48] We reason best from basic truths (Aristotle's first principles) taken in faith, which is fundamental to all knowing. The truth that all truths are reducible to one fundamental truth shows that God moves the mind to assent to the truth before the mind itself gives its assent, which is the mark of faith preceding reasoned knowing. Ultimately, all arguments rest on arguments from authority—but divine authority, not human. Human reasoning is only capable, only able to be trusted, if it, in turn, trusts God. The Muslims who prohibit reason from exploring the faith are fools, for they close themselves off from the merits available to them.[49]

If the articles of faith were demonstrable scientifically, philosophers would already have done so, without the need for revelation. But the articles of faith are difficult, subtle, hidden from natural light. The merit that comes from faith consists in voluntarily and humbly submitting the sensibility to the authority of the Catholic Church and the articles of faith, against which rebellion is a sin. So to view faith and reason as incompatible is premature. Faith is at once an act of believing, a habit, an assent to a truth; since what is known is believed as well, faith and knowing are not really incompatible. One can have both in the same case.[50] Turning to *Moderni* predecessors, the disagreement between Wyclif and Holcot is limited, and

---

[48] Compare to Bradwardine, *De causa Dei* 1.1, corr.32, where he argues against philosophers who believe themselves capable of demonstrating all truths without need of revelation. Bradwardine argues at length of the presence of faith in every act of knowing, continuing on to illustrate Christian history as defined by the concord of faith and reason, pp. 28ff.

[49] *De Trinitate* 4, pp. 33–34.

[50] Here Wyclif's argument with Holcot, if it is with him, becomes more complex. Both agree of the need for the believer to submit himself to the authority of the Church, but the reasons differ. Holcot argued as much because he believed that no natural logic could establish the compossibility of truths evident to empirical experience and the truths of the faith. This is not to say that he believed there to be a need for two separate kinds of logic, but that unassisted reason can only reach so far in its analysis. See Kennedy, pp. 19–21.

in fact the two agree on more than they disagree: both recognize that truths of the faith must be believed on authority of Scripture and the Church, both argue for use of formal reasoning in theological matters, and both appear to suspect that bad reasoning lies at the base of heresy more often than not. The point of divergence is on reasoning within theology; Holcot believes it best for responding to problems within theology, and less useful for *adducendum*, or dialectical exploration, while Wyclif argues in these chapters for its centrality in just that activity.[51] He explicitly says as much in *De dominio divino* 1.6.

> And so the same thing is subject of theology by reason of its dignity and also the subject of metaphysics. But the reasons differ in three ways. For the theologian rightly considers created beings according to the exemplary reasons they have in the Word, and indirectly according to their existence in their proper genera. Thus theology is not perfected before the theologian arrives in paradise. Secondly, the theologian adheres by faith and authority of Scripture to any of the conclusions of his science; indeed, he should explicitly understand this insofar as he is a theologian. Third, the theologian humbly proceeds to the proper highest subject, and understands it as such, but confusedly; barely understanding as distinct knowledge that which he will distinctly know in paradise. And therefore the order of theology will not be reversed in paradise, but will devour every other science, and laying aside perverse ways of proceeding; metaphysics does the contrary. And it is clear that in the Word is sufficient connection to truth, and if the creature knows nothing save the Lord Jesus Christ and that which according to His essence or being is intelligible in the Son, then they [i.e. knower and known] are connected.[52]

---

[51] Wyclif has much more to say about faith in other works, but in these it is considered as the virtue requisite for understanding, without argument as to how it is related to the act of understanding. See, for instance, *De triplici vinculo amoris* 5, in *Polemical Works in Latin*, 2 vols. ed. Rudolf Buddensieg (London, 1883), 1:176–9. Cf. *Trialogus* 3.2, pp. 133–4: "These three theological virtues, faith, hope and love, differ in this, that faith bespeaks supernatural and habitual understanding of the believing, between considering and knowing, and faith has praiseworthy characteristics. But understand that faith is sometimes accepted for the act of believing, sometimes for the habit [of faith] and sometimes for the truth in which is believed. Thus the faithful say that first is the faith *as* [*qua*] we believe, second is the faith *through which* [*per quam*] we believe, and third is the faith *which* [*quam*] we believe. And some faith (as the schoolmen say) is unformed, when "the demons believe and tremble' [James 2.19], while other times faith is formed of charity. It seems to me, though, that the faithful, according to the integrity of [their] faith, necessarily have charity, while demons and anyone lacking it [charity] are accordingly infidels."

[52] *De dominio divino* 1.7 ed. R.L. Poole (London, 1890), p. 43/3–21: "Et sic idem

2.3. *Analogy and God Talk*

Later in the treatise, Wyclif makes a related case for the more specific issue of reason delineating the distinction of persons within the divine essence, leading to his argument for the necessity of care with how language is used in theology. The best way to begin study of doctrinal truth is to look to the different ways terms signify as they are used in theology. To do this, one must first give credal assent to the doctrine one seeks to analyze. The Modalist heresy arose, Wyclif argues, when one presumed to understand the Trinity by analyzing the terms to be used before assenting in belief. "And among all the heresies concerning the divine Trinity, I believe that today things are more perilous because the community of the *Moderni* deny universal truths."[53]

Running throughout Wyclif's argument are references to the utility of analogical predication, the philosophical reference theory most commonly associated with Aquinas. Thomas had argued that the best way of understanding how our language might refer to the transcendent Godhead is through understanding that an ontological difference separates God from creation analogous to the difference between substance and accident.[54] Since Thomas's own understanding

---

est subiectum adequacionis theologie quod et subiectum dignitatis, et idem subiectum theologie et methaphisce. Sed raciones diversificantur in tribus. Nam theologus recte considerat de creatis secundum raciones exemplares quas habet in Verbo, et indirecte secundum existenciam in genere proprio. Ideo non perficietur theologia antequam devntum sit ad patriam. Secondo theologus adheret fide et auctoritate Scripture cuicumque conclusioni sue sciencie; ymo, hoc debet explicite, in quantum theologus, cognoscere. Tercio theologus humiliter procedit a proprio subiecto maxime, primo, et per se cognito, sed confuse; minime autem cognito quoad distinctam noticiam quosque ipsum fuerit distincte cognitum in patria. Et ideo ordo theologice non erit reversus in patria, sed devorabit omnes alias sciencias, et deponet preposterum ordinem procedendi; econtra autem de methaphisica. Et patet uod in verbo est sufficiens connexio veritatum, etsi creatura nichil sciat nisi dominum Iesum Christum et ea que secundum essenciam vel esse intelligible in Filio connectuntur."

[53] *De Trinitate* 9, p. 100: "[E]t inter omnes hereses concernentes trinitatem, credo quod hec esset hodie periculosior quia communitas modernorum negancium veritates et universalia nec non eciam verificancium dicta auctorum solum de signis attribuunt . . ."

[54] The literature on this subject is vast, running from historical studies of the development of the idea in Thomas's own thought, to the theory's comprehensibility and utility in light of contemporary philosophy of language. For Thomas's earlier thought, see *In Sent.* 1, d.19, q.5, a.2, c and ad.1; *In Sent.* 3, d.2, q.1, a.1, ad.3; for later development, see *De Veritate* q.2, a.11; *Summa theologiae* 1.1, Q.13, a.5. For a representative treatment of the theory in light of contemporary interests, see David Burrell, *Analogy and Philosophical Language* (New Haven,1973).

of how this analogical predication functions developed as his own thought evolved, it is not surprising that a host of different approaches cropped up in scholastic theology, well before Cardinal Cajetan's notoriously inaccurate interpretation in the 1490s.[55] Wyclif is clear that univocal and equivocal predication about God, particularly about the divine persons' identity through their relations to one another, is wholly impossible.[56] This is important to bear in mind, not only throughout *De Trinitate*, but in all his theological works. Scotus famously argued for the univocity of being allowing for univocal predication of God and creation. We will see that *De Incarnatione Verbi* is in large part a development of Scotus's christology, and it is difficult to avoid comparisons to Scotus when reading *De ente primo in communi*, the second treatise of Book I of the *Summa de ente*.[57] Wyclif's arguments in this treatise to delineate the right use of analogy in talking about God, while not terribly clear, should at least define the extent to which Wyclif should be identified with Scotism.

Rather than lay out a scheme by which the theologian can best use language for God-predication, organized along recognizable metaphysical lines such as proportionality, Wyclif more commonly describes how our contact with God through language brings us closer to comprehension of the divine. "We cannot cognize God here purely and as a consequence since we cannot impose terms unless proportionate to our knowledge, it is clear that we cannot adapt terms to God for pure signification."[58] Our temporal approach to God is bounded

---

[55] See E.J. Ashworth, "Analogy and Equivocation in Thirteenth-Century Logic: Aquinas in Context," *Mediaeval Studies* 54 (1992), 94–135. Following Aquinas, the next important thinker to explore the topic was Henry of Ghent; see Jos Decorte, "Henry of Ghent on Analogy: Critical Reflections of Jean Paulus' Interpretation," in *Henry of Ghent*, ed. W. Vanhamel, (Louvain, 1996), pp. 71–105. For early fourteenth-century theories, see E.J. Ashworth, "Equivocation and Analogy in Fourteenth-Century Logic: Ockham, Burley, and Buridan," in *Historia Philosophi Medii Aevi: Studien der Geschichte der Philosophie des Mittelalters* 2 vols. (Amsterdam, 1991), 1:23–43. In her "Analogical Concepts: The Fourteenth-Century Background to Cajetan" [*Dialogue* XXXI (1992), pp. 399–413], Ashworth concentrates on Peter Aureol (d. 1322), Hervaeus Natalis (d. 1323), and John of Jandun (d. 1328), Parisian thinkers influential to Johannes Capreolus (d. 1444), Dominic of Flander (d. 1479), and Paulus Soncinas (d. 1494), Cajetan's predecessors. A study of analogy and religious language in Oxford from Ockham through the 1370s would help to explain Wyclif's approach, which is not an original one, but differs from Burley's as described by Ashworth.

[56] *De Trinitate*, p. 99.

[57] See *Johannis Wyclif Summa de ente Libri Primi Tractatus Primus et Secundus*, ed. S. Harrison Thomson (Oxford, 1930), esp. pp. 62–70.

[58] *De Trinitate*, p. 115.

by our inability to breach God's transcendence, but through the fruits of the Spirit we can rejoice in God's love and so enjoy God. We do not enjoy God, but we do enjoy His attributes. The most simple terms connote in signifying God, His being, but they do not signify Him primarily; those most likely to do so would be privative terms composed from the divine transcendence.[59]

Man's passionate nature is analogous to God's, and human passions are attributed to Him in figurative language. "Otherwise it is right for us to understand a term when its primary signification matches God analogously, and elsewhere when its primary signification cannot match God but through analogous properties found in such signs, as regality is in the lion as invincible lord of the beasts. This anthonomastic analogy matches God. Thus God is called a lion in Scripture, and it is clear when the language is figurative and when not."[60] Reason, goodness, knowing, and so on in are causes in God for their realization in creation, so that they are only truly predicable insofar as they relate to God; all created perfections are proportionate to divine perfection by analogy. Anselm's recognition of created being predicates in the divine being leads him to conclude that to find our created good we ought love the simple good of God, which is the good of all.

> This singular goodness of God is infinitely prior in nature to anything universal, and so truth as much as goodness is communicated universally to the creatures of God. Who would say that the source participates in the water of the river or the lake, which could not be water without there already having existed water in the source?[61]

Since prayer is the elevation of the mind to God, it is clear that it assists considerably, as it helps us to recognize that God's glory, holiness, and any other attribute we praise is inseparable from God. This makes expressions of glory and wonder at the greatness of God a kind of prayer, for it unites the mind to God's very being. "[A]nd there can be nothing so fulfilled or replenishing, nor to which the human spirit is so susceptible, than God."[62]

---

[59] In scholastic terminology, 'connotation' means that a term like 'blindness' causes one to think of sight, and thus indirectly signifies it. 'Blindness' is also a privative term, in that it refers to something absent or lacking in the subject.

[60] *De Trinitate*, pp. 124–25.

[61] *De Trinitate*, p. 127. His reference to Anselm is to *Proslogion* 25. Wyclif refers the reader to his fuller treatment of this in *De universalibus*, 4–5.

[62] *De Trinitate*, p. 117.

For analysis of the limitations of language in describing the Trinity, we can do no better than to examine how predicating relations within the divine being is possible. But before we can see how the *Moderni* err in supposing the validity of the syllogism "God is Father, God is Son, therefore Father is Son", we must first be clear about ontology. Wyclif's realism allows him to hold that the syllogism in question is a paralogism of the sort: Animal is Lion; Animal is Horse, therefore Lion is Horse. As the Universal is one common to many singulars, we do not reason from one relation of Universal to singular and another such relation to conclude about the necessity of the relation of the singulars. Theologians unable to distinguish the logical subtlety or engage in precise reasoning will not be able to defend the faith in such arguments. Even worse is the theologian who says that such reasoning should hold in every matter *other* than those of faith. Those who deny natural theology give Muslim theologians free reign to claim their faith to be on a par with our own! "When the Saracen would claim Mohammed as excellent a prophet as our Christ, then unless a defense against their evidence beyond what the Saracens have in their law, we could in no way prevail against the adversaries of our own law."[63]

2.4. *Trinity as Universal*

Realism in Universals makes explaining one being with three persons much easier. Assuming that the differing natures demand a real difference in an 'indivisible being' is the root of Avicenna's mistake that the Trinity entails a divine multiplicity. God is not one person, but one substance, which can be many in one if a Universal is real, for it is as many places as there are particulars. The particulars themselves are not multiple because they are particularlized. "An example of this is in created nature, for according to the way of speaking in Scripture, the nature of the Universal is multiple and numerous according to the multitude of its singulars. The human species is founded in three persons, Adam, Eve, and Cain, and it is

---

[63] *De Trinitate*, p. 133. "Cum Saraceni dicerent Mahometum tam excellentem prophetam sicut fuit Christus noster, ideo nisi assit defensorium contra evidencias ultra hoc quod habent Saraceni in lege sua, in nullo prevalebimus contra adversarium legis nostre."

in three because each of them is a human being, yet none of those three people are threefold themselves because they are in this species [divided up three ways]. And the species is in each of them as a species. A species is in a certain thing as it is in a supposit, but the certain thing is itself in the species as existing in its common cause."[64]

The divine being is not a universal because universals have many singular instantiates, and the divine nature is unified. Later, in chapter 13, he will argue that the divine nature is a universal of which there are three instantiations, G(f), G(s), and G(hs). He is not contradicting himself; here he means to say that the divine being is not a universal in the sense that the persons are instantiations—as created beings are instantiations of their universals—because with created being, the individual instantiations are distinct from one another and the universal in itself, but with the divine persons, there is no separating distinction between one another, or between a person and the divine nature. The distinction appears to be formal, as Scotus and Ockham had earlier said.

Alessandro Conti has shown elsewhere in this volume that Wyclif's conception of the formal distinction changed, and we should pause to see just which type of formal distinction he has in mind. In *Purgans errores circa universalia in communi* he describes the difference between divine persons as really distinct, relegating much less to the formal distinction. In *De universalibus*, the persons are distinct, but the distinction is more complex. Here, the persons are "really but not essentially" distinct as three things, each of the same spirit, but the persons are each formally distinct from the nature.[65] This appears to be the arrangement he presents in *De Trinitate* 13, although he does not refer to his 'real-but-not-essentially' distinction.[66] Ivan Mueller argues for a much later date for *De universalibus* (1373) than Thomson gives

---

[64] *De Trinitate*, pp. 79–80 "Exemplum huius est in natura creata, nam secundum modum loquendi scripture, natura universalis multipliciter numerose secundum multitudinem suorum singularium ut species humana fundata in tribus personis, sicut Adam, Eva, et Cayn, est in tribus quia quilibet horum trium hominum, et tamen nullus illorum est triplex quamvis sit in illa specie, et illa species sicut species est in illo. Species quidem est in illo tamquam in suo supposito sed ipsum est in specie tamquam in suo communi causante."

[65] See Conti, above. Also *Purgans errores . . .* in *De Ente*, ed. M.H. Dziewicki, p. 38.25, and *De universalibus*, ed. Ivan Mueller (Oxford, 1985), pp. 91/135–92/156.

[66] See *De Trinitate* 3, pp. 140–142.

(1368–69).[67] Perhaps if *De Trinitate* (Mueller suggests 1368, Thomson 1370) was written after *Purgans errores circa universalia* (Mueller and Thomson agree that this predates 1368) but before *De universalibus*, then *De Trinitate* would be a good place to look for evidence of the complication of Wyclif's view of distinctions.

Properties do not constitute the person, substance does. Properties serve only as a medium for us by which one person is recognizably distinguishable from another. In the divine being, persons are distinct not according to their properties, but by relation, and speaking of relations within the divine being is difficult. Augustine argues that predicating of relation in God is a middle way between predication according to substance and predication according to accident.[68] Augustine's intent, Wyclif suggests, was to make a formal distinction in eternal being between the subject and that which is not its accident. In God, there is a person, and then that person is G(f), G(s) or G(hs), "because to be a person is to be an hypostasis or substance, and this is said to be in itself and not in regards to some other thing, but to be Father or to be word is relative and is said as regards another, as is clear throughout *De Trinitate* Bk.VII."[69] Each divine person is based in common divine material, and to speak as if the Son is prior to the Father through truth but not causation is just sloppiness and ontologically misleading.

We do not posit a bare divine person devoid of personal nature simply because we recognize the hypostatic nature of the person as a possible basis for accidents. The divine nature causes the persons just as Universals cause singulars, but according to the logic of the Church it does not come into being, so a different sense of causing is involved. We cannot deny that the Son is produced from the substance of the Father, but 'produced' [*produceretur*] must be understood properly. 'Produces' and 'proceeds' [*fit*] must be meant differently, and Wyclif suggests two ways of understanding these verbs. Here

---

[67] See *De universalibus*, introduction, pp. xix–xxxviii.

[68] See Augustine, *De Trinitate* 5.1.3–8.

[69] *De Trinitate*, p. 81. "Secundo patet, ut mihi videtur, quod prius est esse personam quam esse patrem vel filium vel spiritum sanctum, quia esse personam est esse hypostasim vel substanciam, et dici ad se et non ad aliud; sed esse patrem aut esse verbum est relativum et dicitur ad aliud, ut patet VII De Trinitate, diffuse." The reference is to order of knowing, not order of being; Wyclif, following Augustine and the Western tradition, recognizes that by the order of being, nature precedes person.

Wyclif appears to be reasoning about the divine persons' operations using linguistic structure. If predication in being corresponds to predication in words, then it stands to reason that, Latin being the language expressing these truths, there must be ontological declensions.[70] He suggests four ways of ablative predication within God. In the first, [x does m *by/through* y] G(f) knows *by* G(s) and loves *by* G(hs), while G(s) lives, knows, and wills *by* G(f), and G(hs) lives, knows, and wills *through* G(f) and G(s). In the second, the ablative predication is of formal cause [x is Q *through* Q-ness as regards x], and in every such formal predication here Wyclif means for us to think of Q as Divine Nature and x as a person. In the third mode of ablative predication within God, a person acts *through* the nature of the action: the Father 'speaks' the Son through 'wording' or self-expression. This differs from the first in that the relation is between the agent and the nature of the act, rather than between two agents, which the first describes. In the fourth way of ablative predication, x is Q because to be Q is an accident associated *with* x's substance. Confusion arises regarding the relation of persons within the divine nature for those unfamiliar with the difference between 'is' in these predicative senses, and 'is' in identity statements.

More simply, Anselm expresses the triune nature of God in making an analogy to a river, which has three distinct elements: a source, a flow, and the delta. Augustine and Anselm give examples that are useful means of understand the ordering of persons. In our understanding of the relation of the uncreated Trinity to every created nature—whether Universal or singular—there is a base similarity, in that each being is One, True, and Good. For example, the cross is an emblematic symbol of love: the crosspiece demonstrates the width of divine love, the vertical piece the final perseverance from earth to heaven, and the headpiece the celestial hope because Christ is head of the Church.[71] Simply because such created trinities are difficult to recognize in nature, it is not right for philosophers to reject such attempts. If the human mind has the right expression of what is known in the mental word, and the love arising from knowing the truth is right, then is recreated in our minds the uncreated Trinity.

---

[70] This seems to be the substance of *De Trinitate*, pp. 84–86.
[71] *De Trinitate* 8, pp. 91–92.

2.5. *The Father is to the Son as Speaker is to Word*

In the treatise's fifth chapter, Wyclif suggests that understanding the distinction of the persons in the Trinity is best begun by recognizing that the Word expressed by God signifies perfectly the truth of the divine essence. This is the analogy John 1:1 illustrates to show the distinction of God the Father, [G(f)] the speaker, and God the Son [G(s)] the Word. (i.e. Father : Son :: Speaker : Word). Logical discourse communicates truth apart from particular things, for when demonstrating a syllogism one speaks of donkeys and men, but does not mean for the hearer to think that the subject of the statements are animals. So speech is carried not in words, but in what it signifies. Truth is predicated more in the being of things, not words. Accidents "speak" their subject as species do their genus. In man, white is said from whiteness, and whiteness is said from the white man; likewise, if Paul is said to be man essentially from humanity, then humanity "speaks" Paul to be a man. Grosseteste expresses this, "all the world is a statement speaking the art, word and intention intrinsic to God from which it flows."[72] The inherence relation of accident to subject automatically entails self-expression of the particular in which the relation is founded. The argument can best be described:

a. A sentence expresses a truth when it is true, which truth is a statement identical to its ontological subject matter.
b. A statement "Fx" is True if Fx is a part of creation.
c. All creation is a collection of predications related as the form "Fx" suggests.
d. That collection itself is a predication expressive of the Word.
e. Each statement, whether the set (creation), a subset (a branch, or twig of the Porphyrian tree) or an individual (Peter) is analogous "in a certain way" to a correlate truth in the divine mind.
f. The set of all correlate truths in the divine mind, possible, actual, necessary, past, present and future, are the Word, which has a causal agency on all created statements.
g. The identity of the Word with God is undeniable
   Therefore: G(f) : G (s) :: Speaker : word

---

[72] Grosseteste, *Hexameron* 1.1, first version 2–3, p. 48, in Robert Grosseteste, *On the Six Days of Creation*, trans. C.F.J. Martin (Oxford, 1999), p. 48.

If all creation speaks itself, each substance must contain an essential word, and God ordains the limitation of the degree of being that each substance has to its self-expression in just this way. Each substance expresses itself in measure, form, and weight, which expression is analogous to the uncreated Trinity governing it.[73] Objections to this would hold that insensible bodies cannot have appetites or cannot express themselves as do created minds. But earth does have an appetite to move in a straight line, light refracts according to set laws, and these basic physical laws indicate a superior force guiding these bodies, using them to express a regulation greater than the individual bodies. All physical laws, including the laws of motion and physics, have as their basis divine laws enacted and expressing fundamental truths, which illustrates the need for theology to lie at the heart of the physical sciences, as well as of metaphysics. Thus, following a lengthy discussion of how laws of mechanics articulate created being's self expression, Wyclif comes to two conclusions. First, every essential nature desires itself and expresses itself according to its own good. Second, every created nature expresses itself in its accidents and in its Universal as species and genus, and in its essence intrinsically in the form that gives it definition. Each case of self-expression entails use of a word, and this tie of a created being to its word itself "speaks" the primordial tie of Divine being to Word. From this primordial tie simultaneously arises the resolution consequent to an expression of truth, a delight, that completes the uncreated Trinity. This, Grosseteste argues in *Hexameron* 14, is best at explicating the nature of the Trinity for our minds. Philosophers recognize that the same essence is at once possible intellect, agent intellect, and will, which relation of distinction within one thing is analogous, as Augustine holds, and as grammarians and logicians have long recognized.[74] Other scientists, including rhetoricians, arithmeticians, geometricians, astronomers, and so on, all recognize echoes of the Trinity in the created order.

The *Moderni*, by whom Wyclif most likely means Wodeham, Holcot, and their followers, disregard this truth by denying the truth of universals in things, departing from "the ancients" and causing them to misunderstand distinctions within the divine being. The Johannine

---

[73] Grosseteste, *Hexameron* 8.4.4–6, pp. 226–27.
[74] *De Trinitate* 6, p. 61.

phrase "the word was with God" must be understood as positing a distinction between God the speaker and God the word, and John's silence regarding the Holy Spirit here should not be taken as indicative of ignorance of Its identity with G(f) and G(s), see 1 John 5:8.[75] The Holy Spirit is, in fact, the means by which we understand God, as the Gospels affirm repeatedly. To imagine that we see other gods than the Triune God is indeed the grievous sin against the Holy Spirit described in Mark 3:29. Wyclif describes the uncreated Trinity as manifested first in the being of G(s), the second person.

> I believe that John, naming the Son of God 'word', was intending the entire sentence philosophically said about the utterance of the reality, and was intending deep subtlety and through the threefold generation of the word, [was showing] the word [itself] to be threefold: first, the mind concealed and consubstantial with God in the speaking which can be known through the first phrase, 'in the beginning was the word.' The second word is accidental within the speaking as elicited knowledge which can be known through the second phrase, 'the word was with God.' The third is the word spoken from outside, as by the voice or through a work, and this can be known through the third phrase, in which 'the word was made flesh.' These three manners of words are grouped together in Him, and there is no speciousness with this truth, which is the highest spirit expressing itself to be truth, of past or future, either by negation or logical possibility or any other hypothetical truth.[76]

---

[75] This is the famous trinitarian passage proven to be a later addition to the letter by Erasmus. The text of 1 John 5:7–8 in the Latin Vulgate read "There are three on earth that bear witness, the Spirit, the water and the blood, and these three are one. *There are three that bear record in Heaven, the Father, the Word and the Holy Spirit, and these three are One.*" The latter, italicized sentence Erasmus expunged as not original to the Greek. Breck refers to this passage as 1 John 7 without further reference.

[76] *De Trinitate*, p. 74: "Hoc tamen credo quod beatus Johannes nominans filium dei 'verbum' intendebat totam sentenciam philosophiam predicatam de dicencia rei et longe subtiliorem intendebat et per triplicem generacionem verbi, triplex esse verbum: primum mentis magis abditum quod est consubstanciale ipsi dicenti quod notari potest per primam proposicionem, in principio erat verbum. Secundum verbum est accidentale intus dictum ut noticia elicita quod notari potest per secundam proposicionem verbum erat apud deum. Tercium est verbum adextra dictum ut vox vel opus et hoc notari potest per terciam proposcionem in hoc enim quod verbum caro factum est. Congregantur enim in eo omnes iste tres maneries verborum, nec est color apud istam veritatem, que est summum spiritum dicere se esse veritatem, de preterito vel de futuro aut negacionem vel posse logicum vel aliam veritatem hypoteticam."

2.6. *Referring to a (Formally Distinct) Divine Person*

At this point, we must concentrate our attention on how the divine persons are related to one another, and how these relations are described. If God the Father [G(f)] generates God the Son [G(s)], meaning that God generates God, God would have to be distinct from God insofar as Son and Father differ. Otherwise, insofar as G(f) is not the same as G(s), then God is not God. Three results follow. First, God differs from God. Second, God is distinct from God but not different because that would entail real distinction in material essence. Third, God is neither different nor distinct from God.

Regarding the first, holding "God is different from God" would be to say that God is not the same as [God (f), God (s), God (hs)], and the Trinity is other than God. Or if God (f) is not the same as God (s), then God the Trinity differs from God (a Person). If God is not the same as God, then the difference either lies in number within God, or somehow outside of God, with a distinct God. The former, that there is a difference in number within God, cannot be held, but the latter leads to a difference between God as God and God (a Person). The problem rests in how we use the term 'God'. If the analogy were to a man, in that "Fred" refers to Fred the material body and also to Fred's soul, then God differing from God could work because in man body differs from soul in the same man. But 'God' cannot refer to God as such and God (a Person) in this way, because there is one and only one God; nothing can demonstrate real difference within Him, otherwise my God [God (Father)] might have something (generation) that your God [God (Son)] lacks. So, Wyclif, argues, this first suggestion cannot be the way to describe the relation of God to the Trinity of persons in God.

Denying the second (God is distinct from God but not different) entails looking at how to use the personal distinction. John Damascene holds that the three persons differ in number, not nature, while Augustine holds God (the Son) differs from God (the Father) by causality. Who can understand what supports theological truth when the authorities obviously use reference schemes that vary according to their needs? "If a friend is said to be 'another me', how much more is the Son who is the same essence by number with the Father said to be another self!"[77] What of the case of where A thinks of

---

[77] *De Trinitate*, p. 137: "Si enim amicus figurative dicitur 'alter ego', quanto magis

God (Father), B thinks of God (Son) and C of God (Holy Spirit)? Are what each understands different in themselves? Augustine argues that when one person of the Trinity is named, the other two are contained in the essence of the subject of the predication, even if the 'personal' supposition suggests otherwise.[78] Scriptural examples abound, Wyclif continues, in which the need to recognize that [God (f), God (s), God (hs)] is meant when predicating of God (a Person). The term 'person' is not proportionate to 'incommunicable thing.' We must not risk confusing predication of person with predication of essence, Wyclif says, and the means of avoiding the confusion lies in recognizing the need for the formal distinction.

The Divine essence is not caused, communicable, and neither begotten nor begetting. A Divine person is caused, not communicable, and either begotten or begetting. There must be some means of distinguishing between essence and person, and Wyclif follows Scotus and Ockham in invoking the formal distinction to distinguish between them—not that the person is not the essence (or the essence the person) but that the person is not formally convertible with the essence. $G(f)$ is distinct from divine essence in that $G(f)$ is not communicable, while the divine essence is communicable.[79] "I know that the universal is prior by nature to its singular such that any singular whatsoever is bound by it. But it is not thus of the divine nature with regard to its supposit (i.e. [$G(f)$, $G(s)$, $G(hs)$]; but of personal causation there is disagreement, as some concede that the Father precedes the Son in principle but does not cause Him. I think the Father properly causes the Son and both together cause the Holy Spirit, and all three are the first cause of all things."[80]

Augustine agrees, holding that God is the cause of all, including His wisdom; both are the cause of all else sempiternally. Chrysostom holds that $G(f)$ is prior to $G(s)$ not by nature but by cause, and this

---

filius qui est eadem essencia numero cum patre dicitur alter ipse!" A rare Ciceronian reference in Wyclif.

[78] Augustine, *De Trinitate*, 1, p. 2.

[79] Wyclif's use of the formal distinction is by no means uncommon; Adam Wodeham's position is far more fully developed, perhaps because of his more austere ontology. See Hester Goodenough Gelber, *Logic and Trinity: A Clash of Values in Scholastic Thought, 1300–1335* (Ph.D. diss., University of Wisconsin, 1974), pp. 234–64.

[80] *De Trinitate*, p. 143 Compare to *De ente primo in communi* 4, pp. 92–94. Thomson summarizes Wyclif's argument here as denying a formal distinction between persons, (see p. xxxii), but I think this is inaccurate.

is confirmed by Grosseteste, who argues in *De libero arbitrio* that there is no procession in the Godhead, and no causation save that of creation. Grosseteste reports Hilarion as saying that the Father is greater than the Son not through the Son being Incarnated but through Filiation, but to hold that the Son is thus less than the Father is wrong. Grosseteste strives to find agreement between Augustine, Chrysostom, and Hilarion; we ought to emulate him! "Would that the *Moderni* writing now would attend to the words and sense of this good man, whose intention was to agree with the ancient teachers by collecting their catholic senses and expositing them in pious and favorable sense—and not by arguing against dead men in equivocation to equal them in their writing and so be exalted. Very many are guilty of this today."[81]

2.7. *Generation Within God: Wyclif's Commentary on* I Sent. *D.5*

The fullest theological analysis of the treatise lies in Wyclif's exploration of the question 'how can God generate in one person and be generated in another person without compromise in the absolute unity of the divine essence?'. This takes its root in Lombard's fifth distinction of the first book of the *Sententiae*, but the discussion is as much about how language functions in explicating the subtle ontological relations within the divine essence as it is about the relations themselves.[82] Further complicating matters, Wyclif occasionally looks ahead to addressing the metaphysics of Incarnation in this discussion, and refers back again to this discussion in *De Incarnacione*, prompting us to pay close attention to his explanation of how theological language depicts divine reality.[83] Careful analysis of Wyclif's argument on the subject would involve exploring the Trinitarian position of Adam Wodeham; Hester Gelber's study of Wodeham and

---

[81] *De Trinitate*, p. 145: "Utinam moderni scribentes attenderent ad verba et sensus huius boni hominis, cuius intencio fuit concordare antiquos doctores colligendo sensus eorum catholicos et exponendo eos ad sensum pium ac favoabilem. Non enim arguendo contra homines mortuos ad sensus equivocos ut scripture eorum subpeditentur et scripture sic arguencium exaltentur. Sic enim faciun hodie culpabiliter nimis multi."

[82] In Lombard the question is *Hic quaeritur an Pater genuit divinam essentiam vel ipsa Filium, an essentia genuit essentiam vel ipsa nec genuit nec genita est*. Peter Lombard, *Sententiae* 1, dist.5, c.1, (Grottaferrata, 1971), p. 80.

[83] See *De Incarnacione* 9, pp. 150–1.

Holcot's thought lays the foundation for what would be a very welcome comparison between the two great lights of early fourteenth-century Oxford and Wyclif.[84]

One problem that has arisen historically in understanding how the persons are distinct from one another yet identical in the divine essence has been counting the number of entities involved. Are there three, or four, or more? That is, by 'God' do we mean the set [G(f),G(s),G(hs)] or the set {divine essence + [G(f), G(s), G(hs)]}? "There are three divine persons, as there are three things, anyone of which is God. A person is singular when it cannot be communicated to many supposits. The essence is not four things but any of these three . . . The Trinity is not a single of these but all three of these at once."[85] This Wyclif has discussed in *Purgans errores circa universalia in commune.*

> In predication according to essence the singular and its universal are distinct across the board, since the singular is one, as the universal another individual. It does not follow, 'these are distinct things, so to these we assign number' because through most general and most singular demonstrating of its supposit, any things distinct are these, yet they are not held numerable, since one of them remains. Thus they are distinct formally, but not formally distinct things. Nor are they formally 'these two' [indicating this universal and this singular] but they are *this*, and so the differences are to this sense, that these differ, but not through numerical difference are they formally thus; because only by difference formally or according to reason are they 'these'.[86]

---

[84] Hester Gelber, 1974, esp. pp. 235–317.

[85] *De Trinitate*, p. 149: "Sicut ergo tantum sunt tres persona divine, sic tantum sunt tres res quarum quelibet est deus. Persona enim est singularium possibile cum non potest communicari multis suppositis. Essencia igitur non est quarta res sed quelibet harum trium . . . Trinitas vero est non singula harum trium sed omnes tres simul."

[86] *Purgans errores circa universalia in communis, De ente I Tractatus IV,* 5, p. 47/7–22: "Conceditur eciam in predicacione secundum essenciam quod singulare et suum universale sunt quotlibet distincta, cum singulare sit unum, ut universale quotlibet alia individua. Non ergo sequitur: ista sunt res distincte, vel res distincta sunt ista, ergo ista ponunt in numerum, quia demonstrato generalissimo et singularissimo eius supposito, quotlibet res distinct sunt ista, et tamen non ponunt in numerum, cum unum eorum sit reliquum. Et ita ista sunt distincta formaliter, sed non formaliter res distincte. Nec ista sunt formaliter 'ista duo' (demonstrando singulare et suum universale) set sunt 'istud': et sic differencia sunt ista ad istum sensum, quod ista differunt, et tamen nulla numeraliter differencia sunt formaliter ista: quia solum differencia formaliter vel secuncum racionem sunt ista."

If you take Peter and God, you have two; since God is three in one, you also have four. If you count natures, you have two in Peter (body and spirit) and one (Deity), thus three. It follows, then, that 3 and 4 make 2! Obviously, number breaks down as an effective tool of quantification in understanding the divine nature.

A century and a half earlier, Joachim of Fiore wrote a (now lost) treatise criticizing Peter Lombard's innovative analysis of how terms refer to the persons within the Trinity. The Calabrian claimed that Lombard's description of a Trinity that neither begets nor is begotten entailed a fourth entity in addition to the three divine persons. Lombard had emphasized the impossibility of attributing particular actions of the divine persons to the divine essence, and caused Joachim consternation by having used the term 'essence' to mean something other than 'person' or 'hypostasis.' Joachim himself was rebuked by the Fourth Lateran Council for conceiving of the divine unity as a collective, or group of individual persons, guilty of an inability to appreciate Lombard's nuance in reference.[87] He erred, Wyclif explains, by confusing the reference of terms predicated of the divine essence, and terms predicated of persons.

Unlike any other essence-bearing thing, the Divine essence generates Itself; Lombard holds that there is a sense in which essence begets essence as Father begets Son, and another sense in which essence is begotten by essence, as Son is begotten by Father. Some problems arise from this. First, if there is a sense in which G(f) begets the divine essence, and the divine essence includes the being of G(f), then the subset is causally prior to the set. Second, if G(f) understands the begetting, then if G(s) is divine understanding, it must follow that understanding precedes understanding. Third, if there is a sense in which the divine essence neither begets nor is begotten, then in that sense there are four beings referred to by God: The begetting Father, the begotten Son, the spirated Holy Spirit, and the un-begotten non-begetter, a "Quaternity". The Church, Wyclif declares, was right to condemn this line of reasoning about the Lombard.

---

[87] Joachim's *De Unitate seu Essentia Trinitatis* has not been found, and given Wyclif's apparently loose formulation of Joachim's errors, it appears not to have been available to him at Oxford. Joachim's problem lies in his reading of *Sententiae* 1, D.25, c.2. See Giles Emery, *Trintiy in Aquinas* (Ypsilanti, 2003), pp. 12–13.

Any determination of the Church, and especially in matters of faith, is as much to be believed as is the gospel. Something should not be believed to be the saying of Christ or scripturally revealed from the meaning of the Holy Spirit unless brought to bear from information or faith by the Church. So it is right naturally and more to trust the Church as authority, and placed in that state by biblical canon, to be a bold delegate in whatever way by authority of Scripture, as would a sentence spoken by the Savior in any of the gospels boldly pronounce that this sentence would be true because they are the words of Christ.[88]

Wyclif's problem lies not with Joachim, though; his argument is with those who allow linguistic subtlety to derail theological accuracy, although as elsewhere, he names no names in this chapter. The philosophical problem rests in the relation between the divine essence and the generating occurring within the essence. The absolute nature of the divine essence precludes generating or being generated, so the presence of this generating holding between Father and Son cannot be essential to God. Yet to hold that the essence is something beyond the generating and the being generated of the persons seems to lead to positing a Quaternity, a fourth divine being beyond the generating, the generated, and the spirated persons.

At this point it is easy to get lost in the dense thicket of arguments and distinctions around which Wyclif frames his analysis of the problem. Rather than recount each dispute apparent in the chapter, it will be more useful to frame the discussion in terms of a logical phenomenon Desmond P. Henry has recently described.[89] Henry suggests that a useful means of understanding how Wyclif departs from standard medieval thought is through analysis of his mereology, or his understanding of how aggregate or collective terms stand

---

[88] *De Trinitate*, pp. 159–60: "[C]uilibet determinacioni ecclesie et specialiter ein materia fidei est tante credendum sicut evangelio. Patet ex hoc quod non crederetur aliquid esse dictum Christi vel scripture sacre ex sentencia spiritus sancti revelatum nisi ex informacione et fide adhibita ecclesie, ergo prius naturaliter et plus oportet credere ecclesie quam auctoritati et de canone Biblie tamquam loco ab auctoritate ut allegata protervo quacumque auctoritate ut sentencia Salvatoris in quocumque evangelio protervius diceret quod illa sentencia esset vera si esset dictum Christi." This early estimation of the Church's role in regulating dogma at Lateran IV differs markedly from Wyclif's later opinion. See *De Apostasia* 5, p. 69.19–26, wherein he suggests that Joachim had detected defects in the Church and was condemned for largely personal reasons.

[89] D.P. Henry, "Wyclif's Deviant Mereology," *Die Philosophie im 14. Und 15. Jahrhundert*, ed. Olaf Pluta (Amsterdam, 1988), pp. 1–17.

for aggregate beings. It is normal for us to say something like "The Union is preserved!" without presuming there to be something above and apart from the collection of things we call the Union. Wyclif's approach, on the other hand, was to reason that there is an aggregate with identifiable ontological reality that arises from any set of two substantial beings. What follows from this is that for any set of three people (Peter, Paul, and Linus), there are four aggregate beings: the three ordered pairs derived from the set, and the universal Humanity defining each particularized humanity of each member. There cannot be more than this, he argues, for each aggregate being can only arise from substantially real beings.[90] Wyclif devotes considerable effort to refuting the predictable Third Man arguments arising from his position throughout De universalibus, and uses the reality of aggregate beings in his descriptions of how 'a certain man' in the parable of the Good Samaritan serves as an aggregate for all saved people, among other things. Still, Henry remains puzzled as to why Wyclif would have made such an ontological claim, suggesting that the grounds for such a baroque ontology have yet to be identified. His point is well taken; earlier in De universalibus Wyclif objects to Burley's contention that universals are things apart from their particulars, which would put Wyclif in the majority who believed universals to be real, but not really distinct from their particulars.[91] Why, then, would he attribute reality to aggregate beings derivable from any set of two particular objects?

It is possible that evidence for an answer to this question lies in De universalibus 11, where he presents a streamlined description of the argument of De Trinitate 16. Here he says that Joachim's ignorance of the way Universals function led him to conclude that the set [G(f), G(s), G(hs)] is not a true unity, but a collective unity of resemblance, in the way in which many men are a single population.[92] Had he recognized that the Trinity, "that common thing" is what each divine person is, that Itself It neither begets nor is begotten, but contains persons that beget and are begotten and spirated, just as a Universal

---

[90] See De universalibus 9. For a brief, accessible discussion, see Trialogus 2.1.

[91] Ibid., 4, p. 28/50. For Burley's view, which appears closer to Wyclif's than Wyclif might admit, see Elizabeth Karger, "Walter Burley's Realism," Vivarium 37 (1999), 24–40.

[92] Ibid., 11, p. 119/611–17.

like Humanity neither is seated nor is not seated, but contains individuals who are one or the other but not both, his objections would have vanished.[93] There is a sense, Wyclif continues, in which one can say that God begets, or God is begotten, if one refers with the term 'God' to G(f) or G(s) through personal supposition. "But you must not believe that because of the acceptance of these terms, the divine nature begets or does not beget the Son."[94] The more appropriate way of understanding the term 'God' is as referring to that which neither begets nor is begotten; he refers the reader to Avicenna's "*equinitas non est aliquid nisi equinitas tantum*" to encourage our understanding that such universal terms as 'Man', 'Animal', and 'God' refer first and foremost to the universals prior to their instantiates.[95]

As noted earlier, Wyclif is painstaking in his articulation of the idea that the divine essence is a universal of which the divine persons are instantiates. In *De universalibus* he emphasizes that no other universal thinks or acts upon others, and while with all other universals, the particular is ontologically consequent upon the universal, with God, "the nature is not prior to nor more perfect than the person."[96] Further, in the related discussion in *De Trinitate* 16, he says "there is a difference between nature of the universal and the divine nature, because the divine nature moves every created action, but the nature of the universal only causes every action of its supposits."[97] Aware that this same issue would figure in his treatise on the Incarnation, he notes that terms that refer within God to G(s) do not import universals from creation into the divine essence. "If it is conceded that man is God in this way, it must then be conceded that humanity would be deity and that humanity is eternal but deity temporal according to which the Son is less than the Father, and just as the divine essence is common to three persons and consequently a Trinity, thus a man would be common to the three persons and there would be a confusion of persons, since [the essence]

---

[93] This is the substance of Wyclif's argument; the example is my own.

[94] Ibid., p. 120/648.

[95] Ibid., p. 120/655–61; reference is to Avicenna, *Philosophia prima* tract.5, cap. 1, cited in Mueller's edition of *De univeralibus* p. 265.

[96] *De universalibus* p. 121/719.

[97] *De Trinitate*, 16, p. 163: "Et in hoc est differencia inter naturam universalem et naturam divinam, quia natura divina agit omnem accionem creature, natura autem universalis causat omnem accionem sui sarsrrspositi." See also above, n. 58.

would not have been held as common, and he would be a singular in the essence of these persons."[98] Wyclif mentions this issue only in passing, but understanding the relation of the universal 'Man' to God the Son in the Incarnation lies at the very heart of his treatise *De Verbi Incarnacione*, to which we now turn.

3. An Overview of Wyclif's Christology

3.1. Historical Context

Our understanding of fourteenth-century Oxford theologians' arguments about the ontology and logic of the Incarnation is considerably less than it might be. Prior to Wyclif, Ockham appears the last to have made a contribution to what had been a mainstay of thirteenth-century theology. In his pared-down ontology, he rejects the existence of a common nature like humanity apart from individual people. But this easily leads to understanding him to have held that in Christ was an individual human person in addition to the divine nature, making up either a two-person person (that is, the human person Jesus, and with the added Word, the person of the Christ), or a Christ in which a human person and the divine person of the Word are not united by anything into a third composite. Ockham was aware that he could be interpreted as having advocating Nestorianism, and argued vigorously against this interpretation, but the tendency amongst opponents of Ockham's christology seems to have been to press the Nestorian interpretation as the only comprehensible reading of his approach.[99] As we will see, Wyclif's approach is

---

[98] *De Trinitate* 16, pp. 163–64: "Ymmo si conceditur quod homo est deus ita concedendum est quod humanitas esset deitas et quod humanitas est eterna sed deitas temporalis secundum quam filius est minor patre, et sicut essencia divina est communis tribus personis et per consequens trinitas, sic homo esset communis illis tribus personis et esset confusio personarum cum non haberetur ut commune et esset singula illarum personarum essencia."

[99] For the historical evidence of Ockham's struggles against the label of Nestorianism, see Heiko Oberman, *Harvest of Medieval Theology* (Cambridge Mass, 1963), pp. 249–61. For philosophical analysis of Ockham's christology, see Marilyn McCord Adams, "Relations, Inherence and Subsistence: or, Was Ockham a Nestorian in Christology?" *Nous* 16 (1982), 62–75. Her assessment is that Ockham's christology bows to the needs of orthodoxy, a rare instance of his privileging theology over ontological consistency.

to argue both for the existence of a human nature apart from individual people, and for the existence of an aggregate man, a composite of body and soul distinct from both.

Regarding others of Wyclif's predecessors, Nicholas Aston, no fan of Ockham's ontology, appears to have read the *Sentences* after 1350, and he addresses several Christological issues. His treatment of "Whether uncreated Truth could sustain hypostatic union with created truth?" might well contribute significantly to understanding Christological controversy in Oxford during the years just prior to Wyclif's.[100] Another question, "Whether one person incarnated from another not incarnate could be a truth defended by a Catholic?", appears only in Gaudet's summary.[101] Uthred of Boldon, the Benedictine whose opinions aroused an uproar as Wyclif began the *Summa de ente*, appears not to figure in this issue, as none of the censured opinions address the question of the Incarnation directly.[102] In all likelihood, the richest source for Ockhamist arguments against which Wyclif would argue in *De Incarnacione* would be the works of Robert Holcot, (d. 1349) and Adam Wodeham (d. 1358). Unfortunately, neither of these theologians' christological works have been edited.

Holcot was famous as the eminent Dominican theologian in Oxford, and his works were studied well into the sixteenth century. Holcot's theological position is not easy to delineate with terms familiar to the twenty-first century reader. Leonard Kennedy emphasizes his tendency to philosophical skepticism, suggesting that his position inspired with those of Nicholas of Autrecourt and John of Mirecourt.[103]

---

[100] Robson's description of Aston's approach suggests less attention to ontological questions than Wyclif shows, see Robson, pp. 106–108. For a more recent assessment of Aston's place at Oxford, see Courtenay, *School and Scholars*, pp. 334–5, n. 17. Most significantly, see Kaluza, "L'oeuvre Théologique de Nicolas Aston," where he describes Oriel 15 as containing 12 questions of Aston, of which the first is the question listed above. He appends the description of Etienne Gaudet, an early sixteenth-century scholar of English scholasticism, of Aston's works, in which the topics covered in this question are listed, see p. 75. See also Courtenay, *Schools and Scholars*, p. 353, Trapp, "Augustinian Theology of the Fourteenth Century," pp. 230–231.

[101] See Bender, p. 21.

[102] D. Knowles, "The Censured Opinions of Uthred of Boldon," *Proceedings of the British Academy* 37 (1951), 303–42.

[103] Leonard A. Kennedy's *The Philosophy of Robert Holcot, Fourteenth-century Skeptic* (Lewiston, 1993) emphasizes Holcot's influence on the positions of Autrecourt and Mirecourt, condemned in 1346 and 47. "Since Holcot was one of the leading Oxonians to be read on the Continent in the 1340s, and since the doctrines of

Others argue that equating Holcot's unwillingness to recognize human logic's applicability to theological truths is less indicative of skepticism than it is of his evolving understanding of the right approach to ordering reason in the life of faith.[104] Kennedy describes Holcot's christology very briefly, noting that he devoted only a half-page to the Incarnation in his 248 page *Sentences* commentary, and appends a *Quodlibet* (58) 'Whether God can make an impeccable rational nature' to his study.[105] Here Holcot says, "Although the rational creature could be placed in such a disposition such that he could not sin for the time in which he has it, yet this is not to say that he could not sin when the disposition is removed. And so, simply speaking, he is peccable. And so commonly it is said that a creature is made impeccable through grace, not nature."[106] Kennedy describes Holcot as having argued that, had Christ set aside that assumed nature, which was for Him possible, that it could have sinned. Indeed, there is no contradiction in holding that God could have united with a sinful and damned nature, in which case God could be both blessed and damned at once.[107]

I think it likely that Kennedy's description of Holcot's christology is unnecessarily abbreviated, as at least seven earlier *Quodlibet*s address Incarnational theology directly.[108] These include (2) Whether the Son of God assumed the human nature in unity of the supposit?, (4) Whether the history of the conception of Christ is true in totality?, (7) Whether Christ suitably redeemed the genus of humanity?, (8) Whether divinity is a part of Christ?, (9) Whether the incarnate

---

Nicholas and John were akin to his, it is most likely that his influence on them was great, even if it was reinforced by that of many other writers." (p. 139.)

[104] Heiko Oberman, "*Facientibus Quod in Se est Deus non Denegat Gratiam*: Robert Holcot O.P. and the Beginnings of Luther's Theology," *Harvard Theological Review* 55 (1962), 317–42, reprinted in his *The Dawn of the Reformation* (Grand Rapids, 1992), pp. 84–103. See also Gelber, *Exploring the Boundaries of Reason*; and Simo Knuuttila, "Trinitarian Sophisms in Robert Holcot's Theology", in *Sophisms in Medieval Logic and Grammar*, ed. Stephen Read (Dordrecht, 1993), pp. 348–56.

[105] Kennedy, pp. 107–109, and Appendix 4, pp. 164–67.

[106] Kennedy, p. 166: "Licet ergo creatura rationalis posset poni in tali dispositione qua stante non posset peccare pro tempore pro quo eam habet, non tamen fit per hoc talis natura quin poterit peccare, illa dispositione ablata. Et ideo, simpliciter loquendo, ipsa est peccabilis. Et ideo communiter dicitur quod creatura potest fieri impeccabilis per gratiam, non per naturam."

[107] Kennedy, p. 107. These he has culled from said *Quodlibet, Sent* 3, q.1 a.5, and *Sent.III*, q.2, a.6.

[108] Richard Gillespie, "Robert Holcot's *Quodlibeta*," *Traditio* 27 (1971), 480–90.

Christ would have been given had man not sinned? (10) Whether the human will in Christ had conformity with the divine willing?, and (12) Whether Christ established his resurrection through suitable demonstration?[109] Exploring Holcot's arguments in these questions will likely provide a much fuller view of his suitability as a likely opponent of Wyclif in *De Incarnacione*.

Wodeham had a reputation as the equal of Scotus and Ockham, and as an ardent defender of the latter. There are two sources available of Wodeham's thought regarding christology, both arranged in accord with the scheme of the *Sententiae*. The earlier, the Norwich lectures of 1329 and 1332 are briefer, but available in a recently published edition.[110] The later, more theologically complete are the *Oxford Lectures* of 1332, which has yet to be published; William Courtenay provides as an appendix to his study of Wodeham a list of questions from a *reportatio* of the *Oxford Lectures* and from a subredaction of the first book of the *Ordinatio*, showing considerable attention to christology.[111] Until further work on Wyclif's predecessors yields fruit, then, we will have to settle for a summary of Wyclif's christology with little historical context.

Recently, Richard Cross has suggested a useful means of sorting out models for the hypostatic union of God and man in Christ. Some approaches, notably Peter Abelard and Thomas Aquinas, involve recognizing divinity and humanity as being arranged as parts that make up the whole Christ. Peter Lombard described three approaches in *Sententiae* 3.6. In the first, the Word clothed Himself with human nature as a man wears a cloak; this is the *habitus* theory, suggested by Augustine. In the second, a man composed of body and soul was assumed by the Word so that he became identical with the Word; this is the *assumptus homo* theory, endorsed by Hugh of St. Victor and Anselm. In the third, Christ begins to be composed of divinity and (body and soul) in a subsistence relation; this appears

---

[109] Gillespie, p. 487 *2. Utrum Filius Dei assumpsit naturam humanam in unitatem suppositi? 4. Utrum historia conceptionis Christi sit in tota vera? 7. Utrum Christus convenienter redemit genus humanum? 8. Utrum divinitas sit pars Christi? 9. Utrum Christus incarnatus fuisset dato quod homo non peccasset? 10. Utrum voluntas humana in Christo fuit divinae voluntati conformis? 12. Utrum Christus probavit resurrectionem suam convenientibus argumentis?*

[110] Adam Wodeham, *Lectura Secunda*.

[111] See William Courtenay, *Adam Wodeham*, pp. 183–209. See also Rega Wood, "Adam Wodeham," in *A Companion to Philosophy in the Middle Ages*, pp. 77–85.

to have been Lombard's approximation of the position of Gilbert of Poitiers.[112] Aquinas understood both the *habitus* and the *assumptus homo* position as having been condemned by Pope Alexander III in 1170 and 1177, and supposed any theory in which Christ's Humanity is described as accident to have been heretical. Others, including Bonaventure, Giles of Rome, Henry of Ghent, and Scotus, use a "substance-accident" model, in which Christ's Humanity is related to the Word as an accident or property is related to its substance. Ockham's ontology, in which a nature like 'Humanity' is a concept naturally referring to a concrete individual or individuals, denies any sort of further reality to what his predecessors called universals.[113] Given Wyclif's endorsement of a richer realist ontology than most pre-Ockham theologians would have dared embrace, it will likely be best to see him as reacting primarily against Ockham's ontology, using the Scotist "substance-accident" model for his more full-bodied ontological articulation of Humanity being assumed by the Word.

3.2. *What makes a Man?* De composicione hominis *as Prologue*

R.W. Southern describes Robert Grosseteste's *De cessatione legalium* as being a much more profound expression of medieval humanism than Anselm's *Cur Deus homo*, despite its much more abstract argument. This is because Grosseteste envisioned the Incarnation differently than Anslem; it is not rooted in man's having sinned beyond any other form of redemption, but instead is the "final act in the unfolding drama of creation: it made Man and Nature complete, and it bound the whole created universe together in union with God."[114] Grosseteste is notable for having argued that the Incarnation woud have occurred even had man not sinned, on the reasoning that the Incarnation benefits all creation, and to make its occurrence a response

---

[112] Richard Cross, *The Metaphysics of the Incarnation Thomas Aquinas to Duns Scotus* (Oxford, 2002), pp. 1–26. See Lauge Olaf Nielsen, *Theology and Philosophy in the Twelfth Century* (Leiden, 1982), pp. 193ff. for detailed discussion of the period's christology. For Lombard's christology, see Colish, pp. 398–470; also Rosemann, pp. 118–43.

[113] Ockham's approach is best described, I believe, in terms of what today is called trope nominalism. See my "William Ockham and Trope Nominalism," *Franciscan Studies* 55 (1998), 105–20.

[114] R.W. Southern, *Medieval Humanism* (New York, 1970), p. 49. Reference is to Robert Grosseteste, *De cessatione legalium*, c. 1235.

to sin gives it a comparatively diminished place in the order of creation.[115] If we were to assume that Wyclif's title, *De Incarnacione*, is meant to evoke a primarily Anselmian Christology, we would be very mistaken. Anselm's account in *De Incarnacione Verbi* contains very little about what human nature entails, and how it can be assumed by the Word, while Wyclif's account focuses almost exclusively on this subject. Again, Anselm argues extensively for substitutionary atonement in *Cur Deus homo*, emphasizing man's great unpayable debt to God, while Wyclif says comparatively little on the subject.[116] Wyclif's understanding of the Incarnation is more similar to Grosseteste's, who was known as much for his careful scientific understanding of the created world as for his theological acumen.[117] Hence, Wyclif's conception of the ontological make-up of the human person deserves our attention before we can understand how he envisioned the Word becoming a man.

Wyclif likely wrote *De composicione hominis* in 1372, the same year as *De Incarnacione*.[118] He gives three reasons for approaching the subject matter: moral theory relies on a clear understanding of the relation of soul to body, knowledge of this relation of soul to body is the key to understanding the more subtle elements of the faith, and the relation provides insight into what just human *dominium* entails. Of these, only the second reason figures in the treatise, and straightaway Wyclif proceeds to the kind of mereological concern that D.P. Henry mentioned. Scripture shows us, Wyclif argues, that the human soul is a created spirit itself indivisible, able to be unified to

---

[115] See James McEvoy, *Robert Grosseteste* (Oxford, 2000), pp. 127–30.

[116] *De Incarnacione* 6 ed. E. Harris (London, 1886), p. 90 contains his assertion, following Anselm, that because a member of the genus man sinned, a member of the genus would have to redeem that sin. But this is an aside in his explanation as to how Christ is really man.

[117] Wyclif cites Grosseteste not at all in *De composicione hominis*, ed. Rudolf Beer (London, 1904), but frequently in *De Materia et Forma* and elsewhere. A study of Wyclif's theological anthropology in light of Grosseteste's thought would be useful.

[118] Note that neither of these treatises are included in the traditional contents of the *Summa de ente*. Robson describes the arrangement of the *Summa*'s treatises as being first to explicate the metaphysical basis for Wyclif's theology and second to treat the range of questions commonly discussed at Oxford. He describes DCH as a "conflation of Wyclif's opinions on universals and the Trinity and Incarnation, which he had expressed more fully elsewhere." (Robson, p. 139) I think it better to consider DCH and DI as complementary works, and would argue that envisioning Wyclif as emulating Grosseteste's theological anthropology would help considerably in reversing Beer's and Robson's low opinion of DCH's relative worth.

a body, which union results in the integrated human being. Both Augustine and Anselm say that just as the divine essence is a trinity of three singular natures, so in the Incarnation, the same person is three distinct natures—divine nature, human soul, and a body. And by this, it is clear that a man is soul, flesh, and the union of the two. Such a trinity must be unavoidable, the aggregate of (body+soul), which Wyclif calls the integrated nature, having ontological status commensurate to the two considered in themselves.[119]

The created spirit, or soul, animating our corporeal body is what allows us foothold on the horizon of eternity; according to its lower nature, directed to the body, what is real is what is sensible, while according to its higher nature, directed to eternal truths, the reality of intelligible forms shines through.[120] Soul differs from uncreated spirit in three ways. First, the uncreated spirit is the prime creating essence, while the other is accidental to that creator. Second, uncreated spirit is the Word, having being from itself, while created spirit has being from another. Finally, uncreated spirit is beyond all single natural laws, while the created spirit is subject to these laws. The Incarnation did not involve the uncreated spirit assuming a created spirit. "[T]he divine word is said significantly actively to assume a body for itself, not a human spirit, but a human body, which God in the eternal plan had provided that it be joined hypostatically to His creature . . ."[121]

He reports *Moderni* critics of his position as responding with the argument, 'This man is this incorporeal nature, this man is this corporeal nature, therefore the incorporeal nature is the corporeal nature.' Confusing identities in numeration across ontological boundaries, Wyclif retorts, is the cause of constant misunderstanding for these philosophers, commenting that he has dealt with the philosophical grounding for the proper understanding of identity in *De universalibus*.[122]

---

[119] Wyclif refers the reader to *De Civitate Dei* 13.24.2.

[120] *DCH* 1, p. 8.9–18. The phrase "in orizonte eternitatis" is from *Liber de causis* 2, n.22; for earlier use of the phrase in describing the soul's place, see Thomas Aquinas, *Commentary on the Book of Causes*, trans. V.A. Guaglairdo, C.R. Hess and Richard Taylor (Washington, D.C., 1996), p. 17.

[121] *DCH* 1, p. 9/6–10: "[E]t hinc verbum divinum dicitur significanter active assumere sibi corpus, spiritus autem humanus non sic, sed corpori, quod deus eterno consilio disponit a suo creatore ypostatice copulari . . ."

[122] *DCH* 1, p. 10/19. Reference is to *Tractatus De universalibus* 1; see Paul Spade's "Introduction," especially his discussion of Wyclif's theory of identity and distinction,

For just as the nature of the universal is any of its supposits or singulars, which are united in that common being, thus the same singular thing is certainly distinct in itself, which is united with all in the same supposit of species; as any man is a spiritual nature who has a soul; he is the same corporeal nature or essence, who has a human body, and these two are incommunicably distinct. And he is a third nature from body and soul integrated, which is distinguished from both and so, if he wish the first truth, any human person, since he, as man, is completely six and divisible and thus the most perfect prime under the Sun. For by reason of soul he is three, namely memory, reason and will; and by reason of body, which is another qualitative composite part, it appears just as the soul to be three supposits, namely matter, form and their connection. Seven then, as there were seven days in the production of the world, God resting in singular and miraculous new man our Jesus Christ, who with these six would be essentially creator, will be seven . . .[123]

So given that Jesus is seven, every human being is six; three natures (two incomplete and one integrated), and numerically six because the soul has three parts, namely memory, reason, and will. Considered further, man is tenfold, just as the total universe is made up of ten categories: three natures [formal/spiritual, corporeal, and the combination], six things of two incommunicable natures [three of formal/spiritual, i.e. capable of understanding spiritual things, able to be beatified, and able to inform the body, and three of material, namely minimally cognitive, removed from beatification, and able to be formed] and the integration of all these nine which is the com-

---

and his theory of predication in John Wyclif, *On Universals*, Anthony Kenny, trans. (Oxford. 1985), pp. xx–xli.

[123] *DCH* 1, p. 11/2–23: "Nam sicut natura universalis est quodlibet surorum suppositorum vel singularium, que in illo communi quodammodo uniuntur, sic eadem res singularis est valde disparia, que omnia uniuntur in eodem supposito speciei, ut quilibet homo est natura spiritualis, cui accidit esse animam; est iterum natura vel essencia corporea, cui accidit esse corpus humanum, et hec duo incommunicabiliter sunt distincta. Et est tercio natura ex corpore et anima integrata, que distingwatur ab utraque et sic, si prima veritas velit, quelibet persona hominis, cum sit homo integer sex et divisim et sic primus perfectus numerus sublunaris. Nam racione anime est tria, scilicet memoria, racio et voluntas; et racione corporis, quod est altera pars compositi qualitativa, videtur eciam sicut anima supposita esse tria, scilicet materia, forma et earum connexio. Septimo autem, tamquam septimo die produccionis materiarum mundi, deus quiescens in singulariter ac mirabiliter novo homine domino nostro Jesu Cristo, qui cum ad ista sex sit creatrix essencia, erit septem et per consequens omnes vices creature beatificabiles in se tam efficaciter beatificans quam eciam obiective." Compare Christ as seven to the Incarnation as seventh day in Grosseteste quoted in note 139.

mon singular person. The nature composed of these two incommunicable natures is distinct from both considered in themselves. It is a quantity arising from the actualizing power of form on the potential quantity of matter, which should be distinguished as different in kind from both, just as substance is something distinct from the form and matter composing it.

Scripture tells us of the different natures contained within a man; sometimes, the term 'man' refers principally to a soul (Col. 3:10), sometimes, to a body (2 Cor. 4:16), and sometimes to the integrated combination of the two, which philosophers understand to refer to rational animal as composite of body and soul. In a fourth way, Scriptures refer to Christ as man, alternating between the previous senses while still referring to the same God-man.

> [F]or the person or for the substance, which is any of these three natures or things, or indeed all beings contracted [together], which is each of them, and in this way the faith speaks from Scripture that this Man, who created heaven and earth, was born of a virgin, conversed with men, suffered, died, and was buried, descended to hell, and ascended etc. Not according to the assumed nature did He create the kingdom, nor according to Deity did He suffer, nor according to His soul was He dead and buried, nor according to His body or other integrated nature did He descend to hell, but since the same person was all these, according to one of these He did one, and according to another He did the rest, just as it was best suitable.[124]

In a similar fashion Paul refers to his own mystical experience in 2 Cor. 12:3 as something that happened, but Paul is not sure whether it was to himself as ensouled body, or as an extra-corporeal being;

---

[124] *DCH* 1, p. 18/3–22: "[Q]uarto modo accipitur homo prop persona vel pro substancia, que est quelibet istarum trium naturarum vel rerum vel eciam omne ens contraccius, quod est aliqua earundem; et isto modo loquitur fides ex testimonio scripture, quod ille homo, qui creavit celum et terram, fuit natus de virgine, conversatus cum hominibus, passus, mortuus et sepultus, descendit at inferos et ascendit etc. Non autem secundum naturam assumptam creavit seculum nec secundum deitatem paciebatur, nec secundum animam fuit mortuus et sepultus, nec secundum corpus aut aliam naturam integram descendid ad inferos, sed cum eadem persona fuit hec omnia, secundum aliquid fecit unum, et secundum aliud fecit reliquum sicut optime congruebat; et sic loquitur 2 ad Cor.9 de se ipso: Scio, inquit, hominem huiusmodi sive in corpore, sive extra corpus nescio, deus scit, quoniam raptus est in paradiso. Ecce quod scivit se esse raptum et nescivit se in illo raptu esse se corpus vel animam; ideo sequitur, quod scivit se esse commune ad corpus et ad animam." The reference is in fact to 2 Cor. 12:3. See also *Trialogus* 2.7.

yet, Wyclif argues, the term '*hominem*' refers accurately to Paul, in whatever state he experienced paradise.

If body and soul are distinct from one another, what provides the formal basis for accidents for the body that lacks a soul? Wyclif argues for the existence of a corporeal form present in the body prior to ensoulment, but this causes the problem of there being two possible ontological beings contained in one person. One being, a body with a corporeal form considered as such, is distinct from the ensouled integrated man, yet the two are not truly distinguishable, Wyclif argues, because these coextensive bodies communicate equally in the same material essence. This rules out the possibility of an infinite regress of distinguishable essences.

The soul's relation to the body is that of an exemplary form essentially extrinsic to the body that conserves through its virtues the 'complexional form' of the body just as luminosity continually conserves light.[125] The soul requires the pre-existence of the body since its chief act is to animate a body, but not necessarily a temporal priority. In one way, the body causes the soul as material cause, but in other ways, the soul causes the body as final and efficient causality. What of formal causality? The body considered in itself has corporeal formality apart from the formal causality of the soul, which presumably imparts humanity to the body.[126]

> It appears more likely that 'this man' communicates more than 'this body and this animal' for it communicates 'this spirit', which remains human spirit existing as such, even when it no longer remains a body or an animal. It is not the case that these two [spirit and body] are the same animal or the same body in number, for the prior corporeal nature is a body and yet is not thereby an animal. Since man is all three [body, soul, integrated body+soul], he exists, after his body is dead, by virtue of the prior corporeal nature, and he is a composite, prior to being an animal, according to his corporeal nature and the soul.[127]

---

[125] *DCH* 3, p. 46/9: "conservans lumine suarum virtutum formam complexionalem corporis."

[126] This is consonant with *De universalibus* 3, p. 71/20–35.

[127] *DCH* 3, p. 48/10–22: "Ulterius tamen pro materia videtur michi probabiliter posse dici, quod iste homo plus communicatur quam hoc corpus vel hoc animal; nam iste homo communicatur isti spiritui, cum manet homo spiritu per se existente, quando non manet animal sive corpus; et sic negatur, quod ista duo sunt idem animal vel corpus idem in numero; nam prior natura corporea est corpus et

The obvious criticism is to hold that Wyclif might as well be saying that if this soul is this body because of the being of this person, one can as easily say that a man is an ass, or that deity is humanity because Christ is a human person. He refers the reader to *De universalibus* wherein he demonstrates that if this argument were allowed to proceed, anything could be anything, which cannot be so.[128] Yet the paralogism 'God is divine', 'Christ is creature', therefore 'God is creature' is not as easily addressed.

> Deity is essentially, but not formally, a man. I say essentially because the essence of our Lord Christ which He has eternally before assuming man, is deity, and this Person is man formally, because Humanity. And this appears to be denying that this deity is animal, body, and substance or creature, although it might be this [Incarnate Word], which is any of these, because through the same He would be substance and uncreated essence, and consequently a creature, which would not follow from this, that He is a man, unless He were formally a man, as Christ. So although Christ is a man, and this man would be animal and a creature, still Deity is not a man because of this being—animate Word or another creature—but because of this fact—that He is God before being any creature.[129]

This brief discussion on the relation of body and soul in man is meant only to show that Wyclif envisioned a coherent picture of human being in which to portray his understanding of the Incarnation; the reader is advised to look elsewhere for fuller consideration of his philosophical anthropology.[130]

---

non animal . . . homo autem, cum communiter sit ista tria, est post corpus mortuum secundum naturam priorem corpoream, et prius animal secundum naturam ex corpore et anima complete compositam."

[128] *De universalibus* 1, p. 9/220: "Et si sophistice instetur ex dictia sequi 'patrem esse Filium', 'Hominem esse asinum' et sic 'Quidlibet esse quidlibet'—nam in qualibet tali propositione eadem essentia significatur per subiectum et praedicatum, et hoc sufficit ad praedicationem secundum essentiam, igitur et cetera . . ."

[129] *DCH* 3, pp. 48/30–49/5: "[D]eitas est essentialiter, sed non formaliter homo; essencialiter dico, quia essencia domini nostri Jesu Cristi, quam eternaliter habet ante assumptum hominem, est deitas, et illa persona est homo formaliter, quia humanitas. Et sic videtur michi negandum, quod deitas sit animal, corpus et substancia vel creatura, quamvis sit illud, quod est quodlibet istorum, quia per idem essent substancia et essencia increata, et per consequens creatura, quod non sequeretur ex hoc, quod est homo, nisi foret homo formaliter, sicut Cristus. Ideo, quamvis Cristus sit homo, et ille homo sit animal et per consequens creatura, tamen deitas non est homo secundum illud, quod est verbum animal vel aliqua creatura, sed secundum illud, quod est deus ante quamlibet creaturam."

[130] See Emily Michael "John Wyclif on Body and Mind," *Journal of the History of Ideas* 64 (2003), 343–60.

One final element from *De composicione hominis* will add to our understanding of its place in Wyclif's christology. While discussing the relation of corporeal essence to the human form, it occurs to Wyclif to address the question of whether Christ's incarnation preceded creation, a question common in many *Sentences* Commentaries.[131] Lombard had said, 'If you look to the person [of the Word], say confidentally that this man has always been; if to the nature of man, concede him to have come into being."[132] The priority of the created human essence, or humanity as such, to all individual humans allows us to recognize individual humans as instantiations of a universal. Humanity is a universal by community; by virtue of the corporeal presence of the created human essence in Adam, all men are contained in Adam.

Does this mean that there is a sense in which I pre-exist my present existence? In the sense that each being exists in *raciones seminales* contained within first principles being actualized in the earlier creation, yes, but the level of pre-existence is extremely weak. It is more accurate to say that each man exists as intelligible to God, which does not posit any pre-existing man, only God's knowing eternally. This addresses the following paralogism: The Word exists before creation; The Word is human nature, therefore human nature pre-exists creation. We can recognize that the man Christ Jesus was before the world, which He created, but He was not purely a man before the world.

There are three differences between how the human nature becomes instantiated in a particular man and how the Word became man. The nature humanity is united to its particular, and does not unite itself; it is passive in this sense, and does not come together somehow ahead of time with the soul that will occupy the body, but is active in the sense that it acts upon the individual substance realizing the nature of the species therein. The Word, on the other hand, temporally precedes Humanity, because the Word is that which creates, then assumes Humanity. It acts upon Humanity, and remains the Word while also becoming the integrated whole (Word +

---

[131] This question is the subject of *Sentences* 3, D. 12, c.1, and it appears that what follows here is Wyclif's discussion of Lombard's position.

[132] Ibid., p. 81: "Si igitur ad personam respicias, confidenter dic hominem illum semper fuisse; si vero ad naturam hominis, concede eum coepisse."

Humanity) and each of its parts (the number of which varies, depending on how you count the elements and the composites that arise from them, as described above.) Thus, the Word takes up a full man [*plenum hominem suscepit*], as the body through soul and the integrated nature through both body and soul. "One can then philosophically concede that this man was before all creation, because this person, because of His integral excellence, assumed an integrated human nature, so that He had Himself."[133]

3.3. *Christ the Creature and the Triduum*

A good general rule to follow in reading Wyclif is to pay close attention to the opening section of any of his treatises; in most cases, he provides some sort of *vade mecum* to guide the reader through the generally complicated courses of his reasoning. In the case of *De Incarnacione*, he begins by suggesting that many of the difficulties that arise in the christologically oriented study of Scripture can be avoided by remembering that "there are three incommunicable natures in Christ: deity, body, and soul. This is clear in this way. Christ is God and perfect man, as supported by the faith: God is wholly deity, and the perfect man is wholly as much body as soul."[134] We have just described his understanding of what being a man involves: any individual member of the species is body, soul, and the aggregate (body+soul). Christ differs through the addition of Deity to these three components, which addition Wyclif will argue in no way effects the truly human nature of Christ. Wyclif will argue that the Word assumed not *a* human nature, but Humanity as such. Perhaps the right approach is to imagine that Deity, the universal divine nature shared by the persons of the Trinity, needs something more than *a* human nature to offset its magnitude in the Christ: the balance is achieved by the Word's assuming Humanity as such. The questions that result from this are interesting. First, if the Word assumes

---

[133] *DCH* 2, pp. 29/30–30/1: "Digne ergo et philosophice est concedendum, quod homo ille fuit ante omnem creaturam, quia illa persona, que propter sui excellenciam tam integre assumpsit naturam humanam integram, sic se habuit."

[134] *DI* 1, p. 3/6–11: "... Christus sit tres nature incommuicantes: scilicet, deitas, corpus, et anima. Patet sic. Christus est Deus et homo perfectus, ut ex fide supponitur: omnis Deus est deitas: omnis homo perfectus est tam corpus quam anima: ergo conclusio."

Humanity, does this mean that Christ is involved in every relation with each particular of that universal? Is Christ somehow attached to each of us?

Wyclif addresses two issues in the first several chapters of *De Incarnacione*. Was Christ a creature? What happened to Christ's humanity during the triduum, the period between Good Friday afternoon and Easter morning, when tradition holds that Christ harrowed hell? The first question, that of the created being of Christ, may seem redundant, given his brief discussion of Christ's pre-existing creation in *De composicione hominis* 2 Thomas Aquinas addressed this in two places. In *Summa contra Gentiles* 4.48, he argues that Christ must not be called a creature, because "in Christ there is no other hypostasis or person save that of God's word, and that is uncreated."[135] So while it is certainly true that the Incarnation came into being, such that the human nature assumed by the Word was created, to call Christ a creature without qualifications is incorrect. On the other hand, in *Summa theologiae* 3a Q.3 a.3, he explains that we may speak of the Incarnation "as a matter of it coming about in time that a human nature, involving the existence of a human being, came to be assumed by a divine person."[136] The problem lies in whether by "Christ" we refer to the hypostatic union of Deity and Humanity, or to G(s) as that which assumes Humanity. If the first, then Christ is a creature, but if the second, then He is not. Given Wyclif's continued emphasis that Christ is a creature, it is reasonable to ask whether an Ockhamist christology could be construed as denying this.

We cannot pause to explore Ockham's christology in any depth, but a brief discussion of how Ockham diverges from Aquinas will help explain Wyclif's approach.[137] In *Summa logica* 2, Ockham argues that reference to a common nature like humanity in a proposition "Socrates is a man" is really reference to Socrates himself, and nothing more. In this kind of statement, Aquinas and Scotus would hold that the predication "is a man" of Socrates refers to a common

---

[135] *Summa contra Gentiles* 4.48, trans. Charles J. O'Neil (South Bend, 1957), p. 207.
[136] Brian Davies, *The Thought of Thomas Aquinas* (Oxford, 1992), p. 304, see *St* 3a, Q.3 a.3.
[137] See Alfred Freddoso, "Logic, Ontology and Ockham's Christology," *The New Scholasticism*, 58 (1983), 293–330 for philosophical assessment of ongoing attempts to accuse proponents of Ockhamist nominalism of being unable to present a coherent Christology.

nature, humanity, that can be distinguished from the being of Socrates. For Aquinas, the distinction is real, and occurs naturally in our understanding, and for Scotus, the distinction is formal between the common nature Humanity and the *haecceity* of Socrates. Ockham dismisses both, arguing that the humanity arising from predicating "is a man" of Socrates is neither something apart from Socrates nor is it a part of Socrates. "If it were, then real humanity would have remained in Christ in the tomb, and humanity would have been really united to the Word in the tomb, and consequently He would have been a man, which is false."[138] Peter Geach argues that this prevents Ockham from distinguishing between two propositions: "The man Christ began to exist" and "Christ as man began to exist." Aquinas establishes the falsity of the first and the truth of the second in his argument in *Summa contra Gentiles* 4.48, but Ockham, Geach charges, cannot. Freddoso argues that, in most cases, the distinction is possible, but admits that here Ockham is constrained by his theory of reference. The term "Christ" in the second sentence must supposit for G(s) for the sentence to refer properly, and be a true statement, but if it does, then Ockham falls into the Arian heresy, implying that G(s) began to exist.[139]

Wyclif appears to suspect this in his attack on *Moderni* theologians who debase the Incarnation through bad metaphysics. "By scholarly decline from the logic of the *antiqua* about universals and right metaphysics of substantial forms, modern doctors are of one mind in denying that man is a soul, or Christ humanity, and so that Christ is a creature, by understanding through the name [*autonomatice*] Christ only according to the excellence that is Christ; and so although they grasp the truth, many yet fall away from the logic of Scriptures."[140] Not only ancient authorites such as Augustine and Jerome, but Scripture itself, make clear that when Christ refers to Himself in speech in the gospels, it is to Himself as man among men that He

---

[138] William Ockham, *Ockham's Theory of Propositions: Part II of the Summa Logicae*, trans., Alfred Freddoso and Henry Schuurman, (South Bend, 1980), pp. 87–88.

[139] Freddoso, 1983, p. 302.

[140] *DI* p. 12/20–27: "[D]eclinante scola ab antiqua logica De universalibus et a recta metaphisica de formis substancialibus, negarunt doctores moderniores concorditer quod homo est anima, vel Christus humanitas, et consequenter quod Christus est creatura, intelligentes autonmatice Christum solum secundum excellentissimum quod est Christus; et sic licet verum concipiant, multum tamen degenerant a logica scripturarum."

refers, as well as to God the Son. A familiar picture should by now be emerging: in their departure from realist metaphysics and their refusal to recognize the right way of reading Scripture, the foundation of all created truth, the Moderns have lost ability to do theology properly. While he does not explicitly identify his opponents with Arianism, at this point he recounts the Arian heresy, dwelling with ghoulish delight on Arius's ignoble end. He comments that many are now free brazenly to deny the literal sense of Scripture where it suits them, "saying that God was the Word in name only, and that not all things were made through Christ but all things this side of Him, and so He is a god and creature, but neither the God of gods nor a creature in the same univocal sense as we are. Even the heretics [of old] are not so sophisticated, not denying Scripture, as they do today, because [they were] better founded in logic and metaphysics than are our own."[141] Is Wyclif's criticism that of Geach? Is he saying that his opponents' ontology forces them to use the term 'Christ' in an Arian manner? He continues by warning that Eutychism (a species of Monophysite heresy) and Nestorianism loom as real threats for the theologian who, committed to this ontology, attempts to avoid Arianism. That is, the ontological reduction of the *Moderni* force them to refer to Christ as only having a divine nature, which was the Monophysite position. If He has two natures, then their ontology presses them to understand Christ as having assumed a pre-existent human being, which he understands to be Nestorian.

Recall that in *De composicione hominis*, Wyclif describes the distinction between corporeal form in the inanimate body and the soul as form for the human being. He was by no means the first to do this; Matthew of Aquasparta (d. 1302) had argued for the plurality of forms in animate substance in response to Aquinas's assertion that the intellectual soul serves as the form for the human being.[142]

---

[141] *DI* p. 21/14–23: "Scio tamen quod protervus postest, ut hodie, negare quamlibet partem scripture de virtute sermonis, et dicere quod Deus erat verbum nuncupative, et quod per Christum non sunt omnia facta sed omnia citra ipsum, et sic est Deus ac animatus, sed nec Deus deorum nec animatus nobiscum univoce. Sed non sic sophisticati sunt eciam heretici, non sic negantes scripturam ut hodie, quia melius fundati in logica et methaphisica quam nostrates." See also his earlier [1363?] *De Logica Tractatus Tercius* 9, p. 123/5–28, where he explains that the ancient theologians rightly used Platonism to explain the relation of uncreated Word to created Christ.

[142] See Cross, pp. 64ff.

Ockham made a similar distinction in *Quodlibet* 2 Q.11, which Alfred Freddoso translates as "Is the form by which a human being's body is a body distinct from the sentient soul?"[143] Ockham holds that the two are distinct; when an animal dies, the same number of accidents inhere in the corpse as they did in the living body. They can only inhere in a substantial being, which requires both matter and form, so there must be some form remaining in the corpse after the soul leaves. This is the bodily form, or corporeity. Regarding Christ's body during the triduum, "if the corporeity did not differ from the sentient soul in a human being, then Christ's body in the tomb would never have been an essential part of the human nature in Christ, and the living body and the dead body would not have been the same, and the divine nature would not have been united to the body in the tomb [on Easter] except through a new assumption, which is absurd."[144] That is, if there were not a real distinction between Christ's sentient soul and His corporeity, then His corporeity—His human bodily form—would not have been an intrinsic part of the Incarnation, which would be Docetism. Presumably, Ockham means for us to resolve the issue by recognizing that Christ's corporeity held the fort in the tomb during the triduum while His sentient soul descended to hell.

Wyclif's problem with this rests in dividing things so neatly: what about Christ's corporeity entails its retaining human bodily form? The way Wyclif understands the *Moderni* position, Christ's humanity cannot leave Christ's body, nor can it remain. If it descends with Christ's sentient soul, then the corpse is no longer human, no longer that of Christ, for whom the Incarnation did not cease during the triduum. If the humanity does not descend, then G(s) alone descends, which is impossible. It is not that Ockham denies Christ's liberation of hell in His humanity, but that Wyclif thinks that the Ockhamist does not account for the humanity effectively enough. Both the body and the soul need to be human, and Ockham's ontology does not provide for that.

> So every modern doctor of whose writing I have memory of having read, say in agreement that during the triduum the body was the body

---

[143] William Ockham, *Quodlibetal Questions*, trans., Alfred Freddoso and Francis Kelley, (New Haven, 1991), 1:136–39.
[144] Ibid., p. 138, interposition mine.

of Christ just as the soul was then the soul of Christ; because in
remaining outwardly the union of the Word with the assumed nature,
it remained the same union. So they say that it is synedoche [in this
case, using the whole to refer to the part] to say that they buried
Jesus, that is, the body of Jesus. But I do not see how it would then
be the body of Jesus, unless Jesus then were Jesus corporeally, having
every part of the body as His own parts, according to the voice of
Truth, Matthew 26:12, 'sending this ointment here in my body she
has made me for burying.' For certainly I believe that the same Christ
and every part of His body was buried.[145]

The point is to take the opportunity of this critical period of the
Incarnation to understand that humanity and divinity remained hypostatically joined. Taking Lombard's discussion in Bk.3 D.22 as his
starting point, Wyclif explains that Hugh of St. Victor follows Augustine,
Scripture, and philosophical reason in arguing that 'man' refers to
body and soul of man, even when the two are separated in death.[146]
His formal christology begins here, in his clarification of what remained
in the tomb, with endorsement of a modified *assumptus homo* theory
of Hugh and Anselm so that the assumed Humanity, a universal of
kind and not an extant man or particularized human nature, is
united to the Word as accident to substance. That is, he takes up
the *assumptus homo* approach and arranges it by the (post-Aquinas)
substance-accident model using a stronger realism than that coun-
tenanced by any of the previous substance-accident theorists.

Given Augustine's endorsement of the use of the term *habitus*, it
would be startling for Wyclif to have adopted the *assumptus homo*
approach without in some way making the *habitus* model consonant
with it. This he does by describing four senses by which the term
habitus refers. First, it is acquisition of wisdom, the truth which while

---

[145] *DI* 3, p. 39/10–21: "Unde omnes moderniores doctores, quorum scripta mem-
ini me legisse, dicunt concorditer quod in triduo corpus illud fuit corpus Christi
sicut et anima fuit tunc anima Christi: quia manentibus extremis unionis Verbi ad
naturam assumptam, manet eadem unio. Unde dicunt, quod est synecdochica locu-
cio, sepelierunt Iesum, id est, corpus Iesu. Sed ego non video, quomodo foret tunc
corpus Iesu, nisi Iesus tunc foret Iesus corporeus, habens omnes partes illius corporis partes suas, iuxta illam Veritatis vocem Mt. 26 'mittens hec unguentum hoc
in corpus meum ad sepeliendum me fecit.' Pro certo ego credo quod ipse Christus
sicut et quelibet pars corporis sui sepultus est."
[146] *Si Christus in morte fuit homo* in *Sententiae* 3, D.22, c.1, pp. 135–6: "Quibus
respondemus quia licet homo mortuus fuerit, erat tamen in morte Deus homo, nec
mortalis quidem nec immortalis, et tamen vere erat homo." For Wyclif's endorsement of Hugh, see *DI* 3 p. 48/17–29.

not moving, once taken in moves the soul that it informs. Second, it is acquisition of food for nutrients for the body, changing the body that acquires it. Third, the clothing that takes the shape of the wearer's body, and finally, as accoutrements we wear that do not change their shape, as with a ring on the finger. The first changes but is not changed, the second changes and is changed, the third is changed and does not change, and the fourth neither changes nor is changed.[147] Further, there are two other senses of *habitus*, of which the first has two parts: a quality of the body, as with health, or of the soul, as with the moral or intellectual virtues.[148] The second is the sense of *habitus* referred to as the tenth Aristotelian category, "which is to have, possession, or having, and this *habitus* is caused by the third and fourth kinds of *habitus* understood materially: 'riches' [what is had] denominates human riches, possessions, or having formally."[149]

> [H]umanity was assumed by the Word as *habitus* in the third way, since it occurred to a being in act, not changing or making into another person He whom it affected. The saints say that humanity is like clothing uncovering deity, and the religious who put on Christ have *habitus* of the body; knowing this, that humanity happened to God, but not inseparably. Thus says Augustine in his dialogue with Felicianum, that humanity is an accident of the Word, not that it would be a thing inhering as a new kind of accident, since it would be anticipating in created substance; neither that it would be coaeval with the Word or like a passion naturally consequent to the subject, but contingently from our time it is ineffably in the Word not changing the nature to which it comes, but in miraculous form, because the Word of God is identified or hypostatically joined: which according to Augustine in the first book of *De Trinitate*, 'such was the union of incarnation, in which God would have made man and man God.'"[150]

---

[147] Augustine, *De diversibus quaestionibus* 1.73; CCSL 44A, pp. 209–12, see also Peter Lombard, *Sent.* 3, D. 6, c. 6 1–5.

[148] Here Wyclif is referring Thomas's explanation of habits of the body, its sensitive powers, and the soul, and its intellective powers, see *Summa theologiae* 1.2, Q.50 a.1–4.

[149] Wyclif's reference to *habicio* as the tenth category, instead of to affection, which is given in 1b25, is consistent with his list in *De universalibus* 10, p. 234/625.

[150] *DI* 7, p. 119/12–27: "Dicitur ergo quod humanitas assumpta a Verbo est habitus tercii modi, cum accidit enti in actu, non mutans vel faciens ipsam aliam personam quam prefuit. Ideo dicunt sancti quod humanitas est quasi vestis detegens deitatem; et religiosi, qui Christum induunt, habent habitus corporis; hoc notantes, quod accidit Deo humanitas, sed non insearabiliter. Ideo dicit Augustinus

Aquinas rejected both the *assumptus homo* and the *habitus* theories as leading to Nestorianism in *Summa theologiae* 3a Q.2 a.6, because he understood both as requiring a pre-existing man with whom the Word would join. Wyclif argues not for a pre-existing man, but for Humanity itself, the universal by community in which all human beings participate, as that which the Word assumed in hypostatic union. The universal Humanity is what allows the body in the tomb to remain human, and it accompanies Christ to hell in continued union with the Word. He makes the argument by referring to a three-fold distinction in kinds of predication formulated by Bonaventure in his *Sentence* commentary: actual, aptitudinal/habitudinal, and mixed.[151] Actual predication is when the subject is being in act, and the form is predicated in it, as when man is said to exist in the statement 'man is an animal.' Predication by aptitude is when neither subject nor predicated form is in act, but necessarily are ordered to one another based in a higher principle of nature; no red exists on its own in the statement 'the flower is red.' When the subject is in act, and the predicated form is not actually in it, but according to necessity is ordered as based on a higher principle of nature, this is mixed, or part actual, part habitudinal predication. This, Wyclif explains, is the sense in which Christ was man during the triduum, "because the subject, that is the Word of God, then was in act, and the form of humanity was retained in habitude or aptitude of conjunction of soul to body . . . whoever concedes that body and soul were parts of Christ in the triduum, has to concede as a consequence that Christ had human being from them."[152]

---

in Dialogo ad Felicianum quod humanitas est accidens Verbo, non quod sit res inherens ut accidencia novem generum, cum sit precipua creata substancia; nec quod sit coeva Verbo vel sicut passio naturaliter consequens ad subiectum; sed contingenter ex tempore nobis ineffabiliter inest Verbo non mutando naturam, cui advenit, sed formata mirabiliter, quia Verbo Dei ydemptificata vel ypostatice copulata: cum secundum Augustinum primo De Trinitate,, 'talis fuit unio incarnacionis, que Deum faceret hominem et hominem Deum." Reference is to Augustine's description in *De Trinitate*, 13 24.

[151] Harris gives reference to *Sent.* 3, Dist. 22.1.

[152] *DI* 4, p. 49/17–23: "Et sic concedit quod Christus fuit homo in triduo, quia subiectum, quod est Verbum Dei, tunc fuit in actu, et forma humanitatis servata fuit in aptitudine coniuncciionis anime ad corpus. Nec vidi planiorem sentenciam alicuius doctoris in illa materia; quia indubie, quicunque concedit quod corpus et anima fuerunt partes Christi in triduo, habet concedere consequenter quod Christus habet correspondenter esse hominis ex eisdem."

It might be objected that Wyclif's assertion that Christ was univocally man among men can be used to establish change in the Word in experience of the passion.[153] The answer lies in Wisdom 7:24, "Wisdom is more mobile than any motion, because of her pureness she pervades and penetrates all things."[154] This truth, combined with Aristotle's assertion "the motion of the first mover would be the life of the living thing" [Physics 8, 6 259b15] leads Wyclif to assert, "this Wisdom is the first mover in efficacy and dignity in accordance to the assumed Man, by means of whose very first motion of all the whole world, both before and after, is perfected, since any other creature through the passion of Christ is renewed to its primary perfection, by which it serves God and reconciles men to God."[155] In the only scholarly article devoted to Wyclif's christology, Michael Treschow suggests that this indicates the absolute centrality Wyclif attributes to the passion; "[n]ot only did the incarnate Word redeem us from our sins through his Incarnation and Passion, but the incarnate Word also, with his very motion of Incarnation and Passion, gave life to the whole created universe from its very origin, from the beginning."[156] Wyclif's assertion illustrates his determination to champion earlier orthodoxy over what he sees as contemporary attempts to dodge the centrality of Christ in creation.[157] Most likely the earlier view most important to Wyclif was that of Grosseteste, who argued that the Incarnation would have been necessary, even had Adam not sinned, as the act completing all

---

[153] *DI* 6 contains Wyclif's argument for the univocity of Christ's humanity.

[154] NRSV translation; 'omnibus mobilibus est mobilior sapiencia' is Wyclif's version.

[155] *DI* 7 p. 107/19–24: "[S]ic verissime sine ficticia illa Sapiencia est primum mobile efficacia et dignitate secundum assumptum hominem, mediante cuius motu primo omnium totus mundus ante et post perficitur; cum quelibet alia creatura per Christi passionem ad perfeccionem primarium, qua Deo serviret placato et homini instauratur."

[156] Michael Treschow, "On Aristotle and the Cross at the Centre of Creation: John Wyclif's *De benedicta Incarnacione* Chapter Seven," *Crux*, 33 (1977), 28–37, quote p. 33. My thanks are due Prof. Treschow, who kindly sent me a copy of this article.

[157] See Bonaventure, *Breviloquium* 4.4; Anselm, *Cur Deus homo* 2.16 and 22; Thomas Aquinas, *SCG* 4.22; also Dániel Deme *The Christology of Anselm of Cantebury* (Aldershot, 2003) for discussion of this topic, esp. pp. 209–26 for a contemporary approach suggestive of Wyclif's criticism of the *moderni*. For Wyclif on the timing of the Incarnation in human history, see *De veritate Sacrae Scripturae* 28, ed. Rudolf Buddensieg (London, 1905–7), 3:128–9.

creation, as already indicated. Compare Wyclif's argument with that of Grosseteste in *Hexameron* 9:

> "And on the seventh day God ended his work." . . . can be understood allegorically to mean that Christ took on flesh in the sixth age and completed and finished everything. For he brought back all natures as if into the unity of a circle, which before the incarnation had not fully returned into a circle. For God, insofar as he is God, does not have any nature that is common to any creature, or which is said of him and of them in a univocal way. But when God became a human being, the God-man shared in a nature with the rational creature in a univocal way, and the making of the circle was perfect, and the circular return to God was joined up.[158]

2.3. *Criticism of the* Moderni *and Scotus*

The *Moderni* diverge from ancient authority, and hence truth, in three ways. First they reject universals, without which Anselm argues one cannot understand the mysteries of the Trinity, the Incarnation, and many other sacraments of faith. "Just as the divine form or nature is common to three supposits [*i.e.* the persons of the Trinity], so every nature or specific universal form is common in actuality to all of all of its supposits; and the person of the Word is common to the divine nature and hypostatically united to the other two [divine persons] . . ."[159] The further hypostatic union of the Word with the universal Humanity does not result in a further aggregate being, "for the hypostatic union, which is the personal identity, makes it that any of the three uncommunicated natures [Deity, soul, and body] is fully the same common person; although between themselves they are naturally distinguished through all the many testimonies of the saints, as with Gregory, Augustine, and Anselm."[160] The *Moderni* do not understand the close

---

[158] Robert Grosseteste, *On the Six Days of Creation*, 9.8, p. 282.

[159] *DI* 9, pp. 144/30–145/3: "Sicut enim natura vel forma divina est communis ad tria supposita, sic omnis natura vel forma specifica universalis in actu est communis ad omnia eius singularia; et persona Verbi communis ad naturam divinam et alias duas contingenter extranee ypostatice copulatas . . ."

[160] *DI* 9, p. 143/26–31: "Nam unio ypostatica, que est ydemptitas personalis facit quod quelibet istarum trium incommunicancium naturarum est plene eadem communis persona; licet inter se naturaliter distinguantur per totum ex multis sanctorum testimoniis supradictis, ut Augustini, Gregorii, et Anselmi." Wyclif refers the

tie of personal identity and substantial form, foolishly supposing that corporeity can remain as basis for substantial accidents. Wyclif develops his response elsewhere, in *De composicione hominis*.

Just as Christ is of two forms or natures, namely divinity and humanity, so the same person of Peter is corporeity, in which is animality or soul, and with this is the immortal spirit, which some call spirituality. And just as the Word is of a different sort after it became man, then it was when only divinity, so the person of man is something different when it is body, than when it is only spirit, which necessarily it is, if he is. Nor is it against this corporality to be soul, and yet to be indivisible as a mass, since the corporal life is with its way of life, by which the body lives formally. So the Apostle in Col. 2:9 says, that in Christ, 'resides every fullness of divinity corporeally" because (in) Christ, who is a body, divinity formally inheres, and fully everything, which inheres in God, since He is God. And that corporality is humanity, by understanding the term 'man', since it speaks to the union of two natures. Thus, as is clear in what follows, the humanity is said in an equivocal fashion to employ, where it is shown, that not every other thing makes some quiddity, but another complete supposit, which is essential to individual or person. Nor does it follow, that man would have two humanities, of which both are substantial form, but his humanity happens in animation of the body, with which animation this spirit is identified. And from this it is clear, that humanity is to every point of the man according to all of him, and not a simple element of corporeity, which same is indivisible as a mass.[161]

---

reader to Anselm's *De Incarnacione Verbi* 6. The 'three uncommunicated natures' refer to Deity, soul, and body, which Wyclif introduces on p. 3/7.

[161] *DCH* 5, p. 85/5–86/2: "[S]icut Christus est duarum formarum seu naturarum utraque, scilicet divinitas et humanitas, sic eadem persona Petri est corporeitas, que est animalitas et anima, et cum hac est spiritus immortalis, quem quidam vocant spiritualitatem. Et sicut verbum est aliud, postquam fuit homo, quam fuit quando solum erat divinitas, sic persona hominis est aliud quando est corpus, quam est quando est solum spiritus, quod necessario est, si est. Nec obest illam corporalitatem esse animam, et tamen esse indivisibilem quoad molem, cum vita corporalis sit cum huiusmodi vita, qua corpus vivit formaliter. Unde Apostolus ad Coll.2 dicit, quod in Cristo 'habitat omnis plenitudo divinitas corporaliter', quia Cristo, qui est corpus, inest formaliter deitas, et plene omne, quod inest deo, ut deus. Et illa corporalitas est humanitas, intelligendo hominem, ut dicit unionem duarum naturarum. Ideo, ut patebit posterius, humanitas dicitur exercere equivoce, ubi ostendetur, quod non omne aliud facit aliquam quiditatem, sed aliud suppositale completum, quod est essenciale individuo vel persone. Nec sequitur, quod homo habeat duas humanitates, quarum utraque sit forma substantialis, sed humanitati sue accidit animacio corporis, cui animacione ille spiritus est ydentificatus. Ex istis patet, cum humanitas sit ad omnem punctum hominis secundum se totam, et non corporeitas simplicis elementi, quod ipsa est indivisibilis quoad molem." See a condemnation of *Moderni* attitudes on pp. 102–3 of this treatise as well.

The essence of a thing is the same personally as the composite subject, as the intellective soul of man, which is its humanity, is the
same person with the man to which it gives form. Further, the *Moderni*
deny predication according to essence, by which Wyclif means that
the sentence "Socrates is a man" entails predication of a distinct
nature, Humanity, of the individual Socrates.[162] Finally, in their philosophical error they veer into the absurd, considering possibilities such
as the Incarnation of the Word in non-human form. "Nor do I see
how He could have assumed the nature of a pig, or a serpent, or
some other creature than a man. For if one of these could be mon-
strous, He certainly could have been a chimera or a goatstag with
the head of an ass, the tail of a horse, the mane of a lion. He would
in so doing most truly not have been our Jesus . . . It is empty and
dangerous to assert such things."[163] As we will see, this criticism
applies not only to Ockhamists, but they do define Wyclif's philosophical response to Ockhamist thought, although the identity of his
opponents remains unclear.[164] Turning from his arguments against
Moderni theologians, Wyclif believes his own approach is best explained
in light of the model Scotus provided.[165]

---

[162] For an explanation of Ockham's ontological parsimony in his predication theory, see Alfred J. Freddoso, "Ockham's Theory of Truth Conditions," in *Ockham's
Theory of Propositions: Part II of the Summa Logicae*, pp. 1–77; Gyula Klima, "Ockham's
Semantics and Ontology of the Categories," in *The Cambridge Companion to Ockham*,
pp. 118–42.

[163] *DI* 4, p. 65/9–16: "Nec video quomodo posset sumpsisse naturam porci, serpentis, vel alterius creature quam hominis, ut patet posterius. Nam si aliquid potuis-
set esse monstrum, potissime fuisset chimera vel tragelaphus habens caput asininum,
caudam equinam, pectus leoninum. Et sic esset veracissime de Iesu nostro . . . Vacuum
ergo et periculosum est raciones tales asserere." For the intention of Ockham's speculation in this vein, see Oberman, *Harvest*, pp. 255–9.

[164] Adam Wodeham seems a good beginning place. William Courtenay provides
a useful list of Adam's extant christological thought in his *Adam Wodeham*, pp. 194–5.
The incipits he provides from Adam's *Reportatio et Ordinatio Oxoniensis* suggest attention to Christ's knowledge, its relation to divine knowledge, its capacity to know
future contingents, and His ability to know the smallest corporeal part of His physical body. This last question, 3, Q.11, might prove of particular interest for evidence of a position against which Wyclif would have argued.

[165] Wyclif indicates that he has used an "abreviator" of Scotus, "Cowtonus" in
his assessment of the Subtle Doctor's Christology. This was Robert Cowton, an
English Franciscan educated in Paris before 1315. Cowton was a contemporary of
Scotus, but more inclined to the theology of Henry of Ghent. His *Sentences* commentary was later abbreviated by Richard Snettisham and was widely used as a
secondary source during Wyclif's period at Oxford. See William Courtenay, *Schools
and Scholars*, 187, 189, 364. Also, H. Theissing, *Glaube und Theologie bei Robert Cowton
OFM* (Münster, 1969).

Scotus rejects Aquinas's view in which the human nature shares in the existence of the divine person as a concrete part of a thing shares in the existence of the substantial being of the thing, because it suggests Christ's human nature was a constitutive part of the second person of the Trinity, a part perfected by the nature of the Word.[166] This seemed to Scotus to verge on the monophysite heresy. Rather than consider Christ's humanity as a part of the Word's being, Scotus followed the approach of many, such as William of Auxerre, who viewed the relation as like that holding between accident and substance. He identified two characteristics of accident's relation to substance; a substance has a passive potentiality to take on an accident, and the accident, in turn, depends on that substance.

Consider the possibility of becoming blue. Right now, you are not (presumably) blue. Nor am I. We each have the possibility of being made blue, being coated with blue paint, or stained by some dye; this corresponds to the passive potentiality of the substance. But my possible blue is not your possible blue. The blue I might become is mine, and depends on my being, while the blue you might become is yours, and depends on your being. Should I cease to be, the blue I might become will never be, although yours might still come into being. This illustrates the dependence relation of the accident upon the substance; it's being is not anything that affects the being of the substance. Should I become blue, my substantial being will be the support for the being of the blue, which is particularly mine.

The analogy is between the being of the Word and substance, and the possibility of becoming human and blue. In each case, Scotus, argues, the being of the accident has a dependence relation on the being of the substance that does not correspond to a correlate relation in the substance. "Thus Scotus is quite clear that sufficient for the divine person's being human is the actualization of *the human nature's* potentiality for dependence . . . we will have to accept by stipulation that a substance x can have a property F merely in virtue of F's relation to x."[167] Cross's comment underscores his puzzlement about how a thing can acquire an accident without itself being affected; in my example, if my possible blueness is actualized, I become blue. That Christ's human nature's potentiality for dependence

---

[166] *St* 3a, Q.2 a.6, as described in Cross, *Duns Scotus*, pp. 114–16.
[167] Cross, ibid., p. 117, italics his.

is actualized is all that is required: "It is not necessary for a mutation to have existed in anything said to have been made such, but
only in that on account of whose passive change something is said
to be made such; and here that was only the human nature."[168]
Briefly, the metaphysics of the blueness being made real does does
not entail accounting for the possibility of the substance becoming
blue.

Directing all the attention on the individuality of the accident, and
making the human nature of Christ into something having metaphysical properties seems to open one to Nestorianism, the heresy
that held there to have been two separate persons in Christ, one
human and one divine. To avoid this, Scotus and the many other
adherents of the substance-accident approach, had to argue that
Christ's human nature does not count a person. To do this, Cross
describes two approaches. First, one might argue the need for some
further positive feature that needs to be added to the "accident" of
"human nature" to make it a person, and second, one might argue
that a person is different from a nature by virtue of something the
nature lacks, and not something the person has. Scotus opts for the
second approach, since the first suggests that Christ's human nature
is something less than everyone else's human natures. The second
approach holds that being a person is a negative property of a nature.
This seems the counterintuitive approach, but for Scotus it is the
only way of treading the middle ground between Nestorianism and
the Monophysite heresy, and it ends in arguing that all human
nature, from creation onwards, has a negative property, an empty
space, the express purpose of which is to allow the Incarnation.
When this negative property is realized, instead of that human nature
being a person, it inheres in a substance, the Word, *without* being a
separate or separable person.

> [T]he assumed nature [*i.e.* Humanity] has two *habitudes* to the Word,
> either by reason of causation as generally every creature depends on
> the whole Trinity, and this *habitude* presupposes in the creature a nat-
> ural capacity suggesting imperfection, which must have the divine causal
> act inseparably with it. The second *habitude* is [that] by which the
> assumed nature can be the nature of the Word according to obedi-
> ential power, and this power can not be actualized save by miracle,

---

[168] Ibid., quotation from *Ord.* 3.7.2, n. 6.

and bespeaks a certain perfection in the person assuming; to termi-
nate thus the created dependence according to this reason is hypostatically to assume said creature.[169]

Wyclif follows Scotus in adopting the substance-accident model in
which [Substance : Accident :: Divine Nature : Human Nature] is
the analogy for explaining the Incarnation of the Word. In this
model, Scotus describes the relation of accident to substance as having two aspects, namely a relation of ordering and one of ontological dependence. Every creature has a causal dependence to God,
so the causal relation is not a good model for explaining the human
nature's relation as accident to the divine nature's substance. Every
created nature has that relation. The hypostatic union is a union of
order of dependence because the relation holding between the Word
and human nature is a property of the human nature—of the 'accident'—that lacks a corresponding property in the Word that would
make the relation mutual. So the hypostatic union is a non-mutual,
one-sided relation that boils down to a created dependence on uncreated Being structured on something other than causation.[170]

The reference Scotus makes to actualizing this power by miracle
naturally calls to mind other possibilities that might have been mirac-
ulously realized in the Incarnation. We have already noted Wyclif's
scorn for contemporaries who stray into speculation about the Word
having assumed a non-human form, which would have been possible *de potentia absoluta*, by God's absolute power. The terms *potentia
absoluta* and *potentia ordinata* were, by the time of Aquinas, recognized
as useful in distinguishing between divine ability considered in the
abstract and divine ability as actualized in creation.[171] The use of
this distinction acquired political baggage in the 1290s, when conflict
between the pope and mendicant friars introduced the distinction
into arguments about the extent of papal authority. Scotus continued to use the distinction, despite having acknowledged this troublesome mutation in its applicability.[172] This opened the door to his

---

[169] Here, *DI* 11, p. 185/5–23, Wyclif quotes *Ordinatio* 3.d.1.1; Wadding 7.6.
[170] See Cross, *The Metaphysics of the Incarnation*, pp. 121–4 for a careful explanation of Scotus's distinction to which Wyclif alludes here.
[171] William Courtenay, *Capacity and Volition A History of the Distinction of Absolute and
Ordained Power* (Bergamo, 1990); for Aquinas, see pp. 88–89.
[172] Hester Gelber, *It Could Have Been Otherwise: Contingency and Necessity in Dominican
Theology at Oxford 1300–1350*, (Leiden, 2004), p. 313, n. 9; reference is to Scotus's
Ordinatio 1.44, in *Opera Omnia* ed. Charles Balic (Vatican City, 1963), 6:363/17–364/10.

followers' using the distinction to generate possible divine courses of action within creation outside the purview of *potentia ordinata*.

In 1315, regent masters of theology at Oxford condemned several positions making use of the distinction in generating counterfactuals. While not condemning use of the distinction, this effectively limited the scope of possible scenarios theologians might generate.[173] The distinction figured again in 1324–28, during the Avignon commission's investigation and ultimate condemnation of Ockham. Among those most closely following the Scotist approach were the Dominicans at Oxford. Their approaches varied, but two friars in particular subjected ideas in which the distinction figured to careful propositional analysis of the kind that continued to flourish during Wyclif's time. Hugh Lawton and Robert Holcot used analysis of sentences describing God's knowledge, willing, and action modified by the distinction to tease modal subtleties out of problematic statements. Hugh Lawton tended to avoid innovation in summoning hypothetical instances of God's intervening in the created order, but Holcot boldly ventured into this territory, wielding his propositional analysis to engage in real innovation. "Holcot's integration of the vocabularies and logics of contract, of *obligatio*, and of covenant create a sophisticated new context for understanding the deployment of divine power."[174] We cannot yet say whether Wyclif's indictment of those who would dabble in hypotheticals *de potentia absoluta* are directed at Holcot, or some or all of his followers, as texts identifiable with Dominican authors at Oxford in the generation after Holcot and Black Death have yet to be edited. Elsewhere, he writes

> [T]he power of God appears to me to be the highest and greatest and as such self- limited and defined, because other powers are defined through it, though it limits itself through itself . . . indeed He limits Himself insofar as being able, with respect to understanding of extrinsic things in which He can and in which He cannot [act]. But want of ability or a limitation in distinguishing between that which He can [do] and that which He cannot [do] appears to be a place of scholastic exercise in truth or the endless, although to Him it would be most manifest how much He can [do].[175]

---

[173] Courtenay, *Capacity and Volition*, pp. 100–120.

[174] Gelber surveys the rich theological variety of Dominican use of the distinction; see *It Could Have Been Otherwise*, pp. 309–49. Citation, p. 339. for the full flavor of Holcot's analysis, see Robert Holcot, *Seeing the Future Clearly: Questions on Future Contingents*, ed. Paul Streveler and Katherine Tachau (Toronto, 1995).

[175] *De Actibus Anime* 3, in *Miscellanea Philosophica* vol. 1, ed. M.H. Dziewicki (London

2.4. *Christ Assumed Everyman*

Up to this point, it would be understandable to ask in frustration just what Wyclif conceived the Incarnation to involve. His arguments about the triduum suggest antipathy for a *Moderni* approach, although whose is by no means clear. He seems to agree with the Scotistic approach, but only in a limited way; nowhere does he give evidence of agreeing with the Scotistic conception of individuation, in which common nature and *haecceity* define the self. Rather than address Scotus head on, he appears to veer off into a prolonged discussion as to whether the Word could have assumed many humanities at once or successively, noting that Aquinas thought that if the Word had assumed many humanities, He would be many men.[176] Wyclif's response is to argue that the Word assumed the common nature Humanity, a universal having ontological priority to any of its created particulars. "If He were to have assumed all humanities, then He would be one man as such, as the most recent writers have asserted truly enough."[177]

Readers of medieval literature will be familiar with the play 'Everyman', in which the eponymous character, who represents all human beings, goes from carefree ignorance of his place in creation to an awareness of his need for good deeds and the sacraments through the agency of Death. Death says, "Every man I will beset that liveth beastly /Out of God's laws, and dreadeth not folly. . . . Lo, yonder I see Everyman walking;/Full little he thinketh on my coming . . ."[178] Wyclif begins his discussion of the metaphysics of the Incarnation in Chapter 13 by making a jump similar to the one Death has just made. He argues that if every man would be Everyman, then he

---

1902) pp. 109/34–110/8: "[P]otentia dei videtur mihi esse summe et maxime et per se finita et limitata, quia alie potencie finiuntur per illam, et illa per se finit se, sicud patet per theologos concedentes ternarii suppositum esse finem binarii prioris suppositorum; immo finit se quantum ad posse, respectu intelligencia extrinsecorum in que potest et in que non potest. Ideo sicud est per se, sic finite se per se. Sed inercia vel confinium distinguendi inter illa que potest et illa que non potest videtur pro statu opinandi esse scolasticus locus exercitandi in veritate vel demum infinite, quamvis sibi sit manifestissimum quante potest.

[176] *DI* 12, p. 203; Wyclif cites *In Sent.* 3, D.1, a.8–9, but ignores *St* 3a, Q.3, a.7, wherein Aquinas holds that the Word could assume any number of human natures.

[177] *DI* 13, p. 216/8–12: "Si omnes humanitates assumeret, foret unicus homo tantum, ut recentissimi scribentes asserunt satis vere." Wyclif does not disclose the identity of these recent writers, of course.

[178] Everyman, in *Medieval English Literature*, ed. J.B. Trapp (Oxford, 1973), pp. 390–1.

[Everyman] would only be one man, and if Christ assumes Humanity, then Christ, too, would be Everyman.[179] It cannot be that Christ is every man, of course, nor that Christ is more than one man through having assumed the universal Humanity, nor can it be that the universal Humanity is itself a man capable of receiving accidents like individual men are. What Wyclif means is that Christ has the same kind of body and soul as all other men have. In assuming the universal, He did not become the being of the universal by which all its particulars have their being. There need be no posited haecceity by which individualization occurs for Wyclif, and there need be no additional individuating element added to the hypostatic union of the Word and Humanity. In assuming Humanity, Christ did not thereby assume every relation holding between the universal and its particulars.[180]

A problem arises in that the universal Humanity is not something apart from the Godhead, when it is understood as a Divine Idea providing ontological ground for the instantiation of the form in every particular man. How can one person of the Trinity assume an identity of a particular when the divine essence provides the foundation for the universal that defines all particulars? Would not the other two persons be changed thereby? Wyclif argues carefully against change in G(f) and G(hs) by the Word's assumption of Humanity, but he does not address the former question. He gives evidence of awareness of it by arguing that the Word produces the conditions whereby only the Word's Deity is hypostatically united to Humanity; filiation is proper to the Word, and to neither of the other two divine persons, and all the properties of the Word admit of assumption of the flesh, but his arguments for the metaphysical means by which occurs amount to nothing more than assertion. His concluding paragraphs indicate that his intention is to clarify how the term 'Christ' has several referential schema, depending on the sense in which the term demands to be understood.

> [S]ome things are in the Word purely insofar as God; others insofar as man, and others mixed. Insofar as God, He created the world; inso-

---

[179] *DI* p. 216/13–16: "Nam hoc posito, omnis homo foret omnis homo; ergo foret solummodo unus homo. Antecedens patet per exponentes, cum homo Christus sit omnis homo; ut patet per conversionem, omnis homo est Christus."
[180] *DI* 13, p. 220.

far as man, He suffered death; and insofar as God and man, He redeemed man. Nor should a reduplicative sign be understood in each way, so that it expresses a formal logical consequence and cause; just as here Christ insofar as He is man is a creature but in another way He is cause, so that although He can be God and not have produced the world, yet deity was the cause why He produced the world and not His humanity . . .[181]

The treatise, then, appears largely to be an effort to show that *Moderni* christology is best addressed by a philosophical attention to language with a level of depth defined by the approach of Scotus but a richer ontology. At the very simplest level, the Incarnation appears to be the Word having assumed the universal Humanity in the human body born of the Virgin, the integrated whole person resulting from this being the creature Christ. Functioning as a human soul would be the hypostatic union of Word with Humanity. It is possible that such was his plan in 1372; certainly by 1373, when he had begun *De dominio divino*, the idea still figured in his thought.

> . . . Christ is the subject of theology. For which it was considered that in the Word there is a triple unity: first is the unity of essence with Father and the Gift, from which John 10, 'I and the Father are one'; second is the unity of supposition in which according to the blessed Incarnation both natures, namely corporeal and incorporeal, are the same Word; third is unity in common nature by which the same and every creature are one, since every creature is corporeal and incorporeal, and for these two reasons He is communicated to every creature, first according to Ideal Reasons, by which everything, although they are distinct rationally, are the same essentially to the Word of God, and any creature is the same essentially with its Idea. And others have declared that it does not follow, 'this Idea is God, because essentially, and this same Idea is creature, because accidental to it, therefore this creature is God.' But it well follows that any creature according to its intelligible being is God.[182]

---

[181] *DI* 13, p. 230/19–28: "[A]liqua insint Verbo pure in quantum Deus; aliqua in quantum homo; et aliqua mixtim. In quantum Deus, creavit mundum; in quantum homo, passus est mortem; et in quantum Deus et homo, redemit hominem. Nec debet signum reduplicatum intelligi utrobique, ut dicat consequenciam formal logicam et causalem; sicut hic christus in quantum homo est creatura; sed et quomodolibet dicit causam, ut licet potest esse Deus et non produxisse mundum, tamen deitas fuit causa quare produxit mundum et non sua humanitas."

[182] *De dominio divino* 1.6, pp. 42/16–43/2: "[Q]uod Christus sit subiectum theologie. Pro quo considerandum est quod in Verbo est triplex unitas: prima est unitas essencie cum Patre et Dono, de qua Ioh.X, Ego et Pater unum sumus; secunda

Wyclif did not turn completely away from philosophical theology thereafter; his christology continues to factor into his thought through-out the rest of his life. Three examples illustrate this: Christ as ideal Lord in his treatises on human *dominium*, Christ's identity with Scripture in *De veritate Sacrae Scripturae*, and Christ as the paradigmatic teacher of the Christian life in *Opus Evangelicum* and *Trialogus*.

Wyclif's treatises on human justice and its absolute reliance on God's law are ably covered in another chapter, but deserve men-tion because of the centrality of the Incarnation to their argument. Gregory XI had condemned Wyclif's *dominium* writings in May 1377, decrying their expression of the anti-papal monarchism of Marsilius of Padua. I have summarized the inaccuracy of this condemnation elsewhere, but would add here that Marsilius' conception of the role Christ has to play in the just society is rather less than Wyclif's.[183] For Marsilius, the evangelical code of justice as given in the Gospels has less the force of a law, and more that of a doctrine. That is, the evangelical teaching cannot be the basis for coercive legislation in civil government, but only the doctrinal guide by which civil law ought to be inspired. While Christ is indeed the great legislator of salvific law, his heirs are priests only, not kings.[184] Wyclif, on the other hand, envisioned Christ as the paradigmatic just lord in cre-ation, simultaneously just lord and loyal servant, as all true civil lords ought strive to be.[185] Through His restoration of natural *dominium* in His redemption of mankind and the apostolic poverty of the Church, we have the means by which to realize divine justice in civil law. Wyclif's arguments in *De civili dominio* for the centrality of Christ's place in the life and teachings of both species of authority—the civil

---

est unitas suppositalis in qua secundum benedictam incarnacionem utraque natura creata, scilicet, corporea est incorporea, est ipsum Verbum; tercia est unitas in natura communi qua ipsa et omnis creatura sunt unum, cum omnis creatura sit corporea vel incorporea; et sic duplici racione communicatur cuilibet creature, primo secundum raciones ydeales, que omnes, licet distinguantur racinione, sunt idem essencialiter Verbo Dei, et quelibet creatura est eciam idem essencialiter cum ydea. Et alias declaravi, 'Hec ydea est Deus, quia essencialiter, et hec eadem ydea est creatura, quia sibi accidentaliter; ergo hec creatura est Deus.' Sed bene sequitur quod quelibet creatura esse intelligibile sit Deus." see also ibid., 2.5, p. 198.

[183] See my *Philosophy and Politics in the Thought of John Wyclif* (Cambridge, 2003), pp. 63–7.

[184] Marsilius of Padua, *Defensor Pacis* 2.9.

[185] *De dominio divino* 3.6, p. 255/16–21.

lord and the evangelical lord—show the Incarnation as the source of all just human law.

Shortly after writing *De civili dominio*, Wyclif began his monumental treatise on scriptural exegesis *De veritate Sacrae Scripturae* [1377–78]. Here he explains the difference between the eternal truth which is the real nature of Scripture and the physical books to which we usually refer with the term 'Scripture'. While the books themselves are subject to the ravages of time, as are the understandings of individual readers, the Truth they embody is eternal. Further, in John 10:35–36 Jesus teaches that the Scripture cannot be destroyed which God sent into the world, which leads Wyclif to conclude that Christ himself is that truth, the book whom "God the Father sent . . . into the world in order to save the world . . . This book cannot be destroyed, precisely because the divinity and the humanity are insolubly united in the same person in a seven-fold manner."[186] This identity of the Incarnate Word with Scripture compels every Christian to study the Bible, the very image of Christ.[187]

At the end of his life, the Incarnation remained central to Wyclif's thought. In *Trialogus* 3.27 he describes the three natures united in Christ, body, soul and divine nature, just as he had in *De Incarnacione* 1. Here also he warns his lay readers away from the "many wasteful studies and occupations by which the heretics are occupied in formulating and developing responses" in arguments about the metaphysics of the Incarnation. Far better to concentrate on the solid truths Christ Himself teaches.[188] To that end, Wyclif's extended study of Christ's words themselves deserves attention. While much of Wyclif's commentary of Scripture remains unedited, the Wyclif Society has published a number of his later gospel commentaries, including his extensive analysis of Matthew 5–7, in *Opus Evangelicum*, volumes 1 and 2. Here, in his exegesis of the Sermon on the Mount, likely

---

[186] John Wyclif, *On the Truth of Holy Scripture*, trans. Ian Christopher Levy (Kalamazoo, 2001), p. 98. See *De veritate Sacrae Scripturae* 1.6, p. 109; for the seven-fold manner in which divinity and humanity are united, see the Grosseteste-inspired quote in *DCH* given above, n. 116.

[187] See Ian Christopher Levy, "John Wyclif's Neoplatonic View of Scripture in its Christological Context," *Medieval Philosophy and Theology* 11 (2003), 227–40.

[188] *Trialogus* 3.27, pp. 225–6: "[E]t per hoc exonerati sumus a studiis et occupationibus multis superfluis, quibus circa casus et responsiones haeretici occupantur. Salubrius quidem est studere veritates solidas quam inaniter evagari circa fictitias . . ."

written in 1383, we find Wyclif's most sustained argument as the ideal code by which any member of the human race ought live.[189] "Just as in any creature a vestige of the Trinity gleams, thus in any book of the New Testament, which are books of Christ and the Holy Spirit, a certain perfection gleams which is clear in the book to any creature; because just as looking carefully at oneself in the mirror reveals an image of ones face looking back out, so looking in any particular part of scripture, one sees the beginning, middle and end through which one moves to salvation."[190] While the commentary is, in many places, more a patchwork of long quotations from Augustine, Grosseteste, the *Opus Imperfectum*, and the remarkable *De duodecim abusivus*, it shows Wyclif's determination that the Incarnation and Christ's teachings serve as the perennial antidote to all that continues to plague human life.

---

[189] *Opus Evangelicum* 4:33. ed. J. Loserth and F.D. Mathew, 2 vols. (London: 1895–96), 2:368/18–24.

[190] *Opus Evangelicum* 1, 1:1/20–29: "Sicut enim in qualibet creatura relucet vestigium Trinitatis, sic in quolibet libro novi testamenti, cum sit liber Christi et Spiritus Sancti, relucet quecunque perfeccio que patet in libris aliquibus creature; quia, sicut intuens se in speculo videt faciei sue similitudinem quotquot specula intuetur, sic videns quamcunque scripture sacre particulam videt principium, medium et finem per que tenderet ad beatitudinem adquirendam."

WYCLIF'S ECCLESIOLOGY AND POLITICAL THOUGHT

Takashi Shogimen

Introduction

"Since any Christian, theologians in particular, must die virtuously, as (according to the conclusion of St Augustine's *On Christian Discipline*) 'one who lived well could not die badly,' it is time for me to support myself on virtues through the entire rest of my life speculatively as well as practically, according to the capacity God has given, in order to learn to die more salubriously."[1]

Thus began John Wyclif's first treatise on ecclesiastical and political issues, *De dominio divino*. The work was probably written in 1373–74,[2] shortly after Wyclif began royal service at the court of John of Gaunt, Duke of Lancaster. Wyclif, then probably in his late 40s, was preparing to "die virtuously" by turning his literary attention to more practical matters. His engagement with "current affairs" was then a manifestation of his commitment to the moral life. Thus, until his death on St Sylvester's Day (31 December) 1384, he produced a number of tracts on ecclesiastical and political issues.

The circumstance that prompted Wyclif to turn to public issues was probably the national financial crisis, which was triggered by the Hundred Years War. Wyclif was first involved in politics when he was among a delegation sent by King Edward III to Bruges in 1374 in order to negotiate a settlement with papal legates in connection with papal provision to English benefices, taxation of the clergy and the rights of clergy to appeal to papal courts. The secular

---

[1] John Wyclif, *De dominio divino* 1, ed. R.L. Poole (London, 1890), p. 1/3–8: "Cum quilibet Christianus et specialiter theologus mori debeat virtuosus, quia (iuxta conclusionem beati Augustini in De Disciplina Christiana) *non poterit male mori qui bene vixerit*, tempus est mihi per totum residuum vite mee tam speculative quam practice, secundum mensuram quam Deus donaverit, inniti virtutibus, ut sic salubrius discam mori."

[2] Williell R. Thomson, *The Latin Writings of John Wyclyf* (Toronto, 1983), p. 39.

magnates, John of Gaunt in particular, were increasingly critical of the English Church's wealth.[3] There was also a polemical dimension to this conflict, in which Wyclif was to play a part. Ecclesiastical property and the authority of temporal rulers over the Church were to emerge as the predominant themes of his polemical activities.

Wyclif's "polemical" response, however, was neither sporadic nor incoherent; quite the contrary, it was remarkably intense and systematic. Intense because over a period of some ten years until his death he continued to produce highly polemical and controversial works one after another, and systematic because all of his polemical response was built around his theological discourse on the idea of dominion (*dominium*). Wyclif began his engagement with public issues by writing a gigantic theological treatise, *De dominio divino* (1373–74), which offered a comprehensive account of the idea of divine dominion before turning to dominion in its secular aspects. Wyclif's *Summa theologiae*, which was written over the period 1375–1381,[4] was, despite the title, not a work of speculative theology at all; rather it largely comprises a number of substantial writings that tackled political and ecclesiological problems of his day. The works, which have most direct relevance to political and ecclesiological issues, include *De civili dominio* (from late 1375 to late 1376),[5] *De ecclesia* (from early 1378 to early 1379),[6] *De officio regis* (mid-1379),[7] *De potestate papae* (autumn 1379),[8] *De symonia* (early 1380),[9] *De apostasia* (late 1380),[10] and *De blasphemia* (mid-1381).[11]

Some of these works reveal the issues that attracted Wyclif's interest. For instance, *De ecclesia* offers a defense of the Crown's causes and expounds on Wyclif's view of the relationship between Church and State in response to the Haulay-Shakyl Incident; the murder of the knight Robert Haulay and the abduction of John Shakyl in

---

[3] See, for instance, Herbert Workman, *John Wyclif: A Study of the English Medieval Church* 2 vols. (Oxford, 1926), 1:209–32, and K.B. McFarlane, *John Wycliffe and the Beginnings of English Non-conformity* (London, 1952).
[4] Thomson, *The Latin Writings of John Wyclyf*, p. 44.
[5] Ibid., p. 48.
[6] Ibid., p. 58.
[7] Ibid., p. 60.
[8] Ibid., p. 62.
[9] Ibid., p. 63.
[10] Ibid., p. 64.
[11] Ibid., p. 66.

Westminster Abbey by a group of fifty men led by Sir Alan Buxhill.[12] *De blasphemia* alluded to the Peasants' Revolt, which was, in one respect, an imprecise translation of Wyclif's political theory into practice, and condemned the peasants' radical action.[13] In addition to the enormous *Summa theologie*, Wyclif's shorter polemical essays also help us to understand what public issues he tackled. His polemical period overlapped with the beginning of the Great Schism, which of course did not escape his attention. *De dissensione paparum* (*De scismate*; late 1382) was indeed a powerful objection to the Great Schism. Wyclif identified the papacy's worldly desire for temporal power as its cause and denounced those who opposed divestment as the only solution to the ecclesiastical crisis.[14] The concluding section of the work touches upon the so-called Flanders Crusade led by Bishop Despenser of Norwich.[15] The crusading movement came under Wyclif's further scrutiny in *De cruciata* (*Contra bella clericorum*; late 1382),[16] which condemned the military action endorsed by Pope Urban VI as a sign of the reign of the devil.[17]

Although Wyclif's Latin polemical treatises had already been critically edited and published at the turn of the nineteenth and twentieth centuries,[18] they had not received due scholarly attention commensurate with his reputation as one of the late medieval heresiarchs or as the Morning Star of the Reformation. Some of the general surveys of the history of medieval political thought published in the past decade are curiously silent on Wyclif.[19] This forms an

---

[12] *De ecclesia* 7, ed. J. Loserth (London, 1886). See also Joseph H. Dahmus, *The Prosecution of John Wyclyf* (New Haven, 1952), pp. 74–88.

[13] *De blasphemia* 13, ed. Michael Henry Dziewicki (London, 1893), pp. 190ff. See also Workman, *John Wyclif*, 2:221–45.

[14] *De dissensione paparum*, in *John Wiclif's Polemical Works in Latin*, ed. Rudolf Buddensieg, 2 vols. (London, 1883), 2:567–76.

[15] For more on the Despenser Crusade see Margaret Aston, "The Impeachment of Bishop Despenser," *Bulletin of the Institute of Historical Research* 38 (1965): 127–48.

[16] *De cruciata*, in *John Wiclif's Polemical Works in Latin*, 2:588–632.

[17] Ian Christopher Levy, "John Wyclif: Christian Patience in a Time of War," *Theological Studies* 66 (2005), pp. 330–57.

[18] For instance, *De civili dominio liber primus*, ed. R.L. Poole (London, 1885); *De civili dominio liber secundus*, ed. J. Loserth (London, 1900); *De civili dominio liber tertius*, ed. J. Loserth, 2 vols (London, 1903–4); *De dominio divino*, ed. R.L. Poole (London, 1884); *De ecclesia*, ed. J. Loserth (London, 1886); *De officio regis*, ed. A.W. Pollard and C. Sayle (London, 1887); and *De potestate papae*, ed. J. Loserth (London, 1907).

[19] See for instance, Joseph Canning, *A History of Medieval Political Thought 300–1450*

intriguing contrast to the wide attention that Wyclif's near contemporaries, such as Marsilius of Padua and William of Ockham, have
drawn from modern historians. This curious neglect may be attrib-
utable partly to Wyclif's reputation as the second-rate philosopher,
which seems to pervade even in serious scholarship on Wyclif's
thought,[20] and partly to his old-fashioned Augustinian Neoplatonism,
which makes his political conceptualization rather irrelevant to modern readers, who can entertain the proto-modern, rationalist outlook
that is evident in Marsilius and Ockham. However, some specialist
studies exist and a brief survey of them may be required before discussing Wyclif's own thought on ecclesiology and politics.

Wyclif's polemical works were first discussed in biographical accounts
of his polemical career. In 1926, a couple of decades after the introductory accounts offered by the editors of Wyclif's polemical writings, such as Johann Loserth and Reginald Lane Poole, Herbert B.
Workman produced a biographical account of Wyclif with special
reference to the history of the English medieval Church.[21] In 1952,
K.B. McFarlane approached Wyclif from a biographical perspective,
portraying him as a royalist ideologue who served John of Gaunt's
political agenda.[22] In the same year, Joseph Dahmus offered an analysis of the persecution of John Wyclif. These biographical works
focused on Wyclif's polemical career rather than his polemical teachings. It was not until 1960s that monographs on Wyclif's political
and ecclesiological thought first appeared. Lowrie J. Daly, *The Political
Theory of John Wyclif* (1962) is the first book on Wyclif's political
thought.[23] Daly produced a systematic presentation of Wyclif's political conclusions, although he seems to read Wyclif from the standpoint of political thought in general rather than from the standpoint
of Wyclif's own primary motive.

Michael Wilks published a number of papers on Wyclif's politics
and ecclesiology from 1965, which are now collected in a single

---

(London, 1996) and Janet Coleman, *A History of Political Thought from the Middle Ages
to the Renaissance* (Oxford, 2000). However, Antony Black, *Political Thought in Europe,
1250–1450* (Cambridge, 1992) touched upon Wyclif's ecclesiology and political
thought.

[20] See, for instance, Gordon Leff, *Heresy in the Later Middle Ages* (Manchester, 1967)
vol. 2, which occasionally expresses skepticism about Wyclif's philosophical competence.

[21] Workman, *John Wyclif.*

[22] McFarlane, *John Wycliffe and the Beginnings of English Non-conformity.*

[23] L.J. Daly, *The Political Theory of John Wyclif* (Chicago, 1962).

volume.[24] Wilks's studies of Wyclif's political thought are more wide-ranging than anyone else's; indeed, Wilks managed to incorporate analyses of Wyclif's metaphysical and theological writings fully into his discussion on Wyclif's political thought. Gordon Leff's *Heresy in the Later Middle Ages* (1967) was immune from Daly's somewhat "presentist" reading of Wyclif's politics; Leff situated Wyclif in the medieval tradition of heretical movements and accounted for his political and ecclesiological ideas in the wider context of his philosophical and theological views, especially of his metaphysics and biblical scholarship. However, Leff read Wyclif rather unsympathetically; for instance, he dismissed Wyclif's extensive discourse on dominion (*dominium*) as being of mere ornamental significance in his later ecclesiological writings. As we shall see below, dominion is a term that signifies both property ownership and jurisdiction in the general sense, namely the power of ruling. Leff explained away Wyclif's alleged inconsistency relating to divine grace and dominion by emphasizing Wyclif's pragmatism, which "triumphed over theory." William Farr, *John Wyclif as Legal Reformer* (1974), by contrast, took Wyclif's "pragmatism" seriously and pushed this line of enquiry further.[25] While Farr acknowledged the reliance of Wyclif's reform program on his metaphysics, he underlined that the reform program was pragmatically grounded in contemporary legal precedent. In sharp contrast to the conventional understanding of Wyclif as a Utopian at best, an anarchist at worst, Farr's Wyclif is a pragmatic political realist. However, Farr's focus on Wyclif's legal sources allowed him to treat Wyclif's speculative discourses on dominion and grace as marginal as if it were irrelevant to Wyclif's practical political agenda.

Modern scholarship on medieval political thought has often revolved around the question of the relationship between an individual thinker's political ideas and his or her philosophy and/or theology. The turn of the thirteenth and fourteenth centuries witnessed an intellectual volte-face in metaphysics and political thought. In metaphysics, the realist positions of Thomas Aquinas and John Duns Scotus were subject to sharp criticism of nominalists represented by William of Ockham. In political thought, the disputes between the papacy and

---

[24] Michael Wilks, *Wyclif: Political Ideas and Practice*, ed. Anne Hudson (Oxford, 2000).
[25] William Farr, *John Wyclif as Legal Reformer* (Leiden, 1974).

secular powers and the so-called Poverty Controversy between mendicants and secular masters generated a number of polemical treatises on ecclesiastical and secular power. There emerged two camps
of political and ecclesiological views: papalists and anti-papalists. The
so-called "papalists," such as Giles of Rome, James of Viterbo,
Augustinus Triumphus of Ancona and Guido Terreni, asserted the
pope's universal authority in both spiritual and temporal spheres,
whereas "anti-papalists," such as John of Paris, Marsilius of Padua
and William of Ockham, underlined the limits of papal authority.
Neither of the two camps was monolithic: some papalists, such as
Augustinus Triumphus of Ancona argued for papal sovereignty, while
others, such as Guido Terreni maintained papal infallibility. Similarly,
some anti-papalists, such as John of Paris and Ockham proposed a
separation of spiritual and temporal powers while others, such as
Marsilius reduced the Church into an organ of the secular political
community. Wyclif can clearly be categorized as an anti-papalist;
indeed, he was associated with the anti-papal (and allegedly heretical) Marsilius by Pope Gregory XI in 1377 when he declared that
Wyclif's ideas represented the perverted opinion and heretical doctrines of Marsilius of Padua.[26]

It had been conventional to understand the dispute between papal-
ism and anti-papalism with reference to the philosophical debate
between realism and nominalism and to attribute the burgeoning
nominalism to the philosophical underpinnings of anti-papal political doctrines, which were allegedly responsible for the collapse of
the medieval political, ecclesiastical and social order, until Charles
Zuckerman placed a huge question mark over this dualistic interpretation.[27] One of the key thinkers employed to undermine this
dichotomy was in fact John Wyclif, who was a realist and yet a
spearhead of anti-papalism. The relationship between metaphysics
and politics in the thought of John Wyclif was largely left unexplored
by Daly and Farr, while it was discussed but dismissed by Wilks and
Leff. Most recently, Stephen E. Lahey revisited, and shed new light
on, this contentious issue.[28] Lahey asserts that Wyclif's earlier meta-

---

[26] Dahmus, *The Prosecution of John Wyclyf*, p. 48.

[27] Charles Zuckerman, "The Relationship of Theories of Universals to Theories
of Church Government in the Middle Ages: A Critique of Previous Views," *Journal
of the History of Ideas* 35 (1975), 575–94.

[28] Stephen E. Lahey, *Philosophy and Politics in the Thought of John Wyclif* (Cambridge,
2003). See also his "Wyclif and Lollardy," in *The Medieval Theologians* ed. G.R. Evans
(Oxford, 2001), pp. 334–54.

physics about relations formed the foundations for his later thought on ecclesiology, which revolved around the question of the right relation between God and Christian individuals, thus offering an entirely novel interpretation of Wyclif's political thought in relation to his metaphysics.

Thus Wyclif's political thought remains elusive. But it is doubtless that Wyclif's polemical activities centered upon Church reform by means of divestment. Although historians may be divided over the questions of intent behind his reform program and the relationship of his reform agenda to his speculative thought, they agree that the contemporary Church's power and wealth were the target of Wyclif's polemical attack.

The Church's quest for power and its desire for wealth were indeed the recurrent themes in most of Wyclif's polemical writings. Hence he looks forward to a clergy committed to a life far removed from worldly concerns. "It would be the highest privilege in this life were the Church to be liberated from the civil possession of temporal goods, so that she might follow freely after Christ in evangelical poverty."[29] The Church should live by the freely offered alms of the people, rather than perpetual endowments. Such a system would prove more beneficial for all involved, the clergy and the lay alms givers.[30] All clergy, therefore, from friars to monks, to parish priests, should live without property of their own, depending solely on the tithes, offerings and alms given by the laity.[31]

Whether he commented on the Great Schism, the Flanders Crusade or the Haulay-Shakyl Incident, the bottom line was invariably that the Church's power and greed were the source of evil. The Great Schism was caused by papal desire for worldly power and the acquisition of temporal goods.[32] The papal call for, and endorsement of,

---

[29] *De ecclesia* 8, p. 176/19–22: "Ex istis tercio colligitur quod summum privilegium pro statu vie foret ecclesiam esse exoneratam possessione civili temporalium, currendo libere post Christum in evangelica paupertate."

[30] *De ecclesia* 13, p. 274/26–30: "Ex istis incidit declarare sentenciam quam dixi superius scilicet quod humana elemosina temporalis foret elemosina humana perpetua tam clero quam elemosinanti cum paribus magis autentica, magis meritoria et altrinsecus plus secura."

[31] *De ecclesia* 14, p. 308/22–25: "Sic ergo non est quoad hoc distinccio inter fratres, inter possessionatos et inter curatos, viventets de decimis et oblacionibus, quin omnes debemus vivere exproprietarie de elemosinis laicorum . . ."

[32] *De dissensione paparum*, p. 572/1–3: "Primo igitur videtur supponendum tamquam probabile, quod ista dissensio propter cupiditatem mundani honoris et temporalium adiacencium papatui est causata."

the Flanders Crusade were derived from the Church's departure from Christ's example of humility and poverty. Indeed, no one would ever take on the hardship this crusade promises were it not in the hope of earthly honor and riches. The popes and their cardinals have forsaken charity in their quest for vengeance, and thus stand condemned by God, whose very nature is love.[33] Though, it should be noted that Wyclif had originally placed his confidence in the Roman claimant. "We can suppose that our Urban does not authorize this crime, although it seems quite likely that has been seduced by the false friars."[34] Such confidence was short-lived, however.

The view that the Westminster privilege to shelter the knights also stemmed from a misconceived view that the Church should enjoy a variety of privileges and prerogatives that were unfounded in Scripture. "The Church has no genuine privilege that is not founded upon, taught, and drawn from Scripture. This is clear because every law that is useful to Holy Mother Church is taught either explicitly or implicitly in Scripture, and every privilege must be a law of this sort. . . . For, as every truth is contained in Holy Scripture, and every privilege is itself a truth because it is law, so we reach this conclusion."[35] Again, Wyclif attributed such defenses of ecclesiastical privilege to the Church's obsession with temporal power and wealth. The clergy insist upon various exemptions, endowments and worldly forms of power, and prelates esteem merely human charters and privileges above those Christ himself has instituted.[36]

---

[33] *De cruciata* 1, pp. 589/14–590/3: "Alias autem declaravi, quod ista monstruosa dissensio a probabili est causata ex mendaci defectu, quo papa non sequitur viam Cristi. Si enim servaret humilitatem eius et pauperiem, numquam pro causa huiusmodi istam mendacem ficticiam attemptaret. Quis enim attemptaret tam laboriosum et anxium atque certamen cum alio, nisi cupiditas honoris mundani et temporalium sit in causa?" See also *De cruciata* 5, pp. 605–7.

[34] *De dissensione paparum*, p. 574/10–13: "Et cum supponi potest, quod Urbanus noster non auctorizat hoc facinus, licet a pseudofratribus sit seductus, videtur probabile . . ."

[35] *De ecclesia* 8, p. 173/11–18: "Ex istis elicitur quod nullum est verum privilegium ecclesie, nisi de quanto fundatur, docetur vel elicitur ex scriptura. Pater sic: Omnis lex utilis sancte matri ecclesie docetur explicite vel implicite in scriptura, omne privilegium est huiusmodi ex dictis: ergo conclusio. Confirmatur ex sepe dictis: Omnis veritas est in scriptura sacra, omne privilegium est veritas quia lex, ergo conclusio."

[36] *De ecclesia* 8, p. 174/11–13: "Nonne diligencia nostra ostendit quod plus appreciamus cartas et privilegia humana quam scripturam sacram et privilegia que Christus suis instituit?" *De ecclesia* 9, p. 184/1–5: "Secundo videtur quod non licet clero insistere circa privilegia terrena cuiusmodi videntur esse exempciones, prerogative, proprietates et seculares dominaciones, cum videntur repugnare privilegiis Christi que non licet amittere."

So it is that Wyclif sets out to proves that, "the king's decision in this incident in no way violates either the law of God, nor the actual privileges of Westminster. Let someone search the whole of Scripture and he will never find that refuge should be provided for any fugitive fleeing from debt, or from an unjust killing, indeed from any sin whatsoever. For that would mean that God approves of this traitor in his crime; and that is impossible."[37] Scripture does allow for refuge in rare cases, as Wyclif admits, but this case hardly meets those criteria. "If, therefore, in the whole New and Old Law (where this matter is dealt with extensively) a place of refuge is only granted to the innocent and those who accidentally kill their brother, would it not be blind presumption masquerading as piety for Christians to defend the enemies of God, king and country?"[38]

The privilege itself has its limits. "Since it is not in the prince's power to allow something that does injury to God or contributes to the destruction of his own kingdom, or even weakens the royal rights and laws by which he governs his kingdom, it is clear that the incident that we are dealing with here is not included in the general privilege. I ask you, what could be more injurious to God than turning his house into a den of robbers?"[39] The fugitives' appeal to the law also proves to be a dead end. "According to the law of nature," says Wyclif, "it is pointless for the one who breaks the law to then call upon the law to help him. But the fugitives in question have, by rebelling, broken the law of God, as well as the law of Church and that of the kingdom."[40] Haulay and Shakyl are clearly guilty on

---

[37] *De ecclesia* 7, pp. 146/29–147/3: "Quod autem preceptum regis in hac parte non obviat legi Dei nec veris privilegiis Westmonasterii sic ostendo: Scrutetur homo totam scripturam et non inveniet quod pro debito, or occisione iniusta, immo generaliter pro quocunque peccato debet profugus habere refugium, quia tunc Deus foveret proditorem proprium in suo crimine; quod non potest."

[38] *De ecclesia* 7, p. 147/16–21: "Si ergo in tota lege nova et veteri (ubi diffuse tangitur ista materia) non limitatur locus refugii nisi insontibus qui casualiter fratrem suum occiderint, que foret in christianis ceca presumpcio sub colore pietatis defendere hostes Dei, regis et regni?"

[39] *De ecclesia* 7, p. 148/1–8: "Cum ergo non sit in potestate principis concedere quod vergeret ad Dei iniuram, ad destruccionem regni sui, ad enervacionem regalie et legum per quas regeret regnum suum, patet quod illud suppositum in casu nobis exposito non includitur in illo privilegio generali. Quid queso foret magis ad Dei iniuriam quam facere domum suam speluncam latronum?"

[40] *De ecclesia* 7, p. 149/24–27: "Tercio principaliter arguitur sic ad idem de iure nature: *Frustra invocat legis auxilium qui offendit in eam*, sed dicti fugitivi rebellando offenderunt in legem Dei, ecclesie et in legem regni."

all counts according to Wyclif. "We have shown these fugitives to be offenders against God's law through their disobedience to their superiors. Moreover they had broken the law of the Church for various reasons, because (as the canon lawyers say) they have disobeyed the commands of their princes, and in that way committed a certain sort of sacrilege. And since they remained disobedient to the law of God by refusing to obey the laws of their king, what just law could protect them?"[41]

Insofar as Wyclif's polemical target was the corrupted Church, he shared common polemical ground with other anti-papal polemicists such as Marsilius and Ockham. Marsilius of Padua (c. 1275/80–1343), a physician by training, was an innovative Italian political philosopher, whose *Defensor pacis*, completed in 1324, proposed an idiosyncratic vision of the political community based on popular consent and criticized the papal doctrine of the fullness of power (*plenitudo potestatis*). William of Ockham (c. 1285–1347) was an Oxford philosopher and a Franciscan theologian, who was involved in anti-papal polemical activities in the dispute between Pope John XXII and the Franciscan Order. Ockham produced a number of polemical treatises, which demonstrated the heresy of contemporary popes and refuted their misconception and abuse of papal power.

Wyclif's identification of enormous wealth and lust for power (*libido dominandi*) as the main problems that faced the contemporary Church separates him from his anti-papal predecessors. What Ockham observed in the Church of his day, for instance, was that the Christian community was contaminated by heretical doctrinal decisions made by the popes, which, still worse, met no contestation but gained tacit approval from the members of the Church (apart from, of course, Ockham and his "Michaelist" colleagues), due to their ignorance, temerity, and negligence.[42] Ockham lamented and criticized the breakdown of the ecclesiastical institutions, whereas Marsilius questioned the institutional structure of the Church itself. Marsilius's ecclesiol-

---

[41] *De ecclesia* 7, p. 150/10–17: "Dicti autem fugitivi iuxta nobis exposita offenderunt in legem Dei ex inobediencia suis prepositis, offenderant insuper in legem ecclesie racione multiplici, quia (ut dicunt docti in illis iuribus) inobedientes mandatis suorum principum committunt quoddam genus sacrilegii, et cum inobedientes remanserint legi Dei de obediendo legibus regis sui, que lex iusta illos protegeret?"

[42] Takashi Shogimen, "Defending Christian Fellowship: William of Ockham and the Crisis of Late Medieval Church," *History of Political Thought* 25 (2005), 607–24.

ogy is a reverse of the papalist one: the Church is a mere organ of the state and not the other round. Marsilius limited the Church's function to regulating human conduct to conform to the divine law, although such conformity could only be verified in the eyes of God, not in this world. Marsilius accordingly deprived the Church of all coercive power.[43] Wyclif's focus on the allegedly excessive wealth of the contemporary Church clearly differed from Ockham's and Marsilius's criticisms. Unlike Ockham, Wyclif did not think that the contemporary problem of the Church constituted a heretical deviation from the normal operations of ecclesiastical governance. Wyclif considered that the problem was rooted in the misconception of Church government. In this respect, Wyclif was nearer to Marsilius. However, Wyclif was likewise far apart from Marsilius. The Marsilian reduction of the Church into an organ of the state was fundamentally anthropocentric in that the Marsilian proposals for true ecclesiastical institutions were grounded in the notion of popular consent. Wyclif, by contrast, anchored ecclesiastical institutions in the divine will. Exploring these issues further will clarify the unique contributions that Wyclif made to ecclesiology and political thought in the late Middle Ages.

Contexts

Before we examine Wyclif's attack on the excessive wealth of the Church, it is necessary to contextualize his polemical standpoint. We have already seen the political and ecclesiastical circumstances in which Wyclif began his polemical career. The circumstantial contexts alone would not explain why Wyclif began his polemical activities in the way in which he did. First, we need to understand that Wyclif thought it was imperative that the Church should enter a new era of reform. He believed that the time was ripe for radical reform. Wyclif's reform program was underpinned by his cyclical notion of human history. His own time was the nadir of history where the world had reached its worst condition. Wyclif's philosophy of history was unmistakably Augustinian: he assimilated the Augustinian notion of the seven ages of man and applied it to the

---

[43] Marsilius of Padua, *Defensor pacis*, ed. C.W. Previté-Orton (Cambridge, 1928).

history of the world.[44] World history consists of seven stages and the
period described in the Old Testament corresponds to the first three
stages. The lifetime of Christ and the apostolic period constitute the
halfway stage and the summit of history: the early Church was pure
in its pursuit of apostolic poverty. Land and wealth were owned by
the temporal rulers alone and the Church claimed no authority
beyond sacramental power. This pristine state did not last for long:
his schema now turns to the three stages of decline. The first down-
turn in history was the Donation of Constantine: a grant in which
the Emperor Constantine conceded supreme authority in the Church
and unrivalled control over Italy to Pope Sylvester I. The Italian
humanist Lorenzo Valla discovered in the fifteenth century that the
document that recorded the Donation was an eighth-century papal
forgery. But the Donation was widely believed throughout the Middle
Ages as the foundation of the pope's universal authority in the spiritual sphere and his temporal jurisdiction in the Patrimony of St
Peter. Wyclif held that the Donation of Constantine injected poison
into the body of Christ. The Donation marked the beginning of an
era when temporal rulers became patrons of the Church by granting the clergy land and jurisdictional power. Thus began the Church's
fall into things of the flesh and the world. One such sign of deca-
dence, he notes, is the fact there are no martyrs recorded among
the popes from that time forward.[45] What is more, says Wyclif, the
popes now go so far as to claim that the Church had actually received
the empire directly from God, not from Constantine, such that
Constantine was only restoring to Sylvester what he had unjustly
detained.[46]

The grant of the western lands of the empire by the Emperor
Constantine to Pope Sylvester was the first step towards the trans-
formation of the Church into a this-worldly governing institution.
The Gregorian Reform movement in the eleventh century was the

[44] Michael Wilks, "Wyclif and the Wheel of Time," in Wilks, *Wyclif*, p. 208.
[45] *De civili dominio* 3.13, p. 217/1–7: "Postquam autem dotata est dotacione sapi-
ente seculum, decrevit continue tam virtute tam quantitate; cuius causa indubie est
declinacio ad carnem et seculum . . . Unde cronicantes notant quod a tempore huius
dotacionis non successit aliquis papa martir."
[46] *De civili dominio* 3.21, p. 445/15–25: "Et quia post dotacionem ecclesie papa
vendicat temporalia nedum ex elemosina imperatoris . . . et sic non recepit imperium
a Constantino . . . sed immediate a Deo; ad quod imperator instrumentaliter iuvit
ponendo eum in possessionem illius quod prius iniuste detinuit."

incident that manifested the significant growth of earthly Church government, which marked the second stage of decline. Finally, the free-fall of human spirituality had accelerated during and after the pontificate of Innocent III. The late fourteenth century was the age of Antichrist.[47] Indeed, the Great Schism was symptomatic of the end of the world.[48]

But Wyclif believed that the tide of history was changing again. The downward spiral of history has come to an end and the upward trend—"the gradual reconquest of Antichrist"—was about to begin. Wyclif's reform program was thus situated as the first stage that would reverse the tide of history, towards the restoration of the pristine state of the Christian Church.[49] This distinctive philosophy of history explains why Wyclif spoke out when he did, but it does not show what motivated him to engage with the contemporary question of ecclesiastical power and property. This problem can be approached from various angles: the political and ecclesiastical circumstances that Wyclif plausibly witnessed might help to explain his polemical drives. But what made Wyclif engage with polemics over the issues of Church reform, unlike others who witnessed the same political and ecclesiastical reality, is entirely another question. Still another is: what enabled Wyclif to identify ecclesiastical power and property as the single important factor that allegedly corrupted the contemporary Church? The former concerns Wyclif's ideological standpoint and the latter touches upon his political and ecclesiological doctrine. I shall discuss the two issues in turn.

Wyclif's aggressive attack on the Church came from what he perceived as the contemporary derogation of the Bible. At the heart of Wyclif's call for ecclesiastical reform was his desire to restore Scripture to the place of the only, supreme and infallible authority. It is not without reason that his substantial treatise on biblical exegesis, *De veritate Sacrae Scripturae*, is placed immediately after *De Mandatis divinis* and *De civili dominio*, the works that introduce his *Summa theologiae*. The centrality of Scripture in the Church was, in Wyclif's view, seriously undermined by the surging anthropocentric outlook among ecclesiastics. The growth of ecclesiastical wealth and the rise

---

[47] Wilks, "Wyclif and the Wheel of Time," pp. 209–10.
[48] *De dissensione paparum*, pp. 570–2.
[49] Wilks, "Wyclif and the Wheel of Time," pp. 216–17.

of ecclesiastical jurisdictional power were concomitant with the elevation of the status of canon law. Papal statutes, which constituted
the *Decretales*, were increasingly considered to be on a par with the
Bible. Wyclif opposed this development by asserting the superiority
of biblical authority.[50] Were popes of equal authority with the apostles and the authors of Scripture, says Wyclif, it would stand to reason that they could correct Scripture and legislate against the Lord
and his apostles. Indeed the authority of Scripture itself would vary
depending upon papal interpretation.[51] And so it must be affirmed
that Scripture is the absolute standard: "When it comes to papal
laws, bulls and mandates, it is clear that they ought to be obeyed
and believed only to the extent that they are founded upon Scripture."[52]
Furthermore, in the matter of interpreting Scripture itself, the pope
only has the right to interpret it according to the sense that the Holy
Spirit intends, and that the holy doctors have explained; he may not
interpret Scripture anyway he likes. Indeed, if he errs in his interpretation he sins shamefully and then must be resisted.[53]

At the turn of the late thirteenth and early fourteenth centuries,
the status of canon law in the hierarchy of academic knowledge had
already been a contentious issue.[54] From the early fourteenth century onwards, for instance, law became more popular than theology
in the University of Oxford.[55] Probably due to the legal profession's
better employability and lucrativeness, there was a clear tendency

---

[50] *De veritate Sacrae Scripturae* 15, ed. Rudolf Buddensieg, 3 vols. (London, 1905),
1:403. See Ian Christopher Levy, "Introduction," in John Wyclif, *On the Truth of
Holy Scripture*, trans. Ian Christopher Levy (Kalamazoo, 2001), p. 19.

[51] *De officio regis* 9, p. 223/23–29: "Tercio confirmatur ex hoc quod si sunt paris
auctoritatis cum apostolis et scripture sacre auctoribus, cum possunt, ut iniquiunt
seductores eorum, scripturam sacram corrigere et contra apostolum ac dominum
disepensare, videtur quod fluctuat scripture sacre auctoritas, cum ipsi tam fragiles
possint ipsam et eius sensum pervertere."

[52] *De officio regis* 9, p. 224/31–33: "Quod si queratur de legibus, de bullis et mandatis papalibus, quomodo debet obediri vel credi illis, patet quod precipue tante
quante sunt fundabilia ex scripturis."

[53] *De civili dominio* 3.17, p. 331/7–16: "Licet enim dominus papa potest interpretari scripturam sacram ad sensum quem Sanctus Spiritus intenderat et sancti
doctores exposuerant, non tamen quomodocunque voluerit . . . sed si in hoc erravit,
peccat turpiter, ostendens in hoc sibi non esse obediendum sed resistendum."

[54] On this, see Takashi Shogimen, "The Relationship between Theology and
Canon Law: Another Context of Political Thought in the Early Fourteenth Century,"
Journal of the History of Ideas (1999), 417–31.

[55] T.A.R. Evans, "The Number, Origins and Careers of Scholars," in *The History
of the University of Oxford*, ed., J.I. Catto and R. Evans (Oxford, 1992), 2:528–32.

that the number of canon and Roman lawyers increased more sharply than that of the theologians. The popularity of legal studies polarized the attitude of theologians towards canon lawyers. Some theologians were sympathetic to canon law to the extent that that they attempted to juridicize theology, thereby integrating their disciplines into each other. The Dominican theologian Pierre de la Palud won fame for his distinctively "practical" commentaries on Peter Lombard's *Sentences*. Pierre was well versed in canon law and offered a juristic understanding of the *vade mecum* of medieval theology. The work was so successful that it was copied repeatedly in the fourteenth and fifteenth centuries.[56] The fusion of theology and canon law was promoted by canonists as well. The canonist William of Pagula, for instance, wrote a compilation of canon law and theology in five books with two hundred and fifty seven chapters providing every cleric, from parish priests to prelates, with an authoritative response to any question that might arise in the course of their ministrations.[57]

But the amalgamation of the two disciplines was not an option for most of the leading theologians, since theology was superior to canon law. Bonaventure, for instance, argued in Aristotelian fashion that a science, which formed the starting of another, should be regarded as higher. Theology sets the starting point of all the enquiries in canon law and therefore was superior to canon law.[58] The assertion of the superiority of theology was in sharp contrast to the contemporary reality of the increasing influence of canon lawyers. Roger Bacon and Thomas Aquinas had been openly annoyed by the interference of canonists in doctrinal matters.[59] In the early fourteenth century, Dante singled out the decretalists as one of the three groups that poisoned Christendom.[60] Marsilius of Padua lamented that the papal curia had

---

[56] Jean Dunbabin, *A Hound of God: Pierre de la Palud and the Fourteenth-Century Church* (Oxford, 1991), p. 51.

[57] Leonard Boyle, "The 'Summa Summarum' and Some other English Works of Canon Law," *Monumenta iuris canonici*, series C, 1 (1965), 415–56.

[58] Bonaventure, *Commentarium in libros Sententiarum* IV, dist. 18, p. 2, a. 1, q. 3, in *Opera ominia*, vol. 4 (Quaracchi, 1889), p. 488.

[59] Michael Wilks, *The Problem of Sovereignty in the Later Middle Ages* (Cambridge, 1963), p. 305. See also G.H.M. Posthumus Meyjes, "Exponent of Sovereignty: Canonists as seen by theologians in the Late Middle Ages," in *The Church and Sovereignty, c. 590–1918: Essays in Honour of Michael Wilks* (Studies in Church History Subsidia 9) ed. Diana Wood (Oxford, 1991), pp. 299–312.

[60] Dante, *De monarchia* in *Opere minori* (Milan, 1963), p. 701. See also Dante, *Monarchy*, trans. Prue Shaw (Cambridge, 1996), p. 67.

been hijacked by "shyster lawyers."[61] Similarly critical of canon law, William of Ockham deplored the fact that since Innocent III, most of the popes had been lawyers, not theologians.[62] This anti-canonist outlook was subscribed to by thinkers and polemicists beyond the so-called "anti-papalist" camp. The staunch papalist Augustinus Triumphus of Ancona, for instance, regarded theology as "the end and the queen of all knowledge" and asserted the superiority of theology over canon law. Similarly, Giles of Rome advised all the kings to respect theologians over all others. Indeed, he was employed as a theological consultant by the papal curia, which had been dominated by lawyers.[63] Anti-canonist sentiment lingered at the turn of fourteenth and fifteenth centuries. Jean Gerson, for example, maintained that canon law as well as divine law fell into the realm of theology. He also held that canonists were intellectually ill equipped to master theology, whereas theologians were trained to grasp canon law, thereby affirming the superiority of theologians over canon lawyers.[64]

Wyclif was not alien to the long ideological battle between theologians and canonists. He wrote that theology—"the queen of the sciences"—had been "mingled with spurious doctrines, because an exceedingly large part of canon law itself has been mixed up with pagan traditions, though not according to that portion which natural law relates so thoroughly, but rather according to the portion which human traditions and ambitions have taught."[65] He also denounced canon law for having failed to remain evangelical and turned to "a law more vile than the laws of the pagans," especially due to the Donation of Constantine.[66] Indeed, Wyclif accused blasphemous papal

---

[61] Marsilius of Padua, *Defensor pacis*, p. 371.

[62] William of Ockham, *Dialogus* 1.2.30. I have used the British Academy's electronic edition, which is available on the Academy's website.

[63] Walter Ullmann, "Boniface VIII and His Contemporary Scholarship," *Journal of Theological Studies* 27 (1976), 58–87.

[64] John B. Morrall, *Gerson and the Great Schism* (Manchester, 1960), pp. 83–4. See also Louis Pascoe, *Jean Gerson: Principles of Church Reform* (Leiden, 1973), pp. 91–3.

[65] *On the Truth of Holy Scripture*, p. 304; *De veritate Sacrae Scripturae* 24, 2:268/19–24: "Domina scienciarum est commixta cum spurio, cum nimis magna pars iuris canonici permixta sit cum tradicionibus gentilium, non secundum illam partem, quam lex nature edocuit, sed secundum partem, quam tradiciones et ambiciones humane docuerant . . ."

[66] *De veritate Sacrae Scripturae* 2:268/24–28: ". . . quod lex canonica, que debet esse mere evangelica, occasione dotacionis ecclesie versa est in abiecciorem legem civilem quam leges gencium. et totum est ad inducendum, quod clerici debeant civiliter dominari."

lawyers (devoid of a proper understanding of Scripture) of driving bishops mad.[67] Wyclif's anti-canonist outlook, however, was less radical than it might seem. He did not dismiss canon law altogether; he merely rejected the idea that the authority of the papal statutes was on a par with the Bible.[68] This is evident in the fact that he was critical of the *Decretales*, whilst he was rather sympathetic to the *Decretum*, which he considered to be soundly based on Scripture. This forms an intriguing contrast to Ockham, who accused Gratian of making erroneous references to Scripture and included many errors in the *Decretum*.[69] Rather, Wyclif's hostility to the *Decretales* resembled Dante's position.

This is not, however, to downplay Wyclif's anti-legalism. Wyclif's preference for the *Decretum* should be interpreted as his trust in the Church Fathers. Abhorrence towards legalism clearly permeates Wyclif's polemical writings not only in the ecclesiastical but also in the temporal context; for instance, he recommended the king to rule by a minimal number of laws. The more laws the king implements, the more burdensome his rule becomes.[70] In this sense, it may be misleading to describe Wyclif as a "legal reformer." Fundamentally, Wyclif's reform program was intended to be theological, not legal, and so too was his ideological stance.

The Church

In the light of his theological (as opposed to legalistic) standpoint, Wyclif's discourse on the Church makes sense. The most formal and systematic discussion on the Church can be found in the introductory

---

[67] *De ecclesia* 14, p. 321/6–8: "Et in istam blasphemiam ex defectu intellectus scripture incidunt multi iuriste facientes suos prepositos insanire." Cf. Wilks, "Wyclif and the Wheel of Time," p. 216.

[68] Levy, "Introduction," in Wyclif, *On the Truth of Holy Scripture*, p. 19.

[69] Ockham, *Breviloquium de principatu tyrannico* 6.4, in Ockham, *Opera Politica*, vol. 4, ed. H.S. Offler (Oxford, 1997), p. 258. See also Ockham, *A Short Discourse on Tyrannical Government*, ed. A.S. McGrade and trans. John Kilcullen (Cambridge, 1992), p. 167.

[70] *De officio regis* 3, p. 56/6–14: "Et patet prudencia quod leges ille sint pauce. Primo quia sunt principales excedentes statum innocentie; de talibus autem oportet servos dei solum necessariis contentari, quia superhabundancia distraheret multipliciter a lege dei. Secundo quia multitudo legum talium generaret confusionem et intricacionem ad ipsas cognoscendum et exequendum, et per consequens necessitaret ad multiplicandum populum pro ipsis discendis, et subtraheret occupacionem sapientum regni pro ipsis interpretandis."

section of *De ecclesia*. According to Wyclif, the Church was a congregation of all who are predestinate. And this Church may be called "the mystical body of Christ, the bride of Christ, and the kingdom of heaven." Those who are reprobate are excluded from the membership of the Church. Indeed, a member of the body of Christ (*corpus Christi*) would have to be "alive" and those who are reprobate are compared to the members that need to be amputated, though Wyclif also maintained that human beings cannot know who is predestined by God.[71]

Wyclif's definition of the membership of the Church was thus anchored in his doctrine of predestination. "Although the Church is spoken of in many ways throughout Scripture, I think that we can conceive of it in its best known sense, namely the congregation of all the predestined."[72] This means that there are some people who may be within the institutional Church for now without ever being part of the true Church. Either they were permanently bereft of grace or else they had it only for a while before falling away. Like excess food in the stomach of Holy Mother Church, they have been received through the grace of present righteousness only to be spit out later on account of their own hypocrisy and heresy.[73] Indeed, many of the foreknown may be righteous at the moment. "It is clear that a man can be a bishop, a lord and minister of the Church, even as he is foreknown. That man may exist in a state of grace according to present righteousness, and yet he is still not a member of Holy Mother Church."[74] A single most important consequence of this was that the Church was radically de-institutionalized. In

---

[71] *De ecclesia* 1, pp. 1–25. Cf. *De civili dominio* 1.39, p. 288/7–9: "Tercio vero accipitur ecclesia propriissime pro universitate predestinatorum, et ista vocatur corpus Christi misticum, sponsa Christi, et regnum celorum."

[72] *De ecclesia*, p. 2/25–28: "Quamvis autem ecclesia dicatur multipliciter in scriptura, suppono quod sumatur ad propositum pro famosiori, scilicet congregacione omnium predestinatorum."

[73] *De ecclesia* 3, p. 61/2–5: "Illi autem qui sunt intra dictam ecclesiam non ut partes, sunt in gradu duplici, ut quidam in sua infidelitati perpetuo permanentes qui nunquam receperunt caritatem vel graciam." Ibid., p. 61/14–19: "Unde superflua illius cibi sunt infecta duplici, ut aliqui sunt in stomacho sancte matris ecclesie recepti per graciam secundum presentem iusticiam, sed ex eorum ypocrisi vel heresi non sunt propter abhominacionem caritatis operantis digesti, sed in hac vita sensibiliter evomendi, de quibus loquitur spiritus sanctus Apocalypsis 3:16."

[74] *De ecclesia* 6, p. 140/26–30: "Et patet quod homo potest esse episcopus, dominus et minister ecclesie, eciam prescitus, existens in gracia secundum presentem iusticiam, sed homo non est cum hoc membrum sancte matris ecclesie."

Wyclif's vision, no ecclesiastical office or institution can constitute the membership of the Church. Even the holder of the papal office cannot be sure *ipso facto* that he is predestined; still worse, it is impossible for him to know whether he is predestined. "No vicar of Christ should presume to assert that he is the head of the Holy Catholic Church unless he has received a special revelation, nor should he even assert that he is a member."[75] The doctrine of predestination effectively declared that the sacramental power of the ecclesiastical office was null and void and reduced it to the duty of disseminating correctly informed knowledge of the Christian faith. In fact, Wyclif concludes that the sacramental character received at ordination is only temporary among those whose damnation is foreknown, while it is indelible among the predestined.[76] To be sure, in arguing so, Wyclif was not upholding Donatism, which maintained that the unworthiness of the minister affected the validity of sacraments.[77] Wyclif was simply pressing the Augustinian doctrine of predestination to its logical limit. Thus, the legal structure of the Church had effectively crumbled. Wyclif attributed all the authority ascribed previously to priests, rectors, bishops and popes to Christ alone. Christ is the single and only head of the Church. Indeed, against all papal claims, the "rock" upon which the Church was founded is none other than Christ himself.[78] The spiritual Church has been erected with the faith of Christ for its foundation, hope for its walls, and love for its roof.[79]

---

[75] *De ecclesia* 1, p. 5/14–18: "Prima, quod nullus vicarius Christi debet presumere asserere se esse caput ecclesie sancte catholice, ymmo nisi habuerit specialem revelacionem, non assereret se esse aliquod membrum eius."

[76] *De ecclesia* 19, p. 444/4–11: "Tenendo ergo secundam viam de quiditate caracteris dico ulterius quod alius est necessario delebilis, ut caracter ecclesiasticus in prescitis, eo quod non ultra diem iudicii durabit in eis officium dignitatis. In predestinatis autem oportet esse caracterem omnino indelebilem . . ."

[77] *De ecclesia* 19, p. 448/14–16: "Videtur autem mihi quod prescitus eciam in mortali peccato actuali ministrat fidelibus." Ibid., 448/30–32: "Sic ergo sacerdotes mali iniuriantur sed non nocent piis fidelibus non demerentibus ministrando eis ecclesiastica sacramenta . . ."

[78] *De civili dominio* 1.38, p. 281/23–6: "Postquam enim Petrus exclusis heresibus confessus est Christi deitatem et humanitatem, concessit sibi Veritas quod *super hanc petrum*, que secundum apostolum erat Christus . . ." Cf. Matt. 16:18; and 1 Cor. 10:4.

[79] *De civili dominio* 1.39, pp. 288/27–289/2: "Ex istis patet quod domus spiritualis ecclesie edificata habet pro fundamento fidem Christi, pro parietibus spem vite, et pro tecto caritatem. *Super hanc* quidem *petram*, que est fundamentum quo *aliud nemo ponere potest*, fundatur ecclesia."

Glorifying Christ as the head of the Church had direct repercussions on Wyclif's conception of the papacy. He flatly rejected the view that the Bishop of Rome was granted prerogatives that were superior to those of other bishops. "It is quite likely that Christ bestowed the fullness of power on all the apostles so that they might bind and loose, and generally accomplish all that their prelatical office requires in the Church militant, as is clearly stated in Matthew 18:18 and John 20:23. Otherwise, Christ would not have been so prudent as to send out the apostles so that they might each govern their separate provinces. Nor did the rest of the apostles then consult with Saint Peter from their different provinces."[80] But even if Peter did attain to some higher level of excellence beyond his fellow apostles, this does not automatically transfer to his papal successors. Whatever Peter achieved was by the grace of God and on account of his humility. Even the strength of his faith depended upon Christ's grace.[81] Though Peter may be the ideal pope, the Church must now suffer under the present lot. "Just as it is good to have a pope who would follow Christ and Peter in matters of morals and doctrine, so then it is an evil thing to have a pope who would run so contrary to those shepherds in these two things."[82] The situation is so dire precisely because the present popes have misunderstood the nature of Petrine primacy. "Peter's preeminence among the other apostles rests not in honor, nor in worldly power and glory, but rather in their very opposites. It should be clear that his preemi-

---

[80] *De Christo et suo adversario antichristo* 6, in *Polemical Works in Latin*, 2:666/9–16: "Videtur autem probabile, quod omnibus apostolis Christus dedit plenitudinem potestatis ad ligandum et solvendum et faciendum quodcunque prelati officium in ecclesia militante, ut plane dicitur Matth. Duodevicesimo et Ioh. Vicesimo. Aliter enim non fuisset Christus providus mittendo illos apostolos sic solitarie ad tam separatas provincias regulandum. Non enim consuluerunt ceteri apostoli ex suis provinciis sanctum Petrum." See also *De potestate papae* 7, p. 140/12–15: "... Petrus tamquam generalis attornatus gerebat personam ecclesie, ubi recepit potestatem non singulariter pro se et quocumque Romano pontifice sed generaliter ..."

[81] *De Christo et suo adversario antichristo* 6, p. 668/19–23: "Sed si fuit Petri excellencia simpliciter supra alios, hoc fuit ex dei gracia et propter meritum humilitatis que floruit excellencius in hoc Petro. Petrus enim dicitur aliqualiter fuisse firmus in fide, sed notatur ex dicto Christo, quod illa fides fuit fundamentaliter gracia Iesu Cristi."

[82] *De Christo et suo adversario antichristo* 8, p. 673/14–17: "Unde quidam fideles publicant in wulgari, quod, sicut bonum esst, habere papam, qui sequeretur Cristum et Pterum in moribus et doctrina, sic malum esset, habere papam, qui in hiis duobus foret pastoribus istis contrarius."

nence derives from his sincere faith, his humility, and his servitude."[83] Hence a true pope would be the humblest man of all, excelling in every virtue, having put aside all temporal goods, renouncing worldly glory and thus contemplating only heavenly things.[84]

Wyclif, of course, did not endorse the doctrine of papal infallibility. The papal office does not confer any special power on its recipient, just as Judas Iscariot did not receive any special virtue simply for being one of the Apostles.[85] As Wyclif writes: "There are those who claim that the pope cannot commit the sin of simony, thereby attributing to a creature what is proper to God. For Christ, who is both God and man, is the only wayfarer who could not sin."[86] In fact, "no wayfarer is more likely than the Roman Pontiff to be the principal vicar of Satan and the chief Antichrist. It is clear, therefore, that he can easily defraud the Church in his hypocrisy and every sort of lie." And this being the case, "no one should believe the Roman Pontiff in matters of faith, except to the extent that his teaching is founded upon Scripture."[87] Unfortunately for the Church, the pope has taken to inventing his own law. "Christ has prohibited with a grave anathema anyone from adding something that would infringe upon his own law, as is clear in Galatians 1:9 and many other passages. And yet the False One fabricates new laws which have no basis in Holy Scripture, in which Saint Augustine tells us that all truth can be found."[88]

---

[83] *De potestate papae* 7, p. 135/17–21: "... quod preeminencia Petri in alios non stat in honore, in dominatu vel gloria seculari sed in omnino oppositis. Patet primo ex hoc quod stat in fidei sinceritate et humilitate et in servitute, ut patet ex dictis."

[84] *De civili dominio* 2.3, p. 17/24–29: "Ex quo patet quod dominus papa debet esse tocius populi humilimus, mitissimus et effectualissimus ministrator, bonorum fortune strictissimus abdicator, et ut breviter dicatur, omni genere virtutum et potissime in renunciacione secularium negociorum ac contemplacione celestium . . ."

[85] *De blasphemia* 3, p. 42/17–19: "Maior patet de eleccione Scarioth, quem Cristus indubie virtuosius et sic melius elegit, quam cardinales vel alii scirent eligere romanum pontificem."

[86] *De civili dominio* 1.43, p. 372/1–5: "Illi ergo qui dicunt quod 'papa iste non potest committere symoniam' attribuunt creature quod Deo est proprium. Solus ergo Christus, qui est simul Deus et homo, est viator qui peccare non poterit."

[87] *De blasphemia* 3, p. 44/14–18: "Nullus viator est apcior romano pontifice ut sit vicarius principalis sathane et precipuus antichristus. Patet ex hoc quod ipse potest faciliter fraudare ecclesiam in yppocrisi et omni mendacio." Ibid., 44/30–32: "Non est credendum romano pontifici in materia fidei, nisi de quanto se fundaverit in scriptura."

[88] *De potestate papae* 6, 121/10–15: "Tercio, ubi Christi anathemate gravi prohibuit

Finding a genuine pope, who will meet Wyclif's standards, is no easy thing. Papal election requires a special divine revelation and is null if it fails to elect one of God's own elect, that is, one of the predestined.[89] For Wyclif, it only stands to reason that the head of the Church would have to be numbered among the predestined, and it would be nothing short of blasphemy for the electors to attempt to render such a determination.[90] Simply being elected by the college of cardinals proves nothing. "Whoever wishes to be the vicar of Christ or Peter must whole-heartedly follow after their example and imitate their way of life. It is not the mere title, nor some election in the presence of the Church, that makes someone a pope."[91] As it stood, therefore, the contemporary state of the papacy was far removed from the apostolic ideals: the enormous wealth of the papacy, the absence of scriptural foundation for the practice of papal election by the college of cardinals and, above all, the Great Schism clearly demonstrated that the Church could do without the papacy.[92]

Wyclif's conception of the Church has often been compared with Ockham's, since they both reduced the Church to an "invisible" entity. Indeed, Ockham refused to define the Church in institutional terms and identified it with a congregation of believers. However, the ecclesiological implications of "invisibleness" of the Church greatly vary between the two thinkers. Believers are, according to Ockham's definition, those who publicly embrace and manifest the explicit faith (the faith, which the individual is obliged to subscribe to). Ockham's notion of Church membership is based on the individual's external

---

quod non adderetur aliquid impertinens legi sue, ut patet Gal. primo et sepe alibi, iste Pseudo fabricat leges novas, que nusquam reperiuntur in scriptura sacra; in qua secundum Augustinum est omnis veritas . . ."

[89] *De blasphemia* 3, p. 42/26–28: "Sed nulla eleccio electorum pape est valida, nisi de quanto exemplata fuerit ab eleccione divina." Ibid., p. 43/3–6: "Item, foret blasfema presumpcio, in his que concernunt salutem magni populi temere diffinire; sed sic est in quacunque eleccione Romani pontificis, si non esset ad hoc revelacio: ergo, sic eligere foret blasfema presumpcio."

[90] *De blasphemia* 3, p. 43/27–31: "Item, eo ipso quo quis statuit quemquam capud ecclesie, statuit eum predestinatum, cum solum talis sit pars ecclesie, ut hic supponitur. Sed nimis blasfemum esset electores statuere vel diffinire predestinacionem huiusmodi: ergo et suum convertibile."

[91] *De potetstate papae* 7, p. 156/2–6: "Qui igitur voluerit esse Christi vel Petri vicarius, oportet ut ad instar eorum ex animo faciat similiter cum vita imitatoria et non nudum nomen vel eleccio in facie ecclesie facit papam."

[92] See *De Christo et suo adversario antichristo* 8–9, pp. 671–6.

act observable by anyone, thus far removed from Wyclif's theocentric idea of Church membership. Ockham famously argued that heretics might prevail in Christendom and consequently the Church could be reduced to a single individual who continues to maintain orthodox faith: a man, a woman or even an infant.[93] In this argument, however, Ockham does not say that God actually predestines particular individuals to hold the explicit faith. Christ only promised that the true faith remains at all times until the end of time. Ockham logically reduced the indefectibility of the universal Church through time into the permanent presence of, at least, one individual who holds the orthodox faith. In so arguing, Ockham de-mystified the Church as an institution. Of course he did not rule out the possibility of new revelations; however, he asserted on the other hand that no case of new revelations could be found in recent times. Thus, the Church after the time of Christ and the apostles is understood as an institution operated by human beings without clear evidence of divine sanction.

Wyclif's conception of an invisible Church is more emphatically theocentric. It is God who determines the membership of the Church, and human beings as creatures cannot do anything to secure membership. An individual can only believe that he or she be predestinate. Wyclif did not de-mystify the Church in the same way as Ockham did. Wyclif did not regard the operation of ecclesiastical government as entirely human; quite the contrary, he asserted direct divine sanction. On this point, Wyclif is nearer to the majority of medieval political thinkers. Papalist theologians such as Guido Terreni believed that papal doctrinal decision-making was infallible through the work of the Holy Spirit.[94] Likewise, Marsilius of Padua believed that conciliar infallibility was secured by divine intervention through the Holy Spirit.[95] However, Wyclif separated himself from both papalists and Marsilius in that he rejected the idea that the work of God was mediated by ecclesiastical institutions. Wyclif squarely rejected any institutional infallibility and insisted that God sanctioned individual believers immediately, thus depriving the ecclesiastical institutions of

---

[93] See for instance, Ockham *Tractatus contra Benedictum*, in *Opera Politica*, ed. H.S. Offler, vol. 3 (Manchester, 1956), p. 261.

[94] See Takashi Shogimen, "William of Ockham and Guido Terreni," *History of Political Thought* 19 (1998), 517–30.

[95] Marsilius of Padua, *Defensor pacis*, p. 313.

the mystical power that mediates between God and man. The immediacy of the relationship between God and individual believers minimized the institution in order to return it to the simplicity of the primitive Church.

Wyclif often delineated his own vision of the primitive Church and attempted to demonstrate the discrepancies between the primitive Church and the practice of his day. He pointed out that the apostolic Church had been poor and meek, not seeking after temporal dominion.[96] This is another aspect in which Wyclif's polemical writings are in sharp contrast to Ockham. Ockham highlighted the deviation of contemporary ecclesiastical practice from what he understood to be the practice of the Church in the time of Christ and the apostles. But the true Church, against which the state of the Church of the following generations should be assessed, existed *only* in a specific moment in the past. God revealed Himself in certain moments in the past and we have not witnessed any new revelations. In this sense, Ockham's appeal to the primitive Church is strictly historicist.[97] Wyclif, too, often contrasted the primitive Church with the Church of his day; however, he did not think that the true Church existed in the time of Christ and the apostles only. The true Church as the congregation of the Elect had always existed throughout Christian history. Hence, Wyclif's polemical strategy in criticizing the Church of his day differed significantly from Ockham's: Wyclif's identification of the true Church with the congregation of the Elect severed the direct relationship between the true and the visible Church. And the restoration of the true Church in the visible sphere belonged to the (probably distant) future when the time is ripe for it. Wyclif's appeal to the primitive Church does not share the Ockhamist sense of irreversibility of the glorious moments in the Christian past; rather it is undergirded by his doctrine of predestination and his philosophy of history. Wyclif's appeal to the primitive Church, therefore, is not historicist in the same sense as Ockham's.[98]

---

[96] See for instance *De veritate Sacrae Scripturae* 2.22–23.

[97] Takashi Shogimen, "Ockham's Vision of the Primitive Church," in *The Church Retrospective* (Studies in Church History vol. 33) ed. R.N. Swanson (Woodbridge, 1997), pp. 163–75.

[98] Cf. Gordon Leff, "The Making of the Myth of a True Church in the Later Middle Ages," *Journal of Medieval and Renaissance Studies* 6 (1971), 1–15. Among the thinkers

Here a question might arise: if no individual is able to secure his or her own membership, and the institution of the Church is irrelevant to the true Church of the Elect, what would be the significance of the Church on earth? Interestingly, Wyclif's doctrine of predestination did not reduce human effort in ecclesiastical government into something useless and insignificant. Whether or not an individual is predestinate, he still bears the duty to serve God so long as he is a Christian. He must follow and disseminate the words of Christ. Wyclif's attack on the Church of his day was nothing other than the acute criticism of late medieval Christianity as "religion." In Wyclif's vision, contemporary Christianity ceased to be the pristine faith of the apostolic age and had been degraded to an institutionalized religion. Gordon Leff once wrote that Wyclif's denial of the ecclesiastical hierarchy's *raison d'être* was "disruptive" and his rejection of the divine origin of (most of) ecclesiastical institutions including the papacy was his "single most revolutionary step."[99] However, these remarks are misleading because Wyclif had no choice but to be "disruptive" to the institution precisely because he attempted to spiritualize and rehabilitate Christian faith; thus, his reform program represented a constructive project of spiritual reform. Wyclif was confronted by the reality that the Christian faith was jeopardized by the excessive growth of ecclesiastical institutions. The physical growth of ecclesiastical organizations and the maintenance of spiritual well-being were mutually exclusive in the light of the ideal of apostolic poverty; Wyclif was faced with this dilemma and opted for the latter: the spiritual welfare of believers.

The doctrine of predestination renders to God alone all the power that determines eternal salvation or damnation. "Predestination is God's chief gift most freely given, since no one can merit his own predestination." It is a gift that, once received, "cannot be lost, since it is the foundation of glorification or beatitude, which cannot be lost either."[100] Committing mortal sin would not affect the status of

---

who adopted "a new critical historical attitude to the Church," Leff included Wyclif. See also his "The Apostolic Ideal in Later Medieval Ecclesiology," *Journal of Theological Studies* 18 (1967), 58–82.

[99] Leff, *Heresy in the Later Middle Ages*, pp. 519, 531.

[100] *De ecclesia* 6, p. 139/4–14: "Et illa predestinacio cum sit precipuum donum Dei gratissime datum, cum nemo potest mereri suam predestinacionem . . . et sic conceditur quod non potest perdi, cum sit fundamentum glorificacioni vel beatitudini, que nec eciam potest perdi."

the predestined. "No one should doubt the fact that many of the predestined have sinned mortally, as much through original sin as through actual sin, as was the case with David, Peter, and Paul. . . . And so, the grace of predestination may stand along side mortal sin, although it is still opposed to the sin against the Holy Spirit, just as the grace of present righteousness among the foreknown is contrary to damnation." Hence, as Wyclif says, God always loved Peter infinitely more than Judas, even as Peter was denying the Lord.[101] What believers can only know is that the Church is the congregation of the predestinate in the past, present and future. No believer can know that he or she is predestinate. Nor should anyone assert that he or she is predestinate; such an assertion would be utterly blasphemous. It is because the Church must be by definition 'without stain or wrinkle' [Eph. 5:27] that it would be presumptuous to assert without fear that one is a true (namely, predestined) member of the Church. "For no one except for the predestined and the sanctified, those without stain or wrinkle at the proper time, is a member of this Church. But, as no one can, without fear or revelation, assert that he is predestined and sanctified or without stain or wrinkle, the conclusion must follow."[102] Nonetheless, Wyclif insists that believers ought to believe that they are predestinate because they must hope and believe with fear in God's grace.

Wyclif's recognition of the relevance of ecclesiastical life was evident in his call for mutual aid that maintained the spiritual well-being of the body of Christ.[103] For instance, Wyclif underlined the importance of fraternal correction as the normal operation of ecclesiastical institutions. He insisted that priests ought to take the initiative in correcting deviant prelates; however, should the priesthood fail to achieve

---

[101] De ecclesia 6, p. 139/20–27: "Quo ad secundum dicitur, cum nemo dubitat quin multi predestinati peccarunt mortaliter, tam peccato originali quam actuali, ut patet de David, Petro et Paulo, et predestinacio non potest perdi iuxta dicta, manifestum est quod gracia predestinacionis stat cum peccato mortali, verumptamen repugnat peccato in spiritum sanctum, sicut gracia presciti secundum presentem iusticiam repugnat dampnacioni . . ."

[102] De ecclesia 4, pp. 84/29–85/3: "Nam nemo nisi predestinatus et sanctus tempore suo sine macula vel ruga est memborum illius ecclesie. Sed nemo sine formidine vel revelacione assereret quod sit predestinatus et sanctus sine macula vel ruga: ergo conclusio."

[103] Daly, The Political Theory of John Wyclif, pp. 82, 86; Farr, John Wyclif as Legal Reformer, p. 65.

this, laymen are entitled to correct the delinquency of prelates. Who is to judge whether prelates are deviant? Wyclif held that it was the "people" (populus): "It is important . . . . that the people make sure the justice system of the priests does not fail."[104] A salient presupposition in this argument is that the ecclesiastical order is independent of the secular one. Ecclesiastical government should not allow interference from secular government without correcting itself at first instance. Wyclif embraced the duality of spiritual and temporal orders and, in this regard, he resembled Ockham. Ockham only justified the exceptional interference of temporal powers in the spiritual order if the self-corrective procedure had completely failed within the ecclesiastical order. Ockham's radical dissent from papal authority in his battle of words against Popes John XXII and Benedict XII was grounded in his conviction that an informed layman was legitimately entitled to correct popes who had fallen into heretical depravity. Indeed, Ockham and other "Michaelist" Franciscans, who took refuge in Munich, believed that they were defending catholic truths from papal attack. In this sense, their dissent remained a part of the self-corrective process within the ecclesiastical order that they envisaged, although the correctors were no longer holders of ecclesiastical office.[105] Wyclif asserted the same principle: fraternal correction within the Church should precede any interference from secular powers. However, Ockham thought that the Church could still be corrected by some of its members (such as himself). Wyclif, by contrast, diagnosed the corruption of the Church as terminal. A self-corrective process within the Church was, therefore, no longer a viable option. The remedial means were thus sought outside the ecclesiastical institutions: the secular ruler.

Reform

Wyclif maintained that the primary obligation that the king bears is to maintain or restore the well-being of the realm's Church. Serving

---

[104] Wyclif, *On the Truth of Holy Scripture*, p. 309; *De veritate Sacrae Scripturae* 25, 3:15/22–24: "Et dum non deficit iudicium sacerdotum, ad quod iudicum debet populus signanter attendere . . ."

[105] On Ockham's idea of fraternal correction, see Takashi Shogimen, "From Disobedience to Toleration: William of Ockham and the Medieval Discourse on Fraternal Correction," *Journal of Ecclesiastical History* 52 (2001), 599–622.

his kingdom is of only secondary significance because a king cannot maintain the welfare of the kingdom unless the Church is healthy. Identifying kingship with the remedial means for Church reform was central to Wyclif's conception of kingship. For Wyclif, the king is "God's vicar" (*dei vicarius*) and so, even as he is our brother in Christ, he must be honored above all other men.[106] Wyclif will offer a concise summary of the relationship between the royal and priestly powers. "It is fitting that God would have two vicars in the Church, namely the king in temporal affairs and the priest in spiritual matters. The king ought to suppress rebellion with all severity, just as God did in the Old Testament. The priest, on the other hand, should minister to the lowly in all gentleness here in the age of the law of grace, just as Christ had done in his human nature. Though Christ was at once both king and priest. And so it is that Augustine says the king bears the image of God, while the bishop bears the image of Christ for the sake of his ministry.... For the king bears the image of Christ's divinity, just as the bishop bears the image of his humanity."[107]

More specifically, Wyclif argued that the king's duty was threefold: as a man, a father and a king. The king must first be a good individual, wise like Solomon, serving God with fear, and abiding by the teaching of Christ, who is King of kings. He would not constantly seek after riches and victory over his enemies, but would search for the wisdom necessary to rule over God's people. He then must be a good father by administering his household and the royal court, watching over the clergy's behavior and excelling in knowledge of the divine law. Though Wyclif admits that not all kings have wisdom infused into them by God, and so must be willing to seek assistance from the wise men of the realm. The king could then be

---

[106] *De officio regis* 1, p. 4/26–30: "Rex enim est dei vicarius quem proximo dictum est esse timendum, ideo necesse est sibi servari honorificenciam in eius vicario, et per consequens, non obstante quod sit frater noster, differenter ab aliis fratribus honorari."

[107] *De officio regis* 1, p. 13/2–12: "Oportet ergo deum habere in ecclesia duos vicarios, scilicet regem in temporalibus et sacerdotem in spiritualibus. Rex autem debet severe cohercere rebellem, sicut fecit deitas in veteri testamento. Sacerdos vero debet ministrare preceptum miti modo humilibus tempore legis gracie sicut fecit humanitas Cristi, qui simul fuit rex et sacerdos. Et hinc dicit Augustinus quod rex habet ymaginem dei sed episcopus ymaginem Cristi, propter ministerium indubie.... rex gerit ymaginem deitatis Cristi, sicut episcopus ymaginem sue humanitatis."

a good king by administering the smallest possible number of laws and acting as God's vicar.[108]

So, the king is primarily expected to be the instrument of Church reform. How would the king achieve Church reform? Ordinarily, the king would first compel the bishops and other clergy to attend to their spiritual responsibilities. Stamping out heresies serves the common good of the realm and was indeed one of the king's duties. But what the king can do is limited to temporal matters. The king cannot replace bishops or popes as the spiritual leaders of the realm. All he can do is to provide the optimum environment in which the spiritual well-being of the realm can be maintained. And such an environment could only be realized through the divestment of ecclesiastical wealth. One of the king's important functions in Church reform was therefore to take away wealth from the Church if it abuses it.[109] As he writes: "The king possesses the most universal human power of coercion within his own kingdom. And because of this, I would say that it is expedient for him to punish the clergy by forcefully removing their temporal goods."[110] Wyclif's notion of kingship is markedly compulsive and punitive. The king is expected to compel the people to serve God and punish heretics. St Augustine of Hippo considered political authority to be necessary evil—a remedial measure for postlapsarian human beings. Wyclif's idea of kingship is unmistakably Augustinian.

Wyclif's proposal for the king's active intervention in the temporal aspects of the ecclesiastical life, however, has puzzled modern historians in the light of his conception of the Church. Wyclif maintained that the true Church, as the congregation of the Elect, was utterly unknown to any individual believer, thus severing its actual relationship to the Church existent on earth. And, as mentioned, he even embraced a sort of cyclical idea of Christian history and anticipated the recovery

---

[108] *De officio regis* 3, pp. 46–47. Ibid., 46/16–28: "Oportet enim regem, (et specialiter post Cristi instruccionem qui est rex regum) habere specialiter intellectum. . . . non petivit longevitatem divicias vel super inimicos victorias, sed sapienciam ad dei populum regulandum. . . . Sed quia non omnes reges habent sic sapienciam infusam a domino, sed oportet eos habere sapientes tam in iudiciis quam a latere assistentes . . ."

[109] *De potestate papae* 6, pp. 101–2.

[110] *De civili dominio* 1.37, p. 270/12–15: "Item rex habet potestatem coactivam humanam universalissimam regni sui; ergo posito, per possibile, quod expediat clerum per subtraccionem invitam temporalium castigari, hoc principaliter spectat ad regis officium."

from the nadir of history, which he and his contemporaries were in. On the face of it, the Church on earth, as Wyclif envisages it, seems to be alienated from its constituent members. Nonetheless, Wyclif rejected the prophetic expectations of the Franciscan Spirituals; instead, he demanded action from believers as well as the king. This "inconsistency"[111] between the idea of the true Church irrelevant to its empirical reality and the radical reform program he advocated was in fact bridged by Wyclif's idea of dominion. Dominion *is* the term that describes the relation between God and Creation. Divine dominion, therefore, determined the very existence of any created being. A creature's capacity or action of doing anything is predicated on God's dominion. Hence, no justice can be exercised without God willing it. At the heart of Wyclif's metaphysics was the idea that the power exercised by any individual was grounded in, and causally dependent upon, divine dominion. As Stephen Lahey puts it: "God's dominion serves as a universal relation in which all created instances of dominion participate."[112]

Human beings enjoyed true dominion before the Fall; Wyclif named the dominion that prelapsarian human beings enjoyed natural dominion. Natural dominion extended over the whole world (both heaven and earth) where there was neither private, exclusive ownership nor dominative subjugation, whereas civil dominion extends no further than this corruptible sphere.[113] Original sin, however, deprived human beings of the capacity for natural dominion. Natural dominion was replaced by human dominion that assumed human selfishness in desiring exclusive property ownership. But, this does not mean that God has now alienated His dominion from men. God still remains the true lord of Creation. Private ownership is no more than an illusion. Divine dominion remains the universal standard against which every other kind of dominion should be measured. Human dominion over particular individuals results from participation in God's dominion. The relationship between divine and human dominion was tantamount to that between universal and particular.

---

[111] Leff, *Heresy in the Later Middle Ages*, p. 536.
[112] Lahey, "Wyclif and Lollardy," p. 339.
[113] *De civili dominio* 3.13, pp. 228–9. Ibid., 228/1–11 "... primum ex institucione nature per se ante omne peccatum hominis inculpabile ordinatur ... naturale dominium extendit se ad totum mundum: celum, terram et universa que celi ambitu continentur; civile vero dominium non se extendit ultra speram corruptibilium quoad profunditatem terre."

Christ's dominion was a natural dominion restored through the redemption of original sin. "In the state of innocence man had dominion over every part of the sensible world; and thereupon, by virtue of Christ's passion, came the full remission of sins as well as the restitution of dominion to the just. So it is that, here in the age of grace, the just man has full dominion over all things."[114] This is the dominion exercised in the communal life of poverty and simplicity by the apostles, which Wyclif called evangelical dominion.[115] Unlike some of the Franciscan polemicists, however, Wyclif did not envisage his notion of evangelical dominion as merely a state of poverty: the state of using goods "simply" without claiming any positive right of ownership or use (*simplex usus facti*). Evangelical poverty does not pertain to the possession of goods as such, but to the way one relates to them. "This poverty is the true humility which excludes pride and therefore all guilt."[116] Wyclif was clearly not proposing the idea of evangelical poverty as a juristic concept. It was rather a theological notion that was anchored in charity, the chief theological virtue. Wyclif aspired to the restoration of evangelical dominion in the life of the Church.

The idea of being just (*iustus*) was at the center of the poverty dispute in the fourteenth century and Wyclif's understanding can be placed in that context. Pope John XXII's attack on Franciscan poverty was partly grounded in the idea that no act without right (*ius*) can be just (*iustus*). Using consumables such as food and clothing could not be "just" without the right to use them. Ockham, in response, distinguished "just" from "licit" (*licitus*). According to the Franciscan friar, being "just" meant conformity to positive law, while being "licit" meant something sanctioned by natural reason. Ockham thereby discriminated the sphere of positive law from the sphere of morality

---

[114] *De civili dominio* 1.9, p. 62/9–13: "Homo in statu innocencie habuit dominium cuiuslibet partis mundi sensibilis ... et virtute passionis Christi est iustis plena peccatorem remissio ac dominium restitutum; ergo iam tempore gracie habet iustus plenum universitatis dominium."

[115] *De ecclesia* 16, p. 365/21–24: "Tercio notandum quod Deus dedit beato Petro et toti generi suo secundum spiritualem imitacionem dominacionem evangelicam et usufructum super omnia bona mundi, non autem dominacionem vel usum civilem."

[116] *De civili dominio* 3.8, p. 119/34–37: "Sexto colligitur quod paupertas evangelica est inpertinens possessioni temporalium, sed modo habendi respiciens cum augmento diviciarum nunc augeri nunc minui potest." Ibid., p. 120/19–20: "Ipsa enim paupertas est vera humilitas excludens superbiam et per consequens omnem culpam ..."

(more specifically, natural rights), attributing actual use without any right to the latter.[117] Using different terms, Marsilius also expounded a similar argument; Marsilius, who ostensibly eliminated the notions of natural law and natural rights from his legal discourse, also adopted a two-dimensional argument, by differentiating between "licit" (conformity to prescriptive, prohibitive or permissive laws) and "equitable" (neither commanded nor permitted by laws but approved rationally by the legislator), attributing use in cases of necessity to the latter: a position intriguingly similar to that of the "Michaelist" Franciscans.[118] Both Ockham and Marsilius attributed poverty to the realm of morality beyond human positive laws. Wyclif's defense of poverty, by contrast, did not appeal to human reason. Just use is possible only with the consent of a holder of dominion, but use of consumables without the consent of the dominion holder could be just, especially in cases of necessity; for example, in the case of starvation, "all use of comestible presupposes natural dominion."[119] His argument was again theocentric: Wyclif's ideal of poverty required grace as the foundation. Grace restores the lack of solicitude, which prelapsarian humans enjoyed, and therefore lack of property ownership is irrelevant to the Wycliffite state of poverty, which is a grace-founded state of the soul.[120]

This does not, however, exclude actual lack of property from Wyclif's conception of poverty. On the contrary, lack of property (provided it is grace-founded) is preferable to just—grace-founded—civil dominion. Indeed, Christ's redemption enabled the Church to return to a state of enjoying natural dominion, which is sharply distinguished from dominion as a result of original sin. And, with respect to the relationship between sin and dominion, it must be remembered that (as we have seen) Wyclif distinguished between a person's present status and his eternal status. Even the predestined may be in a present state of mortal sin, and thus be unfit for dominion at some point during their earthly life. "Just as an heir lacks dominion when he is still a small boy, even while he is lord of all in due

---

[117] Ockham, *Opus nonaginta dierum* 62, in *Opera politica*, vol. 2, ed. H.S. Offler (Manchester, 1963), pp. 556–67.

[118] Marsilius, *Defensor pacis* 2.12–13.

[119] *De civili dominio* 3.17, p. 340/30–31: "Primo quia omnis usus talis vescibilia presupponit naturae dominium."

[120] Lahey, *Philosophy and Politics*, pp. 133–38.

time, so the predestined man in a state of mortal sin is bereft of dominion, despite the fact that he has dominion at some other time, since God eternally wills that he should have it at the proper time."[121] This is a very important point, because it underscores the fact that the present order of temporal affairs does not depend upon our discerning God's inscrutable plan of eternal election and reprobation.

Among all kinds of dominion, most relevant to the idea of kingship is civil dominion. The idea of civil dominion bridges theological and political discourses and, of course, Wyclif was not unique in introducing the idea. The staunch papalist theologian Giles of Rome was probably the first who employed the idea of dominion in order to analyze the created order. He understood dominion as both private property and jurisdiction and maintained that it required grace as a necessary precondition. Without grace, no one would be entitled to dominion. This idea is not dissimilar to Wyclif's; however, Giles considered that the Church, the pope in particular, monopolized all earthly dominion: a view that Wyclif was to reject flatly.

The direct source of Wyclif's idea of dominion was Richard FitzRalph, Archbishop of Armagh. FitzRalph discussed the idea of dominion extensively in his *De pauperie Salvatoris*. Historians had pointed out similarities between FitzRalph and Wyclif on dominion; however, Wyclif in fact modified FitzRalph's view significantly. While both agree that property and the power of ruling are sub-categories of dominion and that just dominion is only possible through grace, they disagree on the intrinsic nature of property. FitzRalph's notion of property was, as Stephen Lahey argues, the commodity of dominion.[122] FitzRalph's discourse on dominion primarily concerned just possession; it vindicated ecclesiastical property holding and rejected apostolic poverty. This forms a sharp contrast with Wyclif's position. Civil dominion is antithetical to natural dominion; civil dominion is exclusive property ownership or dominative relations resulting from the Fall.[123] It was instituted by human beings, not God. The postlapsarian world requires civil dominion. Wyclif believed, however,

---

[121] *De ecclesia* 6, pp. 140/30–141/4: "Unde sicut heres parvulus caret dominio, dum tamen tempore suo sit dominus omnium, sic predestinatus in mortali caret dominio, dum tamen alio tempore habet dominium, cum Deus eternaliter vult quod illud habeat pro suo tempore."
[122] Lahey, pp. 49–63.
[123] Ibid., p. 117.

that having civil dominion was a grave danger. On the part of
bearers civil ownership involves solicitude, and inevitably leads to
disputes, theft, and war. The Church, therefore, must be free from
civil dominion. Here Wyclif clearly departed from FitzRalph, and
resembles the defenders of Franciscan poverty. Unlike the "Michaelist"
Franciscans, however, Wyclif did not grasp apostolic poverty as the
lack of civil dominion. Indeed, natural dominion was not lost entirely
to human beings. God did not deprive the righteous—the Elect—of
anything that He granted, and Christ's redemption enabled them to
have natural dominion: own nothing and share everything. Still more
importantly, Wyclif did not think that civil dominion was intrinsically and irreversibly unjust dominion. Civil dominion could be just.
The use of civil dominion is just when grace justifies the holder of
the dominion.[124]

Civil dominion, however, is illusory. It is not owned by any civil
lord but truly by God alone. The civil lord is no more than God's
steward, whose property and jurisdictional power were merely loaned
by the Lord. The notion of stewardship explains why the king bears
the special duty to be in charge of temporal property and power.
The civil lord must reject any claim to hold true exclusive dominion. Recognizing civil dominion as loaned from God is nothing other
than participation in divine dominion. This makes a civil lord a just
ruler, who works as a vehicle of grace. In fact, the ideal king is an
earthly image of the Holy Trinity. Just as God the Father creates
the world in his omnipotence, and the Son conserves the created
order, and the Spirit governs it kindly, so then, "the king should
establish his subjects in their ranks, defend them in their goods of
nature, and third, wisely govern them with respect to their temporal
goods by way of his justice."[125] This did not necessarily glorify the
secular ruler but rather redefined all the relationships between ruler
and ruled as "a theological relation between people under God."[126]

---

[124] Ibid., pp. 141–6.
[125] *De officio regis* 3, p. 58/19–27: "Deus autem omnipotenter mundum creat correspondenter ad patrem, sapienter creatum inesse conservat correspondenter ad
filium, et conservatum in suo esse benivolenter in suo processu gubernat correspondenter ad spiritum sanctum. Correspondenter rex debet facere proporcionabiliter
quo ad corporalia comissa suo regimini, debet enim legios suos in gradibus suis
statuere, in bonis nature eos defendere, et tercio quo ad bona temporalia eos in
suo iure provide gubernare."
[126] Lahey, *Philosophy and Politics*, p. 170.

Wyclif identified the king as God's steward of temporal goods in the postlapsarian world. In short, the king is Christ's vicar. It is the king's duty to direct the clergy to serve the spiritual mission by administering the temporal goods including those of the Church and to ensure that the realm is governed in conformity with the divine law. But this is an argument about the king's duty. The king in reality may or may not fulfill his duties. How then can we discriminate "just" civil lords as the vehicles of grace from those who are in fact "unjust"? Wyclif considered that the king's demonstration of the correspondence of his actions with divine justice should evidence his fitness for his duties. In this argument, there is no place for popular consent; in sharp contrast to Marsilius, Wyclif rejects the validity of popular appointment to kingship. However, it is also impossible for anyone to discern grace, which is essential for just civil dominion, in the individual. Again, no one can know or guess the divine will.

Wyclif is well known for his Augustinian view that tyrants should be obeyed rather than resisted. This, however, did not make him a proponent of absolutism. Rather, Wyclif's point was, as Stephen Lahey argued, that those who were wholeheartedly committed to Christ's Law should not pay any attention to tyrants.[127] Living a life of apostolic poverty is more important than the political action of resisting tyrannical princes. Secular tyranny was indeed grasped as divine punishment for sin, which the ruled ought to bear. Wyclif, however, did not advocate unconditional passive obedience to secular tyranny. Indeed, he argued against resistance to tyranny if it concerned temporal matters only. Tyranny should be borne with humility if it touches upon nothing beyond the material wealth of the realm. If a tyrannical ruler persecutes the Church by, for example, legislating against Christ's Law, however, Wyclif advocates resistance to such a ruler. Similarly, the civil lord who allows the Church to indulge itself in private property would need to be resisted by his subjects since he would be effectively allowing the Church to be poisoned spiritually. Royal negligence in executing ecclesiastical reform would generate the rebellion of subjects.[128] What justifies popular resistance, then, is the failure to maintain and promote the spiritual welfare of the Christian community, although Wyclif did not explain fully what constituted spiritual matters.

[127] Ibid., p. 192.
[128] *De officio regis* 3, pp. 59–62. Cf. Lahey, *Philosophy and Politics*, pp. 193–99.

The last question to be addressed is: how should the king execute a reform program? Wyclif insisted that the king's execution of the reform program must be theologically informed. Hence, it was essential for the king to receive the advice of theologians. This also forms an intriguing aspect of Wyclif's ecclesiology and political thought, since, despite his markedly theocentric perspective, Wyclif also paid due respect to the cognitive power of human beings. Before Wyclif, the doctrinal authority of theologians had already been on the rise. In doctrinal matters, theologians such as Godfrey of Fontaines in the late thirteenth century had already asserted the cognitive authority of theologians in opposition to the institutional authority of ecclesiastical officials.[129] Indeed, Ockham asserted the superiority of theologians to canonists on doctrinal issues and Marsilius attributed the role of deciphering heresy exclusively to the doctors of Scripture precisely because they both believed that the cognitive authority of the theologians outweighed the authority of the canonists and theologically ill-informed ecclesiastics. According to Wyclif, not only prelates but also theologians were the physicians of the soul.[130]

Wyclif viewed ecclesiastical office purely in terms of spiritual service. The primary duty of priests was to understand the Bible and to disseminate scriptural teachings. Sacramental functions of the priesthood were not denied but significantly curtailed. The meaning of the hierarchical order accordingly changed: it is no longer a hierarchy of power but a hierarchy of duties. The so-called papal hierocrats such as Giles of Rome maintained that the pope was the source of power, from which all others—ecclesiastics as well as secular rulers—derived their power. In Wyclif's vision, by contrast, ecclesiastical office was nothing other than the duty of spiritual mission. The "disenchantment" of ecclesiastical offices transformed the conception of ecclesiastical duty in a twofold way. First, according to Wyclif, the pope and the hierarchy could no longer declare or legislate on doctrinal issues unless they "conform" to what has been eternally decreed in the Bible and so were already law.[131] Ecclesiastical authority cannot engage in doctrinal decision-making by "the key of

---

[129] Takashi Shogimen, "Academic Controversy," in *The Medieval Theologians*, ed. G.R. Evans (Oxford, 2001), pp. 233–49.

[130] *De potestate papae* 6, p. 133.

[131] Leff, *Heresy in the Later Middle Ages*, p. 540.

power" alone; and ecclesiastical doctrinal decisions are not necessarily divinely sanctioned. This conclusion is identical to Ockham's
position. Ockham understood papal power over doctrinal matters in
terms of mere coercive power. I say "mere" because, according to
Ockham, the pope's doctrinal decision-making does not guarantee
the truthfulness of the decision, but merely authenticates it. This is
why he wrote that the pope's exposition of divine words is, if it is
theologically correct, "a little more authentic than the interpretation
given by another learned man because once the pope's interpretation is given, no one will be allowed to state or hold publicly an
opinion contrary to it."[132] Similarly, Wyclif argued that the pope
should not be believed unless his words are solidly anchored in scriptural authority, which were the "measure of all other things."[133]

The second important change that Wyclif made in the meaning
of the ecclesiastical order was the replacement of the hierarchy of
authority with that of duties: the higher the status one occupies, the
graver the sin one commits. Indeed, status or dignity and sin are
not mutually exclusive. When a spiritual ruler fulfills his duty by
teaching others to follow the divine law, the consequent achievement
would be far more glorious than what secular power can achieve at
its best. However, when spiritual power fails to fulfill its duty, then
the consequence is far more dreadful than when secular power fails
to fulfill its duty. Hence, the vicar of Christ who deviates from the
way of Christ would be the worst Antichrist, whether he be a pope,
a bishop or any other ecclesiastic's[134] Antichrist emerges from the
clergy due to the sin of hypocrisy. "We should be aware of the
necessity that Antichrist would originate from among the clergy. For,
inasmuch as not all priests have been firmly established, it is necessary that some, on account of their positions of dignity, would fall
to even greater depths."[135] Hence the pope and cardinals would be,
in terms of dignity, the most distinguished part of the Church as

---

[132] Ockham, *Dialogus* 3.1.2.24.

[133] *De blasphemia* 3, p. 44.

[134] *De potestate papae* 6, p. 118/6–11: "Romano pontifice vel quocumque alio
fingente se gerere primatum vicarie potestatis Christi in terris, ab eius semita dec-
linante secundum sensum scripture nullus plenius vel periculosius gerit de facto
nomen et opera Antichristi."

[135] *De potestate papae* 6, p. 119/7–11: "Secundo notandum, quod de clero necesse
est Antichristum trahere suam originem; cum enim non omnes sacerdotes confirmati
sunt, necesse est quod aliqui propter status excellenciam cadant profundius."

long as they follow the law of Christ; however, should they fail to do so, they will form a nest of heretics.[136] Wyclif often called some popes "Antichrists," but what he meant was not the same as the Marsilian rejection of papal primacy. On the contrary, he accepted the primacy of Saint Peter's successors and could therefore demand unparalleled holiness in the incumbent that matches such supremacy.[137]

This demand for *noblesse oblige* in the ecclesiastical order was not unprecedented. A number of scholastic giants including Alexander of Hales, Albert the Great, Bonaventure, Thomas Aquinas, Durand de Saint Pourçain, Pierre de la Palud and William of Ockham maintained that the holders of ecclesiastical office are bound to have fuller knowledge of the explicit faith than lay believers.[138] However, Wyclif's position departed from the conventional one in that, whereas Wyclif's scholastic predecessors (excluding Ockham) argued that lay believers were not bound to have any knowledge of explicit faith, Wyclif maintained that every believer should have knowledge of the Bible. The traditional position held that lay believers were bound to have implicit faith, meaning that they ought to be prepared to subscribe to any doctrine authorized by the Church, which was, in effect, the principle of obedience to ecclesiastical authority. Wyclif, by contrast, maintained that all believers ought to read the Bible and become theologians themselves. In Wyclif's vision, lay believers can no longer depend upon the judgment of ecclesiastics for the orthodoxy of the faith, to which they subscribe. They are bound to read and know the Scripture and to vindicate their faith against the biblical truths.

The emphasis on the cognitive authority of knowledge of the Bible (as opposed to official authority of holding ecclesiastical office) had repercussion on Wyclif's idea of heresy. According to Wyclif, "heresy is a false dogma contrary to Scripture which is obstinately defended,"[139]

---

[136] *De ecclesia* 4, p. 88/9–19: "Unde non dubium oratur pro principalissima ecclesia militante quam suppono esse Romanam ecclesiam, verumptamen inter partes eius in comparacione ad quantitatem sunt papa et suum collegium pars precipua dignitate, dum tamen sequantur Christum propinquius et deserendo fastum atque primatum serviant matri sue efficacius atque humilius. Nam faciendo oppositum sunt nidus hereticorum, apostema putridum et ydolum desolacionis cum aliis montrosis nominibus in sacra pagina prophetatis."

[137] Anthony Kenny, *Wyclif* (Oxford, 1985), p. 74.

[138] Shogimen, "From Disobedience to Toleration," 616.

[139] *De Civili Dominio* 2.7, p. 58. See also *De veritate Sacrae Scripturae* 32, 3:275/1–3: "Declaravi autem libro quarto cap. Septimo, quod 'heresis est dogma falsum, scripture sacre contrarium, pertinaciter defensatum.'"

and "a person is not deemed a heretic unless he defends falsehood by word or deed."[140] By arguing so, Wyclif aligned himself with early-fourteenth-century theorists of heresy such as Guido Terreni and William of Ockham. Guido Terreni, a Carmelite theologian and a champion of papal infallibility, argued that heresy was a contradiction of Scripture. It was a break with the thirteenth-century tradition that heresy was defined as opposition to the articles of faith. Similarly, Wyclif departed from the thirteenth-century conception of heresy by identifying heresy as contradiction of Scripture, not the articles of faith.[141]

Perhaps more importantly, Wyclif resembled Ockham in that he singled out obstinacy or pertinacity as the main characteristic of heresy and heretics: "it suffices to define a heretic as an obstinate person, and heresy as obstinacy."[142] To be sure, by the middle of the fourteenth century, it had been widely known that the main characteristic of heretics was pertinacity. However, the meaning of pertinacity or obstinacy changed over time. Since the definition offered by Gratian of Bologna, repeated dissent from ecclesiastical authority was considered as an externally observable action, which was labeled by the Church as pertinacity or obstinacy, and pertinacious adherence to a doctrinal error was considered to turn a believer into a heretic. Pertinacity was in effect disobedience to the authoritative doctrinal decision-making by ecclesiastical office holders.[143] This authoritarian conception was challenged by Ockham. He emphasized that heresy should be defined as opinions that contradict the textual sources of Christian doctrine, thereby attributing the discovery of heresy and heretics largely to theological experts who had cognitive authority on Christian doctrine rather than ecclesiastical office holders, who were often lawyers, not theologians, by training. Nonetheless, Ockham did not ignore, but rather redefined, pertinacity as the main feature of heretics; indeed, he expounded on twenty modes of being pertinacious in his general discourse on heretics.[144] Similarly, Wyclif

---

[140] *On the Truth of Holy Scripture*, p. 353; *De veritate Sacrae Scripturae* 32, 3:275/16–17: "... nec censetur hereticus, nisi denfendat in verbo vel opere falsitatem ..."

[141] Shogimen, "William of Ockham and Guido Terreni," 521.

[142] Wyclif, *On the Truth of Holy Scripture*, p. 357; *De veritate Sacrae Scripturae* 32, 3:280/17–19: "... quin suffict describere hereticum per hoc, quod est pertinax, et heresim per hoc, quod est pertinacia."

[143] R.I. Moore, *The Formation of a Persecuting Society* (Oxford, 1987), p. 68.

[144] William of Ockham, *Dialogus*, Part I, Book 4. On Ockham's concept of heresy,

reduced heresy and heretics to obstinacy and obstinate persons respectively and, importantly, he attributed the task of deciphering heresy and heretics to theologians. "No one can recognize heresy unless they have knowledge of Scripture. . . . only the theologian is suited to judge heresy."[145] Like Ockham, Wyclif regarded the identification of heresy and heretics as an intellectual and cognitive process rather than an authoritative decision-making.

This outlook resulted in a claim that everyone ought to be a theologian.[146] I wrote earlier that negligence in maintaining and promoting the spiritual welfare of the Christian community would legitimate and generate popular resistance against a ruler. Indeed, mutual aid was the self-corrective process of the body of Christ and such rebellions would be an option. But how do we know that priestly or royal leadership is actually damaging the spiritual well-being of the Christian community? The king's failure to deprive the ecclesiastical institutions of this-worldly wealth, for instance, may be evident enough; however, legislation against Christ's law involves interpretation and certitude regarding Christ's law will be a contentious issue. Where all the members of the Christian community can be expected to have sufficient knowledge of Christ's Law, however, they are (supposed to be) cognitively equipped to aid the part of the community in need of correction. Wyclif's contention that every believer ought to be a theologian warrants the cognitive foundation of mutual aid within the body of Christ. Thus, Wyclif's reform program was not exclusively entrusted to the king. Although Wyclif began his conceptualization of a reform program by turning his attention to the king as the major remedial means, he eventually underlined the responsibility of all individual believers to offer mutual aid. The king is required to consult theological experts in order to conform to

---

see especially John Kilcullen, "Ockham and Infallibility," *Journal of Religious Studies* 16 (1991), 387–409 and Takashi Shogimen, "William of Ockham and Conceptions of Heresy, c. 1250–c. 1350," in *Heresy in Transition: Transforming Ideas of Heresy in Medieval and Early Modern Europe*, eds., Ian Hunter, Chris Laursen and Cary Nederman (Aldershot, forthcoming).

[145] *On the Truth of Holy Scripture*, p. 352; *De veritate Sacrae Scripturae* 32, 3:274/24–28: "Ex quo patet, quod solum ad theologum pertinet de heresi iudicare. si enim legista vel decretista ex suo officio discernit de heresi, hoc est, in quantum theologus, et ut de sensu ac contrarietate scripture fuerit a theologis informatus."

[146] *On the Truth of Holy Scripture*, p. 300; *De veritate Sacrae Scripturae* 24, 2:233/15: "Hic dico, quod assumptum est verum, quia, ut ostendi alias, omnem cristianum oportet esse theologum . . ."

Christ's Law in his government. Theological knowledge underpins the legitimate rule of the king not only in his reform of the Church but also in his government of the realm. This is a mirror image of both papalist and Marsilian positions. Wyclif reversed the papalist notion of the superiority of the ecclesiastical order over the temporal one, while he replaced the Marsilian emphasis on popular consent with theological competence and divinely favored grace among the members of a political community. Wyclif's "third way" envisaged a mutually aided community of individuals, possessing theological knowledge and faith in divine grace; more specifically, it was a community of the clergy who aspire to apostolic ideals and believers who thirst for biblical knowledge under the rule of a king who willingly and justly bears the burden of civil dominion as a steward of God. In this vision, only God is glorified.

Conclusion

We have seen that Wyclif's ecclesiology and political thought are markedly dissimilar to such anti-papal predecessors as Ockham and Marsilius in a number of ways. Ostensibly, Wyclif's universe appears deterministic: God predestines the Elect, the true Church is entirely invisible, and history follows a cyclical pattern. And yet, human beings are not God's marionettes. Wyclif's God allows humans to participate in divine dominion—they deserve natural or civil dominion through grace. Humans cannot know the divine will, but can voluntarily establish an immediate relationship with God. Wyclif's ecclesiology and political thought revolves around a variety of such relationships between humans and God, namely the notions of dominion. Wyclif redefined the relationship between ruler and ruled on earth—in both ecclesiastical and temporal spheres—by redefining the relationships between humans and God. This is the course that neither Marsilius nor Ockham took. Marsilius's God intervenes in the works of the principal ecclesiastical institution, the general council, which remains within the quintessentially medieval ecclesiological tradition. Ockham's radical rejection of institutional infallibility, on the other hand, reduced ecclesiastical government into a question of power relationship between men. Ockham's God is removed from ecclesiastical life; He revealed Himself at certain points in the past and may or may not intervene in human affairs by new revelations. Wyclif's God, by contrast, relates immediately to humans. Human

beings cannot know God's will, but the world can be changed by
human beings' spiritual attitude towards God. At the heart of the
discourse on the relationship between human beings and God was
Wyclif's metaphysical idea of dominion. Wyclif's doctrine of predestination destroyed the so-called "papalist" conception of ecclesiastical hierarchy and his realist metaphysics re-established *real* and
immediate relationships between human beings and God in various
ways.[147] The clergy, aspiring to charity in a life of apostolic poverty,
enjoy evangelical dominion and the king, caring for the administration of civil affairs, will serve as a steward of God on earth, who
bears just civil dominion. And all other believers recognize the duty
of learning and defending the Word of God. In this vision, no one
mediates another's relationship with God. Wyclif's ecclesiology and
political thought represent a paradox: the desacralization of the relationships between human beings does not only dissolve but also
redefines these bonds.[148]

---

[147] Hence I disagree with Michael Wilks's view that "in effect, human life could
be considered with but small reference to God." See his "Predestination, Property
and Power: Wyclif's Theory of Dominion and Grace," in Wilks, *Wyclif*, p. 25.

[148] I am grateful to Ian Levy and Stephen Conway for their helpful comments
on this chapter.

WYCLIF AND THE SACRAMENTS

Stephen Penn

Wyclif's reputation as a heretic developed at a relatively late stage in his life, as a consequence almost entirely of his pronouncements on sacramental theology. His conclusions relating to sacramental change in the Eucharist, once made public within and beyond the confines of the Oxford schools, left him in a position of vulnerability without precedent in his academic career. It can be little surprise that these conclusions attracted discussion and debate within Wyclif's own lifetime and in the decades following his death, nor that they have been analyzed at such length by scholars of the present day. Only his views concerning penance, which fuelled Lollard debate concerning the necessity of auricular confession, have been subjected to comparable scrutiny. Yet he was by no means silent concerning the remaining five sacraments (a chapter is devoted to each of them in the *Trialogus*), even if many of his conclusions relating to them were less overtly provocative. How far his ideas contributed to a decline in the perceived significance of the sacraments collectively remains open to question. His conception of the Church as a community of the elect (the *praedestinati*)[1] at least potentially diminished the theological significance of the sacraments, yet such an unexceptional ecclesiology is unlikely to have exerted a significat influence over his broad understanding of sacramental necessity.[2] Moreover,

---

[1] *De ecclesia* 17, ed. Johann Loserth (London, 1886), pp. 408/26–409/19. Here, the three definitions of the Church are provided, the last, the *convocatio praedestinatorum*, corresponding to the universal Church. Wyclif had presented the same argument earlier in *De veritate Sacrae Scripturae*, but *De ecclesia* contains the definitive treatment.

[2] Anthony Kenny argues that Wyclif's belief in predestination "was in no way a peculiar feature of his theological system," and that it would have been shared by all who embraced the teaching of Augustine. See Kenny, *Wyclif* (Oxford, 1985), p. 39. Anne Hudson offers a comparable interpretation in *The Premature Reformation: Wycliffite Texts and Lollard History* (Oxford, 1988), but argues that the concept predestinarianism, though markedly Augustinian, was held by Wyclif "with peculiar tenacity and simplicity." (p. 314). A less measured interpretation is offered by Richard Rex, *The Lollards* (Basingstoke, 2002), pp. 45–6.

he was invariably cautious about denying the significance or necessity of sacramental reception. Though grace may be available without reception of a particular sacrament (as in the case of an innocent child who dies before having been baptized), Wyclif never goes as far as to suggest that the sacraments themselves should be formally dispensed with on a wholesale basis.[3]

Sacraments, Priests and Kings

The sacerdotal duties associated with the sacraments placed priests in a position of spiritual authority that was unrivalled in the late medieval Church. Wyclif's views on the relationship between royal and ecclesiastical power are well known,[4] but what is less widely recognized is that his perception of this relationship rested partially on his controversial understanding of the sacraments and their administration. Priests, unlike kings, had the authority, by virtue of their office, to administer sacraments, which might theoretically bring them greater power (as had been argued by some medieval philosophers).[5] But Wyclif resisted this argument forcefully in De officio regis. Though the priest undeniably possessed the power to consecrate the bread and wine of the Eucharist, his duty was invariably made possible by the king. To authorize any form of sacred activity, Wyclif suggested, entailed a greater degree of power than merely to consecrate (in obedience to such an act of authorization).[6] The relationship between the power of the priest and the power of the monarch, he argued, could be understood as being comparable to

---

[3] This is not to deny, of course, that Wyclif's Lollard followers were often keen to divest the sacraments of their theological glory. See Hudson, *Premature Reformation*, p. 284f.

[4] See the useful discussion in L.J. Daly, *The Political Theory of John Wyclif* (Chicago, 1962), p. 116ff. A more recent analysis, which focuses on Wyclif's theory of civil *dominium*, can be found in Stephen E. Lahey, *Philosophy and Politics in the Thought of John Wyclif* (Cambridge, 2003), p. 148ff.

[5] Giles of Rome in particular. See Daly, *Political Theory*, p. 117.

[6] The point is made concisely by Wyclif in the following comment about the relative status of king and bishop in *De officio regis* 6, ed. A.W. Pollard and C. Sayle (London, 1887), p. 138/3–7: "[E]xcellencior est illa potestas que habet imperare vel mandare quam est potestas que tenetur ad hoc humanitus obedire, sed potestas episcopalis tenetur humanitus obedire regie potestati, non sic e contra, ergo potestas regalis est ad hoc prestancior."

the relationship between the power of Christ's humanity and the power of his divinity, the latter being undeniably greater.[7] It was, he suggested, quite meaningless to argue that the king possessed the greater political, or temporal, power, whereas the priest possessed greater spiritual authority, since the question was not one of different *kinds* of power, but of power *per se*. To draw distinctions of this nature, he believed, would be to prevent us from perceiving power in its simplest terms.[8] Power (*potestas*) or authority (*auctoritas*), he suggested, could be said to be "great" in three quite distinct ways. First, it could be said to be great in absolute terms, such as the power of God, which is infinitely greater than any created power. But it could also be said to be great in two further, inferior senses, which are classified as 'participatory'. In the first of these, power or authority might be communicated to a creature in simple terms; in the second, it could inhere within the creature in respect of a specific office.[9] The power of a created spirit, even a devil, he argues, is inevitably far greater than that of a corporeal being. Human power, the least potent of any, must either be secular (as in the case of God's vicar, the king) or spiritual (as in the case of the priest, vicar of Christ). In respect of these two forms of human power, the king and the priest, respectively, must be pre-eminent. But Wyclif is careful to qualify this point. The priest's spiritual power is greater than the king's, we are told, because he enjoys "a greater grace." But such grace cannot simply be taken for granted, and exists only in proportion to the priest's virtues. Wyclif gestures towards Matthew 11:11:

---

[7] *De officio regis* 6, p. 138/14–18: "[S]acerdos est rege prestancior ex hoc quod conficit vel ministrant ecclesiastica sacramenta, quia maioris potestatis auctoritas est personam precipere conficere quam ipsam conficere. Sic enim deitas precipit Cristo humanitus conficere, et tamen ipsa deitas non potuit conficere vel mori." On the king's status as *vicarius Dei*, see *De officio regis* 6, p. 137/20. See also the illuminating discussion of Wyclif's treatment of this topic in Stephen E. Lahey, *Philosophy and Politics in the Thought of John Wyclif*, pp. 171–99.

[8] *De officio regis* 6, p. 139/26–29: "[D]icitur comuniter quod rex precellit in temporalibus et episcopus in spiritualibus. Sed per hoc non docetur simpliciter que auctoritas sit reliqua maior. Nam si rex est maior, tunc consequens debet concede simpliciter, et per idem concedendum foret quod episcopus est maior."

[9] *De officio regis* 6, p. 140/22–28: "Hic dicam quid ego sencio conformicer ad scripturam. Unde pro declaracione notandum quod potestas vel auctoritas dicitur magna tripliciter; vel absolute penes magnitudinem ex se potentis (et sic potestas eterna dei est equivoce infinitum maior quam alia potesta create; potestas autem participive dicta, creature communicate, potest dupliciter dici magna, vel simpliciter vel quoad speciale officium."

"there has not risen among them that are born of women a greater
than John the Baptist." Here, he suggests, the reference must be to
John's virtues, rather than to any other form of power or authority.
A corrupt priest, therefore, must be a priest whose spiritual power
is diminished in proportion to his corruption. But his authority is
nowhere more massively diminished than if he seeks to assume regal
authority.[10]

The power bestowed by God upon an individual, whether in respect
of spiritual or secular duties, rested fundamentally for Wyclif upon
the biblical principle of adoption.[11] The adopted child who serves
most excellently as heir of his kingdom, he suggests, possesses power
of the highest order. Any heir to the kingdom of heaven, therfore,
necessarily possesses greater power, in absolute terms, than a king
or a priest from among the community of the foreknown (here identified as the *membri diaboli*). Kings and priests who are unworthy to
receive power from God, however, are not, Wyclif suggests, entirely
without value. A priest should be able to perform his priestly duties,
regardless of his own moral condition, by virtue of his office. Priests
or kings among the foreknown, therfore, are in this respect worthy
of *communal* honour.[12] Likewise, as he argues elsewhere, they should
be able to administer sacraments to the faithful.[13] Nevertheless, Wyclif
is in no doubt that a king does a disservice to his people by appointing or retaining priests who are identifiably corrupt or unworthy to
hold office.[14] There is no suggestion in *De officio regis*—or elsewhere
in Wyclif's major academic works—that a priest might ever be unable
to consecrate, though there are traces of Donatism in his *Confessio*,

---

[10] *De officio regis* 6, p. 141/12–18: "sicut ergo homo fit maior coram domino proporcionaliter ut crescit in virtute, sic auctoritas sua est ea racione maior ut crescit
in virtute. Et ad istam racionem debet sacerdos attendere. Unde non plus con-
funderetur, minoraretur vel extingueretur sacerdotis auctoritas quam presumendo
assumere in eodem sacerdote istam duplicem potestatem."

[11] See the discussion in *De officio regis* 6, p. 142/2–8. Wyclif here uses the term
in the extended sense provided in Romans 8:15. In the Vulgate, *adoptio* here translates the Greek *viothesia*, and is used within the context of spiritual adoption of the
viator by God.

[12] See the lengthy discussion in *De officio regis* 1, pp. 20/2–21/24.

[13] *De ecclesia* 19, p. 448/14–16: "Videtur autem mihi quod prescitus eciam in
mortali peccato actuali ministrat fidelibus, licet sibi dampnabiliter, tamen subiectis
utiliter sacramenta."

[14] *De officio regis* 1, p. 61/9f.

prepared at the end of his Oxford career.[15] The priest, Wyclif argues in *De officio regis*, should conduct himself with humility, and should not regard his power to consecrate as a form of authority, as there is no basis for the equation of sacramental power with authority in the text of Scripture. Even if the priest's power were to be treated as such, he is careful to emphasise, then it would be of a lesser kind than that possessed by a secular ruler.[16] Underpinning such a comment, which does not seek in any way diminish the priest's God-given spiritual power, is Wyclif's desire to hold papal authority in check: neither Scripture nor the words of the clergy, he suggests, requires him to magnify the pope above the secular ruler.

Sacraments, Signs and the Sacramental Res

St Augustine had argued that sacraments were a signs of holy things, and that any signs, when they signified holy things, could be called *sacramenta*.[17] This definition, and variations upon it, formed the basis of theological discussions of the sacraments throughout the Middle Ages. Most important among these were two lengthy texts dating from the twelfth century: the *De sacramentis Christianae fidei* of Hugh of St Victor and the *Sentences* of Peter Lombard. The latter text was heavily influenced by the former (which it post-dates by at least a decade), but presents a more focused and systematic analysis of the seven sacraments.[18] In the fourth book of the *Sentences*, the Lombard devoted particular attention to the relationship between signs and

---

[15] See n. 132, below.

[16] *De officio regis*, p. 143/28–34: "Potestas [. . .] sic ministrandi non vocatur in scriptura auctoritas, sed ille terminus ex libris gentilium est extortus. Si autem sit auctoritas, est maior auctoritas civiliter regulandi, cum sit supra temporalitatem immediate a deo, nec sit materia sacerdotis magnificandi se ipsum, sed humilius ministrandi et de inferioritate dampnabile formidandi."

[17] *Epistula* 138, CCSL 44, p. 131: "[signa], cum ad res diuinas pertinent, sacramenta appellantur." A helpfully concise discussion of Augustine's interpretation of the term "sacramentum" can be found in André Mandouze, "*sacramentum* et *sacramenta* chez Augustain: Dialectique entre une Théorie et une Practique," *Bulletin de l'association Guillaume Bude*, vol. 4 (1989), 367–75.

[18] See the edition of *De Sacramentis* in PL 176:173ff. A convenient translation of Hugh's text is provided in *Hugh of Saint Victor on the Sacraments of the Christian Faith*, trans. R.J. Deferrari (Cambridge, MA, 1951). See also Peter Lombard's *Sententiae in IV libris distinctae*, ed. Ignatius Brady, 2 vols. (Grottaferrata, 1971–81).

the sacraments. There are obvious Augustinian echoes in the definition he provides for *sacramentum* in the second chapter of this book:

> A sacrament is a sign of a holy thing. But a sacrament is also called a holy secret, as it is a vestige of divinity (*sacramentum divinitatis*). As such, a sacrament signifies a holy thing, but is also the holy thing which is signified.[19]

Every sacrament, on this interpretation, is a sign, but not every sign is thereby a sacrament. Fundamental to the Augustinian conception of the sign, and a principle readily embraced by the Lombard, was the understanding that it should in no way serve as an end *in itself*.[20] A sign had invariably to be a sign *of something*. Echoing Augustine again, he goes on to paraphrase his definition by suggesting that a sacrament is "the [visible] form of an invisible grace" (*invisibilis gratiae forma*).[21] But a sacrament was not instituted merely to *signify* an invisible grace; its function, in definitive terms, was to sanctify by bestowing the grace of God upon the recipient. The mere signification of grace, therefore, was not sufficient to make a sign into a sacrament. Hence, the Lombard suggests, the sacrificial offerings and ceremonial observances of the Old Law could not be regarded as sacraments.[22] Only the seven sacraments of the New Law could properly be described as such.[23]

A century after Peter Lombard, Aquinas brought the study of signs and sacraments together in his *Summa theologiae* (3a. 60–65).[24] Both authors are conspicuous presences throughout Wyclif's theological writings and, as Williel Thomson has usefully observed, the *Trialogus*

---

[19] *Sententiae* 4.1.2, ed. Brady, 2:232: "Sacramentum est sacrae rei signum. Dicitur tamen sacramentum etiam sacrum secretum, sicut sacramentum divinitatis, ut sacramentum sit sacrum signans, et sacrum signatum."

[20] See *De Doctrina Christiana* 2.1.2. See CCSL 32 for the Latin text. A reliable English translation remains that of D.W. Robertson (New Jersey, 1958).

[21] Ibid.

[22] *Sententiae*, 4.1.4, 2:233: "Sacramentum enim proprie dicitur quod est gratiae Dei, et invisibilis gratiae forma, ut ipsius imaginem gerat et causa existat. Non ergo significandi tantum gratia sacramenta institute sunt, sed etiam sanctificandi. Quae enim significandi gratia tantum institute sunt, solum signa sunt, et non sacramenta; sicut fuerunt sacrificial carnalia, et observantiae ceremoniales veteris legis, quae numquam poterant justos facere offerentes."

[23] See *Sententiae*, 4.1.6 (on the difference between sacraments of the Old and New Laws); 4.2.1 (on the seven sacraments of the New Law).

[24] Throughout this article I have relied upon the Blackfriars edition of Thomas's *Summa theologiae*, ed. Thomas Gilby (London, 1963).

is "structurally similar to late-medieval commentaries on the *Sentences*."[25] This is particularly striking in the final book of the treatise, dedicated to sacramental theology. The significance of sacramental signs in the *Trialogus* is signalled not merely by the frequency of the term *signum* itself, but also by the fact that Wyclif chose to devote the longest of its four volumes—*De signis*—to this subject alone.[26] At the beginning of the book, our attention is drawn to the significance of signs in all aspects of life. The dialogue is opened by the character Alithia,[27] who urges us to attend to the signs around us, suggesting that everything in the created world must be treated—of necessity— as a sign:

> For as long, indeed, as we live here we should attend to signs, since our Samaritan used signs with his apostles; both the sacraments and distinctions of orders and of schools depend chiefly upon signs. It seems, moreover, that a sign and its significate are convertible with being. For every creature is a sign of its creator, just as smoke naturally signifies fire. God, too, is a sign of any signifiable thing, since he is the Book of Life in which every signifiable is written. It follows, likewise, that anything is a sign.[28]

Though apparently embarking on a general excursus on the ubiquity of the sign, Alithia presents in this short passage a very concise summary of Wyclif's entire metaphysical system. Signs and their *signata*, she tells us, are "convertible" with (or equivalent to) being. Signs in nature are signs of their creator, since each creature has intelligible, universal being in the mind of God.[29] This observation leads her to

---

[25] Williell R. Thomason, *The Latin Writings of John Wyclyf* (Toronto, 1983), p. 80.

[26] The Eucharist, which is described by one of the three interlocutors as the "most venerable" of all of the sacraments, is analysed at the greatest length. See *Joannis Wiclif Trialogus cum supplemento Trialogi*, ed. G. Lechler (Oxford, 1869), pp. 244–407.

[27] From the Greek *alétheia* ("truth," fem.). The names of the other two characters, Phronesis and Pseustis, derive from the Greek *phrónesis* ("prudence," masc.) and *pseústes* ("liar," masc.), respectively.

[28] *Trialogus* 4.1, p. 244/3–11: "Quamdiu quidem hic vivemus, oportet ad signa attendere, cum Samaratinus noster usus fuit signis cum suis apostolis; et sacramenta quaecunque et distinctiones ordinum vel sectarum potissime stant in signis. Videtur in primis, quod signum et signatum convertibilia sunt cum ente. Nam omnis creatura est signum creatoris, sicut fumus naturaliter ignem significat. Deus etiam est signum cuiuslibet rei signabilis, cum sit liber vitae in quo quodcunque signabile est inscriptum; et per idem sequitur, quod quodlibet sit signum." When Wyclif says "convertible with," he is suggesting that sign and signified are equivalent in ontological terms.

[29] Intelligible being was the most elevated form of being, coterminous with God.

the fundamental question of the possibility of regarding all aspects of creation as sacraments. It is here that Wyclif first gestures towards a critique of the contemporary "worshippers of signs" (cultores signorum), as he was later to characterize them. The critique is voiced by Phronesis, the second speaker in the dialogue, who attempts to reply to Alithia's observations. The task, he confesses, is not an easy one, since many contemporary pronouncements on the nature of signs have only a fragile foundation. It is not until the third chapter of this text that Wyclif is specific about the nature of some of these pronouncements.[30] The Lombard had suggested that a sacrament was not merely a sign, but a holy thing. It was to this principle that Wyclif adhered throughout his numerous discussions of the seven sacraments. To treat any of the sacraments as mere signs would have been tantamount to blasphemy for him, and he spoke out fiercely against what he perceived as the idolatrous worship of signs in sacramental ceremonies. In his concluding comments in De apostasia, he derides those of the present generation who, in their collective pursuit of signs, were only serving to broaden the range of heretical errors relating to the sacrament of the Eucharist.[31] The misguided worship of the host in itself, rather than as a sign of the body of Christ, was a symptom of what Jeremy Catto has usefully described as the late-medieval "cult of the Eucharist," through which the Mass became, in effect, with the institution of the feast of Corpus Christi in particular, an awe-inspiring public ceremony rather than a process of personal reception.[32]

In the Trialogus, Wyclif lists the traditional seven sacraments that he would have found in the Sentences of Peter Lombard: the Eucharist, Baptism, Confirmation, Holy Orders, Marriage, Penance, and Extreme Unction. Nowhere in his work does he depart from this list, but like

---

Beneath this are four hierarchically-ordered levels of being, from universal being to particular existence. Each level was bound metaphysically to the level above it. See the discussion in De universalibus 7, ed. Ivan Mueller (Oxford, 1985), pp. 126–8; On Universals, trans. Anthony Kenny (Oxford, 1985), pp. 48–50.

[30] Trialogus 4.3, pp. 250–4.

[31] De apostasia 17, ed. M.H. Dziewicki (London, 1889), p. 254/6–8: "Certum, inquam, est, quod multiplicata apostasia generationis signa querencium multiplicanda est errorum varietas in hoc venerabili sacramentum."

[32] See J.I. Catto, "John Wyclif and the Cult of the Eucharist," in The Bible in the Medieval World: Essays in Honour of Beryl Smalley eds. Katherine Walsh and Diana Wood (Oxford, 1985), 269–86. On the origins and development of the feast of Corpus Christi, and of popular late-medieval devotional practices, see Miri Rubin, Corpus Christi: The Eucharist in Late Medieval Culture (Cambridge, 1991).

Aquinas and the earlier scholastics, sees every need to subject it to rigorous interrogation.[33] If, for example, a sacrament is a sign of a holy thing, and if every creature is a sign of its creator, then it would seem that every creature is a also a sacrament. Why should it be, then, that we limit ourselves to the seven sacraments listed by the Lombard? Alithia puts this question to Phronesis at the beginning of the fourth book of the *Trialogus*, and his response is revealing. He makes it clear that he has not suggested that the label 'sacrament" should be restricted univocally to the traditional seven, but in the absence of univocal restriction he limits himself to these alone.[34] Sacraments, as signs of holy things, corresponded to a *res sacramenti* (sacramental thing), a term which is sometimes used by Wyclif, though not systematically. Likewise, he loosely observes the Aristotelian distinction between *materia* (the matter, or "quiddity" of the sacrament) and *forma* (its form, as manifested in the sacramental words or rites) in his work,[35] though his terminology is variable, and is applied with differing degrees of stringency. Whilst his analyses of sacramental theology must necessarily be placed within an Aristotelian and a scholastic context, therefore, they cannot be expected to conform slavishly to popular analytical conventions.

The Eucharist

Wyclif's opinions on the Eucharist were published in the last four years of his life, when the outspoken and occasionally troublesome scholar made the spectacular transition to the life of the secluded heresiarch.[36] The university had been a safe environment in which

---

[33] Wyclif addresses the question as to why the number of sacraments should be restricted to seven in his opening chapter of the final book of the *Trialogus* 4.1, pp. 244–6. Cf. Lombard's enumeration of the seven sacraments of the New Law in the *Sententiae*, 4.2.1, 2:239–40.

[34] *Trialogus* 4.1, pp. 245–46. Cf. Aquinas, *Summa theologiae*, 3a.65.1 ("utrum debeant esse septem sacramenta").

[35] The earliest use of the terms in the context of sacramental theology is thought to date back to William of Auxerre (1150–1231), among the most distinguished and influential scholastic Aristotelians before Aquinas, and one of the fathers of 'scientific' theology. See D.J. Kennedy, "Sacraments," in *The Catholic Encyclopedia* (New York, 1913), vol. 13:295–305. Though inaccurate in places, this remains an authoritative account.

[36] The history of medieval debate surrounding eucharistic presence is examined

to bring forth his theses on dominion, on clerical property, and on the power of the pope. His pronouncements on Holy Orders and Penance, if they were received with hostility by the Church, had not led to formal condemnation (and clearly attracted influential adherents). The university had defended him against the charges laid at his feet by Pope Gregory XI in 1377, and had refused to condemn him as a heretic.[37] But when he began to question the doctrine of transubstantiation, as defined by medieval canon law (in the *Firmiter* decree and the *Cum marthae* epistle of Pope Innocent III), and to problematize the theology of Real Presence in public lectures, the Chancellor of Oxford University, William Barton, had little option but to instigate proceedings against the teaching of his ideas. Barton, though acting in a way that few, if any, of Wyclif's contemporaries would have regarded as either extreme or otherwise exceptional, was by no means a neutral intercessor in the debate, and had opposed Wyclif in academic disputes long before he had ascended to the chancellorship of the university in 1379.[38] The controversy surrounding Wyclif's pronouncements on the Eucharist provided a convenient means by which to silence, through a condemnation of doctrines rather than named doctors, an old and vexatious adversary. According to an account presented in the *Fasciculi zizaniorum*, Wyclif had begun to determine on the Eucharist in 1381 (or possibly a year or more earlier).[39] Twelve conclusions are recorded here, together with three further conclusions which, we are told, the doctor publicly defended. Of these, two were formally condemned by Barton, who had assembled a council of twelve to consider the recent propagation, within and outside the university, of 'pestilential' doctrines.[40] Wyclif had felt

---

in detail in Ian Christopher Levy, *John Wyclif: Scriptural Logic, Real Presence and the Parameters of Orthodoxy* (Milwaukee, 2003), pp. 123–215.

[37] See H.B. Workman, *John Wyclif: A Study of the English Medieval Church*, 2 vols. (Oxford, 1926), 1:132; Rex, *The Lollards*, pp. 29–30.

[38] Workman, *John Wyclif*, 2:141.

[39] A usefully detailed account of Wyclif's condemnation by the council of twelve remains that of Joseph H. Dahmus, *The Prosecution of John Wyclif* (New Haven, 1952), p. 129ff. The date of 1381 is provided in the written record of the trial that survives in the *Fasciculi zizaniorum* (*FZ*, p. 104), though earlier dates have been suggested. On the dating of the condemnation, see Dahmus, p. 129 n. 3.

[40] For a record of the condemnations, including a list of Barton's council of advisors, see *Fasciculi zizaniorum*, pp. 110–114.

it appropriate to offer a response to Barton and the Oxford condemnations, which survives as his lengthy *Confessio* of 10 May, 1381.[41] Shortly after this date, Wyclif left the university to take up residence at his rectory in Lutterworth, Leicestershire, which was to become his last dwelling place. But on 19 May, 1382, only two years before his death, some of his opinions were condemned by the Blackfriars Council (now popularly remembered, after a coinage of Wyclif's own, as the "Earthquake" Council), headed by Archbishop William Courtenay.[42] In the proceedings, as recorded in the *Fasciculi zizaniorum*, we find no less than twenty-four conclusions condemned as heretical or erroneous, ten of which are identifiably Wyclif's own.[43] Among these, only three related to the sacrament of the Eucharist. But it was these three, identical with the three that Wyclif had allegedly been ready to defend earlier in public, that have been remembered, above all of the twenty one others, as the conclusions that led to the demise of the heretic.

The three conclusions recorded at Oxford and then Blackfriars relate to the physical nature of the Eucharistic host, the remanence of the bread and wine, and the impossibility of their annihilation Of these, the first two correspond precisely to those isolated by Barton and his council of twelve. The earlier record of the conclusions is relatively accurate, though its author is not afraid to use the verb *transubstantiare* when describing the process of change (which Wyclif would certainly have avoided), and he does not hesitate to distance the second of the conclusions from the theology of the 'faithful':

1. The sacrament of the Eucharist is, by its nature, a body of bread and of wine, which has within it, by virtue of the sacramental words, the true body of Christ at its every point.
2. The sacrament of the Eucharist is *figuratively* the body and blood of Christ, in which the bread and wine are transubstantiated, and of which something remains after consecration. But in the opinion of the faithful this is sophistry.

---

[41] See *Fasciculi zizaniorum*, pp. 115–32.

[42] A useful account of the findings of the Council, and of Wyclif's use, on more than one occasion, of the term "concilium terrae motus," can be found in Workman, *John Wyclif*, 2:127ff.

[43] See *Fasciculi zizaniorum*, pp. 275–82. The first ten of the *conclusiones haereticae* are Wyclif's (pp. 277–79).

3. That there is an accident without a subject is without foundation. But if it were so, then God would be annihilated and an article of the Christian faith would perish.[44]

The first of the three points stops short of denying sacramental change in the host, but gestures away from the accepted doctrine of transubstantiation (construed as a process of substantial conversion). There is no suggestion here, for example, that the bread and wine are *converted* into the body and blood of Christ (and Wyclif carefully avoids the term *conversio* in his writing); though the bread is "truly" the body of Christ at its every point, it is nevertheless bread *in sua natura*. It is not made clear how the two natures coexist (and the term *consubstantiation* is not used by Wyclif), but we are told that that the host is *figuratively* the body and blood of Christ (a point that was seemingly misconstrued by some as a blasphemous denial of Real Presence, which Wyclif had never sought to question). Elsewhere, he had suggested that Christ was present in three ways: virtually, spiritually and sacramentally.[45] In the second point, the essential presence of the bread and the wine is confirmed when we are told that 'something" of the two remains *after* consecration. The last point, relating to what later became known as *remanence*, follows from the preceding two: bread and wine could only feel, look and taste like bread and wine if that was what they were. The accidents of taste, texture and smell could not exist if the substance of the bread had been destroyed, and such annihilation was itself an absurdity, since God could not act as a destroyer. Annihilation, and the succession of one substance by another in the host, were not, for Wyclif, worthy of consideration as theological realities.

---

[44] *Fasciculi zizaniorum*, p. 106/16–25: "1. Sacramentum eucharistiae est in natura sua corpus panis aut vini; habens virtute verborum sacramentalium, verum corpus Christi ad quemlibet ejus punctum. 2. Sacramentum eucharistiae est in figura corpus Christi et sanguis, in qua transubstantiatur panis aut vinum, cujus remanent post consecrationem aliquitas, licet in consideratione fidelium sit sopita. 3. Quod accidens sit sine subjecto, non est fundabile; sed si sic, Deus annihilator, et perit articulus fidei Christianae." Cf. Archbishop Courtenay's description of the first three conclusions condemned at Blackfriars (*Fasciculi zizaniorum*, pp. 277/26–278/4): "Conclusiones haereticae, et contra determinationem ecclesiae, de quibus supra fit mentio, in haec verba sequuntur: 1. Quod substantia panis materialis et vini maneat post consecrationem in sacramento altaris. 2. Item quod accidentia non maneat sine subjecto post consecrationem in eodem sacramento. 3. Item quod Christus non sit in sacramento altaris identice, vere, et realiter in propria praesentia corporali."

[45] *Fasciculi zizaniorum*, pp. 115/16–116/5.

From these three interrelated claims, it becomes clear that in meta-physical terms, orthodox eucharistic doctrine presented a twofold problem for Wyclif. First of all, there seemed to be a fundamental inconsistency in the belief that the appearance of the bread and wine could be sustained after its substance had been transformed. Such an assumption appeared to run contrary to Aristotelian teaching, which held that accidents (in this case, the *appearance* of the bread and wine, as well as their texture, taste and smell) had to be sus-tained by a substance. This made sense in logical terms, since it was impossible for a predicate in any logical proposition to be used with-out a subject.[46] For a philosophical realist like Wyclif, predicates and subjects had real correlates (accidents and substances, respectively), to which the same rules had to apply. If the bread and wine had been transformed at the point of consecration, its substance could no longer be present. For the Aristotelian, this represented an impos-sibility, since accidents could not exist without a substance. Wyclif's own teaching, as we have suggested, was in many respects at odds with that of contemporary Aristotelians, but he fully endorsed their critique of the accident-without-substance argument. The second half of the problem rested with the belief that the substance of the bread and wine could be reduced to nothing, or *annihilated*. Wyclif had maintained, as a student in the arts, that annihilation was impossi-ble. In the longest of his metaphysical treatises, *De universalibus* (pro-duced a decade before his death),[47] he substantiated this argument at length, drawing upon three interrelated observations. First, since annihilation on an existential level entailed annihilation at the levels of universal and ideal being (the last of which, as we have seen, was identical with divine being), it logically entailed annihilation of the whole of the created universe, which represented an impossibility. Second, annihilation itself required that an accident (nothingness) should exist without its necessary subject (which itself, having been annihilated, would be nothing). Third, if God could annihilate his

---

[46] Medieval philosophers would have known of the crucial dependency of pred-icates upon subjects from Aristotle's *Categories* (1^b25–2^a4), in which a combination of the two is shown to yield a truth value (either "true" or "false").

[47] The date 1374 is suggested by Ivan J. Mueller in his introduction to *De uni-versalibus*, p. xxix, where he argues that *De universalibus* was almost certainly com-pleted after Wyclif and Kynyngham had of Wyclif's likely date of inception. Thomson (pp. 20–4) places the text earlier, in 1369.

subjects, then he could punish them out of any proportion to their deserts. It could not be just to annihilate one sinner whilst punishing another and offering him the prospect of redemption. God, who is by defintion just (*per se iustus*), could not act unjustly. Finally, accidents such as time and motion could not be annihilated before reaching their own natural end (*ante finem suae naturalis periodi*) and neither, therefore, could their subjects.[48] These arguments provided a robust defence against those who might have wished to uphold the doctrine of transubstantiation on philosophical grounds, but Wyclif makes no reference to the Eucharist in this tract.

It was not until he composed the final treatise of the *Summa de ente* in the first half of the 1370s (*Potentia productiva Dei ad extra*) that Wyclif brought his carefully rehearsed objections to the thesis of annihilation and his rejection of transubstantiation explicitly together.[49] That the former is given far greater weight than the latter, however, is a fact so exceptional as to have led J.A. Robson to conclude that this tract must have been composed at "a comparatively early date" (a point with which later scholars have generally concurred).[50] Whilst this must suggest that eucharistic theology had been problematic for Wyclif as a relatively young student of philosophy, it lends urgency to the question of why he was to remain relatively silent about eucharistic presence for nearly ten years. His older Oxford opponent, the Carmelite scholar John Kynyngham, had certainly understood the potential dangers of Wyclif's metaphysical system not long after the *Summa de Ente* had been completed, but his numerous determinations against him focused principally upon his claims about scriptural authority, realist metaphysics and time.[51] In his third determination, however, which was devoted to the latter theme, he expressed

[48] Cf. *De universalibus* 13, pp. 307–16 (Latin text); and *On Universals*, pp. 143–8 (English translation).

[49] See *De ente: librorum duorum excerpta*, ed. M.H. Dziewicki (London, 1909), pp. 287–315.

[50] I am heavily indebted to Robson in my account of Wyclif's early discussion of annihilation. See J.A. Robson, *Wyclif and the Oxford Schools* (Cambridge, 1961), p. 189.

[51] On what little is known of Kynyngham's life, see Anne Hudson, "Kenningham, John (d. 1399)," in *Dictionary of National Biography* (Oxford, 2004) 31:297–8. His three *determinationes* are edited by Shirley in *FZ*, pp. 4–42; 43–72; 73–103. Wyclif's determination against Kynyngham is edited on pp. 453–76 of the same volume. For detailed discussion of the debates between Wyclif and Kynyngham, see Beryl Smalley, "The Bible and Eternity: John Wyclif's Dilemma," *Journal of the Warburg and Courtauld Institutes* 27 (1964), 73–89.

despair at Wyclif's professed opinion that he did not believe that
Christ had said, in the Gospel, that the bread was his body. This
determination is of uncertain date, but was certainly written before
1376, and might conceivably date from as early as 1372.[52] We read
in St John's Gospel, Kynyngham points out here, that Christ said,
"the bread that I will give to you is my flesh, for the life of the
world."[53] "If my Master does not believe the Gospel," he concludes,
"then I will pray for him, just as he offered me the blessing of his
own prayer."[54] If these words, embedded within the discourse of
metaphysical and hermeneutic debate, were to have no effect on
Wyclif's standing within the university, then neither, it seems, were
the early reservations that were almost certainly felt by a younger
contemporary, William Woodford. Though Woodford had spoken
out in 1376 against Wyclif's views on ecclesiastical endowment, he
did not publicly voice his objections to the theologian's controversial views on eucharistic presence until 1383.

Indeed, he was not to present his views in an outwardly controversial manner until the publication of his three tracts on contemporary heresy: *De simonia* (completed early in 1380), *De eucharistia* (his
most extensive analysis of eucharistic theology, probably composed
sometime in 1380), and *De apostasia* (completed late in 1380). He
later reiterated these views in his last published theological *summa*,
the *Trialogus*. It is in the three heresy tracts that he speaks of contemporary eucharistic doctrine in terms of a collective obsession with
the outward nature of the host (a mere *sign* of divinity), and of
upholders of this doctrine as *cultores signorum* ("worshippers of signs").
In *De apostasia*, the *cultores signorum* are said to argue that "the sacrament itself is an aggregate of accidents without a substantial subject."[55]

---

[52] The date 1376, recorded in the *Fasciculus* manuscript by Bishop Bale, has been
uniformly rejected by later scholars. Workman argued for a date as early as 1372
(*John Wyclif*, 2:121), which is consistent with Williel Thomson's suggestion that
Wyclif's three responses to Kynyngham (which survive as the single *determinatio* presented in *FZ*) probably date from 1372. See Thomson, *The Latin Writings of John
Wyclyf*, p. 228. In the last of his determinations, Kynyngham refers to Wyclif as
"doctor," a title which the theologian would certainly have obtained at around this
time. In the two other determinations, he is identified as "magister."

[53] John 6:52. See *FZ*, p. 54.

[54] *FZ*, p. 54: "Et si Magister meus non credit evangelio, tunc orabo pro eo, sicut
ipse promisit mihi beneficium orationis suae."

[55] *De apostasia* 17, p. 254/1–3: "Cultores signorum iuxtaponunt suam sententiam,
quod sacramentum ipsum sit agregacio accidencium sine substancia subiecta."

The absence of the substantial subject, the *cultores* were held to believe, arose out of the annihilation of the substance of the bread and wine. Though the *cultores* might have represented for Wyclif a distinct group of theologians from the schools, it would seem they could equally have included the majority of his Christian contemporaries. All that can be known for certain is that they were "worshippers" of signs, which, for Wyclif, in this context, were the accidental properties of the bread and wine that constituted the eucharistic host.

Wyclif explores the existing alternatives to the position of the contemporary *cultores* in turn in *De eucharistia*. There are, he suggests, three approaches (*viae*) to the problem. He begins with the proposals of Thomas Aquinas and John Duns Scotus. Aquinas had argued in the *Summa theologiae* that the substance of the bread and wine did not remain in the host after consecration, but had resisted the notion of annihilation. After consecration, the substance of the bread and wine, he had suggested, is *converted* (*convertitur*) into the body and the blood of Christ. Conversion, he had been careful to emphasize, does not entail annihilation.[56] It would not be possible, he had suggested, either for the bread and the wine to be annihilated after consecration, or for them to be reduced to their primary elements. This, he had argued, would run contrary to the signification of the words, "This is my body" (*hoc est corpus meum*). It also ran contrary to medieval canon law; transubstantiation (defined as a process of conversion) had become part of Catholic dogma with the assembly of the Fourth Lateran Council in 1215.[57] Aquinas's explanation of eucharistic change, despite its orthodoxy, however, had left him with the problem of explaining how, in the absence of the substance of the bread and wine, its accidental properties could remain. Unlike the *cultores*, he had been unwilling to entertain the possibility of an absent subject (a logical absurdity for an Aristotelian), but his denial of remanence made it necessary to find one beyond the substance of the bread and wine itself. His solution was to argue that the appearance of the Eucharist was sustained uniquely by the *quantity* of the bread and

---

[56] *Summa theologiae*, 3a.75.3, responsio, in vol. 58:66: "[S]ubstantia panis vel vini, facta consecratione, neque sub speciebus sacramenti manet, neque alibi. Non tamen sequitur quod annihiletur: convertitur enim in corpus Christi. Sicut non sequitur, si aer ex quo generatus est ignis, non sit ibi vel alibi, quod sit annihilatus."

[57] The text of Lateran IV can be found in the Vatican edition, *Contitutiones quarti lateranensis una cum commentariis glossatorum* (Vatican City, 1981).

wine, which, though an accident, was sufficiently similar to substance to exist independently. Wyclif summarizes this position as follows:

> The first approach seems to be that of St Thomas and his followers, [who say] that the Eucharist is a mass of the genus of *quantity*, because although it should itself be an accident, quantity is nevertheless the first accident after the genus of *substance*. The sacrament should therefore be a continuous permanent quantity by which the bread, formerly, was formally quantified.[58]

When he suggests that Aquinas had identified quantity as the "first accident after the genus of substance," Wyclif is alluding to a claim made in the third book of the *Summa Theologiae*. Here, "dimensive quantity" (*quantitas dimensiva*) is shown to act as the subject of the remaining accidents after consecration. Accidents are said to inhere in their subject through the mediating presence of quantity (*omnia alia accidentia referantur ad subjectum mediante quantitate dimensiva*), a fact that, for Aquinas, seemed to privilege quantity above the other accidents.[59] Under normal circumstances, however, not even this primary accident could act as the *immediate* subject of the remaining accidents; it could only sustain accidents if it was itself sustained by a substance (as in the case, Aquinas had argued, of a surface sustaining color). The immediacy of the quantitative subject in the Eucharist must therefore be seen to be granted by divine agency.[60] Wyclif would not have endorsed this line of reasoning, but would have been reluctant to address Aquinas in an openly antagonistic way. Indeed, in the fifth chapter of *De eucharistia*, he suggests that the Thomistic denial of remanence is likely to have been a fiction, contrived by fraternal inquisitors after his death.[61]

---

[58] *De eucharistia* 2, ed. Johann Loserth (London, 1892), pp. 29/27–30/5: "Prima [via] videtur esse sentencia sancti Thome cum suis sequacibus quod Eukaristia sit magnitudo de genere quantitatis, quia cum oportet ipsum esse accidens, quantitatis autem est primum accidens post genus substancie, oportet illud sacramentum sensibile esse quantitatem continuam permanentem qua panis perante formaliter fuit quantus."

[59] *Summa theologiae*, 3a.77.2, responsio.

[60] *Summa theologiae*, 3a.77.2, responsio, 58:134: "Accidens per se non potest esse subjectum alterius accidentis, quia non per se est. Secundum vero quod est in alio, unum accidens dicitur esse subjectum alterius, inquantum unum accidens recipitur in subjecto alio mediante, sicut superficies dicitur esse subjectum coloris. Unde, quando accidenti datur divinus per se sit, potest etiam per se alterius accidentis esse subjectum."

[61] *De eucharistia* 5, p. 139ff.

Duns Scotus, whose teaching represented the second of Wyclif's three *viae*, had embraced the Thomistic suggestion that an accident might indeed be capable of sustaining the visible and tangible qualities of the host, but had been ambivalent about annihilation (a process that Aquinas had ruled out emphatically in the *Summa Theologiae*). He had considered the nature of eucharistic change, as was necessary, in his commentary on the *Sentences* (his famous *Opus Oxoniense*), returning to it at a later stage in his quodlibetical questions.[62] His arguments are presented, in each of these texts, in the form of a detailed dialogue with existing authorities on the matter (chief among them, Aquinas), but are ultimately circumscribed by Scotus's adherence to the eucharistic doctrines enshrined in medieval canon law (*Firmiter* and *Cum marthae*). His discussion is structured around three definitions of eucharistic change, which had been recorded, according to Scotus, by Pope Innocent III. According to the first, the substance of the bread could remain *alongside* the body of Christ (consubstantially with it). On the second interpretation, the bread would not remain, but would not be converted; rather, it would cease to be, either through annihilation, or by resolution into its primary *materia*. Only the accidental properties of the bread would remain. Lastly, the bread could be transubstantiated into the body of Christ, and the wine into the blood.[63] Either of the first two explanations would have been sufficient to preserve the truth of the Eucharist, and either form of change could have been chosen by God if he had so wished. The first seemed intuitively attractive because it did not rely on more philosophical assumptions than were rationally necessary, nor upon a superfluous multiplication of miracles.[64]

---

[62] Scotus, *Sententiae* 4.11.3 (on conversion); *Sententiae*, 4.11.4 (on annihilation); *Questiones quodlibetales*, q. 10, dist. 3. All references pertain to the edition contained in *Opera Omnia* vol. 17 (Paris, 1894).

[63] *Sententiae*, 4.11.3, p. 352: "[S]icut recitat Innocentius de Officio Missae part. 2 cap. 26 circa hoc erant tres opiniones. Una, quod panis manet, et tamen cum ipso vere est corpus Christi. Alia, quod panis non manet, et tamen non convertitur, sed desinet esse, vel per annihilationem, vel per resolutionem in materiam, vel per corruptionem in aliud. Tertia, quod panis transubstantiatur in corpus et vinum in sanguinem."

[64] *Sententiae*, 4.11.3, p. 375: "Ad argumenta pro prima opinione et secunda. Ad primum, concedo quod etiam in creditiis non sunt plura ponenda sine necessitate, nec plura miracula quam oportet. Sed cum dicitur in minori, veritas Eucharistiae posset salvari manente pane vel sine transubstantiatione, dico quod bene fuisset possibile intuisse, quod corpus Christivere esset praesens, substantia panis manente, vel cum accidentibus, pane annihilatio, et tunc fuisset ibi veritas Eucharistiae, quia et signum verum et signatum verum."

The second might have been defended on the same basis. Aquinas, however, whose views are represented in Scotus's commentary by an anonymous *Doctor*, had rejected both of these accounts. According to the Doctor's teaching, Scotus had told his readers, nothing of the substance of the bread and the wine could remain after the conversion process. Paradoxically, however, the Doctor had also denied that the bread was annihilated in the course of this process.[65] He had reportedly suggested that if the process of conversion involved annihilation, then the *terminus ad quem* of the process would be pure nothingness. This was equivalent to negation *extra genus* (that is, negation *per se*, beyond any generic constraint), and not negation as otherwise defined (which could inhere, as an accident, in any positive subject). But the *terminus ad quem* here was the body of Christ, in which the negation of the being of the bread inhered (as a *terminus incompatibilis*).[66] If the *terminus a quo* and the *terminus ad quem* of the conversion shared a subject, and if the *negatio* were preserved within it, then annihilation could not be deemed to have taken place.[67]

Though he was himself eventually to reject annihilation, Scotus had considered the *philosophical* objections to its rejection very carefully in his commentary. If conversion were to take place without annihilation, then the desition of the substance of the bread and wine had to be concomitant with the arrival of the body and the blood of Christ. Second, if the bread were to be reduced to nothing,

---

[65] *Sententiae*, 4.11.4, p. 450: "Conclusio Doctoris est nihil substantiae panis et vini manere potest conversionem. Secundo, dicit panem non annihilari: *Vel*, inquit, *quod facilius est, panem ista conversione non annihilari*. Nihil aliud affirmat Doctor in tota quaestione; immerito ergo citatur absolute pro illa sententia, quae dicit panem, ut est terminus huius conversionis, annihilari, prout alii dicunt, tam novi quam antique assertores huius sententiae."

[66] *Sententiae*, 4.11.4, p. 450: "Primam conclusionem seu modum conversionis supponens Doctor, probat panem non annihilari, quia terminus ad quem annihilationis est purum nihil, id est, negation extra genus et non negatio, ut inest alicui positive; sed terminus ad quem transitus panis non est negatio simpliciter, et extra genus, sed corpus Christi, ut habet annexam negationem essendi panis tamquam terminus incompatibilis; ergo panis non annihilator."

[67] *Sententiae*, 4.11.4, p. 451: "Dicit si manere posset respective ad formam corruptam absque eo quod subjectum commune et privatio maneret, esset sufficiens causa, unde corruption non diceretur annihilatio. Et hoc etiam patet in toto substantiali converso in aliud quod dicitur corrumpi; non quod privatio eius manet, sed quod subjectum manet in altero, quod dicit incompatibilitatem et negationem essendi totius corrupti." Cf. Aquinas, *Summa theologiae*, 3a.75.3: "[F]orma quae est terminus a quo non convertitur in aliam formam, sed una forma succedit alteri *in subjecto*: et ideo prima forma non remanet nisi in potentia materiae."

and the body of Christ were to arrive beneath the species of the bread, then this would entail annihilation. Third, desition required an adequate *terminus* if it were not to be equivalent to annihilation; such a terminus could not, however, be identified with the negation of the bread (the Doctor's *terminus incompatibilis*). Scotus had finally rejected annihilation on the basis of a distinction between two kinds of transubstantiation. The first, he had argued, involved the simple desition of the substance of the bread, and the assumption by the host of the substance of the body of Christ—which thereby acquired being (*esse*). This, he had suggested, resulted in the production of the *terminus ad quem*. The second, by contrast, involved not the assumption of being, but of "being here" (*esse hic*). This was not a productive process (that is, a process of bringing into being), but a process by which a particular form of being was being *added* to a pre-existent substance.[68] The first kind of transubstantiation, because productive, could not be applied to a pre-existing substance. Given that the body of Christ had necessarily to be pre-existent, this first process of conversion had to be inconsistent with the change that took place in the Eucharist.[69]

Scotus's rather tentative rejection of annihilation and consubstantiation had rested on his necessary embrasure of Church doctrine, which had defined transubstantiation as a process of conversion. On this interpretation, the body of Christ was present *beneath* the accidental properties of the bread, as a significate beneath a sign. Despite having found philosophical grounds for dispensing with the other possible interpretations of eucharistic change, Scotus had clearly been troubled by the apparently irrational complexity of the dogma of transubstantiation. Like Ockham later, Scotus had been in no doubt that, given the choice between simplicity and complexity, the for-

---

[68] *Sententiae*, 4.11.3, p. 389: "Potest dici quod transubstantiatio (hoc stante quod sit inter terminus positivos, qui sunt substantiae) potest poni duobus modis intelligi. Uno modo quod sit ad substantiam, ut per ipsam accipientem esse; alio modo ut sit ad substantiam, ut per ipsam accipientem esse hic. Prima potest dici productiva sui termini ad quem; secunda adductiva, quia per ipsam adducitur terminus, ut sit hic."

[69] *Sententiae*, 4.11.3, p. 389: "Transubstantiatio primo modo non potest esse ad substantiam quae praefuit, quia non videtur posse poni in substantiam manentem secundum esse suum antiquum; sed secundo modo bene potest esse transubstantiatio in praeexistens, quia potest fieri de novo praesens hic, ubi fuit terminus a quo, manet tamen ubi erat prius."

mer should logically be defended. In this instance, however, the Catholic Church had interpreted Scripture according to the spirit of truth, that same spirit that had guided its compositors.[70] This much was clear from the doctrine laid down under Innocent III at the Fourth Lateran council of 1215 (*Firmiter*).[71] Such an interpretation, Scotus believed, had necessarily to be true, whatever its logical implications. As David Burr has usefully argued, this should not be seen as a slavish and unquestioning adherence to Church authority; Scotus's references to scriptural interpretation rest rather on the assumption that the Council had made explicit and accessible a difficult and possibly obscure piece of biblical teaching.[72]

Scotus's account of eucharistic change, however reliant on foundations established by Aquinas, and however orthodox in its final formulation, had clearly gestured away from an outright rejection of annihilation. But Wyclif finally casts Scotus aside on the related problem of the absolute accident. Here, Scotus had followed Aquinas closely, but, on Wyclif's interpretation in *De eucharistia*, had refused to accept that quantity was sufficient to sustain the other accidents in the host. This, according to Wyclif, was because Scotus had suggested that particular properties of the host—namely, its capacity to be rarefied or condensed—were "inconsistent" with quantity.[73] But Wyclif's representation of this position in *De eucharistia* is not an entirely accurate one. Like Aquinas and many other Scholastics, Scotus had been happy to locate the accidents of quality—colour,

---

[70] *Sententiae*, 4.11.3, p. 376: "Et si quaeras quare voluit Ecclesia eligere istum intellectum ita difficilem huis articuli, cum verba Scripturae possent salvari secundum intellectum facilem et variorum secundum apparentiam de hoc articulo; dico quod eo spiritu expositae sunt Scripturae, quo conditae. Et ita supponendum est, quod Ecclesia Catholica eo Spiritu exposuit, quo tradita est nobis fides, Spiritu scilicet veritatis edocta, et ideo hunc intellectum elegit, quia verus est."

[71] *Sententiae*, 4.11.3, p. 376: "Et tunc ad tertium, ubi stat vis, dicendum quod Ecclesia declaravit istum intellectum esse de veritate fidei in illo Symbolo edito sub Innocentio III in Concilio Lateranensi, *Firmitur credimus*, etc. sicut allegatum est superius, ubi explicite ponitur veritas aliquorum credendorum, magis explicite quam habebatur in Symbolo Apostolorum, vel Athanasii, vel Niceni. Et breviter, quidquid ibi dicitur esse credendum, tenendum est esse de substantia fidei, et hoc post istam declarationem solemnem factam ab Ecclesia."

[72] David Burr, "Scotus and Transubstantiation," *Mediaeval Studies* 34 (1972): 336–60, at p. 354.

[73] *De eucharistia* 2, p. 30/6–11: "Secunda opinio videtur esse Scoti qui improbat opinionem priorem per hoc quod hoc sacramentum potest rarefieri et condensari, quod non potest competere quantitati; ideo cum sit accidens consonum, videtur ipsum ponere qualitatem, cum oportet quod sit accidens absolutum."

texture, taste, etc.—within the unique "absolute" accident, quantity.[74] Indeed, in a later sermon (Sixteenth Sunday after Trinity, 1382), Wyclif had himself placed Aquinas and Scotus together as theologians who had defended this shared position, and had associated the view he later ascribed to Scotus with William of Ockham, its true proponent.[75] The sermon, which addresses itself to the findings of the Earthquake Council, brings Aquinas, Scotus and Ockham together as thinkers who, like Wyclif himself, had ultimately refused to embrace the notion that accidents within the host might exist without a subject. Though each of the three had been rejected systematically in turn in the *De eucharistia*, therefore, Wyclif warns here against a comprehensive heretication of their teaching on the Eucharist.

Wyclif turns finally to the controversial eleventh-century logician Berengar of Tours (d. 1088). Like Wyclif, Berengar had rejected the notion that any kind of accidental separation (or annihilation) could take place at the moment of consecration. His solution, however, was quite at odds with Wyclif's own. Central to Wyclif's argument was the belief that the real body and blood of Christ were present in the consecrated host, just as the substances of the bread and wine—if the theories of annihilation and accidental separation were to be rejected—were present. Berengar had conceded that bread and wine were present materially, but denied that this was true of the body and blood of Christ. The passage that Wyclif cites in *De eucharis-*

---

[74] On the relationship between quality and quantity in Scotus's theory of eucharistic change, see Richard Cross, *Duns Scotus* (Oxford, 1999), pp. 140–41.

[75] *Sermones* 3.50, ed. J. Loserth (London, 1889), p. 436/23–34: "[S]ecundum distincciones fratrum recencium omne accidens respectivum et qualitas subiectatur in quantitate sine informata priori substancia remanente; ergo secundum illos ad omnem punctum sacramenti accidens subiectatur. Et illam sentenciam declarat crebrius doctor communis, doctor subtilis, et alii qui finxerant istam viam. Unde inceptor Ocham videtur dicere quod, si sint accidencia respectiva ut motus vel variaciones distincte in hoc sacramento omnia illis fundantur in qualitate ut in subiecto, ideo videtur nimia presumpcio hereticare fratrum tam probabilium sentencias in hac parte." Cf. Ockham, *De Sacramento Altaris*, ed. T. Bruce Birch (Iowa, 1930), p. 156/7–17: "[D]ico cum doctoribus approbatis ab ecclesia quod remanet ibi color, sapor, pondus, hoc est gravitas, et huiusmodi qualitates; quarum nulla est alia res a quantitate extra omne subiectum situ per se subsistentia divina potentia; quarum nulla est in alia subiective; sed quaelibet per divinam potentiam existit extra subiectum, et simul in eodem loco et situ per divinam potentiam conservatur; et ideo remanet ibi quantitas una habens partem distantem a parte, quae numquam fuit nec umquam erit substantia, sed est simpliciter alia res a substantia."

tia is from the *Ego Berengarius*, in which Berengar declares his belief in both the physical presence of the bread and wine and the Real Presence of the body and blood of Christ. The confession was recorded by Berengar's distinguished opponent, Lanfranc of Bec, whose treatise on the body and blood of Christ was formulated as a corrective to this earlier denial of real presence. Berengar's declaration, which he later retracted, was made at the bidding of Cardinal Humbert of Silva Candida, at a council held in Rome by Pope Nicholas II in 1059:[76]

> I believe that the bread and wine that are placed on the altar are not, after consecration, simply a sacrament, but also the body and the blood of our Lord Jesus Christ. Not as a sacrament alone, but in truth, they are taken and broken in the hands of the priest, and crushed by the teeth of the faithful.[77]

Berengar's words, on Wyclif's interpretation, suggest that the bread and wine are present both before and after consecration.[78] This view, Wyclif argues, was the one that was endorsed by the Roman Church of the time. Berengar's earlier position, which ran contrary to orthodox theology, could not at that time have been defended. Wyclif had chosen to resist Berengar precisely because the earlier theologian, though motivated by logical and metaphysical concerns not dissimilar to his own, had chosen to deny a particular kind of presence within the Host. By denying the physical presence of the body and the blood of Christ in the Eucharist, Berengar had placed himself unambiguously among Wyclif's *cultores signorum*. In his retraction of

---

[76] Details of the *Ego Berengarius*, and of Berengar's confession in the presence of Nicholas II, can be found in Henry Chadwick's useful article, "Ego Berengarius," *Journal of Theological Studies*, n.s., 41:2. (1989), 414–45. On Berengar's sacramental theology see J. Macdonald, *Berengar and the Reform of Sacramental Doctrine* (London, 1930).

[77] *De eucharistia* 2, p. 30/22–27: "Credo panem et vinum que in altari ponuntur post consecracionem non solum sacramentum sed eciam verum corpus et sanguinem domini nostri Jesu Christi esse sensualiter non solum sacramentum, sed in veritate manibus sacerdotum tractari et frangi et fidelium dentibus atteri." See Lanfranc's record of the Confession, *De corpore et sanguine domini nostri adversus Berengarium*, which has been edited by J.A. Giles in *Beati Lanfranci Archiepiscopi Cantuariensis Opera quae supersunt omnia* (Oxford, 1844), 2:147–99 (the relevant passage occurs on p. 151). The text can also be found in PL 150:407–42.

[78] Immediately following the passage, Wyclif remarks in *De eucharistia* 2, pp. 30/27–31/1: "Ubi patet quod ille sensit quod idem panis et vinum remanet post consecracionem tam sacramentum quam corpus dominicum."

the confession of 1059, Berengar was denying what was later to be referred to as Real Presence; for him, the sacrament was a sign which was *not* identical with its *signatum* (namely, the *res sacramenti*).[79] Berengar was certainly among the intellectual *moderni* of his day, and was a very able logician. Like the "modern" logicians of Wyclif's time, he had attracted criticism—most famously from Lanfranc of Bec—about the nature of his philosophical method. His zealous application of the rules of Aristotelian logic to theological problems would in itself have been sufficient to incline the later philosopher to regard him with caution, but his denial of Real Presence would have placed him beyond the resources of theological salvation. Wyclif only considers the relationship between Berengar and his celebrated opponent in the ninth and final chapter of his treatise on the Eucharist. Lanfranc is here described as "first and foremost" among the medieval doctors of law. His views on the Eucharist, we are told, are preserved in his book *contra Berengarium*, but his arguments are held by Wyclif to proceed *inartificiose*.[80]

Berengar, Scotus and Aquinas had produced problematic solutions to the question of eucharistic presence, but had approached the issue in ways that could not easily unite them as a narrow philosophical group. Nevertheless, the obvious advantages of such a grouping have inevitably invited speculation. As a consequence, Ockham and the friars have widely been seen to have been rejected by Wyclif—as sacramental theologians—on the grounds of a shared commitment to nominalist metaphysics.[81] Whilst convenient, such a connection is very difficult to substantiate. Yet there are some tantalizing indications that an aversion to nominalist metaphysics may have fuelled Wyclif's contempt for his sacramental opponents. The errors com-

---

[79] The text of the retraction has been edited by R.B.C. Huygens, *Beringerius Turonensis, Rescriptum contra Lanfrannum*, CCCM 84 (Brepols, 1988).

[80] *De eucharistia* 9, p. 283/18ff.

[81] See, in particular, Penn Szittya, *The Antifraternal Tradition in Medieval Literature* (Princeton, 1986), pp. 156–8. Here, Wyclif's dismissive comments about the *cultores signorum* are seen in terms of a broader rejection of "the friars' nominalist metaphysics." (p. 157) Though nominalism was certainly the province of the friars (Ockham and, in Wyclif's Oxford, Kynyngham), however, such a generalization obscures the philosophical allegiances of two of Wyclif's most distinguished authorities: Aquinas and Scotus. Neither could have been rejected on the basis of any shared commitment to nominalist teaching, nor was either of their positions in respect of eucharistic presence challenged as part of an overtly anti-fraternal gesture.

mitted by contemporary theologians in respect of eucharistic presence are most closely associated with nominalism in *De apostasia*.
Here, Wyclif draws a distinction between things that exist *in actu signato* (as a 'signified actuality" without extra-mental existence) and
those that have "real" being *in actu exercito* (as a "realized actuality").
He speaks disparagingly of the doctors of signs who recognize universals as artificial entities existing only *in actu signato*:

> There is not any strength in that fiction concerning realized and signified
> actualities. For the doctors of signs suppose that there are no univer-
> sals *ex parte rei*; for this reason, in the statements of the philosophers
> to be glossed they would find these terms: as when the philosophers
> say that universals are eternal, always and everywhere, "this is true,"
> they say, "not in an action performed but an action signified."[82]

The distinction between things which exist *in actu exercito* and *in actu
signato* is unexceptional in itself. Here, it merely supplies Wyclif with
another means of characterizing the fundamental difference between
realism and nominalism. He goes on, however, to suggest that the
same distinction is applied by the *doctores signorum* to the substance
of the sacrament:

> "The sacramental bread," [they say,] "is not *in actu exercito* the body
> of Christ, since it is a pure accident, further removed in nature from
> the body of Christ than material bread. But it *is* the body of Christ
> *in actu signato*, that is, it signifies sacramentally the body of Christ."[83]

Superficially, this passage would appear to supply the necessary link
between the *doctores signorum*—a term possibly used to identify philosophical nominalists—and contemporary theologians who were failing to understand sacramental theology.[84] Christ's body, on this
interpretation, has only an imaginary presence within the host, just

---

[82] *De apostasia* 14, ed. M.H. Dziewicki (London, 1889), pp. 186/37–187/5: "Nec
valet ficticia de actu exercito et signato. Ponunt enim doctores signorum, quod non
est dare universalia ex parte rei; ideo pro glozandis dictis philosophorum invenerunt
hos terminos: ut quando philosophi dicunt, quod universalia sunt perpetua, ubique
et semper, "hoc est verum" inquiunt, "non *in actu exercito*, sed *signato*."
[83] *De apostasia* 14, p. 187/10–14: "Panis sacramentalis non est in actu exercito
corpus Christi, cum sit pure accidens longe plus distans in natura a corpore Christi,
quam panis materialis; sed est corpus Christi in actu signato, hoc est, sacramentaliter signat corpus Christi."
[84] M.H. Dziewicki makes this assumption in the introduction to his edition of *De
apostasia*, p. xxxii.

as universals exist, for the nominalist, merely as mental abstractions. The sacramental bread is said to be only an accident, further removed in its nature from the body of Christ than "material" bread (that is, bread which, unlike its sacramental counterpart on this interpretation, has a material base). Wyclif carefully interrogates this position, suggesting that were it to be maintained, then the sacrament would be merely a figure or a sign of the body of Christ (as Berengar had initially suggested, but had condemned as an heretical view in *Ego Berengarius*). The Church, moreover, had offered no recognition of the orthodoxy of such a view, which might conceivably lead any *impositor* to identify himself with God semiotically.[85] We need not necessarily invoke nominalist metaphysics in order to explain Wyclif's hostility to this position, and he is no less markedly opposed to those who would argue, with the Church and the holy doctors, that the substance of the bread is the body of Christ *in acto exercitu*. This position represents the orthodox understanding of transubstantiation of which he has been uniformly critical elsewhere. However the distinction between realized and signified realities be understood, therefore, it seems that it is the semiotic opposition on which it is based, rather than any lingering hostility towards nominalist metaphysics, that frustrates Wyclif. The failings of those who suggest that Christ's body is present only *in acto signato* are better understood, it would seem, from within an Aristotelian framework: there could be no such thing, for the dedicated Aristotelian, as a "pure accident" (as would necessarily exist if Christ's body were present only *in acto signato*). Ockham had known this as well as Wyclif, but he did not turn to philosophical nominalism for an answer; indeed, there was nothing in his own metaphysical system that could have provided one. Instead, he had assumed that quality—the only accident, for him, which could be regarded as a "real" entity[86]—could be sustained by divine

---

[85] *De apostasia* 14, p. 187/15–27: "Sed contra istud instatur, primo, per hoc, quod sacramentum foret solum signum vel figura corporis Christi; ut dicit Berengarius quod sic loquentes ponunt hereticum: Item, cum illud esse quo sacramentum est corpus Christi, non sit aliter ibi quam in signo, magnum foret inconveniens quod haec fides non sit detecta ecclesiae. Item per idem quodcunque signatum quod deus unstituit signari per signum vel terminum, communicaret vere nomen suum illi signo et per consequens sicut quilibet impositor potest facere signum, signans sibi deum omnipotentem, qui creavit mundum ex nihilo, qui summe gubernat ecclesiam quam redemit et qui finaliter iudicabit seculum tamquam summus iudex."

[86] "Quality," for Ockham, was the only accidental term which signified "absolutely"

power (*per divinam potentiam*).[87] If anything, this assumption marks a departure from nominalist metaphysics. On this occasion, like Scotus, Ockham had had to place theology above the demands of a stringent minimalist logic. Indeed, as Paul Spade has suggested, it would seem that the Eucharist may have been Ockham's only justification for preserving the reality of quality.[88]

If we were to accept the possibility of "absolute" accidental entities, and were to apply this principle to the Eucharist, Wyclif argues, then we would have to accept that the sacrament was merely a sign or a figure of the body of Christ.[89] Such a view, as he has learned from Berengar, was plain heresy.[90] It cannot be the case, he argues, that the sacramental being of the body of Christ has no reality except *in signo*; such a belief was nowhere to be found in the Church. Likewise, if the sacrament were merely a sign, then any individual could claim to possess a sign which signified an omnipotent God; the potential for abuse is manifest.[91] Wyclif was emphatically orthodox in his refusal to reduce sacrament to sign *simpliciter*, as is clear from his extensive use of Aquinas's *Lauda Sion salvatorem* at the beginning of *De eucharistia*. In the *Lauda*, Aquinas leaves his audience in no doubt as to the fact that only the host, a sign, is broken at the point of consecration, and not the sacramental body of Christ itself:

> Nor a single doubt retain,
> When they break the Host in twain
> But that in each part remains
> What was in the whole before.[92]

From the first chapter of *De eucharistia*, Wyclif insisted that the sacrament had to be understood in three distinct ways, in order to avoid

---

(i.e. denotatively), rather than by connotation. However, Ockham had argued that even some sub-categories of quality had names that signified denotatively. See Klima, "Ockham's Semantics and Ontology of the Categories," in *The Cambridge Companion to Ockham*, ed. Paul Vincent Spade (Cambridge, 1999), pp. 118–42 (133–4).

[87] William of Ockham, *De Sacramento Altaris*, pp. 156–7.

[88] See Paul Vincent Spade, "Ockham's Nominalist Metaphysics," in *The Cambridge Companion to Ockham*, pp. 100–117 (p. 103).

[89] *De apostasia* 14, p. 187.

[90] Ibid., p. 187.

[91] Ibid., p. 187.

[92] "Fracto demum sacramento/Non vacilles sed memento/Tantum esse sub fragmento/Quantum toto tegitur." See *Analecta hymnica medii aevi*, vol. 1 for the complete Latin text. Wyclif cites these lines in *De eucharistia* 1, p. 12.

any possible confusion of host and the sacramental *res*. First, there
is the "bare sacrament" (*nudum sacramentum*), which is not the sacramental *res*, such as the host. Then, there is the *sacramentum* and the
res sacramenti, which is the body and the blood of Christ. Third, there
is the *res sacramenti* which is not the sacrament (in contrast with the
second definition), and this, Wyclif suggests, is exemplified by the
union of Christ with his mystical body, the Church. This he argues,
is not present to the senses, and cannot be said to 'be' anywhere.[93]
Throughout *De eucharistia*, he was keen to distance himself from the
doctrine of identification, arguing that it cannot be the case that
Christ is *dimensionally* present in the substance of the bread and wine,
since this would lead to absurdities. When the priest utters the word
'*hoc*,' what is signified is the bread, not the body of Christ, and when
he uses the copula '*esse*' to link '*hoc*' and '*corpus meum*,' there is no
suggestion of identity.[94] Though the statement "*hoc est corpus meum*"
is true, it is only figuratively, or "tropically," so.[95] Wyclif traces the
doctrine of identification back to the Lombard (book 4, distinction
11 of the *Sentences*).[96] The evidence supporting such a doctrine, he
argues, is nothing more than sophistry, and is substantiated by the
Lombard largely through the testimonies of saints that have been
misunderstood by him (or by others before him). Identification, he
suggests, must either involve change in a substance (*ydemptificatio indi-*

---

[93] *De eucharistia* 1, p. 11/4–13: "In [haec] materia dixi sepe populo quod in sacramento altaris est tria considerare, scilicet nudum sacramentum sic quod non rem
sacramenti ut hostiam consecratam; secundo sacramentum et rem sacramenti ut
verum corpus Christi et sanguinem; et tertio rem sacramenti et non sacramentum
ut unionem Christi cum corpore suo mistico quod est ecclesia; hoc enim nusquam
est sensibile et per consequens non est alicubi sacramentum."

[94] On the meaning of the demonstrative '*hoc*' in sacramental propositions, see *De
eucharistia* 4, p. 89; *Trialogus* 4.3, pp. 250–54. On '*esse*' and the absence of literal
identity, see *De eucharistia* 7, p. 217ff.

[95] *De eucharistia* 4, pp. 97/29–98/4: "Patet [. . .] quod non obest sed consonant,
ut dicit decretalis *Cum Marthe*, quod in hoc sacramento sint simul veritas et figura;
sacramentum enim figurat Christum et unionem cum ipso atque ecclesia; et vere
facit atque figurat presenciam Christi sacramentalem ultra figures alias."

[96] The Lombard discusses eucharistic change at length, in a properly dialectical
manner. But his opening words suggest that he is merely substantiating an accepted
view. 4.11.1, 2:296: "Si autem quaeritur qualis sit illa conversio: an formalis, an
substantialis, vel alterius generis, definire non sufficio. Formalem tamen non esse
cognosco, quia species rerum quae ante fuerant remanent, et sapor, et pondus.
Quibusdam esse videtur substantialis, dicentibus sic substantiam converti in substantiam, ut haec essentialiter fiat illa. Cui sensui praemissae auctoritates consentire
videntur."

vidualis per motum), or the replacement of one substance with another. If the substance changes, then it must be the case that something is either acquired or destroyed at the level of accidental properties or of the essence of the substance. If something is destroyed in respect of the latter, Wyclif argues, then the thing signified by the pronoun has not been "identified" with anything else, but has simply been destroyed. If something has been acquired essentially, then two discrete essences exist, but are in no way *identical*. If the change is accidental, then the thing signified has not changed.[97] Wyclif demonstrates this with the example of a man and an ass. If a man is identified with an ass, we must ask whether both essences remain. If they do, then no transformation has taken place; if they do not, then the man must have been destroyed if only the ass remains.[98]

Wyclif often remains rather reticent about *how* it can be the case that Christ is present, if *dimensionally* absent, in the sacramental host (which is, as he has emphatically suggested, a mere sign, in no way to be confused with the *res sacramenti*). In *De eucharistia*, he broaches the issue in rather a sporadic manner, employing terms and concepts from the science of optics, then a constituent field of geometry, one of the four mathematical sciences, to explain this apparently paradoxical phenomenon.[99] He appeals to the Pauline distinction between the *oculum mentis* (or *oculum mentale*) and the *oculum corporale* to resolve the problem.[100] When we perceive the body of Christ in

---

[97] *De eucharistia* 7, pp. 190/27–191/12: "[V]el erit ipsa ydemptificatio individualis per motum vel sine motu; si per motum, oportet signare aliquid quod deperdetur vel acquiretur vel utrumque; et signato illo quod acquiretur vel deperdetur, queritur [. . .] utrum erit essenciale vel accidentale ydemptificando, si essenciale signatum non ydemtificatur sed destruetur. Si vero sit accidentale ydemptificando, sequitur quod non obstante illo motu manebit utrumque quidquid prefuit; non ergo ydemptificatur unum alteri, sed manebunt due res tantum essencialiter distincte sicut in principio. Si sine motu fiat ydemptificatio, tunc a neutron fiet ablacio alicuius essencialis vel accidentalis pertinens ydemptificationi, et per consequens remanebunt tante distincta substancialiter et accidentaliter sicut in principio."

[98] See *De eucharistia* 7, p. 191.

[99] On the relationship between optics and geometry in late-medieval education, see Allan Cobban, *English University Life in the Middle Ages* (London, 1999), pp. 156–7. On Wyclif's use of optics in his analyses of eucharistic presence, see Heather Phillips, "John Wyclif and the Optics of the Eucharist," in *From Ockham to Wyclif*, ed. A. Hudson and M. Wilks (Oxford, 1987), pp. 245–58. I am heavily indebted to Phillips in my presentation of Wyclif's position here.

[100] The origin of the distinction between bodily and spiritual vision is usefully summarized in Vivien Law's study, "Learning to Read with the *oculi mentis*: Virgilius Maro Grammaticus," *Journal of Literature and Theology* 3 (1989), 159–72.

the sacrament, he suggests, we do not see it with the bodily eye (the *oculum corporale*) but with the eye of the mind (the *oculum mentis*), which he equates with "faith." This optical principle, Wyclif claims, enables us to see Christ *per speculum enigmate*, as through a mystical mirror, and means that every point of his body can be present without being present dimensionally or physically. The eye of the mind (or "eye of the heart," as Augustinians described it), then, enabled a kind of spiritual vision, analogous to, but in no way identical with, optical vision. To confuse the two would lead to gross metaphysical and theological errors, such as the belief that the body of Christ was broken with the breaking of the bread, and chewed by the teeth of the recipient of the sacrament. It could be assumed, moreover, were the two ways of seeing to be confused, that an animal could eat the body. But this, Wyclif suggested, would be the equivalent of the very obviously absurd conclusion that if a human body were to be eaten by a beast, then that human's soul would also be devoured and destroyed (given that the soul is at every point present in the body, in a similar way to that in which the body of Christ is present at every point of the *nudum sacramentum*). All that the creature would eat were it to chew and swallow the host would be the *nudum sacramentum*, and not the *res sacramenti*.[101]

In this account of the relationship between Wyclif's philosophical realism and his conclusions about the Eucharist, I have made no attempt to claim that his position on the Eucharist arose directly out of his metaphysics. But the compatibility between the two cannot be neglected, and cannot easily be denied. Historians have tended either to downplay the significance of Wyclif's metaphysics as a necessary precursor to his later conclusions on the Eucharist, or to insist on a strong etiological link between the two. The latter position has been questioned very persuasively in studies by Jeremy Catto and Maurice Keen, and has found few adherents since.[102] Keen, in rejecting the earlier, highly influential "philosophical" accounts of Gordon Leff, J.A. Robson and Herbert Workman, complained of an "uncomfortably long gap" between Wyclif's first treatment of the question and the controversial conclusions that he drew years later in *De eucharis-*

---

[101] *De eucharistia* 1, p. 11.
[102] See Catto, "John Wyclif and the Cult of the Eucharist," 269–86; Maurice Keen, "Wyclif, the Bible and Transubstantiation," in *Wyclif in his Times*, ed. Anthony Kenny (Oxford, 1986), pp. 1–16.

tia, De apostasia De blasphemia and the *Trialogus*.[103] Both Catto and Keen took particular exception to Leff's suggestion that Wyclif's metaphysics led to a conclusion about the Eucharist that was ultimately "ineluctable."[104] Leff had further suggested that the conclusions that finally emerged, and that led to Wyclif's condemnation in 1381, might have appeared at any point in the preceding twenty years had he not been so fearful of their likely consequences.[105] I feel less inclined to dismiss these ideas than Catto and Keen had done, particularly given that the relationship between Wyclif's life as a metaphysician and his later position as a theological and political controversialist have been so widely and so conveniently isolated by scholars. Keen is certainly right to suggest that Wyclif's metaphysical teaching was never condemned, and that the Czechs, unaware of his pronouncements on the Eucharist in England, were not in the least alarmed by them; but it seems rather reductive to suggest that the roots of a controversial theological idea should not lie, with any degree of inevitability, in an outwardly innocuous system that had been assembled many years earlier. Metaphysical teaching in the schools was not in any obvious way political, even if it might have contained principles that would lead on closer analysis to problematic, politically sensitive conclusions. The author of the *Fasciculi zizaniorum* seemed to have recognized as much when he suggested that Wyclif's controversial ideas were allowed to develop in the academy precisely because they, like cockles in a cornfield, were inconspicuous, and were sewn *in terram bonam*.[106] This is not, of course, to deny that Wyclif's rejection of transubstantiation took authority from Scripture. And it is certainly true, as Catto suggests in a later study of Wyclif's place among the Oxford schoolmen, that his confidence in his own position on the Eucharist rested heavily on the view of scriptural authority advanced in *De veritate Sacrae Scripturae* (1377–78).[107]

---

[103] Keen, p. 10.

[104] Ibid., p. 10. See also Catto, "John Wyclif and the Cult of the Eucharist," p. 272.

[105] *Heresy in the Later Middle Ages* (Manchester, 1967; reprinted Bath, 1999), vol. 2, p. 550. See also Leff's useful essay, "Metaphysics in Wyclif's Theology," *From Ockham to Wyclif*, pp. 217–32. Here, Leff argues that "one of the main props of Wyclif's later denial of transubstantiation was in place" with the publication of *De universalibus* (1368–9).

[106] *Fasciculi zizaniorum*, p. 1.

[107] See J.I. Catto, "Wyclif and Wycliffism at Oxford 1356–1430," in *History of the University of Oxford* vol. 2, ed. J.I. Catto and R. Evans (Oxford, 1992), pp. 209–13,

It remains the case, nevertheless, that this position—like Wyclif's understanding of Scripture-as-idea—could not have arisen in the absence of a strong realist metaphysic.

Baptism

Baptism, like the Eucharist, could be traced without difficulty by Wyclif to relevant scriptural passages. His treatment of the sacrament addresses mainly those topics that are to be found in the *Sentences*, and in the *Sentences* commentaries of the intervening period. His ideas on the sacrament of Baptism were much further removed from controversy than his views on the Eucharist, and his comments on the sacrament were relatively brief and infrequent (as, correspondingly, are those of his biographers).[108] Yet the *sacramentum tantum* was a sign, open to abuse, like the other six, by idolatrous *cultores*. It was also administered by a priest, who might conceivably be unworthy. Should the layman have the authority to administer the sacrament in the absence of a priest? What would be the consequences for one dying without having received the sacrament? These are quite familiar questions, but might clearly invite potentially difficult answers, as some of Wyclif's certainly were.

Discussion of Baptism by Peter Lombard in the *Sentences* had centered on the Baptism of Christ by St John the Baptist. He had considered the significance of the words of Christ in Matthew 21:25: "The Baptism of John, whence was it?" Here, the Lombard had suggested that the work of John was only that of visible washing, and not of an invisible work by the grace of God. Nevertheless, he argues, the work of John was from God, and the Baptism was therefore from God, and not merely from a man.[109] Matthew also pro-

---

in which Wyclif's understanding of Scripture as "an idea in the mind" is briefly outlined, and then related to his teaching on the Eucharist.

[108] Workman, like Sergeant before him, says nothing of Baptism in his classic biography. Richard Rex, in his recent introductory study of the Lollards, makes only general references to sacraments other than the Eucharist. Hudson explores Lollard teaching relating to Baptism, much of which is more extreme or exceptional than that of Wyclif's own, if identifiably influenced by him. See Hudson's *The Premature Reformation*, pp. 141–2; 291–2.

[109] *Sententiae*, 4.2.4, 2:241: "Ad quid ergo utilise erat baptismus Joannis? Quia hominess usu baptizanti paeparabat ad baptismum Christi. Sed quaeritur quare dictus est baptismus Joannis; sicut Veritas dicit, *Baptismus Joannis unde est?* Quia ibi

vides, for the Lombard, a clear definition of the form of the sacrament (namely, the words that are to be spoken during the baptismal process): "Going therefore, teach ye all nations: baptizing them in the name of the Father and of the Son and of the Holy Ghost (28:19)."[110] The Lombard had turned to Pope Zacharius of the eigth century to indicate that baptismal immersion in the absence of invocation of the Trinity could not be seen to constitute the regenerative sacrament of Baptism.[111] But what of the fact that we read in the Acts of the Apostles that the Apostles baptized in the name of Christ?[112] Here, the Lombard had invoked Ambrose, suggesting that the name of Christ should here be understood to signify the whole Trinity.[113]

As is to be expected, Wyclif does not suggest that Baptism is necessary to salvation. Nor is it possible for the sacramental rites of baptism to relieve the foreknown of the burden of Original Sin, or to free them of their necessary damnation.[114] In the *Trialogus*, the only tract in which Baptism is given more than a passing mention, Wyclif begins with a thoroughly orthodox assessment of the nature and function of baptism, which is offered by Phronesis. This assessment is liberally sprinkled with biblical references, key among which is Christ's statement to Nicodemus in St John's gospel: "unless a man be born again of water and the Holy Ghost, he cannot enter the kingdom of God (3:5)." The faithful, he concludes, are baptized as a general principle, and the ritual is performed by any adult member of the community of the faithful. He then mentions briefly the details of the baptismal process, which, he suggests, may involve complete submersion or simple washing, as local conventions and

---

Joannis operatio tantum visibilis erat exterius lavantis, non invisibilis gratia Dei interius operantis. Sed tamen et illa Joannis operatio a Deo erat, non ab homine . . ."

[110] See *Sententiae*, 4.3.2 ("De Forma Baptismi").

[111] *Sententiae*, 4.3.2, 2:244: "Invocatio igitur Trinitatis verbum dicitur quo Baptisma consecratur; et haec est forma verborum sub qua traditur Baptismus. Unde Bonifacio episcopo Zacharias papa: 'Firmissime praeceptum est in synodo Anglorum ut quicumque sine invocatione Trinitatis, perfectus Christianus non est, nisi in nomine Patris, et Filii, et Spiritus sancti fuerit baptizatus.'"

[112] Acts 10:48: "And he commanded them to be baptized in the name of the Lord Jesus Christ." Peter is here referring to the Gentiles' right to be baptized.

[113] *Sententiae*, 4.3.3, 2:245: "Legitur tamen in Actibus Apostolorum, Apostolos baptizasse in nomine Christi: Sed in hoc nomine, ut exponit Ambrosius, tota Trinitas intelligitur."

[114] *De ecclesia* 19, pp. 467–8.

customs dictate. The key determinant of the validity of any of the different baptismal conventions, he stresses, is the cleansing presence of the Holy Spirit. Baptism by water or baptism of blood (martyrdom), as Wyclif remarks later, are themselves nothing more than signs of the Holy Spirit, or of baptism in its strictest sense, *baptismus flaminis* ("baptism of wind").[115] Alithia accepts the main details of Phronesis's assessment, but has difficulty understanding why any of these accidental trappings of the baptismal process, however generally construed, can be necessary. Why should the salvation of a child of the faithful, she asks, rest upon the material resources and practices of a small number of people? What if the Baptist is himself unworthy?

These questions gesture towards the general critique of the contemporary worship of signs that is present throughout the *Trialogus*. But there was nothing controversial in Alithia's suggestion that God had the power to intercede in the baptismal process, should the requisite materials or conventions be lacking, or should a child die without ever having been baptized (an issue to which Wyclif devotes a later chapter of the *Trialogus*).[116] Aquinas had argued in the *Summa theologiae* that salvation should only be kept from those who had *voluntarily* chosen to avoid baptism. This, he had suggested, constituted "contempt" for the sacrament. However, if Baptism were desired but lacking *in re* (as in the case of death before Baptism), then the unbaptised would only visibly be so, since God would sanctify his subject *interius*.[117] Hence, an unbaptized martyr could be sanctified, but an unbaptized child, who, lacking free will, could have no *desire* to be baptised, could not. It was for the sake of the unbaptised child that Aquinas had introduced the concept of the *limbus puerorum* (the "children's limbo"), a plane midway between Hell and the *limbus patrum*, the limbo of the Fathers. Though the unbaptised child, in the absence of *actual* sin, should not be made to suffer the physical tortures of Hell (the so-called *poena sensus*, "punishment of sense"), he or she was nevertheless denied any prospect of the blessed life.[118] Wyclif's insis-

---

[115] See *Trialogus* 4.12, pp. 285–88, in which the three forms of baptism are discussed in turn.

[116] The chapter, entitled "De infantibus sine peccato actuali decedentibus," can be found on pp. 288–92 of Lechler's edition of the text.

[117] *Summa theologiae*, 3a.68.2, responsio.

[118] I am here indebted to the concise account of Aquinas's position on the *limbus puerorum* offered by Donald Mowbray, "A Community of Sufferers and the

tence that the unbaptised child might be saved by the grace of God must therefore be seen, if not as heretical, then certainly as less than orthodox.

Confirmation

The third sacrament presented a problem for Wyclif. He rejected its doctrinal necessity, and saw no reason why, if it were to be observed, its administration should lie exclusively at the hands of bishops. The sacrament had been subject to debate throughout the scholastic period. The Lombard speaks of confirmation as a sacrament "whose power is customarily examined" (*de cuius virtute quaeri solet*).[119] Aquinas had discussed confirmation at length in his *Summa theologiae*, but had stopped short of suggesting that it was absolutely necessary. Rather, its function was to contribute to the perfecting of salvation (*perfectio salutis*).[120]

In the *Trialogus*, Alithia opens the discussion on a note of doubt, questioning the extent to which confirmation has any scriptural foundation. She and Phronesis discuss the baptism of the people of Samaria *in nomine Jesu Christi*, and their subsequent reception of the Holy Ghost through Peter and John.[121] Does this latter process of reception, Alithia wonders, serve as an adequate indication that *confirmation* should be added to baptism as a necessary condition of salvation? Reception of the Holy Ghost, she argues, is a regular and necessary component of baptism, which would seem to suggest that Confirmation and Baptism are not properly distinct. There is no indication in the scriptural text, moreover, that confirmation—if it may indeed be regarded as a discrete sacrament—should be administered exclusively by bishops. Peter and John placed their hands on the Samaritans, but neither reason nor any physical sign, Alithia

---

Authority of the Masters: the Development of the Idea of Limbo by Masters of Theology at the University of Paris (c. 1230–c. 1300)," in *Authority and Community in the Middle Ages* ed. D. Mowbray, Rhiannon Purdie and Ian Wei (Stroud, 1999), pp. 43–68 (pp. 48–9).

[119] *Sententiae*, 4.7.1.

[120] *Summa theologiae*, 3a.72.1, vol. 57:190: "[O]mnia sacramenta sunt aliqualiter necessaria ad salutem: sed quaedam sine quibus non est salus, quaedam vero sicut quae operantur ad perfectionem salutis. Et hoc modo confirmatio est de necessitate salutis: quamvis sine ea posset esse salus, dummodo non praetermittatur ex contemptu sacramenti."

[121] Acts 8:14–17. See *Trialogus* 4.14, p. 292.

argues, shows that bishops are instrumental in such reception. Moreover, the popular notion—introduced, as Alithia is careful to point out, over and above any apostolic teaching, and in no way endorsed by it—that bishops *give* the Holy Ghost to their *confirmandi* is without scriptural foundation, and seems to be mistaken. Phronesis responds by agreeing with Alithia, but offers some wisdom of his own. To speak of confirmation as a sacrament in very loose terms, he suggests, is acceptable. Here, he appeals implicitly to the Augustinian definition of *sacramentum*, suggesting that when Peter and John walked into the temple and prayed, their actions and speech together constituted "a sign of a holy thing." But there is no reason, he continues, why confirmation should be necessary to the spiritual health or salvation of the faithful.[122] Like Alithia, he is clear in his assumption that confirmation should not be the preserve of bishops alone. Indeed, he goes so far as to argue that "it would be more religious, and more consistent with the scriptural way of speaking, to deny that our bishops give the Holy Ghost, or, furthermore, that they confirm the giving of the Holy Ghost."[123] To make a contrary claim would be to speak without any foundation. Phronesis condemns the "brief" and 'slight" confirmation of contemporary bishops, together with its solemn ceremonial trappings. He is keen to stress, like Alithia, that reception of the Holy Ghost is not subject to the senses, nor in any way the *effect* of the bishop's words or gestures.

Holy Orders and Ordination

Wyclif discussed the sacrament of orders and the ritual of clerical ordination at greatest length in *De ecclesia*, and later returned to it in the *Trialogus*.[124] In both treatises, '*ordo*' is interpreted as an equiv-

---

[122] *Trialogus* 4.14, p. 294/11–20: "Oportet tamen nos sic laxe loqui de *sacramento*, cum Petrus et Johannes ascenderunt in templum ut orarent, fecerunt sacramentum laudabile, quia certum est, quod eorum ambulatio et Petri locutio fuit sacrae rei signum, quia sacri miraculi in sanatione claudi a Spiritu Sancto institutum, ut patet Act. Iii, et sic sancti episcope faciunt vulgo incognita plurima sacramenta. Non tamen video, quod generaliter sit hoc sacramentum de necessitate salutis fidelium, nec quod praetendentes se confirmare pueros regulariter hos confirmant, nec quod hoc sacramentum sit specialiter episcopis Caesariis reservatum."

[123] *Trialogus* 4.14, p. 294.

[124] *De ecclesia* 21, p. 509ff.; *Trialogus* 4.15, pp. 295–302.

ocal term, which signifies in three distinct ways. First of all, it identifies a position or rank (*gradus*) assigned to every creature by God. Each creature, it is argued in *De ecclesia*, has its own order insofar as it necessarily has being (whether or not it actually has existence). Sinners are assigned to a distinct order, the *ordo puniendi*, whose membership consists of those who are to be punished. This ordering arises naturally, since order and goodness, we are told, are equivalent.[125] In the second place, Wyclif suggests that an order can be the position assigned to a cleric, who will then minister to the laity. Here, he lists the familiar seven orders: ostiary, candle-bearer, exorcist, subdeacon, deacon and priest (the latter category must be taken to include bishops). Any of these, he suggests, might be identified by distinct physical characteristics—such as a tonsured head—or by clothing. Very characteristically, he is careful to deny that these signs are themselves, in any way, identical with the order they signify. It is the third definition of "order" to which Wyclif devotes particular attention. In respect of this, he declares, he has interpreted the term in its strictest sense. This sense is expressed with convenient concision in the *Trialogus*: "Order is said to be a power bestowed upon a cleric by God through the ministry of the bishop for the purpose of duly serving the Church."[126] In this simple passage, the distance between the ministering of the bishop and the power conferred on the cleric by God is deliberately highlighted. The bishop performs only the 'sensible" rites that signal the act of divine conferral. When the rights have been performed, we are told that, "God graciously co-assists by granting grace" (*Deus graciose coassistit dando gratiam*).[127]

Grace is the sacramental *res*, which might be withdrawn should the person receiving the sacrament be unworthy in the eyes of God. But the order also consists, most crucially, in the cleric giving himself to the Holy Spirit, and impressing its character (the *character ordinis*) into his soul. In *De ecclesia*, Wyclif dismisses emphatically the popular view—as he perceives it—that the character is only impressed *after* the pronouncement of the sacramental words. We can have no way of knowing precisely when the character of priesthood is offered

---

[125] *De ecclesia* 21, p. 510.

[126] *Trialogus* 4.15, p. 295: "Ordo vocatur potestas data clerico a Deo ministerio episcope ad debite ecclesiae ministrandum." Cf. the discussion in *De ecclesia* 21, pp. 509–10.

[127] *De ecclesia* 21, p. 511.

over by God.[128] Once the character of any one of the seven orders has been impressed, it is, for any but the foreknown (*praesciti*), indelible. But character is more than merely an invisible impression, since every cleric receives from God, according to his degree, a *limitatio oficii ministrandi*, according to which his duties and responsibilities are delimited.[129] In the *praesciti*, character endures only until the Day of Judgement, after which time it is removed. Nobody among the *praesciti* forms a part of the Church, though he may minister effectively within the Church.[130] Indeed, it would be possible for the *praescitus*, even in a state of mortal sin, to minister the sacraments themselves to good effect.[131] This latter position was defended by Wyclif until the last years of his life, but in his *Confessio* of 1381 he went as far as to suggest that it is, in fact, impossible for a member of the foreknown, lacking faith, to consecrate the bread and wine of the Mass.[132] This suggestion is recognisable among the ten condemned at Blackfriars a year later.[133]

Wyclif's interpretation of holy orders is marked by a pressing need to distance the process of ordination from its ceremonial trappings, and to relegate the ordaining bishop to the position, in effect, of an instrumental bystander. In *De ecclesia* Wyclif seems anxious to emphasize that each of the seven orders (as distinguished in his second definition), despite apparent differences, comes together to form a single, unitary order.[134] Like the seven sacraments, or John Chrysostom's

---

[128] *De ecclesia* 21, p. 515/9–14: "Dicitur [. . .] communiter quod non imprimitur caracter sacerdocii ante complecionem verborum sacramentalium, sed veritas est quod ignoramus quando et qualiter Deus imprimit sacerdotalem caracterem nec habent evidencie facte ex legibus ecclesie et scriptura vix corticem coloris."

[129] *De ecclesia* 21, p. 513.

[130] See *De ecclesia*, p. 442/18–24: "Hic videtur mihi indubie quod nullus prescitus est pars vel gerens officium tamquam de sacte matre ecclesia; habet tamen intra illam ecclesiam ad sui dampnacionem et ecclesie utilitatem certa officia ministrandi, ut patet de Scarioth et multis eius vicariis, et ad tantum Deus eligit tales dans eis ad tale officium potestatem."

[131] *De ecclesia* 19, p. 448/14–16: "Videtur [. . .] mihi quod prescitus eciam in mortali peccato actuali ministrat fidelibus, licet sibi dampnabiliter, tamen subiectis utiliter sacramenta."

[132] *Fasciculi zizaniorum*, p. 116/7–9: '[I]mpossibile est praescitum carentem fide secundum justitiam praesentem conficere.' See the discussion in Levy, *John Wyclif*, pp. 305–7 for a detailed analysis. On Donatism among Wyclif's later followers, see Hudson, *Premature Reformation*, pp. 316–18.

[133] *Fasciculi zizaniorum*, p. 278/5–6.

[134] *De ecclesia* 21, p. 513.

seven Churches, he suggests, they are one. The seven orders are not identical with the *sacramentum sensibile*, but rather with its fruit (the sacramental *res*). But since Christ had, without any elaborate celebration, made his apostles into his priests or bishops (as elsewhere, Wyclif here uses the terms *sacerdos* and *episcopus* interchangeably), and since only the order of deacons had been added in the time of the apostles, there seemed little need to dwell on the inferior four orders. The roles of any of the members of these orders, after all, could be adequately carried out by priest, bishop or deacon.[135] Wyclif had emphasized, throughout his discussion of the clerical orders, the propriety of a life without property or material concerns, neither of which could be consistent with membership of one of the seven orders. But in *De ecclesia*, he goes as far as too suggest that the life of poverty is part of the "character" of the clerical life, which must be accepted with the name *clericus*.[136]

The distinctions between orders and the ceremonial trappings of ordination were further diminished in Wyclif's work after the completion of *De ecclesia*. In *De eucharistia*, taking Augustine and Chrysostom as his authorities, he tentatively suggests that *every* predestined layperson posseses priestly character, and that he should be able to consecrate. The power to consecrate, after all, is given by God.[137] (Ceremonial ordination does not seem to warrant mention here.) The concept of the priesthood of all believers was readily taken up by Wyclif's Lollard followers, but the belief in the legimacy of a lay priesthood clearly finds its origins in his own late writing.

Marriage

Among Wyclif's most famous remarks on the sacrament of marriage is found in *De civili dominio*, in which he presents virginity as a more perfect and desirable state.[138] This echoes the more extreme position

---

[135] *De ecclesia* 21, p. 515.

[136] *De ecclesia* 21, p. 517.

[137] *De eucharistia* 4, pp. 98/29–99/2: 'Ymmo videtur iuxta testimonium Augustini, Crisostomi et aliorum sanctorum quod omnis predestinatus laycus est sacerdos, et multo magis devotus laycus conficiens, cum daret ecclesie sacrum ministerium, haberet racionem sacerdotis.' On the development of this idea among the Lollards, see Hudson, *Premature Reformation*, p. 325ff.

[138] *De civili dominio* 1.23, ed. R.L. Poole (London, 1885), p. 167. On this passage, see Workman, *John Wyclif*, 2:45.

he adopted only a little earlier in the first book of his *Summa theolo-giae*, *De mandatis divinis* (1375–6). Here, the primary virtue of mar-riage is said to lie in its prevention of bodily desire (*luxuria*). Any marriage that gives rise to such desire, or which is celebrated for the sake of personal gain, is necessarily sinful. But bodily desire, he suggests, may be manifested in a thought (*luxuria cordis*) or a word (*luxuria verbi*), as well as in a physical act (*luxuria operis*). The physi-cal act of desire arises out of abuse of the *membri genitales*, which may be either natural or unnatural. "Natural" abuse involved both a man and a woman. Its "unnatural" counterparts are said to include mas-turbation, sexual intercourse with a member of the same sex, or sexual intercourse with an animal.[139] Wyclif chooses to say nothing about any of these practices, but directs his reader to the words of the apostle in Romans 1:27.[140] Only for as long as sexual intercourse is practiced as a means of procreation may it be regarded as a legi-timate act. Wyclif therefore regards any other form of sexual activ-ity sinful, and as a breach of the law of marriage. If intercourse takes place for the simple satisfaction of desire, if it runs against nature, if it occurs at forbidden times or places, or during the wife's menstrual period or close to the birth of a child, then it must be regarded as such a breach.[141] Having established each of these points, Wyclif considers the problematic concept of the conjugal debt. When the Apostle speaks of this in 1 Corinthians 7:3, he suggests, he is undoubtedly referring to the debt of physical union. He says little

---

[139] *De mandatis divinis* 25, ed. Johann Loserth and F.D. Matthew (London, 1922), p. 347/16–25: "Loquendo autem specialiter carnalis luxurie potest divide, ut dic-tum est de homicidio, in luxuriam cordis, oris et operis sed descendendo specialius ad luxuriam operis que consistit in abusu membrorum genitalium secundum poten-tiam gignitivam potest divide in luxuriam naturalem inter masculum et femellam, in luxuriam innaturalem hominis cum se ipso, et luxuriam innaturalem unius sexus cum se ipso, vel alio innaturali usu hominis cum bestia vel iumento."

[140] "And, in like manner, the men also, leaving the natural use of the women, have burned in their lusts, one towards another: men with men, working that which is filthy and receiving in themselves the recompense which was due to their error."

[141] *De mandatis divinis* 25, pp. 348/36–349/5: "Peccatur [. . .] excedendo legem matrimonii quinque modis. Primo modo, cum causa satisfaciendi libidini per mere-tricias blandicias irracionabiliter palliatur, secundo cum fit contra naturalem modum, tercio in tempore prohibito, quarto cum fit in loco prohibito, quinto cum accedi-tur ad pregnantem proximam partui vel que est in fluxu menstrui." Wyclif says more on the appropriate times and places for intercourse later in this chapter. In respect of place, he suggests, intercourse should occur in private, and never within the confines of holy office. Likewise, it should occur at times of rest and seclusion, and not at the time of Church festivals. See pp. 360–61.

about the theological debate that has surrounded this concept, but he does mention that those who have discussed it have remained uncertain as to how often, in what place and at what time the debt is to be repaid. There is little, he argues, for the theologian to say about it, and what has already been said in sermons, confessions, and public debates is not worthy of serious attention. Individual cases, he believes, are best left aside. His comments on payment of the debt are predictably severe, and make no concessions to any theory of sexual union that is reliant upon an abstract notion of duty alone. The canonists' moral conception of repayment, introduced by Gratian in the eleventh century,[142] is given no place here. Even in the absence of sexual desire, therefore, intercourse whose motive is perceived obligation cannot, on Wyclif's interpretation, be justified.

Wyclif never abandons his position, but by the time of the *Opus Evangelicum* (c. 1383–4), a text which remained unfinished at his death, he sees marriage as a state that might be compatible with the *vita contemplativa* (to which it is seen to be essentially opposed in *De civili dominio*), and which might also help to lead towards beatitude. Rather than laboring the contrast between marriage and virginity, he presents the two as being fundamentally compatible. In the *Trialogus*, he presents a more structured philosophical account, examining marriage, as he had each of the other six sacraments in this treatise, in terms of its quiddity and accidental properties. The chapter heading, "*Matrimonium: quid proprie sit*," seems to appeal to the need for definition, rather than for a moral account of the function of this sacrament in the life of the wayfarer (*viator*). It can be said, suggests Phronesis, that marriage is the sacrament that allows partners legally to beget children. He also argues that marriage must be understood as a holy union, and one which should not be broken. The words of the Gospel, he argues, supply us with the desired *autenticatio* for marriage.

As for divorce, Wyclif never feels it appropriate to rule out the separation of marital partners, but suggests that it should only be entertained as a possibility when marriage is leading one or both

---

[142] A useful survey of the history of the concept of marital debt in medieval canon law can be found in Elizabeth Makowski's article, "The Conjugal Debt and Medieval Canon Law," reproduced in *Equally in God's Image: Women in the Middle Ages*, ed. Julia Bolton Holloway, Constance S. Wright and Joan Bechtold (New York, 1990), pp. 129–143.

parties towards sin. Given that sin cannot be consistent with God's law, it cannot accepted within a marital relationship (which must therefore be annulled).[143] In the *Trialogus*, nevertheless, he warns against multiplying the possible causes for divorce, suggesting that many are bound to be without foundation. Within the present Church, he argues, friars (or *pseudofratres*, as he terms them) and capitular clerics, together with other selfish individuals, "often divorce people whom God has gladly brought together."[144] But Alithia, recognizing that divorce had been mentioned in Scripture, and that contemporary opinion as to its legitimacy was divided, suggests to Phronesis that they consider it in detail in a chapter dedicated to the topic.[145] Phronesis begins by looking to Christ's words in the Sermon on the Mount, in which any man who would "put away" his wife is exhorted to obtain a bill of divorce (*libellus repudii*).[146] These words, we are told, should not be seen to imply that the bill of divorce is taken from the law of God, but should be understood instead as a practical means of preventing men from killing their wives should they prove unfaithful (a practice, Phronesis suggests, which was common in the time of Moses). In the *Opus evangelicum*, this view is associated with John Chrysostom, whose gloss—cited by Wyclif at length—makes it clear that such practicalities were admitted by the Old Law. But Wyclif turns to Augustine's famous commentary on the Sermon on the Mount for an explanation of how Old and New Laws are interrelated.[147] Here, Augustine directs his readers to a passage in Matthew 19, in which the Pharisees ask Christ why Moses asked his people to give a bill of divorce, and to put away their wives. He replies, "Moses did so because of the hardness of your hearts."[148] A man would not wish to divorce his wife, after all, if it were realized that such a procedure would enable her legally to marry another.

---

[143] *Opus evangelicum* 47, ed. Johann Loserth and F.D. Matthew, 2 vols. (London, 1895–96), 1:170–71.

[144] *Trialogus* 4.20, p. 317.

[145] *Trialogus* 4.21, pp. 319–22.

[146] Phronesis cites the text of Matthew 5:31–32: "And it has been said, Whosoever shall put away his wife, let him give her a bill of divorce. But I say to you, that whosoever shall put away his wife, excepting by cause of fornication, makes her commit adultery: and he that shall marry her that is put away, commits adultery."

[147] The full text of *De sermone Dei in monte* appears in CCSL 35. Wyclif reproduces the text of chapters 14 and 15. See *Opus evangelicum* 46, 1:165–9.

[148] Matthew 19:8.

Though Wyclif had defined marriage in the *Trialogus* as a legal contract that would enable partners to beget children, he is keen to suggest in the *Opus evangelicum* that marriage and virginity are not incompatible. Indeed, virginity within marriage must be seen to be desirable, if not always sustainable. Drawing once again on Augustine's commentary, he suggests that what is good in marriage signifies figuratively the blessedness of heavenly marriage, which is "better" than the begetting of children in this life.[149] Marriage, therefore, in its most elevated sense, must be seen to signify a means to a spiritual end, and, as Wyclif believed, a further aid—for each marital partner—towards the ultimate goal of blessedness.[150]

Penance and Auricular Confession

Wyclif's views on penance were among the most outwardly controversial of his ideas about the sacraments. If they were to have been accepted, the priesthood would have been destined to lose one of its subtlest means of empowerment: private, or auricular confession. Wyclif makes detailed reference to penance in four roughly contemporary texts: *De eucharistia* (1380), *De apostasia* (1380), *De blasphemia* (1381), and the *Trialogus* (1382).[151] His most extensive treatment, however, is found in a brief treatise thought to have been composed shortly before the last of these,[152] *De eucharistia et poenitentia sive de confessione*.[153] The juxtaposition of confession with the Eucharist in the title of this tract was not accidental. These two sacraments, as Workman has pointed out, were closely connected in late-medieval culture, and Wyclif endeavoured to maintain this connection throughout

---

[149] *Opus evangelicum* 46, 1:169.

[150] *Opus evangelicum* 47, 1:171/8–13: "[V]idetur cum cohabitacio coniugum que magis proficeret ad beatitudinem consequendam sit magis notanda quam cohabitacio propter procreacionem, libidinem vel debitum exsolvendum, plus nataret fidelis concordiam coniugum in talibus moribus quam ista carnalia supradicta."

[151] See *De eucharistia et poenitentia sive confessione* 1–6, in *De eucharistia*, pp. 328–43; *De apostasia* 4, pp. 60–61; *De blasphemia* 10, ed. M.H. Dziewicki (London, 1893), pp. 151–4; *Trialogus* 4.23, pp. 326–29. See also the discussion in *De Religione Privata*, whose attribution to Wyclif remains questionable. Buddensieg is unable to date this eccentric tract but, if indeed it were composed by Wyclif, it would be fair to expect that it would be roughly contemporary with the other four. See *Polemical Works in Latin*, ed. Rudolf Buddensieg, 2 vols. (London, 1883), pp. 2:483–518.

[152] Thompson suggests early 1382. See *Latin Writings*, pp. 75–6.

[153] *De eucharistia et poenitentia sive confessione* 1–6, pp. 328–43.

his writings.[154] But his principal concern lay not with penance as a sacramental category, but with the practical, confessional aspect of the penitential process. In order to gauge its importance, however, we need to explore some of the orthodoxies against which he might be seen to have been reacting. These are very conveniently summarized in the *Trialogus*, in the chapter in which Alithia asks for Phronesis for his views on the sacrament. "Penance," he suggests, seems to him to be difficult to define: "While it is commonly said that Penance has three parts, like a harp, namely the contrition of the heart, the confession of the mouth, and the works of satisfaction, it still seems difficult to define the genus of Penance, since those three things belong to different genera."[155] Here, Alithia is presenting what she takes to be an accepted definition. Penance consisted in three separate things: contrition of the heart, confession by mouth, and the completion of works (satisfaction). This definition, by the late fourteenth century, had had a long history, and had been defended by a distinguished line of philosophers and theologians, beginning with Thomists of the thirteenth century.[156] Underpinning it was the assumption that any or all of these three things represented the sacramental quiddity or *materia*, to which a generic label could be assigned. Wyclif's rejection of this formulation was grounded in a simple philosophical problem: it assumed that the sacramental *materia* consisted in three generically distinct parts, each of which was also distinct in temporal terms (since none of the three parts could exist simultaneously). As Phronesis argues here, it seemed paradoxical to assign a single generic label—*poenitentia*—to an entity whose constituent parts so obviously represented distinct *genera*.[157] These *partes*, he suggests, are not penance *per se* (the penitential *quidditas* or *materia*), but merely its accidents, which exist in respect of the penitential substance. Penance itself, he suggests (the *material* to which the accidental elements merely add form), properly exists in the mind, as an act of confession to God; without it, the other parts are without value.[158]

---

[154] Workman, *John Wyclif*, 2:41.

[155] *Trialogus* 4.23, p. 326: "Cum [. . .] dicitur communiter, quod poenitentia habet tres partes ut cithara, scilicet cordis contritionem, oris confessionem et operas satisfactionem, videtur difficile signare genus poenitentiae, cum ista tria sunt diversa in genere."

[156] See Edward J. Hanna, "Penance," in *The Catholic Encyclopedia*, vol. 11:618–35.

[157] Cf. *De eucharistia et poenitentia* 1, p. 330.

[158] *Trialogus* 4.23, p. 326.

Wyclif's critique of penitential doctrine was largely formulated as a response to the famous decrees of Pope Innocent III in the thirteenth century. At the Fourth Lateran Council of 1215, Innocent had assembled seventy decrees, of which one, the twenty-first, was to have particular importance for the laity's understanding of the function of penance. The decree was entitled *Omnis utriusque sexus*, and demanded that every member of the Christian community—"every person of either sex"—should confess to the parish priest, in private, at least once every year.[159] In *De eucharistia et poenitentia*, Wyclif therefore asks how a person can confess to his or her own sins, *except* by confessing orally, in private, to the parish priest. He gestures explicitly here towards the *Omnis utriusque sexus* before responding to the question. It is necessary, he suggests, for the sinner to repent with a contrite heart (*contricione animi*) if his or her sins are to be effaced. But this necessity is not matched by any necessity for verbal confession to a priest.[160] Moreover, no pope could possess the power to institute such a law, which, without biblical foundation, could have no authority.[161] The necessary confession he identifies here, as performed by the contrite individual, is therefore properly a confession to God.[162] It cannot be necessary, he argues, for every *viator* to confess to his or her parish priest once every year, because John the Baptist was saved, alongside many other saints, without ever having made such a confession.[163] Likewise, he suggests, Peter, Paul and Mary Magdalene were saved without that kind of penance.[164] In the *Trialogus*, he presents the same argument in the form of a *reductio ad absdurdum*: if salvation were properly dependent upon yearly confession to a priest, then "everyone who died from the time of the Ascension of Christ until the time of Innocent III would have been damned."[165] Peter, in Acts 2, had made no mention of auricular

---

[159] The text of the twenty-first canon is reproduced in H.J. Schroeder, *Disciplinary Decrees of the General Councils: Text, Translation and Commentary*, (St. Louis, 1937), pp. 236–96.

[160] *De eucharistia et poenitentia* 2, pp. 332–3: "[N]ecesse est peccatori cuius peccata delanda sunt contricione animi penitere; sed ex hoc non infertur quod sit tam necessaria verbalis confession sacerdoti."

[161] *De eucharistia et poenitentia* 3, p. 334.

[162] Cf. *Trialogus* 4.23, p. 327.

[163] *De eucharistia et poenitentia* 2, p. 333.

[164] Ibid., p. 333.

[165] *Trialogus* 4.23, p. 327.

confession, but felt that *poenitentia generalis*—an act of general penance which did not relate to particular sinful acts—was sufficient.[166] It seemed inconsistent, moreover, that such a rule did not emerge explicitly in the teaching of Christ.[167] In *De blasphemia*, Wyclif goes as far as to separate auricular confession from the sacrament of penance, and to suggest that to privilege any of its conventional ceremonies, including all outward signs of priestly absolution, as necessary sacramental practices, would be little short of blasphemy.[168] What seemed more absurd, however, was Innocent's insistence on yearly auricular confession. Whether confession were to be given in general terms (*confessio generalis*), or in relation to a particular sin (*confessio specialis*), the ruling seemed untenable. No confessor could possess sufficient knowledge to grant absolution in general terms, and it seemed absurd to expect every member of the Christian community to remember the details of his or her particular sins over an eleven-month period, given that memories accumulated within the space of one month habitually become divorced from the circumstances that gave rise to them.[169] Moreover, auricular confession could lead the confessor, who was sworn to silence, to depart from a law articulated explicitly in St Matthew's Gospel: "If your brother will offend against you, go, and rebuke him between you and him alone (18:15)." To remain silent, Wyclif suggested, and not to direct the sinner towards virtue, would be to deny this law and to give consent to the offence.[170]

Wyclif's penitential theology served to realign penance with the contrite subject, and hence to restore to him or her a freedom that had been obscured by the papal decrees of Innocent III. It was not

---

[166] Ibid., p. 327.

[167] *De eucharistia et poenitentia* 2, p. 333.

[168] *De blasphemia* 8, p. 114.

[169] *De blasphemia* 8, p. 116/4–13: "[Q]uod omnis fidelis debet sic confiteri omnia peccata sua videtur mirabile, quia nec in generali, nec in speciali. Nam per generalem confessionem non innotescit absolventi quomodo penitenciam injungeret, et de remedio provideret; et si dicta lex exigit confessionem specialem, videtur irracionabilis propter multa. Primo, quia quantumcumque memorati ad minus infra mensem perderet circumstancias agravantes: quomodo igitur datur sibi licencia expectandi per undecim menses?"

[170] *De eucharistia et poenitentia* 5, p. 339/21–26: "[C]um confessor post confessionem non audet culpam confessam prodere nec confessum suum private vel publice ad virtutem oppositam inclinare; et sic necessitatur a lege Domini Matthei XVIII, 15 *Si peccaverit in te frater tuus* consenciendo crimini declinare."

his intention, however, to consign the priest to the realms of redundancy. A good priest, he recognized, might serve to assist the subject in his search for contrition of the heart and, ultimately, for the forgiveness that could properly be conferred only by God.[171] The priest could therefore serve a crucial role in relieving a sinner of his sins, but his status as a confessor gave him no claim to spiritual power. Like St Paul, the pope and his priests received the keys of power and knowledge from Christ to guide sinners in accordance with divine will (the biblical "power of the keys"),[172] but the power of forgiveness and relief from the burden of sin lay with Christ alone. Moreover, such power and knowledge as priests possessed was in no sense exclusively theirs, just as it could not be assumed that every priest possessed this knowledge.[173] *Mandatory* yearly confession to a priest, on Wyclif's interpretation, needlessly limited the freedom of the subject. This much was clear from the Latin term '*confiteor*' itself, which, as Wyclif insists in the tenth chapter of *De blasphemia*, literally means "to acknowledge an error *freely*."[174] Hence, those who would demand that the subject confess to a priest each year were sinning not only doctrinally, but also in their abuse of grammar.[175] More important, however, was the fact that any form of mandatory confession allowed priests and popes to become falsely empowered. As he suggests in his appendix to *De eucharistia*, this might give way to the simonaical sale of penances. If confession to corrupt and ineffectual priests should swell the ecclesiastical coffers, then the ceremony might better be dispensed with and, as he suggests in *De blasphemia*, replaced with a more honest form of yearly taxation. As practiced, confession might lead honest Christians to the misguided belief that the key to salvation or damnation lay at the hands of a

---

[171] See, for example, *De eucharistia et poenitentia* 5, p. 338.

[172] The expression *potestas clavium* enjoyed widespread currency among the scholastics. It derives from the words of Christ to St Peter in Matthew 16:19, in which Peter is promised the keys to the kingdom of heaven.

[173] *De eucharistia et poenitentia* 4, p. 336/20–29: "Concesso [. . .] quod hoc sacramentum tam proficit quam officit diversis hominibus, videndum est primo de clavibus quas Christus concesserat Petro et ceteris apostolis cum suis successoribus; et dictum est diffuse alibi quod iste claves non sunt potestates spirituales date specialiter nostris sacerdotibus ad tollendum peccata hominibus, quia hoc est agno proprium sed iste claves sunt potestates et sciencie ad deviantibus indicandum conformiter voluntati divine secundum iudicium legis Dei."

[174] *De blasphemia* 10, p. 143.

[175] Ibid., p. 143.

pope or a priest.[176] Such a belief would necessarily distance the subject from God, and would mean that his respect for the deity would be diminished.[177] Corruption among the clergy, a problem that Wyclif discusses at length in *De blasphemia*, placed the already questionable institution of confession under further strain, since it seemed anomalous to expect corrupt priests, who might themselves be *discipuli antichristi*, to be able to identify sinful acts.[178] Different priests, moreover, might demand different penances for equivalent acts of transgression. Voluntary confession to God represented a necessary prerequisite for salvation, even if, as Wyclif famously believed, personal salvation was ultimately available only to those who were eternally predestined. It was within no priest's power to grant absolution, however virtuous, and any claim to be able to do so would have amounted to nothing but vain pretence. Priestly conviction about a subject's contrition could be no match for divine certainty. But Innocent's rulings on confession would also create difficulties if the priest were in a state of mortal sin, since it would seem anomalous to argue that such a priest could be responsible for the subject's absolution. It would be equally anomalous, nevertheless, to suggest that no absolution had been achieved in such a case. Wyclif therefore suggested that divine absolution may be granted to a contrite subject regardless of the condition of the confessor.[179]

Though Wyclif's interrogation of orthodox penitential teaching had its grounding in metaphysics, it would be difficult to deny that it received added force from his passionate aversion to the friars, who, since vehemently opposing him on the question of eucharistic change, had become natural enemies. Among abusers of the sacraments and simoniacal profiteers, Wyclif believed, they were without equals.[180] As he suggests in *De blasphemia*, the friars showed little respect for confessional norms, and, solely in the interests of material gain, habitually persisted with unrepentant subjects.[181] A good

---

[176] *De eucharistia et poenitentia* 3, p. 334.

[177] This is a crude paraphrase of the discussion in *De eucharistia et poenitentia* 6, pp. 340–41.

[178] *De blasphemia* 8, pp. 116–17.

[179] *De blasphemia* 9, p. 134.

[180] *De eucharistia et poenitentia* 5, p. 339.

[181] *De blasphemia* 9, p. 167/6–9: "Evidens est quod fraters, per multos annos remanentes affectuose confessors hominum qui non resipiscunt sed pocius peiorantur, consenciunt suo facinori."

confessor, he felt, owed his subject a moral duty to bring him to the appropriate state of repentance, but should not continue should the subject repeatedly fail. St Matthew's Gospel, to which Wyclif directs his readers on this issue, teaches that a man should reproach his erring brother three times, and no more.[182] In *De apostasia*, the friars are once again found to be guided by rapacious instincts. They do their utmost, we are told, to become confessors of kings, princes and secular lords, but offer no guidance about the dangers of sin. Rather, they offer false promises of absolution, or cures for the scars of transgression.[183] Far from deterring their subjects from sinning, and guiding them towards eternal salvation, therefore, they bring the kingdom into a state of corruption.

Extreme Unction

The last of the seven sacraments is passed over relatively quickly in the *Trialogus*, and does not detain Wyclif elsewhere.[184] He devotes relatively little attention to the questions of matter, form and iterability that had interested the Lombard, Hugh of St Victor before him, and later Aquinas, but focuses rather on the question of the validity of the sacrament, and upon its foundations in Scripture. Hugh and the Lombard had gestured towards the passage in James 5:14, in which a sick man is exhorted to invite priests to pray for him, and to anoint him with oil.[185] Both had suggested that the sacrament should therefore be seen to have been instituted by the apostles.[186] Not until the Council of Trent was it formally declared

---

[182] Matthew 18:15–17. See *De blasphemia* 9, p. 167.

[183] *De apostasia* 4, p. 60/26–36: "[P]rocurant se fieri regum, principium, dominorum secularium et dominarum omnimode confessors; et tamen non obstante quod sint custodes anime, nec cognoscunt cibum eukaristie quem propinant, sed ignorancia cecati sunt in ydiotarum capitulo plus quam illi; nec dicunt vel peccati gravidinem, ut prudentes medici, et defensores regni, ac adiudores dei; sed cecis promissionibus absolucionum et falsis ac fictis sanacionibus cicatricum, decipiunt confessos prodicione nimis aspera; et sic regnum."

[184] *Trialogus* 4.24, pp. 333–5.

[185] James 5:14–15: "Is any man sick among you? Let him bring in the priests of the Church and let them pray over him, anointing him with oil in the name of the Lord. And the prayer of faith shall save the sick man. And the Lord shall raise him up: and if he be in sins, they shall be forgiven him."

[186] Under the heading "ab quibus institutum sit sacramentum" the Lombard writes in *Sententiae* 4.23.3, 2:391: "Hoc sacramentum unctionis infirmorum ab Apostolis institutum legitur." Cf. Hugh of St Victor, *De sacramentis* 2.15.2.

that the sacrament had been instituted by Christ himself, though Aquinas had been clear on this point from the outset. Hugh and the Lombard had been in no doubt as to the function and necessity of the sacrament: in the first place, it allowed for the remission of the sick person's sins, and then for the alleviation of his bodily infirmity.[187] The remission of sins was achieved both through the prayers of the priest (the *formal* aspect of the sacrament), and the application of the oil (the *material* aspect). Wyclif did not deny that the oil might relieve bodily suffering, though he had some doubts about its sacramental efficacy. More important, however, were his views about the nature of its institution. In the *Trialogus*, Phronesis is asked by Alithia to consider the passage from James, but concludes that it is too slight to constitute a foundation for the sacrament. It might be said, he argues, that the apostle does not specify that an act of prayer and anointment should take place *in extremis*, but only that a sick man should be consoled and prayed for by a priest. If the physical oil were a sacrament, he suggests, then Christ and his apostles would not have chosen to remain silent about it.[188] Much remains unncertain in this discussion, and Phronesis gestures towards questions such as that of iterability, desirability and time of annointment without offering definitive answers.[189] Finally, Phronesis concludes that it would be nothing less than an antichristian presumption to suggest that nobody would be saved who had not received such a sacrament.[190] In many respects, these words constitute a very typical dismissal by Wyclif, but his treatment of the last of the sacraments is also markedly less precise, in dialectical terms, than those of the preceding six. Yet it is undoubtedly true that the last of the sacraments, if its rejection would not be associated famously with the reformer, would be remembered as one whose status at the hands of the later Lollards and Hussites was to be more emphatically, if no less decisively questioned.

---

[187] *Sententiae*, 4.23.3, 2:391: "In quo ostenditur duplici ex causa sacramentum hoc institutum, scilicet, ad peccatorum remissionem, et ad infirmitatis alleviationem." Cf. Hugh of St Victor, *De sacramentis* 2.15.2.

[188] *Trialogus* 4.25, p. 334.

[189] *Trialogus* 4.25, p. 335.

[190] *Trialogus* 4.25, p. 335.

Conclusion

John Wyclif began life as a philosopher and a theologian, as his biographers have been keen to emphasize. Yet it is arguably less than useful to construct him as an academic uncomfortable in his role as reformer and controversialist (after McFarlane), or as a reformer held back by his academic roots (after Kenny); he was neither of these. His position in the political and intellectual climate of late-medieval England was a unique one, and one that ultimately lost him friends both within and outside the walls of the university. The anti-clerical nature of many of his pronouncements about sacramental abuse was often pushed to extremes, and his suggestions relating to Penance—itself a controversial topic at the time—were more subtly provocative than has often been recognized. His late retreat into Donatism, had his other teaching proved less contentious, might have proved more perilous than it did. Nevertheless, it was only the rejection of transubstantiation that led to the condemnations of the council of twelve, to the most damaging conclusions of the Blackfriars synod (more damning, for sure, than its condemnation of Donatism), and to Wyclif's eventual withdrawal from the university. Though this momentous rejection finds stable foundations within Wyclif's realist metaphysics, it remains difficult to believe that, if purely philosophical in nature, it should have taken the many years that it did to emerge. The safest compromise, as has been suggested, sees Wyclif answering a metaphysical concern by appealing to a hermeneutic theory that had been committed to paper in precise terms with the composition of *De veritate Sacrae Scripturae* (completed only shortly earlier). Like any compromise, this is bound to be unsatisfactory, but it offers, at the very least, an alternative to the supposition that Wyclif—such an extraordinarily elusive figure, despite his scholarly legacy—should have acted without good reason.

WYCLIF AND THE CHRISTIAN LIFE

Ian Christopher Levy

John Wyclif was a moral idealist, and like idealists in every age he often proved inflexible. He was both a champion and a scourge whose tracts and sermons are filled with religious directives informing the English people as to how they should properly honor their God. This essay will examine Wyclif's directives, and his complaints, within the larger religious and doctrinal context of his own day. In his magisterial study of the late medieval English Church, Eamon Duffy presents a generally devout people whose religious aspirations found expression within the larger community of the faithful. This was a society quite content with many of the devotional practices which would then be attacked by the Lollards.[1] That seems to be a fair assessment, though it also seems fair to say that, for all of his invective, the substance of John Wyclif's critique of these devotional practices was generally moderate, and his attacks on abuses often quite commonplace. Wyclif was not a revolutionary in search of the sort of doctrinal and devotional upheaval that was to be introduced during the sixteenth century. No puritanical iconoclast, he was very much the late medieval Catholic theologian firmly fixed in centuries of tradition.

And yet we see that he managed to arouse the ire of ecclesiastical officials, even to the point of enduring papal condemnation in 1377, some three years prior to the eucharistic controversy which spelled the end of his Oxford career. This condemnation had nothing to do with Wyclif's views on saints and pilgrimages, nor funerals, prayer or images. Rather, it concerned Wyclif's attacks upon clerical wealth and privilege, and the power of excommunication to enforce the ecclesiastical will. The irony is that Wyclif at his most traditional was Wyclif at his most radical. For the most explosive aspect of Wyclif's reform program was also the most deeply rooted aspect of

---

[1] Eamon Duffy, *The Stripping of the Altars: Traditional Religion in England 1400–1580* (New Haven, 1992).

Wyclif's entire theology, and ultimately lay at the heart of his own personal devotion: conformity to the poor and suffering Christ. There is no dimension of Christian piety more ancient or more sacred than this. Once John Wyclif sought to impose this model of poverty and meekness upon the clergy as a whole—from parish priest to archbishop and pope—that is when he became a dangerous man.

Wyclif began to address matters pertaining to the Christian life by about 1374 with the publication of his *De dominio divino*, thus two years after receiving his doctorate. For the next ten years he issued a steady stream of tracts and sermons which became increasingly polemical, especially after his expulsion from Oxford in 1381. Many of these works were overtly political or theological, in the sense that their discussions had less to say about everyday devotional practices, and more to say about the abstract theories which undergirded them. But even those massive works devoted to a precise comprehension of civil dominion, the nature of the Church, biblical exegesis, and eucharistic presence, still had real implications for what was happening "on the ground." And in that sense, one could reasonably contend that there was nothing Wyclif wrote in these years which was not ultimately concerned with the ordering of a Christian society and the living out of the Christian life. We will look mainly at works cutting across that last decade of his life, from his relatively straightforward treatise on the Ten Commandments to those especially polemical, even apocalyptic, tracts written in the final years of his life, where he details the advent of Antichrist.[2] We should see that, for all of Wyclif's haranguing, there is a deeper affective piety which emerges from the pages of his works. Driving Wyclif's quest to improve the devotional life of his fellow Catholics was his own commitment to the poor Christ. In the end, Wyclif's idealism yields to a personalism: devotion to the Person of Jesus Christ, the Word Made Flesh.

---

[2] Unless otherwise noted, I have followed the dating of Wyclif's works as recorded in Williell R. Thomson, *The Latin Writings of John Wyclyf* (Toronto, 1983). One must remember, though, that Wyclif likely revised a number of his earlier works when at Lutterworth. On this see Anne Hudson, "The Development of Wyclif's *Summa Theologie*," in *John Wyclif: Logica, Politica, Teologia*, ed. M. Fumagalli, B. Brocchieri, S. Simonetta (Florence, 2003), pp. 57–70.

The Mendicant Orders

Wyclif's view of the mendicant orders may be a good place to start when assessing his conception of the Christian life, for it is in the course of his various disputes with the friars that much of his own program for properly ordered religious devotion emerges. This is not surprising, inasmuch as the mendicant orders played such a significant role in virtually every aspect of late medieval religious life: preaching, confession, indulgences, eucharistic piety, alms giving, the cult of saints, and burials. The friars were not only involved in the "field work" of medieval devotion, however; the many theologians from among their ranks were integrally involved in the formation of the doctrines they subsequently propagated. In short, for Wyclif the secular university cleric, there was no getting around the friars, precisely because there was no dimension of late medieval religious life and thought which they had not touched. More to the point, though, the friars were in many ways representative of the greater anomalies of late medieval Christianity itself, with its contradictory tendencies of charity and venality often subsisting side by side in the service of God and the struggle for salvation.

Wyclif is often remembered for his blistering attacks on the friars, launched with an unflagging zeal after his falling out with them over the doctrine of transubstantiation in 1381. But until that time he had counted some of them as allies in his fight against clerical wealth and dominion. He held the Franciscans in especially high regard, extolling their original commitment to Christ-like poverty. And even in his last years, convinced as he was that this order had forsaken its evangelical ideal, he held out hope for a faithful remnant within its ranks, though by then lamenting that a good friar is as rare as a phoenix.[3] Wyclif recounted how William of Ockham, along with other faithful friars, had labored to cleanse the order and restore it to the primitive rule from which it had fallen away, complaining that present-day friars only observe poverty in the most superficial manner, as Ockham and St Bonaventure had rightly pointed out years before.[4] Wyclif believed there had been, and indeed

---

[3] *De fratribus ad scholares*, in *Opera Minora*, ed. Johann Loserth (London, 1913), p. 16/18–20.

[4] *De ordinacione fratrum* 2, in *Polemical Works in Latin*, ed. Rudolf Buddensieg, 2 vols. (London, 1883), 1:92–94. Though Wyclif was an ardent metaphysical realist, he

still are even now, some genuine friars. Hence in 1378 we find him protesting the treatment of a certain Oxford Franciscan forced to retract his remarks about apostolic poverty and ecclesiastical endowment.[5] He also tells of faithful friars forbidden to preach, and even persecuted, by superiors who will only commission "false friars" in their quest for temporal goods.[6] In fact, Clopper makes the case for there having been renegade Franciscans in England at this time preaching the absolute poverty of Christ and calling for a strict adherence to the Rule and Testament of St Francis.[7] It seems safe to say, therefore, that when Wyclif employs his frequent epithet of "false friars" (*pseudofratres*) this ought not to be taken as a condemnation of all friars as such, but rather the majority he reckons to have forsaken their original mission. There are still a few faithful friars out there preaching the poor Christ and facing the wrath of their superiors for doing so. The Rule commands that the deeds of the friars shine forth with holy poverty, and yet most, Wyclif laments, now seek only to display their riches. They have abandoned their calling to serve as models of evangelical poverty and humility. While bound to the observance of "Christ's religion" by preaching the poor life in word and deed, their luxurious convents and churches only move the laity to delight in the friars' riches and worldly glory.[8] Even as Wyclif will blame the friars for introducing unscriptural customs which infringe upon gospel liberty and hinder the law of Christ (e.g. habits, vows and rules), the Franciscan Rule is itself laudable insofar as it affirms the primitive ideal of evangelical poverty, and in that way functions as an expression of gospel law.[9] Would that the little brothers only return to it!

For all their vitriol, Wyclif's antimendicant diatribes were hardly unique among secular theologians. Already by the middle of the thirteenth century, the secular Parisian master, William of St Amour,

---

forgave Ockham his nominalism, holding him in high esteem for his attacks on the Pope John XXII in the name of apostolic poverty.

[5] *De veritate Sacrae Scripturae* 1.14, ed. Rudolf Buddensieg, 3 vols. (London, 1905–7), 1:356.

[6] *De fundatione sectarum* 10, in *Polemical Works*, 1:51; See also *Sermones* 2.8, ed. Johann Loserth, 4 vols. (London, 1887–90), 2:57–59.

[7] Lawrence M. Clopper, "Franciscans, Lollards, and Reform," in *Lollards and Their Influence in Late Medieval England*, ed. Fiona Somerset, Jill C. Havens, Derrick G. Pitard (Woodbridge, 2003), pp. 177–96.

[8] *De blasphemia* 15, ed. M.H. Dziewicki (London, 1893), p. 236.

[9] *De ordinatione fratrum* 1–3; 1:89–96.

was attacking the new mendicant orders as heralds of Antichrist.[10] Secular resentment of the friars and their privileges was also prevalent in fourteenth-century England. In 1309 the rectors of London presented a petition to the Canterbury provincial council complaining that the mendicants were abusing their various privileges, whether preaching, confession or burial. Moreover, they argued that the hearts of the laity were being hardened by the friars against their parish churches, such that some had stopped attending and were failing to pay tithes, thereby reducing the local priest to penury. At the Convocation of Canterbury in 1356 a bill of complaint was lodged against the friars accusing them of being lax confessors, slanderers of the secular clergy, and adulators of the powerful. Riding the finest horses, wearing the best clothes, and filling their bellies, these friars not only have no fear of bishops and other prelates, but they conduct their secular and spiritual affairs to the detriment of the English Church. It was also at this time (June 1356 to March 1357) that one of Wyclif's favorite theologians, Richard FitzRalph, was preaching against the friars on the familiar topics of poverty, mendicancy and their abuse of privileges.[11] The role of friars as confessors was especially vexing to the parish clergy who reckoned that they used their office to curry favor with penitents, as evinced in the *Memoriale Presbiterorum*, a 1344 confessional manual, which criticizes the friars for not imposing sufficient penances and for absolving without authority in reserved cases.[12]

According to Erickson, there were five basic charges leveled against the friars in Wyclif's day: their excessive number, their hypocrisy, abuse of their own poverty vow, the usurpation of the rights of seculars, and their defense of their own orders while attacking others.[13] And yet, despite such charges and all the secular ill-will, the friars actually remained very popular among the people throughout the fourteenth century. In fact, the antimendicant literature, as well as

---

[10] John Moorman, *A History of the Franciscan Order* (Oxford, 1968), pp. 128–30.

[11] W.A. Pantin, *The English Church in the Fourteenth Century* (Cambridge, 1955), pp. 156–62. See also John Doyne Dawson, "Richard FitzRalph and the Fourteenth-Century Poverty Controversies," *Journal of Ecclesiastical History* 34 (1983), 315–44.

[12] Michael Haren, *Sin and Society in Fourteenth-Century England* (Oxford, 2000), pp. 185–89.

[13] See Carolly Erickson, "The Fourteenth-Century Franciscans and their Critics I," *Franciscan Studies* 35 (1975), 107–35; and "The Fourteenth-Century Franciscans and their Critics II," *Franciscan Studies* 36 (1976), 108–47.

the satire, seems to testify to this. For, as Erickson observes, had the friars been generally despised there would have been little point in attacking them. Opponents (such as Wyclif) chalked their popularity up to hypocrisy, but the fact remains that one-third of the known wills in Oxford at the time contain bequests to Franciscans, and many among the laity were also becoming tertiaries. Thus, even while Gower portrays the friars as seeking after profit and bilking the poor, he must admit the friar draws a crowd wherever he goes.[14] Wyclif, therefore, would only have been venting the frustration of many of his peers. Indeed, as Catto notes, for an educated cleric to speak of the friars as agents of the devil was not the unique province of Wycliffism. Only by the 1390s, when Lollardy was regarded as an increasing threat, did the Church seek to curtail open criticism of the mendicant orders.[15]

The friars were consistently being accused of favoring the rich and giving them easy penances and fraternal letters. Pope Benedict XII even had to mandate that the Franciscan superiors see to it that their friars hear the confessions of the poor and not just the wealthy. So well-ensconced were some of the mendicants with the rich and powerful that the English Franciscans often provided lodging for the nobility; kings had apartments at Greyfriars in York.[16] Wyclif would also attack the friars on this account, reckoning it all especially nefarious, precisely because the friars seem to court the wealthy at the expense of the poor. He complains that they despoil the people and build sumptuous houses on the most fertile lands, and then only give hospitality to rich men and women.[17] The friars target the poor, he says, confident that they can take advantage of their ignorance. The people flock to the spectacle of their new grand churches where they are primed for yet further seduction. And all the while, the collective charity for neighbors in the parish church is abandoned. Through this subtle rapine the old parish church falls into disrepair and is destroyed, only to make way for one of the new mendicant structures.[18]

---

[14] Erickson, "Franciscans II," pp. 144–46. See also Moorman, p. 349. Cf. Gower, *Vox clamantis* 1130–34, ed. H.O. Coxe (London, 1850), p. 242: "Sic, ubi se volvit frater, sibi mundus abundat, Quicquid et ipse manu tangit adhaeret ei."

[15] J.I. Catto, "A Radical Preacher's Handbook," *English Historical Review* 115 (2000), 893–904.

[16] Erickson, "Franciscans I," pp. 128–31.

[17] *De fundatione sectarum* 14, 1:69.

[18] *De quattuor sectis novellis* 4, in *Polemical Works* 1:254.

Wyclif hardly broke new ground either when charging the friars with sexual misconduct. The Franciscans' own statutes lamented cases of sexual impropriety and tried to limit the friars' contact with women. One observant Franciscan, John Brugman, rebuked his fellow friars for blatant fornication and the siring of children.[19] And so, we find Wyclif accusing the friars of entering the homes of widows to further their subtle hypocrisy, where they not only eat well, but also beg, and even go so far as to defile noble women.[20] It is customary, Wyclif reports, for the lady to have a friar for a confessor when her husband is away. Widows, and especially nuns, are seduced by their confessors in private rooms as the friars feign sanctity all the while.[21] That is all old news and, other than a few asides, Wyclif was not especially exercised by such goings-on. He would rather detail a whole host of injustices perpetrated by the friars which strike at the very core of Christian charity, and thus the Christian life. Chief among these is the immense wealth amassed by the supposedly poor mendicant orders, a wealth he reckoned to have been built up on the backs of the poor.

When Wyclif attacked the friars for their excessive wealth, once again, he was not alone. By the middle of the fourteenth century the Franciscans were rich; they had rentals and a steady flow of donations, meaning that they no longer needed to beg at all. Hence the charge that they were fleecing the poor by their begging. Now known for their elaborate buildings, their poverty was no more than a legal technicality.[22] Even the prohibition against accepting money was no longer enforced; the friaries were mostly run by this time on a system of income and expenditure. Decrees handed down to prevent friars from having their own money were also of no avail.[23] Wyclif will echo the standard charges of greed and hypocrisy: that in amassing homes, books, hidden wealth, and large stores of food, they render any lack of dominion a mere pretense.[24] But there is more to this than hypocrisy and deceit; as we have mentioned, Wyclif considered it an affront to Christian charity. The friars have not

---

[19] Erickson, "Franciscans I," pp. 126–27.
[20] *De fundatione sectarum* 8, 1:44/9–12.
[21] *Opus evangelicum* 3.11, ed. Johann Loserth, 2 vols. (London, 1896), 2:40/25–32.
[22] Erickson, "Franciscans II," pp. 108–9, 114–15.
[23] Moorman, pp. 350–65.
[24] *De fundatione sectarum* 8, 1:42/6–18.

only forsaken the life of evangelical poverty, they have made themselves rich at the expense of the poor. Caring only for themselves, they seek after worldly gain to the detriment of the public good. Driven by their cupidity they plunder the poor and seduce the people, all for the sake of constructing their tall domes and opulent houses.[25] "They rob the truly needy, defraud Christ's paupers, and subvert the law of the gospel," devouring the goods of the Church which evangelical law has reserved for the sustenance of the destitute.[26] This clamorous begging is contrary to both evangelical and natural law. The former because the apostles had lived by the labor of their hands; and the latter because in the state of innocence (where there is no superfluity) nothing would have been taken from those in need without equivalent recompense. Not only do the mendicants beg from the poor, but now the truly poor will go without the alms they might have otherwise received. These are the blind and lame poor who divine law recognizes must beg by necessity, the poor souls who deserve all that is going to those mendicant sturdy beggars. It is precisely because the begging of the friars is utterly superfluous that it proves even more culpable than robbery.[27] Wyclif can only conclude that the begging of the friars was introduced by the devil, as they seek to despoil the poor until they have reduced them to complete destitution.[28]

The unleashing of the devil emerged as a persistent theme in Wyclif's last years, and we will have more to say about his apocalypticism later. Not only the papal schism, but the rise of the friars, had signaled to Wyclif that he was living in the End Time. Szittya has observed how Wyclif's use of Scripture gave his writing an eschatological theme reminiscent of the thirteenth-century opponents of the mendicants. Though, unlike the fiercely antimendicant William of St Amour, who had placed the friars at the center of his eschatology, Wyclif saw them as one symptom among others. While he would never fix an exact date for the End Time, he believed that many biblical prophecies were being borne out in his own age. Chief among them was the emergence of the mendicant orders, those

---

[25] *De fundatione sectarum* 7, 1:39/1–8.
[26] *Sermones* 4.13, p. 109/16–18: "... specialiter cum ipsi sepe spoliant egenos simplicies, defraudant Christi pauperes et subvertunt legem evangelii ..."
[27] *Sermones* 1.9, pp. 64–5; *Sermones* 1.33, p. 226.
[28] *De dyabolo et membris eius* 3, in *Polemical Works*, 1:366–67.

prophesied as the dangerous hypocrites whose arrival signals the end of the world.[29]

The friars were often singled out for the most withering attacks, but Wyclif placed them within a larger category of disrepute: the "four sects" comprising the endowed clergy, monks, canons, and friars, all of whom were to blame for corrupting the simple law of Christ with their new regulations. They all stand guilty of schism and idolatry for rejecting Christ in favor of their religious patrons Augustine, Benedict, Francis and Dominic.[30] The Saracens and pagans may be to blame for not taking on the yoke of Christ, but the four sects are even worse; they have deserted the true sect of Christ to take on some new yoke.[31] This massive apostasy, this rejection of Christ's pure and simple rule, is a prime symptom of the apocalypse. While Wyclif will admit that many antichrists have appeared over time, none can compare with the four sects. The devil may have already been unleashed to some extent in the first millennium, but he rages all the more now in his lying sects, most notably among those false friars who seduce the Church with their hypocrisy.[32]

That the mendicant orders come in for the sharpest criticism in Wyclif's later years is perhaps because their ideal was all the more noble, the very ideal which had initially commended them to Wyclif. He observes how the friars were instituted in the spirit of poverty, to instruct the people through the dissemination of the divine word, setting before them the evangelical form as a mirror of virtue and honesty. But now their preaching just lays snares that lead people to ruin rather than the crown of salvation. They are pseudo-prophets, ravenous wolves in the vestments of sheep, demons transfigured as angels of light.[33] The false friar has already been revealed in this age; he is the devil incarnate, coming with his sensible signs, ready to sow the seeds of discord in the Church Militant.[34] Wyclif will come to brand the four mendicant orders as a whole with the acronym CAIM, murderer of his brother Abel: there are the Carmelites,

---

[29] Penn Szittya, *The Antifraternal Tradition in Medieval Literature* (Princeton, 1986), pp. 152–54; 167–80.

[30] *Descripcio fratris*, in *Polemical Works*, 2:440/2–5.

[31] *Opus evangelicum* 2.47, 1:417–18.

[32] *De solutione satanae* 1, in *Polemical Works*, 2:392–93.

[33] *De fratribus ad scholares*, p. 17.

[34] *Descripcio fratris*, 2:409/1–4.

Augustinians, Jacobites (Dominicans) and Minorites (Franciscans). Moreover, he will equate them with the four beasts Daniel saw ascending from the sea, singling out the Carmelite order as the fourth, ten-horned beast, perhaps because of the prominent role they played in the condemnation of his views at the Blackfriars Council in May of 1382.[35]

Preaching

Much of Wyclif's conflict with the friars revolved around preaching; not only did he loathe their preaching, he viewed them as hindering the true preaching of others. Prolific writer that he was, Wyclif produced a large set of Latin sermons broken into the distinct categories of Sunday Gospel readings, Epistles, and Saints' Days. While he may not have preached each of these sermons personally, there is a further set known as the *Sermones Quadraginta* which does represent his own preaching. Whether these sermons, though written in Latin, were preached in English, cannot be established, but in light of some of the references it seems that the audience would have been a mixture of clerics and laymen. That Wyclif was an active and well-known preacher in the late 1370s is clear, and his opponents noted that it was mainly through preaching that he spread his ideas to the laity.[36] Though the friars could not really get in the way of Wyclif's own preaching, he often complained of the treatment given his protégés as they set out to preach. Despite the reservations of earlier scholars such as McFarlane,[37] it seems clear that Wyclif was integrally involved with those he termed the "simple priests" (*sacerdotes simplici*). Hudson notes that the first wave of preachers would have consisted largely of Oxford scholars dispersed among the neighboring towns when Wyclif was still active at the university or had just retired to his parish at Lutterworth.[38] Wyclif envisioned these preachers addressing various ecclesiastical ills and counter-acting the

---

[35] *De fratribus ad scholares*, pp. 15–16. See Thomson, 241–42.

[36] Anne Hudson, *The Premature Reformation: Wycliffite Texts and Lollard History* (Oxford, 1988), pp. 64–67.

[37] Notably K.B. McFarlane, *John Wycliffe and the Beginnings of Nonconformity* (London, 1952), pp. 100–1.

[38] Hudson, *Premature Reformation*, pp. 62–81.

preaching of the friars, whom he charged with concealing "Christ's meaning" (*sensus Christi*) beneath their own diabolical interpretations of the gospel.[39] Just how Wyclif conceives this evangelical or divine sense we will soon consider, but clearly he believed that such a sacred sense was readily comprehensible to the laity without recourse to the friars' exegetical skills.

Central to this conflict was the right to preach. But just who had the right to preach was not entirely clear in Wyclif's day. In the words of one canon law handbook, the *Regimen Animarum*, priests, deacons and subdeacons may lawfully preach, but only on the condition that, "they have preferment (*prelationem*) and the care of souls, because those so entitled preach by reason of their preferment, not by reason of their order." In other words, only bishops and beneficed clergy have the unqualified right to preach.[40] Church officials feared, perhaps understandably, that by granting preaching rights *ex officio* to unbeneficed clergy the less educated priests might end up teaching error and heresy. Thus, when Wyclif complained that his "simple priests" were prevented from preaching without a license, he would likely have been referring to those unbeneficed clergymen lacking any other title, those who were simply priests. We see that one of the erroneous (though not heretical) propositions condemned at Archbishop Courtenay's Blackfriars Council, stated that any priest or deacon could preach without a license by virtue of his ordination.[41] But one should remember that, prior to Archbishop Arundel's 1407 Constitutions, there does seem to have been some ambiguity as to whether all priests possessed the right to preach *ex officio*, even if Courtenay would have denied them that right already in 1382.[42]

We find Wyclif complaining bitterly, therefore, that the false friars attempt to thwart his own preachers by insisting that it is unlawful for a priest to preach without a license. And he rejects their claim that the apostles had received their license to preach from

---

[39] *De dyabolo et membris eius* 4, 1:371/13–15: "Quod autem fratres fingunt quecunque sensum, quem ipsi aptare voluerint, esse sensum ewangelii . . . quia sic possent sensum Cristi abscondere . . ."

[40] G.R. Owst, *Preaching in Medieval England* (Cambridge, 1926), pp. 1–4.

[41] The condemned propositions are printed in the *Fasciculi Zizaniorum Magistri Johannis Wyclif cum Tritico*, ed. W.W. Shirley (London, 1858), pp. 275–82. See proposition fifteeen on p. 280.

[42] H. Leith Spencer, *English Preaching in the Late Middle Ages* (Oxford, 1993), pp. 173–74.

Peter (the first pope), noting that Paul had already been doing so prior to their first meeting.[43] Though many from among the earliest wave of preachers would have been Oxford scholars, some of these men may not have advanced very far in their degree programs. Hence Wyclif's complaint that his preachers were reproached by the friars for being insufficiently trained to interpret the Bible correctly. An important theme throughout is Wyclif's belief that what these "simple priests" may lack in formal education they more than make up for in divine inspiration; these are a group of holy men confident that God will imbue them with a true understanding of the gospel message. "And so it is that whenever these simple priests manage to comprehend the divinely bestowed evangelical sense, the friars upbraid them, calling them heretical idiots who are incapable of understanding the sense of Scripture. For [they claim] the treasury of the Lord's sense has been hidden away among the friars."[44] Actually, Wyclif is willing to concede that some of his priests are relatively uneducated, pointing out in their defense, however, that Christ had ordained "the uncultured and the uneducated" (*rudes et idioti*) to preach the gospel. Only Antichrist, therefore, would limit preaching to those with university degrees, when God would be so pleased to see "evangelical preaching" (*predicacio evangelica*) dispensed freely to the people.[45] The false friars hate when "simple priests" rise up and preach the gospel. But, even as they attempt to restrict this holy task, the true cleric, moved as he is by divine inspiration, will not be hindered by mere human jurisdiction.[46] The powers-that-be continue to conspire against "faithful priests" (*sacerdotes fideles*), the very ones who prove themselves in word and deed to be the true pugilists on behalf of God's law.[47] Persecution thus becomes part of Wyclif's apocalyptic drama. These faithful priests never cease to evangelize despite the censures and excommunications of Antichrist.

---

[43] *De mendaciis fratrum*, in *Polemical Works*, 2:405/1–13.

[44] *De dyabolo et membris eius* 5, 1:371/25–372/2: "Et sic ubi simplices sacerdotes habent sensum ewangelicum divinitus eis datam, fratres improperando eis dicunt, quod sunt heretici ydiote, cum ipsi non sciunt sensum scripture, sed thesaurus sensus domini est absconditus apud fratres."

[45] *Exposicio textus Matthei XXIII* 6, in *Opera Minora*, pp. 331–32, at 332/2–5: "Et hinc non graduatorum sacerdotum predicacio evangelica gratis data populo, sicut gratis a Deo est accepta, est a satrapis suspendenda."

[46] *Sermones* 1.43, pp. 288–9; *Sermones* 1.57, p. 377; *Sermones* 2.60, p. 448.

[47] *De ordinacine fratrum* 3, p. 95.

With their celestial treasure assured they are all the more obedient to God who strengthens those who sing out his word. And because all Christ's priests have received their commandment and license to preach directly from God, any prelate who would prohibit their evangelizing efforts reveals his own diabolical nature, depriving the people of that spiritual life by which they may live unto God.[48] All this while the pseudo-friars have been licensed by the devil to sow their lies among the nations.[49] Hyperbole aside, Wyclif made a more cogent charge which would have resonated among his fellow seculars, namely that the friars themselves sin when claiming exemption from episcopal jurisdiction.[50] Wyclif the secular priest was on firmer ground here actually, for he seems to have had local precedent on his side.

In 1300 Pope Boniface VIII issued the bull *Super cathedram*, which later entered into the 1317 Clementine Constitutions. It granted the friars the right to preach freely in their own churches, as well as in public spaces, unless it be at the very hour when the local prelate was preaching. They only needed a license from the local clergy to hear confession.[51] Kedar has studied the rather ambiguous situation prevailing in England throughout the fourteenth century, pointing out that many English bishops still required a license *ad predicandum*. In fact, the licenses issued were often stated in a way to prove their conformity to *Super cathedram*, even as they violated the spirit of the law. Such interpretations may have stemmed from the fact that preaching and confession naturally went together, inasmuch as preaching would call the audience to repentance, and the hearing of confession was indeed limited by the statute. In 1367 some friars protested that by the common law of the Church they had the right to preach wherever they liked without a license. In 1382, the same year of the Blackfriars Council, the English Parliament declared that all preaching must be licensed, although this did not apply to those already authorized to preach under canon law, a stipulation which should have exempted the friars. And yet, because the English bishops had

---

[48] *Sermones* 3.10, pp. 73–75.
[49] *De mendaciis fratrum*, 2:406/1–3.
[50] *De fundatione sectarum* 14, 1:69.
[51] Emil Friedberg, ed., *Corpus iuris canonici*, 2 vols. (Lepizig, 1879–91), 2:1162–4, at 1162: "... ut dictorum ordinum fratres in ecclesiis et locis eorum, ac in plateis communibus libere valeant clero et populo praedicare ac proponere verbum Dei, hora illa duntaxat excepta, in qua locorum praelati praedicare voluerint ..."

been requiring a license all along, it could be argued that the friars
were not so covered under canon law. Indeed, many secular priests
continued to argue that the friars were not permitted to preach
within their parish.[52] It seems quite likely that, as Spencer observes,
Wyclif and his cohorts were only too happy to make the most of
this confusion regarding the exact nature of mendicant rights.[53]

Preaching rights aside, another point of contention for Wyclif was
the homiletical style employed by the friars. Wyclif's own style was
not in keeping with that modern form often associated with the friars, one which focused on a single verse of biblical text to be elaborated by various distinctions and sub-distinctions, all designed to
delight the listeners and impress them with the preacher's erudition.
Believing that such sermons were all for show, Wyclif adhered to an
older form modeled on patristic sermons, one which lacked such
clear divisions and was designed to let the preacher closely explicate
an entire passage of Scripture.[54] In fact, Wyclif lamented that in his
own day it seems as if the chief requirement for the preaching office
was skilful argumentation reminiscent of the university lecture halls.
And he specifically dismisses all the attention paid to the arrangement of questions and thematic divisions, claiming that anyone who
intends to edify the Church will be preaching the word of God,
choosing Bede and Francis as a worthy examples.[55] The preacher,
says Wyclif, should proclaim the truth plainly with a clear intention,
speaking by divine inspiration (*ex Deo*), unencumbered by irrelevant
distractions. Devices such as the use of meter, he argues, may be
fitting for songs of praise, but when used by modern preachers it
only serves to obscure the meaning, as the delighted audience pays
more attention to the outward signs than to what they are meant
to signify.[56] Here one encounters a consistent theme to be found

---

[52] B.Z. Kedar, "Canon Law and Local Practice: The Case of Mendicant Preaching
in Late Medieval England," *Bulletin of Medieval Canon Law* n.s. 2 (1972), 17–32.

[53] Spencer, pp. 167–70.

[54] Spencer, pp. 228–46.

[55] *De veritate* 2.24; 2:241/19–26: "unde solet esse verbalis contencio, quid requiritur ad officium predicandi. et certum est, quod multa cerimonialia introducta sunt
quoad locum, quoad formam divisionis thematis et quoad formam vel circumsta-
nias dicendi, que non sunt essencia predicandi, ut eo ipso quid predicat, quo dicit
intencione edificandi ecclesiam verbum dei. Et sic Beda et Franciscus dicuntur predicare saxis et avibus . . ."

[56] *Sermones* 4.31, pp. 268–69, at p. 269/11–16: ". . . sed quoad secundum non
dubium quin colores moderni confundunt intelligenciam sentencie . . . tum eciam

throughout Wyclif's works: outward signs, be they verbal or visible, are too often valued more than their insensible and eternal significates.

No matter his complaints, people clearly enjoyed hearing the friars preach, and the crowds they drew must have been galling to Wyclif. The message of their sermons notwithstanding, that their preaching methods were extremely effective was undeniable. Wyclif chalks up much of this popularity to what he sees as their penchant for vacuous anecdotes, fables, and even outright lies. Despite Wyclif's own contempt for the flamboyant and the entertaining, the mendicants were very conscious of the predilections of their audience. Smalley has noted how the friar doctors drew up aids for preaching in the form of *artes predicandi* and *exempla* collections, as well as manuals for instruction on doctrine and morals. Jokes and *exempla*, and a touch of classical allusion, were all called upon for the sake of getting the moral point across to the audience. But among the friars themselves there was some debate as to how much of this sort of thing was too much. Some, such as Archbishop Pecham, forbade his fellow Franciscans to use any jokes, while others held that one could tell a fictitious story without committing a mortal sin if done for the purpose of keeping the audience awake. But then again, the fourteenth-century Dominican, Pierre de Baume, attacked the new sermon methods, arguing that Christ preached the gospel of God's kingdom, not jokes and poems.[57] Such words could easily have come out of the mouth of Wyclif himself. Indeed, one can concur with Wenzel that so many of the homiletical abuses that Wyclif and the Lollards complained about had long been condemned by orthodox churchmen.[58]

Wyclif will blast the friars for preaching their fables and rhymes to curry favor with the people, and extolling their own methods over that of the simple priests who preach Christ's law freely and purely.[59] The friars not only preach ludicrous stories, but even heretical doctrines, all for the sake of pleasing the crowd.[60] As for heresy, it is the preaching of transubstantiation which comes in for the severest

---

quia auditus assistencium senciens pruriginem in verbis metricis plus attendit ad signa sensibilia quam signata . . ."

[57] Beryl Smalley, *English Friars and Antiquity in the Early Fourteenth Century* (Oxford, 1960), pp. 28–44.

[58] Siegfried Wenzel, *Latin Sermon Collections from Later Medieval England* (Cambridge, 2005), pp. 343–45; 393–94.

[59] *Super textus Matthei XXIII* 6, p. 331.

[60] *Speculum secularium dominorum* 1, in *Opera Minora*, p. 77/30–37.

criticism, primarily because Wyclif reckons it a metaphysical fiction that leads the people into idolatry, teaching them to worship the bare accidents of bread and wine, rather than Christ in his spiritual presence.[61] But it also involves so many of the fables he despises. By Wyclif's day there was a proliferation of miracle stories involving the host, whether concerning its adoration or desecration. Such stories were the stock and trade of the friars, who had various *exempla* prepared as would befit the purpose of their sermons. Some involved sensory perception of the real substances as a reward for faith or as a cure for doubt, while others involved the appearance of the flesh and blood as punishment meted out to someone who abused or profaned the host.[62] Wyclif recounts one story in which a host descended from the altar, crept into the heart of a sick man and immediately cured him. It is not the story itself which so rattles Wyclif as much as the fact that the narrator later admitted it was really just a *pulchrum mendacium*. There are no "lovely lies" as Wyclif sees it, and no grounds for anything remotely deceitful. He fears that the laity can be manipulated to believe just about anything; the very fables the friars employ to increase eucharistic devotion might just as well seduce the people into worshipping moles and bats rather than God.[63]

Everyone recognized that preaching was a vital component in forming the Christian life of the laity. Preaching was a highly effective form, not only of moral motivation, but of basic education; and the value of education was not lost on late medieval bishops. The moral and spiritual formation of the laity through frequent preaching was at the heart of reform efforts dating back to the twelfth century. And, while it may be hard to ascertain just how frequently the average lay person would have heard a sermon, there can be no doubt that the duty to preach was considered an essential aspect of the pastoral office.[64] Hence, despite the impression Wyclif may give, there were in fact many conscientious churchmen very keen on seeing that the local parish priest effectively cared for the souls committed to

---

[61] On Wyclif's reaction to popular eucharistic piety see J.I. Catto, "John Wyclif and the Cult of the Eucharist," in *The Bible in the Medieval World: Essays in Honour of Beryl Smalley*, ed. Katherine Walsh and Diana Wood (Oxford, 1985), pp. 269–86.

[62] Miri Rubin, *Corpus Christi: The Eucharist in Late Mediaval Culture* (Cambridge, 1991), pp. 108–29.

[63] *De eucharistia* 1, ed. Johann Loserth (London, 1892), pp. 19–20.

[64] See Wenzel, pp. 229–42; 333–45. The Fourth Lateran Council (1215) speaks of nourishing souls with the spiritual food of God's word. Cf. Friedberg 2:192.

his charge. A notable example of this effort was Archbishop of York, John Thoresby's 1357 *Instruction*, circulated in English as *The Lay Folk's Catechism*. Thoresby's manual was itself modeled on Archbishop of Canterbury, John Pecham's 1281 *Ignorantia sacerdotum*. The priest was to instruct the laity in the Fourteen Articles of Faith, the Ten Commandments, seven sacraments, seven works of mercy, seven virtues and seven sins.[65] That the clergy themselves needed to be reasonably well educated was not lost on medieval bishops either, and various measures were taken throughout the thirteenth and fourteenth centuries to ensure that the local parish priest was fundamentally competent. To this end various manuals for confessors were designed to help those parish priests who did not otherwise have access to the larger scholastic works. They offered the priest, and thus the lay penitent, a detailed account of Christian faith, morals and practice.[66] One rather successful educational effort was William of Pagula's *Oculis sacerdotis* (1320–28), a manual directing parish priests on how to hear confession as well as offer proper instruction to the laity.[67]

The common reason given for restricting preaching to the most basic instruction in faith and morals was that this is all the Christian really needs to know in order to attain salvation. While an uneducated adult could be saved apart from knowledge of the biblical text, he or she was responsible for knowing the Creed and the Lord's Prayer. Wyclif's chief objection to the educational system, at least as conveyed through preaching, was that it limited the content to the so-called *pastoralia*. And this meant, said Wyclif, that the people were not hearing the Gospel narratives themselves and thus were being diverted from the Law of Christ expressed within those narratives. One argument made against preaching the Gospel texts in

---

[65] *Lay Folk's Catechism* in EETS, o.s., vol. 118. On the Lambeth Provincial Council of 1281 see Pantin, pp. 193–94.

[66] Leonard Boyle, "The *Summa* for Confessors as a Genre and its Religious Intent," in *The Pursuit of Holiness in Late Medieval and Renaissance Religion*, ed. Charles Trinkhaus and Heiko Oberman (Leiden, 1974), pp. 126–30.

[67] Leonard Boyle, "Aspects of Clerical Education in Fourteenth-Century England," *The Fourteenth Century. Acta IV. Center for Medieval and Early Renaissance Studies* (Binghampton, NY, 1977), pp. 19–32; reprinted in *Pastoral Care, Clerical Education and Canon Law: 1200–1400* (London, 1981). See also Boyle, "The *Oculus Sacerdotis* and Some Other Works of William of Pagula," *Transactions of the Royal Historical Society*, 5th series, 5 (London, 1955), pp. 81–110; reprinted in *Pastoral Care*.

English was that they could easily be misconstrued. But Wyclif reckons the real reason is the fear that a clear explanation of Christ's life, to which all the faithful should be conformed, would then expose many ecclesiastics as disciples of Antichrist.[68] He complained that, while the friars may be free to tell the people jokes and lies in the hope of despoiling them after the sermon, they will persecute anyone who dares preach the gospel in English.[69] In fact, though, when Wyclif complained of the friars and bishops restricting preaching to the *pastoralia* and prohibiting the reading or preaching of the gospel in the vernacular, it was really not so clear cut. There was not as yet any general consensus on this issue; not all friars and bishops would have held that line.[70] One must also remember that the related question of allowing the laity greater access to vernacular bibles was also very much alive at this time, and was being debated among perfectly orthodox schoolmen.[71] Nevertheless, much of the preaching done by Wyclif's Oxford companions would have been in the vernacular. And, as Aston observes, what made this especially threatening to clerical power was their insistence upon using English to speak of such contentious issues as the Eucharist. The mysteries of the faith were now being disseminated to the laity by way of a burgeoning English theological vocabulary.[72]

Wyclif will also take issue with those churchmen who neglect their preaching duties in favor of more pressing affairs, justifying their inattention on the grounds that preaching is no longer even necessary, since everyone has been sufficiently instructed in the Creed and the Lord's Prayer, and thus possesses all the salvific knowledge they need. To Wyclif's mind this is to misunderstand the very principle of salvation, which is based upon conformity to the whole evangelical life as depicted in Holy Scripture.[73] He complains that the prelates and friars do not want the gospel preached in its entirety, but only

---

[68] *De nova praevericancia mandatorum* 4, in *Polemical Works*, 1:126.

[69] *Opus evangelicum* 3.31; 2:115/4–10.

[70] Spencer, pp. 156–59.

[71] On the debate over translating the Scriptures into the vernacular see Mary Dove's "Wyclif and the English Bible," in this present volume. See also Anne Hudson, "The Debate on Bible Translation, Oxford 1401," *English Historical Review* 90 (1975), 1–18.

[72] Margaret Aston, "Wyclif and the Vernacular," in *From Ockham to Wyclif*, ed. Anne Hudson and Michael Wilks (Oxford, 1987), pp. 299–305.

[73] *De veritate* 2.21; 2:179.

in bits (*non ex integro sed curte*), precisely because the gospel speaks of sacrifice, the penitential life of Christ. Worst of all, though, is that, in their fear of exposing their own hypocrisy, they end up endangering the souls of the laity, who will not otherwise learn how to follow after Christ.[74] For Wyclif, salvation is not attained through knowledge of the Creed, but through personal conformity to Christ, the poor Christ of the Gospels.

Wyclif may have been demanding that the word or law of God be preached to the people, but many would have thought they were already doing just that. To Wyclif's contemporaries preaching the word of God did not necessarily refer to biblical instruction; it could just as easily refer to the Church's moral law and the precepts grounded in Scripture.[75] Yet when Wyclif called for the preaching of God's law, or Christ's law, he thought it was to be found principally in the Gospel narratives. That is where one encounters the poor and humble Christ, and that is why Scripture must form the content of Christian preaching. Christ is the Wisdom of God the Father, "the kernel hidden within the leaves of the words of Holy Scripture," and the faithful who elucidate such Wisdom will have eternal life (Eccl 24:31). This means that all the faithful, especially those whom God has given the gift of knowledge, must take great pains to proclaim this gospel of Christ.[76] For Wyclif, to speak of the law of Christ is not to speak of some abstract principle designed to govern human affairs; it is the expression of a personal will, the will of the Second Person of the Trinity. And, as Christ the Word is God, so the law of Christ and the law of God are the same thing. The eternal law of Christ demands loyalty on the part of the believer, loyalty grounded in love for Christ himself. As an expression of Christ's will, the *lex Christi* is infinitely more honorable than any human tradition, for it is a law handed down by uncreated Wisdom. It is the cause of all true peace, inasmuch as it is the worship of the true God; where it is not implemented there can only be strife. And here again are the apocalyptic overtones; just as the commingling of human traditions with the Mosaic law heralded the demise of the Jews in the time of Christ, so now the dissolution of Christ's law in the time of Antichrist

---

[74] *De officio pastorali* 2.4, ed. Gotthard Lechler (Leipzig, 1863), p. 39.
[75] Spencer, pp. 145–46.
[76] *Exposicio textus Matthei XXIII* 2, p. 313/1–11, at p. 313/1–2: "Cum sapiencia Dei Patris sit nucleus veritatis in foliis verborum scripture absconditus..."

attests to the destruction of the Christian people.[77] There is no spiritual profit to be acquired apart from the teaching of Holy Scripture,
for it is there that one encounters the love of God made manifest
in the poor Christ. It is love which is both taught and acquired
through the Christ's law.[78] Thus to believe in Christ, says Wyclif, is
to believe in his gospel as testified to throughout the entire Bible.
Here is the Lord's most immaculate and salubrious law which, in
its abbreviated form, is nothing other than love itself, the fullness of
the law (Rom. 13:10).[79]

This law of love makes plain that priests should attend to the
work of preaching above all else, for that is where the true dignity
of their office rests.[80] Preaching is all about the loving conveyance
of God's word to one's fellow Christians and may even be considered a more solemn act than consecrating the Eucharist. In an age
when the laity rarely communicated, Wyclif exalted preaching over
eucharistic consecration as a far more effective way to convey Christ's
saving power to the many. He came to identify the preached word
with the truth itself, indeed to the point that it is God the Word
who is encountered in preaching. And it is for this reason that preaching must be the most dignified work a creature can perform, thereby
making gospel preaching the chief task of the priesthood.[81] For Wyclif,
God the Word is at his most efficacious in preaching, rivaling, if not
surpassing, the power of the consecrated host. There can be no work
so perfect as preaching God's word, he says, for it nourishes the
inner man, thereby enabling him to grow into a child of God. Hence,
by the time that Wyclif had come to reject transubstantiation, he
could argue that preaching was a worthier activity than celebrating
the Mass. "For the consecration of the Eucharist only makes the
bread become Christ's body sacramentally, while proclaiming the

---

[77] *De veritate* 2.20; 2:129–30.

[78] *De veritate* 2.20; 2:142–43.

[79] *De veritate* 1.7; 1:156.

[80] *De veritate* 2.20; 2:150/15–17: "sic igitur ex lege caritatis et principiis fidei
demonstratur, quod sacerdotes precipue debent arti operis predicandi attendere,
cum ex isto habent officii dignitatem."

[81] *De veritate* 2.21; 2:156/3–7: "patet secundo, quod predicacio verbi dei est actus
solempnior quam confeccio sacramenti, cum tantum sit unum recipere verbum dei
sicut corpus Cristi. igitur multo plus est, populum recipere verbum dei, quam uni-
cam personam recipere corpus Cristi." We should remember that a long line of
perfectly orthodox churchmen considered the task of preaching to be equal, if not
superior, to a priest's sacramental duties. On this see Wenzel, pp. 333–36.

gospel brings a more noble nature into being, inasmuch as the human soul will in some manner be transformed into Christ himself."[82] The word of preaching conveys the Person of Christ the Word, the Word that does not return void, but instead effects an ontological transformation in the hearer who is united to the Savior in faith. All of this is, of course, very Pauline: "It is no longer I who live, but Christ who lives in me (Gal. 2:20)." Preaching is a sacramental act for Wyclif precisely because the words of the preacher make present the Word they signify.

Wyclif's sense of intimacy between the act of preaching and the preached Word itself naturally led to a great deal of emphasis being placed on the preacher's own conformity to Christ the Word. To draw a connection between the preacher's task and his own moral standing was certainly nothing new; it had been a topic of discussion throughout much of Christian history. Patristic writers such as John Cassian emphasized the preacher's need for a pure heart and a body subdued by ascetical practices.[83] And in the late Middle Ages Robert Basevorn's 1322 *Forma praedicandi* listed three essential requirements for preaching: pure life, competent knowledge, and authority. While it was generally recognized that a notorious sinner should not preach, lest he scandalize his audience, the medieval schoolmen did make a point of distinguishing the qualities of the office from those of the man; a sinful preacher could still preach to the benefit of the people. And it is precisely this distinction which Minnis thinks Wyclif had rejected when he coupled sanctity of life with effective preaching.[84]

Indeed, Wyclif would insist that the priest shine forth in the sanctity of Christ; he must be holy if he is to illumine his flock with his preaching. Not only would an unclean life render his preaching "worthless" (*inutilis*), it would pollute the word of God itself. Thus, while the pastor's principal duty is to declare the word of God to his sheep, it will be his own way of life that proves the most effective

---

[82] *Sermones* 1.16; 110/16–19: "Iterum, eucaristie confeccio non facit nisi panem esse sacramentaliter corpus Christi, evangelizacio vero facit naturam dignoriem, quia animam humanam esse quoddammodo ipsum Christum." See also *De officio pastorali* 2.2, p. 36.

[83] See C. Colt Anderson, *Christian Eloquence: Contemporary Doctrinal Preaching* (Chicago, 2005), pp. 11–16.

[84] Alastair Minnis, "Chaucer's Pardoner and the 'Office of Preacher'," in *Intellectuals and Writers in Fourteenth-Century Europe* (Cambridge, 1986), pp. 88–119. See also Spencer, pp. 98–100.

means of preaching, rather than bare words alone.[85] Thus prelates must not only preach Holy Scripture, they must live in conformity with its precepts. Holy Scripture itself has established a rule for Christians; priests, like the Apostles before them, are to live by it.[86] In a sermon on the Parable of the Sower (Luke 8:4–15), Wyclif lays down the requirements for the task of preaching. It first requires an assiduous preacher with whose living voice the Trinity cooperates. He cannot be lacking in charity, for the word cannot derive power from a contrary heart. Secondly, the content of his preaching must be the true word of God, rather than the lies and fables which are the seeds of Antichrist. Finally, the earth must be adapted for reception, namely the earth of body and soul well tilled with good works, free from the poisonous weeds of sloth.[87]

One is so often struck by Wyclif's intimate bond with Christ the Word. "Every Christian is obliged to ponder God's Word and cherish it in his heart, intellect and will, for it is in that way that the Christian must conceive Christ in his soul, since He is the Principal Word of God. And so it is that one is also bound to beget and nurture Christ, and by doing the will of his Father, become a mother to Christ." Christ, in turn, is not only our God, but our parent and our teacher. "For he created us out of nothing, begot us from Mother Church by his blood, and instructed us until that time when he took his place upon the royal throne. Surely, then, we are chiefly bound to him by the law of gratitude."[88] As Christ is the Living Word which comes to the hearer, one must also have an experience of that genuine transformation to be sure that the preaching has been effective. It is by experiencing the gift of the Holy Spirit that one can trust that Christ abides within (1 John 4:12). But this is not a purely mystical realization of the divine presence. Wyclif consistently

---

[85] *De officio pastorali* 2.1, pp. 34–35.
[86] *De veritate* 2.22; 2:181.
[87] *Sermones* 4.30, p. 257.
[88] *Sermones* 4.37, p. 309/11–35: "Dictum est dominica proxima quomodo omnis christianus tenetur audire verbum Dei et custodire illud mente, sensu et voluntate, et per consequens omnis christianus tenetur concipere Christum in animo, cum ipse sit precipium verbum Dei, et per consequens tenetur Christum gignere et nutrire, et tunc faciendo voluntatem patris Christi fit mater Christi, ut ipsemet dicit Matthei XII°, 50 . . . Ipse enim produxit nos ex nichilo, genuit nos ex matre ecclesia sanguine suo et instruit nos quousque collocet in regni solio. Ideo sibi tenemur precipue ex lege gratitudinis."

asserts that faith without works is dead; works testify to a living faith
(James 2:17). One's manner of life and a willingness to proclaim the
gospel will bear testimony to the fact that Jesus has called someone
and now dwells within. For God is love and his greatest gift is that
infusion of love into the faithful heart.[89] Divine love springs forth
into action after its initial implanting. As the house of virtues is
founded upon Christ, so one must first come to Christ by imitating
his ways; then he should hear the words of Christ, and finally put
the words he has heard into action. Wyclif insists that no one can
be saved unless he follows these three steps. While the standards of
lay education would have everyone learn the Fourteen Articles of
Faith, a set of creedal principles, Wyclif has personified these principles. Every article of faith, he says, belongs to the discourse of
Christ (*sermo Christi*). Only by interiorizing this inner word, only by
letting it resonate in one's soul, can one be saved. That is just the
beginning though; one must still fulfill that word, for it is by doing
Christ's word that one arrives at ultimate perfection and is finally
divinized (*deificatur*).[90] The articles of faith are an expression of the
Law of Christ, which is itself an extension of the person of Christ.
To know and internalize the articles of faith is to enter into the
Divine Person and thus be made like him.

Wyclif makes it clear that there is no love for God where there
is not conformity to God's law. And as that law finds its fulfillment
in Christ, to live in opposition to him is to be at odds with the
divine life and thus the Holy Trinity itself.[91] If Christ is at the heart
of Wyclif's preaching, this means, in turn, that his cross is there as
well. Wyclif's own sermons can be a call to a piety of abnegation,
conforming oneself to Christ in his crucifixion, spiritually extending
our flesh upon his cross, mortifying our flesh by rooting out sins and
vices, joined in mystical similitude to the crucified God/man.[92] The
faithful preacher must be "an evangelical man" (*vir evangelicus*), drawing sinners away from their vices through love, there amid the pains
of hell and the joys of heaven.[93] He will lead the way, personally
observing Christ's gospel, the infinitely effective and authoritative

---

[89] *Sermones* 3.35, pp. 291–93.
[90] *Sermones* 1.59, pp. 385–86.
[91] *De nova praevaricancia* 4, 1:129.
[92] *Sermones* 3.68, p. 420.
[93] *De citacionibus frivolis* 7, in *Polemical Works*, 2:561.

word of the Word Made Flesh.[94] To preach from the Gospel Books, therefore, is to recount the narrative of the Incarnate Word, the standard of perfection for Christian life. True preaching places Christ at the center, a life lived in conformity with a Living Person, not simply a set of theological principles.

The Good Priest

We have just looked at Wyclif's emphasis on affective piety as conveyed through preaching. It was evangelical preaching above all else which he took to be the hallmark of the good priest; the ideal priest lives for Christ and preaches Christ to others. The true pastor, says Wyclif, must be instructed in faith, hope and love, which is nothing less than being conformed to Christ himself. Only when conformed to the likeness of the who laid down his life for the flock, will he be able to tend to his sheep.[95] We have also seen that, for Wyclif, a life in Christ is a life lived in good works; Christ's indwelling blossoms in sanctity. Renna is right in this regard that Wyclif considers action to be a means of contemplation, the action of imitating Christ, attaching oneself to Christ and his law in deeds rather than ecstatic prayer. Hence Wyclif's attacks on the monks who he claims only pretend to genuine contemplation in order to avoid an active apostolate. This is in keeping with Wyclif's interest in the twelfth-century mystic, Joachim of Fiore's idea of a coming *ordo contemplativus* replacing the existing monastic orders. Though again, for Wyclif, this would be an order dedicated to active service.[96] For the time being, however, it will have to be the work of the faithful few, his poor and simple priests. This new age would be ushered in by a small and persecuted order of preachers proclaiming the Eternal Evangel.[97]

For the clergy a life of service would invariably mean a life lived in Christ-like poverty, which stands at the heart of Wyclif's call for clerical disendowment. Living like Christ in evangelical poverty, the

---

[94] *Sermones* 1.54, pp. 358–59.
[95] *De officio pastorali* 1.1, p. 7.
[96] Thomas Renna, "Wyclif's attacks on the Monks," in *From Ockham to Wyclif,* pp. 267–80.
[97] See Michael Wilks, "Wyclif and the Great Persecution," in *Studies in Church History, Subsidia* 10 (1994), pp. 39–63; reprinted in Wilks, *Wyclif: Political Ideas and Practice* (Oxford, 2000); see there pp. 188–90.

pastor would ask only for the alms sufficient to nourish him with the food and drink needed to sustain him in his work.[98] We have noted that, despite his later attacks on the mendicant orders, Wyclif had a special affinity for those strictly observant Franciscans who had labored so heroically for the cause of evangelical poverty. But, as we mentioned at the outset, Wyclif then took the radical step of demanding that this principle be applied to the entire clergy, thereby prompting Pope Gregory XI to condemn a series of his propositions in May of 1377.[99] Wyclif's theory of dominion, or lordship, will be covered in separate essay in this volume; suffice it to say here that Wyclif believed that, while Scripture allows Christ's priests the simple use of life's necessities, it forbids them all civil dominion.[100] The entire clergy would come to resemble a religious order and its rule would be the *lex Christi*. The Lord's chief disciples would be poor like "our abbot Christ," who was himself the poorest man of all.[101] Wyclif found support for his reform program not only within the Gospel books, but among the folios of the canon law collections. Thus, despite that fact that Pope Nicholas III's 1279 bull *Exiit qui seminat* was intended only to protect the poor life of the Franciscans, Wyclif read it as an endorsement of across-the-board clerical poverty. This decretal, he said, had confirmed Christ's intentions for the whole Church as it ratified the most perfect form of the evangelical life.[102] Hence the prelates of Wyclif's new, ideal Church would soon come to recognize the life of poverty as one more closely approximating the state of innocence, thereby leading them to embrace the counsel of evangelical poverty as a privilege.[103] It is no wonder that Pope Gregory wanted him imprisoned.

We have remarked on Wyclif's concern for society's truly destitute, a concern he often voiced in conjunction with his attacks on clerical wealth. That there are some in Christ's household who suffer such need belongs to the reality of a fallen world; their condition is

---

[98] *De officio pastorali* 1.2, p. 8.

[99] For the list of condemned propositions see Henry Denzinger, ed., *Enchiridion Symbolorum* 36th ed. (Rome, 1976), 1121–39.

[100] *De civili dominio* 3.9, ed. Reginald Lane Poole and Johann Loserth, 4 vols. (London, 1885; 1900–4), 3:137.

[101] *De civili dominio* 3.1; 3:10; 3.8; 3:114.

[102] *De potestate papae* 5, ed. Johann Loserth (London, 1907), p. 81. Cf. Friedberg 2:1109–21.

[103] *De ecclesia* 8, ed. Johann Loserth (London, 1886), pp. 177–80.

the result of others' sinful greed. Thus, even as Wyclif deplored the murder of Archbishop Sudbury during the Peasants' Revolt as "excessively cruel," he contended that the rebels had been provoked by the fact that the goods of the poor remained in the hands of the prelates, rather than being distributed to the community. In fact, the revolt could have been avoided had the temporal lords disendowed this delinquent Church. That would certainly have been preferable to the peasants taking a man's life.[104] Wyclif never advocated such an uprising, but even his disavowal of the violence was not given without a foreboding caveat. If the next archbishop had reason to worry, Wyclif offered him cold comfort.

Wyclif's emphasis on the ideal of poverty, as well as his care for the destitute poor, was by no means unusual in his day. Aston has pointed out that concern for the poor in the fourteenth century was a very powerful issue that transcended distinctions of clerical and lay, orthodox and heterodox.[105] Aers believes that Wyclif's response to the gospel message, like Langland's, was "part of a neo-Franciscan heritage," observing how Wyclif equates voluntary poverty and non-violence with the way of Christ. The way of the cross is an absolute which all disciples must bear if they are to be saved. On the strength of this universal call to abnegation, Wyclif came to reject (at least in principle) the traditional medieval distinction between precepts and counsels as unscriptural. Aers argues, though, that it is most often the priests who are vilified as heretics for not abiding by the evangelical counsels and living out this Christ-like life, while the secular lords seem to receive a pass. The lords are instead called upon to defend the Church by force, thereby relieving them of the responsibility to follow after Christ's humble human nature.[106] And it is along these lines that Aers also believes the centrality of poverty in Wyclif's theology is more complicated than Aston realizes, inasmuch as Wyclif sidesteps its application to the nobility and winds up advocating the concentration of wealth in the hands of the few for the

---

[104] *De blasphemia* 2, p. 33; ibid. 13, pp. 190–91. See Anne Hudson, "Poor Preachers, Poor men: Views of Poverty in Wyclif and his Followers," in *Haeresie und Vorzeitige Reformation in Spätmittelalter*, ed. F. Smahel (Munich, 1998), pp. 41–53.

[105] Margaret Aston, "'Caim's Castles': Poverty, Politics and Disendowment," in *Faith and Fire: Popular and Unpopular Religion: 1350–1600* (London, 1993), pp. 95–131.

[106] David Aers, "John Wyclif's Understanding of Christian Discipleship," in *Faith, Ethics, and the Church: Writing in England, 1360–1409* (Cambridge, 2000), pp. 119–48.

good of the many.[107] To this one can only say that Wyclif did indeed hold the clergy to an especially high standard of Christian conduct. In that sense he perpetuated the traditional medieval distinction between the spiritual and temporal classes, expecting more of the former than the latter. Though, in the process, he had denied to the clergy all the power that the Church customarily claimed for herself based upon the supposed ontological superiority of those who had received the sacrament of holy orders.

In expecting the clergy to live a life of poverty and meekness, bereft of civil dominion, Wyclif may have garnered the support of powerful laymen such as John of Gaunt, but among the Church's prelates he found little sympathy. Asking the clergy to live without civil power and rights is one thing, however, and asking them to live honest and chaste lives in keeping with their vows was quite another. In supporting the latter he was hardly alone; calls for moral reform had rung out from within the clerical ranks for centuries. At the Fourth Lateran Council in 1215, Pope Innocent III placed the blame for religious corrosion and the eruption of heresy squarely on the clergy's shoulders. The people's corruption proceeds from their priests, he said, for as the anointed sin, so the laity follows.[108] In Wyclif's own day Richard FitzRalph had chastised his fellow prelates in a synodal sermon for being fornicators, gluttons and thieves who seize the fruits of churches without rendering service. They are almost all simoniacs who nourish themselves to the ruin of their subjects. And the Cistercian, William Rymyngton, a later opponent of Wyclif, would recite all manner of clerical crimes, observing how the laity defends its own criminal behavior by pointing to that of the clergy. Rather than provide a good example, he says, clerics are blinded by their own simony and avarice.[109]

No one would have been the least bit shocked, therefore, to hear Wyclif complain that the laws against clerical cohabitation with women are multiplied to no avail, since they are simply not observed.[110]

---

[107] David Aers, "John Wyclif: Poverty and the Poor," *Yearbook of Langland Studies* 17 (2003), 55–72.

[108] *Sacrorum conciliorum, nova et amplissima collectio*, ed. G.D. Mansi, 54 vols. (Graz, 1960–61), 22:971–72.

[109] G.R. Owst, *Literature and Pulpit in Late Medieval England* (Oxford, 1961), pp. 243–44, 273–74.

[110] *De mandatis divinis* 29, ed. Johann Loserth and F.D. Matthew (London, 1922), p. 445/1–3.

He would have been in keeping with his contemporaries in demanding more of the clergy, precisely because they had followed a higher calling. Hence his belief that fornication committed by a priest is a worse sin than that of the layman, inasmuch as the priest has taken a vow to his bride the Church, and so has entered into a union surpassing the carnal marriage of a secular lord; to break his vow of chastity is to be guilty of spiritual adultery. This is not to say that the layman is excused, of course, for he too sins mortally when fornicating, even if the priest's sin is all the more evil.[111] To this end, Wyclif recommends three remedies against fornication: the priest must put aside voluptuous thoughts, keep away from female company, and mortify his flesh.[112] It is always better to flee from the company of women than to struggle against the flames of lust.[113] And, while Wyclif thinks female charms are the greatest threat to clerical chastity, he adopts the traditional line in reckoning sodomy the gravest sexual sin, since it is the most unnatural.[114]

The problem of clerical concubinage was centuries old; reformers since the days of Peter Damian and Pope Gregory VII had been combating it. So there was no shortage of legal material for Wyclif to draw on when making his further case that the offending clerics be censured. That sanctions were in order was a basic legal principle; the question was what constituted legitimate sanctions and who should enforce them. Wyclif thought the most effective means of sanctioning incontinent priests would be for the laity to withhold their tithes. When making his case he appealed to the canonical statutes which not only called for the excommunication of priests living in concubinage, but forbade the laity to hear their Mass. On this basis, Wyclif reasoned that, inasmuch as such a priest is suspended from his benefices, he must also be unfit to receive the goods of the church by which he sustains the divine office. In fact, for the laity to continue funding this priest is to be complicit in his crime.[115]

Tithing was mandatory in the Middle Ages and tithes seem to have been paid by most citizens most of the time without any accom-

---

[111] *De paupertate Christi* 27, in Opera Minora, p. 58/18–27.
[112] *De mandatis* 29, p. 438/1–4.
[113] *De mandatis* 29, p. 444/2–7.
[114] *De mandatis* 25, p. 351/10–13.
[115] *De officio pastorali* 1.8, pp. 16–17; 1.17, p. 29; *De paupertate Christi* 27, p. 60. Cf. Friedberg, 1:117; 2:454–55.

panying anti-clerical sentiment.[116] People might grumble, but there was never any widespread resistance to tithes; where there were disputes they tended to be over interpretations of what was subject to the tithe requirements, not the tithes themselves. Resistance to tithing, therefore, was most often the province of dissenting groups, whose primary objection concerned their misuse at the hands of a corrupt clergy, which is not to deny that many orthodox reformers also voiced strong opposition to their abuse.[117] The freedom of the laity to withhold tithes from sinful clerics was a mainstay of Wycliffism, and was condemned as erroneous by the 1382 Blackfriars Council.[118] Wyclif's arguments from law and tradition were not unsound, though, and perhaps that is why his position could not be judged outright heresy. Where he went astray of the law was in assigning the determination of clerical fitness to the laity, although he deemed it another of Antichrist's lies to deny them that right.[119] Nevertheless, Wyclif may have been aware of the tenuous nature of his legal arguments, prompting him to withdraw this question from the strict confines of ecclesiastical statutes and make it a point of natural law. It is the fornicating priest's violation of natural law under God, the *ius poli*, and not merely human law, which renders him intrinsically (*per se*) unfit to dispense the sacraments.[120]

Notorious sinners aside, Wyclif wanted to make sure the parish priest was meeting his official obligations. The curate, he says, is like a physician who attends to the care of souls by applying the appropriate medicines, namely preaching and penance. Those who fail in that regard lack the very title under God's law by which they can demand tithes.[121] Sometimes, though, matters are not so clear cut. Tithes are indeed the goods of the poor, he says, and so it would be no sin to withhold them from a curate who abuses them. But he also cautions that evangelical prudence must be employed when assessing specific cases. If a priest is faithfully ministering to his parish then the laity would definitely be in the wrong in withholding the

---

[116] Norman Tanner, *The Church in Late Medieval Norwich: 1370–1532* (Toronto, 1984), pp. 5–7.

[117] Giles Constable, "Resistance to Tithes in the Middle Ages," *Journal of Ecclesiastical History* 13 (1962), 172–85.

[118] See proposition eighteen in *Fasciculi Zizaniorum*, p. 280.

[119] *De officio pastorali* 1.8, p. 17.

[120] *De paupertate Christi* 27, p. 60.

[121] *Opus evangelicum* 3.15; 2:54/15–20.

stipend he needs to live.[122] Though, as Wyclif observes, poor parishioners often believe their curate can get by with less than he really
needs, or they want him to take up worldly cares and labor just like
the rest of the poor and in this way pay for his own food and clothing. But then, says Wyclif, he would have to forsake his pastoral
duty and embroil himself in secular business, which is precisely what
tithing was meant to forestall. The priest needs his tithes, albeit freely
offered, so that he may devote his time to the care of souls. The
honest curate should have enough to live on; but, providing that the
parishioners' judgment is sound, it is lawful, and even meritorious,
to withhold tithes from those who abuse them, thereby allowing the
money to be put to more pious use.[123]

Just what constituted the abuse of parochial privileges was not so
clear. The rights of absentee benefice holders to the revenues of their
office were a mainstay of the late medieval Church. Nor should we
forget that, until Wyclif retired to his parish in Lutterworth at the
end of 1381, he spent the better part of his adult life as one of those
absentee curates in need of parish revenues to sustain his university
career.[124] To channel the financial benefits of one's ecclesial office
into the quest for higher learning was a long established practice
given special impetus in 1298 when Pope Boniface VIII issued the
bull Cum ex eo. This legislation, which was frequently utilized by fourteenth-century English bishops, provided for rectors who were not
yet priests to study for as long as seven years at university, provided
that they found a suitable replacement who would then be paid out
of the parish revenues. That the revenues of a local parish might
be used to fund a young man's education was not looked upon
askance, inasmuch as the education of promising clerics was seen to
benefit the wider Church (ad utilitatem communem ecclesiae). Noteworthy
here is that such licenses did not limit the course of study to a
specifically clerical regimen; the only requirement was that the recip-
ients actually spend their time studying something. Moreover, for
those who already possessed a master of arts degree, the license
allowed them to pursue still higher degrees in law or theology. Boyle

---

[122] De officio pastorali 1.14, p. 24.
[123] De peccato in Spiritum Sanctum, in Opera Minora, pp. 14–15.
[124] On Wyclif's various prebends and livings see Anne Hudson, "John Wyclif,"
in The Dictionary of National Biography vol. 60 (Oxford, 2004), p. 617.

believes that Wyclif was a recipient of a *Cum ex eo* license, and notes that he generally approved of them.[125]

Doubtless there were those who abused the system outright, or spent a good deal of their energy looking for ever more lucrative appointments. That is only to be expected, and Wyclif does not miss an opportunity to complain of those curates (*curati*) who, rather than tending to their parishes, spend so much time in Rome pleading for benefices and privileges extracted from the alms of the poor laity, or else are in London, among other comfortable locales. Yet, as one who personally benefited from such provisions, Wyclif could hardly label all absentee curates as selfish climbers. Perhaps a bit defensively, he will even make a strong case for absenteeism. A pastor may in good conscience be away from his parish provided that he is doing something of greater assistance to the Church, though he must see to it that his flock is not neglected in his absence. In fact, the curate has a greater obligation to Mother Church in her entirety than to his own particular parish. It would be perfectly acceptable, says Wyclif (likely with himself in mind), if a man of pure doctrine was thereby instructing the laity in the law of Christ; or if he went off to the university for a time in order to gather up the spiritual food to feed his flock. But not all university men are so noble, he laments, for rather than studying theology, many curates are instead learning canon and civil law. And if that is how they choose to spend their time, the parishioners would be right to withhold their tithes.[126] Wyclif the theologian may have had a personal aversion to lawyers, but there was nothing improper according to the statute in using parish revenues to pursue such degrees.

Prayer and Worship

Wyclif's comments on prayer can range from the pastoral to the scholastic all within the same work: in this case his 1375 treatise on the Ten Commandments. In his more scholastic mode, he notes that

---

[125] Leonard Boyle, "The Constitution 'Cum ex eo' of Boniface VIII," *Mediaeval Studies* 24 (1962), 263–302; reprinted in *Pastoral Care*. See Boyle's comments on Wyclif in "Aspects of Clerical Education," pp. 23–24. For *Cum ex eo* see Friedberg 2:964–65.

[126] *De officio pastorali* 1.17, p. 29; *De blasphemia* 12, pp. 178–9; *De veritate* 3.26, 3:37–39.

prayer is necessary, because God eternally ordains that what he grants should happen by way of such secondary causes. Prayer, therefore, functions as a secondary cause when the good of the creator is more abundantly communicated to creatures through intercession. In an especially un-pastoral remark, however, Wyclif says that God is never really so moved by the human voice as to grant someone's prayer; instead, God wants to see human beings extend to him the adoration he is due. In the process, though, prayer also serves to enflame one's own devotion and affection for God.[127] Wyclif the scholastic theologian, working out the fine points of necessity and contingency, recognizes that it may seem pointless to pray that God's will be done, as one does in the Lord's Prayer, since it is an absolute necessity that the will of God's good pleasure be fulfilled. Hence this petition must be read as a plea only to discern God's will (Ps. 142:10). Wyclif turns here to the standard scholastic distinction between God's will of good pleasure (beneplacitum) by which the omnipotent God governs the universe, and God's signified will (signum voluntatis) borne out in the specific precepts God communicates to his creatures. While none can resist God's good pleasure, sinners do resist his signified will when they fail to carry out his commands.[128] What all of this means for private devotion is that we must submit ourselves entirely to the will of God and ask for nothing beyond our own beatitude. But Wyclif also exhorts his fellow Christians to follow the gift of counsel and let their prayers be determined by the will of the Holy Spirit.[129]

We have already noted that Wyclif equates the contemplative life with some form of active devotion manifested in virtuous practice. This comes through in a sermon on Psalm 121:6 (Pray for the peace of Jerusalem . . .) where he extols the contemplative life of virtuous living as that which brings one closest to true peace. And peace itself is more stable in a life lived uprightly in both word and deed. Righteous works, therefore, prove far greater supplications than mental devotion and vocal prayer. Both good work and prayer please the Holy Trinity, but many people go wrong in imagining that prayer alone is sufficient. Soldiers, for example, worship God in the wrong way, living wickedly and yet expecting their prayers to help them.

---

[127] De mandatis 20, pp. 256–57.
[128] De mandatis 21, pp. 278–79. Cf. Hugh of St Victor, De sacramentis 1.2–4.
[129] De mandatis 21, p. 280/1–7.

So often people pray for peace and victory, for good weather and good crops, when it would please God far more were they to emend their lives and make satisfaction for their sins. Thus the wayfarer who merely wants to see his own desires fulfilled winds up blaspheming Christ and tempting God. Wyclif's words are those of the moralist preacher, less interested here in extolling God's compassion than in calling his flock to repentance as well as trust in God's eternal providence. Here he tells the faithful that they should not offer specific prayers, for whether we like it or not we are all subject to God's will, and so are better off simply striving to conform to his law. Ignorant as we are of all the particulars it would be presumptuous to pray for specific things as if we shared in God's omnipotence and omniscience. But, lest people come to the conclusion that they should give up on prayer entirely, Wyclif the preacher evokes Christ's example of praying night and day, and extols the Lord's Prayer as the principal example for Christians to follow. The Church would do well to stick to this simple and humble prayer, though he admits that others are also good (which he does not name). Positively sinful, however, are those prolix prayers which only serve to distract people from doing the good works that mean far more than mere vocal orations.[130] Prayer is a good and useful thing when kept simple. In fact, the power of prayer can be so great, says Wyclif, that it would be impossible for God to deny a righteous petition. This is not to say that all prayer requests are granted, however. There are various conditions under which prayer will not be effective: if the person praying is unworthy, the one prayed for unworthy, the person praying is not devout, the request itself unhelpful, or the form of the prayer defective.[131]

Despite Wyclif's emphasis on the action of good works, he does find room for meditation, and recommends meditating on death as an especially effective antidote to the enticements of the flesh, the javelins of the demons, and the flattery of the world. He points as well to the love of God, calling on the faithful to meditate upon the immense mercy of God, lest prayer grow tepid; for God's mercy is infinitely greater than the creature's misery. Here is the pastoral Wyclif, observing how the contemplation of God's infinite mercy will

---

[130] *Sermones* 4.3, pp. 25–28.
[131] *De mandatis* 20, pp. 257–58.

fill us with confidence. For we can find in the works of the Trinity
our hope and means to reconciliation through Christ's passion. One
must always remember that God can hate nothing but sin, since he
is filled with an "ineffable love" (*ineffabilem dileccionem*) through which
he loves human nature to the point of assuming it unto himself and
being crucified for the sins of humankind.[132] At times, if not too
rarely, Wyclif can speak eloquently about the redemptive mercy of
God, as he does in a Good Friday sermon from 1378. His words
of exhortation and comfort take on a monastic tone, calling Christians
to meditate on the Lord's passion. Not even the most "stony hearted"
(*cordis saxei*) could fail to be moved, says Wyclif, by the thought of
God's natural son dying for our sins, and thereby overcoming the
world, our flesh and Satan himself. If the temptations of the world
lead one into the concupiscence of the eyes, consider how the Lord
of the World was suspended naked on a cross. If one is led into the
concupiscence of the flesh, then consider how the King of Heaven
suffered so many pains for the sake of that concupiscence. And if
one is afflicted by pride, then meditate upon the fact that the Lord
of Hosts humbly subjected himself to his servants. There is no reason why anyone should sin, therefore, unless he fails to meditate on
Christ's sufferings. As the devil was conquered by way of Christ's
cross, so too must Christians take up this same cross in love, for this
is the surest way to overcome all demonic assaults. And as Christ
himself had to suffer before entering into his glory, so too must
Christians suffer if they are to achieve this end.[133]

Prayer must be conformed to what it was in the state of innocence,
which means praying constantly (Deut. 6:7). Thus Christians are to
pray always and everywhere, not just in church or at festivals.[134]
Having said that, though, Wyclif does advocate prayer in church
and lists many good reasons for it. Prayer is harder and thus more
meritorious when one has had to travel; and when made to God
there in obedience it accrues greater merit. The cleansed soul is
more devout in church when one has left behind servile chores and
cares. Moreover, when the faithful gather together to pray they help
one another. And because the church is consecrated it weakens the
power of the devil when he tries to tempt those who are praying.

---

[132] *De mandatis* 19, pp. 242–44.
[133] *Sermones* 4.39, pp. 327–28.
[134] *De mandatis* 20, p. 253/1–7.

In a more mystical vein, visiting God's house of prayer anagogically symbolizes the journey to the heavenly Jerusalem, while the material church building tropologically symbolizes the pure heart, and the walk to church reflects this present life of pilgrimage.[135]

In liturgical matters Wyclif was no Puritan. He genuinely appreciated the sublime beauty and dignity of the late medieval Mass. Only when the liturgy becomes an obstacle to prayer and worship does he voice his dissatisfaction. He concedes the point of those who argue that the otherwise uninterested laity may be roused to devotion by the ringing of bells and the singing of choirs, but fears that such things can also impede that very goal. Nevertheless, such rites can be used and moderated according to their proven efficacy. Wyclif would not abolish the Church's many prayers, but only demands that they prove their worth by exciting, rather hindering, devotion to God. He laments, however, that in his own day the people have been seduced into preferring new prayers, subtle songs and splendid locations, rather than the ancient prayers and rites which Christ had established. Once again, it is a case of dismissing the greater and more useful good for what is splendid in the eyes of the world.[136] Wyclif's liturgical criticisms are not very specific, but he was likely reacting to ceremonial elaborations such as those suggested in the "new" Sarum ordinal, which had been introduced in the early fourteenth century, and was employed throughout much of England, including Wyclif's own diocese of Lincoln. Indeed, the Sarum Use was becoming increasingly elaborate, continually being adapted to new feasts, each class of which had specific liturgical requirements.[137]

Wyclif will express his appreciation for ecclesiastical music and commends clerics for alternating between plainsong and instrumental accompaniment, since it makes prayer more pleasant for both the laity and clergy. He does critique the clergy's musical skills, however, complaining that clerics do not always accent the music correctly, thereby failing to give each syllable its proper time and the right pause in the middle of a verse or end of a sentence. Some of them just "bark like dogs in a sack," for their minds are in the law court

---

[135] *De mandatis* 20, pp. 248–49.
[136] *Opus evangelicum* 2.6; 1:262–63.
[137] See Jonathan Black, "Sarum Use," in *The Dictionary of the Middle Ages* vol. 10, ed. Joseph Strayer (New York, 1988), 655–6. I am indebted to Professor Richard Pfaff and Professor Anne Hudson for their help on this matter.

even as their bodies are in the choir; their tongues are in the hymnal, but their affections are in the carnivals, rendering them woefully unprepared to ask anything of God. Hence the very purpose for which the music is designed, namely to help the laity worship more devoutly, is undermined.[138]

Neither are the laity exceptionally devout in church. True Sabbath observance means fostering one's desire for God and reining in one's sin. It would be a lesser evil, therefore, if lay people spent their time plowing and weaving on the Sabbath, rather than just sitting around idly in church.[139] Many who should be headed for church are instead headed to the tavern. Rather than giving alms they are eating to excess, or they are giving away the goods of the poor to actors and prostitutes, all the while forgetting about the needs of their neighbor. No wonder, he says, that the Jews and pagans deride Christian Sabbath-keeping, seeing as we chiefly worship our own bellies.[140] Wyclif's own abstemiousness comes through at those times when he rails against excessive eating and drinking. In an Ascension Day sermon he protests that when Christ had fed the multitude there were only a few things on the menu and no strong drink, probably just water, and likely no tables or any of the other things that accompany worldly feasts nowadays. Sumptuous meals were introduced as a punishment for sin after the Fall, since it would have been unfitting in the state of innocence to care for such carnal luxuries. In fact, in the state of innocence there was no cooking at all; one would eat what nature herself had prepared from the fruits of the earth.[141]

The Cult of the Saints

Up until the twelfth century most of the venerated saints belonged to the patristic era, but then after 1150 there was a dramatic rise in the number of recent saints, most of whom had been dead for sixty years or less. Between the years 1198 and 1268 there were twenty-three canonizations, though this was followed by a steep drop as the process became much lengthier and more complicated, espe-

---

[138] *De mandatis* 20, p. 251.
[139] *Sermones* 1.49, pp. 325–26.
[140] *De mandatis* 18, pp. 221–24.
[141] *Sermones* 2.60, p. 445. Cf. *De statu innocencie* 3, in *De mandatis divinis accedit tractatus de statu innocencie*, pp. 493–95.

cially at the curial stage. This is not to say that the canonization of recent saints did not continue well into the fifteenth century. And besides, any such decline only reflects what was occurring at the papal level where saints were officially recognized. On the local scene cults were constantly springing up; and the bishops, who had traditonally been in charge of regulating the cult of the saints in their diocese, frequently acquiesced to the laity in the creation of new cults and pilgrimage sites, aware of the financial benefits to be reaped. The people naturally tended to prefer saints who were closely connected to them both in time and space, which meant that recent local saints were considered to be especially effective intercessors.[142] As an expression of their devotion the laity often left bequests in their wills to honor favorite saints with lights before their images, masses said at their altars, and the commissioning of pilgrimages. It was understood that saints were pleased by visits to their shrines where one would offer a coin or candles; and those who had benefited from such pilgrimages were then expected to spread the word.[143]

One did not have to be a heterodox dissenter to be dismayed by some of the current trends. In the first half of the fourteenth century, Bishop Grandisson of Exeter was exasperated by so many miracle accounts, which he did not believe, and considered impossible to prove. What is more, he thought that many people were being driven to idolatry by a lethal combination of superstition, diabolical prompting, and their own cupidity. Some of the leaders of the orthodox reform movement which resulted in the Council of Constance (1414–18) were also troubled by so many recent canonizations. Henry of Langenstein not only thought too many people were being canonized, but objected that the solemnity of veneration they received seemed to surpass even that afforded the Apostles. Pierre d'Ailly called for reform measures that included limiting the number of shrines and canonizations. And Jean Gerson argued that miracles stories tended to proliferate only when the candidate's holiness was in doubt.[144] Thus, as we go on to discuss Wyclif's views, we should keep these orthodox voices in mind, aware that d'Ailly and Gerson

---

[142] André Vauchez, *Sainthood in the Later Middle Ages*, trans. Jean Birrell (Cambridge, 1997), pp. 61–67; 87–110; 132–33.

[143] Duffy, pp. 156–200.

[144] Jonathan Sumption, *Pilgrimage: An Image of Medieval Religion* (London, 1975), pp. 273–74.

sat in judgment of Jan Hus at Constance and condemned the forty-five Wycliffite errors.[145]

Wyclif was not opposed to the cult of the saints; as with many aspects of popular devotion, he feared its excess. He was even willing to tolerate relics, though he feared that too often the people's obsession with them only fueled the desire to capitalize financially on the creation of new saints.[146] That being said, he did allow that saints canonized by the Church may have indeed attained heavenly blessedness, only cautioning that this should not be taken as an article of faith. Given Wyclif's consistent emphasis on the authority of Holy Scripture over and against extra-scriptural tradition, it is not surprising to hear him say that the only saints one should believe in as a matter of faith are the apostles, St Paul, Mary Magdalene, and others whose sainthood is implied in Scripture. As for those not mentioned in the Bible, no matter how great their sanctity, one is under no compulsion to believe that they are really in heaven.[147] Given those basic criteria, perhaps Wyclif's cynicism regarding recent canonizations is not surprising. Despite all the evidence marshaled by the Roman Church, one can never be sure of someone's ultimate status, especially as the alleged evidence of miracles may prove a mere illusion. Wyclif's position on saints ties in neatly with his ecclesiology, notably his suspicion of claims to prelatic authority. If the Church excommunicates many who are in fact acceptable to God, it stands to reason that she lists some within the catalogue of saints whom God has condemned. And the logical corollary of this is that one is entitled to believe explicitly in the sainthood of someone who lacks the Church's official approval. Better, though, just to stick to the apostles, martyrs, and saints of the primitive Church.[148]

Wyclif's comparatively measured tones can give way at times to outright contempt for the whole canonization process, however; one he believes to have run amok. It is rife with corruption; personal affections and cupidity have so infected the Church that the devil himself could be canonized and there would be plenty of fools ready to adore him. The "private religions" (i.e., monks and friars) beseech

---

[145] For the Wycliffite condemnations see Denzinger, 1151–95.

[146] *Sermones* 1.28, pp. 187–88.

[147] *Dialogus sive Speculum ecclesiae militantis* 14, ed. Alfred W. Pollard (London, 1886), p. 27/5–11.

[148] *De ecclesia* 2, p. 44.

Rome to canonize their brothers, all driven by a combination of avarice and faithlessness. The curia blasphemously presumes to canonize saints despite lack of divine revelation and thus with no real knowledge of the deceased's sanctity. The deposition of witnesses proves nothing, Wyclif insists, since the whole process is tainted by lies and filled with conflicting accounts. Miracle stories are often mere illusions, which is hardly surprising, seeing as the devil is quite capable of transforming himself into an angel of light and working great feats through the person of the damned. Here again Wyclif's deep suspicion of the sensible realm comes to the fore. The people are fascinated with prodigies and the devil is only too happy to cook up all sorts of fabulous signs designed to seduce the ignorant into worshipping some parvenu pseudo-saint, thereby forsaking the true worship of Jesus Christ.[149] Preying upon the people's obsession with sensible signs, these outward shows are the work of Antichrist who wants to lead the people away from the realm of true faith, namely that insensible, and thus most real, domain of true contemplation. This is not to say that there are no genuine miracles, of course, but they are the proper work of God. The saints themselves do not perform them, though they may sometimes provide the occasion for God's action. But even here the problem is that people become caught up with the miracle itself, thus losing sight of its ultimate purpose. Wyclif can only lament the multiplication of so many ceremonies and signs. For the deeds of the saints, like the Church's liturgy and rituals, are only laudable insofar as they elevate the soul to love Christ more fervently.[150]

Thus, even when it is right to venerate a given saint, Wyclif insists that the saint be considered in due proportion to Christ. The saint must exhibit Christ-like qualities; that is what makes him or her worth venerating. No saint, however, is so praiseworthy in word and deed as Christ. That may go without saying, but Wyclif insists that when one prays to a saint one's words should be directed principally towards Christ, not the saint. Nor should one celebrate the feast of any saint unless it serves to honor and magnify Christ. The honoring of saints is pointless unless it leads one to love Christ and prepares one to pray all the more for his assistance. Indeed, it might

---

[149] *Trialogus* 3.30, ed. Gotthard Lechler (Oxford, 1869), pp. 234–38.
[150] *De ecclesia* 2, pp. 45–46.

do the Church more good, he says, to abolish the saints' festival days altogether and just honor Christ's own feast, since that would focus the laity's devotion on Christ the Head, rather than diffusing it to his members.[151] Wyclif even wagers that the saints would pray for the faithful all the more effectively were their cults abolished, thereby allowing the people to love Jesus with greater fervor. Once more, we are back to idea that true sainthood remains a mystery; for there are many as-yet unrecognized saints doing the faithful more good with their prayers than those so-called saints whose feast days receive so much devotion.[152]

Truth be told, therefore, even as Wyclif acknowledges the genuine status of some saints, and is willing to see them venerated within proper parameters, he often gives the impression that the whole cult of the saints is superfluous. It seems almost pointless to petition the saints for anything, he says, since it is Christ who is the true mediator between God and humanity; he is the one who will grant whatever we may ask of the saint. And if Christ is the greatest mediator and intercessor, the one filled with the greatest love and kindness, it hardly makes sense for anyone to choose some lesser intercessor. It is Christ who lives eternally in the Father's presence, he who is prepared to intercede on behalf of the devout wayfarer. No need, therefore, to call on the saints when Christ is gentler and more prone to help.[153] Yet Wyclif was not making a merely dogmatic point; rather, it was born of a genuine affection for the person of Christ the Savior. Christ is the loving friend of the wayfarer. One must never imagine, says Wyclif, that Christ is so exalted as to be untouched by our prayers of sorrow, for there is no saint so merciful and ready to listen to our anguished cries than Christ.[154]

It is not surprising to find that Wyclif's devotion to the Blessed Virgin Mary is quite pious and traditional. Prescinding from whatever special place of honor she would rightfully claim as the Mother of God, she is a biblical saint, thus placing her sanctity and authority beyond doubt. But Mary is also worthy of Wyclif's praise precisely because, among all the saints, she best exemplifies Christ-like humility

---

[151] *Trialogus* 3.30, pp. 234–35.
[152] *De ecclesia* 2, p. 45/13–20. On Wycliffite ideas of sainthood see Christina von Nolcken, "Wyclif, Another Kind of Saint," in *From Ockham to Wyclif*, pp. 429–43.
[153] *Trialogus* 3.30, pp. 234–38.
[154] *Dialogus* 14, p. 27.

and patience. Thus his insistence that there is no better way to please the Virgin and her Son than to imitate their way of life. More specifically, the three best ways to please Our Lady are through humility, chastity and reticence. And this, in turn, means to clothe oneself with the humility of Christ, who was the most humble person of all, and the Blessed Virgin the most humble woman. It was Mary's humility that pleased God and disposed her to conceive the Word of God. As for chastity, it is essential for salvation, whether it be the celibacy of the clergy, the chastity of the married, or the continence of the unmarried laity. And reticence, finally, is that virtue between the two extremes of loquacity and muteness.[155]

There are also certain things that the Christian must believe about the Virgin Mary: that she was assumed into heaven and that she is the most blessed person this side of Christ. The bodily assumption into heaven of the Blessed Virgin Mary was not declared Roman Catholic dogma until 1950. And so, while Wyclif will affirm her assumption, he does so in the broadest terms. Whether she was assumed in body or only in soul is an issue that has not been settled, he notes, which means that one is not compelled to believe either position. Here it is better to bridle one's curiosity, he cautions, for God has hidden such matters from Christians so that they might humbly recognize their ignorance and stay focused on the necessities of the faith. Mary clearly holds a place for Wyclif that the rest of the saints simply cannot match, though in this regard he was in perfect conformity with the late medieval tradition. Hence we find him insisting that Christians believe that Mary is an advocate for those who truly venerate her. She sees our need and we should trust that by her great love and mercy she will provide for us. Everyone should be imploring the Virgin for help, since there is no one who will merit beatitude, nor anyone she will pray should obtain it, who does not follow her path. Here again Wyclif insists that true veneration is borne out in deeds. If we seek her assistance we must be willing to imitate her in humility, poverty and chastity, for she is not going to intercede for those she knows to be unworthy.[156]

The Immaculate Conception of the Blessed Virgin Mary was hotly debated in the later Middle Ages, often with the Franciscans supporting

---

[155] *Sermones* 2.20, pp. 149–51.
[156] *Sermones* 4.48, pp. 388–90.

this doctrine and the Dominicans opposing it. No one doubted that Mary had lived a life without sin; the only question was whether her being conceived without sin derogated from Christ's universal salvific efficacy. But, seeing as the Immaculate Conception was not rendered Roman Catholic dogma until 1854, Wyclif could proceed cautiously when counseling the faithful not to argue, as the friars do, over whether Mary was conceived in original sin or graciously preserved from it. The fact remains, he says, that neither group of friars can make the case either way.[157] For his own part, Wyclif thinks it quite likely that, just as Mary was free from actual sin, so she was also free of original sin. But, insofar as we have no idea which opinion the Blessed Virgin herself favors, it seems better not to make a full-fledged academic assertion either way.[158]

Images

A significant part of the cult of saints was the devotion to their images. The place of images in Christian devotion has a long and tumultuous history, even erupting in violence with attempted settlements by way of imperial legislation, and then counter-legislation, most notably during the iconoclast controversy of the eighth century.[159] Central to the issue at that time, as in later centuries, was the status of the created order within the sphere of Christian devotion. Wyclif's neoplatonic bent left him deeply suspicious of the temporal realm, often afraid that, rather than being a window into the spiritual, it instead proves an obstacle, a blinding distraction. He would often complain that human beings love temporal visible things more than invisible goods, and love buildings, vestments and ornaments, and other such artificial creations more than their uncreated exemplars. Much of the Church, he laments, is now infected by this idolatry, loving such things even more than God.[160]

Aston provides some excellent analyses of Wycliffite attitudes towards images of various kinds. She concludes that Wyclif himself was no extremist on the matter of images, allowing for their proper use not only in teaching the laity, but for arousing in them love for God.

---

[157] *De salutacione angelica* 1, in *Opera Minora*, p. 396.
[158] *Sermones* 2.8, p. 54.
[159] For the decisions of Nicea II (787) see Denzinger, 605–9.
[160] *De mandatis* 15, pp. 165–66.

It is the excessive ornamentation which he condemned, as well as the adoration of images, which he reckoned to be a violation of the First Commandment.[161] Wyclif takes a cautious, though perfectly orthodox, stand on images. Following Origen, he notes that worship (*cultus*) consists of a mental disposition, and adoration (*adoratio*) of bodily reverence. He then breaks adoration down into the three categories of latria, which is due to God alone; dulia, which is reverence due the creature; and hyper-dulia, which is owed to Christ's human nature on account of its hypostatic union with the divine.[162] What Wyclif fears here, as is so often the case, are the excesses of lay piety, excesses which he thinks are often fostered by the clergy. Thus, while images may arouse faithful hearts to an even more devout worship of God, they may also lead people away from the truth of the faith, as when the image itself ends up receiving the adoration rather then the person depicted. The common portrayal of the Holy Trinity consisting of an old bearded Father, his crucified Son, and the Holy Spirit descending between them in the form of a dove, also aroused his ire. Here is a case, he says, where both the laity and the ecclesiastical authorities err in the faith, thinking that they can depict the Father and the Holy Spirit in corporeal form.[163] It is worth noting that the theologians of Nicea II (787) had also maintained that God the Father cannot be depicted in images, precisely because he never became incarnate.

At any rate, even where Wyclif does allow for the use of images he warns against the tendency of many to think that the divine is actually contained within the image, thereby adoring one image more than another on the grounds that it will have even greater effect, as that does amount to idolatry. Here, though, Wyclif's abiding concern comes to the fore: misunderstanding the role of images is an occasion for diabolical deception. No merely human production should be adored as if it could perform a miracle. All too often, he says, pilgrims are cheated out of their money, unaware that the image is effective only insofar as it rouses one's mind and stirs one's affections to the contemplation of heavenly things. Nor does Wyclif

---

[161] Margaret Aston, "Lollards and Images," in *Lollards and Reformers: Images and Literacy in Late Medieval Religion* (London, 1984), pp. 137–43; and Aston, "Lollards and the Cross," in *Lollards and Their Influence*, pp. 99–113.

[162] *De mandatis* 15, pp. 160–61. Cf. Origen, *In Exodum homilia* 8; PG 12:354.

[163] *De mandatis* 15, p. 156.

accept Thomas Aquinas's argument that the image may be adored
inasmuch as such adoration redounds to the prototype; for that line
of reasoning smacks of the paganism current in Old Testament times.
People deceived into mistaking signs for things, the classic error
Augustine commented upon almost a thousand years earlier, is for
Wyclif an all too real state of affairs.[164]

Purgatory and Indulgences

Seeing as purgatory was where most medieval Christians expected
to find themselves after death, and given the fact that it was not
going to be very pleasant, people made arrangements to get out as
fast as possible. St Bonaventure describes it as a place of suffering
inflicted by material fire where people are punished according to the
measure of their misdeeds. In fact, the pain may be so great at times
that they are unaware this is not hell itself.[165] By the late Middle
Ages purgatory and indulgences were often spoken of in the same
breath, inasmuch as the latter could significantly shorten the length
of one's stay in the former. This is because purgatory was the place
where one had to endure all the temporal punishment accruing to
the sins which had not been effectively discharged here on earth;
indulgences were a form of debt relief. That indulgences could be
a contentious issue was not merely because they were prone to abuse,
but because the abuse itself often stemmed from a misunderstanding of the very nature of indulgences themselves. Precisely speaking,
an indulgence is the relaxation of the temporal penalty (*poena*) which
accompanies a mortal sin, since the guilt (*culpa*) is remitted in the
sacrament of confession when the priest pronounces God's absolution. Yet, despite the fact that the theologians confirmed that God
alone can forgive this guilt, the general populace usually believed
that in acquiring an indulgence they had not only procured the
remission of punishment, but of guilt as well. By the end of the
twelfth century, it was also being made clear that indulgences applied
only to those who were contrite and had received absolution from
their guilt in the sacrament of penance. That is why Aquinas could

---

[164] *De mandatis* 15, p. 157. Cf. Aquinas, *Summa theologiae* 3.25. 3–4. On Robert
Holcot's reaction to Aquinas's theory see Aston, "Lollards and Images," pp. 155–58.
[165] *Breviloquium* 7.2.

say that indulgences are of no benefit to those in a state of mortal sin, since the penalty cannot be relaxed while the guilt still remains. But it was not just the pardoners who misconstrued this theology; even some otherwise responsibly-minded popes found occasion to offer full pardon without recourse to contrition or confession.[166]

Indulgences had long accompanied the sacrament of penance as a form of commutation, but they cemented their place within the panoply of medieval devotion when the doctrine of purgatory began to be more formally developed. In 1274 the Second Council of Lyons affirmed the existence of purgatory, stating that those who die in a state of charity before having rendered satisfaction for their sins are purged after death by purificatory penalties, and that these penalties may be alleviated through the suffrages of the pious faithful in their prayers, masses, alms and other good works.[167] Aquinas not only held that such suffrages of the living can be useful to the dead, he also believed that indulgences could be applied to the dead in purgatory, since there is nothing to prevent the Church from transferring her common merits (upon which indulgences are based) from the living to the dead. Aquinas cautioned, however, that prelates cannot liberate souls on a whim; there must be a fitting reason for the indulgence.[168] Nevertheless, in the Jubilee Year of 1300 Pope Boniface VIII was liberally granting indulgences which effected the immediate liberation of souls from purgatory.[169]

In 1343 Pope Clement VI issued the famous bull *Unigenitus Dei Filius* in which he formally declared that all the merits accumulated by Christ and the saints were at the disposal of the papacy to be dispensed in the form of indulgences.[170] Wyclif, on the other hand, argued that this is to misunderstand the very essence of an indulgence. To grant an indulgence one must first have the power to indulge, which Wyclif defined as "graciously granting, showing care, or forgiving." And this power to indulge, or have mercy upon, sinners belongs to God alone, just as it is God alone who forgives sins.

---

[166] Henry Charles Lea, *A History of Auricular Confession*, 3 vols. (New York, 1968), 3:60–62. See Aquinas, *ST*, suppl. 27.1.

[167] Jacques Le Goff, *The Birth of Purgatory*, trans. Arthur Goldhammer (Chicago, 1984), pp. 285–305.

[168] Aquinas, *ST*, suppl. 71.6; 71.10.

[169] Le Goff, pp. 330–31.

[170] Denzinger, 1025–27.

Wyclif complained, therefore, that the term "indulgence" has been uprooted from its original meaning and is now used by both theologians and canonists to denote the remission of punishment, which they have put squarely in the hands of prelates.[171] At the heart of this system is that alleged storehouse of merits under the control of the papacy, which has spawned the buying and selling of sins for cash, a thoroughly impossible exchange designed to line the pockets of an already avaricious clergy.[172] When Wyclif spoke about indulgences he focused on their abuse, the fact that they had been turned into a commodity, and are now far removed from whatever genuinely pastoral function they might have had in the earlier medieval Church.

Wyclif knew of Aquinas's position on indulgences, but no matter the respect he often accorded the Angelic Doctor, he rejected out of hand the idea that they could be applied by the papacy to those in purgatory. Wyclif's own position on purgatory and indulgences was often driven by his anti-papalism. He directly attacked the program outlined in Clement's bull, countering that there is no such treasury of superogatory merits to begin with, let alone one at the disposal of the pope to dispense from as he sees fit.[173] In fact, says Wyclif, the superogatory merits of Christ and the saints are things past, and thus do not exist; but even in their own time they would have remained outside of the pope's ordinary power. The pope simply cannot distribute works which are not in his control, nor may he take from the blessed the rewards due their good works and distribute them to sinners.[174] Clearly, the feature of the indulgence system that most bothered Wyclif was the pope's claim to be able to release souls from purgatory, thereby further extending his power of the keys. We should remember, though, that the question of papal power relative to the realm of purgatory was not settled when Wyclif was writing in the late fourteenth century. Indeed, he raises some principled objections which touch on the exact parameters of that rather murky relationship between the living and the dead. The

---

[171] *De ecclesia* 23, p. 549/7–10: "... ita quod indulgencia non sit aliud nisi habentem ad hoc potenciam indulgere, et est indulgere gratis concedere, operam dare, sive remittere ..."

[172] *De ecclesia* 23, p. 551/25–28.

[173] *De ecclesia* 23, p. 551. Wyclif quotes Aquinas at length on pp. 552–53.

[174] *De ecclesia* 23, p. 564.

notion that the pope could extend his judiciary power to the souls in purgatory and the saints in heaven would mean that even a damned pope would have the power to communicate the merits of the just to whomever he wished, thereby granting him judiciary power over Christ and the saints.[175] Furthermore, if the pope really does possess this infinite power, such that he can grant indulgences to an infinite number of people over an infinite period of time, one would expect him to perform this act of spiritual mercy constantly.[176]

Wyclif appealed to canon law to prove that the power of the keys was strictly limited to the Church Militant here on earth. And he pressed his case by arguing that indulgences cannot function in hell, inasmuch as there is no redemption there, nor in paradise, since those souls have no need of prayers.[177] As to whether the suffrages of the living might at least mitigate the pains of the damned, there seemed to be some division between theologians and canonists; the former ruling this out, and the latter admitting its possibility. Wyclif pointed out that the noted canonist Hostiensis had approached this issue cautiously and declined to take a definitive stand, though he (like Raymond of Penafort) conceded that the opinion of the theologians was more widely held.[178] When objecting to the outright release of souls from hell, Wyclif would have not encountered any opposition from his fellow theologians either; Bonaventure and Aquinas said the same.[179] There was precedent for the idea, however. Pope Gregory the Great had believed that masses offered for the dead could confer absolution after death and thus release souls from hell. Wyclif would have been in line with his fellow schoolmen, though, in rejecting as impossible the legend of St Gregory's prayers securing the Emperor Trajan's release from hell. Neither Gregory, nor any other saint, can alter the divine will through prayer. If Trajan was saved it was because God had eternally predestined him to glory, and thus eternally ordained that he would be saved by means of Gregory's intercessions.[180]

---

[175] *De ecclesia* 23, p. 565.
[176] *De ecclesia* 23, p. 571.
[177] *De ecclesia* 22, pp. 522–23. Cf. Dec. 2, C.24, q.2, c.1–6; Friedberg 1:984–86.
[178] *De ecclesia* 22, pp. 518–19. See also Lea, 3:333–34.
[179] Bonaventure, *Breviloquium* 7.3; Aquinas, *ST*, suppl., 71.5; 71.8.
[180] *De ecclesia* 22, p. 533; *Sermones* 4.3, p. 33.31–38. Cf. Gregory, *Dial.* 4.55; PL 77; 416–21. See also Lea, 3:329–34.

No matter his misgivings, Wyclif was hardly going to stem the tide of indulgences. By this time there had been a great leap, not only in the number of indulgences being granted, but in the amount of pardon offered for comparatively small deeds.[181] That the power of indulgences had reached grotesque proportions is evinced by a 1370 vernacular English account of the "Stacions of Rome" listing the indulgences offered at various Roman churches. To visit St Peter's from Holy Thursday to Lammas (August 1) meant a daily indulgence of fourteen thousand years, likewise at San Tommaso, while at San Anastasio one could get seven thousand years. Compare this to Peter the Chanter in the late twelfth century who spoke of the two or three years to be had for visiting Rome on Holy Thursday.[182]

In the face of all this, Wyclif tried to rally his faithful priests to enlist the best arguments they could muster against what he reckoned the current fraud of indulgences, these sophisms of Antichrist designed to delude the laity with vain hope. Because Wyclif had concentrated both forgiveness of sin and remission of punishment in the more immediate relationship between God and the penitent, the only sure course of action for wayfarers is to live righteously and place their confidence in the portion of merit which God has given them.[183] As it is God alone who forgives sins, so then he alone may grant an indulgence, and only then to those of his beloved whom he has first made worthy. Hence the bishop's indulgence only works to the extent that one has been previously disposed by God's grace to receive it. It is the bishop's duty, therefore, to instruct the people in the faith of Christ, so that they might ascend in their love for God and thus be worthy of his indulgence. Wyclif makes it clear that he is not attacking the entire sacrament of penance here, only its various abuses. Priests do indeed have the power to absolve the laity of punishment and guilt, he says, but ought not to do so unconditionally short of a special revelation. Nor should a layman demand absolution, as if it were some sort of guarantee that he was now pure in God's eyes. Wyclif's larger point here, as elsewhere, is that outward rites and signs count for nothing where the spiritual significate is ignored. Reliance on ritual as an end unto itself is what Wyclif fears;

---

[181] R.N. Swanson, *Church and Society in Late Medieval England* (Oxford, 1989), p. 293.
[182] Lea, 3:279–80.
[183] *Opus evangelicum* 1.12; 1:39.

thus his emphasis on the interior qualities of sacramental and devotional practices. The sacrament of penance is valuable and necessary, he says, but it is only effective where there is true contrition, which is known to God alone.[184] Wyclif may seem to be introducing a level of uncertainty into a sacrament which was designed to provide the assurance of pardon to anxious souls. But what he was saying is perfectly orthodox; the very reason for a priest to ask such penetrating questions was to illicit a full and frank confession which ultimately led to contrition, apart from which the penitent remained in his sins. The real problem arises when the system becomes so distorted that the laity come to assume that sin can be commuted for money, thereby placing God in the position of selling his righteousness. This, says Wyclif, would be tantamount to God auctioning his own dominion, meaning that the creature is put on equal footing with God, such that God can no longer demand his servitude. The truth is that each person who sins against God must make satisfaction for his or her own transgression. God does not remit sin without satisfaction, nor does he communicate such power to his vicar.[185]

Funerals, Prayers, and Masses for the Dead

Preparing for one's own death became a principal concern for many late medieval Christians. This meant putting one's estate in order, making out a will, and arranging for a proper funeral. Funerals could be quite extravagant: a formal procession, the ringing of bells, money doled out to the poor and a feast given for the entire parish.[186] We have noted the strife between secular and regular clergy on a range of issues, not the least of which was burial rights; this is because the burial house often received more money than the rest of the churches named in the will. Add to this the funeral costs and the elaborate tombs of the gentry, and the church chosen for burial made out very well.[187] Given the popularity of the friars it is not surprising

---

[184] *De ecclesia* 23, pp. 583–85.

[185] *De ecclesia* 23, p. 561/11–18.

[186] Andrew D. Brown, *Popular Piety in Late Medieval England: The Diocese of Salisbury 1250–1550* (Oxford, 1995), pp. 100–1.

[187] Joel T. Rosenthal, *The Purchase of Paradise: Gift Giving and the Aristocracy 1307–1485* (London, 1972), p. 100.

that they fared better than the other orders when it came to deathbed bequests, with the Dominicans and Franciscans out-pacing the Carmelites and Augustinians.[188]

When drawing up their wills people were eager to make donations for a variety of purposes. To leave money for masses, for the poor, the incarcerated, and even for road repairs, was thought to be meritorious and, as such, could hasten one's journey through purgatory. The seven works of mercy, which the faithful layman would have learned, figured prominently in funeral arrangements with bequests to the poor made in the form of gifts and always with the implicit (if not explicit) obligation to pray for the donor.[189] For a fee the local poor also served as part of the funeral procession and were often allowed to keep their ceremonial garments which were usually worth more than the penny cash payment.[190] While all pious and charitable donations were meant to aid the deceased, none was more valuable than masses and prayers. Tanner's study of late medieval Norwich reveals that testators left more money for masses and prayers than for any other activity. Even the less well-to-do who could not afford perpetual chantries left money for masses and prayers as they could afford them, usually asking for a large number immediately after death and then a few dispersed over intervals for years to come.[191] Yet, despite what may appear to be expressions of anxiety over purgatory's terrors, Duffy and Heath have concluded that there really was no sense of panic. People simply made out their bequests, often with detailed liturgical instructions, and trusted this would get them safely through. The rich were all the more scrupulous about this, inasmuch as they expected to face a stiffer judgment.[192] People placed their trust in a well-tried system which had been carefully set in place to minimize future pain. And it was this belief in the effectiveness of the Mass for easing the pains of purgatory that led to an explosion in the number of non-beneficed clergy to staff the chantries or serve as guild chaplains. It also led to the decoration

---

[188] Rosenthal, pp. 121–22.

[189] J.A.F. Thomson, "Piety and Charity in Late Medieval London," *Journal of Ecclesiastical History* 16 (1965), 178–95.

[190] Rosenthal, pp. 106–7.

[191] Tanner, pp. 106–8.

[192] Duffy, pp. 347–49; Peter Heath, "Between Reform and Reformation: The English Church in the Fourteenth and Fifteenth Centuries," *Journal of Ecclesiastical History* 41 (1990), 647–78, at p. 673.

and construction of churches as a sign of one's piety, a good work that would count for something on the Judgment Day.[193] To some modern scholars, such as Rosenthal, the gentry's chantries were an instance of individualism in an age of collective devotional practice, selfish endeavors which provided for the testator, his friends and family, with scant resources devoted to helping the poor at set times of the year.[194] Certainly, there was a lot of self-interest involved, but this should not be taken as a sign of theological shallowness on the part of the nobility. While noble wills of the later fourteenth century may have been primarily concerned with leaving money for prayers and chantries, Catto has pointed to the educated laity's keen interest in contemplative literature as evidence of genuine devotion and spiritual reflection.[195]

Whatever Wyclif's feelings about indulgences, he fully accepted the reality of purgatory and readily admitted the propriety of praying for the dead, especially parents and relatives, seeing as we received so much from them when we were as yet unable to help ourselves. Now they are the ones in no position to help themselves and so require our assistance. Yet Wyclif was wary of the calculated aspect of the whole process, one that seems to divorce prayer from piety. Thus, rather than simply praying for the dead, or arranging for someone else to do so, we can be of greater service to them by disseminating corporeal and spiritual works of mercy. This will be a far more productive activity, he says, than having so many masses celebrated on behalf of the dead each day.[196] This is not to say that Wyclif denied the Mass is a true and efficacious sacrifice, or that there is merit to be gained from its celebration (at least for the devout faithful). He only objected to treating the Mass as though it were some sort of merit-machine to be put at one's disposal as a substitute for humble acts of mercy.

Earnestly praying for one's relatives and friends is one thing, paying to accumulate the prayers of others to speed you through purgatory is another. Of course, vast sums were often left to religious

---

[193] Duffy, pp. 301–2.
[194] Rosenthal, pp. 51–52.
[195] J.I. Catto, "Religion and the English Nobility in the Later Fourteenth Century," in *History and Imagination: Essays in Honor of Hugh Trevor-Roper* (New York, 1981), pp. 53–55.
[196] *De mandatis* 23, pp. 322–23.

orders to pray for the deceased. But Wyclif is clear that prayers must
not be bought or sold, and he warns the wayfarer against imagining
that he has the capacity to manipulate the power of his own prayer,
let alone someone else's. In fact, God wants the efficacy of our prayer
to remain hidden from us, lest we try to buy his favors. And while
we cannot be certain how much God loves us, we can be sure that
the more beloved one is to God, the more effective the prayer. This
is why Wyclif warned against falling victim to the monks who deceive
rich and poor alike in commending the merit of their prayers on
behalf of the dead, and contends that the prayers of sinful monks
are useless, since they will not be heard by God.[197] This last point
is noteworthy, for there was some debate in the Middle Ages as to
how effective the prayers and sacraments of sinful priests were, but
here it is a question of an otherwise righteous testator making a provision for a meritorious act. Aquinas concluded that, because the
principal agent (the testator) was in a state of grace when com-
manding that these suffrages be offered on his behalf, they will still
be effective despite the fact that the one praying is in a state of sin.
Though he does note that the prayers would be even more effective
were both parties in a state of grace.[198]

In this vein, Wyclif attacks the popular letters of fraternity whereby
the friars granted the laity a portion of their merits. First of all, he
notes that, as no one can be certain of his own salvation, one can
hardly guarantee that someone else will have a share of such salvific
merits. To buy these letters is the height of foolishness, therefore,
since the friars are simply in no position to grant what they are selling. He notes that even the proponents of the system were willing
to concede an element of uncertainty despite their guarantees, though
they maintained that these letters do at least prompt people to perform good deeds. Needless to say, Wyclif is unimpressed by such
equivocal promises, pointing out that no one should lie even to save
the entire world, let alone make a profit in the process. At root,
though, Wyclif's objections strike a moral tone, reproving not only
the friars, but the laity as well. Letters of fraternity constitute one
more instance of people attempting to skirt their Christian duties,
foisting off the hard work of a virtuous life onto the supposed mer-

---

[197] *Dialogus* 23, pp. 46–47.
[198] *ST*, suppl., 71.3.

its of the friars who, by the way, he thinks are motivated solely by greed with not a care for their neighbor's salvation.[199] Wyclif is under no illusions; the laity are not angels, but they are desperately in need of spiritual guidance. The clergy, however, have abdicated their responsibility and now foster a culture which is unwilling to bear the cross of genuine discipleship.

Given Wyclif's general mistrust of outward displays of piety, believing they are too often distractions from the requisite inward conformity to Christ, it is only natural that he would disparage the funeral customs of the well-to-do. People ought to be buried at moderate expense, he contends, while in fact most are spending far too much. These lavish ceremonies amount to no more than occasions for worldly glory. The ideal simplicity and purity of the Early Church always remains the standard by which Wyclif will judge the practices of his own day. As such, he cannot abide all the customs attached to the funeral, such as the sermons, feasts, distributions, probations, and lavish tombs, when so many glorious martyrs had no such fare. Piece by piece he dismantles the ceremony. The sermons are usually a sham concocted by a friar who mendaciously recounts the life of the deceased. And even if the friar were to utter a single genuine word it would do the dead no good, seeing as this person is no longer in a position to merit. As for the feasts, they are given for the deceased's rich friends despite the fact that Christ called on us to invite the poor. What distribution of money to the poor there is, he says, is just a fraudulent show designed to win worldly honor and praise, none of which can help the dead. The probation of the will amounts to a giveaway to the bishop or archdeacon who already holds the goods of the Church by way of simony. The great tombs do no good for either the corpse or soul of the dead; better that such riches were distributed to the needy. And the payments given the friars for masses are also rife with fraud, not only because the same friar already has many salaries, but because it is contrary to the faith to think that such masses can be of any avail beyond what the dead have merited in this life. As for the perpetual alms given to monasteries, secular lords think that they can buy their reward from God. But, as these endowments savor of pride, and will only end up damaging the Church anyway, the soul cannot

---

[199] *Sermones* 3.42, pp. 356–58.

expect any suffrage to come of them. Behind all of these errors, says Wyclif, is the notion that one can earn merit after this life is over. But once the soul has been separated from the body the possibility of merit has come to an end. Hence the great memorial tombs of the gentry are useless, merely the stuff of worldly spectacle. Those belonging to the damned are the fruit of their sin against the Holy Spirit, and those belonging to the elect are the fruit of their affection for property, and so must be expurgated. The poor are the ones who will die in a greater grace, since they have made better use of their temporal goods, free as they were from such worldly affections.[200] Funeral rites, far from being meritorious, therefore, actually end up harming both the living and the dead: the former because they are vain attempts to gain worldly favor when such wealth could be distributed to the poor, the latter precisely because the suffrages of the surviving friends are negated by the evils of the funeral rites themselves. The wishes of the rich are undone; the dead poor will have a greater share in the merits of the Church Militant than the wealthy who have left their possessions to the friars. All of this is to demonstrate the vanity of storing up treasures on earth in the hope that one's soul will benefit from them after death. The Catholic merits as he lives in this life, while God proportionately distributes the merits of the living to him after death in keeping with divine justice, thereby rendering the friars' intercessions meaningless.[201]

It must be admitted that Wyclif had a certain affinity for secular magnates, and he was not calling on them to divest themselves of their property. God, in his immense goodness, furnishes secular lords with earthly riches and offers them just ways to distribute these riches for the greater good. Such alms giving falls into three categories: for the captives of Christ, namely the blind and lame; tithes to curates as the law allows; and the repair of bridges, roads and churches.[202] Wyclif cautions, though, that such giving should not be put off until after one's death; it should be done now so as to merit eternal life. He suspects that some among the rich fear for their own salvation and are hoping that posthumous distributions to the poor will save their souls, prompting his warning that only by giving away their goods in this life can they merit eternal beatitude. Echoing the com-

---

[200] *De ecclesia* 22, p. 547.
[201] *Sermones* 4.11, pp. 93–94.
[202] *Sermones* 1.41, p. 274.

mon sentiment, he notes that the best a posthumous donation can do is take some time off purgatory.[203] Wyclif is well aware that it is easier to part with one's money and possessions after death, than to be without them now. Thus his insistence that the smallest act of loving distribution during one's lifetime is infinitely more effective for salvation than any post-mortem bequests.[204]

Wyclif also offers advice on the proper Christian response to death itself. The faithful must regulate their emotions, learning how to die and how to grieve. He admits that when someone dies there is room for natural affection, as when a mother grieves the death of her son. Yet one must not wallow in grief, but instead rejoice as Christ and the martyrs rejoiced at their own deaths. Christians have to use their rational faculties to control the soul's natural impetus, just as Mary mitigated her own grief. This means that when Jesus wept for Lazarus, whose death would lead to glory, he did so only indirectly, weeping more for the sin of the human race than for his friend. All too often, however, it is love for the temporal realm that forms the real source of anxiety, as people weep primarily for the worldly benefits they will now be missing.[205] Adopting a rather stoical attitude, Wyclif notes that as death is inevitable, and God determines what will become of the dead, all sorrow amounts to grief over the divine will, and so proves to be the height of unfaithfulness. Real sadness ought to be saved for the errors of the living who fall away from the law of Christ; these are instances which really can be remedied. As for the dead, we should just have faith that their merits will be sufficient for them to rise on the final day and claim their reward.[206]

We do not know much about Wyclif's own funeral other than that it would have been a proper Catholic burial at his Lutterworth parish, having died in communion with the Church. Only later, in 1427, on the orders of the Council of Constance, was his body eventually exhumed and his bones burnt. There is no record of exactly where he was buried, whether in such standard locations as the chancel, by the west door, or beneath the processional path. There must have been a stone marker, though, because some of his Czech admirers took chips of it back home to Prague. There is no surviving will,

---

[203] *Sermones* 1.40, p. 270.
[204] *Sermones* 4.55, pp. 432–33.
[205] *De ecclesia* 22, p. 544.
[206] *Sermones* 4.1, pp. 1–2.

so it is impossible to know what sort of funeral Wyclif asked for, or how he distributed his assets.[207] But we do know that the recanted Lollard, and later Bishop of Lincoln, Philip Repingdon, asked that his own funeral ceremony be held for the remission of his sins of worldly vanity. All of his money was left to the poor and not a penny for masses or any religious foundation.[208] This is a far cry from Wyclif's nemesis, Archbishop Courtenay, who provided for fifteen-thousand masses and two-thousand matins of All Saints.[209]

Sin and Grace

Everything we have looked at so far, from preaching to prayer, has as its goal the salvation of the wayfarer, the pilgrim on route to the heavenly Jerusalem. It is appropriate, therefore, to say something about Wyclif's more precise theory of salvation—his soteriology.[210] Wyclif was a professor of theology, after all, and thus steeped in the high scholastic debates about the role of divine grace and human free will in the salvific process. Medieval theologians generally agreed that God is both omniscient and omnipotent; there is nothing that happens in the world that God does not know and will. Just how this could be reconciled with human freedom and moral responsibility was much discussed by theologians from Augustine to Anselm, and never more so than in the fourteenth century. Wyclif realized that two of his favorite theologians, Richard FitzRalph and Thomas Bradwardine, were sharply divided on the question of human freedom. And, while Wyclif was wary of openly criticizing Bradwardine, his sympathies were with FitzRalph, whose position would have been more in keeping with the prevailing thought of the fourteenth-century schools. Even as Wyclif would concede to Bradwardine that all things happen by necessity, he insisted on making a distinction between absolute and hypothetical necessity (a distinction which Bradwardine did not accept). Wyclif notes that absolute necessity has to do with

---

[207] Herbert B. Workman, *John Wyclif: A Study in the English Medieval Church* 2 vols. (Oxford, 1926), 2:317–20.

[208] Aston, "'Caim's Castles'," pp. 129–31.

[209] Swanson, p. 298.

[210] For a more detailed treatment of Wyclif's soteriology see Ian Christopher Levy, "Grace and Freedom in the Soteriology of John Wyclif," *Traditio* 60 (2005), 279–337.

things which cannot not exist, such as God or the eternal truths within the divine essence. Hypothetical or conditional necessity (*necessitas ex suppositione*), on the other hand, deals with eternal contingent truths. This means that, while there is an absolutely necessary connection between an eternal causal antecedent and its temporal consequent, the antecedent is still contingent.[211] When applied to God's will, therefore, we would say that, on the condition that God eternally wills something, it must come to pass; but it might have been that God never willed such a thing at all.

Though the distinction between absolute and hypothetical necessity was itself not new, Wyclif was following a fourteenth-century trend which applied it in such a way so as to guarantee a good deal of human freedom, even to the point of making the decision of the free rational creature determinative of divine knowledge.[212] Wyclif makes no bones about the fact that a temporal truth can be the cause of an eternal truth. For instance, Christ said that God the Father loves the disciples because they had loved Christ himself. Thus the eternal love of God the Father was caused by the disciples' temporal expression of love for Christ.[213] In other words, while the love of God for the disciples is eternally constant, and in that way necessary, God might never have loved them at all; and in that sense his eternal love remains contingent. As one might expect, the fact that human beings have the power to cause divine volitions has serious implications for moral theology, insofar as it is meant to preserve human freedom, and thus human responsibility as well. The whole notion of meritorious action would be meaningless, says Wyclif,

---

[211] *De dominio divino* 1.14, ed. Reginald Lane Poole (London, 1890), pp. 115–16. Here Wyclif appealed to Aristotle and Aquinas. Cf. Aristotle, *Physics* 2,9; 200a–200b; and Aquinas, *ST* 1.19.3. Cf. *De universalibus* 14, ed. Ivan Mueller (Oxford, 1985), p. 334. See also Anthony Kenny, "Realism and Determinism in the Early Wyclif," in *From Ockham to Wyclif*, pp. 165–77. Note, however, that Alessandro Conti (in his essay in this volume) maintains that Wyclif's proposed distinction does not actually hold up within the larger context of his realist metaphysical system.

[212] For studies of these fourteenth-century developments see Maarten J.F.M. Hoenen, *Marsilius of Inghen: Divine Knowledge in Later Medieval Thought* (Leiden, 1993); Chris Schabel, *Theology at Paris 1316–1345* (Aldershot, 2000); Bartholomew R. De la Torre, *Thomas Buckingham and the Contingency of Futures: The Possibility of Human Freedom* (Notre Dame, 1987).

[213] *Sermones* 1.29, p. 194/21–25: "Ex quibus convincitur, cum amor patris sit eternus et amor discipulorum quo humanitatem Christi dilexerant, incepit in tempore, quod unum temporale potest esse causa eterni contingit a temporali huiusmodi dependere."

were not many effects in the control of the rational creature.[214] In
fact, God only loves or hates someone conditionally, depending upon
his knowledge of whether that person would act well or evilly.[215]
There could be no moral virtue if everything occurred by absolute
necessity, he says, since we can neither be praised nor blamed for
things that are not in our power.[216] On the other side of this moral
coin, the creature's freedom must be emphasized to avoid implicat-
ing God in evil. Wyclif thinks it contrary to Scripture to say that
all things occur by absolute necessity; for if sin occurred in this way
then God would become the author of sin.[217]

In keeping with his emphasis on human freedom as the lynchpin
of a genuinely moral system, Wyclif argues that, while God could
have prevented human sinfulness altogether, it is a greater good for
the human race that the rational creature be permitted to sin. Indeed,
it would have been unbecoming of divine goodness to rule out the
possibility of human sin entirely.[218] Sin had to be a real possibility
for the human race, but the choice to sin always has to remain free.
Because God is just, says Wyclif, he will not condemn anyone except
on account of his own evil deeds. It is impossible for God to condemn the innocent, precisely because God never acts against his own
good and just nature.[219] Wyclif's theory of hypothetical necessity
comes into play here when he argues that God only willed to damn
Lucifer because he sinned, meaning that Lucifer could have chosen
to refrain from sinning and so made it that God never willed to
damn him at all. Wyclif insists that it is because God created creatures to be free that he must allow that their free volitions determine his own. "That is why I can make it such that God never
willed my damnation;" though, inasmuch as God's will is eternally
constant, I cannot prevent God from willing this when he does.[220]

---

[214] *De universalibus* 14, p. 343.

[215] *De volucione Dei* 1, in *De ente: librorum duorum excerpta*, ed. M.H. Dziewicki (London,
1909), pp. 116–17, at p. 117/8–10: ". . . 3° sequitur, quod omnis volucio dei est
determinata, et per consequens deus neminem amat vel odit, solum conditionaliter,
si bene vel male se gesserit."

[216] *De universalibus* 14, pp. 348–49.

[217] *De universalibus* 14, p. 349.

[218] *De dominio divino* 1.14, pp. 121–2.

[219] *De statu innocencie* 2, p. 480. Cf. Augustine, *Contra Iulianum* 3.18; PL 44.721.

[220] *De volucione* 7, p. 192/13–17: "Ideo possum facere quod deus nunquam voluit
dampnacionem meam vel aliam quacunque penam ego demerior pro peccato existente in libertate mee potencie; set non impedire deum ne hoc velit, set cavere possum ne deus hoc velit."

Thus, despite the debilitating effects of original sin, people always maintain the innate ability to avoid evil, albeit with the help of God's unfailing grace. Not even the devil can tempt someone to sin to the extent that he could not resist. The divine nature, says Wyclif, dwells within the creature's free will and cannot be expelled unless the free will itself first decides to reject God. Anyone, therefore, who has been overcome by the devil must first have abandoned God, meaning that his own guilt had preceded the punishment.[221]

For all of this talk about human freedom, one must not forget that Wyclif placed the emphasis squarely on God's grace in the salvific process. Human beings are free, but they are free to respond to God's offer of grace, apart from which they could never overcome sin and be saved. It is God's grace, Wyclif insists, that brings about the aversion from evil and the conversion to the good, as well as perseverance in that good. Following an analogy borrowed from Robert Grosseteste, Wyclif contends that eternal uncreated grace assists the human soul just like the heat of the sun excites a seed to grow, while infused created grace is like the moisture of the soil, and the seed's intrinsic germinative power corresponds to the free will of the person who merits.[222] Human nature never merits without the concurrence of created grace. The grace of God not only takes the chief role in the meritorious action, but the creature is even disposed to merit by grace in ways impossible for its own unaided natural disposition.[223]

Wyclif's God is a saving God whose principal desire is to redeem all people; and that means that God extends grace to all. Wyclif paints the picture of God knocking on the door of people's hearts; some resist and refuse to let him in, while others let him in only to cast him out later. No one can be excused, therefore, since all people have the capacity to receive God's grace. Those who do accept this divine offer, however, can count on Christ's assistance so long as they will to be saved.[224] Christ is the great physician, but even

---

[221] *De volucione* 3, pp. 144–46.

[222] *De dominio divino* 3.5, pp. 240–41. Wyclif's discussion of grace here is deeply indebted to Robert Grosseteste's *Dictum* 134 (*De gracia et iustificacione hominis*). MS Bodley 798 (SC 2656), fols. 108rb–108vb.

[223] *De dominio divino* 3.5, p. 241.

[224] *Sermones* 3.19, pp. 145/35–146/1: "... gracia enim est bona voluntas Dei qua antecedenter vult omnes homines salvos fieri. Primo ergo talis obsistit Deo pulsanti ad hostium mentis et ingredi volenti, secundo admissum aut receptum abicit...."

as his medicine is thoroughly sufficient for human salvation, this does not rule out the need for concurrent causes. The medicine designed to cure sin only cooperates for full healing if the heat of charity and the humidity of contrition are also active. For it is the very nature of merit that it be voluntary, and thus cooperative.[225]

The principle of merit dominated late medieval soteriology. The theologians made a basic distinction between two different sorts: *meritum de congruo* and *meritum de condigno*, the former being a sort of half-merit, and the latter a full merit worthy of eternal reward. Speculations regarding the parameters of God's absolute power notwithstanding, no one believed that human beings did actually merit eternal life apart from divine grace. But a controversy did arise in the fourteenth century as to whether the wayfarer can, by his own efforts, obtain the gift of sanctifying grace needed to merit eternal life. The traditional position was no; a person's will must first be prepared for the gift of sanctifying grace (*gratia gratum faciens*) through the action of freely bestowed prevenient grace (*gratia gratis data*).[226] In other words, there was no merit of any kind to be had apart from grace. William of Ockham, on the other hand, argued that, by their own natural faculties (*ex puris naturalibus*), human beings could in fact perform those works which God would deem sufficient for the infusion of sanctifying grace. That is, apart from divine assistance, a person could attain that first level of merit (*meritum de congruo*), and thus receive the grace which will enable him to perform works worthy of eternal life (*meritum de condigno*).[227] Despite Ockham's insistence that unaided human effort only pertained to the initial stage of the soteriological process, and that no one can merit eternal life apart from grace, this all rang of Pelagianism in the ears of Thomas Bradwardine, and then later, Wyclif.[228]

Wyclif, no less so than any other medieval theologian, regarded the whole system of merit as indispensable. The invariable law of

---

146/21–33: "Nec sunt excusandi qui dicunt quod non est in potestate sue graciam Dei recipere, quia Isaie XLIX°, 8 . . . Christus enim assistit sic viantibus qui volunt efficaciter se salvari . . ."

[225] *Sermones* 4.54, p. 423/17–19: ". . . eo quod medicina redempcionicis Christi non proderit nisi voluntarie ipsam acceptanti et humiliter cooperanti . . ."

[226] Cf. St Bonaventure, *Breviloquium* 5.2–3; Aquinas, *ST* 1:2.112.2.

[227] See Ockham's *Quaestiones Varia* 6.11; and *Reportatio* 4.10–11.

[228] For Bradwardine's response see his massive *De causa Dei contra Pelagium* ed. Henry Saville (London, 1618; reprint, Frankfurt, 1964).

God dictates that no one is rewarded with beatitude unless he first merits worthily. Indeed, God cannot beatify a creature unless he becomes worthy of such beatitude, since it would be a contradiction for someone to be beatified if God (whose will is always just) were to allow that person to be blessed even as he remains unworthy. Thus a created spirit cannot be purely passive in this process, but must be active in making itself worthy, cooperating with grace.[229] And yet when Wyclif explains the process of merit it becomes clear that, despite the requisite human effort, the glory always remains with God. So adamant was Wyclif in stressing divine power and initiative in this process, that he went as far as to reject the possibility of someone meriting condignly before God. People can and should earn merit on the basis of their good deeds, but the best they can hope to attain is the lesser *meritum de congruo*, defined as an instance of a lord freely and graciously rewarding his humble servant. Wyclif reckons *meritum de condigno*, on the other hand, to be an exchange between two equals based purely upon justice and apart from all grace.[230] But this latter situation cannot possibly attain between God and humanity, inasmuch as Wyclif insists that God furnishes both the merit and the means to merit, even inciting the person to merit in the first place. God, in his great lordship, gives his servants all they need to merit and then later graciously rewards them. Because it is impossible for a creature to offer anything to God apart from the initial offer of divine grace, there can be no fully condign merit. Wyclif remains adamant that there is nothing that human beings have which they have not first received by God's grace (1 Cor. 4:7).[231] Like Augustine, therefore, he maintains that all merit is the result of grace, as God crowns the good works he has already bestowed.[232]

There can be no doubt, then, that Wyclif held God's grace to be essential to the salvific process from beginning to end. But, despite this utter dependence upon divine grace, the whole process still hinges on accruing merit by means of good works and thus earning one's final salvation. Hence, whatever reputation Wyclif may have as a

---

[229] *De dominio divino* 3.4, pp. 229–30.
[230] *Sermones* 3.38, pp. 315–16.
[231] *De dominio divino* 3.4, pp. 226–28.
[232] *Opus evangelicum* 3.70; 2:263. Cf. Augustine, *Epist.* 194; CSEL 57:190.

"Pre-Reformer," Lechler was surely correct over a century ago in his observation that Wyclif adhered to the traditional medieval notion of faith formed by love (i.e., works of charity) and thus cannot be counted as holding to the Reformation principle of justification by faith alone.[233] Indeed, one will find that Wyclif fully accepted the traditional medieval understanding of faith as the foundation upon which the salvific edifice is built. It is the foundation of the soul's spiritual house, he says, and humility is the cement. The walls are the four cardinal virtues of justice, prudence, fortitude and temperance, while charity and hope make up the roof.[234] Along these lines, he makes the classic medieval distinction between formed and unformed faith (rejected by the Reformers). We are only joined to Christ, says Wyclif, if we believe in him with a fully formed faith (*fides formata*), as opposed to the unformed faith which is merely an assent to doctrinal principles.[235] But this faith which believes in Christ is always a faith which must be built up, actualized, formed by the love which is borne out in good works. God demands a life led according to his justice, and Wyclif never grows tired of telling his audience that "faith without works is dead (James 2:17)."[236] That is what it means to live by the *lex Christi*: to serve Christ in humility and charity, but all the same, to adhere to a law. Wyclif's faith is still the faith of scholastic theology; it is not the trusting faith or confidence (*fiducia*) of the Wittenberg Reformers, which relies solely upon God's gracious promise in Christ to save sinners without regard to works.[237] As we have just seen, God's grace is central to the life lived righteously, and Wyclif is confident that God in his wisdom prepares what is useful for the wayfarer. Always, though, it is a cooperative effort, never Martin Luther's *iustificatio sola gratia*. For, as Wyclif says, the just God will reward the person who lives justly.[238] Justice does not come through faith alone, however; it is the product of a life lived in conformity with divine law, albeit with the indispensable help of grace, apart from which all merit is impossible.

[233] Gotthard Lechler, *John Wyclif and His English Precursors* trans. P. Lorimer (London, 1904), p. 304.
[234] *Opus evangelicum* 3.60; 2:221.
[235] *De ecclesia* 1, p. 4.
[236] *De oracione et ecclesie purgacione* 1, in *Polemical Works*, 1:343.
[237] Cf. Philip Melanchthon, *Loci Communes* in *Melanchthons Werke* 2:1, ed. Hans Engelland (Gütersloh, 1952), pp. 92–94.
[238] *De oracione* 1, pp. 343–44.

The Saved and the Damned

Related to Wyclif's ideas on grace and merit, and indeed integral to much of his thinking in general, is his doctrine of predestination: God's eternal acts of election and reprobation. First of all, we should never forget that every medieval theologian believed in predestination in one form or another. What set Wyclif apart from his fellows was only his willingness to make this doctrine such a driving theme of his ecclesiastical and political reform program. But behind all the bluster is a rather benign doctrine. It is noteworthy that he speaks of the damned only as the "foreknown" (*praesciti*), those whom God foreknew he would punish on account of the sins they freely committed. They are not actively predestined to damnation in the way that the saved are predestined to glory, but rather are permitted to remain fallen. In that sense he holds to the traditional medieval doctrine of single predestination as opposed to the double form advocated in the sixteenth century by John Calvin.[239] Taking an even milder tone than some of his medieval contemporaries, however, Wyclif did not think that the damned were intentionally passed over by God, and thus refused even the possibility of salvation.[240] Instead, he believed that, while all were lost in sin, the elect are those whom God has eternally willed to save based upon his knowledge that they would accept his universal offer of grace; while the damned are those whom God eternally willed to condemn because they had freely rejected that grace.[241]

The offer of grace to a fallen human race is by definition wholly gratuitous, a free act of mercy which no one is entitled to receive. There can be no question, therefore, of anyone meriting predestination for himself, nor even the first grace, since merit implies that one is worthy of future reward, and merit is itself impossible apart from grace.[242] To say this is not to exclude human free will on the part of the saved or the damned, however, but to underscore God's initiative and effectiveness against all human presumption. Nor does

---

[239] Cf. Calvin, *Institutes of the Christian Religion* 3.23.

[240] Cf. Aquinas, *ST* 1.23; and Scotus, *Ordinatio* 1.41.

[241] In fact, Wyclif's theory seems closest to that of the fourteenth-century Franciscan, Peter Aureol. For Aureol's theory see James L. Halverson, *Peter Aureol on Predestination: A Challenge to Late Medieval Thought* (Leiden, 1998), pp. 83–90.

[242] *De veritate* 3.30; 3:201–2.

this exclude the possibility that the foreknown could have been saved. For while the number of saved and damned is eternally fixed, these numbers are not determined by absolute necessity, but rather by hypothetical necessity, and in that way remain contingent.[243] Wyclif makes it quite clear that the damned did have the possibility of responding to grace, but having refused that offer God then withdraws himself and no longer incites them to merit. Now that the opportunity has passed for the damned, they have locked themselves into a sinfulness from which they cannot desist, and thus remain perpetually rooted in a deficiency of faith, hope and love. But again, it is only by way of hypothetical necessity that they perpetually will evil in an evil way. For, while it is now the case that they cannot desist from that evil volition, they might never have had such volition at all.[244] Wyclif will even argue that if the damned were capable of being contrite for their past sins they would receive the grace of salvation, but it is their perpetual obstinacy which prevents this. It is their great pride which does not permit them to humble themselves, for they are obstinate people who do not wish to forgive and love others.[245] It is their own character that seals their fate, a character freely chosen, and now ineluctable.

For the saved, the certainty of their predestination is founded upon the steadfastness of the elector. Christ eternally chooses every member of the Church, which is why no one can cease to be predestined; to suggest otherwise is to cast doubt on the elector himself.[246] Unfortunately, this objective assuredness remains beyond the grasp of the believer, thus offering none of the comfort that Christ's certain purpose might grant to the anxious conscience. And yet, while it is true that we do not know our predestination by either faith, demonstration, or intuition, we can still make an educated guess based upon our way of life and by the virtues God has graciously given us, especially if we are humble and rejoice in the divine law.[247] Nor will God reveal to someone his or her own damnation, since

---

[243] *Sermones* 1.34, pp. 231–32.

[244] *De veritate* 3.30; 3:219/22–27: "et sic necessaria necessitate ex supposicione volunt perpetuo malum male . . . nec possunt ab illa volucione deistere, licet illam potuerunt non habere."

[245] *De veritate* 3.30; 3:216–17.

[246] *De ecclesia* 4, p. 74.

[247] *Opus evangelicum* 3.54; 2:197.

that would drive one to despair, leading the person to cast aside virtue and enter into the devil's service. And so, seeing as nobody can know his or her final status, everyone who lives a virtuous life should do so with the hope of acquiring eternal beatitude. Indeed, all people, whether among the predestined or the foreknown, should hope for their own beatitude, seeing as God could not damn someone unless that person's own demerit were the cause, for this would violate God's own just nature. The fact remains, however, that while both the predestined and the foreknown should hope for salvation, the foreknown person is hoping for what is false; but then he is the very reason for its falsity.[248]

Wyclif was hardly alone in denying the wayfarer insight into his final destiny. It was generally accepted throughout the Middle Ages that, short of a special revelation, no one can know whether he or she is among the elect.[249] Despite all the uncertainty of election, however, Wyclif does not want to sow doubt in the minds of pious Christians. Thus, while it is true that no wayfarer can know for certain that he is not of the devil, he should still hope that he is not. And when he sees others doing good he ought to suppose that they are also numbered among the saved. Indeed, says Wyclif, the Christian should believe as a matter of faith that if he perseveres in God's commandments he will be saved.[250] The faithful Christian need not be burdened by nagging doubts regarding his relationship to God, therefore; the more steadfastly someone keeps God's law, the more confident that person can be that he loves his God. For just as the commandments of God are all inter-connected, so is their observance connected to one's love for God, who is himself the lovable object of this law.[251] One need not despair, therefore, unless one freely chooses to distrust God, thereby joining the devil in voluntary obstinacy. No one is condemned if he is willing to be converted to the Lord; and were the person so willing, God would receive him unto his mercy. For God is both fair and merciful, and cannot hate any creature except for reason of sin; and every sin is born of human free will. Hence, if those who were otherwise damned would

---

[248] *De statu innocencie* 9, p. 514.
[249] Cf. Aquinas, *ST* 1.23.1. This was also upheld at the Council of Trent (Denzinger, 1540).
[250] *De dyabolo et membris eius* 2, p. 1.
[251] *De amore*, in *Opera Minora*, p. 9.

willingly turn to God, then, in keeping with the fruits of repentance, God would lovingly accept them unto grace, provided that their own pride does not get in the way. So great is God's mercy that it extends itself even among the ranks of the damned, for he punishes them mercifully, still granting them not only their very being, but many subsequent benefits that exceed their merits.[252]

Human beings may not know their eternal status, but Wyclif thinks they can be reasonably certain whether they are in a present state of sin or grace. If we love anything more than God we are outside of grace, while if we love him above all creatures then we abide in grace.[253] Wyclif sums up the whole Christian religion as being based upon the love of God, such that every faithful Christian must learn the art of love upon which rests all human salvation and the principle of every good. The more a person knows of the art of love the wiser he is; and the one who abides by it will never fall from the path, since it is the most secure charter for all those seeking the kingdom of heaven.[254] Charity must be extolled, therefore, above all other virtues, since it exceeds them all in its necessity, usefulness, and stability. It is the root of all good, the supreme virtue which makes all the other gifts better, informing them all. Everything leads back to Christ, though, for he is that uncreated charity whose way of life must always be imitated. As we observed earlier, to follow the law of Christ is to be conformed to Christ in love; this is the path to salvation. And while it is true that no wayfarer can know whether his is the charity of predestination, there is no surer sign that one really does have the habit of charity than to observe and defend the freedom of Christ's law. Thus, even if the soul's possession of the habit itself cannot be verified, the acts of the soul are very well known to us, and that knowledge can form the basis of our hope, trusting that if we ultimately persevere in Christ's law we will be saved.[255] For Wyclif, the whole question of grace and merit, and the mystery of predestination itself, only finds its fulfillment in the human being's ontological transformation. The Christian life is about conformity to the triune God. If our works are conformed to

---

[252] *De mandatis* 19, p. 245.

[253] *Differentia inter peccatum mortale et veniale* in *De mandatis*, p. 528. Cf. Augustine *Ennarationes in Psalmos* 80, 21; CCSL 39:1133–34.

[254] *De mandatis* 11, p. 93.

[255] *Sermones* 3.18, pp. 138–42.

the vestige of the Holy Trinity then, on account of that likeness, they must be pleasing to God. If not, they must be hateful owing to their deformity. In fact, all works are reducible to these three: the love of the Father who accomplishes such great deeds, the grace of the Son who knows the will of the Father, and the perseverance of the Spirit through whom we may perfectly live.[256]

Last Things

We have noted that in Wyclif's later years he came to view the mendicant orders as accomplices of Antichrist, their popularity and power sure signs of the final age. In addition to the emergence of the mendicant orders, Wyclif believed that the Great Schism (1378–1417) was a prelude to Armageddon and the final battle against evil. Here again one may detect the influence of Joachim of Fiore, as well as the Franciscan Spirituals, as Wyclif attempted to combine Augustine's world-week schema with Joachim's three ages.[257] But even as Wyclif was convinced that he lived in the last and worst days, he was prudent enough not to make any exact predictions. In fact, he reckoned it futile to predict the precise time of the Lord's second coming and thought Joachim and many others were deceived in their vain prognostications.[258] Christ conceals from the faithful not only their own predestination and time of death, but also the hour of the Final Judgment, which is why presumptuous calculators of the last day, like Joachim, have all failed so miserably.[259] This is not to say that Wyclif did not value Joachim's teachings, however. For he had specifically appealed to the Calabrian Abbot when predicting that the fourth apocalyptic plague would be a clerical assault upon the laity through the exaction of temporal goods, all the while stoked by that fervor of malice which precedes the advent of Antichrist.[260] It is true that Christ has not informed the faithful just how long Antichrist's persecution will last, but Wyclif finds some consolation in knowing that it shall last only as long as Christ has determined.[261]

---

[256] De mandatis 10, p. 83.
[257] Wilks, "Great Persecution," pp. 189–92.
[258] Super textus Matthei XXIV 7, in Opera Minora, p. 375.
[259] Opus evangelicum 3.58; 2:216.
[260] De civili dominio 1.41; 1:325–26; ibid., 3.14; 3:258.
[261] Opus evangelicum 3.52; 2:191.

Confident that God's will be done, the faithful are not going to mur-
mur against God, but will instead accept all that befalls them with
patience and joy, resting assured that God has ordained it for their
good. The heresy and schism wrought by Antichrist will all work to
the good of the Church, especially for those who stand firm in the
faith.[262]

We have seen Wyclif complain bitterly of the treatment meted
out to his poor gospel preachers, itself another sign of the End Time.
Just as Christ was called a blasphemer, so now the faithful remnant
who stand firm in the truth of God's law are persecuted as heretics
by Antichrist. All the while Magog is subverting the faith in the private schools where his accomplices congregate. But even though
Antichrist hides his hypocrisy and heresies now, the day will come
when his falsehoods will be brought to light. And then the soldiers
of Christ, like children of light, will withdraw their temporal support from him (i.e., disendow the Church), and the true light of the
orthodox faith will once again shine.[263] That glorious day has not
arrived yet, and until it does the faithful remnant will have to suffer.
Indeed, as Wilks has pointed out, the prospect of martyrdom was
very much in keeping with Wyclif's apocalypticism, and it coincides
with his idealization of the primitive Church. Wyclif complained that
martyrdom is little valued now, though he and his band of poor
priests were prepared to suffer in these final days to secure England's
redemption. But Wilks has also noted that, for all of Wyclif's talk
about the great persecution and impending martyrdom, there is little to show that the Wycliffites actually faced such serious dangers
in the late fourteenth century. Most bishops at this point moved very
cautiously against them and no one was put to death.[264]

The End Time may be drawing nigh, but Wyclif assures his followers that no matter how grim things look now, God will finally
prevail against the devil. And it is under that hope that the faithful
should patiently bear their injuries, believing that they will find justice. Like most of his contemporaries, Wyclif maintained that, just
as we cannot know exactly when the judgment will take place, nor
can we know where. Perhaps, as was the common expectation, it

---

[262] *Opus evangelicum* 3.53; 2:196.
[263] *De solucione satanae* 1; 2:397–400.
[264] Wilks, "Great Persecution," pp. 180–82.

will be in the Valley of Jehoshaphat (Joel 3:2), though Wyclif will not venture a guess. It is enough to have faith that the day will come, and to hope that our meritorious lives will bring us to salvation.[265] Also in keeping with the general consensus, Wyclif believed that the dead will rise with the very same body which was actuated by their soul when they lived here on earth, as God will be able to gather up all the atoms of that body. Again, like most, he held that the bodies of the saints would attain a new level of subtlety, clarity, impassibility, and agility since, of the four primal elements, these bodies will be composed of less water and earth, though more air and fire. And this leads him to conclude that presently corpulent people will end up carrying around less matter in heaven following the resurrection.[266]

Wyclif looks as well to the Apocalypse of St John for guidance on the final state of the Church. The descent of the New Jerusalem refers to the souls of the saints coming down to collect their bodies in preparation for the Final Judgment (Rev. 21:1–8). This is the holy city of saints united by perfect charity. It seems likely that both the saved and the damned will know their sentences before that day, lest those descending from heaven be miserable and those coming up from hell retain the hope of salvation. After they all hear the general sentence, however, the damned will be all the more sorrowful and the saved all the more joyous. When the spirits of the saved make their descent they will then prepare to be invested with that subtle, agile, radiant, and immortal body. At this time there will no longer be any stones, minerals, herbs or vegetables, nor beasts, reptiles or birds; there will only be two types of bodies, those of the blessed and those of the damned. With respect to the physical universe, Wyclif concludes that the two parts of the sublunary sphere which are currently stirred up and irregularly mixed will finally be restored. Following the Day of Judgment these elements will be separated and each put in its proper place. At that time the whole sphere of fire and air and earth will be purged so that it may then exist in due proportion and complete clarity. The individual elements will be

---

[265] *Trialogus* 4.40, pp. 389–90. Aquinas (*ST* suppl., 89.3–4) also said that the time of the judgment is known only to God. But he thought it likely, though not certain, that it would take place in the vicinity of the Valley of Jehoshaphat.

[266] *Trialogus* 4.41, pp. 393–97. Cf. Aquinas, *ST* suppl., 79–85.

clearer than they are now and all the darkness and turbulence will be cast into hell. This, in turn, will mean that the whole sensible world outside of hell will be more radiant, purer, and more stable.[267]

As for the lot of the damned, Wyclif's description of hell is basically in keeping with other medieval theologians: a dark netherworld at the center of the earth where the damned suffer both the lack of the beatific vision and the pain of unceasing material flames.[268] The damned will be as locked into their punishment as the blessed are secure in their bliss. And as the blessed will enjoy gifts in body and soul, so the damned will endure perpetual punishment in both. Wyclif cautions, though, that one must read those Gospel passages figuratively which speak of the many pains like gnashing of teeth (Matt. 8:12), even though it is still true that the damned will experience a bodily distress greater than anyone here on earth can feel. Whether their bodies will be crowded into a small space, or will be composed of more earth and water than other elements, Wyclif leaves to others to figure out. There, at the center of the earth, far removed from heaven and thus bereft of light, the damned will endure more than physical pain. It is the loss of the beatific vision that will be the root of their punishment, filling their souls with sorrow. Nor will they even enjoy the consolation of the mutual charity, but instead must face the desolation of their own accursed fellowship. Yet, for all the punishment they have to endure, it is still better for the damned to suffer than not to exist at all, since even as they abide eternally condemned they continue to reap many gifts from God.[269]

While the damned endure such woe the blessed will gaze upon the face of Christ and finally rest in the eternal understanding of his divinity. All the powers of the blessed soul will abide perpetually in their most perfect operation without dormition. And Christ, who is the bread of life, will satiate them with his everlasting gospel.[270] It is in that blessed country that the faithful will finally be conformed to Christ, the very goal of the entire Christian life. This hope is expressed movingly in Wyclif's own personal confession: "I am cer-

---

[267] *Sermones* 4.63, pp. 492–94. Compare similar accounts in Bonaventure's *Breviloquium*, 7.4; and Aquinas, *ST* suppl., 74.1–5.

[268] Again, Compare Wyclif with Bonaventure's *Breviloquium*, 7.6; and Aquinas, *ST* suppl., 97.4–5.

[269] *Trialogus* 4.43, pp. 400–2.

[270] *Trialogus* 4.44, pp. 403–4.

tain that if I were to persevere in confessing the truths of the gospel even unto death, and so order my life according to that perfect end, forsaking earthly vanities by having crucified both my flesh and the world, then I would become a friend to the Church's bridegroom, dwelling with her in his house forever. It is in this way that I will be a friend to Holy Mother Church, having been perfectly incorporated into her bridegroom. That is why I must forsake the conclusions of the flesh and the world, following Christ in poverty, if I am worthy to be crowned."[271]

---

[271] *De veritate* 1.14, 1:357/2–11: "certus sum enim, si vixero in confessione earum [veritates evangelicae] usque ad mortam et habeam consumatam conversacionem correspondentem, quod relinquam mundum et temporalia per carnis et mundi crucifixionem et per consequens fiam amicus sponsi ecclesie per eternam domus sue cohabitacionem, et sic ero amicus sancte matris ecclesie, quia sponsi per consumatam incorporacionem. conclusiones itaque carnis et seculi oportet me deserere et sequi Cristum in pauperie, si debeam coronari."

WYCLIF AND THE ENGLISH BIBLE

Mary Dove

Wyclif and the text of Scripture

In the England in which John Wyclif grew up, there was a Bible in French, and English versions of biblical material were increasingly available as English began to rival French as a vernacular, but there was no English Bible.[1] The late-medieval Latin Bible was a descendant of translations of the Jewish and Christian Scriptures made by Jerome (c. 346–420) and earlier translators.[2] Having been commissioned by Pope Damasus to revise the existing Latin translations of the Greek New Testament,[3] Jerome completed his revision of the Latin Gospels by 383/4 and continued to work on translation of the biblical text until 405.[4] By the early fifth century, the Latin Bible incorporating Jerome's translations consisted of the following elements: Jerome's revision of the Old Latin translations of books of the Jewish Scriptures made from the Greek of the Septuagint;[5] Jerome's translation of all

---

[1] On the French Bible completed c. 1235–60, and the *Bible historiale*, see Clive R. Sneddon, "The 'Bible du XIIIᵉ siècle': its Medieval Public in the Light of its Manuscript Tradition," in *The Bible and Medieval Culture*, ed. W. Lourdaux and D. Verhelst (Louvain, 1979), pp. 127–40.

[2] On Jerome's translation of Scripture, and other early Latin translations, see H.F.D. Sparks, "Jerome as Biblical Scholar," in *The Cambridge History of the Bible*, vol. 1: *From the Beginnings to Jerome*, ed. P.R. Ackroyd and C.F. Evans (Cambridge, 1970), pp. 510–41; E.F. Sutcliffe, "Jerome," in *The Cambridge History of the Bible*, vol. 2: *The West From The Fathers To The Reformation*, ed. G.W.H. Lampe (Cambridge, 1969), pp. 80–101, and H.J. White, "Vulgate," in *A Dictionary of the Bible*, vol. 4, ed. James Hastings (Edinburgh, 1902), pp. 873–90.

[3] The first clear evidence for a Latin translation of the NT is c. 180, Pierre Nautin, "Bibelübersetzungen I," *Theologische Realencyclopëdie* 6 (1980), p. 172.

[4] On Damasus's commission, see Sparks, *The Cambridge History of the Bible*, 1:513–14, and White, "Vulgate," pp. 873–74. White provides a useful chronology of Jerome's biblical translations, p. 876.

[5] Including at least Job and Psalms (twice); Jerome's first translation of Psalms may be the text now known as the "Roman Psalter;" the second is the "Gallican Psalter," and the third the "Hebrew Psalter," see Sparks, *The Cambridge History of the Bible*, 1:514. Raphael Loewe argues that Jerome's revision of the Old Latin was available *in toto* to Cassiodorus, *The Cambridge History of the Bible*, 2:116; see also White, "Vulgate," p. 875.

the books of the Jewish Scriptures from the Hebrew (a Latin translation without any precursors); Jerome's translations of Tobit and Judith from Aramaic; unrevised Old Latin translations of the rest of the Old Testament (included in the Septuagint but not in the Jewish Scriptures); Jerome's revision of the Old Latin translations of the Gospels from Greek;[6] and the rest of the New Testament in an Old Latin translation from Greek—revised, but perhaps not by Jerome.[7]

Wyclif, in his *De veritate Sacrae Scripturae,* "On the Truth of Holy Scripture," 1377–8, reminds his readers of the well-known fact that "Blessed Jerome . . . in his own time was harshly criticized [as a translator] by Augustine and his other rivals."[8] Familiar with Old Latin translations, and believing the Greek textual tradition of the Jewish Scriptures to be superior to the Hebrew tradition, Augustine regarded as unsound Jerome's decision to translate the Jewish Scriptures from Hebrew.[9] Old Latin translations from the Septuagint and alternative Old Latin translations of the Gospels continued to exist alongside Jerome's translations, so that the Latin Bible entered the Middle Ages in a state of considerable textual complexity. Awareness of the wide variety of texts and readings preserved in biblical manuscripts resulted in several attempts at establishing a correct and homogeneous text of the Latin Bible, notably by Cassiodorus in the mid sixth century, the Northumbrian Alcuin (commissioned by Charlemagne, in 797), Alcuin's contemporary Theodulf of Orleans, Lanfranc of Bec in the late eleventh century and Stephen Harding in the middle of the twelfth century.[10]

---

[6] See Sparks, *The Cambridge History of the Bible,* 1:527–29.

[7] Sparks argues that Jerome did not revise the other books of the NT, *The Cambridge History of the Bible,* 1:519–20, 522, but for a contrary view see White, "Vulgate," p. 874.

[8] *De veritate Sacrae Scripturae* 1.11, ed. Rudolf Buddensieg, 3 vols. (London, 1905–7), 1:232/17–20: "beatus Ieronymus . . . tempore suo passus est ab Augustino et aliis emulis suis calumpniam."

[9] On the reception of Jerome's translation, see Sparks, *The Cambridge History of the Bible,* 1, 544–46; Loewe, *The Cambridge History of the Bible,* 2:102; White, "Vulgate," p. 876. On Augustine's response, see Gerald Bonner, *The Cambridge History of the Bible,* 1:544–46.

[10] On the history of the text of the Latin Bible, see Samuel Berger, *Histoire de la Vulgate pendant les premiers siècles du moyen âge* (Paris, 1893) [to the end of the Merovingian period]; H.H. Glunz, *The History of the Vulgate in England from Alcuin to Roger Bacon* (Cambridge, 1933) [on the Gospels only]; Laura Light, "Versions et revisions du texte biblique," in *Le Moyen Age et la Bible,* ed. Pierre Riché and Guy Lobrichon (Paris, 1984), pp. 55–93 [from the 9th to the 13th cent.]; Raphael Loewe, "The Medieval History of the Latin Vulgate," in *The Cambridge History of the Bible,* 2:102–54; White, "Vulgate," pp. 877–79, 886–69.

Until 800, nearly half of all biblical manuscripts were manuscripts of the Gospels alone; pandects (manuscript-volumes containing all the books of the Old and New Testaments) were enormous and rare.[11] Developments in the technology of manuscript-production in France in the late twelfth century enabled pandects of a practical size to be produced,[12] and from the 1230s multiple copies of portable Bibles written in a tiny hand on ultra-thin ("uterine") vellum were sold by the Paris stationers to friars, monks and seculars.[13] The Franciscan polymath Roger Bacon lamented in the late 1260s that what he calls the "exemplar Parisiense" (Parisian copytext) of the Bible, and dates to the late 1220s, was more corrupt than earlier texts of the Latin Bible, and that the *Correctorium Bibliae* (a list of variant readings rather than a "corrected" text) produced by the Dominicans of St.-Jacques at the University of Paris, and promulgated by the Dominican General Chapter in 1236, only multiplied error.[14]

Bacon's opinion is cited by Richard Ullerston of the Queen's College, Oxford, in his *determinacio* on biblical translation (1401), as one of the reasons against translating the Latin Bible into English: "If formerly the translation was faithful and is now corrupt, it is dangerous to translate according to it."[15] Bacon, says Ullerston, attributes the corrupt nature of the translation to ignorance of the original languages, "apparent [according to Bacon] throughout the Bible."[16]

---

[11] Florence, Biblioteca Medicea-Laurenziana Amiatino 1 [Codex Amiatinus], written in Northumbria around 700, has 1030 large folios, see Christopher De Hamel, *The Book: A History of the Bible* (London, 2001), pp. 33–34 and pls. 16–17; the leaves measure 505 by 340mm, p. 34.

[12] Laura Light, "French Bibles c. 1200–30: a new look at the origin of the Paris Bible," in *The Early Medieval Bible: Its Production, Decoration and Use*, ed. Richard Gameson (Cambridge, 1994), pp. 155–76, esp. 158–59.

[13] De Hamel argues that it was in particular the Dominican and Franciscan friars who created the demand for these portable Bibles, *The Book: A History of the Bible*, pp. 129–33; see also Beryl Smalley, *The Study of the Bible in the Middle Ages*, 3rd ed (Oxford, 1983), pp. 196–263.

[14] *Opus Tertium* (ca 1266–8), J.S. Brewer, ed., *Rogeri Bacon Opera Quedam Hactenus Inedita* (London, 1859), pp. 92–7. See also Gilbert Dahan, *L'exégèse chrétienne de la Bible en Occident médiéval: XII⁰–XIV⁰ siècle* (Paris, 1999), pp. 161–238; Loewe, "The Medieval History of the Latin Vulgate," pp. 147–51, and Smalley, *The Study of the Bible in the Middle Ages*, pp. 329–33.

[15] Vienna, Osterreichische Nationalbibliothek MS 4133, fol. 195v: "si ab olim translacio erat fidelis et modo corrupta, periculosum est secundum illam transferre." Ullerston's tract is unedited; the contents of his *determinacio* are discussed by Kantik Ghosh, *The Wycliffite Heresy: Authority and the Interpretation of Texts* (Cambridge, 2002), pp. 86–93, 102–111; also Anne Hudson, "The Debate on Bible Translation, Oxford 1401," in *Lollards and their Books* (London, 1985), pp. 67–84.

[16] Ullerston, ibid.

Bacon himself knew some Hebrew, as well as Greek.[17] Ullerston argues, against Bacon, that an established text will always be preferred to a new text, until the new text becomes established in its turn. Augustine, he says, thought Jerome's translation of the Jewish Scriptures from the Hebrew inferior to translations from the Septuagint, but "because the Church prefers Jerome's translation, Augustine, if he were alive now, would have chosen it above all others."[18] Sympathetic to Wyclif, although not himself a Wycliffite, the orthodox Ullerston determines in favor of translation, while at the same time upholding the authority of the Church, and scarcely understanding the linguistic issues Bacon is raising.[19]

Bacon's harsh words about the text of the "Paris Bible" properly relate to late-medieval French Bibles more generally; they characteristically include a considerable degree of interpolation, derived from glosses and from the writings of the Fathers, as well as textual errors and inferior readings.[20] Ignorance of the original languages of Scripture was, however, beginning to be remedied. Bacon greatly admired Robert Grosseteste (1175–1253, Bishop of Lincoln from 1235), who learnt Greek late in life, and promoted, among other linguistic projects, an interlinear translation of Psalms from the Hebrew.[21] The Cistercian Stephen Harding had consulted Jewish rabbis when preparing his recension,[22] but in the thirteenth century interest in the Hebrew biblical text was predominantly the preserve of Franciscans.[23]

The most significant work of biblical textual scholarship in the later Middle Ages, Nicholas of Lyra's *Postilla litteralis et moralis in Vetus*

---

[17] On Bacon's Hebrew, see Deeana Copeland Klepper, "Nicholas of Lyra and Franciscan Interest in Hebrew Scholarship," in *Nicholas of Lyra: the Senses of Scripture*, ed. Philip D.W. Krey and Lesley Smith (Leiden, 2000), pp. 295–96, and Smalley, *The Study of the Bible in the Middle Ages*, pp. 332–33.

[18] Fol. 200r: "quia ecclesia prefert translacionem Ieronimi, ipsam pre ceteris preeleg[eret] Augustinus, si modo uiueret." See Ghosh, *The Wycliffite Heresy*, pp. 104–5.

[19] Ullerston's Wycliffite sympathies are discussed by Hudson, "The Debate on Bible Translation," pp. 79–80. Ghosh notes that Ullerston concedes Bacon's point that "translaciones longius deriuate sunt imperfecciores," but Ullerston falls back on arguing that knowledge of things signified is more important than changing verbal signs, *The Wycliffite Heresy*, p. 105.

[20] Light, "French Bibles c. 1200–1230," p. 157.

[21] Klepper, "Nicholas of Lyra and Franciscan Interest in Hebrew Scholarship," pp. 292–93, and Smalley, *The Study of the Bible in the Middle Ages*, p. 343.

[22] Smalley, *The Study of the Bible in the Middle Ages*, pp. 79, 81. Harding's Bible is now Dijon, Bibl. de la Ville 9bis.

[23] Klepper, "Nicholas of Lyra and Franciscan Interest in Hebrew Scholarship," pp. 297–302.

et Novum Testamentum, 1322–31, is informed throughout by Lyra's familiarity with the writings of Rashi (Solomon ben Isaac of Troyes, 1045–1105) and other medieval Jewish scholars of Scripture.[24] Following Bacon, Lyra cautions his readers against trusting the Hebrew tradition uncritically: he believes that the Jews have deliberately corrupted their own ancient texts where they referred openly to the divinity of Christ.[25] Special cases excepted, Lyra's commentary strongly reinforced Bacon's argument that biblical scholars needed to return, in the Old Testament, to Jerome's translation of the *hebraica veritas*, the authentic Hebrew text.[26] When Wyclif, at the height of his academic career in Oxford, decided to take the ambitious step of lecturing on the entire Bible, for advanced university students, he was heavily dependent on Lyra,[27] whom Wyclif regarded as a "recent and yet copious and clever interpreter of the Bible."[28]

Wyclif does not, however, follow Lyra in commenting on the Bible from Genesis to the Apocalypse; no doubt he wanted the shape of his commentary (and perhaps also the lecture series from which it derived) to appear quite different from Lyra's. His unprinted, incomplete commentary on the Bible, *Postilla super Totam Bibliam* (which Williell Thomson dates c. 1371–6, but which Pamela Gradon suggests was completed and revised during Wyclif's years in Lutterworth, 1381–6), divides the Bible into eight parts, a division borrowed from the Franciscan Peter Aureol and resting on Aristotelean determinations about the *causa formalis*, that is, the generic and stylistic characteristics of biblical books.[29] The five surviving parts of Wyclif's

---

[24] Ed. Conradus Sweynheym and Arnoldus Pannartz, 5 vols. (Rome, 1471–72). There is no modern edition. On Lyra's life (1270–1349) and works, see Krey and Smith, *Nicholas of Lyra: the Senses of Scripture*, pp. 1–12.

[25] This is "a charge almost as old as Christian scholarship itself," Klepper, "Nicholas of Lyra and Franciscan Interest in Hebrew Scholarship," p. 296; see also p. 384, below.

[26] *Opus Minus*, p. 332; Smalley, *The Study of the Bible in the Middle Ages*, p. 331.

[27] Gustav A. Benrath says "[d]ie Benutzung der Postille Lyras ist in Wyclifs Bibelkommentar vom Anfang bis zum Ende auf Schritt und Tritt nachweisbar," *Wyclifs Bibelkommentar* (Berlin, 1966), p. 10. Smalley points out that the inc. and expl. to Wyclif's postill on Job are same as Lyra's, "John Wyclif's *Postilla super Totam Bibliam*," *Bodleian Library Record* 4 (1953), p. 190.

[28] *De veritate Sacrae Scripturae* 1.12; 1:275: "novellus tamen copiosus et ingeniosus postillator scripture."

[29] On Wyclif's *Postilla*, see Benrath, *Wyclifs Bibelkommentar* and Smalley, "John Wyclif's *Postilla super Totam Bibliam*," pp. 186–205. On the date, see Williell R. Thomson, *The Latin Writings of John Wyclyf* (Toronto, 1983), pp. 192–215, and Pamela Gradon, "Wyclif's *Postilla* and his Sermons", in Helen Barr and Ann M. Hutchison,

commentary are Job/Ecclesiastes, books which teach, according to Aureol, "dialectically and disputatively," Psalms/the Song of Songs/ Lamentations, which teach "hymnically and as if poetically and singingly (*decantative*)," the Prophets, who teach "prophetically and declaringly (*declarative*)," and, more conventionally, the Gospels, and the other books of the New Testament.[30] There are two postills on the Song of Songs, the prologue to the second postill being, as Smalley demonstrates, the inaugural lecture Wyclif delivered when he incepted as a Doctor of Divinity in 1372.[31]

If Wyclif does not make a great deal of the generic and stylistic determinants of the parts derived from Aureol, it is doubtless because his chief concern is with interpretive issues relating to the Bible as a whole. The biblical commentary is not an ideal mode for him; for each biblical book he depends on Lyra for an overall framework of interpretation, and comes into his own only in discussions of the issues raised by individual verses.[32] The postill on the Prophets contains some of the most interesting material in the surviving commentary. In the prologue to the postill, Wyclif argues, following Augustine, that biblical rhetoric is different from pagan rhetoric in that the sense does not depend on rhetorical flourishes, which rhetoricians in his own day, too, labor over at the expense of meaning.[33] Again following Augustine, Wyclif gives the first verse of Genesis as an example of the multiple meanings of unembellished Scripture. Wyclif has learned from Lyra and from Richard FitzRalph, Archbishop

---

Text and from Wyclif to Bale: Essays in Honour of Anne Hudson (Turnhout, 2005), pp. 75–77. The eight-part division of the Bible occurs in Aureol's *Compendium sensus litteralis totius divinae scripturae*, ed. P. Seeboeck (Quaracchi, 1896). The three parts that do not survive in Wyclif's *Postilla* are the Pentateuch, the historical books and Proverbs/Wisdom/Ecclesiasticus; see Benrath, *Wyclifs Bibelkommentar*, p. 4. On the influence of Aristotle on biblical *accessus*, see A.J. Minnis, *Medieval Theory of Authorship: Scholastic Literary Attitudes in the Later Middle Ages*, 2nd ed. (Aldershot, Hants, 1988).

[30] *Compendium sensus litteralis*, pp. 28–29.

[31] St John's Coll. Oxf. 171, fols 323v–326v; "Wyclif's *Postilla* on the Old Testament," pp. 271–79. The second postill finishes at the end of Song of Songs 3.

[32] Beryl Smalley whimsically describes Wyclif's recipe for the *Postilla* as "use Auriol's *Compendium* as a mould, pour in Lyre, flavour with Augustine, and sprinkle with Grosseteste," "Wyclif's *Postilla* on the Old Testament and his *Principium*," *Oxford Studies presented to Daniel Callus, O.P.* (Oxford, 1964), p. 256. Richard FitzRalph is also frequently cited.

[33] Magdalen Coll. Oxf. lat. 55, fol. 1r; Benrath, *Wyclifs Bibelkommentar*, pp. 64–65, and Rita Copeland, "Rhetoric and the Politics of the Literal Sense in Medieval Literary Theory: Aquinas, Wyclif, and the Lollards," in *Interpretation: Medieval and Modern*, ed. Piero Boitani and Anna Torti (Cambridge, 1993), p. 6.

of Armagh, to enlarge the domain of the literal sense to include all manner of figurative senses intended by the author.[34] In this first, brief verse of Genesis there is a threefold allegorical sense, a sixfold tropological (moral) sense and a twofold anagogical sense, Wyclif explains, citing Grosseteste's *Hexameron*, and because "the author undoubtedly intended all these catholic senses" they should all be called "literal senses."[35]

Later in the postill on the Prophets, Wyclif, following Lyra, makes a more elementary point about authorial intention, pointing out that both the Old and the New Testaments "often speak figuratively (*parabolice*), when there is no literal sense," as in Judges 9:8 where the trees of the wood are said to speak.[36] This "parabolic" sense, intended by the human author of Scripture, should also be understood as literal. In his commentary on Daniel, Wyclif refers to cases where there is more than one literal sense, what Lyra calls the double (or triple, or quadruple) literal sense, but Wyclif's point here is that some literal senses take precedence over others, though all are authentic. His example, taken from the second prologue to Lyra's *Postilla litteralis*, is that God says concerning Solomon "I shall be to him a father and he shall be to me a son (1 Chron. 17:13)," whereas the same verse is cited in Hebrews 1:5 as said literally of Christ, and this literal sense is therefore *principalior* ("more principal," a deliberate catachresis), though the literal sense according to which the son is Solomon is still a principal sense.[37] In his commentary on Galatians, Wyclif cites the same example, but his point is now that the literal sense is identical with the fullness of God's authorial intention, so that one cannot speak of "grades of authenticity of senses" in Scripture.[38] Students hearing Wyclif lecture on the Bible must sometimes have nodded as

---

[34] See A.J. Minnis, "'Authorial Intention' and 'Literal Sense' in the Exegetical Theories of Richard FitzRalph and John Wyclif: An Essay in the Medieval History of Biblical Hermeneutics," *Proceedings of the Royal Irish Academy*, vol. 75, Section C, no. 1 (Dublin, 1975).

[35] Magdalen Coll. Oxf. lat. 55, fol. 1r–v; see Benrath, *Wyclifs Bibelkommentar*, p. 65.

[36] Commenting on Jer. 31:12, Magdalen Coll. Oxf. lat. 117, fol. 107v; see Benrath, *Wyclifs Bibelkommentar*, p. 76, and Mary Dove, "Literal Senses in the Song of Songs," in *Nicholas of Lyra: the Senses of Scripture*, p. 132.

[37] Commenting on Dan. 8, Magdalen Coll. Oxf. lat. 117, fol. 201v; see Benrath, *Wyclifs Bibelkommentar*, p. 76.

[38] Gal. 4:24, Vienna, Österreichische Nationalbibliothek 1342, fols 227v–228r; see Benrath, *Wyclifs Bibelkommentar*, pp. 371–73, and Ghosh, *The Wycliffite Heresy*, pp. 41–42.

he made familiar points about the senses of Scripture, but they could never afford to assume that he would rest in the familiar.

While he was delivering his lectures on the Bible, between 1372 and 1374, Wyclif was involved in a disputation on the truth of Scripture with the Oxford Carmelite John Kynyngham.[39] Among the texts discussed by Kynyngham and Wyclif are the words of the prophet Amos to Amaziah the priest "I am not a prophet, neither am I the son of a prophet, but a herdsman, pulling up sycamore trees (Amos 7:14)."[40] Wyclif discusses the same text in his postill on the Prophets, depending on the same theory of *ampliacio temporis* ("extension of time") which he elaborates in the disputation.[41] Amos, argues Wyclif, is extending the present of the verb "to be;" he cannot mean what Gregory the Great and the *Glossa ordinaria* take him to mean, that he is not a prophet at the moment of speaking because he is not experiencing a prophetic vision.[42] Wyclif likes Lyra's explanation, that Amos means that he is not (has not been and will not be) a false prophet, but he also suggests to Kynyngham that Amos may mean that he is not a prophet by "kind," that is, by being the son of a prophet.[43] At any rate, what Amos says must be true, and true of past and future as well as present, because all times are simultaneously present to God.[44] It is unthinkable that Scripture should ever be false *de vi sermonis*, "by virtue of what it says," even if it seems to be false from a grammatical point of view and from the point of view of common sense.[45] Scripture has its own specialized mode of speaking, and always speaks the truth.

---

[39] Ian Christopher Levy, "Defining the Responsibility of the Late Medieval Theologian: the Debate between John Kynyngham and John Wyclif," *Carmelus* 49 (2002), 5–29.

[40] *Fasciculi Zizaniorum Magistri Johannis Wyclif cum Tritico*, ed. W.W. Shirley (London, 1858), 7–8, 21–29, 48–55, 458–59; see Smalley, "Wyclif's *Postilla* on the Old Testament," pp. 284–86, and Levy, "Defining the Responsibility of the Late Medieval Theologian," pp. 16–20.

[41] Magdalen Coll. Oxf. lat. 117, fols 237v–238r; see Benrath, *Wyclifs Bibelkommentar*, pp. 77–79.

[42] Magdalen Coll. Oxf. lat. 117, fols 273v, cf. Shirley, *Fasciculi Zizaniorum*, pp. 7–8; see Levy, "Defining the Responsibility of the Late Medieval Theologian," p. 17.

[43] Shirley, *Fasciculi Zizaniorum*, p. 459; see Levy, "Defining the Responsibility of the Late Medieval Theologian," pp. 18–19.

[44] See Levy, "Defining the Responsibility of the Late Medieval Theologian," pp. 10–11, and Smalley, "The Bible and Eternity: John Wyclif's Dilemma," *Journal of the Warburg and Cortauld Institutes* 27 (1964), 73–89.

[45] Shirley, *Fasciculi Zizaniorum*, p. 459; see Levy, "Defining the Responsibility of the Late Medieval Theologian," p. 19.

Wyclif's commitment to the truth of Scripture becomes the subject of his major work on the Bible, *De veritate Sacrae Scripturae*. In chapter ten of the first book of *De veritate*, Wyclif makes a powerful and subtle case for both the Old and the New Testaments being the word of God and totally authentic, "for the law contained in the Church's manuscripts, commonly called 'writ' (*scriptura*), is the law that God gave to his Church" (Church, that is, including the Jews of the Old Testament), and God would never permit his Church to be deprived of his law.[46] The chapter is a dazzling exegesis of biblical intertextuality. Wyclif goes on to rehearse the points his opponents make about the long history of textual corruption.[47] First, even if the text of Jewish Scripture had originally been given *indefectibiliter*, incorruptibly, "it does not seem necessary to believe that Ezra correctly restored it" after the return from the Babylonian exile (4 Ezra 14).[48] Second, "it is not necessary to believe that Blessed Jerome translated incorruptibly": Augustine and others certainly did not think so.[49] Third, the corrupt nature of modern scribes makes it impossible to be sure that the text of the Latin Bible has been corrected where it was in error.[50]

Contra, Wyclif maintains that there are three things it is necessary for himself and his readers to believe: first, that the Jewish Scriptures (the twenty-two books accepted by both Jews and Christians, as detailed by Jerome in his prologue to 1 Kings) are *autentici*, completely authentic,[51] and that "there is no difference in sense found in our Latin books and the books of the Jews."[52] Second, Jerome's translation is commended by the "the holiness of his life" to which Augustine testifies, as much as by his linguistic expertise and faithful rendering of the original languages of Scripture.[53] Third, the deficiencies of

---

[46] 1.10; 1, p. 206/15–17: "lex codicum ecclesie , vocata vulgariter scriptura, sit lex, quam deus dedit sue ecclesie." On the meaning of *ecclesia*, see 1, 228/12–13.

[47] See Ghosh, *The Wycliffite Heresy*, pp. 57–59.

[48] 1.11; 1, p. 232/13–16: "non videtur oportere credere quod Hesdras recte restituit scripturam hebraicam." According to 4 Ezra 14, Ezra dictated a perfect text by divine inspiration to five scribes for forty days.

[49] 1.11; 1, p. 232/16–19: "nec oportet . . . credere, quod beatus Ieronymus indefectibiliter transtulit." Wyclif refers to Augustine's *Epist.* 82 [to Jerome], ed. Alois Goldbacher, CSEL 34.2 (Vienna, 1898), pp. 351–87.

[50] 1.11; 1, p. 232/21–23.

[51] 1.11; 1, p. 233/22–24. On Jerome's prologue to 1 Kings, the *Prologus Galeatus*, see F. Stegmüller and N. Reinhardt, *Repertorium Biblicum Medii Aevi*, vol. 1 (Madrid, 1950), no. 323.

[52] 1.11; 1, p. 234/2–3: "inter nostros libros latinos et suos hebreos non est in sensu diversitas."

[53] 1.11; 1, p. 234/24. The letter of Augustine "De Sanctitate Ieronymi," 233/25, is not otherwise known.

contemporary texts of the Bible are the consequence of the sin of the Church. "Manuscripts," that is, particular texts of the Bible, "are nothing but substitutes, necessary for a limited time only; the meaning, however, is always required, and thus it is necessary that the catholic faith should reside within the entire Mother Church."[54]

Kantik Ghosh argues that Wyclif "takes the easy way out" here; that he "is indeed aware of the central relevance of textual matters to his ideology of authority, but refuses to acknowledge this relevance."[55] This seems unjust to Wyclif, who is concerned to defend the overall veracity of the Bible against assertions that textual errors undermine its holiness. He did not reach the position he espouses in *De veritate* easily: it was partly because of the textual problems associated with the late-medieval Bible, highlighted by Lyra, that the young Wyclif was exercised about the lack of congruence between the Bible as physical book and the nature of the writing contained in it. Wyclif recalls that in his immaturity, perhaps while a boy at grammar school,[56] he "was painfully entangled in understanding and defending Scripture *de virtute sermonis*," which evidently means, in this context, "according to the literal, grammatical sense."[57] He had not realized at that stage that Scripture should be interpreted "entirely according to the sense intended by its author (*pure ad sensum autoris*);" not its human author, but God.[58] God, Wyclif says, later made it clear to him that what is written in a Bible is not in itself holy; it is "no more than the trace of a tortoise-shell on a stone" unless it can be called holy "on account of the way in which it leads the faithful by hand into knowledge of heavenly Scripture."[59]

Ghosh observes in this passage "the characteristic vertical movement of Wyclif's thought: 'Scripture' is identical with Christ and the

---

[54] 1.11; 1, p. 235/12–15: "codices non sunt nisi supposicione pro tempore necessarii, semper autem sensus requiritur, et sic necesse est in tota matre ecclesia esse fidem catholicam."

[55] *The Wycliffite Heresy*, p. 59.

[56] *De veritate* 1.4; 1:87.

[57] 1.6; 1, p. 114/1–3: "fui anxie intricatus ad intelligendum ac defendendum istas scripturas de virtute sermonis." On Wyclif's use of the phrase *de uirtute sermonis* to mean "strictly literal sense" and "intended literal sense," see Ian Christopher Levy, trans., *John Wyclif: On the Truth of Holy Scripture* (Kalamazoo, 2001), p. 33.

[58] 1.9; 1, p. 183/15. See Ghosh, *The Wycliffite Heresy*, pp. 42–45.

[59] 1.6; 1, pp. 114/25–115/3: "non plus quam vestigium testudinis super saxum . . . sacra autem nullo modo dicitur, nisi propter manuduccionem qua inducit fideles in noticiam scripture celestis."

will of God . . . the book itself is quite irrelevant."[60] It is true that only according to the fifth and lowest of Wyclif's modes of Scripture is "Holy Scripture taken to be the manuscripts . . . which are designed to recall the first truth,"[61] while the highest of Wyclif's five modes of Scripture refers to Scripture as an "open book" (Dan. 7:10), identified as the "book of life" (Rev. 20:12), in which is inscribed all truth.[62] In a highly elusive discussion of the biblical apocrypha, Wyclif says we should not think of the "book of life" as being limited to the biblical canon.[63] He has in mind the New Testament apocrypha as well as the Old Testament apocyrypha, for he specifies the Gospel of Nicodemus as well as Wisdom, Ecclesiasticus, Judith, Tobit and the Maccabees, claiming (not without justification) that what Jerome says about the books of the Old Testament apocrypha applies in the same way to "the Gospel of Nicodemus and those others which the Church has decided neither to condemn explicitly, nor explicitly canonize."[64]

Yet although the Bible as book is Scripture in the fifth and lowest mode, it cannot be called insignificant. Wyclif's neo-Platonist concept of Scripture is grounded in the material presence of the Latin Bible, the most highly-valued of books in the medieval West. His search for the truth of Holy Writ seems to have originated in an awareness of the incommensurability of material and spiritual value: he realized, he says, that truth was not to be found *de pellis bestiarum*, that is, in the vellum of manuscript pages.[65] Twice during his discussion of textual matters he asserts that individual biblical manuscripts are of no more worth than the beasts from which they were made.[66]

---

[60] *The Wycliffite Heresey*, p. 56.

[61] 1.6; 1, pp. 108/15–109/2: "quinto modo sumitur scriptura sacra pro codicibus . . . que sunt signa memorandi veritatem priorem."

[62] 1.6; 1, p. 114/9–12. On Wyclif's five modes of Scripture, see Ghosh, *The Wycliffite Heresy*, pp. 54–6; Levy, *John Wyclif: On the Truth of Holy Scripture*, pp. 14–16; A.J. Minnis, "'Authorial Intention' and 'Literal Sense'," pp. 25–7; Smalley, "The Bible and Eternity." Levy maintains against Ghosh, Minnis and Smalley that "Wyclif . . . fits quite comfortably within a continuum of biblical exegesis stretching from Augustine to Aquinas;" *John Wyclif: On the Truth of Holy Scripture*, p. 8.

[63] 1.11; 1, pp. 241–42.

[64] 1.11; 1, p. 242/9–11: "ewangelio Nichodemi et aliis, quos decrevit ecclesia nec dampnare nec explicite canonizare." On Wyclif and the apocrypha, see Anne Hudson, *The Premature Reformation: Wycliffite Texts and Lollard History* (Oxford, 1988), p. 230.

[65] 1.6; 1, p. 114/4.

[66] 1.11; 1, pp. 238/3–4, 244/8–10.

Yet it seems to this reader that he protests too much. If the potentially defective biblical text is where enquiry into the truth of Scripture begins, it surely follows that each and every Bible is a pearl without price.

Wyclif and the debate about biblical translation

Part Four of *De veritate Sacrae Scripturae* (1378) for the first time implies a context of arguments against biblical translation. Wyclif prophesies woe to the Church whose clerics are more concerned with temporal dominion and with human traditions of their own making than with preaching the law of God, which is the totality of Scripture.[67] "Spiritual profit is infinitely better than temporal," he concludes, "and spiritual profit cannot be acquired apart from the teaching of Holy Scripture."[68] An argument sometimes advanced against the necessity of preaching, says Wyclif, is the "lie that it is no longer necessary," and the reasons given are twofold: that "every old crone knows the Creed and the Lord's Prayer well enough, and that is sufficient for salvation," and that "theologians are generally said to be heretics."[69] His *contra* is that "it is necessary to preach to the very end of the earth."[70]

Although there is no mention in *De veritate Sacrae Scripturae* of translating the Bible into English, the arguments Wyclif cites against preaching the law of God are commonly encountered in the debate about biblical translation:[71] that only what is necessary for salvation needs to be known, and that exposure to the text of Scripture can lead to heresy.[72] John Kynyngham, the Oxford Carmelite who debated

---

[67] 4.20, vol. 2, pp. 129–42.

[68] 4.20; 2, p. 142/18–20: "infinitum melius [est] lucrum spirituale quam temporale . . . spirituale autem non potest acquiri sine doctrina scripture sacre," cf. 1,10; 1, 205/14–17.

[69] 4.21; 2, p. 179/7–11: "ficticia . . . quod iam non oportet predicare . . . quelibet vetula scit satis simbolum et oracionem dominicam, et hoc sufficit ad salutem . . . ut inquiunt, theologi communiter sunt heretici."

[70] 4.21; 2, p. 179/14–15: "necesse est predicare usque ad finem mundi."

[71] That the one implies the other is recognized in John Trevisa's "Dialogus inter Dominum et Clericum," see p. 389, below, and in tract 7 in Cambridge UL Ii. 6. 26, fol. 42r, ed. Simon Hunt, "An Edition of Tracts advocating Scriptural Translation and of Some Texts connected with Lollard Vernacular Biblical Scholarship," DPhil thesis, University of Oxford (1994), 2, 313/10–14.

[72] Ullerston's *determinacio*, fol. 195v, quotes Jerome to the effect that when Scripture

the senses of Scripture with Wyclif in the early 1370s, makes the point that notorious heresies have arisen from biblical verses being interpreted according to the strictly grammatical sense when they in fact invite interpretation according to the full sense intended by the author (Kynyngham here seems to be taking a leaf out of Wyclif's book).[73] If, during the 1370s, it became generally known in Oxford that Wyclif and his companions were at work on a translation of the Bible into English (more on this below), one would expect an intensification of the debate about biblical translation. In the *Trialogus* (1382/3), Wyclif for the first time unambiguously argues that readers literate in English but not in Latin should have access to Scripture in the vernacular. His desire for an English Bible is put into the mouth of the Holy Spirit, who (Wyclif says) "wishes manuscripts of the New Testament or the Old Testament to be read and studied in the common tongue," because Scripture contains all truth.[74] A new kind of reader, situated outside the university, will then be in a position to share Wyclif's detestation of those "new-fangled doctors" who claim that infinitely truthful Scripture contains logical falsehoods.[75]

Wyclif has often been associated with the principle of *sola scriptura* ("Scripture alone"), the principle that only the text of the Bible has the authority of revelation, and that tradition does not share that authority. Although Heiko Oberman shows that Wyclif accepted what he calls Tradition I, the ongoing interpretation of Scripture by the Church faithful to Christ, and rejected only Tradition II, extra-scriptural tradition,[76] the Carmelite Thomas Netter, in his *Doctrinale* (1420–30), Michael Hurley and Alastair Minnis all contend that Wyclif set himself apart from the Church and tradition in his exegesis of

---

is available in the common tongue a "garrula anus" or "delirus senex," among other incompetent or sophistical readers, may fail to understand Scripture and "depravare sententias et ad voluntatem suam scripturam trahere repugnantem," *Epistola 58, ad Paulinum*, ed. Lindberg, *The Middle English Bible: Prefatory Epistles of St. Jerome*, vol. 1 (Oslo, 1978), pp. 99–101/22–41; see also Ghosh, *The Wycliffite Heresy*, p. 88.

[73] *Fasciculi Zizaniorum*, pp. 41–2; the point is well discussed by Levy, "Defining the Responsibility of the Late Medieval Theologian," 23–26.

[74] Ed. Gotthard Lechler (Oxford, 1869), p. 240/12–13: "vult vulgares codices de lege nova vel veteri studeri et legi;" see Hunt, "An Edition of Tracts," 1, 11–12.

[75] *Trialogus*, p. 241/3–4: "doctores novelli." On Wyclif's hatred of sophists, see Levy, *John Wyclif: Scriptural Logic, Real Presence, and the Parameters of Orthodoxy* (Milwaukee, 2003), pp. 102–5.

[76] Heiko A. Oberman, *The Harvest of Medieval Theology: Gabriel Biel and Late Medieval Nominalism* (Cambridge, Mass., 1963), pp. 371–78.

Scripture.[77] Ian Levy, on the other hand, reminds us that "Wyclif considered himself loyal to the Catholic Church," and he makes the excellent point that "the decisive issue is not respect for tradition, but the assignation of authority in determining the nature of that tradition."[78] As Malcolm Lambert has argued, the translation of the Bible into English "was a natural outcome of Wyclif's doctrinal position. If the visible Church had lost its authority to mediate salvation to the people, then the word of God, properly interpreted, was the one remaining certainty."[79] Not *sola scriptura*, then, but a renewal of the authentic tradition of biblical interpretation.

Claiming direct authorization from the Holy Spirit for the work of translation looks like Wyclif's response to indications that a Bible in English would be unwelcome. The debate on the Bible in English was by no means confined to Oxford academics; the earliest unambiguous reference to Wyclif as biblical translator implies the context of a widespread discussion. Henry Knighton, writing at the Augustinian abbey of St Mary at Leicester no later than 1396, claims in his Chronicle:

> Master John Wyclif has translated from Latin into the English language—which is very far from being the language of angels—the Gospel that Christ gave to the clergy and doctors of the Church, so that they might administer it to laypeople ... As a result, because of him the content of Scripture has become more common and more open to laymen and women who can read than it customarily is to quite learned clerks of good intelligence, and thus the pearl of the gospel is scattered abroad and trodden underfoot by swine (Matt. 7:6).[80]

The editor of Knighton's Chronicle, G.H. Martin, argues that Knighton was "a close observer of the phenomenon [of Lollardy] with access to

---

[77] Hurley, "'Scriptura sola': Wyclif and his Critics," *Traditio* 16 (1960), 275–352; Minnis, "'Authorial Intention' and 'Literal Sense'," pp. 25–28.

[78] Levy, *John Wyclif*, pp. 112–22, quotation at 122.

[79] *Medieval Heresy: Popular Movements from the Gregorian Reform to the Reformation*, 2nd ed. (Oxford, 1992), p. 239; see also Gordon Leff, *Heresy in the Later Middle Ages: The Relation of Heterodoxy to Dissent c. 1250–c. 1450* (Manchester, 1967), vol. 2, pp. 511–16.

[80] Ed. G.H. Martin, *Knighton's Chronicle, 1337–1396* (Oxford, 1995), pp. 242–45: "Hic magister Iohannes Wyclif euangelium quod Cristus contulit clericis et ecclesie doctoribus, ut ipsi laycis ... ministrarent, transtulit de latino in anglicam linguam non angelicam. Vnde per ipsum fit vulgare et magis apertum laicis et mulieribus legere scientibus quam solet esse clericis admodum litteratis et bene intelligentibus, et sic euangelica margarita spargitur et a porcis conculcatur." On the date of Knighton's composite entry on Wyclif and the Wycliffites, see Martin, pp. xvi–xvii.

some particular sources of information about it."[81] We should therefore take his testimony about the authorship of the translation—the
earliest testimony there is—very seriously. The name of Wyclif, however, is not mentioned in the surviving academic *determinaciones* on
biblical translation dating from the turn of the fifteenth century,
Ullerston's, in favor, and those of two friars, the Franciscan William
Butler and the Dominican Thomas Palmer, against.[82] Only Palmer
associates translation of the Bible with the Lollards.[83]

Evidently Knighton had been privy to debates about biblical translation, since he rehearses here two of the arguments recorded elsewhere: that translation derogates from the privilege of the clergy,
and that it renders Scripture liable to fall into disrepute.

For Knighton "laymen and women who can read" are the swine
who tread the pearl of the gospel underfoot; he is not troubled by
any doubt that the gospel was one of the privileges Christ reserved
for "clericis et ecclesie doctoribus." (In his *Opus evangelicum*, 1384,
Wyclif characteristically contests this conventional reading of Matthew
7:6, associating those unworthy of the word of God with the friars,
who "argue aimlessly and uselessly about the biblical text.")[84] Knighton
recognizes, however, that in England at the end of the fourteenth
century even "quite learned clerks of good intelligence" have less
access to the gospel in Latin than literate laypeople have to the
gospel translated into English. Since biblical translation makes Scripture
"open" and "common," smudging the traditional boundaries between
clergy and laity, it is patently (in Knighton's view) a bad thing.

Palmer, who is also anxious to keep the boundaries clearly marked,
argues for a better-educated clergy. Every nation needs *clerici* who
are sufficiently learned in the language in which Scripture is preserved

---

[81] "Knighton's Lollards," in Margaret Aston and Colin Richmond, eds, *Lollardy
and the Gentry in the Later Middle Ages* (Stroud and New York, 1997), p. 1.
[82] On Ullerston, see n. 15, above. Butler's *determinacio* is preserved in Oxford,
Merton Coll. 68, fols. 102r–204v, ed. Margaret Deanesly, *The Lollard Bible and Other
Medieval Biblical Versions* (Cambridge, 1920), pp. 401–18, and discussed by Hudson,
"The Debate on Biblical Translation," pp. 67–68, and Ghosh, *The Wycliffite Heresy*,
pp. 86, 93–100, 109–10. Palmer's *determinacio* is preserved in Cambridge, Trinity
Coll. 347, fols. 2v–47v, ed. Deanesly, *The Lollard Bible*, pp. 418–37, and discussed
by Hudson, ibid., and Ghosh, *The Wycliffite Heresy*, pp. 86, 100–2.
[83] Ed. Deanesly, *The Lollard Bible*, p. 421/13–15, p. 425/22–5; see Ghosh, *The
Wyliffite Heresy*, p. 100.
[84] Ed. Johann Loserth, vol. 2 (London, 1895), p. 387/34–35: "circa textum scripture diffuse et inutiliter altercantur." Matt. 7:6 is the core text of Book 3, cc. 38–39,
pp. 383–90.

to be able "to interpret Scripture to the people by way of circumlocution."[85] Circumlocution is necessary, in Palmer's view, because access to the naked text, uninterpreted Scripture, provoked the Arian, Sabellian and Nestorian heresies, and *a fortiori* could lead "simple people" into error.[86] For fear of heresy, laypeople should not be allowed to read Scripture *ad libitum* even in Latin, according to Butler.[87] Another of Butler's fears is that the dissemination of translations of Scripture might result in inaccurate texts (*libri mendosi*), as happened in the early Church.[88] To the argument that not all Latin Bibles are free from misreadings, either, he replies that the Church has ensured that Scripture is now taught and written in universities, so that if Bibles "contain errors, they can easily be corrected."[89] One senses his relief that the Latin Bible is controlled within a clerical enclave. As Ghosh argues, Butler's model of the relation between clergy and laity is uncompromisingly hierarchical and supervisory.[90]

The *determinaciones* of Butler and Palmer both exemplify the traditional model of pedagogy identified by Rita Copeland, according to which there is a symbolic boundary between simple people, who understand Scripture on the literal, grammatical level, and "those assumed to be endowed with reason and hermeneutical perspicacity (men, clergy, *litterati*)," for whom the "higher," spiritual senses of Scripture are reserved.[91] How, given this model, could a translation of the Bible into English, without circumlocution, fail to lead the "simple people" Palmer calls *idiote circa scripturam* ("illiterate idiots as far as Scripture is concerned,") astray?[92] Unsurprisingly, those advo-

---

[85] Ed. Deanesly, *The Lollard Bible*, p. 435/13–17: "populo per circumlocutionem scripturas interpretari."

[86] Deanesly, p. 422/9–12.

[87] Deanesly, p. 401/14–15.

[88] Deanesly, p. 401/6–7.

[89] Deanesly, p. 401/12: "si . . . falsi sunt, facile possunt corrigi;" see Ghosh, *The Wycliffite Heresy*, pp. 92–3.

[90] *The Wycliffite Heresy*, pp. 93–100. Ghosh underlines the contrast between Butler's "concept of a mediated, rhetorically appropriate faith which discourages any intellectual engagement with the Bible on the part of the laity," and Wyclif's insistence on the accessibility of the biblical text, pp. 99–100.

[91] "Childhood, Pedagogy and the Literal Sense," in *New Medieval Literatures* 1, ed. Wendy Scase, Rita Copeland and David Lawton (Oxford, 1997), pp. 131–8; quotation, p. 138; also Copeland, *Pedagogy, Intellectuals and Dissent in the Later Middle Ages: Lollardy and Ideas of Learning* (Cambridge, 2001), pp. 55–98. Central to Copeland's argument is Palmer's exegesis of Deut. 22:6–7, ed. Deanesly, *The Lollard Bible*, p. 424; see Ghosh, *The Wycliffite Heresy*, p. 102.

[92] Deanesly, p. 425/22–25.

cating biblical translation retaliated with the charge that the friars were afraid of translation because they did not want the common people to see how "þei prechen sumwhat of þe gospel and gloson (gloss) it as hem likeþ," to their own temporal advantage (in the words of the of the seventh of the twelve tracts advocating biblical translation in Cambridge University Library Ii. 6. 26, c. 1410).[93] Worse, "þei pursuen (persecute) symple pepel for þei wolde[n] lerne, rede and teche þe lawe of God in here moder tonge."[94]

Crucially, as advocates of the English Bible point out, the history of the transmission of Scripture was a history of translation. "Sume [opponents of translation] seyne," according to the first of the Cambridge tracts, "þat Crist tauȝtte þe peple þe gospel and þe *pater noster* ("Our Father") frist in Latyn, and þerfor it schulde not be translated into Englische, but it is not so." Because the king of heaven wanted his law and gospel to be taught "opinly to þe pepel," Christ taught in Hebrew, the language of the people to whom he preached. Therefore, "as nedeful as it was to translate þe gospel from Ebrewe in to Grwe (Greek) and in to Latyn for helpe of þe peple þat couden noon (knew no) Ebrwe, now it is nedful and leful (lawful) to translate in to Englysche for helpe of Englisch peple."[95]

The translators of the Wycliffite Bible claim that their opponents ask "what spiryt makiþ idiotis hardi to translate now þe bible into English, siþen (since) þe foure greete doctouris [Ambrose, Augustine, Jerome and Gregory the Great] dursten (dared) neuere do þis? (*The Wycliffite Bible*, 1, 59/4–6; see n. 117)." As the translators say, this is a "lewid" (idiotic) question, no doubt introduced to enable them to remind their readers that the doctors "ceessiden neuere til þei hadden holy writ in here modir tunge of here owne puple," that is,

---

[93] Inc. "þis tretty[se] þat folewþ proueþ þat eche nacioun may lefully haue holy writ in here moder tunge," fol. 43r, ed. Hunt, "An Edition of Tracts," 2, 314/29–30. Hudson points out that the friars are also specified as opposing biblical translation in the Wycliffite *Opus Arduum* (1389–90): "docent eciam isti falsi fratres quod gradu laici quamuis litterati non debent studere scripturam sacram, nec eam habere in lingwa materna nec alias informare," Brno University Library 28, fol. 136r, *Selected English Wycliffite Writings* (Cambridge, 1978), p. 190.

[94] Fol. 45v, ed. Hunt, 2, 317/113–14. Hudson says these lines may suggest a date after 1407, *Selected English Wycliffite Writings*, pp. 190–1, but Ian Forrest shows that earlier canons anticipate Arundel's 1407/9 *Constitutiones*, "Ecclesiastical Justice and the Detection of Heresy in England, 1380–1430," DPhil thesis, University of Oxford (2003), pp. 92–99.

[95] Fol. 6r–v; ed. Hunt, 2, 261/160–262/168.

Latin, for "Latyn was a comoun langage to here puple ... as Englishe is comoune langage to oure puple (*WB*, 1, 59, 13–14)." The history of the Bible in the vernacular, in England and in Europe, is sketched in several texts arguing for biblical translation.[96] The Prologue to the Wycliffite Bible introduces this history with the exclamation: "Lord God, siþen at þe bigynnyng of feiþ so manie men translatiden into Latyn,[97] and to greet profyt of Latyn men, lat oo (one) symple creature of God translate into English, for profyt of English men (*WB*, 1, 59/26–8)." The "simple creature" (the writer's periphrasis for himself) will, after all, be following the precedent set by Bede, who translated the Bible into "Saxon," the English vernacular of his time,[98] and by King Alfred, who translated "þe bigynning of þe Sauter" [Psalms 1–50].[99] He will also be giving English people the access to Scripture in the vernacular already enjoyed by the French, the Czechs and the "Britons" (*WB*, 1, 59/29–33).[100]

Copeland attributes to the Lollards a new pedagogical model, one that refuses to acknowledge a boundary between lay and clerical potential for learning.[101] The first of the Cambridge tracts advocating biblical translation argues that "lewed curatis," men who have care of souls but little or no education in Latin, need Scripture in English to enable them to teach the people, for "now it is fulfillid þat þe prophete seid, *the little ones looked for bread and there was no one to break it for them* (Lam. 4:4)."[102] There are those who argue, says the

---

[96] Notably the tract "First seiþ Bois [Boethius]," which is closely related to Ullerston's *determinacio*, ed. C.F. Bühler, "A Lollard Tract: On Translating the Bible into English," *Medium Aevum* 7 (1938), 167–83.

[97] The writer has just quoted Augustine's *De Doctrina Christiana* on the innumerable translations of Scripture into Latin, 2.11.16, ed. J. Martin, CCSL 32 (Turnhout, 1962), p. 42/21–26.

[98] Trevisa and the tract "First seiþ Bois" say Bede translated the Gospel of John, on the authority of Higden, *Polychronicon* 5.24, ed. Joseph Rawson Lumby, *Polychronicon Ranulphi Higden*, vol. 6 (Kraus reprint, 1964), p. 224. See also Deanesly, *The Lollard Bible*, pp. 133–35.

[99] Higden, *Polychronicon* 6.1, ed. Lumby, 6, 356, and William of Malmesbury, *Gesta Regum Anglorum* 2.123. See also Deanesly, *The Lollard Bible*, pp. 134–36, and Geoffrey Shepherd, *The Cambridge History of the Bible*, 2, pp. 370–71.

[100] On vernacular translations of the Bible in medieval Europe, see *The Cambridge History of the Bible*, 2:338–491. Andrew Breeze argues that "Britons" means Welsh, in "The Wycliffite Bible Prologue on the Scriptures in Welsh," *Notes and Queries* XLVI (244) (1999), 16–17, but there was no translation of the Bible into medieval Welsh.

[101] *Pedagogy, Intellectuals and Dissent in the Later Middle Ages*, pp. 99–140.

[102] Inc. "All[e] cristine peple stant in þre maner of folke," fols 3r–v, ed. Hunt, 2, 258/72. The argument is made on the authority of the text *sicut populus sic sacerdos*,

tract (and Butler and Palmer were among them), that "lewid peple" (laypeople) should not read the Bible because it "haþ so manye vnderstondynges litera[l] and spiritual þat þe lewid pepel may not vnderstonde it."[103] The writer replies that "þe most part" of priests "vnderstonden not holy write ne þe gospel neiþer literalliche ne spiritualiche," neither in English nor in Latin, and even the wisest clerks living do not understand "al þe gospel ne al þe sauter ne al holy write litterallich and spiritualiche." Learned laypeople may understand both Latin and English better than unlearned priests do.[104]

If the laity do not know God's law, and are therefore "redi to rebelle aʒens here souereyns" and commit all manner of unlawfulness, the Church is to blame.[105] This point is evidently made in response to an implied argument given voice in the second Cambridge tract advocating translation:[106] "wordely (worldly) clirkis crien and seyn holy writt in Englische wolde make men at debate, and sougitis (subjects) to be rebel aʒeyns here soueryns."[107] The uprising of 1381 certainly raised the level of clerical anxiety about the potentially radical consequences of the teachings of Wyclif. Michael Wilks argues that the rebels were demanding the *reformatio regni* (reform of the kingdom) that Wyclif's writings ask the king to undertake,[108] and according to the St Albans chronicler Thomas Walsingham, John Ball, whom the rebels liberated from the Archbishop of Canterbury's prison, was a long-time teacher of Wyclif's perverse doctrines.[109] William Courtenay,

---

2, 258/67–68 (Isa. 24:2; Hos. 4:9). On this tract, see Hudson, *The Premature Reformation*, p. 424.

[103] Fol. 7r; ed. Hunt, 2, 262/188–263/191.

[104] Fol. 7r–v; ed. Hunt, 2, 263/194–6, 199–202. See Ghosh, *The Wycliffite Heresy*, pp. 97, 108, and Hudson, "Lollardy: the English Heresy?" in *Lollards and their Books*, p. 156. On the concept of the laity in the later Middle Ages, see Rudi Imbach, *Laien in der Philosophie des Mittelalters: Hinweise und Anregungen zu einem vernachlässigten Thema* (Amsterdam, 1989).

[105] Fol. 19v; ed. Hunt, 2, 276/571–72.

[106] Inc. "þis preueþ þat þei ben blessed þat louen goddis lawe," Cambridge UL Ii. 6. 26, fols. 22r–25r, ed. Hunt, 2, 282–8 (also *WB*, 1.xiv–xv). This tract is found in 7 MSS, Hunt, 1, 92.

[107] Fol. 24r–v; ed. Hunt, 2, 284/68–70.

[108] "*Reformatio Regni*: Wyclif and Hus as leaders of religious protest movements," in Hudson, ed., *Wyclif: Political Ideas and Practice: Papers by Michael Wilks* (Oxford, 2000), pp. 63–84, esp. 81.

[109] *Chronicon Angliae*, ed. V.H. Galbraith (Oxford, 1937), pp. 320–1. On Ball's role in the uprising, see Steven Justice, *Writing and Rebellion: England in 1381* (Berkeley, 1994), pp. 103–11.

who was successor to Thomas Sudbury, the Archbishop of Canterbury murdered by the rebels in June 1381, argued that heresy must be ruthlessly suppressed to avoid further unrest.[110] The availability of the Bible in English was drawn into the orbit of clerical anxiety not because Scripture advocates dissension—to say so, says the writer of the second Cambridge tract, would "sclaundre God, auctor of pees"[111]—but because the English Bible was associated with Wyclif, and because the *clerici* were fearful that laypeople who became familiar with the book invoked as the source and justification of all authority might well feel confident to discuss questions going to the heart of the Church as an institution and the relationship between Church and state.[112]

Wyclif's assertion, in *De veritate Sacrae Scripturae*, that the truth of the Latin Bible is guaranteed by the holiness of Jerome's life, put a weapon into the hands of opponents of translation. In the final chapter of the Prologue, they are represented as arguing that "if men now weren as holi as Jerom was, þei miȝten translate out of Latyn into English, as he dide out of Ebru and out of Greek into Latyn, and ellis (otherwise) þei shulden not translate now . . . for defaute (lack) of holynesse and of kunnyng (wisdom) (*WB*, 1, 58/22–5)." The translators' reply is that Jerome was less holy than the apostles and evangelists, that the translators of the Septuagint were not nearly as holy as Moses and the prophets, and that the Church has approved even translations by "open eretikis" (that is, Jews cunningly mistranslating their own Scriptures, *WB*, 1, 58/26–35).[113] Therefore, "myche more lat þe chirche of Engelond appreue þe trewe and hool translacioun of symple men þat wolden for no good in erþe, bi here witing (their knowledge) and power, putte awei þe leste truþe, ȝea þe leste lettre eiþer title (jot or tittle) of holy writ (58/35–8; cf. Matt. 5:18)."

[110] Joseph Dahmus, *William Courtenay, Archbishop of Canterbury* (Philadelphia, 1966), p. 297, and Aston, "Lollardy and Sedition, 1381–1431," *Past and Present* 17 (1960), 1–44.
[111] Fol. 24v; ed. Hunt, 2, 284/72–3. See Ghosh, *The Wycliffite Heresy*, p. 239.
[112] See Glending Olson, 'Geoffrey Chaucer," in David Wallace, ed., *The Cambridge History of Medieval English Literature* (Cambridge, 1999), p. 585.
[113] The authorities cited for Jewish mistranslation are Jerome's first prologue to Job and his prologue to Daniel; *Repertorium Biblicum Medii Aevi*, nos. 344 and 494. This charge is repeated in the additional prologue to John's Gospel in Cambridge, Emmanuel Coll. 1. 4. 33: "as Lire seiþ, we cristen men moten be weel war of þe orignals of ebrew in summe poyntis, for now þe Jewis han corrupt her olde lettre in þo placis where it spekiþ openly of þe godhede of Crist, and þei haue do þis for hatrede to cristen men," *WB*, 4.685ᵇ/12–14.

In spite of this moving plea, the advocates of biblical translation lost the legal battle to be allowed open access to the law of God in their mother tongue in 1409. Archbishop Arundel's *Constitutiones* promulgated in that year inhibited the reading of translations of the Bible "by way of a book, pamphlet or tract . . . newly composed in the time of the said John Wyclif, or since then, or that may in future be composed, in part or in whole, publicly or privately."[114] The inhibition is to remain in place until such time as a translation is approved by the diocesan or by a provincial council.[115] As he said in a letter to Pope John XXIII in 1412, accompanying a copy of the *Constitutiones*, Arundel believed that "the pestilent and wretched John Wyclif, of cursed memory, son of the old serpent . . . endeavoured by every means to attack the very faith and sacred doctrine of Holy Church, devising, to fill up the measure of his malice, the expedient of a new translation of the Scriptures into the mother tongue."[116]

The association of the English Bible with a man whom the Church regarded as a notorious heretic made it impossible for the those advocating translation to persuade the ecclesiastical authorities to approve it, in spite of the fact that the opponents of translation had not offered any specific criticisms of the text of the Wycliffite Bible, and in spite of the fact that the arguments put forward for Scripture in the vernacular were extremely strong.

---

[114] Ed. David Wilkins, *Concilia Magnae Britanniae et Hiberniae*, vol. 3 (London, 1737), p. 317: "per viam libri vel libelli aut tractatus . . . iam noviter tempore dicti Johannis Wycliff, sive citra, compositus, aut in posterum componendus, in parte vel in toto, publice vel occulte." The wide-ranging implications of Arundel's *Constitutiones* are discussed by Peter MacNiven, *Heresy and Politics in the Reign of Henry IV: The Burning of John Badby* (Woodbridge, Suffolk, 1987), pp. 114–16, and Nicholas Watson, "Censorship and Cultural Change in Late Medieval England: Vernacular Theology, the Oxford Translation Debate, and Arundel's *Constitutiones* of 1409," *Speculum* 70 (1995), 822–64.

[115] The only evidence surviving for the approval of a translation, by two successive masters of Whittington College, London, not by a bishop or provincial council, is in Machester, John Rylands Library Engl. 77, fol. 267v; see Ralph Hanna, "English Biblical Texts before Lollardy," in *Lollards and Their Influence in Late Medieval England*, ed. Fiona Somerset, Jill C. Havens and Derrick G. Pittard (Woodbridge, 2003), pp. 150–51, and Hudson, *The Premature Reformation*, pp. 23–24.

[116] Wilkins, *Concilia Magnae Britanniae et Hiberniae*, 3, 350: "ille pestilens et damnandae memoriae miserrimus Johannes Wycliff, serpentis antiqui filius . . . ipsam ecclesiae sacrosanctae fidem et doctrinam sanctissimam totis conatibus impugnare studuit, novae ad suae malitiae complementum scripturarum in linguam maternam translationis practica adinventa."

Authorship of the "Wycliffite Bible"

The title of Josiah Forshall and Frederic Madden's fine edition of the first complete Bible in English, published in 1850, claims that it was "made from the Latin Vulgate by John Wycliffe and his followers."[117] Although "it may be impossible to determine with certainty the exact share which Wycliffe's own pen had in the translation," Forshall and Madden believe "there can be no doubt that he took a part in the labor of producing it, and that the accomplishment of the work must be attributed mainly to his zeal, encouragement and direction."[118] Madden first called this Bible the "Wycliffite Bible" in his diary-entry for 24 April 1832: "[Forshall and I] intend to devote every day to the collation of our Wycliffite Bible" (while the British Museum, where they were both employed, was closed for the annual holiday).[119] This title of convenience, associating the earliest English Bible with Wyclif but not specifying him as translator, has become customary.

As though wishing to reassert Wyclif's role, Conrad Lindberg's edition of the de luxe copy once owned by King Henry VI calls it "the Wyclif Bible."[120] Lindberg, the modern scholar who has done the most extensive textual work on the Wycliffite Bible, had argued that Wyclif's role was "probably restricted to initiating and supervising the work," which, in his view, began around 1370 in Oxford with a translation in the form of an interlinear gloss.[121] Lindberg now believes that Wyclif was responsible for the whole textual trajectory of the translation. The "first finished version" was the highly literal, word-by-word translation identified by Forshall and Madden

---

[117] *The Holy Bible, The Old and New Testaments, With the Apocryphal Books, In the Earliest English Versions, Made* [etc.] 4 vols (Oxford, 1850) [*WB*].

[118] *WB*, 1. vi. Similarly, Hudson says "if not the immediate cause, Wyclif was the ultimate effective cause of the versions that have come to be known as the Wycliffite Bible," "Wyclif and the English Language," in Anthony Kenny, ed., *Wyclif In His Times* (Oxford, 1986), p. 85.

[119] Bodl. Engl. hist. 148, p. 111. Work on the edition had begun in 1829, see p. 391, below.

[120] *King Henry's Bible, MS Bodl 277: the Revised Version of the Wyclif Bible*, 4 vols. (Stockholm, 1999–2004; Stockholm Studies in English 89, 94, 98 and 100). Previously, Lindberg had used the customary title; *The Early Version of the Wycliffite Bible* (Stockholm, 1959–97: Stockholm Studies in English 6, 8, 10, 13, 20, 29, 81 and 87).

[121] *The Middle English Bible* [vol. 2]: *the Book of Baruch* (Oslo, 1985), p. 50. Lindberg has, however, associated Northern dialectal elements in the earliest version of the translation with Wyclif himself, *The Middle English Bible* [vol. 3]: *The Book of Judges*, vol. 3 (Oslo, 1989), p. 74.

as the "Earlier Version [EV],"[122] completed, according to Lindberg, around 1380.[123] This was followed by the more idiomatic "Later Version [LV]," completed, according to Lindberg, not later than 1390, and finally by the revised text of the Later Version that Lindberg calls "King Henry's Bible" and dates around 1400 (although the date of Bodl. MS. 277 is c. 1425–35).[124]

In fact, there are several partially-revised texts of the Later Version, of which "King Henry's Bible" is but one, and some of these certainly belong to the first quarter of the fifteenth century.[125] Making any one of the revisions of the Later Version the endpoint of the translation of the Bible projected by Wyclif would seem to be going a step too far. On the other hand, Lindberg is surely right to emphasize that from the outset the translation of the Bible was envisaged as a process, culminating in a text that could be understood by readers whose only language was English. Starting with a "construe" and revising in the direction of readability in the target language was, after all, a recognized method of translation.[126] The final chapter of the English Prologue to the Wycliffite Bible (*WB*, 1, 56–60) details some of the ways in which the Latinate idiom of the Earlier Version has been Anglicized, and boldly describes the resulting text (that is, the Later Version) as a "trewe and hool translacioun" of the Bible into English (58/36).[127]

---

[122] *King Henry's Bible*, vol. 1, p. 47. EV exists in various versions, discussed by Lindberg in *The Early Version of the Wycliffite Bible* (n. 120, above).

[123] *The Middle English Bible*, vol. 3, p. 74.

[124] Lindberg does not discuss the date of the MS in his edition; Forshall and Madden's date, "perhaps 1440," *WB*, 1. xlvii, is almost certainly too late.

[125] Forshall and Madden's base MS of LV, London, British Library Royal 1. C. VIII, c. 1400–10, is itself a partial revision. From Psalms to the end of the OT translational alternatives are usually omitted, and *WB* relegates LV's readings to the apparatus. Lindberg's title *King Henry's Bible* is not a happy one, given that the Royal MS was also owned by a King Henry [Henry VIII]. There is no edition of an unrevised LV. See further my review of Lindberg, *King Henry's Bible*, vol. 3, *Notes and Queries* 51 (2004), 436–7.

[126] See Smalley's review of Margaret Deanesly, *The Significance of the Lollard Bible* (London, 1951), *Medium Aevum* 22 (1953), 51, and Christina von Nolcken, "Lay Literacy, the Democratization of God's Law and the Lollards," in *The Bible As Book: The Manuscript Tradition* ed. John L. Sharpe III and Kimberly Van Kampen (London, 1998), p. 189.

[127] The following MSS include the complete Prologue: Cambridge, Corpus Christi Coll. Parker Library 147, fols. 1r–18r (with Bible in LV); Cambridge UL Mm. 2. 15, fols. 275r–290v (with Bible in LV); Dublin, Trinity Coll. 75, fols 218r–251r (with NT in EV, and other Wycliffite Bible [henceforth WB] material); Oxford, University Coll. 96 (with lections in LV); Princeton, William H. Scheide 12, fols. 1r–17r (with Bible in LV).

Lindberg's 1390 date for the completion of the Later Version seems slightly late, since it was nearly finished when the Prologue to it was written in 1387/8.[128] Work on the English Bible must have begun in the early 1370s, for the project cannot have taken much less than twenty years.[129] Assuming for the moment that Wyclif was the instigator, he was simultaneously taking the first steps towards making the word of God accessible to the laity, incepting as a doctor of theology and composing his ambitious *Postilla super totam Bibliam* for his Oxford colleagues. At this stage, there was no reason to suppose that a translation of the Bible instigated by him would meet with opposition.

Wyclif argued, as we know, that the whole of the law of God should be preached, read and studied in English, but was he involved in the translation? To add to the evidence from Knighton and Arundel already rehearsed, in 1411 in Prague, a city in which a number of English Wycliffites had taken refuge from persecution, John Hus commented that "English people say that [Wyclif] himself translated the whole Bible from Latin into English."[130] This must be an exaggeration, whether on the part of Hus or on the part of the English in Prague, but it is at least as unlikely that Wyclif played no personal role at all in the translation that was, according to Arundel, his (devilish) "invention." Other significant early evidence naming the translation as Wyclif's comes from the Reformation printer Robert Crowley, who says in his editions of *Piers Plowman* in 1550 that Wyclif "translated the holye Bible into the Englishe tongue,"[131] and from the bibliographer John Bale, who says in 1557 that Wyclif "translated the whole Bible into English, with prologues and synopses attached to each book" (one of the copies he had seen, a complete Bible in the the Later Version, including the Prologue, can still be identified).[132]

---

[128] On the date of the Prologue, see pp. 391–92, below.

[129] See further p. 395 below, and Hudson, *The Premature Reformation*, p. 242.

[130] "Contra Iohannem Stokes," ed. Jaroslav Eršil, *Magistri Iohannis Hus: Polemica* (Prague, 1966), pp. 61–2: "per Anglicos dicitur quod ipse totam bibliam transtulit de latino in anglicum." Hus is refuting the claim made by John Stokes that Wyclif was German ("quod autem Wigleff non fuit Theutonicus sed Anglicus patet ex suis scriptis," p. 61).

[131] STC 19906, 19907, 19907a (London, 1550), sig. *ii; see Hudson, "No Newe Thyng," in *Lollards and their Books* (London, 1985), pp. 247–48.

[132] *Scriptorum Illustrium Maioris Brytanniae . . . Catalogus* (Basel, 1557), *Centuria Sexta*, 1, p. 456: "Transtulit in Anglicum sermonem Biblia tota adhibitis praefationibus atque argumentis cuisque libro suis." Bale's MS *Index Britanniae Scriptorum* (from which his

The only other candidate for the authorship of the whole Middle English Bible is John Trevisa, who is said by William Caxton to have translated the Bible "atte request of Thomas Lord Barcley [Berkeley]," his patron.[133] In the Translators' Preface to the Authorized Version of the Bible (1611), Miles Smith claims that "in our King *Richard* the seconds dayes, *Iohn Trevisa* translated [the Scriptures] into *English*, and many *English* Bibles in written hand are yet to be seene."[134] Trevisa argues for biblical translation in the "Dialogus inter Dominum et Clericum," prefixed to his translation of Ranulf Higden's *Polychronicon* (1387).[135] He translated the apocryphal Gospel of Nicodemus.[136] He was admitted as a fellow of the Queen's College, Oxford, in 1369, the same year as Nicholas Hereford,[137] who is named in Bodl. Douce 369 as the translator of the Earlier Version as far as Baruch 3:20 (fol. 250r).[138] Wyclif also lived in Queen's College from 1374 (probably until 1381).[139] Trevisa was expelled in 1378–9, with other "southerners," who took with them several books relevant to the translation project, including Lyra on Psalms and Proverbs.[140] Taken together, these facts make it not unlikely that Trevisa was one of the translators involved in the production of the Earlier Version.

---

catalogue derives) makes it clear that he had seen Princeton, William H. Scheide 12, then owned by Bower, fol. 94r, *John Bale's Index of British and Other Writers*, ed. Reginald Lane Poole and Mary Bateson (Woodbridge, Suffolk, 1990), p. 266.

[133] In the prologue to Caxton's edition of Trevisa's translation of Ranulf Higden's *Polychronicon* (London, 1482). Bale repeats Caxton's assertion in *Scriptorum Illustrium Maioris Brytanniae*, p. 518. On Trevisa as translator of the Bible, see David Fowler, "John Trevisa and the English Bible," *Modern Philology*, 58 (1960), 81–98, and *The Life and Times of John Trevisa, Medieval Scholar* (Seattle, 1995), pp. 225–32. Fowler demonstrates that Bale had not seen an MS of Trevisa's translation, p. 82.

[134] Ed. David Daniell, *The Bible in English: Its History and Influence* (New Haven, 2003), p. 783. Daniell restates with approval Fowler's case for Trevisa as translator, pp. 91–95.

[135] Ed. R. Waldron, "Trevisa's Original Prefaces on Translation: A Critical Edition," in *Medieval English Studies Presented to George Kane*, ed. E.D. Kennedy, R. Waldron, and J.S. Wittig (Woodbridge, Suffolk, 1988), pp. 285–99. See Fiona Somerset, *Clerical Discourse and Lay Audience in Late Medieval England* (Cambridge, 1998), pp. 64–68, 78–93.

[136] On this translation, see Fowler, *The Life and Times of John Trevisa*, pp. 120–45.

[137] Fowler, "John Trevisa and the English Bible," pp. 88–89.

[138] Henry Hargreaves, *The Cambridge History of the Bible*, 2, 400; De Hamel, *The Book: A History of the Bible*, p. 171.

[139] Fowler, "John Trevisa and the English Bible," p. 89.

[140] Fowler, pp. 93–94. Hudson finds these facts intriguing, *The Premature Reformation*, pp. 394–97, but concludes her discussion of Trevisa's Wycliffism with a verdict of "not proven," p. 397.

In manuscripts of the Wycliffite Bible, the translation is habitually attributed to Wyclif from the Reformation onwards—by Andrew Cook, for instance, who was given Oxford, Bodl. Laud misc. 33 (part of the New Testament in the Later Version) in 1615.[141] During the course of the seventeenth century, ecclesiastical historians and cod-icologists began to recognize that there were two distinct versions of the Wycliffite Bible. Thomas Fuller attributes the earlier of the two to Wyclif and the later to Trevisa.[142] Henry Wharton argues that the Prologue's commination against abuses at the University of Oxford (*WB*, 1, 51/7–52/25) could not have been written by Wyclif,[143] and observes that the Prologue belongs to the version to which it is (some-times) prefixed because of the absence of 3 Ezra, rejected in the Prologue on the authority of Jerome but present in the other ver-sion,[144] and because the biblical verses translated in the final chap-ter of the Prologue accord exactly with what is now known as the Later Version. The Prologue-version, Wharton concludes, is not Wyclif's, and must therefore be Trevisa's.[145]

Not surprisingly, Protestant scholars were anxious to reinstate Wyclif's claim to the version they call the "common" version (that is, the Later Version). Proposing the first edition of the Wycliffite Bible in 1719 (a proposal that came to nothing), John Russell says that Trevisa's "pretensions" to authorship will be "considered and con-futed."[146] Ignoring Wharton's observations, Russell clings to the fact that Bale's description of Wyclif's Bible "agrees exactly" with the "common" version—"unless it be in this, that it does not deserve the many slanders which [Papists] have been pleased to throw upon it." The "other" version, with Jerome's prologues (that is, the Earlier

---

[141] Attribution, fol. 2v; date, fol. 145r (not 1635, the date given in *WB*, 1. xlvi).

[142] *The History of the Worthies of Britain* (London, 1662), 1, 204. Fuller greatly exag-gerates the linguistic differences between the two.

[143] *Auctarium Historiae Dogmaticae Jacobi Usserii*, appended to *Jacobi Usserii, Armachani Archiepiscopi, Historia . . . de Scripturis et Sacris Vernaculis* (London, 1690), pp. 424–25. Wharton quotes from Robert Crowley's edition, *The pathwaye to perfect knowledge* (London, 1550), which attributes the Prologue to Wyclif.

[144] This apocryphal book [also known as 1 Esdras] is rejected on Jerome's authority, *WB*, 1, 2/18–19; see further p. 398, below.

[145] *Auctarium Historiae Dogmaticae Jacobi Usserii*, pp. 426–27; see also C. Oudin, *Commentarius de scriptoribus ecclesiae antiquis*, vol. 3 (Leipzig, 1722), 1044–48, and *WB*, 1. xxi.

[146] *Proposals for Printing by Subscription, the Holy Bible . . . Translated into English by John Wickleffe*, 1 August 1719, pasted onto fols. i^r–ii^v of Oxford, Lincoln Coll. Lat. 119. Russell says that the text will be transcribed from the Lincoln MS in the OT and from Robert Keck's MS (now BL Harl. 5017) in the NT.

Version), should, Russell thinks, be dated "many years before Wickleffe." In his edition of the New Testament, in 1731, John Lewis agrees with Russell about Wyclif's authorship of the version he prints, the "common" version, but supposes that this is the earlier of the two, and that the "revised" version is "more rare and scarce."[147] This confusion is reproduced in the introduction to Henry Hervey Baber's reprinting of Lewis's text of the New Testament, in 1810.[148] When Baber visited Madden in May 1829 "respecting the publication of Wickliffe's Old Test[ament]," Madden had difficulty in convincing him that he, Lewis and Daniel Waterland (who had collaborated with Lewis) had the versions the wrong way round, but Madden's knowledge of the the manuscripts enabled him to prove that the "common" version of the Old Testament "is *not* that of Wiclif but of the writer of the Prologue."[149]

Waterland realized that the Prologue could not have been written by Wyclif, since the writer castigates the University of Oxford for attempting to introduce, in 1387, a statute inhibiting students from beginning the study of Divinity until they had become regents in Arts, a nine or ten-year process. This would have meant that men who went to Oxford with little previous education, and who could afford only a short time there, would never have proceeded from Arts to Divinity (*WB*, 1, 51/8–15, 52/1–3).[150] Lewis dates the Prologue post-1395, on the grounds that the passage also mentions the "sodomy and strong mayntenaunce þereof" practiced in the University and "knowen (made known) to many persones of þe reume (realm) and at þe laste parlement," apparently a reference to the third of *The Twelve Conclusions of the Lollards* attached to the doors of Westminster Hall during the parliament of 1395 (*WB*, 1, 51/38–9).[151]

---

[147] *The New Testament of Our Lord and Saviour Jesus Christ Translated out of the Latin Vulgat* (London, 1731), pp. 5–9. The base text of the gospels is Bodl. Gough Eccl. Top. 5 (then owned by Lewis).

[148] *The New Testament Translated from the Latin In the Year 1380 By John Wiclif* (London, 1810), pp. lii–lxxii; see *WB*, 1, xxi.

[149] 31 May 1829, Bodl. Engl. hist. c. 147, fols 118r–119r; see also *WB*, 1, xxi–xxiii. At first, Baber was was going to be one of the editors of *WB*, but he resigned in Nov. 1829 (fol. 135v). It was not until 1842 that Forshall and Madden decided to edit the whole WB, Bodl. MS Engl. hist. c. 155, pp. 10–11.

[150] *The Works*, vol. 10 (Oxford, 1823), pp. 360–61, 395. On the intended statute, see Anthony à Wood, *The History and Antiquities of the University of Oxford*, trans. John Gutch, vol. 1 (Oxford, 1792), p. 517, and *WB*, 1, xxiv. The writer also alludes to a riot probably in April 1388 (*WB*, 1, 51/22), see à Wood, p. 518.

[151] *The New Testament of Our Lord and Saviour Jesus Christ*, p. 9; see Hudson, *Selections*

Waterland disagrees with Lewis about the date of the Prologue, on the grounds that a reference to the statute of 1387 "would have been very impertinent so late as 1396."[152] Hudson rightly points out that the terms of the third of *The Twelve Conclusions* are "less specific than the reference in the Prologue would lead one to expect."[153] For me, the clinching evidence is that the Prologue's commination against abuses at Oxford is framed around Amos 1:3, the four abominations of Damascus, with the 1387 statute represented as the fourth and worst abomination (Amos 1:3); sodomy is only the second of the four (the first is worldliness and the third is simony). Because the statute is what matters to the writer most, I agree with Waterland (and with Forshall and Madden) that the passage must have been written no later than 1388.

Knowing that the only early Wycliffite writer with works attributed to him in Bale's Catalogue, apart from Wyclif himself, is John Purvey,[154] Waterland guessed (his own word) that Purvey was the author of the Prologue-version: "[Purvey] is the man I pitch upon, for the Translator of the Bible, and composer of that Prologue."[155] In fact, the only evidence that Purvey may have been one of the translators of the Bible is the inventory of his books made in 1414, while he was in prison after the Oldcastle uprising. This includes items that could been used by the translators of the Wycliffite Bible.[156] The note in one manuscript "Here endiþ the translacioun of N and now bigynneþ þe translacioun of J and of oþere men (Bar. 3:20)" could refer to John Purvey, John Wyclif, John Ashton, or many another.[157]

---

from English Wycliffite Writings (Cambridge, 1978), p. 25/5–7, 30–31. Deanesly argues for the date 1395 in *The Lollard Bible*, p. 257.

[152] *Works*, 10, 385; see also *WB*, 1, xxiv.

[153] *Selections from English Wycliffite Writings* p. 174. In *The Premature Reformation*, however, she accepts the date 1395, p. 247.

[154] *Scriptorum Illustrium Maioris Brytanniae, Centuria Septima*, 50, pp. 541–43. Bale says Purvey was "theologus facundus, & legis prudentia clarus . . . Lollardorum librarium & Vuicleui glossatorem," p. 542; Bale's information is derived from Knighton's Chronicle, the *Fasciculi Zizaniorum*, and Thomas Netter, *Doctrinale Antiquitatum Fidei Cathholicae Ecclesiae* (1423–30), see Hudson, "John Purvey: A Reconsideration of the Evidence," in *Lollards and their Books*, pp. 86–95.

[155] *The Works*, 10, 361. Waterland attempts to bolster his argument for Purvey as author with the motto in Dubin, Trinity Coll. 75, "Christus homo factus J.P. prosperet actus," fol. 1r, and the monogram "Peruie", fol. 217v, but it is improbable that these refer to the follower of Wyclif; see Hudson, "John Purvey," pp. 102–3.

[156] Including Bede and Lyra on the Pauline Epistles, Maureen Jurkowski, "New Light on John Purvey," *English Historical Review* 110 (1995), 1184.

[157] Cambridge UL Cc. 1.10, fol. 61v; the noted was discovered by Hargreaves in 1956, see *The Cambridge History of the Bible*, 2, 400.

The evidence for Purvey's participation is not as strong as the evidence for the participation of Trevisa.

When Forshall and Madden began work on their edition, they surmised that Purvey's role was limited to his being one of the translators responsible for the later part of the Earlier Version.[158] In the introduction to their edition, however, they follow Waterland in attributing the Prologue and the Later Version to Purvey,[159] arguing that the Prologue must have been written by the same person who wrote *The Thirty-Seven Conclusions* [*Ecclesiae Regimen*],[160] and that the content of this Wycliffite text "very nearly coincides" with the articles Purvey abjured in 1401, and with the Carmelite Richard Lavenham's list of Purvey's errors and heresies.[161] In 1850, English Wycliffite writings were only just beginning to be studied, and the shared content and style that seemed to Forshall and Madden to indicate common authorship are now known to be characteristic of these writings.[162] Forshall and Madden's edition, however, turned Waterland's guess into accepted fact, and the Later Version of the Wycliffite Bible has been attributed to Purvey ever since.[163]

A "trewe and hool translacioun"?

Wyclif and his fellow-translators did far more than turn the Latin Bible into English. Their hugely ambitious project involved editorial, hermeneutic and linguistic biblical scholarship. Aware that one of the most telling arguments against biblical translation was the danger of translating from a corrupt text of the Latin Bible, the translators wanted to give their English readers a Bible they could rely upon

---

[158] 20 June 1829, Bodl. Engl. hist. c. 147, fol. 120r.

[159] In spite of finding Waterland's evidence unsatisfactory, *WB*, 1, xxiv–xxv; Hudson, "John Purvey," p. 103.

[160] *WB*, 1. xxv; ed. Josiah Forshall, *Remonstrances against Romish Corruptions of the Church: addressed to the people and parliament of England in 1395, 18 Ric II* (London, 1851).

[161] *WB*, 1, xxvi–xxviii; *Fasciculi Zizaniorum*, pp. 383–99.

[162] On the significant differences between the texts cited by Forshall and Madden, see Hudson, "John Purvey," pp. 103–4. On shared content and style in Wycliffite writings, see Hudson, "A Lollard Sect Vocabulary?" in *Lollards and their Books*, pp. 165–80.

[163] Hudson, "John Purvey," pp. 105–8. Lindberg also attributes the revision of LV tentatively to Purvey, *King Henry's Bible*, 1, 47.

as an apt and accurate rendering of a carefully-edited original. The project is outlined in the final chapter of the Prologue, written after Wyclif's death but, in my view, recalling a process Wyclif played an important part in determining and developing. First, "þis symple creature hadde myche trauaile wiþ diuerse felawis and helperis to gedere (collect) manie elde (old) biblis" in order to establish a corrected and authoritative Latin text. Second, they studied this authoritative text with the aid of commentaries and glosses, "and especially Lire [Nicholas of Lyra] on the old testament;" third, they consulted linguistic authorities in order to elucidate "harde wordis and harde sentencis," and, fourth, they produced a clear and accurate English translation (*WB*, 1, 57/7–15).[164]

What is being sketched here in the final chapter of the Prologue, as Anne Hudson recognizes, is the whole trajectory of the Wycliffite Bible enterprise,[165] although, as we shall see, there is evidence that to some extent the translators put textual criticism and biblical scholarship on hold until the Earlier Version was being revised. We shall also see that this "symple creature" seems to have been responsible for some editorial decisions reversing what had been decided during the production of the Earlier Version. Nevertheless, his arrogation of responsibility should not be read too literally: he is the translators' mouthpiece, blowing the trumpet for what has been achieved by them all after some twenty years' labor, a "trewe and hool translacioun."

With a task of such magnitude, several scholars must have been involved at any one time.[166] In *De veritate Sacrae Scripturae*, Wyclif (as we have seen) professes a lack of concern with textual minutiae, and his own writings must have occupied the larger part of his time, but the very strong contemporary evidence linking him with the translation implies that at the least he initiated the project and actively supervised it. From his claim that manuscripts of the Bible are

---

[164] See Hudson's notes on these four stages, *Selected English Wycliffite Writings*, pp. 162–63.

[165] *The Premature Reformation*, p. 243. As she points out, *WB*, 1, xxii, Sven L. Fristedt, *The Wycliffe Bible, Part I. The Principal Problems Connected with Forshall and Madden's Edition* (Stockholm, 1953), p. 137, and Hargreaves, "The Latin Text of Purvey's Psalter," *Medium Aevum*, 24 (1955), p. 73, all assume that this passage relates to the production of the Later Version only.

[166] Hunt, "An Edition of Tracts," 1, 54–55, and Hudson, "Wyclif and the English Language," p. 92, and *The Premature Reformation*, p. 242.

Scripture in the fifth and lowest mode it does not follow that he lacked interest in the accuracy and reliability of the English Bible: on the contrary, the way the project was formulated suggests that Wyclif and the translators were determined to prove to the opposition that an English Bible could be more reliable and accurate than most Latin Bibles.

Hudson argues that Wyclif's attitude towards translation was "amazingly nonchalant," and he was certainly less aware than Trevisa shows himself to be of the difficulties of replacing one language with another,[167] but over-confidence was probably a virtue during the early stages of the enormous project. Wyclif was well-placed to organize the gathering of the necessary resources (Bibles, commentaries, lexicons, a place to keep these and for the translators to work), and while Wyclif was in Oxford the translation was surely made there. The naming of Hereford substantiates this: he seems to have been in charge of the Earlier Version of the translation as far as Baruch 3:20, but the work of at least five scribes and revisers is apparent in Bodl. 969, and Wyclif was probably a contributor. It would be odd if he did not want to take a turn at translation, having set the project up.

There were probably fewer translators at work in the 1380s than in the 1370s, and there are signs of haste in the production of the Later Version. The nature of some of the errors in the Later Version (see below) suggests that the translators did not carefully check it either against the Earlier Version or against a Latin Bible before it went into production. There is also a relative lack of revision in the latter part of the Old Testament, the final part of the work to be completed (after the translation of the New Testament had been revised). In chapter twelve of the Prologue, the writer says he does not have access to Isidore's *De Summo Bono*, or the prologues to Lyra's *Postilla litteralis*, or Richard FitzRalph's *Summa in Questionibus Armenorum* (*WB*, 1, 48/21–6). In the following chapter he says "Lyre cam late to me (Lyra's *Postilla* has recently arrived)," and at once he launches into what Lyra says about the senses of Scripture (52/24–5). The content of the Prologue makes it clear that the writer is still managing the project and overseeing its completion, but he was evidently

---

[167] "Wyclif and the English Language," p. 90; Hudson cites Wyclif's *De Contrarietate Duorum Dominorum*, in *Polemical Works in Latin*, ed. R. Buddensieg, vol. 2 (London, 1883), p. 700/29. For Trevisa's "Dialogue", see n. 135, above.

working without the resources the translators had enjoyed in Oxford.[168]

To us, who take for granted the Bible as book, it seems obvious that a decision to translate Scripture into English meant a decision to translate all the books of the Bible. In Wyclif's Oxford, however, this was a surprising decision, in view of the long history of highly selective translation.[169] The fact that followers of Wyclif revised Rolle's English commentary on the Psalms and compiled Glossed Gospels in English strongly suggests that Wycliffites, in common with their orthodox contemporaries, conceived of an inner canon of biblical books most necessary for the laity to know.[170] The pattern of extant manuscripts of the Wycliffite Bible (more than 250 in total) tends to confirm this.[171] Twenty complete Wycliffite Bibles survive, but the New Testament, as a whole or in part, was copied far more frequently than the Old. The most frequently-copied Old Testament book, Psalms, survives in forty-two manuscripts, while 177 manuscripts contain solely books from 'þe testament of crist' (110 of these being complete New Testaments, 33 of these containing Gospels only and 34 of these containing books from Romans to the Apocalypse only). This is in line with the recommendation made in the first chapter of the Prologue to the Wycliffite Bible, that "cristen men and wymmen, olde and ȝonge, shulden studie fast (intently) in þe newe testament, for it is of ful autorite and opyn to vndirstonding of simple men (*WB*, 1, 2/31–2)."

Yet in the same chapter the reader literate in English but not in Latin is reassured that, according to Augustine, anyone who maintains meekness and charity truly understands "al holi writ," and therefore the "simple man of wit" should not be too frightened to study it (2/36–8). Contrariwise, says the Prologue, Augustine threatens the "clerk," the Latin-literate reader, that if he reads the Bible blinded

---

[168] But chapter 10 indicates that Purvey did have Guido de Baysio's *Rosarium super Decreto* and Grosseteste's sermons.

[169] Geoffrey Shepherd, *The Cambridge History of the Bible*, 2, 362–87.

[170] On the Wycliffite revision of Rolle, see Hudson, *The Premature Reformation*, pp. 259–64. On the Glossed Gospels see Hargreaves, "Popularising Biblical Scholarship: the Role of the Wycliffite *Glossed Gospels*," in *The Bible and Medieval Culture*, pp. 171–89, and Hudson, *The Premature Reformation*, pp. 251–58.

[171] My own list of MSS (forthcoming in *The First English Bible: The Text and Context of the Wycliffite Versions*) adds to those recorded in Lindberg, "The Manuscripts and Versions of the Wycliffite Bible: a preliminary survey," *Studia Neophilologica*, 42 (1970), 333–47, revised in Hunt, 2, 557–63.

by pride in his "verrey (true) vndirstondyng of hooly writ, wiþouten charite," he will "go quyk (alive) in to helle (2/42–3/1)."[172] The person who decided to make the entire Bible available in the vernacular, so that "simple men of wit," the growing body of people literate in English but not in Latin, would have full access to God's law without the need for a Latin-literate intermediary, was someone with rare boldness and tenacity. I believe this person was Wyclif.

The model for the elements the Bible as book should contain, and the order in which they should appear, was evidently the Latin Bible as it was customarily written in France from around 1230 (the "Paris Bible"). Like "Paris Bibles," all Wycliffite Bible manuscripts have the new chapter divisions and numbers devised in the university of Paris at the end of the twelfth century, probably by Stephen Langton.[173] By 1230, the order of the biblical books had become standardized, and this is the order found in the Wycliffite Bible.[174] In the Old Testament, the order derived from the Hebrew Scriptures was superseded by the order derived from the Septuagint:[175] the Pentateuch, the historical books (Joshua, Judges, Ruth, 1–4 Kings, 1–2 Chronicles, 1–3 Ezra, Tobit, Judith, Esther), Job, Psalms,[176] the Sapiential books (Proverbs, Ecclesiastes, the Song of Songs, Wisdom, Ecclesiasticus),[177] the major prophets (Isaiah, Jeremiah-Lamentations-Baruch, Ezekiel, Daniel-Susanna-Bel and the Dragon), the twelve minor prophets and 1–2 Maccabees.

All surviving manuscripts of the Wycliffite Bible containing the Old Testament have the books in this "Paris Bible" order, including,

---

[172] *Enarrationes in Psalmos*, 54:16; ed. E. Dekkers and J. Fraipont, CCSL 39, 2 (Turnhout, 1956), pp. 668–69.

[173] These replace the "*capitula* lists" (summaries of contents) found in French Bibles c. 1200–30, Light, "French Bibles c. 1200–1230," pp. 168–70. WB MSS do not, however, contain the alphabetical list of Hebrew names, inc. "*Aaz* apprehendens," usually found in "Paris Bibles," Light, p. 156.

[174] On the standardization, see Light, "French Bibles c. 1200–1230," pp. 155, 161–63, and De Hamel, *The Book: A History of the Bible*, pp. 120–22. The characteristic components of the Vulgate before the thirteenth century, including the prologues, are conveniently detailed by De Hamel, pp. 22–24.

[175] The Septuagint order is that in which Augustine lists the OT books in *De Doctrina Christiana* 2.8.13, ed. Martin, CCSL 32, pp. 39–40; see Light, "French Bibles c. 1200–1230," p. 161. Theodulfian Bibles and Stephen Harding's Bible order the OT books according to Jerome's discussion in his *Prologus Galeatus*, see n. 51, above.

[176] Thirteenth-century Latin Bibles sometimes have parallel Hebrew and Gallican Psalters; WB has the Gallican Psalter only.

[177] "Paris Bibles" sometimes include the Prayer of Solomon, Ecclus. 52 = 2 Chron. 6:13–20, but WB does not.

therefore, books and parts of books deemed apocryphal by Jerome,[178] as the Prologue to the Wycliffite Bible explains (1, 1/16–21): Tobit, Judith, Wisdom, Ecclesiasticus, 1–2 Maccabees, the Prayer of Manasseh (2 Chron. 37),[179] the non-Hebrew portions of Esther and Daniel,[180] and the Greek appendices to Jeremiah known as Baruch[181] and the Epistle of Jeremy (Bar. 6).[182]

The Later Version, however, as Wharton noted, omits 3 Ezra. The writer of the Prologue says that Jerome "biddeþ þat no man delite in þe dremis of þe iij. and iiij. Book of Esdre þat ben apocrifa, þat is not of autorite of bileue (WB, 1, 2/14–15)," and therefore he "translatide not þe þridde neiþer þe fourþe book of Esdre (2/18–19)."[183] Since the Earlier Version contains 3 Ezra and the Later Version does not, an editorial decision to omit it must have been made during the production of the Later Version, and the unique 3 Ezra in Bodl. 277 must be the work of an independent reviser.

The inferior status of the apocryphal books and portions of books is written into the first chapter of the Prologue to the Wycliffite Bible and into the prologues of Jerome defining the canon included in the Old Testament in the Earlier Version. Hudson claims that there would seem to be "a logical inconsistency" here, since the selection of canonical texts depended upon the Church's authority, an authority which the Wycliffites disputed.[184] This is a telling criticism, yet what is most evident in the Prologue to the Wycliffite Bible is the great esteem in which the translators (following Wyclif) hold Jerome. They do not simply imitate the canon of "Paris Bibles." Carefully,

---

[178] In the *Prologus Galeatus*, see n. 51, above, and in Jerome's prologue on the Books of Solomon, *Repertorium Biblicum Medii Aevi*, no. 457.

[179] Sometimes omitted in Latin Bibles of the thirteenth and fourteenth centuries, but included in WB.

[180] All WB MSS of Esther and Daniel include Jerome's rubrics specifying the portions of the text lacking in Hebrew.

[181] Frequently omitted in Latin Bibles pre 1200, P.-M. Bogaert, "Le nom de Baruch dans la litterature pseudépigraphique: L'Apocalypse syriaque et la livre deutéro-canonique," in *La littérature juive entre Tenach et Mischna*, ed. W.C. van Unnik (Leiden, 1974), p. 66.

[182] The order Jeremiah, Lamentations, Baruch, Epistle of Jeremiah (Bar. 6) is new in "Paris Bibles," Bogaert, "Le nom de Baruch," p. 61.

[183] *Repertorium Biblicum Medii Aevi*, no. 330, cf. WB, 2, 477/25–29. Some Latin Bibles of the thirteenth and fourteenth centuries also omit 3 Ezra [1 Esdras], e.g. Bodl. Lat. bibl. e. 7, Bodl. Laud Lat. 13 and Bodl. Lyell 7.

[184] *The Premature Reformation*, p. 230. Hudson notes that Netter recognized this inconsistency; *Doctrinale Antiquitatum Fidei Ecclesiae Catholicae* 2.20, ed. B. Blanciotti, vol. 1 (Venice, 1757), pp. 344–46.

even pedantically, the writer of the Prologue presents the English reader with a digest of all the relevant evidence concerning the canon from Jerome's writings.

When applied to the New Testament, the Prologue says, the term "apocryphal" means that the Church "doutiþ of þe treuþe þerof." The examples given are the [Gospel of] the Infancy of the Savior and "þe book of þe takyng up of þe body of Seynt Marie to heuen" [the *Transitus Mariae*] (*WB*, 1, 2/25–8).[185] There is no suggestion of a blurring of the boundaries between canonical and non-canonical, as there is in Wyclif's discussion of the apocrypha in *De veritate Sacrae Scripturae*. The usual order of books in the New Testament in the Wycliffite Bible, following the customary "Paris Bible" order, is: the Gospels, the Pauline Epistles, the Acts of the Apostles, the Canonical Epistles, and Revelation.[186] A decision was evidently made to omit the epistle to the Laodiceans, which is sometimes found in "Paris Bibles"; it was translated c. 1425, and is placed between Colossians and 1 Thessalonians in thirteen manuscripts of the Later Version. The first four verses of Luke are missing in all but three manuscripts; this omission must have been accidental, and it is surprising that it was not rectified in the Later Version.[187]

Nearly all manuscripts of the Earlier Version and a few manuscripts of the Later Version include translations of the prefatory epistles of Jerome (*Epistola 58* and *Praefatio in Pentateuchum*), and also the prologues to portions of the Old Testament and to individual Old Testament books, by Jerome, Hrabanus Maurus and others, customarily found in "Paris Bibles" (omitting, however, all the prologues after the prologue to Baruch). In the New Testament, some manuscripts of the Earlier Version and nearly all manuscripts of the Later Version contain translations of the prologues customarily found in "Paris Bibles."[188]

---

[185] As his authority, Purvey cites *Catholicon*, the twelfth-century dictionary composed by Johannes Balbus of Genoa, *WB*, 12/21, 28.

[186] Acts sometimes follows the Canonical Epistles (which are also called Catholic Epistles, or Epistles of the Christian Faith, or the Seven Epistles, or "smalle pistils").

[187] BL Addit. 11858, Oxford, New Coll. 67 and Pennsylvania UL e. 6, all revised EV MSS, in which the translation is borrowed from Glossed Luke, *WB*, 1, xvii. The Later Version also accidentally omits part of Wisd. 12:9, Hab. 1:12, and Rev. 20:12.

[188] For the customary OT and NT prologues, see *Repertorium Biblicum Medii Aevi*, nos. 284–842; De Hamel, *The Book: A History of the Bible*, pp. 22–24, 123–24, and Light, "French Bibles c. 1200–1230," pp. 164–67. On the prologues in WB, see *WB*, 1, 29–30; there are slight differences between the NT prologues in EV and LV. Hunt details additional NT prologues found in some LV MSS, "An Edition of Tracts advocating Scriptural Translation," 1, 47.

It looks as though Wyclif and the translators considered this material "an integral part of the translation," as Simon Hunt says.[189] Yet
when the translation of the Old Testament in the Earlier Version
was nearing completion (Baruch is five-sixths of the way through the
Old Testament) a decision was made to translate nothing thereafter
but the words of Holy Writ, and the short prologue to Baruch is
the only prologue from the Latin Bible preserved in the Later Version
of the Old Testament.[190] Because the prologue to Ecclesiasticus, an
integral part of the book, was wrongly understood to be an added
prologue, that was omitted as well.[191]

Surprisingly, when the translators revising the Earlier Version
reached the beginning of Isaiah, having omitted all prefatory materials to that point, they included a new English prologue, to serve
as "þe prologe of Ysaie and of oþere profetis (WB, 3, 225–6)." This,
the only Wycliffite prologue which is a fully integral element of the
Wycliffite Bible,[192] advocates interpreting Scripture according to the
literal sense, and warns against the dangers of a spiritual sense rooted
not in the words of Scripture or in plain reason but in "moral fan-
tasye" (WB, 3, 226/16). Interpreting the text in this dangerous way,
the writer says, "haþ disseyued grete men in oure daies, bi ouer
greet trist to her fantasies (excessive trust in their fabricated interpretation)" (226/19–20). The writer invites his reader to agree that
contemporary princes of the Church have misled themselves, preferring their own imaginings to the open sense of the Bible. These
impolitic words were written by the same writer as the Prologue to
the Wycliffite Bible, not long before that Prologue was written.[193]
The Wycliffite biblical prologue was a very natural extension of the
translation project. Nevertheless, we may doubt whether Wyclif would
have approved of the omission of Jerome's and other customary prologues and the substitution of new ones. The content of the Earlier
Version suggests that Wyclif chose to have the Latin Bible in its post-

---

[189] "An Edition of Tracts," 1, 46.
[190] *Repertorium Biblicum Medii Aevi*, no. 491; WB, 3, 484. This prologue probably
survived in LV accidentally, because it was seen as a rubric rather than a prologue.
[191] Inc. "Multorum nobis et magnorum;" it is included in one LV MS, Cambridge.
Dd. 1. 27.
[192] It is found in all LV MSS containing Isaiah, whereas the Prologue is only
occasionally present, see n. 127, above.
[193] He says he intends to write a prologue "on þe bigynnyng of Genesis (WB, 3,
226/24–25)," and that in it he will discuss the senses of Scripture.

1230 manifestation translated "hool" into English, without addition or subtraction.

How "trewe" a translation was the Wycliffite Bible? The Prologue claims that "þe English bible late (newly) translatid (*WB*, 1, 58/3),"[194] the Later Version, is freer from error than most "comune Latyn biblis (58/2)," in spite of what the enemies of translation predicted. There are no contemporary comments on the accuracy of the translation, but one of the earliest references to Wyclif as translator is a marginal note, in an early-sixteenth-century hand, accusing Wyclif of not knowing his Latin because he translates "erodii domus dux est eorum (Psa. 103:17, Gallican Psalter)" as "þe hous of þe gerfaukun is þe leader of þo (them)," whereas [every schoolboy knows] *erodius* means stork.[195] This is patently clutching at anti-Wycliffite straws, but enemies of Wyclif could have identified gaffes if they had looked carefully.

Egregious errors were usually corrected during the process of revision, as one would expect: for example, one of the earliest manuscripts, Bodl. 969, reads "Kyng Dauiþ smellede in his bed (3 Kings 1:47)," which is corrected in all other Earlier Version manuscripts to "honourde" (*adoravit*, "worschipide" in the Later Version).[196] In numerous cases, the Later Version corrects a translation in the Earlier Version based on an inferior or inaccurate reading in the Latin text. Often, in the Old Testament, the translators were alerted to an inferior or incorrect reading by their study of Lyra's *Postilla litteralis*. In the Earlier Version, Jacob asks Laban "why vnderputtis þu Lya to me? (why did you secretly bring Leah to my bed?) (Gen. 29:25)" whereas in the Later Version he asks "whi hast þou disseyued me?" A marginal gloss in the Later Version explains: "þis is þe verie lettre as Lire seiþ here, but comyn latyn bokis han þus 'whi hast þou priuyly put Lya to me,' but þis is fals lettre [*falsa est litera*], as Lire seiþ here."[197]

---

[194] Hargreaves understands this to be a reference to EV, *The Cambridge History of the Bible*, 2, 410, but the Prologue is concerned with the merits of the finished translation.

[195] But in the Hebrew Psalter the reading is *milvus*, bird of prey ("gerfaukun"). The note is found in Cambridge, Corpus Christi Coll. Parker Lib. 147; in Lambeth Palace Lib. 1033 the note is now invisible. See *WB*, 1, xlvi (where the biblical reference is, however, incorrect).

[196] Lindberg, *The Early Version of the Wycliffite Bible*, vol. 3 (Stockholm, 1963), p. 319. Nicholas Hereford has been blamed for several gross errors pre-Bar. 3:20, but no doubt several translators were to blame.

[197] This gloss is in 4 MSS, Cambridge UL Mm. 2. 15, Hereford Cathedral Lib.

A telling instance in the New Testament shows the revisers restoring a reading Wyclif himself argues for. In *De veritate Sacrae Scripturae*, he says that "in accurate manuscripts (*in correctis codibus*)" the reading of John 10:35–6 is "the Scripture cannot be destroyed, *whom (quem)* the Father sanctified and sent into the world," thus equating the text of the Bible (the word) with the person of Christ (the Word); this equation is central in Wyclif's writings.[198] The Later Version rightly reads "Scripture may not be vndon, *þilke þat* (whom) þe fadir haþ halewid and haþ sent in to þe world (*WB*, 4, 267)," whereas the Earlier Version has the *facilior lectio* "þe Scripture which þe fadir halwide." Work on establishing an accurate text would seem to have taken place largely during the revision process, and this example hints that Wyclif may possibly have been involved.

Not all errors or inferior readings, however, were corrected. Herbert B. Workman points out that both versions mistranslate *pauperes evangelizantur* as "pore men ben taken to prechynge of þe gospel [+ or ben maad keepers of þe gospel, EV] (Matt. 11:5, cf. Luke 7:22)." This is an error "in favour of Poor Priests," in Workman's view, and it causes him to "regret that Wyclif did not abandon his polemics, and devote himself to the supreme task of doing the Bible into the vernacular instead of handing it over to his assistants."[199] In the parable of the royal wedding feast, in both versions the king tells his guests "my bolis (bulls) and my volatilis (winged creatures) ben slayne (Matt. 22:4)." "Volatilis" is corrected to "fatte beestis (*altilia*)" in five late manuscripts of the Earlier Version, indicating that this version was being corrected (in the Gospels, at least) independently of the Later Version, after the Later Version was complete.[200]

O. 1.17, BL Cotton Claudius E. II and Oxford, Lincoln Coll. Lat. 119. Both the *Correctorium* of the Dominicans of St.-Jacques and the *Correctorium* of Hugh of St Cher note that "quare Lyam supposuisti me" is an incorrect reading, but it is common in thirteenth- and fourteenth-century Bibles.

[198] *De veritate* 1.6; 1:109/21–110/2; see Levy, *John Wyclif: Scriptural Logic*, pp. 87–91, and Ghosh, *The Wycliffite Heresy*, p. 55. Levy points out that Wyclif had "been equating Scripture with Christ as early as 1372," p. 87.

[199] *John Wyclif: A Study of the English Medieval Church* (Oxford, 1926), vol. 2, p. 176. In the English Wycliffite Sermons, Matt. 11: 5 is translated "poore men ben preysud of God" in all MSS except Pembroke Coll. Camb. 237, where "preysud" is corrected to "prechud," Pamela Gradon and Anne Hudson, *English Wycliffite Sermons*, vol. 1 (Oxford, 1983), p. 336/22, but Luke 7:22 is correctly translated: "pore men ben / prechid gode," *EWS*, vol. 3 (Oxford, 1990), p. 17/19–p. 18/1.

[200] Lindberg, *The Early Version of the Wycliffite Bible*, vol. 7 (Stockholm, 1994), p. 63. No variant *alates* has been recorded, but BL Royal 17. E. VII (*Bible historiale*) has "mes toraux et mes uolailles sont occises." Other examples of correction in late EV

There are also places where the Earlier Version has a "trewe" translation and the Later Version an incorrect one. "Vp on a shreude womman good is a signe (*super mulierem nequam bonum est signum*, Ecclus 42:6) inexplicably becomes "A seelyng is good on a wickid man."[201] "By þe mydil of þee (*in medio tui*, Amos 5:17)" becomes "in þe myddil of þe see."[202] Nevertheless, it is substantially true that the Later Version was freer from error, inaccuracy and inferior readings than the Earlier Version.

But was it freer from error than most "comune Latyn biblis," as the Prologue boasts? Like the Earlier Version, it contains nearly all the interpolations commonly found in late-medieval Latin Bibles (most notably in Kings and Proverbs). At Proverbs 4:27, for example, all the words following "fro yuel (*a malo*)" are an interpolation, as a marginal gloss in BL Cotton Claudius E. II, translating Lyra, points out: "al þis til to þe ende of þe chapitre is not of þe text, for it is not in ebreu." In spite of Lyra, the interpolated passage remains in the Wycliffite Bible, in every late-medieval Latin Bible I have seen, and in the first printed edition of the *Glossa Ordinaria*.[203] In several other cases, the interpolation is signalled as such in the *Correctoria* of the Dominicans of St.-Jacques and of Hugh of St Cher, and also in Bodl. Laud Lat. 13, an Oxford *correctorium*, c. 1240–50,[204] but there is no signal in the Wycliffite Bible. In one remarkable case, the Later Version has attempted to omit an interpolation present in the Earlier Version, following Lyra (and the *correctoria*), but instead it succeeds in preserving the interpolation and omitting a portion of "trewe" text (1 Kings 24:7–8).[205]

MSS but not in LV MSS are Matt. 4:16 and Luke 1:1–4; see also Lindberg, pp. 19–21. Hargreaves understands one of these revised EV MSS, Oxford New Coll. 67, to be intermediate between EV and LV, "Marginal Glosses to the Wycliffite New Testament," *Studia Neophilologica* 33 (1961), 285–300, but it is probably an independent revision.

[201] The error is corrected in 2 LV MSS, BL Cotton Claudius E. II and Royal 1. C. VIII. No Latin variants have been recorded.

[202] Two LV MSS have the correct reading, Cambridge UL Dd. 1. 27 and Lambeth Palace 25. At Ecclus 43:15: "briddes (EV, *aves*)" becomes "bees (LV)." No variants have been recorded in either case.

[203] *Biblia Latina cum Glossa ordinaria*, ed. Adolph Rusch (Strassburg, 1480/1).

[204] Illuminated by William de Brailes, who worked in Catte Street, Oxford; J.J.G. Alexander, "English or French? Thirteenth-century Bibles," in *Manuscripts at Oxford: an exhibition in honour of Richard William Hunt*, ed. A.C. de la Mare and B.C. Barker-Benfield (Oxford, 1980), p. 71, fig. 46.

[205] "*crist of þe lord*, in summe bokis it sueþ, and Dauyþ brak hise men bi siche wordis and suffride not hem þat þey risiden aȝenus Saul (= 24:8) but þis lettre is not in ebreu neþer in bokis amendid, Lire here," BL Cotton Claudius E. II.

In respect of interpolated material, the Wycliffite Bible is no worse than "comune Latyn biblis," but not significantly better, either. The same may be said of the Earlier Version in respect of inferior or inaccurate readings, but the Later Version, thanks largely to Lyra, is a better-than-average, though by no means outstanding, text. Apart from the errors and omissions already mentioned, it still includes many of the inferior or inaccurate readings characteristic of late-medieval Bibles. For example, the *correctoria* and Lyra make it perfectly clear that the Hebrew text says the Midianites sold Joseph for twenty pieces of silver, not thirty (Gen. 37:28), but the Wycliffite Bible, in common with about half the late-medieval Latin Bibles I have seen, prefers the reading that links the sin of the Midianites with the sin of Judas.

To this point, we have been considering whether the Wycliffite Bible is a "trewe" translation purely in textual-critical terms, but how successfully did it fulfill Wyclif's intention that the entire Latin Bible should be available to English readers or hearers? After all, the format and layout of complete Wycliffite Bibles, and the fact that they often include lectionaries and indicate the beginnings and endings of lections in the margins, suggests that they may have been intended to be read aloud in place of the Latin Bible in churches, as well as read privately or in small groups.[206] A.I. Doyle says BL Egerton 617/618 (part of a Wycliffite Bible in the Earlier Version, owned by Thomas of Gloucester at his death in 1397) "must be meant for use on a lectern."[207] An English reader with elementary Latin (whether a layperson or a priest) would have been able to use the Earlier Version alongside the original; with no Latin, however, the syntax of the Earlier Version would have been a serious obstacle. The syntax of the Later Version is considerably friendlier to the non-Latin-literate reader, and the writer of the Prologue proudly lists some of the ways in which Latin syntax was translated into English (*WB*, 1, 57/15–41).[208]

---

[206] De Hamel, *The Book: A History of the Bible*, pp. 183–86, and David Lawton, "Englishing the Bible: 1370–1549," in Wallace, *The Cambridge History of Medieval Literature*, p. 472.

[207] "English Books In and Out of Court from Edward III to Henry VII," in *English Court Culture in the Later Middle Ages*, ed. V.J. Scattergood and J.W. Sherborne (New York, 1983), pp. 168–69.

[208] Hudson, *Selected English Wycliffite Writings*, pp. 173–77. The methods described do not always reflect the actual syntax of LV, see Lilo Moessner, "Translation Strategies in Middle English: The Case of the Wycliffite Bible," *Poetica: An International Journal of Linguistic-Literary Studies* 55 (2001), 123–54.

One of the ways involves changing the variable object-subject order possible in Latin to the subject-object order required in English: the revisers alter the impossible "Two folkis [object] hateþ my soule [subject] (*duas gentes odit anima mea*, Ecclus 50:27, EV)" to "My soule hatiþ twei folkis (LV)."

Wyclif and the translators recognized early on in the enterprise that an accurate literal translation would not always be "open" enough for the reader who did not have at hand (as they, in Oxford, had) books interpreting "harde wordis," and commentaries and postills interpreting the biblical text. Explanatory glosses were therefore added, always within the text, not in the margin: "wymmen mournynge, *a mawmet* (idol) *of letcherie þat is clepid* (called), Adonydes (Ezek. 8:14, EV);" "þer was not place to birie, *for þe multitude of careynes* (corpses) (Jer. 7:32, EV)." In the Later Version, there are numerous, often expansive, glosses within the text (and, in a few manuscripts, in the margins, but the translators intended that marginal glosses would be reserved for textual commentary, as the Prologue indicates, *WB*, 1, 58/4–7.) The Latin Bible's own gloss on Judges 1:17, "Horma, *id est anathema*" is further expanded: "*þat is cursyng eþer* (or) *perfit distriyng* (complete destruction), *for þilke citee was distried outerly*," a gloss derived (as most were) from Lyra. The translators intended that these glosses would be underlined in red, but the underlining is often in black ink, and in most manuscripts it is sporadic.

There is a very fine line between a gloss that helps the reader to understand the literal sense of the biblical text and a gloss that interprets the literal sense of the biblical text. In the Earlier Version, the translators are clearly wary of glosses, for they err on the side of not helping their readers enough, especially in the Old Testament. It is not that they are suspicious of glosses that make the text intelligible (it is glosses that distort the text for worldly purposes that trouble Wyclif and the Wycliffites); rather, they are acting on the Augustinian conviction that the "open" sense of Scripture will speak to the "simple man of wit" reading in a spirit of charity and happily ignorant of the sophistry of worldly clerics. The writer of the Wycliffite Old Testament prologues asserts this conviction explicitly.[209]

There are, however, several places in the Later Version where the translators gloss the text in such a way that the literal sense of the

---

[209] See further Rita Copeland, *Rhetoric, Hermeneutics and Translation in the Middle Ages* (Cambridge, 1991), pp. 44–51.

words is overridden by what Karlfried Froehlich calls their "true literal sense," which encompasses all the figurative senses intended by the writer and all the christological significations the Holy Spirit has inscribed within the text.[210] This is the way in which Lyra and the writer of the Prologue to the Wycliffite Bible (translating Lyra) understand "literal,"[211] and Wyclif's identification of the literal sense with the divine authorial intention is distinguishable from Lyra's only insofar as combatting the reductionism of the sophists involves him in paying less attention to the human author than Lyra does. When Psalm 44:3 opens with the words *speciosus forma prae filiis hominum*, "fair in form befor þe sonus of men (EV)," the divine authorial intention could not, in late-medieval eyes, be clearer: it is Christ of whom the Psalmist is speaking. The Lyran gloss on the title of this psalm, included in most manuscripts of the Later Version, states: "þis salm is seid of Crist . . . for Poul in (Hebr. 1:8–9) aleggiþ þis salm seid of Crist to þe lettre (*ad litteram*)."[212] Yet when the Later Version reads "*Crist*, þou art fairer in schap þan þe sones of men," the translator oversteps the mark.[213]

Wyclif undoubtedly understood Psalm 44 in this way, but when he claimed that the Holy Spirit wants the whole Bible to be read and studied in the vernacular, he trusted that the same Holy Spirit would initiate uneducated or minimally-educated readers into the authentic tradition of exegesis of Scripture, as long as he and his fellow-translators co-operated with the Spirit by producing as "trewe and hool" a translation of the Latin Bible as they could. There would have been no English Bible without Wyclif's trust in English readers, uncontaminated by clericalism. Even if he was, or would have been, unhappy with some of the decisions taken by the translators towards the end of the production of the Wycliffite Bible, the first English Bible and the name of Wyclif properly belong together.

---

[210] " 'Always to Keep the Literal Sense in Holy Scripture Means to Kill One's Soul': the State of Biblical Hermeneutics at the Beginning of the Fifteenth Century," in *Literary Uses of Typology from the Late Middle Ages to the Present*, ed. Karl Miner (Princeton, 1977), p. 47.

[211] See esp. *WB*, 1, 54/12–24.

[212] See Theresa Gross-Diaz's discussion of Lyra's christological reading of the Psalms by way of the New Testament, "What's a Good Soldier to Do? Scholarship and Revelation in the Postills on the Psalms," in *Nicholas of Lyra: the Senses of Scripture*, pp. 126–28.

[213] Hargreaves gives other examples in Psalms (but not this one), "The Latin Text of Purvey's Psalter," *Medium Aevum* 24 (1955), 73–90.

THE OPPONENTS OF JOHN WYCLIF

Mishtooni Bose

Is not this excuse for mere contraries,
Equally strong; cannot both sides say so?

> John Donne, *Satyre III* (ll. 98–99)

Why do you not cite yourselves in support of your arguments, since
you are doctors, as Jerome and Augustine were?

> (attributed to Reginald Pecock)[1]

In 1428, forty-four years after his death, the body of John Wyclif was
exhumed and burned, and the ashes were thrown into the River
Swift, which flows through his former parish of Lutterworth. Writing
about what would then have been a recent event in the final instalment
of his *Doctrinale antiquitatum fidei*, the Carmelite Thomas Netter, one
of Wyclif's most vehement opponents, notes with some relish that "the
flames . . . consigned the vile corpse to hell, and the streams absorbed
the ashes."[2] Commenting in a marginalium on the word "cadaver,"

---

[1] "Quare vos non allegatis vosmet, cum estis doctores, ut Jeronimus et Augustinus?"
Quoted by Thomas Gascoigne in his *Liber Veritatum* (Lincoln College, Oxford, MS
118, f. 596) and printed in *Loci e Libro Veritatum* ed. James E. Thorold Rogers
(Oxford, 1881), p. 217/25–26. I am grateful to the following for permission to quote
from manuscripts in their possession: The British Library, London; The Bodleian
Library, Oxford; the Warden and Fellows of Merton College, Oxford; and the
Provost and Fellows of Worcester College, Oxford. I am also grateful to Julia
Walworth, librarian, and Julian Reid, archivist (Merton College); and to Joanna
Parker, librarian (Worcester College) for facilitating access to their respective col-
lections. I have expanded manuscript abbreviations throughout. All translations from
Latin are my own, unless otherwise stated.

[2] *Doctrinale antiquitatum fidei ecclesiae catholicae* [henceforth *DAF*], ed. Bonaventura
Blanciotti, 3 vols. (1757–59; repr. Farnborough, 1967), 3:830B: "flammae . . . vile
cadaver praejudicaverunt ad inferos, & flumina cineres absorbebant." On the composition and dissemination of the work, see Margaret Harvey, "The Diffusion of
the *Doctrinale* of Thomas Netter in the Fifteenth and Sixteenth Centuries," in *Intellectual
Life in the Middle Ages. Essays Presented to Margaret Gibson*, eds. Lesley Smith and
Benedicta Ward (London and Rio Grande, 1992), pp. 281–94 (p. 282). On Netter,
see Anne Hudson, "Netter, Thomas (c. 1370–1430)," in *Oxford Dictionary of National
Biography*. 60 vols. (Oxford, 2004), 40:444–47 (further references to the *Dictionary*
will be given as *DNB*); Kirk S. Smith, "The Ecclesiology of Controversy: Scripture,
Tradition and Church in the Theology of Thomas Netter of Walden, 1372–1430"
(Ph.D. thesis, Cornell University, 1983); Kantik Ghosh, *The Wycliffite Heresy: Authority*

Netter's eighteenth-century editor, Bonaventura Blanciotti, is appropriately gleeful: "It had to be exhumed because of the decree of the
Council of Constance; but over and above this, through the zeal of
the faithful, and with the permission of the Bishop of Lincoln, it was
thrown into the river in the year 1418 [*sic*]."[3] The actions were precipitated by an order from Pope Martin V (9 December 1427), who
added to the condemnation originally pronounced at the eighth session of the Council of Constance (1415) in stipulating that Wyclif's
body was not merely to be exhumed, but burnt, and the ashes to
be "disposed of so that no trace of him shall be seen again."[4]

Blanciotti's mistaken dating of the event to 1418 unwittingly draws
attention to the fact that it had been a long journey from the condemnation at Constance to the eventual exhumation and burning.
That is not the only way in which his footnote exposes faultlines, or
at least barely healed sutures, in the orthodox ranks assembled against
Wyclif. The Bishop of Lincoln to whom instructions for the exhumation were originally given was Philip Repingdon; but Repingdon,
one of several distinguished members of the clergy who had formerly
been supporters of Wyclif, "took no action" to carry them out.[5] The
Bishop of Lincoln who belatedly presided over the event was Richard
Fleming, who, despite his long-standing orthodox credentials (he had
founded Lincoln College, Oxford, in the previous year), had once
briefly been suspected of heresy.[6] Rather than putting a decisive end
to the Wycliffite controversies, therefore, this piece of orthodox the-
atre reveals rather more than was intended about the history and
heterogeneous composition of the avowedly orthodox establishment
ranged against Wyclif. The conflagration was intended as the symbolic

---

and the Interpretation of Texts (Cambridge, 2002), pp. 174–208; Kirk S. Smith, "An
English conciliarist? Thomas Netter of Walden at the Councils of Pisa and Constance,"
in *Popes, Teachers and Canon Law in the Middle Ages*, eds. James R. Sweeney and Stanley
Chodorow (Ithaca and London, 1989), pp. 290–99.

[3] *DAF* 3:830 (footnote): "Ex Decreto Constantiensis concilii exhumari debebat:
sed insuper ex fidelium zelo & Episcopi Lincolniensis permissu, in flumen projec-
tum est, an. 1418."

[4] Herbert B. Workman, *John Wyclif. A Study of the English Medieval Church*, 2 vols.
(Oxford, 1926), 2:319–20; Edith C. Tatnall, "The Condemnation of John Wyclif
at the Council of Constance," in *Councils and Assemblies*, eds. G.J. Cuming and Derek
Baker (Cambridge, 1971), pp. 209–18; Anthony Kenny, "The Accursed Memory:
The Counter-Reformation Reputation of John Wyclif," in *Wyclif in His Times*, ed.
Anthony Kenny (Oxford, 1986), pp. 147–68.

[5] Simon Forde, "Repyndon, Philip (c. 1345–1424)," *DNB* 46:503–5 (504).

[6] R.N. Swanson, "Flemming, Richard (d. 1431)," *DNB* 20:78–80 (79).

annihilation of Wyclif, with his opponents, whom Netter had characterized as a second Israel challenged to single combat by Wyclif's Goliath, having the last word.[7] But the last word was an elusive prize in these controversies. Wyclif's death had not interrupted the sequence of exchanges between his supporters and opponents, and neither the conflagration of 1428 nor the *Doctrinale* could quite bring the Wycliffite controversies to an end.

In a sympathetic assessment of the intellectual liveliness of Netter's *Doctrinale*, Anthony Kenny contrasts this mode of response to Wyclif with the condemnations produced at Constance and concludes that "it was not Netter's scholarship and sensitivity that was to shape Catholic reaction to Wyclif, but the crude anathemas of 1415."[8] This frank and melancholy appraisal of the situation after Constance has a great deal to tell us about the developments that had led up to 1415, and thus it establishes both the tone and the context of this essay. While I will concentrate here on discussing the strategies adopted in texts written against Wyclif rather than the wording of official condemnations against him, it must be acknowledged at the outset that academic refutations of his ideas were only ever one "arrow in the quiver" of his opponents (to use the imagery deployed by "Brother John," the semi-anonymous Dominican author of an anti-Wycliffite treatise on the Eucharist, *Pharetra Sacramenti*). When reading the sequence of extant responses to Wyclif, we are obliged to remember that, diverse in matter and content as they are, what most of these treatises, determinations and dialogues have in common is the fact of their having been written in the temporal interstices of the escalating phases of opposition driven by ecclesiastical and state legislation. Lists of propositions for condemnation could never achieve—indeed, did not seek to achieve—the degrees of subtlety displayed in the writings of the most intellectually gifted of Wyclif's opponents, such as those of the Franciscan William Woodford. But Netter identified a perennial problem inherent in the Church's long history of confrontations with heretics, and offers a melancholy reflection on the development of the particular controversies in which he was embroiled. Using the words of Bernard of Clairvaux, he asserts that heretics will not be convinced through the use of reasoned arguments, because

---

[7] *DAF* 1:7, referring to the episode in 1 Samuel 17:8–9.
[8] Kenny, "The Accursed Memory," p. 157.

they do not understand them; nor will they be corrected through the
use of authorities, because they do not accept them; nor will persuasion work with them, because they are perverse. In fact, Bernard
concludes (and Netter with him), they would rather die than be converted.[9] In these controversies, therefore, disputation and legislation
ran along generally parallel lines that occasionally met. The disputations
and other kinds of written response to be considered here were often
generated by specific, discrete, local and occasional circumstances,
whereas the motives behind condemnations and other forms of official
legislation ranged from broader attempts at building a strong ecclesiastical consensus against Wyclif (as at the Blackfriars Council of
1382) to the brokering of power between Crown and Church (as
expressed in the 1401 statute *De haeretico comburendo*).[10] But it was a
hallmark of these controversies that they would call into question the
already porous boundaries between the worlds in and beyond the
schools, and the production of certain major anti-Wycliffite texts can
be tied to specific events.[11] Thus, the *Liber contra duodecim errores et
hereses lollardorum* (1395), by the Dominican Roger Dymoke, was written in response to the publication of the Wycliffite *Twelve Conclusions*.
Likewise, the condemnation by Convocation in 1397 of propositions
derived from Wyclif's *Trialogus* was accompanied by a "commissioned"
response, William Woodford's *De causis condempnationis*, written at the
behest of Thomas Arundel, Archbishop of Canterbury. Netter's
Doctrinale, begun at the instigation of Henry V and addressed to Pope
Martin V, was the culmination of this collaboration between academic and extramural needs and interests.

   The relationship between disputation and condemnation was not
always a natural one, however and they are at their most distant in

---

[9] *DAF*, 1:2: "Nam quantum ad istos, nec rationibus convincuntur, quia non intelligent; nec authoritatibus corriguntur, quia non recipiunt; nec flectuntur suasionibus,
quia subversi sunt. Probatum est: mori magis eligunt, quam converti." The words are
taken from Bernard's *Sermon 66* on the Song of Songs; on which, see further below.
   [10] A.K. McHardy, "De Heretico Comburendo, 1401," in *Lollardy and the Gentry
in the Later Middle Ages*, eds. Margaret Aston and Colin Richmond (Stroud and New
York, 1997), pp. 112–26. Peter McNiven, *Heresy and Politics in the Reign of Henry IV:
The Burning of John Badby* (Woodbridge, 1987).
   [11] On the distinctive, extramural reach of these controversies, see Jeremy Catto,
"Wyclif and Wycliffism at Oxford 1356–1430," in *The History of the University of
Oxford, Vol. 2: Late Medieval Oxford*, eds. J.I. Catto and Ralph Evans (Oxford, 1992),
p. 211. The consequences for the relationships between Latin and vernacular literature of the period are pursued in Fiona Somerset, *Clerical Discourse and Lay Audience
in Late Medieval England* (Cambridge, 1998).

Archbishop Arundel's *Provincial Constitutions* (1407–9). It has recently been suggested that this is a piece of legislation aimed in the first place at academic practice within Oxford.[12] Certainly the eighth Constitution is explicitly hostile to the scholastic culture that had generated the diverse writings that are our concern here, specifically identifying some of the standard scholastic practices that previous generations of Wyclif's opponents, in keeping with academic custom, had used. Referring to God as the "determiner" or "limiter of all things" (*omnium terminator*), the Constitution points out that he cannot be enclosed in "philosophical terminology" (*terminis philosophicis*). Since Augustine often revoked his conclusions because, although true, they were offensive to pious ears, the Constitution forbids anyone from:

> asserting or proposing, in the schools or outside, by disputing or communicating, conclusions or propositions that sound contrary to the catholic faith or good morals, beyond the teaching necessary for his faculty, whether with or without a prefatory protestation, even if they can be defended by a certain ingenuity in words or terms; for, in the words of Hugh of St. Victor on the sacraments, "Very often what is well said is not well understood."[13]

Remarkably, therefore, the *Constitutions* implicitly put academic dissidents such as Wyclif and any of his remaining supporters on the same side as his opponents, suggesting that the very enterprise of academic theology had the potential to run counter to the defence of the faith. It is a tightening in the definition of orthodoxy, whereby argumentative practices, as well as the ideas that they generate, hone and disseminate, can be anathematized and marginalized.[14] While in

---

[12] Fiona Somerset, "Expanding the Langlandian Canon: Radical Latin and the Stylistics of Reform," *Yearbook of Langland Studies* 17 (2003), 73–92; "Professionalising Translation at the Turn of the Fifteenth Century: Ullerston's *Determinacio*, Arundel's *Constitutiones*," in *The Vulgar Tongue: Medieval and Post-Medieval Vernacularity*, eds. Fiona Somerset and Nicholas Watson (University Park, PA, 2003), pp. 145–57. But for a different view of the *Constitutions*, which evaluates them as part of the history of ecclesiastical legislation rather than as negative catalysts in intellectual history, see Ian Forrest, "Ecclesiastical Justice and the Detection of Heresy in England, 1380–1430," (D.Phil. thesis, Oxford, 2003).

[13] *Concilia magnae Britanniae et Hiberniae*, ed. David Wilkins. 3 vols. (London, 1737), 3:317: "[N]e quis, vel qui . . . conclusiones aut propositiones in fide catholica seu bonis moribus adverse sonantes, praeter necessariam doctrinam facultatis suae, in scholis, aut extra, disputando aut communicando, protestatione praemissa vel non praemissa, asserat vel proponat, etiamsi quadam verborum aut terminorum curiositate defendi possint. Nam teste beato Hugone, de sacramentis, 'Saepius quod bene dicitur, non bene intelligitur.' "

[14] Rita Copeland, *Pedagogy, Intellectuals and Dissent in the Late Middle Ages. Lollardy and Ideas of Learning* (Cambridge, 2001), pp. 119–24, 198–99, 201–4, 208–14.

important respects, therefore, the *Constitutions* must continue to be seen as "the summation and enforcement of episcopal vigilance on this front since at least 1382," their language reopens the centuries-old wound in academic theology, an issue that the twelfth- and thirteenth-century theologians had been obliged to confront in their opening questions on the *Sentences*: the need for a fundamental justification of the academic "science" of theology.[15] Writing years before these *Constitutions* were drawn up, the Benedictine Nicholas Radcliff had included just such a *protestatio praemissa* in the first of his *Dialogi* written against Wyclif, and identifies it as such:

> In my writings, I do not intend to assert, declare, and teach anything that might be contrary to Sacred Scripture, offensive to pious ears or dissonant or repugnant to the determination of the Church in its authentic teaching of the Catholic faith.

He submits himself "with all humility" to reformation and correction by the Archbishop of Canterbury and other prelates and doctors if necessary.[16]

In a later generation, Reginald Pecock, the mid-fifteenth-century Bishop of Chichester, was a prominent exponent of an alternative approach, the attempt to convert heretics, and pre-empt lapses into heresy among the spiritually ambitious, by engaging them in rigorous dialogue and providing them with written instruction as well as with other forms of doctrinal mediation.[17] An anti-Wycliffite who was nevertheless arraigned for heresy and deposed from his see, Pecock and his fate exemplify the way in which the two spheres of anti-heresy, the academic and the legislative, could pull sharply away from one another, and in some respects it may seem surprising that this did not happen more often.[18] As one would expect, the possibility of a

---

[15] For continuity with previous legislation, see Alan J. Fletcher, *Preaching, Politics and Poetry in Late-Medieval England* (Dublin, 1998), p. 15; Forrest, "Ecclesiastical Justice." On the effects of the *Constitutions* on preaching, see H. Leith Spencer, *English Preaching in the Late Middle Ages* (Oxford, 1993), pp. 163–88.

[16] Nicholas Radcliff, *Dialogus primus de primo homine*, London, British Library, Royal 6.D.X, fol. 2v: "non intendo in scriptis meis aliqui assertive asserere, ponere & docere quod sit sacre scripture contrarium, piis auribus offensivum, determinacioni ecclesie fidei catholice autentice disciplina dissonum aut repugnans." On Radcliff, see James G. Clark, "Radcliffe, Nicholas (d. 1396 × 1401)," *DNB* 45:745–46.

[17] For discussion, see Margaret Aston, *Faith and Fire: Popular and Unpopular Religion, 1350–1600* (London and Rio Grande, 1993), pp. 73–93.

[18] For the political circumstances surrounding Pecock's fall, see Wendy Scase, *Reginald Pecock* (Aldershot, 1996), pp. 103–16, and Jeremy Catto, "The King's Government

plurality of approaches, together with the independence of academic institutions—in this case, Oxford in particular—were rendered vulnerable by these controversies. It has been observed that "orthodoxy is *constructed*, in the processes of both theological and political conflict."[19] In the *Sermon* from which, as we have seen, Netter had quoted, Bernard of Clairvaux went on to emphasize that "faith is a matter of persuasion, not coercion" (*fides suadenda est, non imponenda*).[20] This attitude was to come under particular pressure during the Wycliffite controversies, but the texts that we will consider here do much to protect discursive space and to solicit independent judgment. With the privilege of hindsight, we can see that the independence of mind displayed by Roger Rygge, Chancellor of Oxford in the pivotal year of 1382, in the face of the demands of Archbishop Courtenay, was getting to the heart of the matter.[21] Even Netter, who attempts to distance the *Doctrinale* from a *scholasticus ludus*, had nevertheless assembled in it the encyclopaedic record of a scholastic culture rooted in an increasing appreciation of the value of patristic arguments considered *in situ*. Thus one important question to be asked of these controversies is what cumulative effect they had on intellectual freedom, both within and beyond the schools, and particularly on the possibilities for frank discussion by English writers of clerical abuses and ecclesiastical reform, and I will conclude this essay with some remarks on that subject.

Because it had become possible to conflate "Lollardy" and the spread of Wyclif's ideas with the threat of sedition, events in this field of intellectual history were condemned to take place in the narrowing spaces left by events in the wider world.[22] Enforcement of religious (and thus, political) orthodoxy could not happen as effectively, and conclusively, through academic discussion as it could through intransigent legislation, for the very good reason that Wyclif and his

---

and the Fall of Pecock, 1457–58," in *Rulers and Ruled in Late Medieval England: Essays Presented to Gerald Harriss*, eds. R. Archer and S. Walker (London, 1995), pp. 201–22.

[19] Rowan Williams ed., *The Making of Orthodoxy: Essays in Honour of Henry Chadwick* (Cambridge, 1989), p. ix.

[20] *S. Bernardi Opera*, eds. J. Lerclerq, C.H. Talbot and H.M. Rochais (Rome, 1958), 2:126/3.

[21] For the events in question, which I discuss further below, see Jeremy Catto, "Wyclif and Wycliffism," p. 219; *Fasciculi Zizaniorum Magistri Johannis Wyclif Cum Tritico* [henceforth *FZ*], ed. The Rev. Walter Waddington Shirley. Rolls Series 5 (London, 1858), pp. 298–301.

[22] Margaret Aston, "Lollardy and Sedition, 1381–1431," in *Lollards and Reformers. Images and Literacy in Late Medieval Religion* (London, 1984), pp. 1–47.

academic opponents were often arguing over the interpretation of
the same sources and materials. It is for this reason that John Donne's
question from *Satyre III* serves as one of the epigraphs to this chapter. It is not intended to suggest, in a trivial and dismissive fashion,
that Wyclif and his opponents were merely trading sterile and
exhausted quotations (though this may well have been Pecock's view,
as we shall see), but rather to focus another important issue to be
addressed in this essay, namely that what was at stake in the Wycliffite
controversies was an uncomfortable confrontation between two branches
growing from the same stem, two argumentative positions nourished
and supported by the same sources. However much Wyclif's opponents liked to present him in their writings as a fully-formed heretic
and an outcast, they were obliged to trace and critically refute his
use of sources upon which they themselves were dependent. In one
of the earliest debates with Wyclif, the Carmelite John Kynyngham
pointed out that "literary authorities can easily be interpreted in such
a way as to provide support for either side."[23] Notoriously, Jan Hus
defended himself at Constance by pointing out that the doctrine that
the Church was the "whole body of the predestined" (*praedestinatorum
universitas*) is present in St. Augustine's writings, and that the Council
was thus "putting itself in the ironic position of condemning as heretical one of the Fathers of the Church."[24] Despite the prolonged and
vehement nature of the controversies, therefore, they exposed, but
could not have been expected to resolve, the longer-standing question of the role and status of textual interpretation in establishing
and defending Church doctrine.[25] It has been noted, however, that
Wyclif's mode of procedure in *De veritate Sacrae Scripturae* suggests that
the approaches of some of his more gifted critics had hit home: "the
arguments of opponents like Kenningham and Woodford may have
forced him, however reluctantly, towards historical criticism."[26] What
would distinguish Wyclif's approaches from those of his opponents

---

[23] *FZ*, 12/1–2: ". . . [A]uctoritates pro utraque parte de facili possunt glossari."
[24] Tatnall, "The Condemnation of John Wyclif," p. 218. Wyclif's assertion that
"[E]cclesia catholica sive apostolica sit universitas predestinatorum" ("The catholic or
apostolic Church is the whole body of the predestined") is stated in *De civili dominio*,
eds. R.L. Poole and J. Loserth 4 vols. (London, 1885; 1900–04) 1:358/29–30 and
can also be found as early as his dispute with Ralph Strode: *Responsiones ad Argumenta
Radulfi Strode*, in *Opera Minora*, ed. Johann Loserth (London, 1913), p. 176/4–7.
[25] This is the central theme of Kantik Ghosh, *The Wycliffite Heresy*.
[26] Catto, "Wyclif and Wycliffism," p. 209.

was often not material, therefore, since many of them accommodated his tendency to use a restricted canon of authorities (*auctoritates*), but method. We will consider the implications of these controversies for theological method at the end of this essay.

It is first necessary to trace the development of opposition to Wyclif and his supporters, from his earliest interlocutors to those who, like Netter, "exhumed" him and his ideas only to condemn him afresh. The sequence of events in Wyclif's career, and in particular the development and nature of academic responses to his writings and arguments, have already been traced in detail by others, beginning with the accounts of contemporary chroniclers and continuing with the fifteenth-century compiler of the anti-Wycliffite *Fasciculi Zizaniorum*, who binds together accounts of some of the condemnations, declarations and disputations generated by the controversies with his own interpretative narrative.[27] I will first provide a chronologically-driven narrative that concentrates largely on placing the emergence of written refutations of his views in historical sequence, commenting on features of some individual works. I will then discuss at greater length some compelling issues raised in particular texts, placing them within the broader contexts that I have already outlined. I will use the early debate between Wyclif and Kynyngham to explore the anxiety aroused in several of Wyclif's opponents regarding the possible implications of his arguments for different audiences, and the way in which his opponents' definitions of orthodoxy were often driven by the desire, and indeed the necessity, of building and drawing on a *consensus fidelium*. This particular debate touches on several issues that are fundamental to the Wycliffite controversies, not least the way in which they brought into question the relationship between doctrinal orthodoxy and tradition, and the precarious authority of texts and interpretations in establishing that tradition. Anne Hudson has pointed out that the anonymous researcher who was involved in the drafting of the 267 Oxford articles against Wyclif (1410) observes that "some of Wyclif's statements could be defended scholastically 'quo ad verba,' but that, preached or taught openly or secretly, they could

---

[27] Anne Hudson, *The Premature Reformation. Wycliffite Texts and Lollard Hisory* (Oxford, 1988), pp. 92–103; Catto, "Wyclif and Wycliffism"; Anne Hudson and Anthony Kenny, "Wyclif, John (d. 1384)," *DNB* 60:616–60. On the Carmelite compilation of *Fasciculi Zizaniorum*, see J. Crompton, "*Fasciculi Zizaniorum*," *Journal of Ecclesiastical History* 12 (1961), 13–45, 155–65.

lead the hearers to error."[28] In this he is with some of Wyclif's earliest opponents, most notably Kynyngham; and in general the relationship between the context in which ideas were uttered and their
effects on putative audiences was to loom very large in the considerations of Wyclif's opponents. With this in mind, I will then turn
to developments in the fifteenth century, and in particular to the
methodological choices of Thomas Netter, a comparatively late opponent. Netter's method of proceeding will be compared and contrasted
with the tactics adopted by Nicholas Radcliff and the Franciscan
William Woodford, opponents of an earlier generation. This will lead
to a consideration of the radical discontinuity between the approach
taken in Netter's *Doctrinale* and in Reginald Pecock's later, vernacular anti-Wycliffite writings. I will turn in conclusion to an appraisal
of the areas of overlap between anti-Wycliffism and reform, and will
offer some final remarks on the implications of the controversies for
the theory and practice of theological method in this period.

Several remarks are necessary at the outset. First, in order to avoid
merely reduplicating the echo-chamber of these controversies, it is
necessary to view them from a critical vantage-point. Jeremy Catto
rightly points out that "the period of Oxford history which lasted
from 1356 to 1430 was an era of controversy," and a yet broader
perspective is provided by R.N. Swanson's comment that "because
Western Christianity developed, indeed was transformed, between
1100 and 1500, heresy was almost a necessary concomitant."[29] Most
of this controversy was generated by, and around, the writings and
intellectual afterlife of Wyclif and his supporters, but it is also true that
the Wycliffite controversies themselves grew out of earlier disputes
such as the antimendicant controversies. The compiler or compilers
of *Fasciculi Zizaniorum* certainly seems to have viewed the controversies surrounding Wyclif as part of a *longue durée*, since the manuscript
from which the materials in the widely-used but abbreviated printed
edition were taken also contains lists of errors condemned at Oxford

---

[28] Anne Hudson, "Notes of an Early Fifteenth-Century Research Assistant, and
the Emergence of the 267 Articles against Wyclif," *English Historical Review* 118
(2003), 685–97 (690).
[29] Catto, "Wyclif and Wycliffism," p. 180; R.N. Swanson, "Literacy, Heresy, History
and Orthodoxy: Perspectives and Permutations for the Later Middle Ages," in *Heresy
and Literacy, 1000–1530*, eds. Peter Biller and Anne Hudson (Cambridge, 1994), pp.
279–93 (280).

in the time of Robert Kilwardby, errors condemned by William, Bishop of Paris and errors of the Greeks.[30]

Second, it has to be recognized that the episodic nature of the production of anti-Wycliffite writings, which I have briefly mentioned, makes it difficult to place them in a coherent, unfolding "grand narrative" of opposition. It is possible, for example, to imagine a parallel narrative about Wyclif's opponents that assesses the impact of the controversies on the internal histories of each religious order respectively, and elucidates the differences between approaches taken by men from different orders.[31] It is not otherwise easy to assess the degree of influence exercised on successive generations by men such as Kynyngham, who were prominent, and even distinguished, early in the disputes. By contrast, the works of others, such as Woodford, the Cambridge theologian and Irish secular priest John Deveros, and Netter, were carefully preserved and thus may have enjoyed a lease of life greater than they might have expected. Codicological evidence shows, as one would expect, that the works of some opponents were more widely distributed than others, and this makes it difficult to speak of a concerted, systematic attempt to destroy Wyclif's arguments and influence.[32] Likewise, some issues preoccupied one generation more than another and took time to emerge (such as the topic of image-worship in the 1390s), while others (transubstantiation, clerical endowment) were present from the outset and continued to dominate the controversies. Thus, to survey the range of responses from Kynyngham to Pecock is to be struck rather by an overall impression of discontinuity, with each writer approaching his task rather as if beginning the demolition of Wyclif afresh.

---

[30] FZ, p. lxxiv. The manuscript is Oxford, Bodleian Library e. Musaeo 86 and the errors listed are on fols. 149v–156r.

[31] See, for example, Patrick J. Horner, "The King Taught Us the Lesson: Benedictine Support for Henry V's Suppression of the Lollards," *Mediaeval Studies* 52 (1990), 190–220. It is well known that the Carmelites "kept at the heels of the heterodox for some sixty years." On some aspects of their activities, see Ann Eljenholm Nichols, *Seeable Signs: The Iconography of the Seven Sacraments, 1350–1544* (Woodbridge, 1997), pp. 106, 114–28 (the quotation is taken from p. 115).

[32] For all works and extant manuscripts associated with the opponents discussed in this essay, see Richard Sharpe, *A Handlist of the Latin Writers of Great Britain and Ireland Before 1540* (Turnhout, 1997).

Chronology of the Controversies

A complete roster of Wyclif's opponents would have to include writers who will not be considered here, such as the Carthusian, Nicholas Love, whose *Myroure of the Blessed Lyfe of Jesu Christ* contains anti-Lollard observations; bishops such as Robert Hallum and Henry Bowet, who zealously sought out heretics in their dioceses; and figures such as Arundel, who coordinated the ecclesiastical and state action against the supporters of Wyclif.[33] It would also have to recognise those who did not engage in theological controversy, confining their anti-Wycliffite activities to attendance at heresy trials, or participation in interrogations; in certain notable cases, such as those of Netter and the Dominican Thomas Palmer, these two categories overlap.[34] Although I shall focus here on academic treatises in different genres (disputations, determinations, *quaestiones*, culminating in the very different *summae* produced by Netter and Pecock), it is important to note that a significant amount of opposition to Wyclif was articulated through other genres, such as chronicles and sermons. The recent work of Siegfried Wenzel, in particular, has made it easier to grasp the evolution of anti-Wycliffite preaching.[35] For the fullest possible appraisal of the range of views that could be marshalled against Wyclif and his followers, significant sermon collec-tions should be taken into account, such as the *Festial* of the Augustinian Canon, John Mirk, whose sermons contain several anti-Lollard observations, or another collection by an anonymous Augustinian Canon in Hereford, Cathedral Library, MS O.iii.5.[36] To these should be added several collections by Benedictines, such as the preacher whose sermons are contained in Oxford, Bodleian Library MS 649 (some of which also appear in Laud Misc 706, another Benedictine collection), or Robert Rypon, whose sermons are collected in British Library, MS Harley 4894.[37] Wenzel's reappraisal of the relations between "orthodox and

---

[33] On Love, see Ghosh, *The Wycliffite Heresy*, pp. 147–73. On Arundel and the bishops, see McNiven, *Heresy and Politics*, and Forrest, "Ecclesiastical Legislation."

[34] Anne Hudson, "Palmer, Thomas (fl. 1371–1415)," *DNB* 42:536–37.

[35] *Latin Sermon Collections from Later Medieval England. Orthodox Preaching in the Age of Wyclif* (Cambridge, 2005). See also Spencer, *English Preaching* and Fletcher, *Preaching, Politics and Poetry*.

[36] On anti-Lollard observations in the *Festial*, see Wenzel, *Latin Sermon Collections*, p. 65. On the Hereford manuscript, see pp. 159–65.

[37] Ibid., p. 71. On the previous two Bodleian collections, see pp. 84–90. On Benedictine anti-Lollardy, see Patrick J. Horner, "The King Taught Us the Lesson."

heterodox" points of view in this genre leads us to a more complex question, namely the fate of what has been termed "radical orthodoxy," a strongly reforming mentality among anti-Wycliffite preachers, and this is an important theme to which I will return when appraising the character and legacy of anti-Wycliffism in the conclusions to this essay.[38]

It is useful to distinguish between different phases in opposition to Wyclif, and to observe the relationship between the official condemnations of his ideas and the motives behind the production of written works by individual opponents. For the sake of convenience and coherence, opposition to Wyclif can be seen as falling chronologically into eight phases:

> I. 1372–1377: from Wyclif's earliest debates with contemporaries such as Strode and Kynyngham until his condemnation by Pope Gregory XI (1377).
>
> II. 1377–1381: from the exchanges between Wyclif and opponents such as Woodford and Crump, whose arguments fed into the writing of *De civili dominio*, to William Barton's condemnation of Wyclif's views on the Eucharist and Wyclif's *Confessio* of 1381.
>
> III. 1382–1384: from the Blackfriars Council of 1382 to Wyclif's death, this phase also incorporating his exchanges with William Rymington.
>
> IV. 1384–1395: from Wyclif's death to the publication of the Lollard *Twelve Conclusions* and Dymoke's reply to them.
>
> V. 1396–1401: from the condemnation of views extrapolated from the *Trialogus* to the statute *De heretico comburendo*.
>
> VI. 1401–1410: from *De heretico comburendo* to the condemnation of Wyclif's views at Oxford, this phase also incorporating Arundel's *Constitutions* (1407–9).
>
> VII. 1410–1430: from the Oxford condemnation of 1410–11 to the death of Netter, incorporating the Oldcastle rebellion, the Council of Constance and the burning of Wyclif's bones in 1428.
>
> VIII. 1430 onwards: the decline of academic Wycliffism and the work of Pecock.

In the *Doctrinale*, Netter characterizes Wyclif as an eager combatant challenging the Church to a series of disputations concerning fraternal

---

[38] For a subtle discussion of the complex relationship between orthodoxy and heterodoxy, see Hudson, *Premature Reformation*, pp. 421–30, especially p. 429 on "radical orthodoxy"; Wenzel, *Latin Sermon Collections*, pp. 370–94.

oaths, religion, the Eucharist and the Pope: "*Disputemus de voto; disputemus de Religione, de Eucharistia, vel de Papa.*"[39] This does some justice to the range of topics covered by Wyclif's contemporary and posthumous opponents. The first phase of the controversies occupies the period between the early 1370s, when Wyclif was in disputation with Ralph Strode, John Kynyngham and others, and the papal censure that Wyclif received from Gregory XI in 1377, on account of the views expressed in *De civili dominio*. Tracing the sequence of response to Wyclif during this early period enables us to feel the pace at which he became a controversial figure in Oxford circles and beyond. The earliest extant example of his participation in a disputation with an opponent is the sequence of his Oxford disputations (c. 1372–73) with Kynyngham, a written record of which was preserved in *Fasciculi Zizaniorum*, and which will be given more detailed consideration later in this essay, as it is substantial, subtle and in important respects anticipates the trajectory of subsequent responses to Wyclif. Also preserved from this early phase are Wyclif's responses to arguments by William Binham O.S.B. (c. 1374–77), Strode (late 1370s) and Uthred of Boldon, O.S.B. (1377–78).[40]

In c. 1376, the Cistercian Henry Crump preached against Wyclif, provoking him to respond in Book Two of *De civili dominio*, which was written by 1377.[41] Although not strictly the record of a disputation with his opponents (as other works collected in the *Opera Minora*, such as the *Responsiones* to William Rymington, clearly are), *De civili dominio* should therefore be read as the product of dialogue in the broadest sense, since, in addition to those sections written in response to Crump, two chapters of Book Three were written in response to the first thirty arguments of William Woodford's *De dominio civili*

---

[39] *DAF* I:7D.

[40] *Opera Minora*, pp. 175–200, 398–430. The works of Binham and Strode are no longer extant. Uthred of Boldon's works are preserved in Durham Cathedral Library. MS A.IV.33 and MS B.IV.34, Jesus College, Cambridge, MS 41, and BN Paris MS Lat. 3183.

[41] Katherine Walsh, "Crump, Henry (fl. c. 1376–1401)," *DNB* 14:536–37. Crump is an interesting example of a comparatively rare phenomenon, the opponent who later becomes an adherent of Wyclif's ideas; Wycliffites who later conformed, such as Nicholas Hereford and Philip Repingdon, were rather more common. On the transformation of members of this academic generation from supporters of Wyclif to reformers within the ecclesiastical establishment, see Jeremy Catto, "Fellows and Helpers: The Religious Identity of the Followers of Wyclif," in *The Medieval Church: Universities, Heresy, and the Religious Life*, Studies in Church History, Subsidia 11, eds. Peter Biller and Barrie Dobson (Woodbridge, 1999), pp. 141–62.

clericorum.[42] When searching for evidence of the impact that academic opposition made on the development of Wyclif's thought, therefore, it remains necessary to remain alert to the presence of what might be regarded as "embedded disputation" of this kind in his extant written works, and the *Opera Minora* is a rich source for evidence of Wyclif honing his thoughts in response to sustained and diverse opposition. Woodford's early intervention in the development of academic opposition to Wyclif, lecturing in Oxford (1376) on ecclesiastical endowments, inaugurated a particularly distinguished twenty-year career of opposition to Wyclif, characterized by the production of thoughtful and immensely pithy responses that never succumb to polemical sclerosis but explore the topic in hand, whether disendowment, eucharistic theology, or ecclesiastical authority, from the standpoint of a markedly historicist sensibility that suggests ways out of the methodological impasse that threatened to build up in the more vehemently polemical works of Wyclif's other opponents.[43] In both content and method, Woodford's responses stand out from the general run of written opposition to Wyclif in that they manage to roam widely through their subject while being amongst the least prolix, and we will return to him later in this essay. The last of Wyclif's opponents associated with this first phase is Adam Easton OSB, who was prominent among Wyclif's early Benedictine critics, and who wrote the substantial anti-Wycliffite work *Defensorium ecclesiasticae potestatis*, dedicated to Pope Urban VI.[44]

The next opponent of note, William Barton, Chancellor of Oxford, is a crucial transitional figure who precipitated the crisis of 1381–82. Barton's determination against Wyclif's views is no longer extant, but it provoked a response from Wyclif in *De veritate Sacrae Scripturae*

---

[42] Eric Doyle, O.F.M., "William Woodford's 'De dominio civili clericorum' against John Wyclif", *Archivum Franciscanum Historicum* 62 (1969), 377–81. Wyclif's response is in *De civili dominio*, 3:351–405.

[43] Jeremy Catto, "Woodford, William" (d. in or after 1397), *DNB* 60:179–80; J.I. Catto, "William Woodford O.F.M. c. 1330–1397" (D.Phil. thesis, Oxford, 1969); Doyle, "William Woodford's 'De dominio civili clericorum'" and "William Woodford, O.F.M. (c. 1330–c. 1400) His Life and Works Together With a Study and Edition of His 'Responsiones Contra Wiclevum et Lollardos,'" *Franciscan Studies* 43 (1983), 17–187.

[44] R.B. Dobson, "Easton, Adam (c. 1330–1397)," *DNB* 17:599–600; Margaret Harvey, "Adam Easton and the Condemnation of John Wyclif," *English Historical Review* 113 (1998), 321–35; S.L. Forte, "A Study of Some Oxford Schoolmen of the Middle of the Fourteenth Century with special Reference to Worcester Cathedral MS. F. 65" (B.Litt. thesis, Oxford, 1947). The prologue and first six books of the *Defensorium* survive as Vatican City, Biblioteca Apostolica Vaticana, Vat. Lat. 4116.

(Barton's identity having been revealed in a manuscript marginalium).[45] Barton was instrumental in orchestrating the first phase of official condemnation, bringing together a group of doctors of theology and canon law (1380–81) who condemned two propositions that encapsulated Wyclif's views concerning the eucharist (although he was not named).[46] It was this condemnation that in turn provoked Wyclif's *Confessio* (10 May 1381). Barton was among those present at the Canterbury session of the Blackfriars Council in which propositions imputed to Wyclif were condemned on 1 July 1382. Wyclif's *Confessio* generated an *Absolutio* from the Augustinian Thomas Winterton.[47] This treatise will be considered in greater detail below.

As might be expected, a number of opponents, who either wrote treatises refuting Wyclif's views or provoked written responses from him, were involved in the activities of 1382. Barton, as mentioned above, was one; another was the Carmelite Peter Stokes.[48] Nicholas Radcliff, whose series of dialogues countering Wycliffite positions on a range of topics will also receive further examination below, was present, as were the protean Henry Crump, later to be accused of sympathy with Wyclif's ideas, and the Benedictine John Wells, known as the "Hammer of the Heretics" (*Malleus Hereticorum*), whose many anti-heretical works are, unfortunately, lost to us.[49] Stokes was employed as the agent of Archbishop William Courtenay in Oxford, with a brief specifically to monitor support for Wyclif's views. In standard narratives of these heightened times, Stokes features as a somewhat pusillanimous figure, easily outflanked by Philip Repingdon (in his incarnation as an early supporter of Wyclif) and Robert Rygge, Chancellor of the University, an admirer of Wyclif and an active supporter of his associates.[50] Rygge stalled Stokes's attempts to have the condemnation of Wyclif's views, which had been pronounced at the Blackfriars Council on 17 May, publicly pronounced in Oxford before Repingdon preached on Corpus Christi Day (5 June). Although Rygge's support for Wyclif's associates was relatively easily curtailed by Courtenay, his case brings into focus the important issue of the

[45] Jeremy Catto, "Barton, William (d. after 1382)," *DNB* 4:214–215. The manuscript in question is Cambridge, Peterhouse 223, fol 230r.
[46] *FZ*, 110–112; Catto, "Wyclif and Wycliffism," pp. 213–14.
[47] Anne Hudson, "Winterton, Thomas (d. 1400 × 02)," *DNB* 59:800–1.
[48] Anne Hudson, "Stokes, Peter (d. 1399)," *DNB* 52:872.
[49] Christina von Nolcken, "Wells, John (d. 1388)," *DNB* 58:64–65.
[50] Jeremy Catto, "Rygge, Robert (d. 1410)," *DNB* 48:468–69.

extent to which Oxford's privileges, including its immunity from ecclesiastical jurisdiction, were perceived to have been called into question by the spate of condemnations initiated outside the university against Wyclif and his supporters. This brings to the fore the pressures to which academic disputations were subjected extramurally as well as intramurally, and, as we will see, anxieties surrounding this question were to become a prominent feature in literary responses to Wyclif.

Nicholas Radcliff was later Archdeacon of St. Albans, which was to remain a focus of opposition to Wyclif at least until the time of John Whethamstede's two periods of abbacy, some eighty years later.[51] Radcliff is the author of a series of works, including six dialogues: *De immortalitate primi hominis, De dominio naturali, De obedienciali dominio, De dominio regali et judiciali, De potestate Petri apostoli successorum, De eodem argumento.*[52] Although Radcliff's involvement in anti-Wycliffite activities date from 1382, the six dialogues have been dated to the period 1378, and though it has been claimed that his works "were known outside St. Albans," it has also been asserted that they do not seem to have been widely consulted beyond the monastery.[53] The significance of Radcliff's contribution to anti-Wycliffite writings will be more fully considered in the discussion of Netter below, but for now it should be noted that they are a surprisingly overlooked resource for those hoping to understand the argumentative resourcefulness of anti-Wycliffism in its earliest decades. Radcliff writes copiously and approaches his topic with some agility. His preference is for the dialogue form, which enables him to pit his own arguments from natural reason, and from his patristic sources, against the arguments of

---

[51] James G. Clark, "Whethamstede, John (c. 1392–1465)," *DNB* 58:455–58. For Radcliff, see Clark, "Radcliffe, Nicholas" and Forte, "Some Oxford Schoolmen."

[52] These dialogues are preserved in London, British Library Royal 6.D.X, fols. 1–283r. The manuscript also includes Radcliffe's extensive anti-Wycliffite treatise on the Eucharist (*De viatico salutari animae*), which is also composed in the form of a dialogue with Stokes, and two shorter treatises, *De voto religionis* and *De imaginum cultu.* An *Invectio Contra errores Wyclif,* a digest of Radcliff's arguments, is also extant in BL Harley 635. Clark notes in his *DNB* entry that these works "were probably written at the request of the abbot, Thomas De la Mare, and not only tackle many of the theological questions raised by Wyclif but also reflect De la Mare's concern to counter Lollardy in the local community."

[53] For the dating of Radcliffe's *Dialogi* to c. 1378, see Catto, "Wyclif and Wycliffism," p. 206; for the dating of the treatise on images to 1387–95, see Hudson, *Premature Reformation*, p. 93. Clark claims that the works were known outside St. Albans; Catto (p. 206) is less convinced.

Wyclif, which his interlocutor, "Petrus," amplifies with a range of possible refutations of Radcliff's position. There is much to be gleaned from the *Dialogi* concerning Radcliff's understanding of the relative degrees of authority possessed by his sources. For example, "Nicholaus" appraises some arguments that his interlocutor has drawn from Peter Lombard and Hugh of St. Victor in refutation of one of his own arguments, and respectfully concludes that under the terms of the prefatory protestation that he appended earlier, which we have already considered, "and with all humility and reverence" (*sub protestacione premissa cum omni humilitate et reverentia*), the sayings of those particular doctors or of other saints are not of such great authority that they can serve the purposes of the current argument.[54] At times he tailors his arguments to refutations of specific passages in Wyclif's writings on dominion.[55] It is contributions such as Radcliff's—those of Deveros are another good example—that invite speculation as to the range and kind of intellectual activity that Arundel would attempting to curb some years later.[56]

Also from the early 1380s, spanning the period just before and just after the death of Wyclif in 1384, are the writings of the Cistercian William Rymington.[57] Although these are not confined to controversial literature, his exchange of arguments with Wyclif is instructive in that, unlike in the case of the earlier disputation with Kynyngham, this is one exchange in which the views of both participants are extant and can be compared. It is also thus possible to see how each opponent "voices" the other, and to assess how generously, or otherwise, each participant represented the other's position, since we have Wyclif's *Responsiones* to compare with Rymington's ventriloquising of Wyclif's position. The exchange began with Rymington's promulgation of his *Quadraginta quinque conclusiones*, to which Wyclif replied in the *Responsiones*. Shortly after Wyclif died, Rymington incorporated abbreviated forms of the *Responsiones* in his *Dialogus inter catholicam veritatem et haereticam pravitatem*.[58] A close comparison of the Rymington

---

[54] London, British Library, Royal 6.D.X, fol. 7r.

[55] For example in the *Dialogus secundus* concerning dominion, where Radcliff also turns Grosseteste, one of Wyclif's favoured authorities, against him (fol. 31v).

[56] This line of enquiry is pursued suggestively in Somerset, "Expanding the Langlandian Canon."

[57] Jeremy Catto, "Rymington, William (d. in or after 1385)," *DNB* 48:497–98.

[58] Rymington's contributions to the exchange are preserved in Oxford, Bodleian Library 158 (from which the references below are taken), although in reverse chrono-

manuscript with Wyclif's *Responsiones* (in *Opera Minora*) shows that each man represented, paraphrased or summarised the other's accurately. Rymington's having fortuitously had the last word in the disputation inevitably meant that "*Catholica veritas*" was able to refute "*Heretica pravitas*" at far greater length in the final exchange.[59] It could be dispiriting to see how swiftly Wyclif's positions have been demonized by Rymington as expressions of "heretical depravity"; on the other hand, Rymington's commitment to the dialogue form shows that he still regarded his opponent's arguments, as well as his own, as deserving of adjudication by the anonymous "impartial judge" (*quilibet iudex indifferens*, a putative reader of the dialogue) to whom he habitually appeals. This is made clear in the prologue to the *Dialogus*, where he states that he will lay out their arguments "as if between interlocutors in a dialogue . . . so that it may be possible to adjudicate between us" (*velud inter colloquentes . . . ut iudicare possit inter nos*).[60] The reader of Rymington's initial *Conclusiones* is also struck by the range of topics on which he sought to engage Wyclif: civil dominion, the sacrament of the altar, private religion (a topic that would also exercise Woodford), lay and clerical relations, poverty.[61] Rymington's anti-Wycliffite writings thus communicate, and preserve, a sense of discursive space, even if, as Netter was to do a few decades later, he cannot resist pointing out that Wyclif's arguments may be as harmful to their originator as Goliath's sword had been to him.[62]

More of William Woodford's writings are threaded through this post-1382 phase, and include his anti-Wycliffite treatise on the Eucharist, written in Framlington Castle in 1383, and his *Quattuor*

---

logical order, with the *Dialogus* followed by the *Conclusiones*. Wyclif's *Responsiones* to Rymington are printed in the *Opera Minora*, pp. 201–57. For some suggestive remarks on Rymington, see Somerset, "Expanding the Langlandian Canon," pp. 81–82 and Fiona Somerset, "Here, There, and Everywhere? Wycliffite Conceptions of the Eucharist and Chaucer's 'other' Lollard Joke," in *Lollards and Their Influence in Late Medieval England*, eds. Fiona Somerset, Jill C. Havens, and Derrick G. Pitard (Woodbridge, 2003), pp. 127–38 (pp. 129–31).

[59] Close comparisons may be made, for example, between the wording of Rymington's several conclusions on fols. 188v (Christ was both rich and poor; concerning the respective powers of the Pope and the Emperor) and Wyclif's representations of them (*Opera Minora*, pp. 202–3); see also Rymington's seventh and eighth conclusions concerning the Eucharist (fol. 191v), and Wyclif's discussions of these on p. 209.

[60] Fol. 188r.

[61] These are listed on fols. 198v–200v. Wyclif's "heretical or erroneous" conclusions are listed on fol. 198v.

[62] Fol. 188v.

determinationes in materia de religione (1389–90).[63] This brings us to the 1390s, a period in which the temperature of the Wycliffite controversies increased considerably. From 1390–92 dates the disputation of the Carmelite Richard Maidstone with John Ashwardby. Maidstone's works comprised *determinaciones* against heretics and concerning the role of the priest; a more substantial work, *Protectorium pauperis* (preserved in Oxford, Bodleian Library e. Musaeo 86, but not included in the printed version of *FZ*), was provoked by the sermons of John Ashwardby, the vicar of St. Mary's, Oxford, as was a series of sermons by Maidstone, of which only one survives.[64] None of Ashwardby's contributions to this ongoing disputation survives and, as is so often the case in the Wycliffite controversies, they have to be deduced from the tenor and content of Maidstone's responses. In her reading of Maidstone's response, Valerie Edden identifies "rules of engagement" that were to mark other contributions to these controversies, principally Maidstone's concern to "distinguish between authentic and inauthentic authorities"; his interest in complete quotations— *"auctoritatibus integris non truncatis"*—is also interesting in that it anticipates the long quotations in Netter's *Doctrinale* several decades later.[65] Maidstone's reply is robust and full of methodological nuggets: when criticizing his adversary for drawing on FitzRalph's arguments in his descriptions of the mendicant life, he not only criticizes Ashwardby for preferring the testimony of a "new" doctor (*doctor novellus*) over an "authentic" doctor (*doctor autenticus*), but also accuses FitzRalph of spouting arguments that are wilful (*voluntaria*) and directly contrary to the mode of speaking common to authentic doctors (*modum loquendi doctorum*).[66] Maidstone's treatise makes clear how "authority" was being constructed around a patristic consensus by many of Wyclif's opponents. When presenting the fifth of his conclusions—namely, that it is an indifferent proposition, rather than heretical or blasphemous, to

---

[63] M.D. Dobson, "Quattuor Determinaciones Fratris Willelmi Woodford de Ordine Fratrum Minorum contra Wyclyff in Materia de Religione," (thesis, Oxford, c. 1932).

[64] Richard Copsey, "Maidstone, Richard (d. 1396)," *DNB* 36:164–65. "*Protectorium pauperis*, a defence of the begging friars by Richard of Maidstone," ed. A. Williams, *Carmelus* 5 (1958), 132–80 and reprinted in *Carmel in Britain: Essays on the Medieval English Carmelite Province*, ed. Patrick Fitzgerald-Lombard O. Carm. 2 vols. (Rome, 1992), 2:35–83; Valerie Edden, "The debate between Richard Maidstone and the Lollard Ashwardby," *Carmelus* 34 (1987), 113–34, and reprinted in *Carmel in Britain*, 2:84–105.

[65] Edden, "The debate," p. 89.

[66] Williams, "*Protectorium Pauperis*," p. 60/120–21.

say that Christ had been able to beg "in his own person" (*in propria persona*)—Maidstone responds by pointing out that there are plausible arguments on both sides (*ad utramque partem sint verisimiles rationes*), but that when it comes to the testimony of the holy doctors, the evidence points in one direction: "the authorities of the holy doctors incline more to the proposition than to its opposite" (*auctoritates . . . sanctorum doctorum magis sonant ad propositum quam ad oppositum*).[67] When we examine Kynyngham's arguments against Wyclif, we will see how Maidstone's fellow Carmelite was similarly perturbed by what appeared to be Wyclif's estrangement from the "soundings" (the verb *sonare* is repeatedly used in this context) of an interpretative community.

Woodford's next important anti-Wycliffite treatise was the *Responsiones*, written in 1395, a year which also saw the publication of the *Twelve Conclusions*, and the literary response that they provoked from the Dominican Roger Dymoke in the form of the *Liber contra xii errores et hereses Lollardorum*. This substantial response, written in an often impassioned and characteristically elaborate Latin, has recently attracted attention from scholars seeking to understand Dymoke's role in a number of academic, social and political developments during this period, notably the extramural circulation of academic ideas and the framing and reception of Wycliffite views by the clergy.[68] Where one reading sees Dymoke's *Liber* as "halfhearted" in its commitment to addressing a wider audience than that composed solely of clergy, another proposes that "it is helpful to view Dymoke's *Liber* as an example of the process of clerical reception of the *Conclusions*," noting that the book is written in what could reasonably be regarded as "obscure scholastic language."[69] Dymoke's style has been discussed at some length, and it has been noted that whereas in some respects he has "made some effort to pitch his text to a non-academic audience," his style nevertheless contains many examples of "the machinery of argumentation."[70] I agree with this reading of the stylistics of

---

[67] Ibid., p. 61/4–6.
[68] The *Responsiones* have been edited in Eric Doyle, "William Woodford O.F.M." On Dymoke, see Anne Hudson, "Dymoke, Roger (fl. 1370–1400)," *DNB* 17:503–4. *Rogeri Dymmok Liber contra XII errores et hereses Lollardorum*, ed. H.S. Cronin (London, 1922).
[69] The first view is explored in Somerset, *Clerical Discourse*, pp. 103–34, the second in Wendy Scase, "The Audience and Framers of the *Twelve Conclusions*," in *Text and Controversy from Wyclif to Bale. Essays in Honour of Anne Hudson*, eds. Helen Barr and Ann M. Hutchison (Turnhout, 2005), pp. 283–301 (pp. 289–90).
[70] Somerset, *Clerical Discourse*, p. 128.

the *Liber*, but would also agree with the view that on balance it reflects the priorities of a predominantly clerical readership absorbed in processing the provocative document. Among Dymoke's range of *auctoritates*, patristic literature, and in particular the writing of John Damascene, is prominent: there is a particularly rich quotation from Damascene in praise of the value of the Cross as an object of veneration.[71] As might be expected, Dymoke draws on the authority of Aquinas repeatedly, and on several occasions, significantly, to the *Summa contra Gentiles*, a work through which Aquinas demonstrates the rhetorical efficacy of argument aimed at natural reason.[72] When arguing in the *Pars Quarta* in defence of the theology of transubstantiation, Dymoke argues for the doctrinal authority of doctors as "belated" as Aquinas and Peter Lombard, the former included not only on the strength of his arguments *contra Gentiles* but also because of his having composed the office for the feast of Corpus Christi.[73]

In February 1397, a list of Wyclif's views extrapolated from the *Trialogus* were condemned by Convocation, and Archbishop Arundel commissioned William Woodford to compose a refutation of these views. This resulted in *De causis condempnationis*, to which Deveros refers in his own collation of anti-Wycliffite arguments preserved in Worcester College, Oxford, 233.[74] Woodford died during the late 1390s, and the last years of the fourteenth century saw the production of a cluster of anti-Wycliffite writings on the closely related subjects of the veneration of images and the defence of pilgrimages. These included works by Deveros, the Dominican Thomas Palmer and Robert Alyngton, as well as an anonymous tract sometimes ascribed to Walter Hilton.[75] As written opposition to Wyclif continued into the fifteenth

---

[71] Dymoke, *Liber*, pp. 188–89. On this topic, see Margaret Aston, "Lollards and the Cross," in *Lollards and Their Influence in Late Medieval England*, pp. 99–113.

[72] As for example in the *Pars Prima* (a defence of Church temporalities): *Liber*, pp. 34–36, 44–45.

[73] Ibid., p. 92.

[74] Woodford's *De causis condempnationis articulorum 18 damnatorum Joannis Wyclif* have been printed in *Fasciculus rerum expetendarum ac fugiendarum*, ed. Edward Brown (London, 1619), 1:191–265. Deveros's reference to Woodford occurs in Worcester College, Oxford, 233, fol. 134r.

[75] On this phase of the controversies, see Hudson, *Premature Reformation*, pp. 92–94. Deveros was a particularly prominent contributor to this topic: on his works, see J. Crompton, "Lollard Doctrine, with special reference to the Controversy over Image-Worship and Pilgrimages" (B. Litt. Thesis, Oxford, 1949), pp. 133–202 and A.B. Emden, *A Biographical Register of the University of Cambridge to 1500* (Cambridge, 1963), p. 186. On Alyngton, see A.B. Emden, *A Biographical Register of the University of Oxford*

century, alongside the intensification of ecclesiastical and royal legislation intended to counter the spread of heresy (notably *De heretico
comburendo* in 1401 and Arundel's *Constitutions*), Richard Ullerston
joined the debate, producing *Defensorium dotacionis ecclesie* (1401), a
defence of ecclesiastical temporalities that draws on the arguments
of Uthred of Boldon and conducts a dense and detailed interpretation of passages from Leviticus and the books of Kings.[76] It is necessary to conclude this survey of theological response to Wyclif by
marking the events of 1410–11, when eighteen conclusions and then
267 propositions derived from Wyclif's works were drawn up at
Oxford.[77] These would, in turn, feed into the composition of the
articles of condemnation at Constance, which returns us to our starting-point.[78] It is now time to reflect on the important issues addressed
in some of these writings.

Theology in the World:
Kynyngham, Tissington and Winterton contra *Wyclif*

The writings of many of Wyclif's opponents have a singular value in
that they enable us to trace quite precisely the growth of anxiety
about the fate of scholastic discourse in the world beyond the schools.
This was an anxiety born of acute awareness of the change in the
currency value of scholastic terminology beyond the comparatively
protective environment of a university. To make such an observation,
however, is not to romanticise the degree of intellectual freedom

---

to A.D. 1500. 3 vols. (Oxford, 1957–59), 1:30–31; Catto, "Wyclif and Wycliffism,"
pp. 227, 231. Hilton's authorship of a tract entitled *De adoracione ymaginum* (Merton
College, Oxford 68, is disputed: it appears in *Walter Hilton's Latin Writings*, eds. John
P.H. Clark and Cheryl Taylor. 2 vols. (Salzburg, 1987), 1:175–214, but the certainty of this ascription questioned by Nicholas Watson, "'Et que est huius ydoli
materia? Tuipse': Idols and Images in Walter Hilton," in *Images, Idolatry and Iconoclasm
in Late Medieval England. Textuality and the Visual Image*, eds. Jeremy Dimmick, James
Simpson and Nicolette Zeeman (Oxford, 2002), pp. 95–111 (p. 97).

[76] Margaret Harvey, "Ullerston, Richard (d. 1423)," *DNB* 55:867–68; Catto,
"Wyclif and Wycliffism," pp. 239, 245. For discussion of Ullerston's views on the
translation of the Scriptures into English, see Somerset, "Professionalizing Translation."

[77] On this phase, see Catto, "Wyclif and Wycliffism," pp. 244–48.

[78] For further discussion of the drafting of the 267 conclusions, see Hudson, "Notes
of An Early Fifteenth-Century Research Assistant." On the process whereby these
were turned into the "crude anathemas" of Constance, see Kenny, "The Accursed
Memory."

possible within the medieval university, a topic that remains a subject of inquiry among modern scholars. Thijssen, for example, contends that "the medieval concept of academic freedom was much narrower than ours. It neither comprised the freedom of learning for students nor the freedom to teach, but was based only on the principle of the freedom of the academic institution to manage its own affairs."[79] This conclusion certainly bears out the facts concerning the University of Oxford's clashes with Canterbury between 1382 and 1411. Thijssen's further contention that "freedom of thought and expression did not lie heavily on the minds of medieval academics"[80] is somewhat at odds, however, with the proposal of John Birch of Oriel College, Oxford, that the committee that had been convened to examine Wyclif's writings should be disbanded and that "the faculty of arts should be free to hold probable opinions as in the past."[81] William J. Courtenay's exploration of the same topic has further resonance for the subject of our inquiry. While asserting that "freedom of thought and expression within the university community were judged primarily by the masters themselves," he goes on to point out that "only if the topic of controversy had wider ecclesiastical or political meaning, as in the cases of mendicant privileges, apostolic poverty, *dominium*, papal authority, and major points of doctrine, was the issue adjudicated outside the university."[82] The implications for the course taken by the Wycliffite controversies, and the way in which they brought university and extramural authorities into conflict, are self-evident.

These observations about the contexts in which university disputations took place do not, however, directly address the ways in which concerns about the interpretation and public resonance of academic language were internalized and expressed by the disputants themselves. In the more sensitive and ambitious of these writings we find men sharply aware of their roles as (to use a phrase coined to describe modern teachers of literature) "custodians of a discourse."[83] This

---

[79] J.M.M.H. Thijssen, *Censure and Heresy at the University of Paris 1200–1400* (Philadelphia, 1998), p. 91. The issue is pursued in relation to earlier generations of schoolmen in Heinrich Fichtenau, *Heretics and Scholars in the High Middle Ages 1000–1200*, trans. Denise A. Kaiser (University Park, PA, 1998).

[80] Thijssen, p. 91.

[81] Catto, "Wyclif and Wycliffism," pp. 248–49.

[82] William J. Courtenay, "Inquiry and Inquisition: Academic Freedom in Medieval Universities," *Church History* 58 (1989), 168–81 (180).

[83] Terry Eagleton, *Literary Theory: An Introduction* (1983), p. 201. Eagleton seeks to

awareness among the writers themselves is matched by a growing interest among modern scholars in the significance of the Wycliffite controversies as part of the broader, evolving culture of European scholasticism. In the theological literature generated by these controversies we can hear, increasingly clearly, the accents of scholastics aware of their roles as "public intellectuals," communicating with each other, and with their various publics, in literary genres loosely derived from academic models but increasingly attuned to the demands of extramural interpretative communities. Tracing the evolution not merely of these controversies but of late-medieval intellectual life *tout court*, we find that it is possible to construct a critical narrative of this period that begins with Wyclif and ends with Jean Gerson, so that these men may be seen not as occupying contrasting points on a putative spectrum of late-medieval intellectuals, but as occupying common ground.[84]

The partial transcript of Wyclif's earliest recorded debate with John Kynyngham, preserved in its incomplete form in *Fasciculi Zizaniorum*, brings these concerns fully into focus.[85] It has been noted that this is a debate "concerning the role and responsibilities of the theologian," conducted by men unable "to conceive of the theologian as a detached figure, separated from the community of faith . . . Theology is a public task, exercised in and for the Church, and thus requires a corresponding awareness of the ways in which the faithful public hears and responds to the proclamation of their faith."[86]

make a distinction between "purveyors of doctrine" (a term that he finds inapt to describe literary theorists) and "custodians of a discourse," but it could be argued that both phrases suit the medieval theologians with which we are concerned.

[84] For a ground-breaking discussion of this topic, see Daniel Hobbins, "The Schoolman as Public Intellectual: John Gerson and the Late Medieval Tract," *American Historical Review* 108 (2003), 1308–37.

[85] Although it is printed as part of Shirley's edition of *FZ*, Wyclif's part of the debate with Kynyngham is not in the *Fasciculi* manuscript, but in Cambridge, Corpus Christi College MS. 103. I am grateful to the anonymous reader of the present volume for pointing out that this needs to be emphasized.

[86] Ian Levy, "Defining the Responsibility of the Late Medieval Theologian: The Debate between John Kynyngham and John Wyclif," *Carmelus* 49 (2002), 5–29 (6, 28–29). On Kynyngham, see Anne Hudson, "Kenningham, John (d. 1399)," *DNB* 31:297–98. For further analysis of this debate, see also Stephen Penn, "Antiquity, Eternity and the Foundations of Authority: Reflections on a Debate between John Wyclif and John Kenningham, O. Carm.," *Trivium* 21 (2000), 107–119; J.A. Robson, *John Wyclif and the Oxford Schools. The Relation of the "Summa de Ente" to Scholastic Debates at Oxford in the Later Fourteenth Century* (Cambridge, 1961); Beryl Smalley, "The Bible and Eternity: John Wyclif's Dilemma," *Journal of the Warburg and Courtauld Institutes* 27 (1964), 73–89.

In an essay that argues for a measure of continuity between Kynyngham's concerns and those of Jean Gerson in a later generation, Maarten
Hoenen sees Kynyngham as one concerned "with orthodoxy and
common understanding."[87] In this, as in many other respects, Kynyngham skilfully anticipated the concerns of Wyclif's later critics. The
leitmotif of "common understanding" not only plays forcefully through
his resourceful and always courteous engagements with Wyclif, but
also occurs significantly in the other extensive responses to Wyclif
preserved in *FZ*, those of the Franciscan John Tissington and the
Augustinian Thomas Winterton, both of whom, with varying degrees
of subtlety, addressed Wyclif's rejection of the doctrine of transubstantiation. It is important, therefore, to note that it was increasing
concern for the way in which Wyclif's arguments might play in the
wider world, rather than disagreement simply with his arguments,
that fuelled the opposition to him.

In order to trace the growth of this awareness, therefore, and to
appreciate its significance as a fundamental plank of opposition to
Wyclif's ideas, we can turn in the first place to the arguments of
Kynyngham, Tissington and Winterton. In particular, I will trace
Kynyngham's arguments in some detail here, as they serve as a par-
adigm of concerns that would re-surface among successive generations
of Wyclif's opponents. In evaluating and criticising the root and
many branches of Wyclif's arguments concerning the restriction and
ampliation of the present tense, which was fundamental to his interpretation of statements in Scripture, Kynyngham points out that
Wyclif's use of the present tense invites a response that is neither
taught by philosophers nor approved by academic discourse in general (*nec docuerunt philosophi, nec approbat communis scola*).[88] In an argumentative manoeuvre that would come to be a hallmark of responses
to Wyclif's language, Kynyngham accuses his opponent of using
"curious and subtle inventions . . . in difficult sentences and logical
deductions" from which the only refuge is the "rock of solid truth."[89]

---

[87] Maarten J.F.M. Hoenen, "Theology and Metaphysics. The Debate between
John Wyclif and John Kenningham on the Principles of Reading the Scriptures,"
in *John Wyclif: Logica, Politica, Teologia*. Atti del Convegno Internazionale Milano,
12–13 Febbraio 1999, eds. Mariateresa Fumagalli Beonio Brocchieri and Stefano
Simonetta (Florence, 2003), pp. 23–55 (55).

[88] *FZ*, p. 13/6–8.

[89] *FZ*, p. 14/25–15/2: "[C]uriosis et subtilibus adinventionibus . . . arduis sententiis
et deductionibus . . . refugium mihi est humilis petra solidae veritatis."

In pursuing his interpretation of Scriptural terms, Wyclif was constantly running the risk of violating the interpretations agreed upon by a notional interpretative community, whether of scholars or of the Church in general. One of Kynyngham's most trenchant arguments against Wyclif is that "we should not imitate the manner of speaking that Scripture uses, but expound the sense of Scripture by speaking accurately."[90]

If, when in the schools, theologians keep strictly to using the mode of speaking used in the Scriptures, "we would not be doctors [i.e. teachers] but reciters, and all interpretations beyond those adequate for preaching would be superfluous."[91] Kynyngham is concerned to police the boundaries of acceptable discourse, well aware of the contexts in which terms that doctors might permit among one another might arouse unwelcome suspicion. Thus he points out ominously that in settings such as the Curia at Rome, positions that resound against the faith are rebuked, even if they fulfil the criteria for acceptability established by logic; all the more should new opinions of the kind that Wyclif is holding be rebuked, since these are neither logically nor catholically acceptable—and they certainly do sound against the faith.[92]

Although Kynyngham was speaking from within the same scholastic culture as that of Wyclif, it is worth pausing here to weigh the way in which the terms of the warning that he offers here would later acquire a different resonance in a new setting: the eighth of Arundel's *Constitutions*. As Rita Copeland's attention to the rhetoric of this legislation shows, its language is dense throughout with the accumulated weight of intellectual and institutional history.[93] In this particular Constitution, it will be remembered, Arundel condemns anyone who

---

[90] *FZ*, p. 27/26–28: "Non debemus imitari modum loquendi Scripturarum, sed proprie loquendo Scripturarum sensum exponere."

[91] *FZ*, p. 28/3–6: "Non essemus doctores sed recitatores, et superfluerent omnes glossae praeter illas quae sufficient ad praedicandum."

[92] *FZ*, p. 58/12–15: "[I]n quibusdam universitatibus solemnibus, et praecipue apud curiam Romanam, solebant positiones reprobari quae sonant contra fidem, quantumcumque subtiliter essent positae justa logicalem sententiam terminorum; multo magis hujusmodi opinions novellae, quae nec logice nec catholice sunt verae, cum contra fidem sonent, sunt penitus abjiciendae."

[93] The rhetorical strategy of the *Constitutions* as a whole is to appropriate and consolidate a formulaic discourse whose keywords are rooted in long-established intellectual tradition. For discussion of the fifth, seventh and eleventh Constitutions in this respect, see Rita Copeland, *Pedagogy, Intellectuals and Dissent*, pp. 120, 201–2, 209.

asserts propositions that "sound contrary to the catholic faith or good morals" (*in fide catholica seu bonis moribus adverse sonantes*). When we turn back to Kynyngham's *Determinatio*, we find a similar concern with argumentative positions that "sound contrary to the faith" (*sonant contra fidem*). Kynyngham takes pains to point out that his strictures here do not apply solely to Wyclif, but to many other opinions that have arisen at this time, and that his own position is one authorized by many wise men before him. His concern, as ever, is to preserve a common mode of understanding (*juxta communem modum intelligendi*) as opposed to the individual, and hence possibly erroneous, interpretations of the faithful, and particularly doctors, who might utter such interpretations publicly.[94] Kynyngham argues that the holding of his opponent's position would require denying the interpretations of "common expositors" (*communes exponentes*) and the introduction of a "new logic," when in fact the old logic was perfectly sufficient.[95] The problem with Wyclif's mode of speaking is that, however subtle it is, it is not fruitful nor to be generally observed: "I know that if such things were to be said in the face of the Church, error or sophistry would be imputed to one who spoke in such a way."[96] Later still, Kynyngham asserts that "it seems preferable to me to choose a mode of speaking that is unrefined but correct, than subtly to state those things that are in conflict with the faith."[97] Kynyngham's arguments thus spell out clearly the limits of acceptability in Wyclif's originality.

Ultimately, Kynyngham is concerned to preserve an interpretative consensus that extends beyond the preserve of academic theologians, and while he is willing to engage with Wyclif's arguments in the schools, we see here the beginning of a concern here about the changed currency of academic arguments in the extramural world. Kynyngham responds with one ear cocked towards a less forgiving environment such as the Papal Curia, and it is thus no surprise that wording similar to that of his responses was to resurface in Arundel's *Constitutions*.

---

[94] *FZ*, p. 58/25–26.

[95] *FZ*, p. 62/4.

[96] *FZ*, p. 64/4–5: "Scio quod si talia dicerentur in conspectu ecclesiae, sic dicenti imputaretur error vel sophisma."

[97] *FZ*, p. 86/19–23: "[P]raeeligendum mihi esse videtur uti quodammodo rudi modo loquendi, sed tamen proprio, quam subtiliter pronunciare quae contra fidem sonant." On this passage and its implications, see also Hoenen, "Theology and Metaphysics," p. 44.

To observe this is not to tar Kynyngham with the same brush as Arundel, who was working with a very different agenda, but rather to draw attention to the extent to which Kynyngham's worst fears regarding the resonance of Wyclif's arguments were ultimately realized. It is also necessary to acknowledge here, therefore, how successful the *Constitutions* were in drawing on the web of locutions established within the very community whose activities they sought to curtail.

The debate between Wyclif and Kynyngham thus established the faultlines crossed by subsequent phases of the Wycliffite controversies. They broach the question of the theologian's responsibility in maintaining an interpretative discourse more sophisticated than that required purely for preaching but nevertheless free from error and endorsed by a broad interpretative community that included both the Fathers and current exegetes. They are permeated with an acute sense of the theologian's responsibilities as a public intellectual. Furthermore, they raise the perennial questions of the appropriate relationship between philosophy and theology, and between conclusions acceptable within academic theology on one hand and ecclesiastical determinations on the other.

Kynyngham was not alone in his concern to keep Wyclif within a community of interpreters that included both professional theologians and more broadly defined *fideles*. The Franciscan John Tissington put the matter rather less subtly: "Holy Mother Church is accustomed to approving those doctores who maintain the simplicity of faith, and work at defending it. She reproves those who try to change the faith of the Church, whether in sense or sound, or soften the teachings of the ancient fathers in matters of faith, since it is not possible to correct those."[98] Further on, Tissington deals candidly with the fact that the ordinary language of the *fideles* when dealing with the terminology of the sacraments is elliptical and, hence, superficially misleading: "The faithful . . . accept 'to be' for 'to exist,' or 'to be' for 'being,' in the way that all men speak of existence; 'bread and wine' for 'bread and wine in respect of their species'; and this is the logic of Scripture and of Augustine. They accept 'to put' for 'to put mentally,' as when we put it that God is in heaven, and other conclusions

---

[98] *FZ,* pp. 133/23–134/4: "[S]ancta mater ecclesia illos doctores consuevit approbare, qui simplicitatem fidei supponunt, et quomodo defendatur laborant. Illos quoque reprobat, qui fidem ecclesiae, vel sono vel sensu, mutare contendunt, aut antiquorum patrum sententias in materia fidei, cum non possint corrigere, molliuntur."

in the schools."[99] In discussing the dangers attendant on erroneous uses of language, Tissington is obliged to acknowledge the fragile intelligibility of scholastic discourse, which works well as a professional dialect among the initiated but crumbles when exposed to the harsh light of common understanding. The ellipses of ordinary language work well as a commonly understood shorthand for more precise terms, but fall short of the full rigor that "good logic" and orthodox understanding require.

The Augustinian Thomas Winterton, whose *Absolutio* also forms a substantial part of *FZ*, deals with a closely related issue vividly, taking as his point of departure the common use of *est* for *significat* on which Tissington had commented. He argues that although theologians speaking in broad and metaphorical terms (*large loquendo, et tropice*), say that the bread "is" the flesh of Christ. Problems arise when they have to explain the sacrament to laymen, or those less learned than themselves, since such people do not know how to distinguish tropological or figurative speech from other kinds.[100] Once again the question of the extramural reach, and interpretation, of theological terminology is broached. An increasing self-consciousness about the ramifications of the debate's percolations into the extramural world would be the hallmark of Thomas Netter's response to Wyclif. On the other hand, Reginald Pecock's belated vernacular experiments, which were provoked by the Wycliffite controversies without ever wholly being circumscribed by their concerns, are marked by a reaction not only to the dissemination of Wycliffite ideas in the wider world, but by what he judged to be the inadequacy of earlier, avowedly orthodox responses. It is to these later developments in the history of opposition to Wyclif that we now turn.

Netter's Doctrinale

The withering of academic Wycliffism in fifteenth-century England has long been a matter for consensus among historians and literary

---

[99] *FZ*, p. 156/15–22: "Fideles . . . accipiunt[que] esse pro existere, sive esse pro essentia, quomodo omnes homines loquuntur de esse: panem vero et vinum pro pane et vino secundum speciem; et haec est logica Scripturae et Augustini. Ponere vero accipiunt pro ponere mentaliter, quomodo ponimus quod Deus est in coelo, et alias conclusiones in scholis."

[100] *FZ*, p. 197.

scholars.[101] The broader significance of the Wycfliffite controversies in shaping the landscape of late-medieval religious life in England has, however, become a contested issue, with some scholars more eager than others to downplay the extent and the impact of popular Lollardy, in particular.[102] This does not, however, detract from the equally important fact that anti-Wycliffism remained a distinctive and sometimes substantial component in the mentality of fifteenth-century theologians, and in particular among those who took an active role in institution-building and in the professional and doctrinal formation of the young.[103] This fact may be readily appreciated from the sequences of book acquisitions and bequests that are important threads binding institutional and intellectual history in fifteenth-century England.[104] Several of the most valuable anti-Wycliffite codices that remain to us show the zeal of fifteenth-century anti-heretics in the collecting, preserving and transmitting fourteenth-century theology, and thus serving, at least hopefully, to keep its issues alive. It is possible that these codices were intended as a kind of preventative medicine: as we have seen, their stated intention was often not to confront avowed heretics directly, but to prevent the impressionable from succumbing to their arguments. It is thus that the writings of Deveros, Woodford and Radcliff, for example, were preserved. John Whethamstede, Abbot of St. Albans for the first time between 1420 and 1440, had been prior of Gloucester Hall, Oxford (the Benedictine house), and was responsible for the building of its library, to which he gave the manuscript that is now Worcester College, Oxford, 233, which

[101] For example, Rita Copeland argues that "Lollardy is marked as a failed revolution" as early as 1407 and that this realization is expressed in *The Testimony of William Thorpe* (*Pedagogy, Intellectuals and Dissent*, p. 200).

[102] J.A.F. Thomson, "Orthodox Religion and the Origins of Lollardy," *History* 74 (1989), 39–55 usefully complicates our understanding of what constituted English "orthodoxy" in this period. Eamon Duffy, *The Stripping of the Altars. Traditional Religion in Late-Medieval England*. Second edition (New Haven, 2005), argues that "there is no convincing evidence that [Lollardy] served as *the* shaping factor in any of the major developments of late medieval English piety" (p. xxiii). For a similar view, see Richard Rex, *The Lollards* (London, 2002). Hudson, *The Premature Reformation*, pp. 390–517, offers a nuanced account of the issues.

[103] Ian Forrest's concentration on "anti-heresy" among the legislators as a way of understanding this period is also salutary ("Ecclesiastical Justice").

[104] In what follows I am chiefly indebted to Crompton, "Lollard Doctrines." The age of Crompton's thesis inevitably means that some of its codicological and other conclusions have had to be revised, but it remains a valuable, systematic account of some of the works and codices generated by the controversies, particularly those of Deveros. For the manuscripts referred to here, see also Sharpe, *Handlist*.

contains a portion of Netter's *Doctrinale*, Woodford's *De causis con-dempnationis*, and Deveros's treatises in support of image-worship and pilgrimages. It also contains Deveros's exchange with his Oxford opponent on a number of controversial topics. Merton College, Oxford, 175, which also contains writings by Deveros, was among the manuscripts given to the college by Henry Sever, Warden of between 1455 and 1471. Previously, Sever had spent two years (1440–42) as the first Provost of Eton. This new foundation also numbered among its early Fellows John Mabelthorp (himself a former fellow of Fleming's foundation, the avowedly orthodox Lincoln College, Oxford), who was responsible for the compilation that is now British Library MS Harley 635, which contains works by Woodford and Deveros as well as others attributed to Nicholas Radcliff. Robert Wyght, a contemporary of Warden Sever of Merton, gave to the college the manuscript that is now Merton 68 as part of a bequest of six books in 1468. This contains Butler's determination against the translation of the Bible into English, as well as works by Deveros and Robert Alyngton.

Rather than forcing us to contend that "Wycliffism continued to be an important determinant in the religious character of fifteenth-century England," however, such examples enable us to put forward a more nuanced proposition, namely that *anti*-Wycliffism continued to be a part of the essential fabric of academic orthodoxy during this period, and that the burning of 1428 was not felt to have put matters to rest. This certainly tells us more about the preoccupa-tions of particular theologians than it does about the impact of pop-ular heresies, but given the extent of these theologians' institutional influence, such evidence is no less important for that. These bequests, and others like them, show that the debates of the 1390s, in par-ticular, exercised the intellects of a quite different generation who sifted the literature of that earlier period and selected for retention what might prove most useful to it: indeed, Netter, as we shall see below, was a casualty of this process in at least one instance. It is largely thanks to the efforts of fifteenth-century theologians that we are able to trace the development of earlier opposition to Wyclif.

Our examination of Netter's *Doctrinale*, a relatively accessible and monumental contribution to the history of anti-Wycliffism, takes place in the shadow of recent analysis that has not been favorable to him. In particular, his theological method and positivistic understanding of the role played by textual interpretation in the establishment of orthodox tradition have been seen as constituting a retreat from

Woodford's treatment of this fundamental topic: "for a thinker such as Woodford, with his sceptical dialogic vision of meaning, 'tradition' poses no problem. For a positivist such as Netter, it does."[105] The *Doctrinale*'s theological method has been critically appraised as an anxious and ultimately inconclusive response to the implications of Wycliffite hermeneutics, having "no pragmatic awareness of itself as one kind of rhetorical gesture among several."[106] It is not difficult to see why it might be suggested that Netter and Wyclif might be regarded as "hermenutic *confrères*," with Wyclif, rather than Woodford, having determined the methodological agenda and canon of authorities followed by his posthumous opponent. Is it possible that this judgment corroborates fifteenth-century views concerning the usefulness, or otherwise, of Netter's work? It is certainly telling that fifteenth- and even sixteenth-century anti-Wycliffite "market forces" could on occasion favour the teacher over the pupil. As Vincent Gillespie has shown, despite the fact that "overtly anti-Wycliffite materials" were retained in the library at Syon Abbey into the sixteenth century, "surprisingly (especially given Syon's contact with the Carmelites early in its history), there is no sign that Thomas Netter's compendious assault on Wyclif's teachings in the *Doctrinale fidei* was ever present in the Syon collection. Instead the anti-Wycliffite charge was led by an opponent from a slightly earlier generation, the Franciscan William Woodford."[107]

Rather than reprising the reasons behind the suggestion that Netter may be Wyclif's hermeneutic *confrère*, I offer here a discussion that complements, and to a certain extent complicates, such a view by approaching the issue from a diachronic perspective and inviting Netter's method to be compared not with that of Wyclif but with his anti-Wycliffite predecessors, beginning with Woodford.[108] The differences between their approaches mark out the effects of time on the development of opposition to Wyclif. Where Woodford, even after Wyclif's death, is clearly still framing his arguments as if for a debate in the style of Rymington and earlier opponents, Netter, from a later

---

[105] Ghosh, *The Wycliffite Heresy*, p. 183.

[106] Ibid., p. 174.

[107] Vincent Gillespie, "The Mole in the Vineyard: Wyclif at Syon in the Fifteenth Century," in *Text and Controversy*, eds. Barr and Hutchison, pp. 131–61 (p. 155).

[108] I discuss further aspects of the *Doctrinale*'s method in "Netter as critic and practitioner of rhetoric: the *Doctrinale* as disputation," in a volume of essays on Netter eds. Richard Copsey, O. Carm. and Johan Bergstrom-Allen (forthcoming).

generation, is concerned solely to reduce heretical arguments to rubble. Nevertheless, despite the fact that most of Woodford's surviving
written work was generated by the need to respond to Wyclif, he
continually keeps a broader perspective in mind. This may account
for the durability of his charisma even in modern scholarship. Thus,
J.J.M. Bakker points out that in Woodford's *Septuaginta duae quaestiones* on the Eucharist, his argument with Wyclif's positions plays a
naturally important role but does not determine the character and
content of the treatise as a whole. By contrast, in the treatment of
the Eucharist in *De sacramentis* (Book V of the *Doctrinale*), the battle
with Wyclif determines everything about the scope and tone of
Netter's discussion.[109] The *Tabula questionum* to Woodford's treatise
announces a wider-ranging, more disinterested and practical discussion that interrogates the sacrament from a variety of stances.[110] He
asks, for example, whether a priest is able to consecrate one part of
the host without another (q. 11); what condition the wine should be
in (q. 16); whether vinegar, claret or unfermented wine can be used
(q. 13); whether an individual in a state of mortal sin should under
any circumstances abstain from receiving the sacrament (q. 33); why
the mass is celebrated daily in the Church (q. 60); and so on. He
does not avoid thornier questions that confront Wyclif's arguments
directly, but Wyclif is only a part of the picture. It might be said
that the *Septuaginta duae quaestiones* put Wyclif in his place as effectively
by breaking up his monopoly of the discussion as they do by direct
confrontation with his arguments; and the changes in Wyclif's views
regarding the interpretation of the formula of consecration are drily
and extensively traced by Woodford.[111] Bakker helpfully contrasts the
ways in which Woodford and Netter confront Wyclif's interpretation of the formula of consecration, that is, the words of Christ—
"This is my body" (hoc est corpus meum)—pointing out that whereas
Woodford sees the crucial analysis of "hoc" as the occasion to col-

---

[109] Paul J.J.M. Bakker, "Les *Septuaginta duae quaestiones de sacramento eucharistiae* de
Guillaume Woodford O.F.M. Présentation de l'ouvrage et edition de la question 51,"
in *Chemins de la Pensée Médiévale. Etudes offertes à Zenon Kaluza*, ed. Paul J.J.M. Bakker
with Emmanuel Faye and Christophe Grellard (Turnhout, 2002), pp. 439–91 (p. 441).
[110] Bakker, "Les *Septuaginta duae quaestiones*," pp. 461–66.
[111] Bakker quotes this passage from Woodford in full on pp. 442–48. For further discussion of Woodford's treatise, see Jeremy Catto, "William Woodford O.F.M.,"
pp. 202–300. Catto, too, notes that it has an encyclopaedic as well as a polemical
function (p. 227).

late the opinions of previous theological masters such as Richard of Middleton, Aquinas, Durandus of St. Pourçain, Petrus Aureolus and others, Netter contents himself with characterising Wyclif as another Berengar and therefore reprising Guitmund d'Aversa's *De corporis et sanguinis Christi veritate* in refutation of Wyclif's overly "grammatical" interpretation.[112]

Granted that the atmosphere of the *Doctrinale*, littered as it is with extensive quotations from the Fathers, is very different from the uncluttered distillations of scholastic thought offered by Woodford, it remains to be seen what, if anything, Netter had absorbed from his other anti-Wycliffite predecessors, and we might recall at this point Richard Maidstone's strictures about the uses of literary authority in his *Protectorium Pauperis*. It has been suggested that Netter's bibliographical fervor, which is expressed in these long citations, should be seen as an "anxious display of textual, and contextual, fidelity."[113] It must also be seen, however, as emanating from Netter's profound ambivalence towards the language of scholastic "sublimities" (*sublimitates*). This is exhibited in a passage in which, despite his evident mastery of philosophical theology, he waives aside the opportunity for a detailed philosophical discussion:

> I hand over this subtle matter of faith to experienced theologians, lest I seem to go against my brief by weaving in sublime matters and, beyond the remit of the plain style, . . . to lead people to the pinnacle of the temple, as it were; and lest it also be said that I lead ordinary people astray, vainly hiding the little snares laid for the innocent.[114]

The terms used in this passage reveal much about Netter's sense of the *Doctrinale* as having some of the qualities of an "extramural" text intended for *populares*, rather than solely for professional theologians. His resulting decision to rely heavily on patristic literature when composing his arguments can be located within the context of an evolving "patristic turn" and concomitant disaffection from certain scholastic techniques and terminology that had come to be identified as

---

[112] Ibid., pp. 458–59. Bakker prints Woodford's *Quaestio 51* on pp. 471–91.

[113] Ghosh, *The Wycliffite Heresy*, p. 203. Catto asserts that in Netter's thought authority has completely displaced philosophy or reason as a guide to the revealed truth: "William Woodford," pp. 293–94.

[114] *DAF*, 1:75A: "Dimitto hanc fidei subtilitatem peritis scholasticis, ne videar contra promissum sublimia texere, & ultra quam stylus pauper pretendit . . . ducere populares quasi super pinnaculum Templi, & capere viros etiam mediocres dicar, abscondens tendiculas contra insontem frustra."

"sophistry." Netter's theological method has thus been identified as the recognizable product of the kind of "lengthy patristic scholarship . . . cultivated at Oxford from Wyclif's generation onward" and his contextualist approach has rightly been viewed as both impressive and distinctive in that "[he] took further than any of his colleagues or predecessors the careful study of the *originalia* from which the standard quotations derived."[115] This fundamental aspect of Netter's intellectual temperament enables us to understand why it was insufficient for him simply to seek to prove that Wyclif's logic and metaphysics were inherently flawed. Rather, he sought to demonstrate Wyclif's isolation from a tradition of "orthodox" logic that had its roots in patristic practices. When attempting to drive a wedge between Wyclif and his own preferred authorities, the Fathers, Netter unleashes a string of arguments to prove that Wyclif's logic was not the *logica Sancti*.

It is instructive to compare Netter's rhetoric, and the whole thrust of his approach here, with Kynyngham's arguments concerning the value of "antiquity" in relation to religious authority. Kynyngham had argued against Wyclif's view that "antiquity is the great cause of truth, and of its authority" (*FZ* 15).[116] Kynyngham's response to Wyclif can be interpreted as an attempt to warn his opponent in as courteous a way as possible of the risks he was running by espousing interpretations of Scripture that ran counter to those "commonly" (*communiter*) accessible. What in Kynyngham's response is the sober and painstaking uncovering of Wyclif's singularity has, in Netter's *Doctrinale*, become enshrined as an accusation: Wyclif's logic is not that of Augustine, nor are his interpretations those of the Church as constituted by the "*concors Patrum.*"

It could be argued that, in restricting himself only to those patristic sources accepted by his opponent, Netter was following an established scholastic tradition and one to which, moreover, previous opponents of Wyclif had adhered.[117] Aquinas had argued that scholas-

---

[115] Catto, "Wyclif and Wycliffism," p. 260; on signs of a growing "detachment from academic theology" and revival of patristic scholarship among fifteenth-century English theologians, see Catto, "Theology after Wycliffism" in the same volume (pp. 263–65). On Netter's fostering of a "patristic movement" in Oxford theology, and his influence on Thomas Gascoigne, see R.M. Ball, "The Opponents of Bishop Pecok," *Journal of Ecclesiastical History* 48 (1997), 230–62, (243–45).

[116] "Antiquitas est magna causa veritatis, et auctoritatis ejusdem": *FZ*, p. 15/12–13.

[117] I expand here an argument taken from my "Vernacular Philosophy and the Making of Orthodoxy in the Fifteenth Century," *New Medieval Literatures* 7 (2005), 73–99.

tic discourse should be sufficiently flexible, sufficiently endowed with a sensibility that can only be called "rhetorical," to be modulated so that the orthodox and their heretical opponents could occupy the same argumentative ground:

> In a theological disputation of this kind, it is most important to use those authorities that are accepted by those with whom you are disputing. Thus, if you are disputing with Jews, you must take your authoritative statements from the Old Testament; if with Manichees, who reject the Old Testament, you must only take authoritative statements from the New Testament; if with schismatics (for example the Greeks), who accept both Testaments, but not the teaching of our Fathers, you must dispute with them using authorities from both Testaments, and from those Doctors whom they accept. If they do not accept any authority, you must resort to the use of natural reason in order to convince them.[118]

More closely at hand, there is nothing in Netter's canonical self-restriction that would have surprised Winterton or Radcliff. In his *Absolutio*, Winterton had announced that he would restrict his *auctoritates* to those acceptable to his opponent:

> The Master of the Sentences writes expressly against this first conclusion in Book Four, as do almost all doctors endorsed as authorities after him in the schools and in the Church. But he does not value any of these, accepting only the authority of Augustine, Jerome, Ambrose and Gregory, with other ancient writers of the early Church, the text of the Bible and the determination of the Church. Thus one must proceed against him on that basis.[119]

Tone can be difficult to judge in such cases, but Winterton's methodological concession here may be viewed as one sign among several

---

[118] *Quodlibet* 4 q. 9 a. 3. in *Quaestiones Quodlibetales*, ed. R. Spiazzi (Turin and Rome, 1949), p. 83: "[In] tali disputatione theologica maxime utendum est auctoritatibus, quas recipient illi cum quibus disputatur; puta, si cum Iudaeis disputatur, oportet inducere auctoritates veteris testamenti; si cum Manichaeis, qui vetus testamentum respuunt, oportet uti solum auctoritatibus novi testamentis; si autem cum schismaticis, qui recipient vetus et novum testamentum, non autem doctrinam Sanctorum nostrorum, sicut sunt Graeci, oportet cum eis disputare ex auctoritatibus novi vel veteris testamenti, et illorum doctorum quod ipsi recipient. Si autem nullam auctoritatem recipient, oportet, ad eos convincendos, ad rationes naturals confugere."

[119] *FZ* p. 186/12–19: "Contra quam [*i.e.* Wyclif's first conclusion, concerning the eucharist] est expresse Magister Sententiarum [*i.e.* Peter Lombard] libro IV., et quasi omnes doctores ipso posteriores auctenticati in schola et in ecclesia. Sed . . . omnes istos minus appreciat, et solum accipit Augustinum, Hieronymum, Ambrosium, Gregorium, cum aliis antiquis primitivae ecclesiae, cum textu Bibliae et determinatione ecclesiae. Ideo ex illis ex procedendum contra eum."

of the apparently courteous and mutually respectful atmosphere of this early debate.[120] As we have seen, Kynyngham had likewise been acutely aware of the ease with which the wax nose of authority could be twisted by either side on this debate.

There are aspects of Nicholas Radcliff's method that Netter may have found less congenial, notably the former's willingness to recapitulate extended arguments, based on natural reason and the terminology of the liberal arts, that occupy long sections of the *Dialogi* and *De viatico*.[121] More significantly, Radcliff's ubiquitous and enterprising use of the dialogue form never loses contact with the genre and atmosphere of the *scholasticus ludus* that Netter would later reject. The relationship between "Petrus" and "Nicholaus" is generally represented as a pedagogically straightforward one between pupil and master, whereby Petrus requests guidance on particular topics; but as in so many of these literary relationships, Petrus goes further and models possible refutations of Nicholaus's position in order to elicit further instruction: Radcliff is explicit about his interlocutor's role, as when, in the prologue to *De viatico*, he announces the presence of his "disciple," to whose "opposing and inquiring" (*opponenti & inquirenti*) he will respond.[122]

This does not, however, prevent Radcliff's writings from being a significant conduit for the patristic literary culture that would nourish the *Doctrinale* even more explicitly. He keeps largely to the patristic canon that Wyclif and opponents such as Rymington and Winterton had staked out; in *De viatico*, for instance, Nicholaus invokes the collective authority of "blessed Augustine, blessed Ambrose, John Damascene, Jerome and Hilary," and this is followed by Petrus asking Nicholaus to recapitulate what Hilary, "this marvellous disputant" (*hic mirabilis disputator*) said concerning the sacrament of the Eucharist in his book on the Trinity.[123] A little further on, Petrus states that he finds Hilary's arguments difficult and this elicits further clarification from Nicholaus. Further on still, another chain of patristic authorities is endorsed: Ambrose, Augustine, Gregory, Benedict.[124] Radcliff segues

---

[120] Hudson, "Winterton, Thomas," p. 800.
[121] See for example the sequence of eleven arguments in *De viatico*, cap. 3 (London, British Library, Royal 6.D.X, fols. 147r–148r).
[122] Ibid., fol. 144v.
[123] Ibid., fol. 153v.
[124] Ibid., fol. 156v.

between lengthy paraphrases of his own and extended passages of direct quotation from patristic sources. This contribution to anti-Wycliffite discourse is, therefore, an intriguing balancing act in which the evolving dialogues between Petrus and Nicholaus frame what often amounts to a seamless *catena* of lengthy patristic quotations. The dialogue constitutes an act of critical appreciation as the participants mull over the effectiveness of different patristic responses to heresy and enjoy the distinct, rich textual culture by which, in their view, orthodox doctrine is fortified. Netter's approach is hardly without precedent, therefore, even within the comparatively narrow canon of previous anti-Wycliffite writings. Reading his work in the wake of Radcliff is to feel that the *Doctrinale* has taken the Benedictine's commitment to staging patristic disputation *contra* Wyclif several steps further. Crucially, from this perspective Netter's contribution appears as the readily explicable product of methodological evolution. In the trio of anti-Wycliffite opponents with which we have been concerned in this section, it is Woodford, with his far sparser *quaestiones*, who seems to be the odd one out. When seeking to evaluate Netter's contribution to the development of anti-Wycliffite argument, therefore, we must take into account the question of his diachronic relationship with his anti-Wycliffite forebears and appreciate the extent to which he developed, theorised, and modelled a commitment to patristic literature that has its roots in the writings of earlier generations. Such an approach does not preclude critical engagement with his hermeneutic "positivism," but it does offer a different perspective on it.[125]

In distinguishing between his idioms and practices and those of Wyclif, Netter chose to endorse a "pure" theology in which logic and rhetoric were more closely connected with patristic models than with the practices of the schools. In this way, the concerns and practices enshrined in the *Doctrinale* make contact with intellectual developments in the world beyond it, recalling Jean Gerson's dissertations on the subject at Constance and elsewhere. The rhetoric of anti-scholasticism (as distinct from that of proto-humanism) thus appears as one of the embedded discourses of fifteenth-century orthodoxy. The *Doctrinale* was poised at a particular moment in intellectual history

---

[125] Catto, "Wyclif and Wycliffism" (p. 221), points out that the "new generation of scholars" (in which he includes Netter, Woodford and Radcliff, as well as Wyclif) shared characteristics, including wide reading (Woodford, Netter) and a "critical and historical attitude to texts" (Radcliff, Woodford).

when the language of orthodoxy was beginning to blend with a disavowal of sophistry.[126] Pecock's anti-Wycliffism, to which we shall now turn, is a radical and provocative contrast.

Pecock and the rejection of patristics

When we survey the trajectory of opposition to Wyclif across the decades, it is not difficult to perceive the pressure that had built up in this controversial discourse, pressure that would eventually result in the bursting-forth of Reginald Pecock's vernacular experiments, which turn pointedly away from the method of citing authorities and patiently working through the interpretations of Scripture and the Fathers in Wyclif's writings and those of his followers. Pecock would sidestep the textual culture of scholasticism altogether, finding in universal "doom of resoun," and a discourse accommodated to it, a method of tackling Wycliffism that in effect reduces the edifice of texts to rubble.[127] Whereas Netter's *Doctrinale* builds an edifice of orthodoxy from the stones of scriptural citations, individual tracts, determinations, letters and other discourses, Pecock's works efface textuality altogether. He insists instead that it is not necessary for any books other than his own to be read in order that orthodoxy may be safeguarded and he is notoriously sparing in his acknowledgement of scholastic and other predecessors to whose arguments he may be indebted.[128]

Pecock's extant vernacular writings show him to have been engaged in a dispute on two fronts: first, with Wycliffite thought and culture,

---

[126] An important conjunction between nascent English humanism (as opposed to Netter's anti-scholasticism) and anti-Wycliffite thought may be seen in a Latin poem by John Whethamstede, abbot of St. Albans (1420–40 and 1452–65), on which see David R. Carlson, "Whethamstede on Lollardy: Latin Styles and the Vernacular Cultures of Early Fifteenth-Century England," *Journal of English and Germanic Philology* 102 (2003), 21–41.

[127] On Pecock, see Wendy Scase, "Pecock, Reginald (b. c. 1392, d. in or after 1459)," *DNB* 43:382–386 and *Reginald Pecock* (Aldershot, 1996); Hudson, *Premature Reformation*, 440–443; V.H.H. Green, *Bishop Reginald Pecock* (Cambridge, 1945); Mishtooni Bose, "Reginald Pecock's Vernacular Voice," in *Lollards and Their Influence*, pp. 217–36.

[128] This need not, however, prevent the reconstruction of plausible intellectual contexts for the emergence and development of Pecock's ideas. In "Vernacular Philosophy," I identify a possible source of "doom of resoun" (the central feature of Pecock's attempts to engage heretics and the curious laity in dialogue) in well-known medieval theories of optics and logic.

which he represents as being very much alive in mid-fifteenth-century England; and second, and scarcely less explicitly, with other modes of orthodox theological method. He saw the threat of heresy as closely connected to the failure of the avowedly orthodox to meet lay curiosity more directly and to provide for intellectual, as well as spiritual, hunger among the laity, a topic that he explores in the *Book of Faith*.[129] What Pecock invalidates is not merely the use of patristic authorities in such a context, but the rhetorical manoeuvres that the citation of *auctoritates* permits and the stalemate in which they trap those who use them.[130] In his most overtly anti-Wycliffite book, *The Repressor of Over Much Blaming of the Clergy*, he expressed his conviction that, were he to rely on patristic arguments, he might be arming himself with a "Goliath's sword."[131] No passage more neatly encapsulates the swiftness with which Pecock frees himself from the terms under which his anti-Wycliffite predecessors such as Winterton and Netter had been content to argue.

Such discontinuity might naturally leads us ask to what extent Pecock may have been familiar with any of the writings of Wyclif's earlier opponents. It is intriguing to note the few fleeting occasions on which his arguments seem to make contact with those of his unacknowledged predecessors. In the *Repressor*, for example, he mocks the Lollards' literalism by pointing out that the argument concerning the translation of Scripture into English cannot itself be found in Scripture.[132] This approach had been anticipated by Deveros. Confronted by the argument that something should not be believed because it was not grounded (*fundantur*) in Scripture, Deveros counters this by saying that it is only by repute (*secundum vulgi opinionem*) that paternity, and thus legitimate inheritance, can be established.[133]

A single example of Pecock's singularity can serve to show how provocatively he departs from the approaches of his predecessors. For such an expansive writer, he is curiously muted on the subject of the Eucharist. Neither in terms of method nor materials does Pecock follow any of his anti-Wycliffite predecessors in their Latin treatises

---

[129] *The Book of Faith*, ed. J.L. Morison (Glasgow, 1909), p. 191.
[130] On this stalemate, see Ghosh, *The Wycliffite Heresy*, p. 212.
[131] Ed. Churchill Babington. 2 vols. Rolls Series 19 (London, 1860), 1:71. I discuss this manoeuvre at greater length in "Vernacular Philosophy," pp. 84–85.
[132] *Repressor*, 1:119.
[133] Deveros, *De adoratione et veneracione ymaginum*, London, British Library, Harley 635, fols. 191r–v.

on this subject: not for him the conspectus of scriptural and patristic authorities on the nature and value of the Eucharist that absorbed
Radcliff, for example. We know from a single observation in *The
Reule of Crysten Religioun* that he regarded Wyclif as having gratuitously
led laypeople into error because of the rejection of transubstantiation
and he preferred to believe that laypeople would never have fallen
into this particular error without such a notorious academic precedent.[134] Pecock prefers to discuss the Eucharist as one sacrament
among many, and he takes a broader view of the purposes of "sacra-
mentyng" as a whole, arguing that "sacramenting is not ellis þan
such an outward worschiping."[135] In the *Repressor*, he states that:

> Mankinde in this lijf is so freel, that forto make into him sufficient
> remembraunce of thingis to be profitabli of him remembrid he nedith
> not oonli heereable rememoratijf signes (as ben Holi Scripture and
> othere deuoute writingis), but he nedith also therwith and ther to seable
> rememoratijf signes . . . And also, if hereable rememoratijf signes had-
> den be sufficient to Cristen men into al her needful goodstli remem-
> brauncingis, wherto schulde Crist haue ʒeue to Cristen men undir
> comaundement seable rememoratijf signes, as ben hise sacramentis of
> the Newe Testament?[136]

The argument concerning frailty and the utility of images in rein-
forcing the Church's repertoire of signs has identifiable analogues in
the argumentative *topoi* used by opponents in earlier generations,
such as Deveros and Alyngton (though Pecock characteristically sup-
presses any suggestion that his arguments here might not be original).[137]
The implications drawn by Pecock for the purpose of the Eucharist
are at the least provocative, particularly in the vernacular: he argues
that since the Eucharist has been ordained to enable Christians to
recall Christ's life and passion, it should be viewed as a "remem-

---

[134] *The Reule of Crysten Religioun*, ed. William Cabell Greet. E.E.T.S. o.s. 171 (London,
1927), p. 96/6–8: "þei camen into her erring bi summe clerkis, namelich Johan
Wiccliffe and his disciples."

[135] Ibid., p. 374/75–6.

[136] *Repressor*, 1:209/3–9, 14–15.

[137] In *De adoracione et veneracione ymaginum*, for example, Deveros speaks of the usefulness of images in addressing three perennial problems: the simplicity of the
unlearned, the tardy behaviour of the emotions and the weakness of memory
("propter simplicium ruditatem, propter affectuum tarditatem & propter memorie
labilitatem"): London, British Library, Harley 635, fol. 179v. Exactly the same formula is used by Thomas Palmer in his (now incomplete) tract on images (London,
British Library, Harley 31, fol. 183v) and by Robert Alyngton in *De adoracione
ymaginum*: Oxford, Merton College 68, fol. 35r.

brauncyng tokene, or sygne, of witnesse therof."[138] I do not agree
with the contention that Pecock has necessarily "slipped" into wholesale error here.[139] It is true that one might at least have expected a
formula that insisted on the material conversion of the elements into
the body and blood of Christ, and it would surely not have been
beyond Pecock to have attempted the "translation" of such a formula
into a workable English version. Nevertheless, as with Netter, so with
Pecock, a diachronic perspective is illuminating. When defending
himself and others against Wyclif's charge that they were mere "doctors of signs," Kynyngham had insisted that the Church did use
signs, and that sacraments could legitimately be regarded as such,
but that this did not mean that its sacraments were of purely metaphorical value.[140] Likewise, Dymoke's *Liber* includes a particularly powerful
chapter in which he explicates the way in which the sacrament of
the Eucharist may be understood as a memorial of Christ's passion
(*hoc sacramentum . . . est commemorativum Dominice passionis*).[141] Pecock is
with Kynyngham insofar as he, too, wishes to emphasise the value
of signs to the Church.[142] What is missing here is any attempt to
defend himself from possible misunderstanding of the term "rememo-
ratijf," as it could be all too easily objected that he believes the
sacrament of the Eucharist to have no value other than this—and
indeed it appears from what might be a rather gleeful sixteenth-century marginalium ("Transsubstantiation not knowne") in the single
surviving manuscript of the *Poore Mennis Myrrour*, a work closely related
to *The Donet*, that this is how at least one sixteenth-century reader
interpreted him on this subject.[143]

It could be suggested that the fact that Pecock's remaining works
are all in English does him the favor of making him seem more deviant,
more original, than is in fact the case. But it is difficult to concur
with this. Pecock is a demystifier, a compelling figure in intellectual

---

[138] *The Donet*, ed. Elsie Vaughan Hitchcock. E.E.T.S. o.s. 156 (London, 1921),
p. 35.
[139] V.H.H. Green (*Bishop Reginald Pecock*, p. 168) contends that Pecock's wording
with regard to the Eucharist followed "closely along the ordinary orthodox lines."
The view that Pecock has "slipped" here is that of R.F. Green, *A Crisis of Truth.
Literature and Law in Ricardian England* (Philadelphia, 1999), pp. 286–87.
[140] *FZ*, p. 64/27–30.
[141] *Liber*, 105.
[142] On the role of sacraments as signs in late-medieval culture, see Nichols, *Seeable
Signs*.
[143] *The Donet*, p. 35.

history because he was able to see what was not working in scholastic argumentation, while seeking out his own path and not embracing
nascent humanism as Whethamstede, a contemporary anti-Wycliffite,
and others would. Moreover, he went further in proffering the results
of his critique of theology to a lay audience, initiating them into a
rudimentary understanding of the intellectual plate tectonics with
which fifteenth-century clerks were gradually becoming familiar. This
brings us finally to a consideration of the second epigraph to this
essay, and its implications for the trajectory of anti-Wycliffite discourse that we have been considering. In the account by Thomas
Gascoigne from which the quotation is taken, Pecock's challenging
question was aimed at his opponents when he was arraigned on charges
of heresy. It is the instinctive response of a radical revisionist, human-
ising the Fathers while cutting them down to size; and it is a back-
handed compliment to the theologians who were his contemporaries.
In using reason as a way out of the patristic labyrinth, Pecock may
have been courting yet more methodological problems, but his question is quirkily humanist in its attempt to dignify the living authority of active judgment.[144] Netter's rejection of "sophistic" culture had
been resoundingly rejected in turn. He had thus unwittingly inaugurated a late phase of response to Wyclif in which, as I have argued
elsewhere, orthodoxy was as much in dialogue with itself as it was
with identifiably Wycliffite views.[145]

The Survival of Reform

The spectacle of orthodoxy in dialogue with itself leads us to some
final considerations regarding the remaining possibilities for the nur-
turing of reforming sensibilities in England after the most vigorous
phase of the Wycliffite controversies. Jeremy Catto has explored the
developments whereby former supporters of Wyclif, such as Philip
Repingdon, matured into Churchmen whose reforming energies found
other outlets, and he has also suggested how "the fervour of the

---

[144] On the fundamental but problematic role of reason in Pecock's anti-Wycliffite
theological method, see Kantik Ghosh, "Bishop Reginald Pecock and the Idea of
'Lollardy'," in *Text and Controversy from Wyclif to Bale*, pp. 251–65.
[145] "Vernacular Philosophy," p. 74.

Lollard preachers . . . might almost have been a model for these con-
sciously orthodox scholars and evangelists [of a later generation]."[146]
Thomas Gascoigne's *Liber veritatum*, which is full of hostile comments
regarding Pecock, is an invaluable source for revealing mid-fifteenth-
century English "orthodoxy" to be a distinctly polychromatic phenomenon whose different shades play through and shape its author's
predilections and prejudices.[147] His hostility towards Archbishop
Arundel, which is given added emphasis through the repetition of
an anecdote about the Archbishop's death from an obstruction of
the throat, is balanced by his piety towards the memory of Netter.[148]
Arundel's solutions to the problem of heresy are given short shrift
by Gascoigne, who sees his insistence on the licensing of preachers
as contributing to a general dearth of priests, and thus seriously
weakening the pastoral support available to the laity. For him, Arundel
was nothing more than a careerist and censor. Netter, on the other
hand, offered a model of patristic scholarship that was far more in
tune with Gascoigne's own intellectual temperament, and particularly appealing to him as an admirer of Augustine and Jerome.

It is instructive to compare Gascoigne and a reformer from an
earlier generation: Thomas Brinton OSB, Bishop of Rochester (1373–
89), who had made distinguished responses to the emergence of
Wyclif in several of his sermons.[149] Brinton, as his editor points out,
was "vehement in his criticism of the prelates and clergy who did
not preach, or preached poorly because of ignorance, laziness, or the
immorality of their lives."[150] Henry Summerson identifies in Brinton
a compelling radical conservatism: "Though accepting divisions in
society . . . he outspokenly denounces the wealthy and powerful,
whether lay or ecclesiastical, who fail to meet their responsibilities."[151]
Brinton provides a salutary reminder of the possibilities that existed in
the late fourteenth century for a flourishing, independently reforming

---

[146] Catto, "Fellows and Helpers"; "Wyclif and Wycliffism," pp. 257–59 (p. 258).

[147] Christina von Nolcken, "Gascoigne, Thomas," *DNB* 21:587–89; Winifred A.
Pronger, "Thomas Gascoigne," *English Historical Review* 53 (1938), 606–26; 54 (1939),
20–37; Ball, "The Opponents of Bishop Pecock."

[148] For the anecdote about Arundel, see *Loci e Libro Veritatum*, ed. Rogers, p. 180;
on Netter, see pp. 2, 11, 141, 186.

[149] *The sermons of Thomas Brinton, bishop of Rochester, 1373–1389*, ed. M.A. Devlin,
2 vols., Camden Society 3rd series 85–86 (1954); Henry Summerson, "Brinton,
Thomas (d. 1389)," *DNB* 7:669–70.

[150] *The sermons of Thomas Brinton*, 1:xxi.

[151] Summerson, "Brinton, Thomas," p. 670.

position during the period of Wyclif's rise to notoriety, but he was among Wyclif's opponents, having been present at Blackfriars in 1382, and he preached several sermons against Wyclif. In a sermon from July 1382, he identifies as "pseudoprophets" those who espoused Wyclif's views concerning the sacraments of the Church (here, baptism, confession and the Eucharist). He responds to these positions as if in a disputation and ends by noting that these heresies and errors have been publicly condemned.[152] It is not difficult, particularly when reading the sermons in which Brinton attempts to enjoin a self-critical, ascetic cast of mind on his audience, to understand how frustrating and possibly pre-emptive the emergence of Wyclif and his supporters must have been to a bishop of such a distinctively reforming sensibility.

To pass from reading Brinton to reading Gascoigne is to be struck by the vehemence and passion with which a reforming voice and sensibility have survived in a very different world. The argument that Arundel's *Constitutions* were a cultural watershed, stalling any adventurous or vigorous thinking about reform, is fundamentally challenged by Gascoigne's *Liber*, which shows that it was still possible to entertain fully-fledged reforming ideas in the decades after their promulgation.[153] In his loathing of Pecock, Gascoigne is aggressively orthodox; yet in certain respects he can sound startlingly like a Wycliffite preacher, repeatedly listing and castigating ecclesiastical abuses and advocating preaching as the best means of disseminating religious doctrine. Gascoigne praises a dynamic, authentic parish life and laments the non-residence of priests in appropriated parishes, vehemently criticizing monasteries for taking them over. His stated concern for the care of souls is congruent with this mentality, and it appears that he was scrupulous about living on his inheritance rather than from the wealth provided by an ecclesiastical sinecure.[154] As Christina von Nolcken points out, he was "in many ways a typical representative of a piety

---

[152] *The sermons of Thomas Brinton*, 2:466 (Sermon 101, 22 July 1382).

[153] The most influential of such readings of the *Constitutions* is Nicholas Watson, "Censorship and Cultural Change in Late-Medieval England: Vernacular Theology, The Oxford Translation Debate and Arundel's Constitutions of 1409," *Speculum* 70 (1995), 822–64. Watson is chiefly concerned to measure the impact of the *Constitutions* on the writing and dissemination of "vernacular theology" in England, but this inevitably results in a partial picture of what was possible in English culture during this period: my concern here is to mark the survival of a reforming sensibility in a different context.

[154] *Loci e Libro Veritatum*, ed. Rogers, pp. 30–31.

that the Church had encouraged partly as a means of countering Wycliffism. Yet he vehemently deplored the prevalent clerical abuses of his time, and many of his emphases echo those of Wyclif and his followers."[155] It is true that our evaluation of Gascoigne needs to take into account the problematic status of the *Liber*: while Netter and Pecock sought to make their works public, albeit via very different cultural networks, the *Liber* may well have been written for Gascoigne's eyes only, at least until his death. This makes it difficult to speak of Gascoigne as the wholehearted voice of reform in mid-century. Nevertheless, the *Liber* remains a record of thought, and in these terms it provides ample evidence to suggest that theologians in the wake of the Wycliffite controversies continued to explore the latitudes of orthodoxy.

Conclusion

Writing in 1515, Thomas More offered an extremely critical appraisal of the usefulness of scholastic theology as a tool in the confrontation with heresy:

> [W]hen I see a theologian of this sort, I wonder just what useful service such problems can ever equip him to do for the Church.
> Perhaps to dispute against heretics; for this is their principal selling point. But the heretics are either learned or unlearned. If they are unlearned, as the great majority of them are, then they would understand neither those subtleties which are his only weapon nor the outlandish words which are his only means of expression ... But if the heretics are learned, indeed learned in those very problems (for they are almost never heretics with reference to anything else), when will they be refuted? Will there be any end to disputing? For the very problems with which they are assaulted afford them no end of material with which to strike back, ... Now then, pitted against the sort of theologians I have mentioned, how soon are the heretics going to succumb, since they have been trained in the same school of tactics? Not very soon, to be sure, in my view, were they not more intimidated by one little bundle of faggots than daunted by many large bundles of syllogisms.[156]

---

[155] Von Nolcken, "Gascoigne, Thomas," p. 589.

[156] Thomas More, "Letter to Dorp" [1515], in *In Defense of Humanism*, ed. Daniel Kinney. *The Yale Edition of the Complete Works of St. Thomas More*, 15 vols. (New Haven and London, 1986), 15:70–71: "... [Q]uibus miror, quum sit talis, qua in re possit ecclesiae esse usui. Disputando fortasse aduersus hereticos, (nam hoc nomine

It is salutary to remember that years after regaling Martin Dorp with his insights into the futility of anti-heretical disputations, More would not be able to prevent himself from becoming embroiled in just such a sequence of exchanges with Tyndale, thereby participating in a spilling of words that has led one modern scholar to observe that:

> More's own glosses, and his glosses of Tyndale's glosses, are reduplicated in Tyndale's *Answer unto Sir Thomas More's Dialogue*, and then again, at ever-greater length, in More's *Confutation of Tyndale's Answer*. Not even a million words can give More the last word on English meaning. Only death . . . could interrupt the endless glossing.[157]

What is asserted here about a later phase of English religious controversy serves as a useful reflection on the intellectual culture that preceded it. Despite the energy expended on literary responses to Wyclif, most notably after his death, it is salutary to reflect, not least when confronted by the extensive writings of Radcliff, Netter and Pecock, that what took the momentum away from the Wycliffites were not "bundles of syllogisms" but the combined assertions of royal, legal and ecclesiastical will, culminating not merely in successive legislative acts, but sometimes actually in "bundles of faggots." Discursive responses to Wycliffite arguments were increasingly produced to protect the *fideles* and *simplices*, rather than actually to convert real or imagined heretics.

The *Letter to Dorp*, however, also prompts further reflections on another theme, namely the contribution of anti-heretical discourse to the evolution of theological method. The former had long been instrumental in the evolution of the latter: indeed, as all of these controversialists knew, the foundations for the relations between reason and faith had been laid down in the Scriptures, with the injunction to the early Christians that they should "always be ready to satisfy those who ask with a reason concerning the hope that is in

---

praecipue sese solent uenditare.) At his aut docti sunt aut indoct. Si indocti (ut est multo maxima pars) neque acumina ista, quibus iste solis ualet, neque uerba tam insueta, quibus iste solis assueuit, intelligerent . . . Sin docti sint heretici idque in illis ipsis questionibus (neque enim fere accidit ut alias sint heretici) quando iam redarguentur? Quis erit disputandi finis? Quum ex illis ipsis questionibus, quibus oppugnantur, ipsis quoque referiendi ministratur inexhausta material . . . Heretici ergo cum talibus compositi, quales ante dixi Theologos, quum sint in eodem docti ludo, quando succumbent? Non cito hercle opinor, si non unum magis lignorum fasciculum uererentur, quam multos syllogismorum fasces pertimescerent."

[157] Brian Cummings, *The Literary Culture of the Reformation: Grammar and Grace* (Oxford, 2002), p. 196.

them."[158] What part, therefore, did the Wycliffite controversies play in the evolving dialogue between scholasticism and humanism? As this essay has sought to suggest, the answers are various. Netter's *Doctrinale* could be seen as the culmination of the attempt to expose Wyclif's problematic relationship with an interpretative community (comprising both contemporary theologians and the Church Fathers) whose consensual custodianship of terminology was crucial for the continued construction of orthodoxy. Pecock's experiments with method were isolated and not influential, but his was a distinctive, radical and original attempt to break with the attitudes towards patristic authority enshrined in the *Doctrinale*. Ultimately, however, Netter's work would be displaced by a radically different appropriation of patristic culture: contemporary with the earliest printed copies of the *Doctrinale* in the 1520s was Erasmus's edition of Irenaeus.

---

[158] 1 Peter 3:15: ". . . parati semper ad satisfactionem omni poscenti vos rationem de ea quae in vobis est spe."

CONCLUSION

The history of John Wyclif cannot be read without addressing the larger issue of orthodoxy itself. Orthodoxy is literally "right belief." In the eyes of the late medieval ecclesiastical authorities John Wyclif was profoundly unorthodox, a man who propounded doctrines which contradicted the body of right belief that made up the received catholic tradition. Needless to say, Wyclif did not see himself in this way, nor did the future generations of Lollards and Hussites. Rather, they saw themselves as the defenders of a pristine faith which had been disfigured by years of satanically inspired corruption. All reform movements, whether Gregorian or Lollard, believe one thing above all else: that they are restoring the apostolic ideal, recovering that sacred primitive order which Christ had taught to his disciples and had envisioned for his Church.

And so it is that all sides of the Wycliffite debate reckoned that they, and they alone, were the protectors of orthodoxy, this "right belief" which was equated with the original deposit of eternal truth—a body of holy teachings that is continually under attack by the devil's forces. One need not have espoused a Lollard apocalypticism to have viewed the history of the Church as a titanic struggle between Christ and the devil; a battle Christ and his faithful were surely destined to win, but frightful and perilous nonetheless. If this sounds strange to modern ears, it did not to medieval Christians. The writings of churchmen, from Athanasius in the fourth century to Thomas Netter in the fifteenth, unmistakably display that conviction.

An orthodox statement is a statement made about an eternal truth. In order for such a statement to be true, therefore, it must accurately represent that eternal truth. If this is the case there will have to be a gauge by which to measure the accuracy of all doctrinal pronouncements. Here, then, we are confronted with the question of authority. It would seem that an eternal truth could only be safeguarded by an infallible authority, one which operates under the guidance and protection of the Holy Spirit. John Wyclif and his opponents would have agreed that God's saving truth has been revealed to the Church and that this truth can be ascertained with a high degree of certainty. Prescinding from the question of an extra-scriptural tradition, all sides concurred that Holy Scripture is an infallible repository of truth; the point of contention was the authoritative interpretation and application of that truth. It was a question of locating the authentic magisterium, the genuinely authoritative teaching office. Wyclif's opponents located this office among the bishops who maintained their role as defenders of the sacred tradition. But Wyclif had lost confidence in the bishops' ability to preserve that tradition; they ceased to be genuine successors to the apostles once they distorted the content of the apostolic faith. All sides agreed that there is a body of eternal truth to which we have access. A determination of the truth is possible; now it is a matter of who will render that determination.

This was hardly a new dilemma; it had been with the Church since its inception. But it does take us to heart of the Wycliffite saga. John Wyclif's posthumous reputation has depended largely upon how one views his place within this larger question of authority in the Church. Well known is the later Protestant portrayal of Wyclif as the "Morning Star of the Reformation," who placed his confidence solely in the authority of Scripture amid the coercive power of human traditions. But Wyclif has also found a place in various modern "histories of heresy." Both of the these categorizations are unfortunate, however, inasmuch as Wyclif was neither a proto-Reformer, nor a heretic. He was a thoroughly medieval theologian engaged in long-standing debates over a number of contentious issues, not the least of which was the proper ordering of a Christian state.

And yet it must be admitted that Wyclif generated an enormous amount of controversy in his own day, and spawned a movement that brought the sort of religious unrest to England that had previously been confined to the European continent. There was something very special about John Wyclif. What made him so exceptional was his willingness and ability to plum the depths of the catholic tradition (which he cherished) in order to make the most forceful and unrelenting case for recasting the Church's position in Christian society. At a time in England when the Church and the State had a achieved a functional—albeit antagonistic—relationship, Wyclif advocated a fundamental restructuring of this otherwise stable system. He envisioned an England in which a poverty-stricken clergy would serve a Christian king who ruled over his subjects on the basis of the grace he had received directly from God.

When one keeps this larger vision in mind it is easier to see how so much of what Wyclif said within the university walls could quickly become super-charged. Debates over scriptural hermeneutics, and even the issue of eucharistic presence, all flowed back into the larger question of authority—not only within the Church itself, but more crucially, with respect to the authority and power of the Church within society as a whole. Wyclif wanted the leading ecclesiastic potentates of the realm to exchange their temporal power for a spiritual authority born of holy living. He wanted them to move men to good action based not upon threats of censure and excommunication, but rather by stirring a desire to imitate those who were themselves genuine imitators of the Apostles. Wyclif pressed Scripture and canon law into service to achieve this goal, and did so with a measure of zeal and intellectual heft that made him a formidable figure to contend with, and thus impossible to ignore. Pope Gregory XI had recognized this already back in 1377, prior to the unrest which was soon to manifest itself in the Great Western Schism and the English Peasants' Revolt.

We said that Wyclif was not a proto-Reformer; indeed, Luther and Melanchthon were well aware of that. They knew that Wyclif was too much the medieval schoolman to advocate a doctrine of "justification by faith alone." Nor, despite his high view of biblical authority, did Wyclif grasp the Lutheran dialectic of law and gospel which facilitated an evangelical reading of Scripture. When Wyclif turned to Scripture in order to promote his vision of a reconstituted Christendom, it remained for him exactly what it was for his opponents: a law designed to regulate the entirety of Christian life. None of Wyclif's opponents, from Kynyngham to Netter, questioned the absolute authority of Scripture in the life of the Church. The point of contention (as we have noted) was an authoritative reading of the text, one which would also entail a correct assessment of the Church Fathers, whose counsel was universally held to be essential for navigating the intricacies of the Sacred Page. Wyclif was never condemned for exalting too highly the place of Scripture, but for failing to accept the "received interpretation" of the text, whether having to do with rightful dominion, ecclesiastical power, or eucharistic presence.

Wyclif was no heretic either, despite the "heresiarch" label attached to him not only by the likes of Thomas Netter, but also perpetuated in some modern studies. It should be remembered that Wyclif died in communion with the Catholic Church. The closest he came to official condemnation in his own lifetime was when Archbishop Courtenay's 1382 Blackfriars Council condemned twenty-four propositions as either heretical or erroneous. And while these were clearly directed at Wyclif and his Oxford cohorts, Wyclif was never actually named. Moreover, there is a difference between condemning a proposition and a person; in order for someone to be formally considered a heretic he would have to defend such a proposition obstinately in the face of direct and clear refutation. This is not the place to review each proposition, but with respect to the first three, which deal with Christ's presence in the consecrated host—the very issue that spelled the end of Wyclif's career at Oxford—we should recall that Wyclif never denied that Christ's body is truly present; the conflict turned on *how* that body is present. Here again, the issue boiled down to one of authority, as Wyclif had rejected the standard interpretation of this divine mystery, refusing to yield to the authoritative explanation on the grounds that it was at once unscriptural and metaphysically impossible. When considering Wyclif's legacy, therefore, it would be inappropriate to treat him as a heretic, especially in light of the fact that he was never accused of violating any of the central tenets of the Christian faith as embodied in the Nicene Creed. On that score he was by all accounts impeccably orthodox.

Nevertheless, Wyclif certainly stood under the threat of condemnation in his own day. Some of his views on the Eucharist and rightful dominion were deemed heretical not only by the canon lawyers, but by his fellow theologians. Though it is also true that other theologians, notably among his Oxford colleagues, were perfectly content with the orthodoxy of his views and deeply resented Archbishop Courtenay's intrusion into the sacrosanct precincts of the university. It is one of history's unanswerable questions as to how the eucharistic issue might have been settled had Wyclif been an otherwise quiet schoolman espousing no radical theories of dominion and ecclesiastical poverty. Would there have been the will within the university to censure this brilliant and popular logician? Would his case have moved beyond the university walls to demand the attention and energy of the Archbishop of Canterbury? No one can say for certain. But when one surveys the list of twenty-four condemned propositions another, perhaps more important, question comes to mind. Had the definition of what constitutes theological orthodoxy now expanded to the point that it created an equally expansive realm of heresy?

What the essays in this volume should have made abundantly clear is that John Wyclif was one of the foremost thinkers of his age: the sheer range and volume of his works testify not only to his indefatigable spirit, but they exhibit an expertise and originality which would make him a force for many years to come. Rooted as he was in the catholic and scholastic tradition he was able to think through long-held positions and apply them in cogent new ways. One might say that Wyclif was a traditionalist, but he was no antiquarian clinging to outmoded theories. He was well-versed in the most current theological and philosophical trends, but he put them to work within his larger Augustinian vision. To be sure, everyone in the Middle Ages was deeply influenced by St Augustine, but medieval "Augustinianism" was marked by a special veneration for the role of grace and divine illumination in practically every facet of human action and cognition. Coupled with this is a strong metaphysical realism which pervades the whole of Wyclif's thought from ecclesiology to biblical hermeneutics to sacramental theology, not to mention his fundamental philosophical works. In this vein, then, Wyclif stands as one of the last great exponents of what we would call Late Medieval Augustinianism.

What makes Wyclif extraordinary, however, is not only that he was able to expound on such a variety of topics, but that he channeled his ideas into matters of direct concern to the wider world outside of the university. He articulated what might otherwise have been a traditional medieval vision of divine-human relations in terms of a bold vision for Christian society in his own day. This is precisely what made him such a formidable foe to the ecclesiastical powers-that-be: his dynamic and original expression of some of the most revered and long-standing principles in the Western Church. In an age when all sides of the debate equated novelty with heresy, Wyclif presented some very old ideas in new, even radical, ways. While this proved compelling and invigorating to his followers, it looked dangerous and destructive to his opponents—men who took with utter seriousness their role as protectors of Christ's flock. When the ecclesiastical authorities at the Council of Constance consigned Jan Hus to the flames they were acting to protect the Church from what they saw as the inevitable chaos which would result from a Wycliffite ecclesiology. The irony is that they too were reformers with a new vision for the medieval Church, a conciliarism which might have proved quite congenial to Wyclif. As it was though (and however unfairly) Wycliffism had the ring of Donatism in the ears of the Conciliarists.

Nevertheless, Wyclif's name would go on to be cherished among the Hussites, who copied and preserved the bulk of his writings. Wyclif was a prolific writer whose works engaged virtually every aspect of medieval life and thought, and so, is clearly worthy of modern scholarly attention, not only from those engaged in the history of ideas, but those in social and literary history as well. Wyclif deserves to be read, therefore, but more importantly he deserves to be re-read—reconsidered by a new generation of scholars. For he was not only a first rate and original thinker, but one who thought on a grand scale. Wyclif constructed a thoroughgoing and coherent vision which embraced Church, Scripture and Sacrament within a comprehensive divine metaphysic meant to be actualized in the world. If we are still willing to speak of a "medieval synthesis," then this is nowhere more evident than in Wyclif's writings. And if there is a rich crop still to be "harvested" from the Late Middle Ages, we can choose no place better to begin than with John Wyclif.

SELECT BIBLIOGRAPHIES

John Wyclif, c. 1331–1384 (Andrew E. Larsen):

Primary Works
Henry Knighton, *Knighton's Chronicle*, ed. and trans. G.H. Martin, (Oxford, 1995).
Fasciculi Zizianiorum, ed. W.W. Shirley (Rolls Series 5, London, 1858).
Thomas Walsingham, *Chronicon Angliae, 1328–88*, ed. E.M. Thompson, (Rolls Series 64, London, 1874).
———, *Historia Anglicana*, ed. H.T. Riley, (Rolls Series 28, London, 1863–64).

Secondary Works
Jeremy Catto, "Wyclif and Wycliffism at Oxford 1356–1430," in *The History of the University of Oxford*, ed. J.I. Catto and Ralph Evans, (Oxford, 1992), 2:175–261.
William J. Courtenay, *Schools and Scholars in Fourteenth Century England*, (Princeton, 1987).
Joseph H. Dahmus, *The Prosecution of John Wyclyf*, (New Haven, 1952).
Aubrey Gwynn, *The English Austin Friars in the Time of Wyclif* (Oxford, 1940).
Anne Hudson, "Wycliffism in Oxford 1381–1411," in *Wyclif in his Times*, ed. Anthony Kenny (Oxford, 1986), pp. 68–84.
———, "Wyclif, John," in *Oxford Dictionary of National Biography* (Oxford, 2004), 60:616–30.
Anthony Kenny, *Wyclif*, (Oxford, 1985).
J.A. Robson, *Wyclif and the Oxford Schools*, (Cambridge, 1961).
Michael Wilks, "John Wyclif, Reformer, c. 1327–1384," in *Dictionnaire de Spiritualité*, xvi, cols. 1501–1512 (repr. in *Wyclif: Political Ideas and Practice: Papers by Michael Wilks*, (Oxford, 2000), pp. 1–15.
H.B. Workman, *John Wyclif: A Study in the English Medieval Church*, 2 vols. (Oxford, 1926).

Wyclif's Logic and Metaphysics (Alessandro D. Conti):

Primary Works: Wyclif
De logica (*On Logic*—ca. 1360), in *Tractatus de logica*, ed. M.H. Dziewicki, 3 vols. (London, 1893–99), 1:1–74.
Continuatio logicae (Continuation of <the Treatise on> Logic), in Tractatus de logica, 1:75–234, and vols. 2–3 (date of composition: about 1360–63 according to W.R. Thomson, *The Latin Writings of John Wyclyf: an Annotated Catalog* [Toronto, 1983], pp. 5–6; but between 1371 and 1374 according to I.J. Mueller in the philological introduction to his critical edition of Wyclif's Tractatus de universalibus [see below], pp. xxxv and xxxvii–xxxviii).
De ente in communi (On Universal Being—ca. 1365), in S.H. Thomson ed., Johannis Wyclif Summa de ente, libri primi tractatus primus et secundus (Oxford, 1930), pp. 1–61.
De ente primo in communi (*On Primary Being*—ca. 1365), in *Summa de ente, libri primi tractatus primus et secundus*, pp. 62–112.
De actibus animae (On the Acts of Soul—ca. 1365), in M.H. Dziewicki ed., Johannis Wyclif miscellanea philosophica, 2 vols. (London, 1902), 1:1–160.

Purgans errores circa universalia in communi (*Amending Errors about Universals*—between 1366 and 1368), in M.H. Dziewicki ed., *Johannis Wyclif de ente librorum duorum excerpta* (London, 1909), pp. 29–48.

Purgans errores circa universalia in communi, chs. 2–3, in S.H. Thomson, "A 'Lost' Chapter of Wyclif's *Summa de ente*," *Speculum* 4 (1929), 339–346 (The MS Cambridge, Trinity College, B.16.2, used by Dziewicki for his edition of the work, lacks the second chapter and the first section of the third chapter. S.H. Thomson integrated the text on the basis of the MS Wien, Österreichische Nationalbibliothek, 4307)

Purgans errores circa veritates in communi (Amending Errors about Truths—ca. 1367–68), in Johannis Wyclif de ente librorum duorum excerpta, pp. 1–28.

De ente praedicamentali (*On Categorial Being*—ca. 1369), ed. R. Beer (London, 1891).

De intelleccione Dei (*On the Intellection of God*—ca. 1370), in *Johannis Wyclif de ente librorum duorum excerpta*, pp. 49–112.

De volucione Dei (*On the Volition of God*—ca. 1370), in *Johannis Wyclif de ente librorum duorum excerpta*, pp. 113–286.

Tractatus de universalibus, ed. Ivan J. Mueller (Oxford, 1985) (date of composition: about 1368–69 according to W.R. Thomson, *The Latin Writings*, pp. 20–24; but between 1373 and 1374 according to Mueller in the philological introduction to his own edition of the treatise, pp. xix–xxv)—English Translation by A. Kenny, with an Introduction by P.V. Spade, *On Universals* (Oxford, 1985).

De materia et forma (*On matter and form*), in *Johannis Wyclif miscellanea philosophica*, 1: 163–242 (date of composition, between late 1370 and early 1372 according to W.R. Thomson, *The Latin Writings*, pp. 35–36, but about 1374–75 according to Mueller in his introduction to the critical edition of the treatise on universals, p. xxxviii).

Secondary Works

P.J.J.M. Bakker, "Réalisme et rémanence. La doctrine eucharistique de Jean Wyclif," in *Wyclif: logica, teologia, politica*, ed. MT. Fumagalli, Beonio Brocchieri, and S. Simonetta (Florence, 2003), 87–112.

J.I. Catto, "Wyclif and Wycliffism in Oxford, 1356–1430," in *The History of the University of Oxford*, ed. J.I. Catto and R. Evans, (Oxford, 1992), 2:175–261.

L. Cesalli, "Le 'pan-propositionnalisme' de Jean Wyclif," *Vivarium* 43.1 (2005), 124–55.

Alessandro D. Conti ed., Johannes Sharpe, *Quaestio super universalia* (Florence, 1990) (philological introduction, pp. i–xxxii; critical edition of Sharpe's treatise, pp. 1–145; textual appendices, pp. 149–207; critical essay on Sharpe's theory on universals viewed in its historical context, pp. 209–336).

———, "Logica intensionale e metafisica dell'essenza in John Wyclif," *Bullettino dell' Istituto Storico Italiano per il Medioevo e Archivio muratoriano* 99.1 (1993), 159–219.

———, "Linguaggio e realtà nel commento alle *Categorie* di Robert Alyngton," *Documenti e studi sulla tradizione filosofica medievale* 4 (1993), 179–306 (at pp. 242–306 partial edition of Alyngton's *Litteralis sententia super Praedicamenta Aristotelis*: chs. 2: de subiecto et praedica-to; 3.1: de regulis praedicationis; 3.2: de complexo et incomplexo; 4: de numero et sufficientia praedicamentorum; 7: de relativis; and the first section of ch. 5: de substantia).

———, Esistenza e verità: Forme e strutture del reale in Paolo Veneto e nel pensiero filosofico del tardo medioevo (Rome, 1996).

———, "Analogy and Formal Distinction: on the Logical Basis of Wyclif's Metaphysics," *Medieval Philosophy and Theology* 6.2 (1997), 133–65.

———, "*Annihilatio* e divina onnipotenza nel *Tractatus de universalibus* di John Wyclif," in *Wyclif: logica, teologia, politica*, ed. MT. Fumagalli, Beonio Brocchieri, and S. Simonetta (Florence, 2003), pp. 71–85.

———, "Johannes Sharpe's Ontology and Semantics: Oxford Realism Revisited," *Vivarium* 43.1 (2005), 156–86.

N.W. Gilbert, "Ockham, Wyclif and the *via moderna*," in *Antiqui und Moderni: Traditionsbewubtsein und Fortschrittsbewubtsein im späten Mittelalter*, ed. A. Zimmermann, (Berlin, 1974), pp. 85–125.

V. Herold, "Wyclifs Polemik gegen Ockhams Auffassung der platonischen Ideen und ihr Nachklang in der tschechischen hussitischen Philosophie," in *From Ockham to Wyclif*, ed. A. Hudson and M. Wilks (Oxford, 1987), pp. 185–215.

M.J.F.M. Hoenen, "Jean Wyclif et les *universalia realia*: le débat sur la notion de *virtus sermonis* au Moyen Âge tardif et les rapports entre la théologie et la philosophie," in *La servante et la consolatrice. La philosophie dans ses rapports avec la théologie au Moyen Âge*, ed. J.-L. Solère and Z. Kaluza (Paris, 2002), pp. 173–92.

Zénon Kaluza, "La notion de matière et son evolution dans la doctrine wyclifienne," in *Wyclif: logica, teologia, politica*, ed. MT. Fumagalli, Beonio Brocchieri, and S. Simonetta (Florence, 2003), pp. 113–52.

Anthony Kenny, *Wyclif* (Oxford, 1985).

——, ed., *Wyclif in his Times* (Oxford, 1986).

——, "Realism and Determinism in the early Wyclif," in *From Ockham to Wyclif*, ed. A. Hudson and M. Wilks (Oxford, 1987), pp. 165–77.

Gordon Leff, *Heresy in the Later Middle Ages*, 2 vols. (Manchester, 1967), 2:494–573.

——, "The Place of Metaphysics in Wyclif's Theology," in *From Ockham to Wyclif*, ed. A. Hudson and M. Wilks (Oxford, 1987), pp. 217–32.

Emily Michael, "John Wyclif on Body and Mind," *Journal of the History of Ideas* 64 (2003), 343–60.

Stephen Read, "'I promise a penny that I do not promise'. The Realist/Nominalist Debate over Intensional Propositions in Fourteenth-Century British Logic and its Contemporary Relevance", in *The Rise of British Logic*, ed. O.P. Lewry (Toronto, 1985), pp. 335–59.

J.A. Robson, *Wyclif and the Oxford Schools* (Cambridge, 1961).

Paul Vincent Spade, "Introduction," in John Wyclif, *On Universals*, trans. A. Kenny, with an Introduction by P.V. Spade (Oxford, 1985), pp. vii–l.

——, and G.A. Wilson, "Introduction", in *J. Wyclif Summa insolubilium*, ed. P.V. Spade – G.A. Wilson (Binghamton, NY,1986).

W.R. Thomson, *The Latin Writings of John Wyclyf: an Annotated Catalog* (Toronto, 1983).

Wyclif's Trinitarian and Christological Theology (Stephen E. Lahey):

Primary Works
Robert Grosseteste, *On the Six Days of Creation*, trans. C.F.J. Martin (Oxford, 1999).
Peter Lombard, *Sententiae in IV Libris Distinctae*, ed. Ignatius Brady, 2 vols. (Grottaferata 1971–81).

Primary Works: Wyclif
De actibus anime, in *Miscellanea Philosophica* vol. 1, ed. M.H. Dziewicki (London, 1902).
De composicione hominis, ed. R. Beer (London, 1884).
De Incarnacione, published as *Tractatus de Benedicta Incarnacione*, ed. E. Harris (London, 1886).
Purgans errores circa universalia in communis, in *De Ente: Librorum Duorum Excerpta*, ed. M.H. Dziewicki (London, 1909).
De Trinitate, ed. Allen duPont Breck (Colorado, 1962).
Summa de Ente Libri Primi Tractatus Primus et Secundus, ed. S.H. Thomson (Oxford, 1930).
Trialogus cum Supplemento Trialogi, ed. G. Lechler (Oxford, 1869).
De universalibus, ed. I. Mueller (Oxford, 1985).

Secondary Works
Marilyn McCord Adams, "Relations, Inherence and Subsistence, or, Was Ockham a Nestorian in Christology?," *Nous* 16 (1982), 62–75.
William J. Courtenay, *Adam Wodeham* (Leiden, 1978).

——, *Schools and Scholars in Fourteenth-Century England* (Princeton, 1987).

Richard Cross, *The Metaphysics of the Incarnation Thomas Aquinas to Duns Scotus* (Oxford, 2002).

Alfred Freddoso, "Logic, Ontology and Ockham's Christology," *The New Scholasticism* 58 (1983), 293–330.

Hester Gelber, *Exploring the Boundaries of Reason, Three Questions on The Nature of God by Robert Holcot O.P.* (Toronto, 1983).

——, *Logic and Trinity, A Clash of Values in Scholastic Thought, 1300–1335* (unpublished Ph.D. dissertation, University of Wisconsin, 1974).

D.P. Henry, "Wyclif's Deviant Mereology," in *Die Philosophie im 14. Und 15. Jahrhundert*, ed. Olaf Pluta (Amsterdam, 1988), pp. 1–17.

Zénon Kaluza, "L'Oeuvre Théologique de Nicolas Aston," *Archives D'Histoire Doctrinale et Littéraire au Moyen Age* 48 (1978), 45–82.

——, "L'oeuvre théologique de Richard Brinkley, OFM," *Archives D'Histoire Doctrinale et Littéraire du Moyen Age* 56 (1986), 169–273.

David Knowles, "The Censured Opinions of Uthred of Boldon," *Proceedings of The British Academy 37* (1951), 303–42.

Simo Knuuttila, "Trinitarian Sophisms in Robert Holcot's Theology," in *Sophisms in Medieval Logic and Grammar*, ed. Stephen Read (Dordrecht, 1993), pp. 348–56.

Gordon Leff, "Wyclif and the Augustinian Tradition," *Medievalia et Humanistica*, ed. Paul M. Clogan (Cleveland, 1970), pp. 29–39.

Ian Christopher Levy, "John Wyclif's Neoplatonic View of Scripture in its Christological Context," *Medieval Philosophy and Theology* 11 (2003), 227–40.

Emily Michael, "John Wyclif on Body and Mind," *Journal of the History Of Ideas* 64 (2003), 343–60.

J.T. Muckle, "Utrum Theologia Sit Scientia A Quodlibetal Question of Robert Holcot, O.P.," *Mediaeval Studies* 20 (1958), 127–153

Heiko Oberman, *Archbishop Thomas Bradwardine: A Fourteenth Century Augustinian* (Utrecht, 1957).

Paul Vincent Spade, ed., *The Cambridge Companion to Ockham* (Cambridge, 1999).

Damasus Trapp, "Augustinian Theology of the Fourteenth Century," *Augustiniana* 6 (1956), 146–274.

Michael Treschow, "On Aristotle and the Cross at the Centre of Creation, John Wyclif's De Benedicta Incarnacione Chapter Seven," *Crux* 33 (1977), 28–37.

Wyclif's Ecclesiology and Political Thought (Takashi Shogimen):

Primary Works: Wyclif

De civili dominio liber primus, ed. R.L. Poole (London, 1885).

De civili dominio liber secundus; liber tercius, ed. J. Loserth (London, 1900–4).

De dominio divino, ed. R.L. Poole (London, 1890).

De ecclesia, ed. J. Loserth (London, 1886).

De officio regis, ed. A.W. Pollard and C. Sayle (London, 1887).

De potestate papae, ed. J. Loserth (London, 1907).

On Simony, trans. T.A. McVeigh (New York, 1992).

De veritate Sacrae Scripturae, ed. R. Buddensieg, 3 vols (London, 1905–07).

Secondary Works

L.J. Daly, *The Political Theory of John Wyclif* (Chicago, 1962).

William Farr, *John Wyclif as Legal Reformer* (Leiden, 1974).

Stephen E. Lahey, *Philosophy and Politics in the Thought of John Wyclif* (Cambridge, 2003).

——, "Wyclif and Lollardy," in *The Medieval Theologians*, ed. G.R. Evans (Oxford, 2001), pp. 334–54.

Gordon Leff, *Heresy in the Later Middle Ages*, 2 vols (Manchester, 1967).
Ian Christopher Levy, "Introduction," in *John Wyclif, On the Truth of Holy Scripture*, ed. I.C. Levy (Kalamazoo, 2001), 1–40.
D.E. Luscombe, "Wyclif and Hierarchy," in *From Ockham to Wyclif*, ed. A. Hudson and M. Wilks (Oxford, 1987), pp. 233–44.
Michael Wilks, *Wyclif: Political Ideas and Practice*, ed. Anne Hudson (Oxford, 2000).
H.B. Workman, *John Wyclif: A Study of English Medieval Church*, 2 vols (Oxford, 1926).

Wyclif and the Sacraments (Stephen Penn):

Primary Works
Peter Lombard, *Sententiae in IV Libris Distinctae*, ed. Ignatius Brady, 2 vols. (Grottaferrata, 1971–81).

Primary Works: Wyclif
De apostasia, ed. M.H. Dziewicki (London, 1889).
De ecclesia, ed. J. Loserth (London, 1886).
De eucharistia tractatus maior, ed. J. Loserth (London, 1892).
Trialogus cum Supplemento Trialogi, ed. G. Lechler (Oxford, 1869).

Secondary Works
Paul J.J.M. Bakker, "Réalisme et rémanence: La doctrine eucharistique de Jean Wyclif," in *Wyclif: logica, teologia, politica*, ed. MT. Fumagalli, Beonio Brocchieri, and S. Simonetta (Florence, 2003), pp. 87–112.
D. Burr, "Scotus and Transubstantiation," *Medieval Studies* 34 (1972), 336–60
J.I. Catto, "John Wyclif and the Cult of the Eucharist," in *The Bible in the Medieval World*, ed. Katherine Walsh and Diana Wood (Oxford, 1985), pp. 269–86.
——, "Wyclif and Wycliffism at Oxford 1356–1430," in *History of the University of Oxford*, vol. 2, ed. J.I. Catto and R. Evans (Oxford, 1992), pp. 175–261.
H. Chadwick, "Ego Berengarius," *Journal of Theological Studies* n.s., 41:2. (1989), 414–45.
Joseph H. Dahmus, *The Prosecution of John Wyclyf* (New Haven, 1952).
L.J. Daly, *The Political Theory of John Wyclif* (Chicago, 1962).
Dyan Elliott, "Marriage," in *The Cambridge Companion to Medieval Women"s Writing* (Cambridge, 2003), pp. 40–57.
Joseph Goering, "The Invention of Transubstantiation," *Traditio* 46 (1991), 147–70.
Michael Haren, *Medieval Thought: Western Intellectual Tradition from Antiquity to the Thirteenth Century* (London, 1985).
Maarten J.F.M. Hoenen, "Theology and Metaphysics: the Deabte between John Wyclif and John Kenningham on the Principles of Reading the Scriptures," in *Wyclif: logica, teologia, politica*, ed. MT. Fumagalli, Beonio Brocchieri, and S. Simonetta (Florence, 2003), pp. 23–56.
Anne Hudson, *The Premature Reformation: Wycliffite Texts and Lollard History* (Oxford, 1988).
——. "The Mouse in the Pyx: Popular Heresy and the Eucharist," *Trivium* 26 (1991), 40–53.
——, and M. Wilks, eds., *From Ockham to Wyclif* (Oxford, 1987).
Maurice Keen, "Wyclif, the Bible and Transubstantiation," *Wyclif in his Times*, ed. A. Kenny (Oxford, 1985), pp. 1–16.
Anthony Kenny, *Wyclif* (Oxford, 1985).
——, ed., *Wyclif in his Times* (Oxford, 1986).
Gyula Klima, "Ockham's Semantics and Ontology of the Categories," *The Cambridge Companion to Ockham*, ed. P.V. Spade (Cambridge, 1999), pp. 118–42.
Stephen E. Lahey, *Philosophy and Politics in the Thought of John Wyclif* (Cambridge, 2003).

Gordon Leff, "Metaphysics in Wyclif's Theology," in *From Ockham to Wyclif*, ed. A. Hudson and M. Wilks (Oxford, 1987), pp. 217–32.

——, *Heresy in the Later Middle Ages* (Manchester, 1967; reprinted Bath, 1999).

Ian Christopher Levy, "*Christus qui Mentiri Non Potest*: John Wyclif's Rejection of Transubstantiation," *Recherches de théologie et philosophie médiévales* 66:2 (1999), 316–34.

——, *John Wyclif: Scriptural Logic, Real Presence and the Parameters of Orthodoxy* (Milwaukee, 2003).

J. Macdonald, *Berengar and the Reform of Sacramental Doctrine* (London, 1930).

Gary Macy, "A Re-evaluation of the Contribution of Thomas Aquinas to the Thirteenth-Century Theology of the Eucharist," in *The Intellectual Climate of the Early University*, ed., Nancy van Deusen (Kalamazoo, 1997), pp. 53–72.

Elizabeth Makowski, "The Conjugal Debt and Medieval Canon Law," reproduced in *Equally in God's Image: Women in the Middle Ages*, ed. Julia Bolton Holloway, Constance S. Wright and Joan Bechtold (New York, 1990), pp. 129–43.

André Mandouze, "*Sacramentum* et *sacramenta* chez Augustain: Dialectique entre une Théorie et une Practique," *Bulletin de l'association Guillaume Bude*, vol. 4 (1989), pp. 367–75.

Heather Phillips, "John Wyclif and the Optics of the Eucharist," in *From Ockham to Wyclif*, ed. A. Hudson and M. Wilks (Oxford 1987), pp. 245–58.

J.A. Robson, *Wyclif and the Oxford Schools* (Cambridge, 1961).

Miri Rubin, *Corpus Christi: The Eucharist in Late Medieval Culture* (Cambridge, 1991).

Beryl Smalley, "The Bible and Eternity: John Wyclif's Dilemma," *Journal of the Warburg and Courtauld Institutes*, 27 (1964), 73–89.

Richard W. Southern, "Lanfranc of Bec and Berengar of Tours," in *Studies in Medieval History Presented to Frederick Maurice Powicke*, ed. R.W. Hunt, W.A. Pantin and R.W. Southern (Oxford, 1948), pp. 27–48.

Paul Vincent Spade, ed., *The Cambridge Companion to Ockham* (Cambridge, 1999).

——, "Ockham's Nominalist Metaphysics," *The Cambridge Companion to Ockham*, ed. P.V. Spade (Cambridge, 1999), pp. 100–117.

Wyclif and the Christian Life (Ian Christopher Levy):

Primary Works: Wyclif
De mandatis divinis, ed. J. Loserth and F.D. Matthew (London, 1922)
De officio pastorali, ed. G. Lechler (Leipzig, 1863).
Opus evangelicum, ed. J. Loserth, 2 vols. (London, 1896).
Opera minora, ed. J. Loserth (London, 1913).
Polemical Works in Latin, ed. R. Buddensieg, 2 vols. (London, 1883).
Sermones, ed. J. Loserth, 4 vols. (London, 1887–90).
De veritate Sacrae Scripturae, ed. R. Buddensieg, 3 vols. (London, 1905–07).

Secondary Works
David Aers, *Faith, Ethics, and the Church: Writing in England, 1360–1409* (Cambridge, 2000).

Margaret Aston, *Lollards and Reformers: Images and Literacy in Late Medieval Religion* (London, 1984).

Leonard Boyle. *Pastoral Care, Clerical Education and Canon Law: 1200–1400* (London, 1981).

Eamon Duffy. *The Stripping of the Altars: Traditional Religion in England 1400–1580* (New Haven, 1992).

Carolly Erickson, "The Fourteenth-Century Franciscans and their Critics I&II," *Franciscan Studies* 35 (1975), 107–35; and 36 (1976), 108–47.

B.Z. Kedar, "Canon Law and Local Practice: The Case of Mendicant Preaching in Late Medieval England," *Bulletin of Medieval Canon Law* n.s. 2 (1972): 17–32.

Jacques Le Goff, *The Birth of Purgatory*, trans. Arthur Goldhammer (Chicago, 1984).
W.A. Pantin, *The English Church in the Fourteenth Century* (Cambridge, 1955).
H. Leith Spencer, *English Preaching in the Late Middle Ages* (Oxford, 1993).
Penn Szittya, *The Antifraternal Tradition in Medieval Literature* (Princeton, 1986).
André Vauchez, *Sainthood in the Later Middle Ages*, trans. Jean Birrell (Cambridge, 1997).
Michael Wilks, *Wyclif: Political Ideas and Practice*, ed. A. Hudson (Oxford, 2000).

Wyclif and the English Bible (Mary Dove):

Primary Works
Forshall, Josiah and Frederic Madden, eds. *The Holy Bible, The Old and New Testaments, With the Apocryphal Books, In the Earliest English Versions Made from the Latin Vulgate by John Wycliffe and his Followers*. 4 vols. (Oxford, 1850).
Conrad Lindberg, *The Early Version of the Wycliffite Bible*. 8 vols. (Stockholm, 1959–97. Stockholm Studies in English 6, 8, 10, 13, 20, 29, 81 and 87).
———, *King Henry's Bible, MS Bodl 277: the Revised Version of the Wyclif Bible*. 3 vols. (Stockholm, 1999–2002. Stockholm Studies in English 89, 94 and 98).
John Wyclif, *De veritate Sacrae Scripturae*, ed. R. Buddensieg, 3 vols. (London, 1905–07).

Secondary Works
P.R. Ackroyd and C.F. Evans, eds. *The Cambridge History of the Bible, Volume 1: From the Beginnings to Jerome*. (Cambridge, 1970).
Samuel Berger, *Histoire de la Vulgate pendant les premiers siècles du moyen âge* (Paris, 1893).
Rita Copeland, *Rhetoric, Hermeneutics and Translation in the Middle Ages* (Cambridge, 1991).
Christopher De Hamel, *The Book: A History of the Bible* (London, 2001).
Margaret Deanesly, *The Lollard Bible and Other Medieval Biblical Versions* (Cambridge, 1920).
David Fowler, *The Life and Times of John Trevisa, Medieval Scholar* (Seattle, 1995).
Richard Gameson, ed. *The Early Medieval Bible: Its Production, Decoration and Use*. (Cambridge, 1994).
Kantik Ghosh, *The Wycliffite Heresy: Authority and the Interpretation of Texts* (Cambridge, 2002).
Anne Hudson, *Selections from English Wycliffite Writings* (Cambridge, 1978).
———, *Lollards and their Books* (London, 1985).
———, *The Premature Reformation: Wycliffite Texts and Lollard History* (Oxford, 1988).
Simon Hunt, "An Edition of Tracts advocating Scriptural Translation and of Some Texts connected with Lollard Vernacular Biblical Scholarship." (DPhil thesis. 2 vols. University of Oxford, 1994).
Philip D.W. Krey and Lesley Smith, eds. *Nicholas of Lyra: the Senses of Scripture* (Leiden, 2000).
G.W.H. Lampe, ed. *The Cambridge History of the Bible, Volume 2: The West From The Fathers To The Reformation* (Cambridge, 1969).
Ian Christopher Levy, trans. *John Wyclif: On the Truth of Holy Scripture* (Kalamazoo, 2001).
———, *John Wyclif: Scriptural Logic, Real Presence, and the Parameters of Orthodoxy* (Milwaukee, 2003).
Pierre Riché and Guy Lobrichon, eds. *Le Moyen Age et la Bible* (Paris, 1984).
Beryl Smalley, *The Study of the Bible in the Middle Ages*. 3rd ed. (Oxford, 1983).
H.J. White, "Vulgate," in *A Dictionary of the Bible*, ed. James Hastings, vol. 4 (Edinburgh, 1902), pp. 873–90.

The Opponents of John Wyclif (Mishtooni Bose):

Primary Works

Eric Doyle, O.F.M., "William Woodford's 'De dominio civili clericorum' against John Wyclif",' *Archivum Franciscanum Historicum* 62 (1969), 377–81.

——, "William Woodford, O.F.M. (c. 1330–c. 1400) His Life and Works Together With a Study and Edition of His 'Responsiones Contra Wiclevum et Lollardos,'" *Franciscan Studies* 43 (1983), 17–187.

Fasciculi Zizaniorum, ed. W.W. Shirley (Rolls Series 5, London, 1858).

Thomas Gascoigne, *Loci e libro veritatum*, ed. James E. Thorold Rogers (Oxford, 1881).

Thomas Netter, *Doctrinale antiquitatum fidei catholicae*, ed. Bonventura Blanciotti, 3 vols. (1757–59; repr. Farnborough, 1967).

Reginald Pecock, *The Repressor of Over Much Blaming of the Clergy*, ed. Churchill Babington. 2 vols. Rolls Series 19 (London, 1860).

Secondary Works

R.M. Ball, "The Opponents of Bishop Pecok," *Journal of Ecclesiastical History* (1997), 230–62.

Helen Barr and Ann M. Hutchison, eds. *Text and Controversy from Wyclif to Bale. Essays in Honour of Anne Hudson* (Turnhout, 2005).

Jeremy Catto, 'Wyclif and Wycliffism' and "Theology after Wycliffism," in *The History of the University of Oxford*, vol. 2, ed. J.I. Catto and R. Evans (Oxford, 1992), pp. 175–261, 263–80.

J. Crompton, "Lollard Doctrine, with special reference to the Controversy over Image-Worship and Pilgrimages" (B. Litt. Thesis, Oxford, 1949).

Kantik Ghosh, *The Wycliffite Heresy: Authority and the Interpretation of Texts* (Cambridge, 2002).

Anne Hudson, *The Premature Reformation: Wycliffite texts and Lollard History* (Oxford, 1988).

Peter McNiven, *Heresy and Politics in the Reign of Henry IV: The Burning of John Badby* (Woodbridge, 1987).

Richard Rex, *The Lollards* (London, 2002).

Richard Sharpe, A Handlist of the Latin Writers of Great Britain and Ireland Before 1540 (Turnhout, 1997).

Fiona Somerset, *Clerical Discourse and Lay Audience in Late Medieval England* (Cambridge, 1998).

——, Jill Havens and Derrick G. Pitard eds., *Lollards and Their Influence in Late Medieval England* (Woodbridge, 2003).

Siegried Wenzel, *Latin Sermon Collections from Later Medieval England: Orthodox Preaching in the Age of Wyclif* (Cambridge, 2005).

INDEX OF WORKS CITED

GENERAL INDEX

Brill's Companions to the Christian Tradition

Volumes deal with persons, movements, schools and genres in medieval and early modern Christian life, thought and practice. Written by the foremost specialists in the respective fields, they aim to provide full balanced accounts at an advanced level, as well as synthesis of debate and the state of scholarship in 8-15 substantial chapters. Volumes are in English (contributions from continental scholars are translated). 2-3 volumes of 350-600 pages will be published each year. The series is expected to comprise 20-30 volumes.

1. Schabel, C. (ed.). *Theological Quodlibeta in the Middle Ages*. The Thirteenth Century. 2006. ISBN-13: 978-90-04-12333-5, ISBN-10: 90-04-12333-4
2. Cox, V. & J.O. Ward (eds.). *The Rhetoric of Cicero in Its Medieval and Early Renaissance Commentary Tradition*. 2006. ISBN-13: 978-90-04-13177-4, ISBN-10: 90-04-13177-9
3. McGuire, B.P. (ed.). *A Companion to Jean Gerson*. 2006. ISBN-13: 978-90-04-15009-6, ISBN-10: 90-04-15009-9
4. Levy, I.C. (ed.). *A Companion to John Wyclif*. Late Medieval Theologian. 2006. ISBN-13: 978 90 04 15007 2, ISBN-10: 90 04 15007 2
5. Swanson, R.N. (ed.). *Promissory Notes on the Treasury of Merits*. Indulgences in Late Medieval Europe. 2006. ISBN-13: 978-90-04-15287-8, ISBN-10: 90-04-15287-3
6. Stayer, J.M. & J.D. Roth (eds.). *A Companion to Anabaptism and Spiritualism, 1521-1700*. 2006. ISBN-13: 978-90-04-15402-5, ISBN-10: 90-04-15402-7